# INSTANT ALL WAS DARK

NORDESTE — A beleza do Sertão!
O povo … trabalhando,
Regando o terreno e plantando.
… santa …
… cuidar … plantação
… desigual,
Tempo vario, carestia em geral.
… indecisão.
"HOROSCOPO PARA TODOS"
Autor MANOEL … SILVA

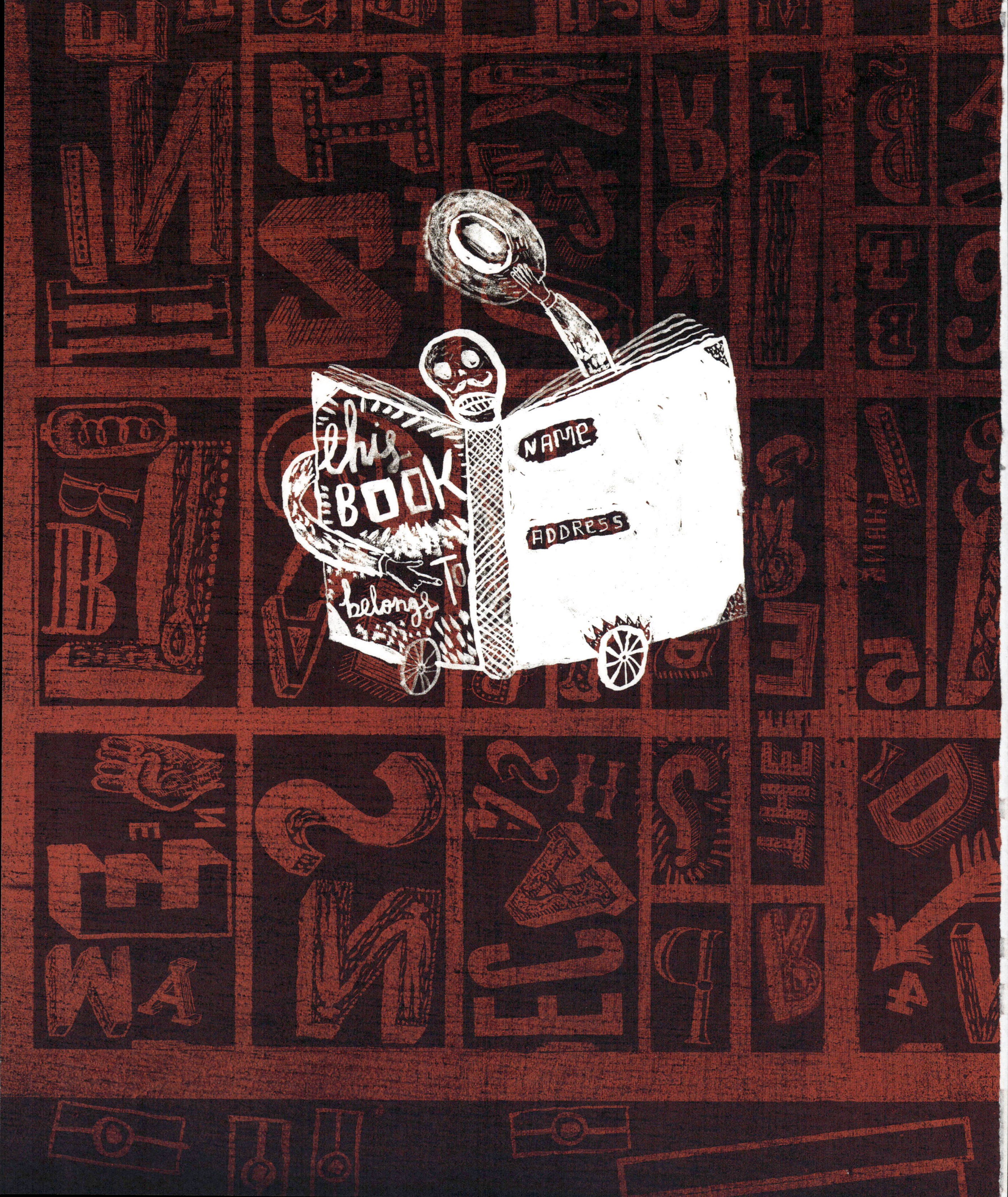
this BOOK belongs To
NAME
ADDRESS

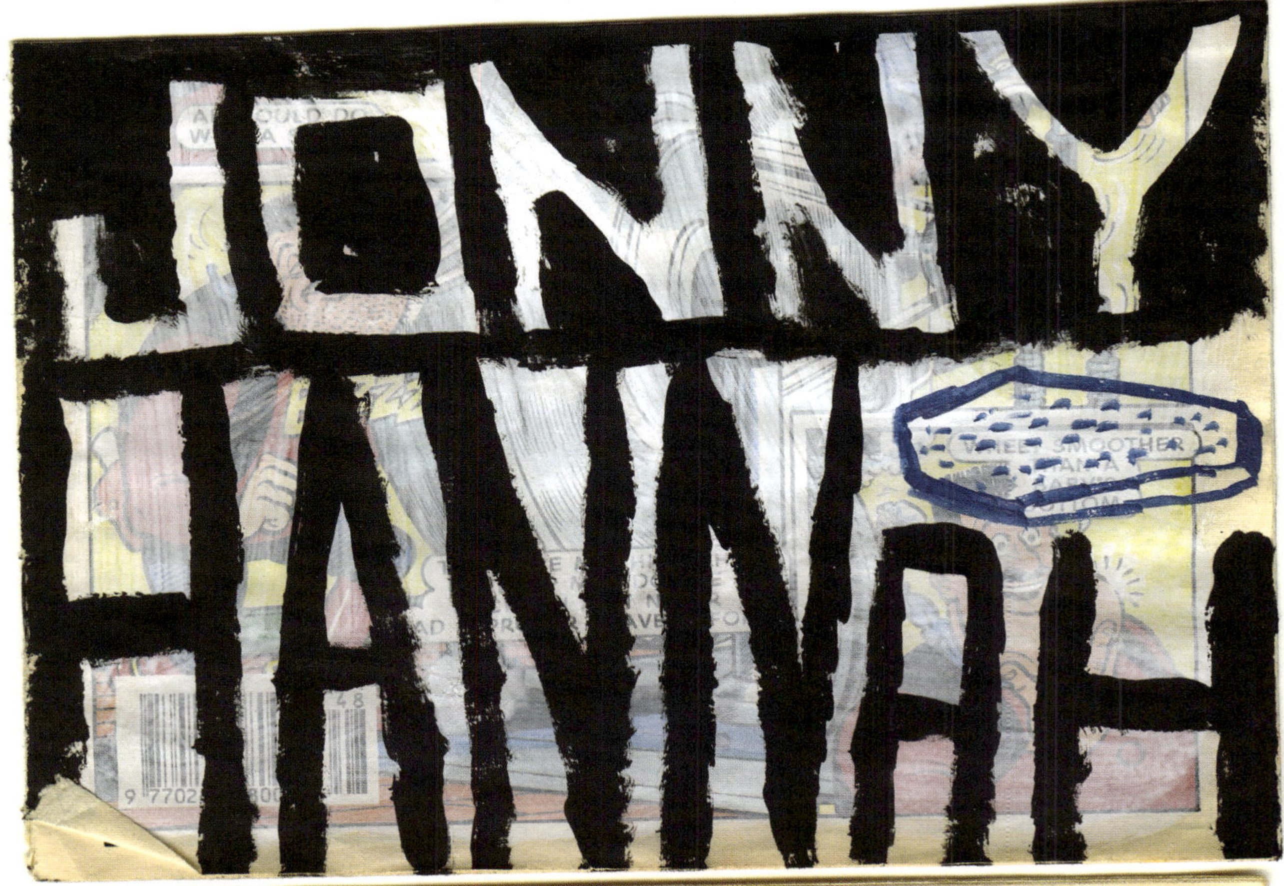
JONNY
HANNAH

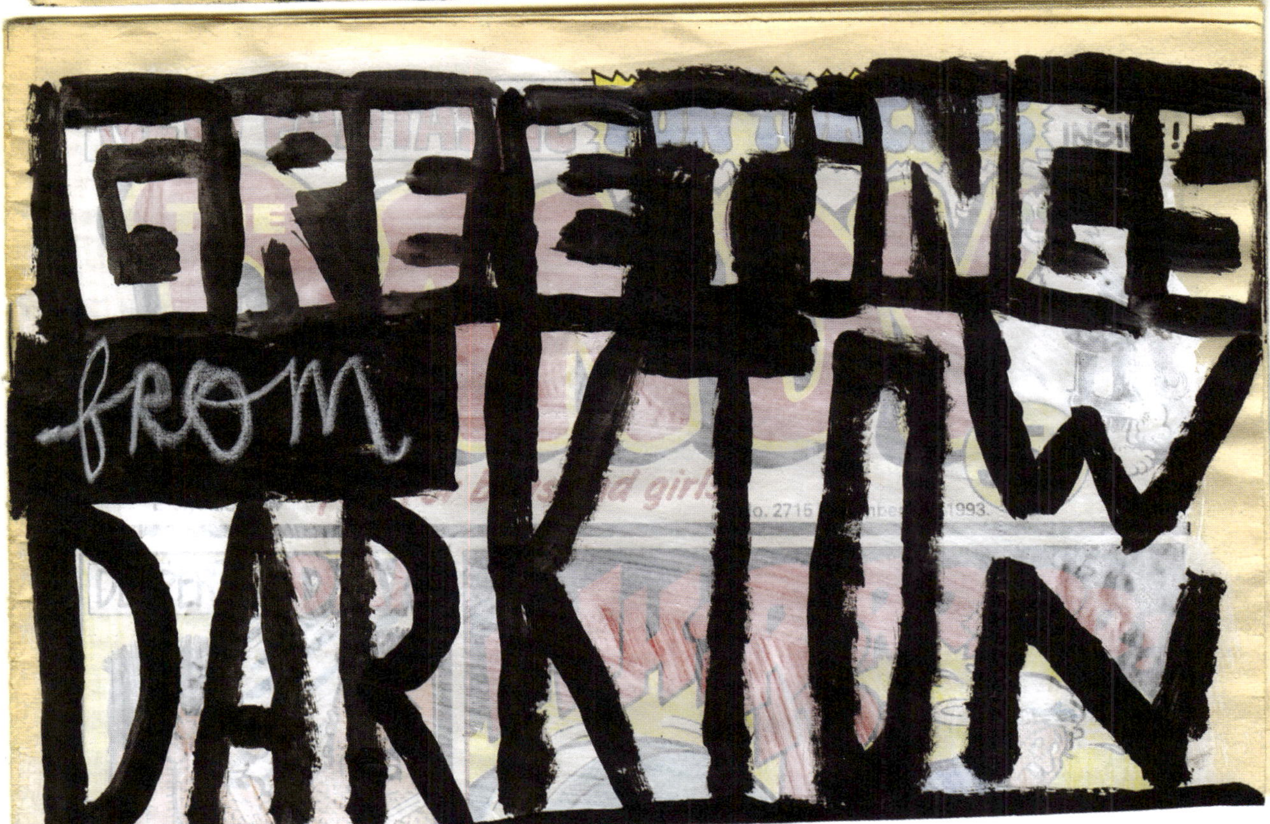
GREETINGS
from
DARKTOWN

# Jonny

# GREETINGS DARKTOWN

## AN illustrator's MISCELLANY

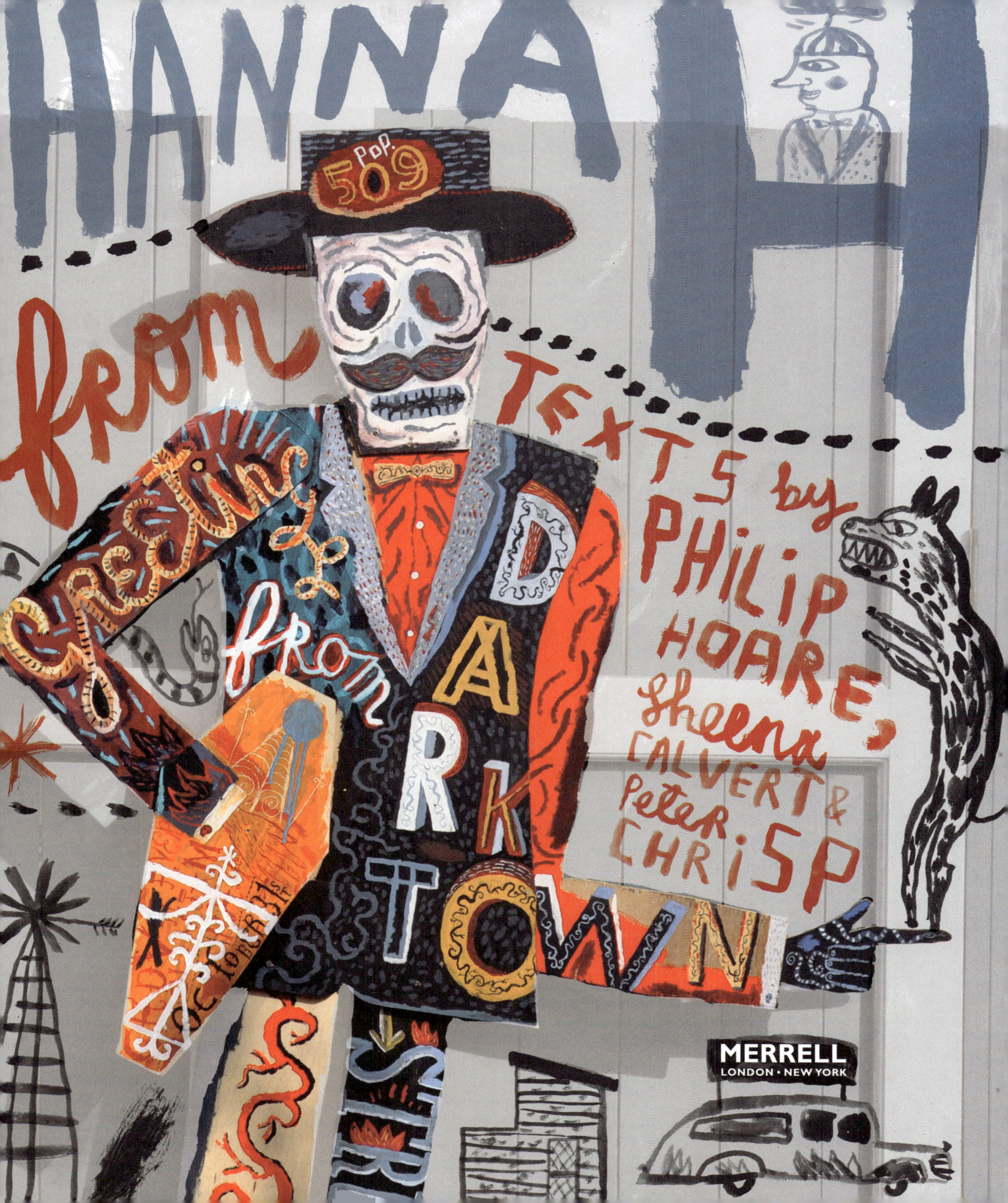
HANNAH
from
TEXTS by
PHILIP HOARE,
Sheena CALVERT &
Peter CHRISP
Greetings from DARKTOWN
POP. 509
MERRELL
LONDON • NEW YORK

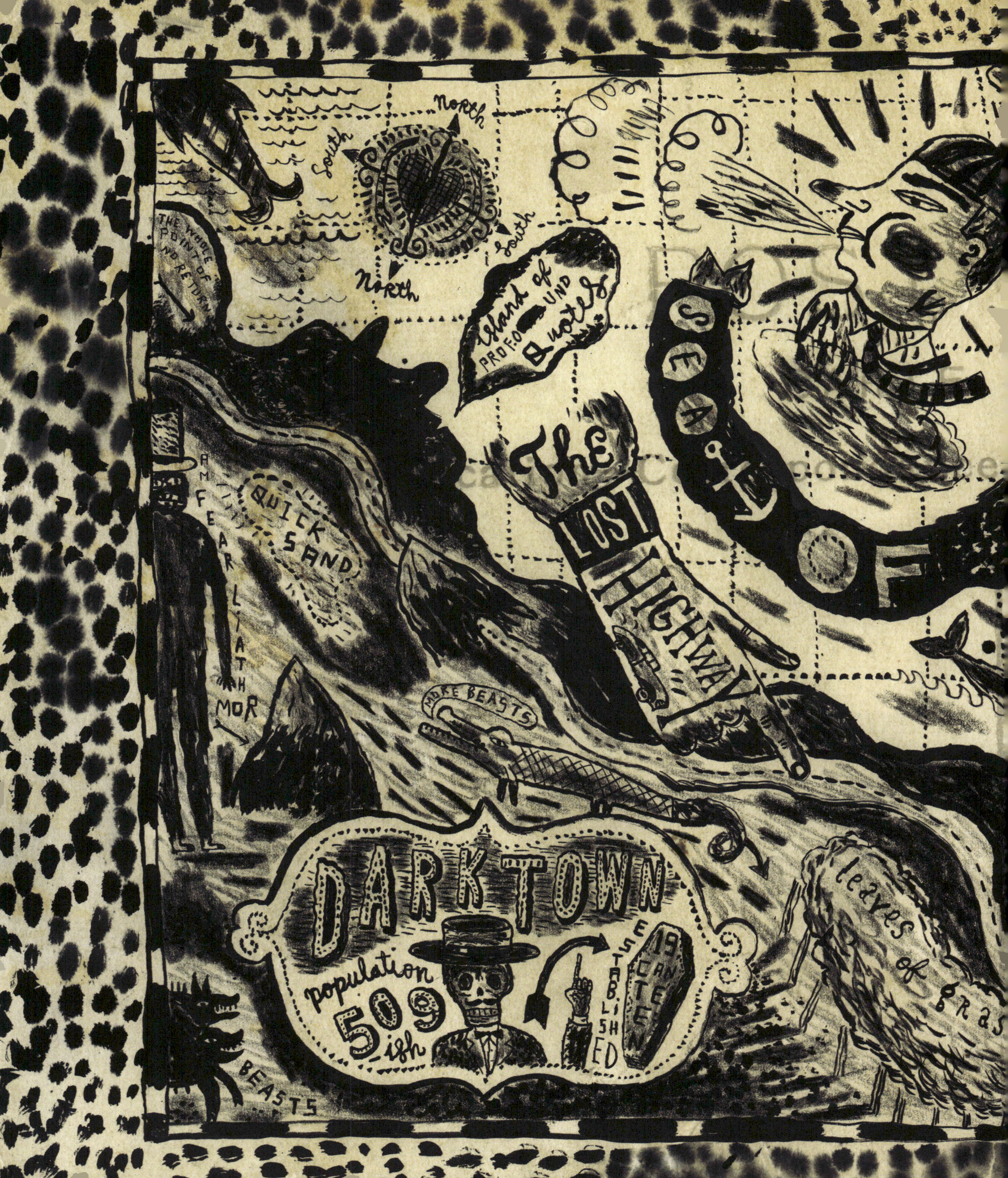
North
South
South
North
THE WHOLE POINT OF NO RETURN
Island of PROFOUND Quotes
SEA OF
The LOST HIGHWAY
QUICK SAND
AM FEAR LIATH MOR
MORE BEASTS
DARKTOWN
population 509 ish
ESTABLISHED
19 CANTEEN
leaves of gras
BEASTS

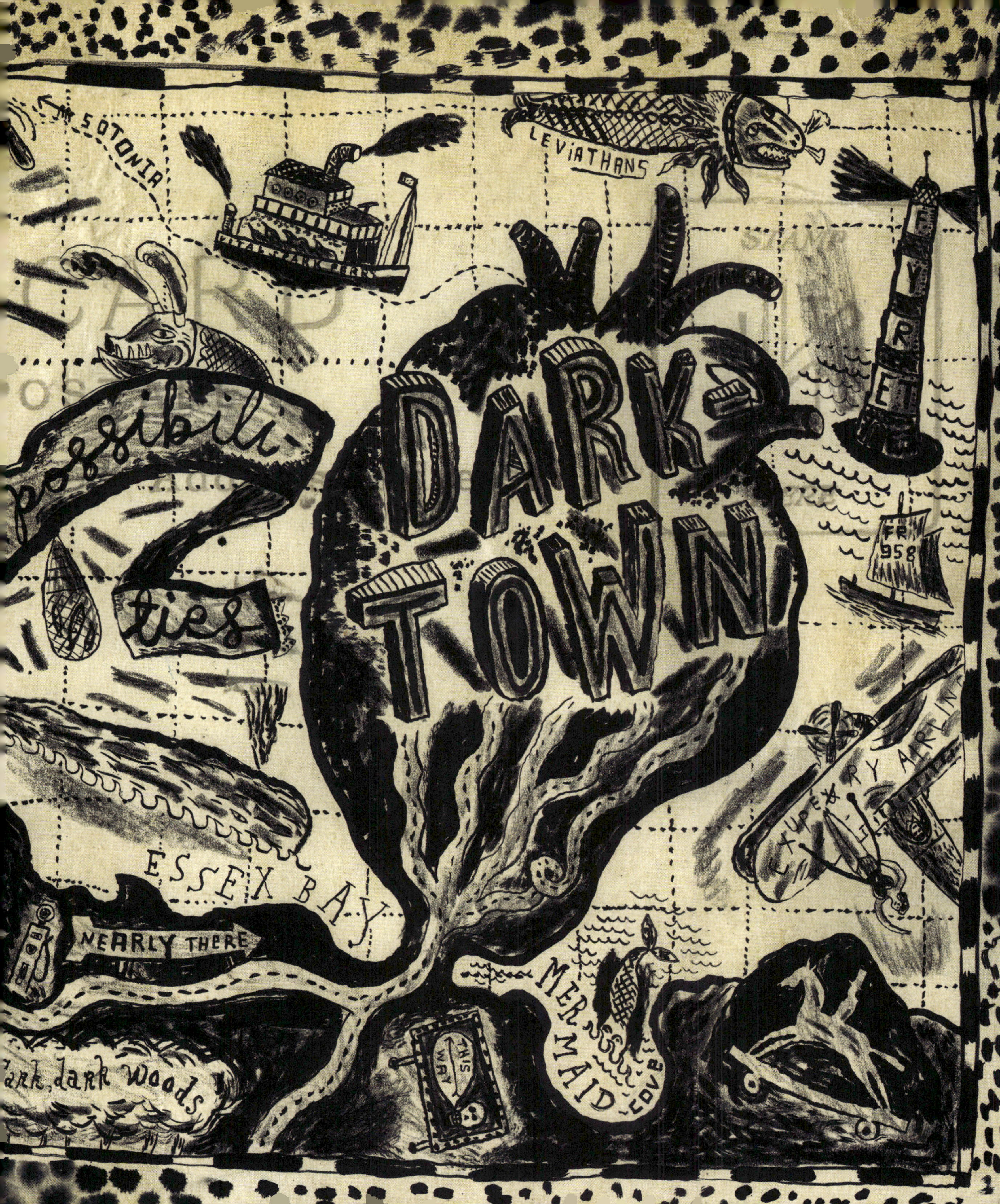

SOTONIA
LEVIATHANS
VITAL SPARK FERR
FYRET
possibili-
ties
DARK-
TOWN
FR 958
EXUPERY AIRLIN
ESSEX BAY
NEARLY THERE
ark, dark woods
THIS WAY
MERMAID COVE

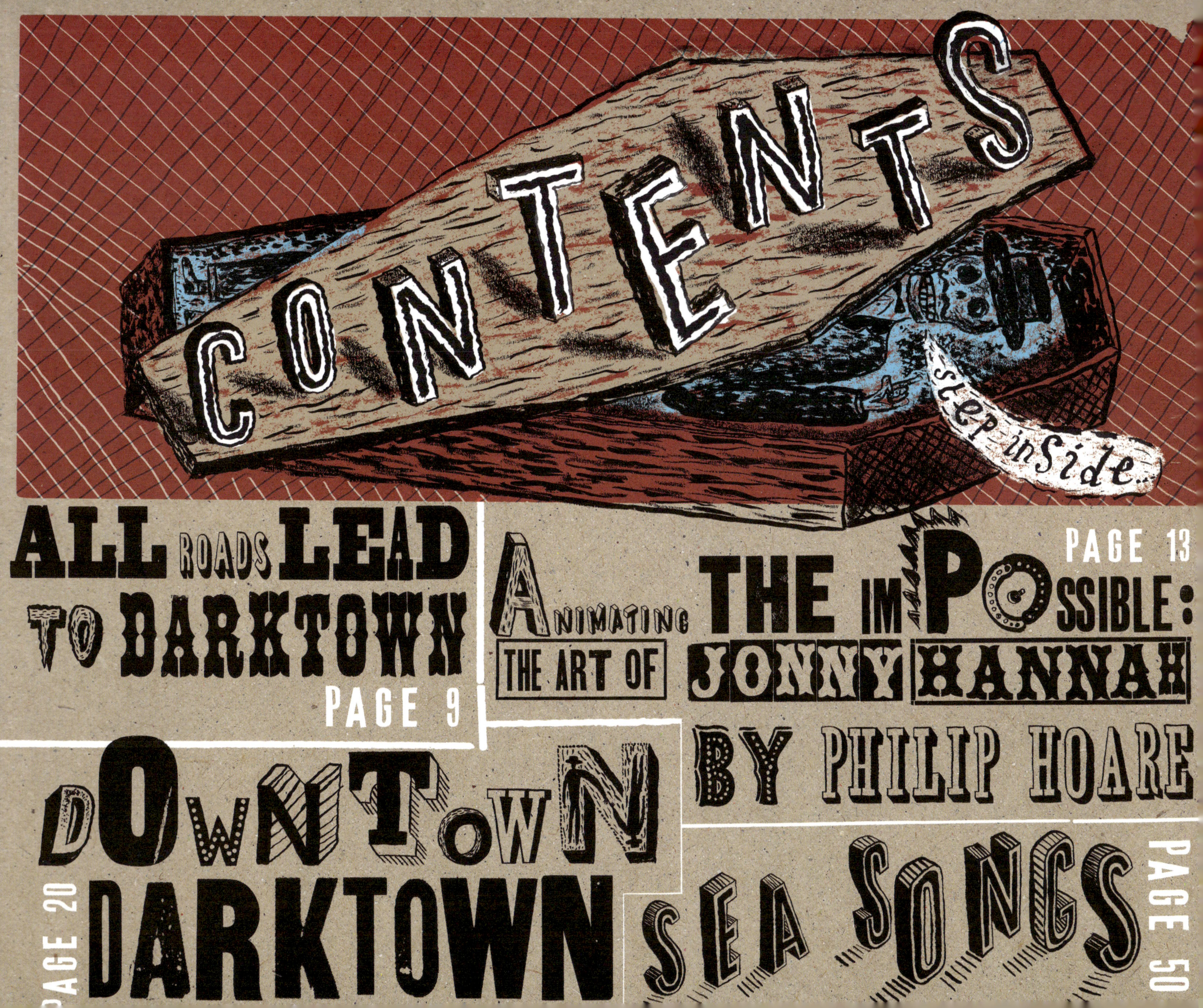

CONTENTS
step inside..
ALL ROADS LEAD TO DARKTOWN
PAGE 9
ANIMATING THE IMPOSSIBLE: THE ART OF JONNY HANNAH
PAGE 13
BY PHILIP HOARE
DOWNTOWN DARKTOWN
PAGE 20
SEA SONGS
PAGE 50

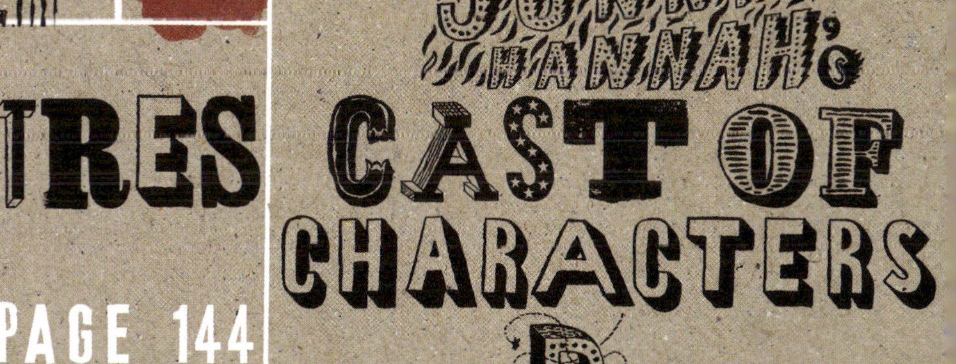

Ole Whitman's
Type Specimen
Catalogue
Off the Page:
Jonny Hannah's
Typeface
Designs by
Dr. Sheena Calvert

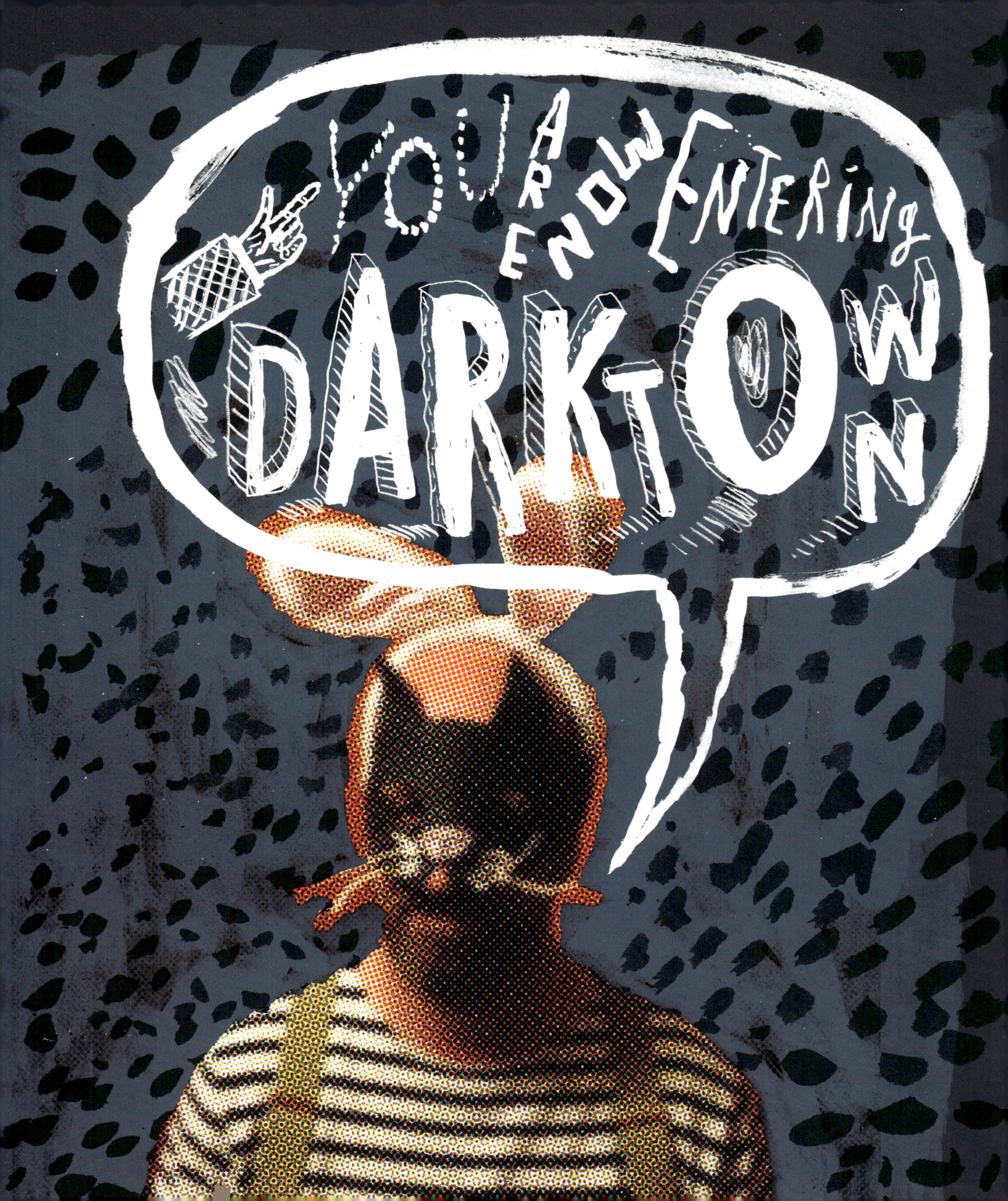
YOU ARE NOW ENTERING DARKTOWN

# ALL ROADS LEAD TO DARKTOWN

## by JONNY HANNAH

Herein lies mostly junk. A miscellany of debris, mainly from the collection of Mr Emmett Miller, proprietor of downtown Darktown's Unquiet Grave emporium. He himself came by it from a variety of sources: leftovers from the Collyer brothers' apartment and charity shops on Shirley High Street; flotsam and jetsam from the shores of Fife and Coney Island, carried on the Sea of Possibilities, exhumed from the long-lost towns of yesteryear. What makes it all come together is the fact that I made it all – printed, drawn, hurriedly painted, cut out with a jigsaw, hammered together with cheap nails.

Dunfermline legend has it that I first drew Korky the Cat. Everybody was impressed, so I moved on to Desperate Dan. That pleased more, and I've kept copying ever since; appropriating, stealing, borrowing, but only sometimes giving back. The need to draw and make a mess took me over the Forth Bridge, first to Auld Reekie, then Liverpool Art School, then the Royal College of Art. I'm now a resident of sunny Southampton, where I teach and paint and draw. My studio is partly in a damp Victorian arch, under a bridge, where I work like a mole in the ground, and partly at home, at the Cakes & Ale Press HQ – a shed in our Shirley garden. Actually, the press itself is a movable feast, and often functions from the printroom in the downtown School of Art and Design, where I try my best to do a 'proper' job.

My many clients have included the *New York Times*, Penguin Books and the *St Kilda Courier*. Monies from these odd jobs led me to buy a second home in Darktown. Not the main street, you understand, but just off it, on rue Zigzag. That's where I first met Emmett, who had recently relocated from Smithville. He began buying my work, then I started giving it to him too. So all this stuff is a guide, a compass-less map to the heart of a grumpy Scot who likes fine wines and Tricker's shoes. Open this book at any page and you'll see a self-contained fragment: a pin-up girl (I'm married to one), a jazz artiste, a tattooed sailor (don't ask). But whatever page you see first, it all comes from the same place, with the same sentiment, with the same nosiness that made me look again, read listen thrice and put my brush to a blank bit of paper or board. The urges came from an inner Darktown long before I started going there. It's a

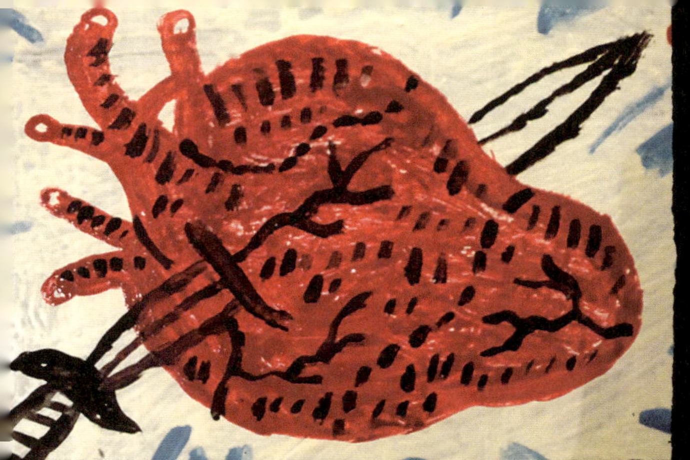

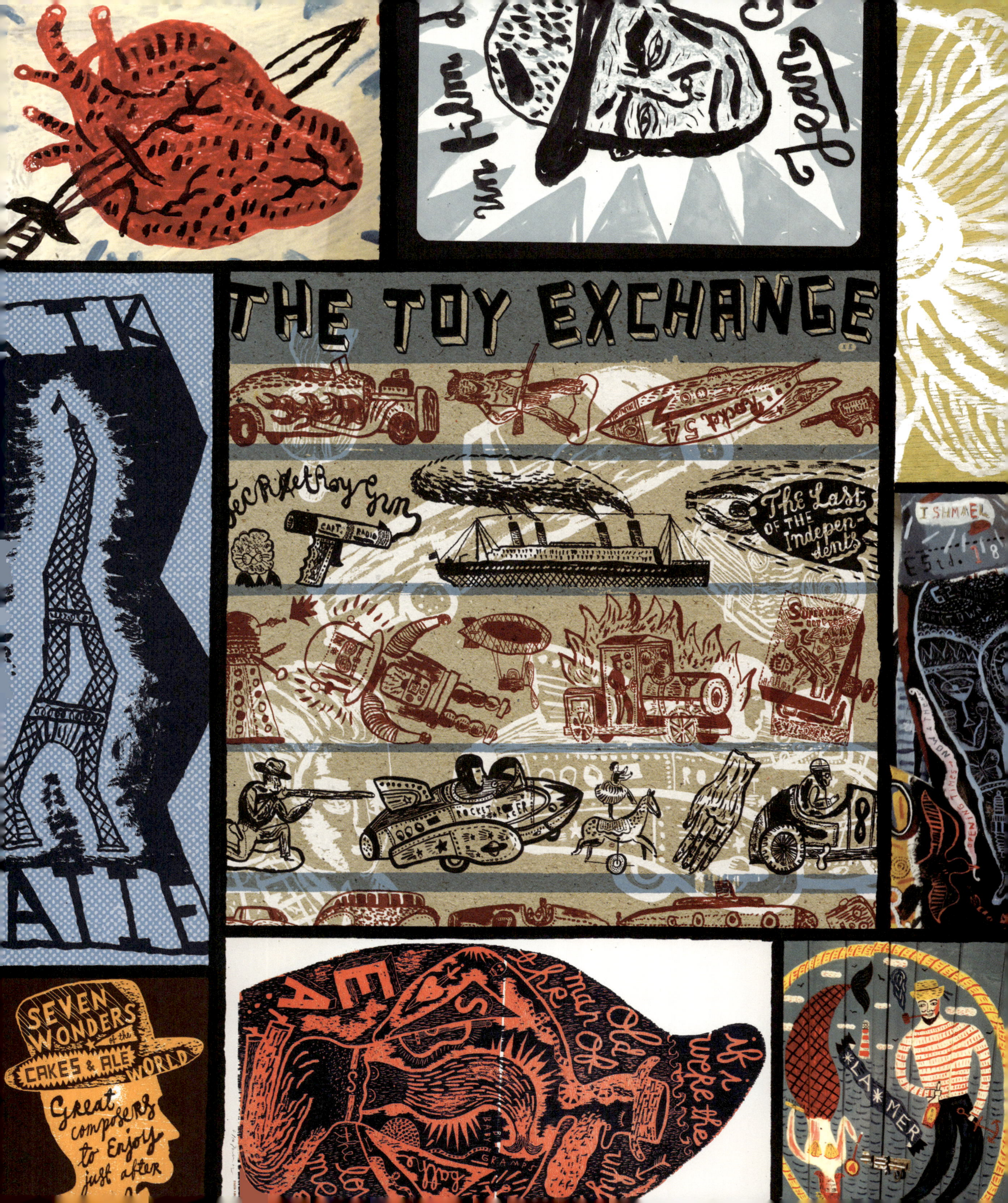

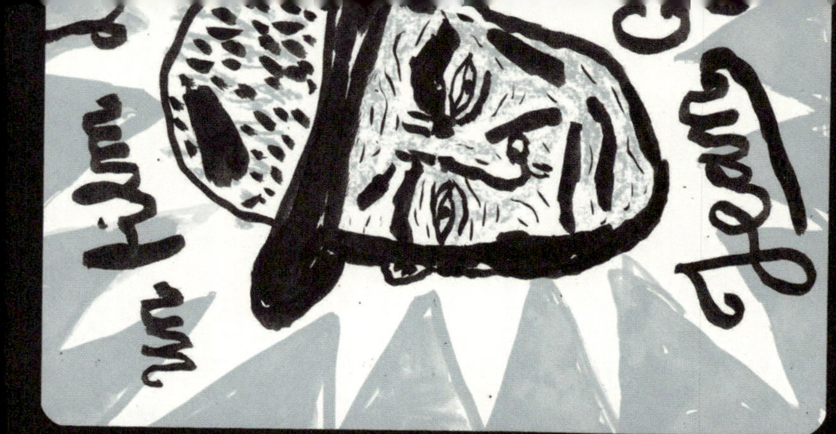

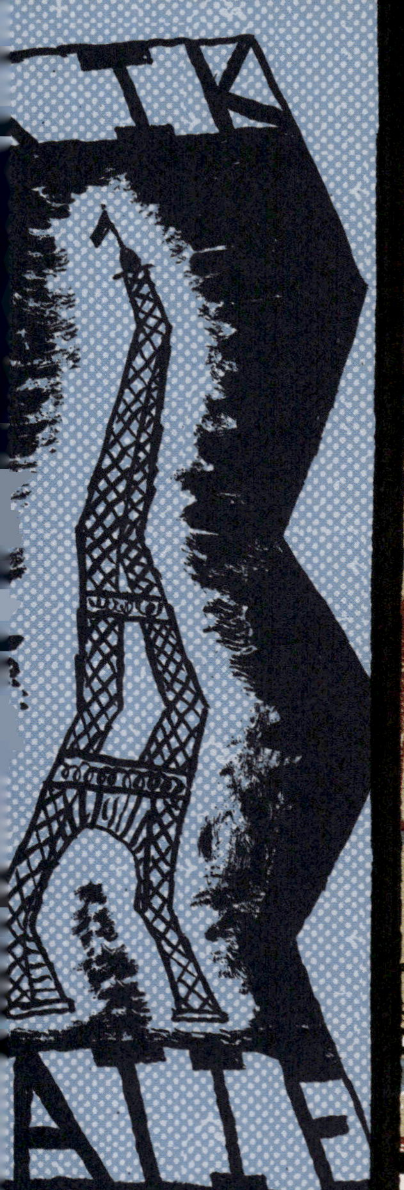

THE TOY EXCHANGE

Rocket 54

The Last of the Independents

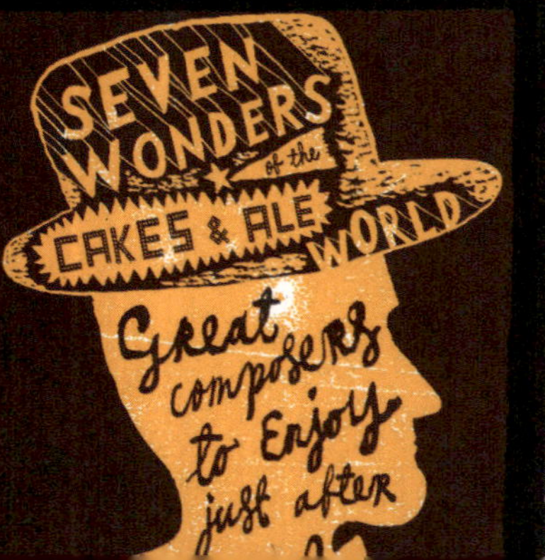


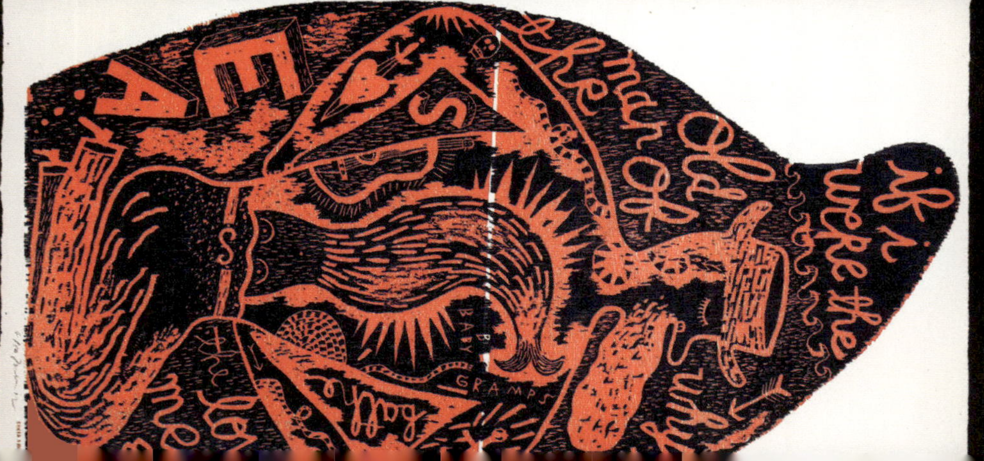

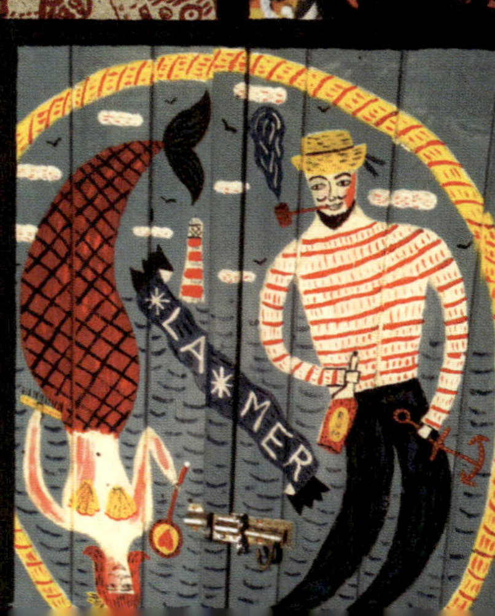

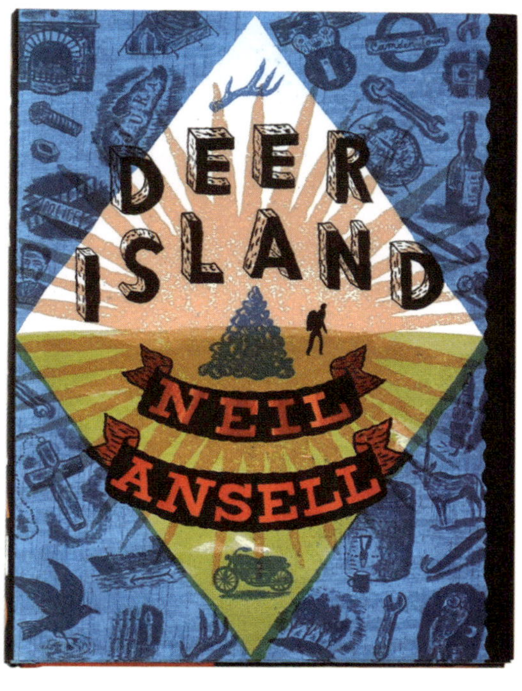


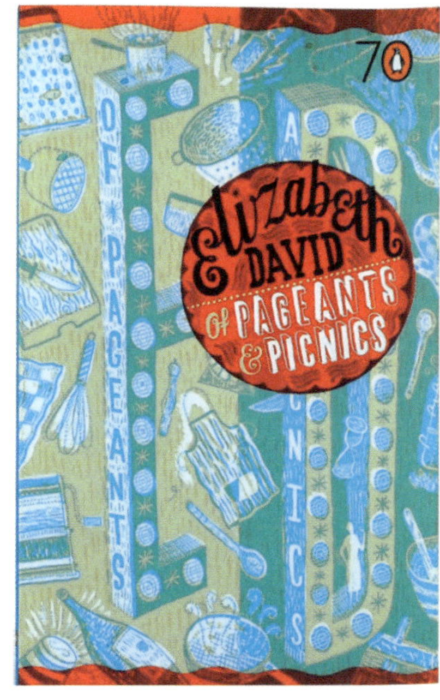


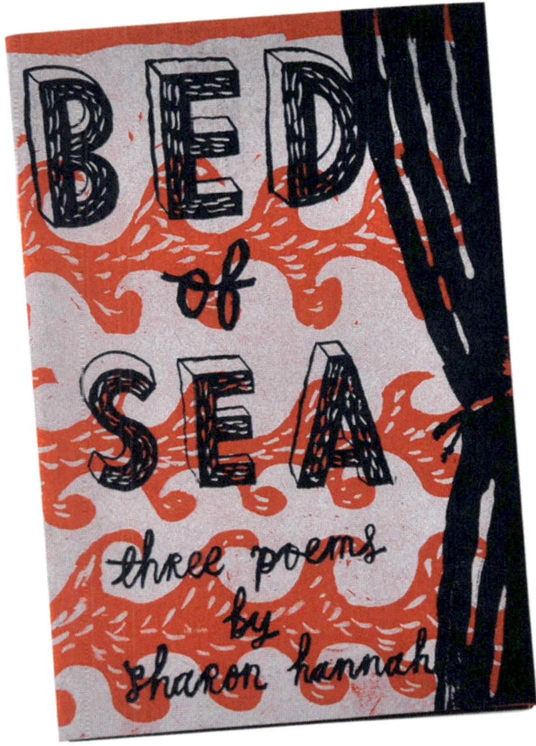


cesspool, a mire of love and death; a circle, unbroken. A great big plate of stovies. And it all has the soundtrack of a mix tape, equally varied and lacking the same continuity. Mad Dogs and Englishmen (I'm neither). Quel Temps fait-il à Paris? (It's about to rain). Tiptoe through the blues. *Flânez* among the *chansons*. Navigate your way through songs to sirens. Oceans of ballads that send Ouija messages to inform, entertain and warn. Roller coasters of emotional, honest words, designed to make you laugh and cry in unequal measures. A map turned upside down and taped back together so it will never truly make sense.

So step inside, have a peek. There's no right or wrong way to begin. But once you set off on this Lost Highway, there's no turning back. All roads lead to Darktown. At least, they do for me …

---

Three covers for three great publishers:
Little Toller, 2013; Penguin, 2005;
Cakes & Ale Press, 2009.

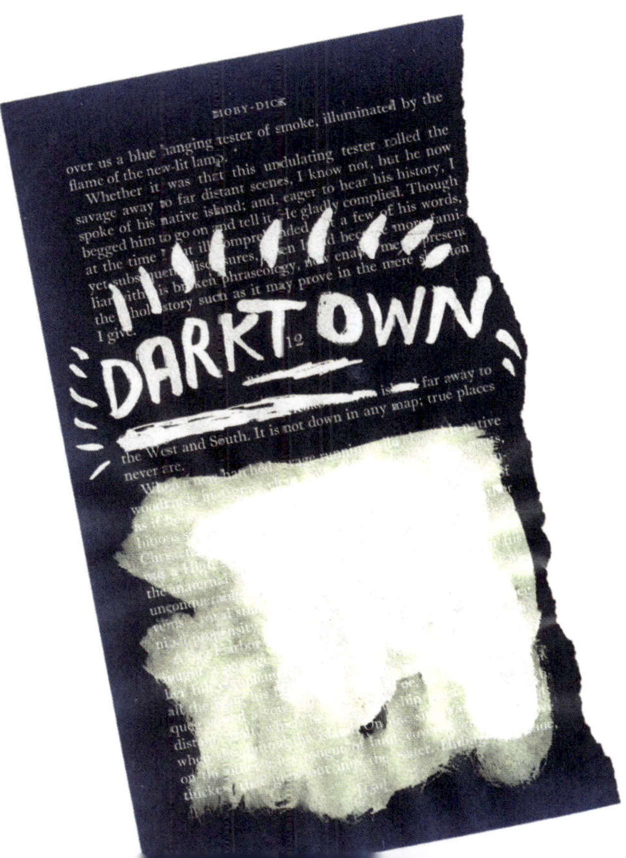

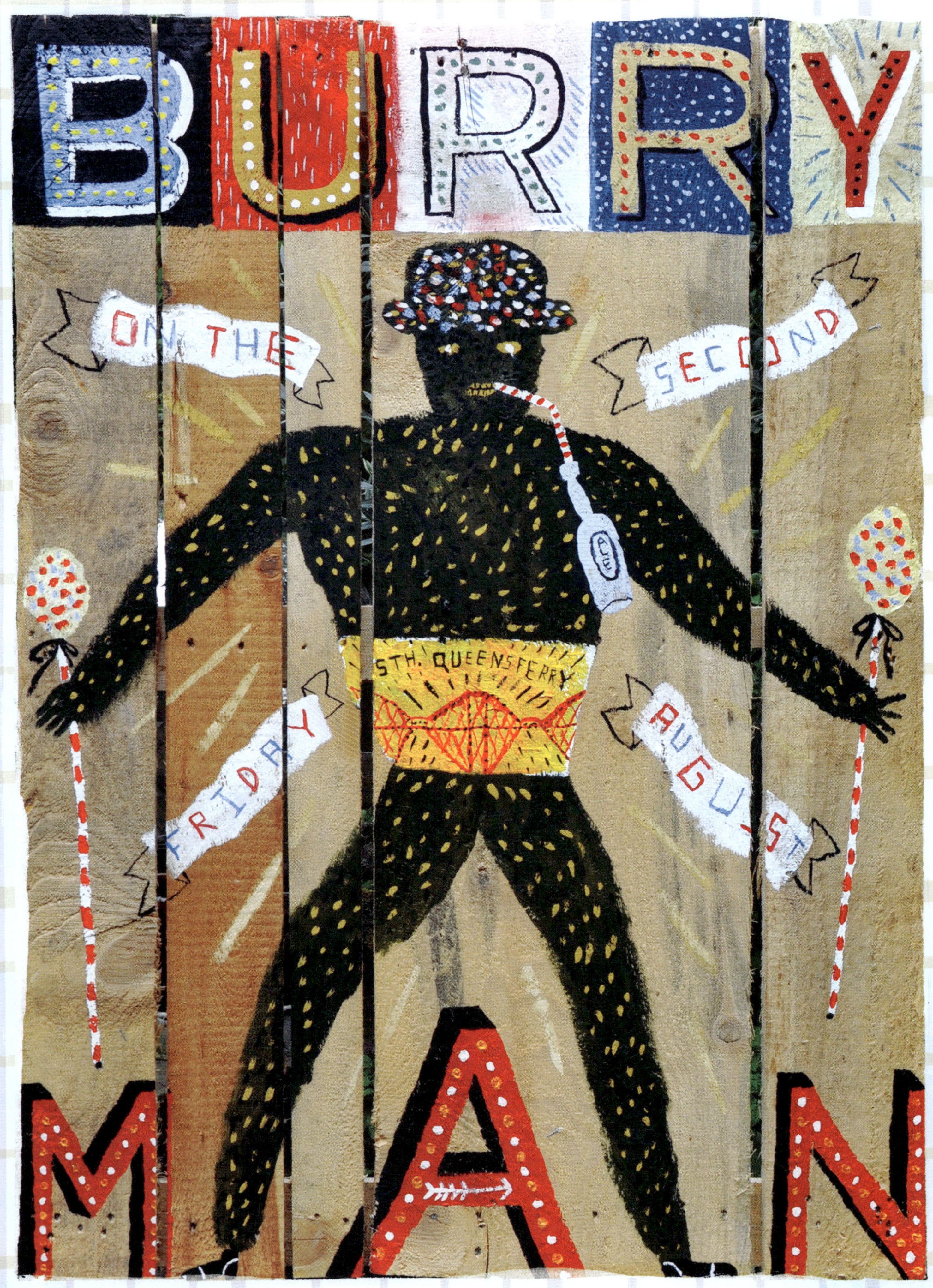
BURRY
ON THE
SECOND
FRIDAY
AUGUST
ALE
STH. QUEENSFERRY
MAN

# ANIMATING THE IMPOSSIBLE:
## THE ART OF JONNY HANNAH
## BY PHILIP HOARE

Jonny Hannah doesn't live in quite the same world as you and I. Oh, yes, he does apparently reside in a town on the south coast, rather far from the Scottish place that gave him birth. But in reality, in the world he has created, he wanders through the streets of somewhere entirely other, a collection of memories and impressions, bad jokes and strange birds, obscure books and cheap stores, long-dead singers and black-and-white movies. Hannah is not content with the ordinary, everyday world. He has to invent something different – or perhaps it is we who are the inventions.

Hannah's art is applied in the best sense. It bursts out of his brain and on to the page, on to wood, through a silk or even a computer screen. It is provincial, anachronistic, transatlantic, European, futuristic, international. Prolific, self-propagating, it is full of pattern and surface, sliding over entire time zones: from nineteenth-century sailors and whalers, through 1920s movies and French *nouvelle vague*, from smoky jazz dives in Harlem to salty promenades of semi-forgotten resorts and haunted ports.

Hannah's is a new vernacular, a folk art for the twenty-first century, entirely closed-in (almost claustrophobically so) yet far-ranging and unlimited by mere practicalities, for all that it is sourced in the apparently commonplace. It is somewhere on the edge of things, a place where the Burry Man is still paraded through the streets of South Queensferry, near Edinburgh, every August, a golem-like figure, surreally covered in burrs (from the burdock plant), who has to drink through a straw.

As in the case of other peculiar cults of British folk – such as the hobby horse of Padstow's May Day Cornish tradition, or the carved white chalk horses and other figures of the southern English downlands – one gets the impression that Hannah has merely animated the impossible, from the weirder margins of popular culture. His work is far removed from the quotidian demands of contemporary life, from reality television, uPVC windows and the digital coma that threatens to overcome us.

---

A pallet, courtesy of John Purcell Paper, seemed to have the right texture for this painting of the Burry Man, a folklore phenomenon from South Queensferry, in my original neck of the woods. Simon Costin bought it for the collection of the Museum of British Folklore at an exhibition at Hornseys, Ripon, in 2011.

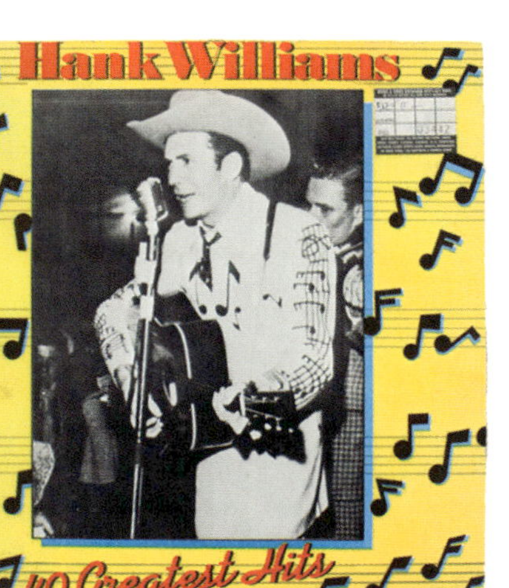


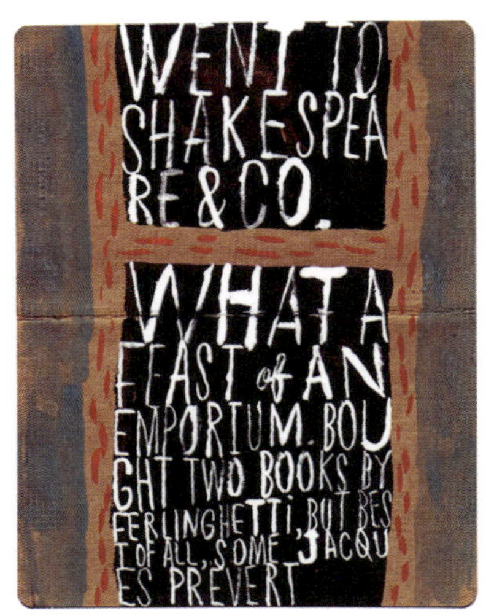


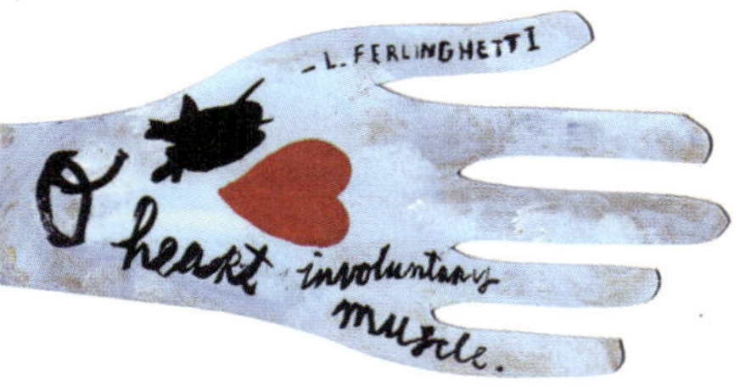


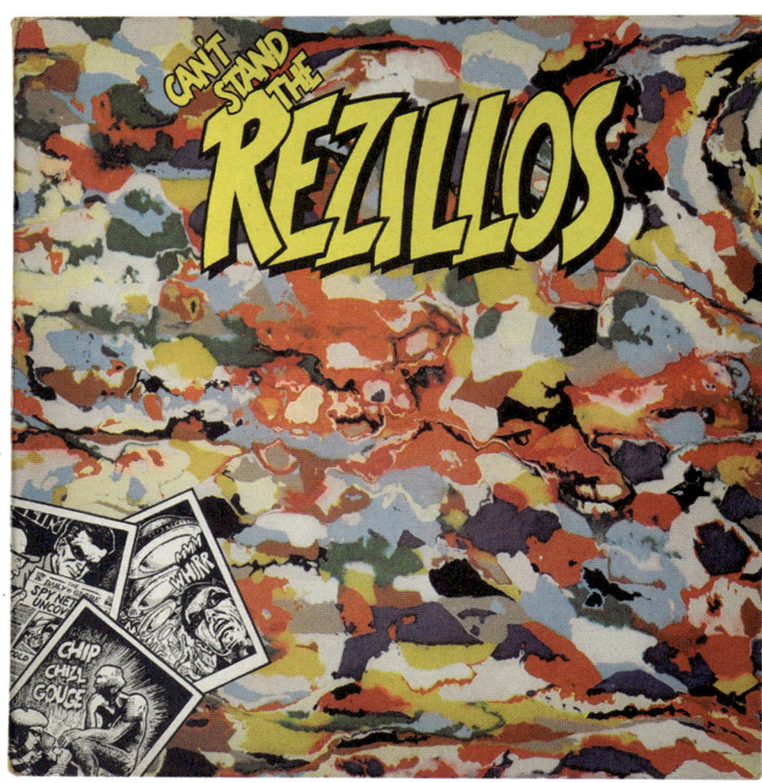


I've never actually seen Hannah's place of work, but I imagine his art to be made in a shed, spilling over with ink and imagination, bespattered rare copies of Herman Melville and Charles Bukowski editions to hand, crumbed with fruitcake and stained with tea and whisky; the whiff of the intangible past as re-imagined in an indie ethic. Hannah's Scottishness puts me in mind of the make-do aesthetic of such post-punk record labels as Postcard and Fast Product, with their own intangible links to obscure pop culture. Indeed, one of his favourite bands is, or was, The Rezillos, a frenetic, comic-strip Scottish creation born of punk into sci-fi kitsch, fronted by the mini-skirted and Sixties-made-up lead singer Fay Fife and Eugene 'Don't touch that dial' Reynolds, in ever-present wrap-round shades.

Be in no doubt, Hannah's is an analogue, retro, vintage, vinyl, tweed and buffed-leather world. It rejoices in textures and references, the then and the now, all mashed up and assimilated into Darktown's eerie alleys and arcane establishments. It is a little utopia of its own, somewhere you might reach through the lanes of a Paul Nash or an Eric Ravilious landscape, via Peter Blake, along Route 66, in the company of Charlie Parker and Hank Williams. I'm sure Jonny Hannah must have been there when Roy Rogers rode his horse Trigger through the lobby of the grand South Western Hotel in Southampton as a publicity stunt. (I'm also reminded of the plangent Scottish taste for country and western music, with an underlying sense of the mordant, if not the gothic. It is no coincidence that among Jonny's favourite short stories are those of M.R. James and their 1970s television adaptations.)

Hannah's is a pop-art, twenty-first-century update on the neo-romantics of the 1930s and 40s, the same spirit in which Sir Clough Williams-Ellis created the architectural fantasy village of Portmeirion – famously the setting for the archly mysterious 1960s TV series *The Prisoner*. There is much of the seaside and the salty air in Hannah's work; a little of *Brighton Rock*, perhaps; the tragic heroine, the bathetic plot. Certainly, it is no coincidence that he has set up shop in a south coast port. That sense of fluidity, of coming and going, of jaunty airs and darker intent, suits his purposes.

Every image that Hannah creates has its own narrative; each picture and illustration and assemblage is its own short story. If he weren't an artist, Hannah would be a

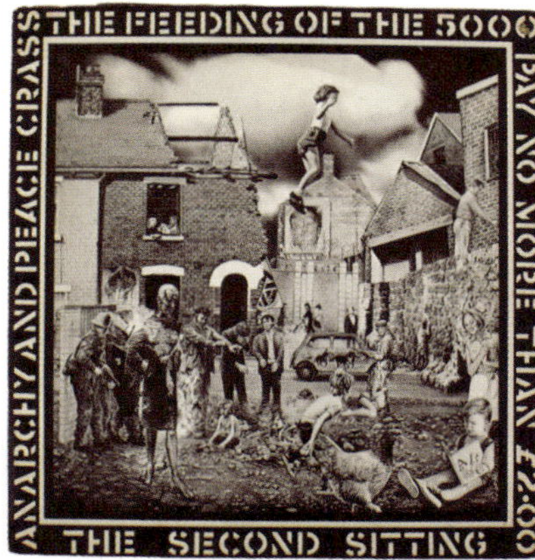


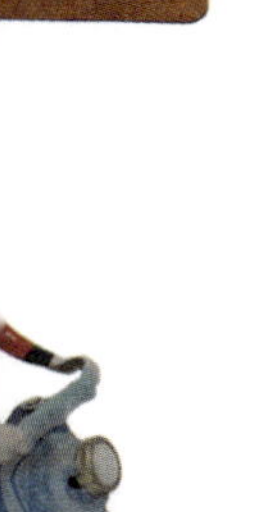

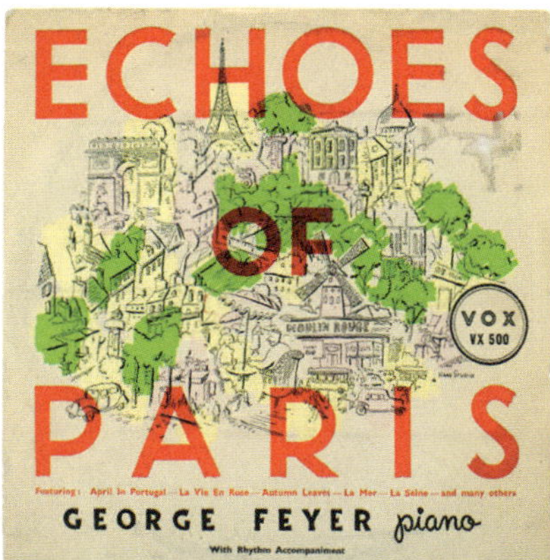


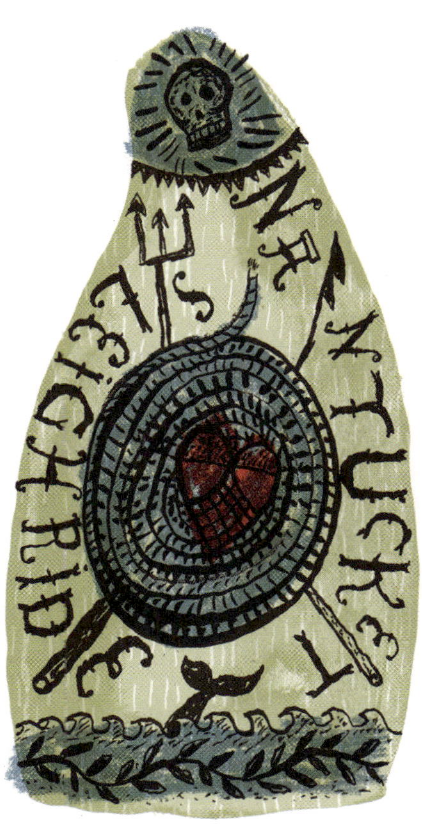


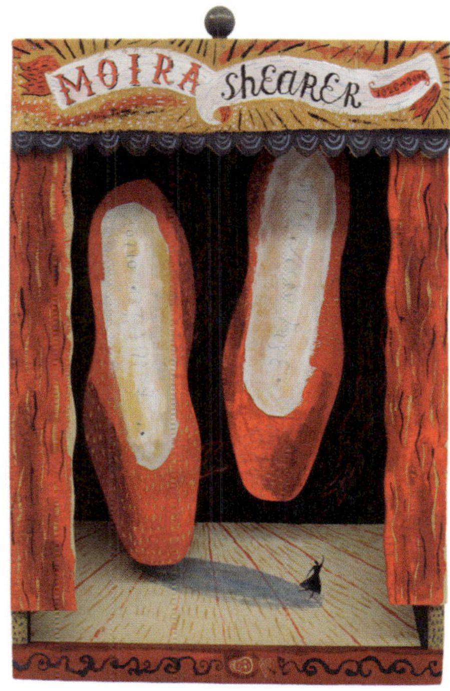


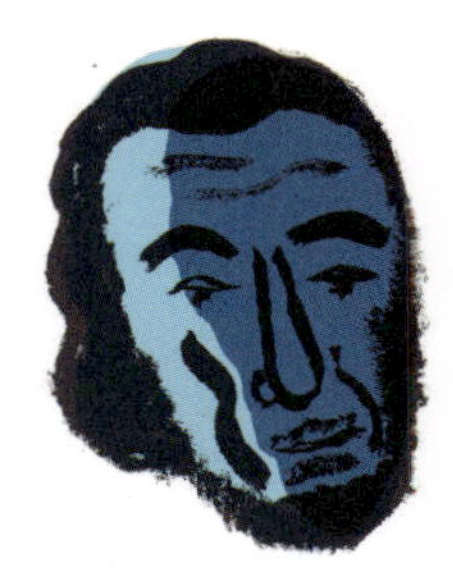

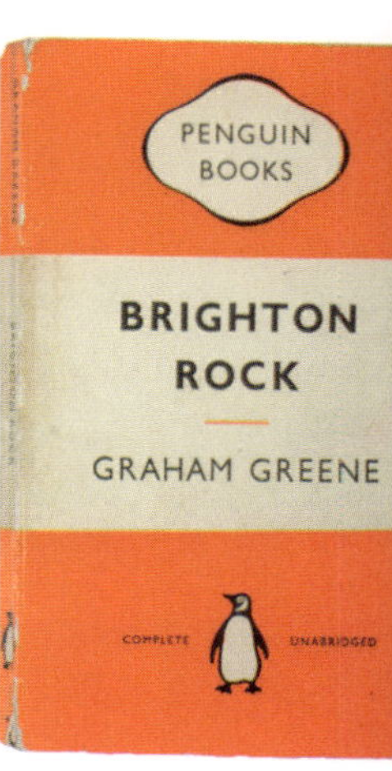


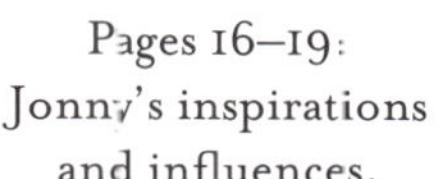
Pages 16–19:
Jonny's inspirations
and influences.

writer or a British version of the French *flâneur*, a dandy figure wandering the streets in search of new sensation. He is the only man I know who can wear co-respondent shoes with conviction. In another life, he might have strolled the streets of 1940s Soho in the company of Julian Maclaren-Ross (himself sporting a silver-topped cane and a teddy-bear fur coat). Along the way, passing posters of pin-up girls and celebrated boxers, they might meet up with Jean Vigo, Moira Shearer or Gene Kelly. But Hannah is only a shade in such company, since he is also a puppet-master, a Hitchcock directing his charges to perform his will.

Above all, it is his love of the typographic that runs through Hannah's work, drawn from past decades of packaging, styling, decoration and advertising, from shop signs to beer-bottle labels, from scrimshaw to psalters, from vintage toys to dead men's suits. Propagated through his Cakes & Ale Press, posters, graphics and wooden sculptures, his characteristic typefaces are woven through his pieces as a continuing theme: a Victorian or Edwardian sampler, a Powell and Pressburger film, a sideshow at the Festival of Britain, a speakeasy in New York. Both transatlantic and European, there's an element of Dadaism at work here, too – especially the collages of Kurt Schwitters. Perhaps Hannah might yet create his own *Merzbau* in his Southampton suburb.

Minimal it is not: Hannah's world revolves around his fertile, magpie imagination, picking up that which history and our contemporary culture have left behind. His is the jumble sale, all those things in our remote and recent past that we thought had been forgotten, yet which tumble out of Jonny Hannah's head and into a world he has created anew. His imagination might be graphic, but

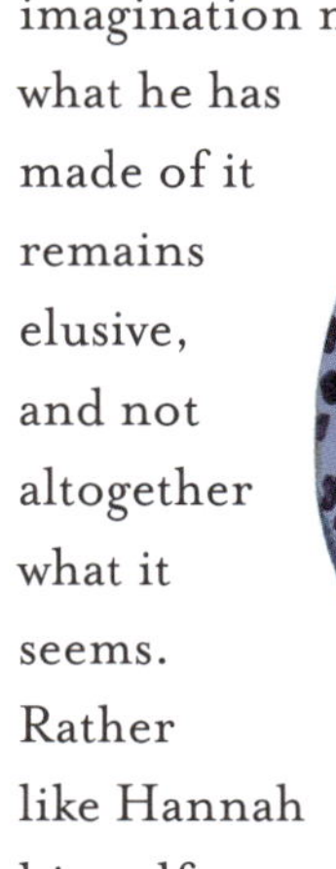
what he has made of it remains elusive, and not altogether what it seems. Rather like Hannah himself.

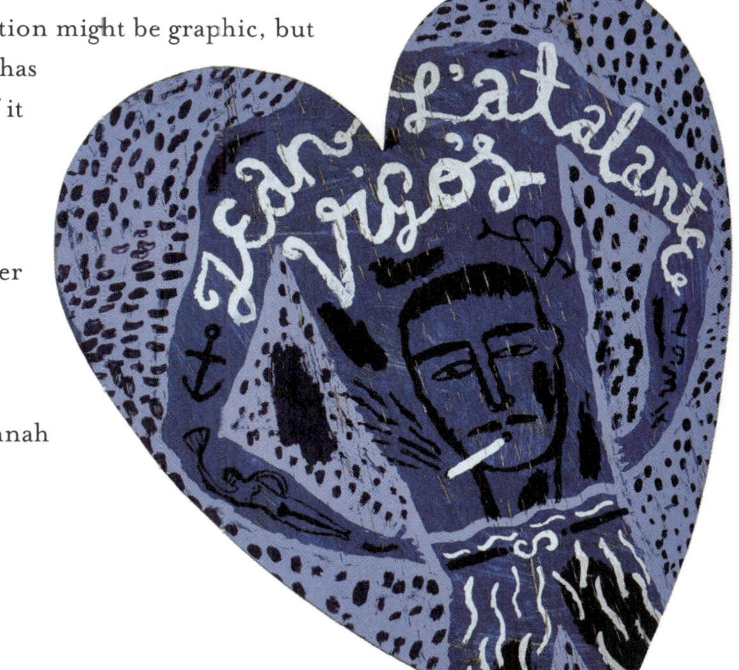

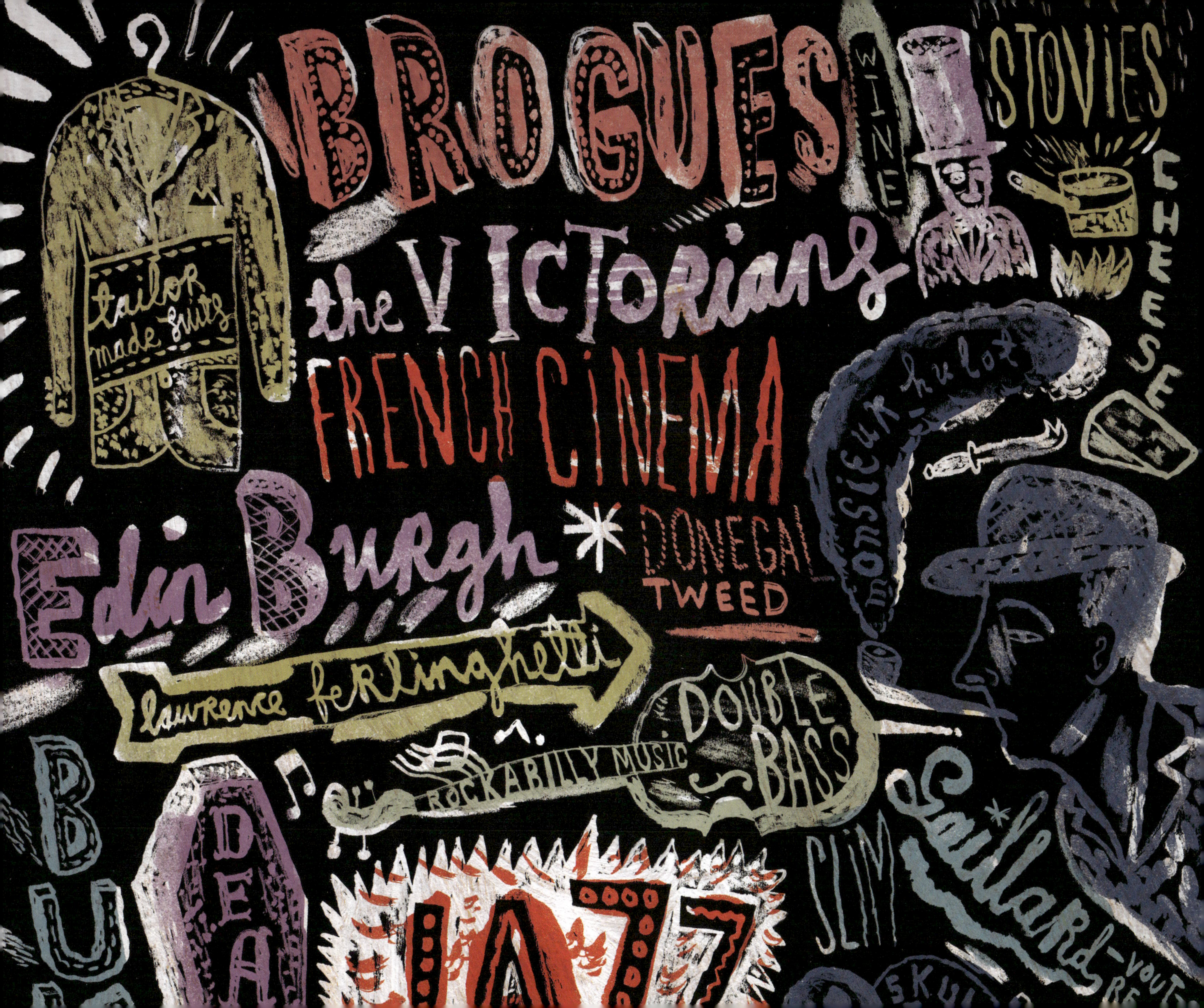

BROGUES
WINE
STOVIES
CHEESE
tailor made suits
the VICTORIANS
FRENCH CINEMA
EdinBurgh
DONEGAL TWEED
lawrence ferlinghetti
DOUBLE BASS
ROCKABILLY MUSIC
SLIM
Gaillard

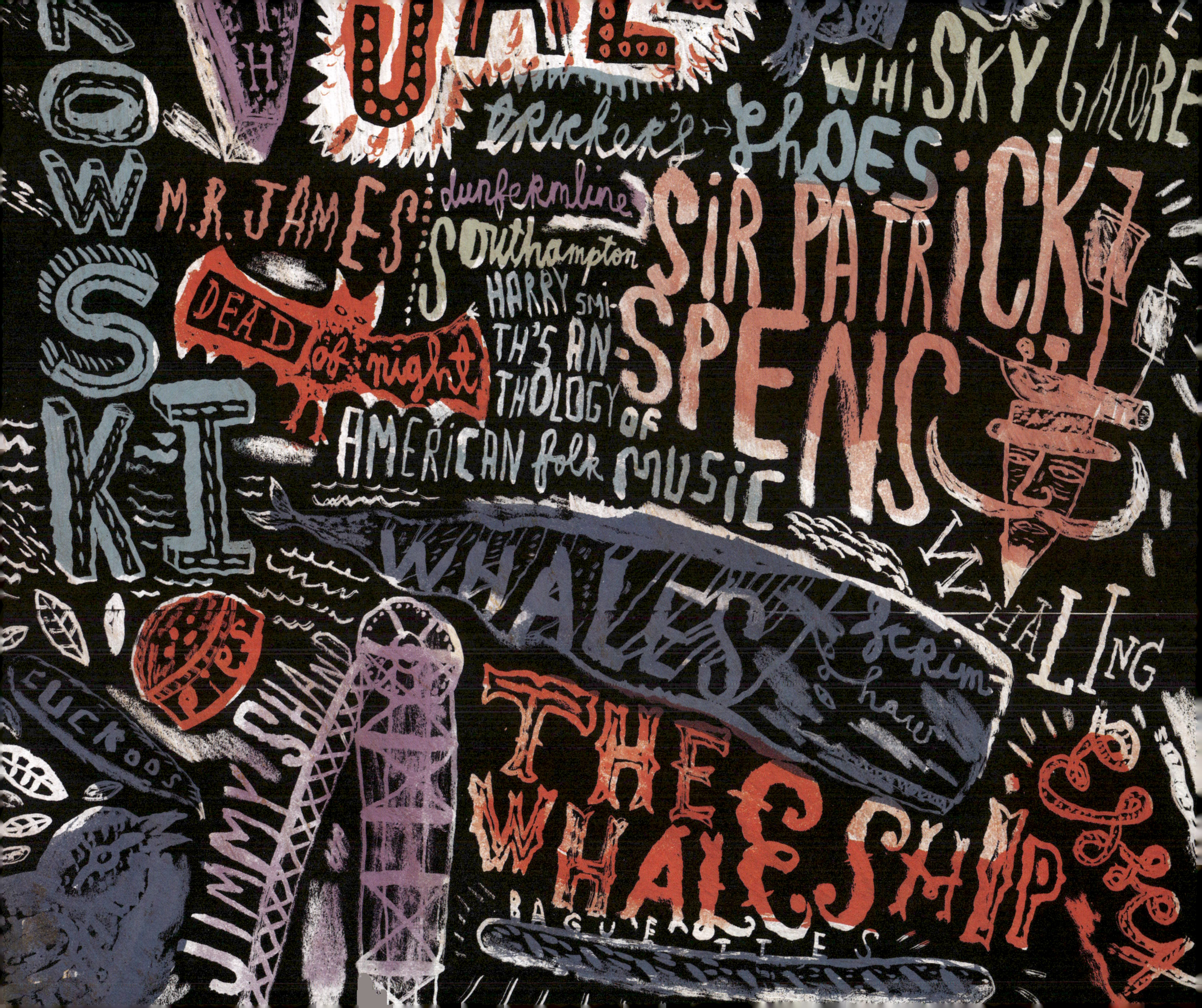

WHISKY GALORE
brucker's shoes
M.R. JAMES
dunfermline
Southampton
HARRY SMITH'S ANTHOLOGY OF AMERICAN folk MUSIC
DEAD of night
SIR PATRICK SPENS
WHALING
WHALES
scrimshaw
THE WHALE SHIP
BAGUETTES
JIMMY SHAND
CUCKOOS

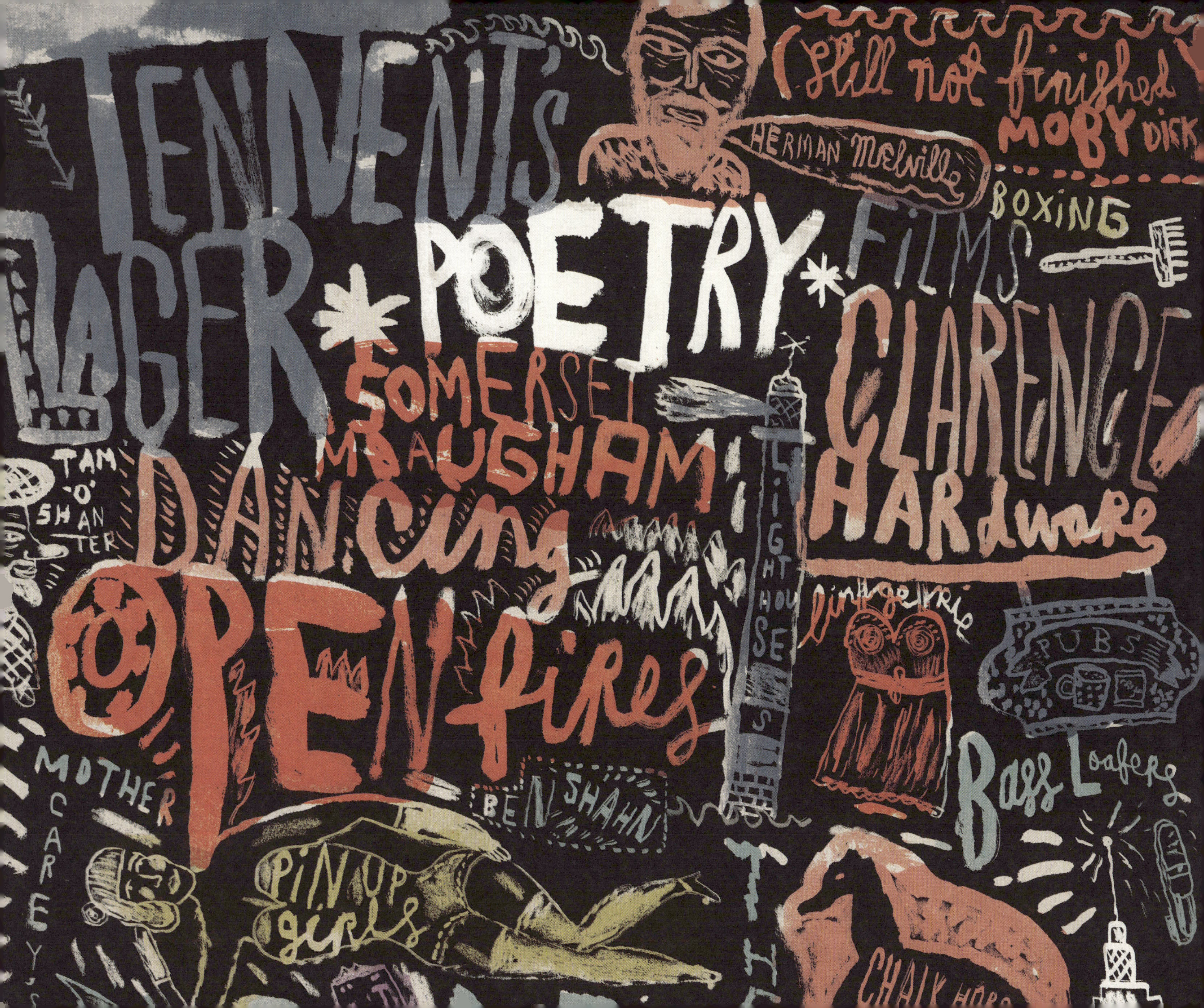

TENNENT'S LAGER
(Still not finished
MOBY DICK
HERMAN Melville
BOXING
POETRY
FILMS
CLARENCE
HARdware
SOMERSET MAUGHAM
DANcing
OPEN fires
TAM 'O' SHANTER
LIGHTHOUSES
PUBS
Bass Loafers
BEN SHAHN
MOTHER CAREY'S
PIN UP girls

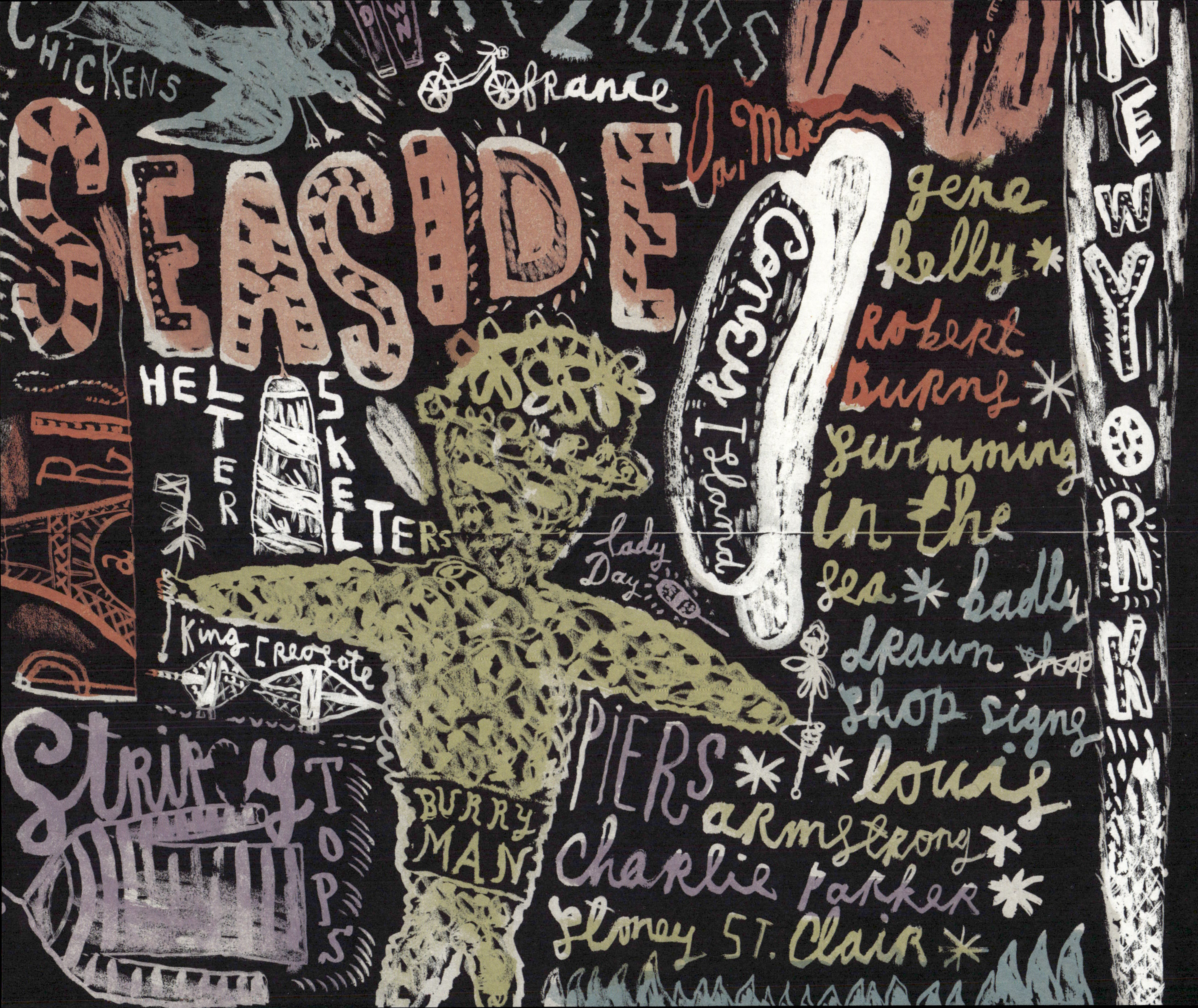
CHICKENS
france
la Mer
SEASIDE
HELTER SKELTERS
Coney Island
gene kelly
robert burns
swimming in the sea
badly drawn shop signs
louis armstrong
charlie parker
stoney st. clair
lady Day
King Creosote
PIERS
BURRY MAN
Stripy TOPS
NEW YORK

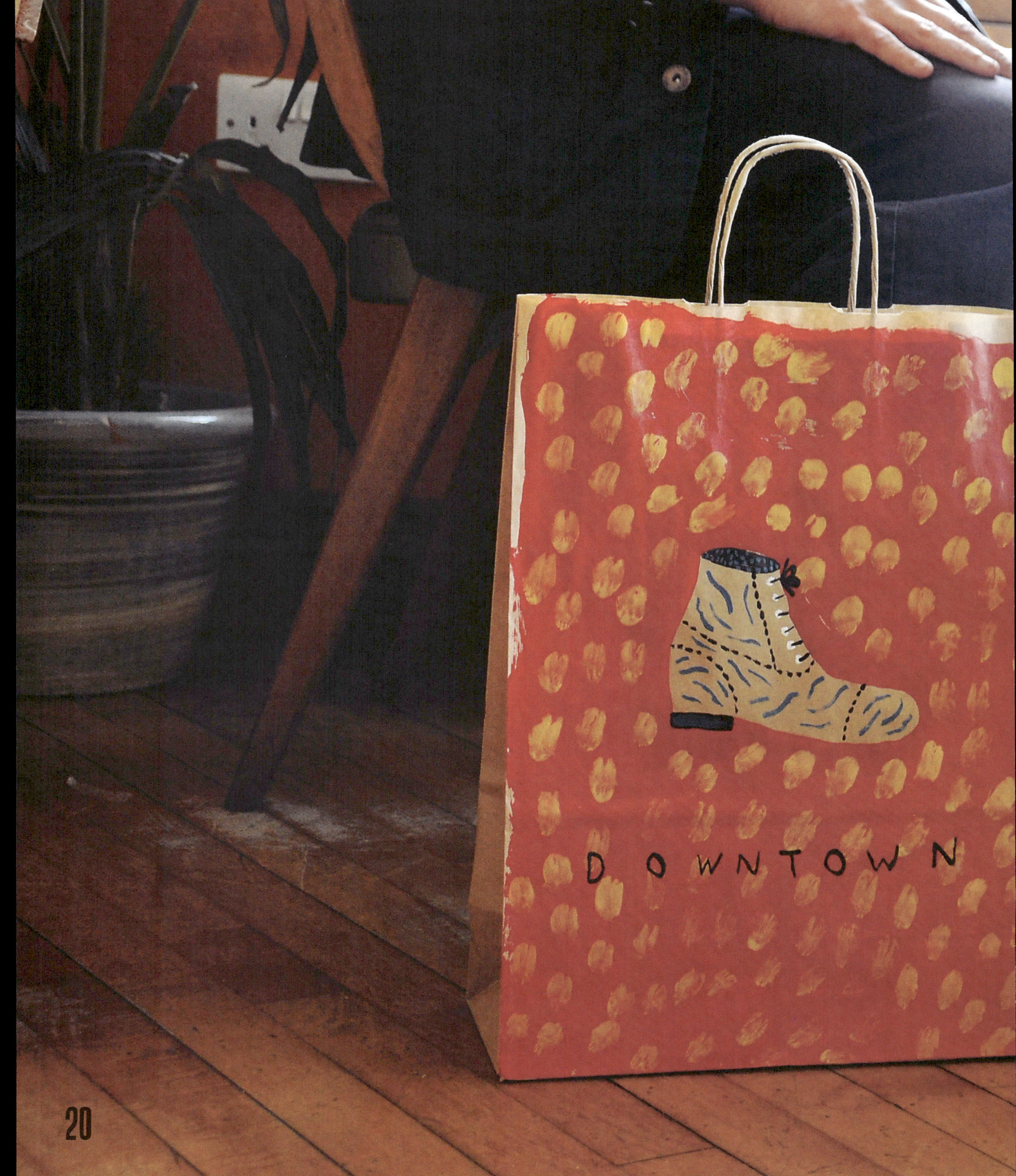
DOWNTOWN

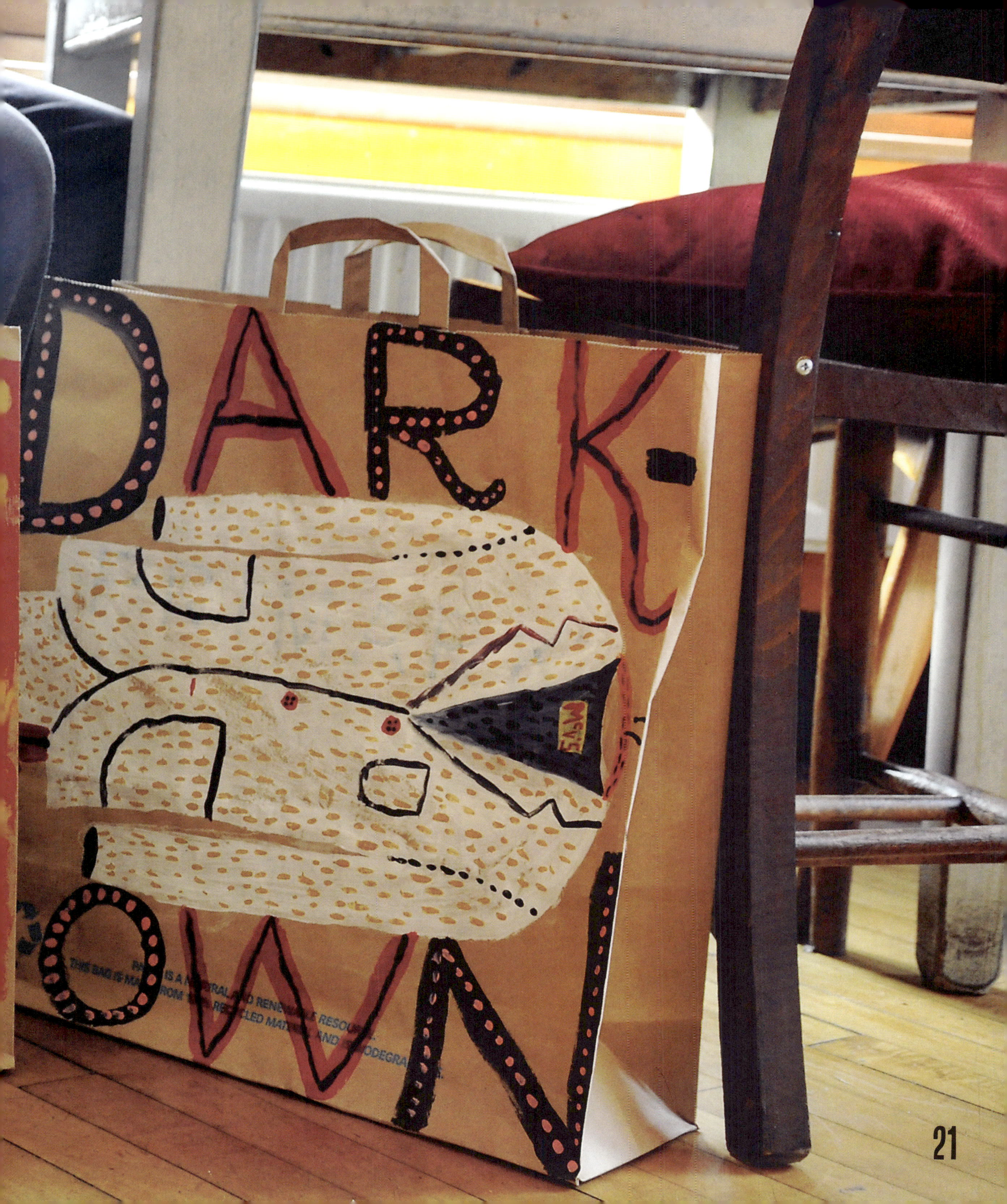
DARK-
OWN

# DOWNTOWN DARKTOWN

Oh, the wonders of a high street. Go to your nearest one. Among the cheap shoe shops and opticians, there'll be treasures to uncover. I grew up in a town where such streets and braes held marvels. The magic of Miss Kay Bruce's half-toy, half-sweetie shop. Bright-blue denims from Donaldson's, otherwise known as 'the household'. These days, it might not be the same ('It were better back then' – or was it?), but there's still magic in the air of any parade of shops, and nowhere more so than the main street in Darktown.

It began when the Mermaid Café relocated from Coney Island. It's nothing fancy, mind. Just good, old-fashioned grub, great coffee and a soupçon of exotica, such as carbolic milkshakes. Woody Guthrie still plays most Sunday afternoons, and it's never too busy. Then McVouty arrived with his smorgasbord of second-hand quality goods. His top-notch vintage clothing collection was best of all, though: traditional guayabera shirts, Pendleton Hollywood jackets, even knitted bow ties. He kitted out the entire hipster population of Darktown, then moved on to the squares too, of which there are very few.

As news spread of this more-than-ordinary main street, other shops arrived. Owen Coffin opened another of his chandler's; Clarence Hardware too, selling only the finest foam, cut to size for any caravan. Chinaski's Poetry Store does decent business, but as long as he has enough money for cigarettes and wine, he's not too bothered either way. Many of his chapbooks and pamphlets are churned out at Ole Whitman's Print Shop. Then there's the Black Shuck Bookshop, with extra-special books on folklore, hoodoo men and other jiggery-pokery. The shopping experience that Darktown offers is truly exceptional. You just never know what you'll find.

Emmett Miller's Unquiet Grave has to be the bee's knees, though. People travel from miles around to see what this old minstrel keeps, and they are rarely disappointed. Legend has it, this is where Hank Williams bought his deck of cards and jug of wine before that last Cadillac ride. Vivian Maier buys her black-and-white camera film only here. And Harry Smith left his entire 78 rpm collection to old Emmett when he moved into the Chelsea Hotel, so there are top tunes to boot, every time you rummage through the boxes and shelves.

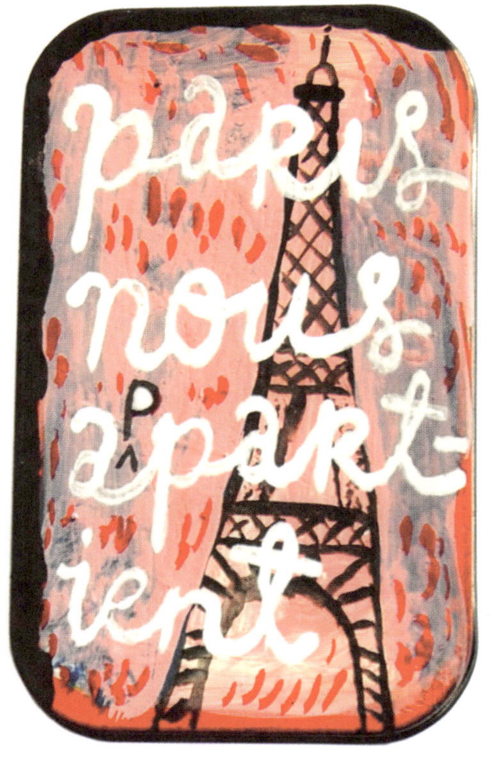


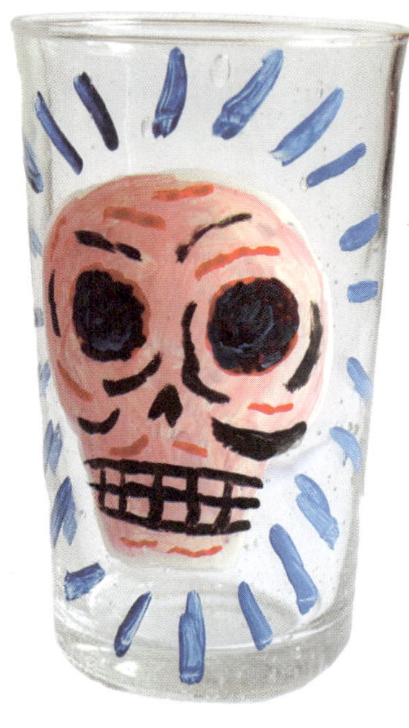

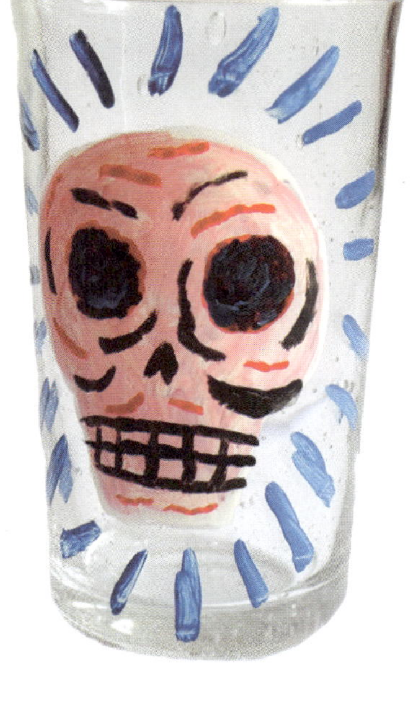

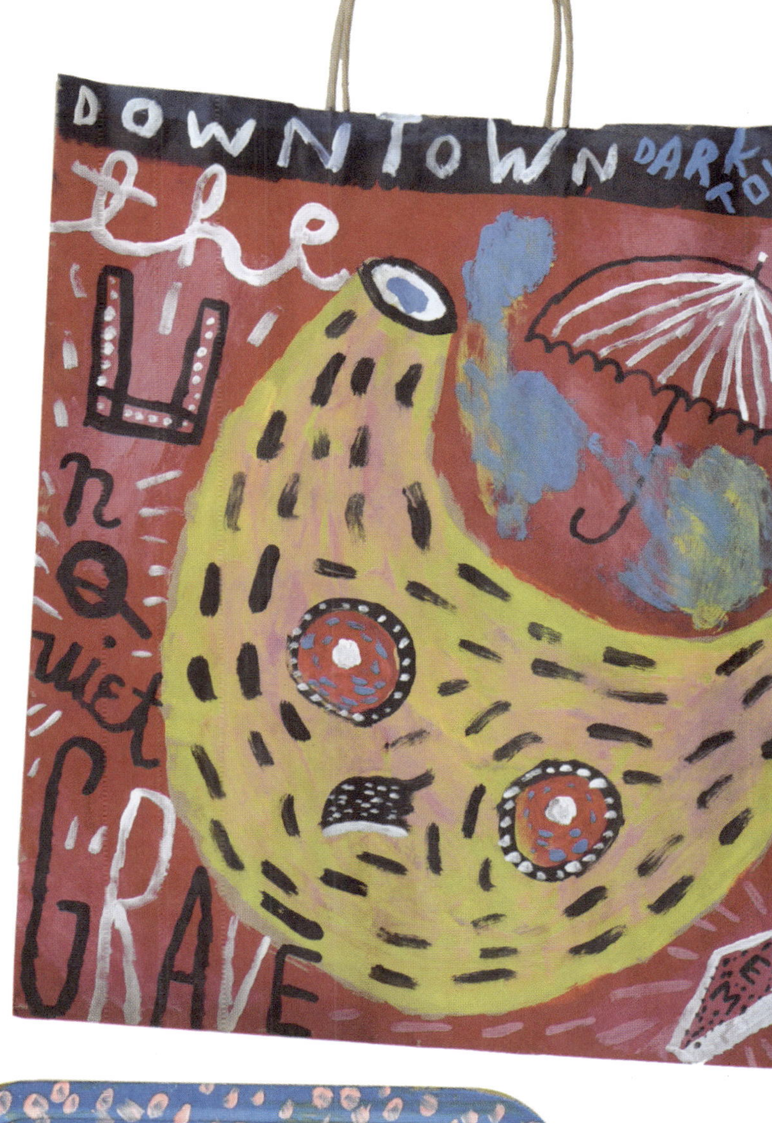


The Unquiet Grave first opened some time ago in Smithville, where there's a constant air of gloom and the chilly winds most certainly blow. Emmett moved, as he needed the fresh sea air that Darktown offers. The fact that Jane Russell owns the apartment upstairs probably also had something to do with it. Jacques Tourneur runs the Roxy Cinema. Henry Thomas owns the bait and tackle store, to help you lose those fishin' blues. Fresh scallops and the like may be found at the Cullen Skink Fishmongery. Just around the corner from my teeny wee house is the Jolly Scrimshander Tavern. It has all you could want from a bar, even live music now and again. Roy Smeck and Baby Gramps are never shy, and will happily entertain anyone who'll listen. The bigger acts often play the Starlight Hotel. But if it's complete, enjoyable silence you want, and a great bowl of mussels, Hulot's Hôtel de la Plage is the place to go after a hard day. And it's ideal if, like me, you love to look out at the sea.

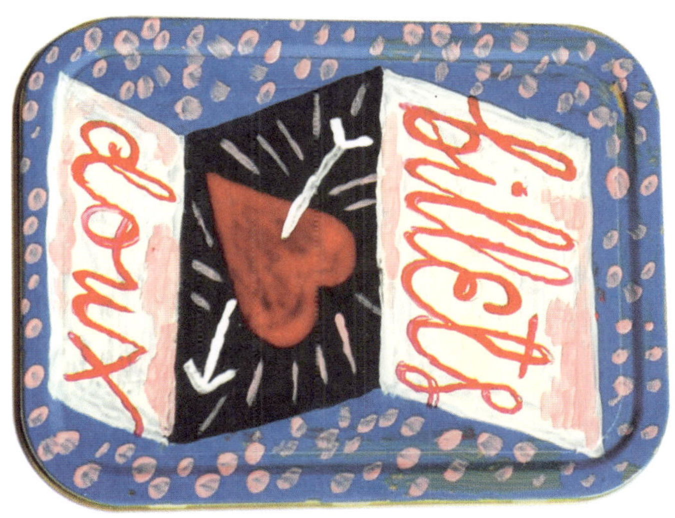


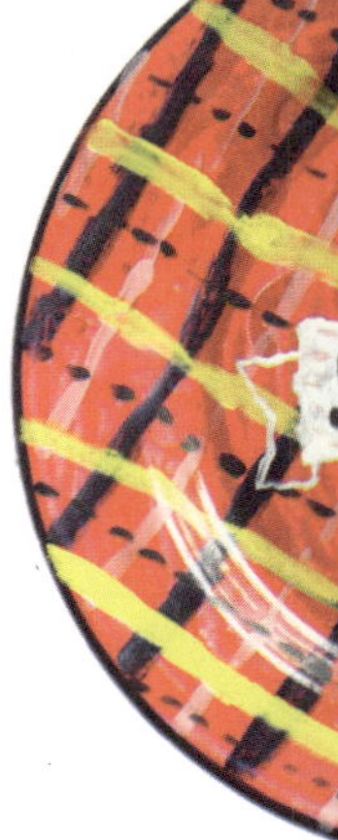

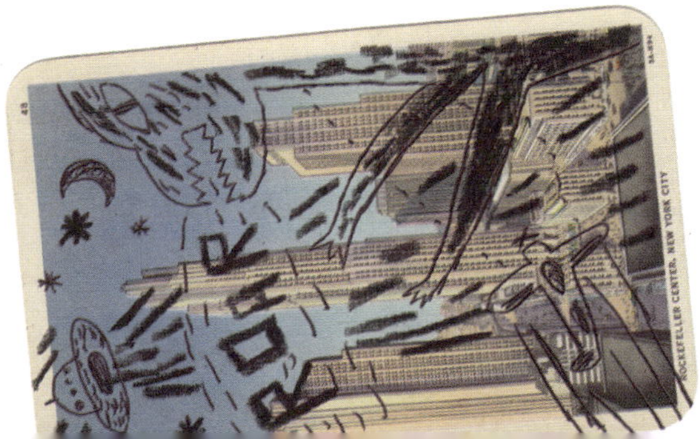

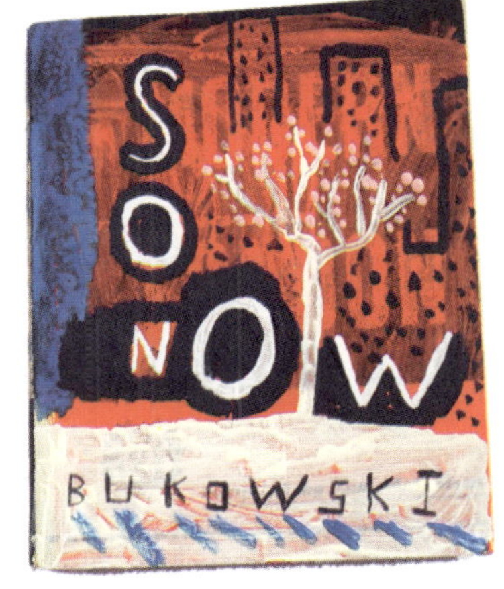

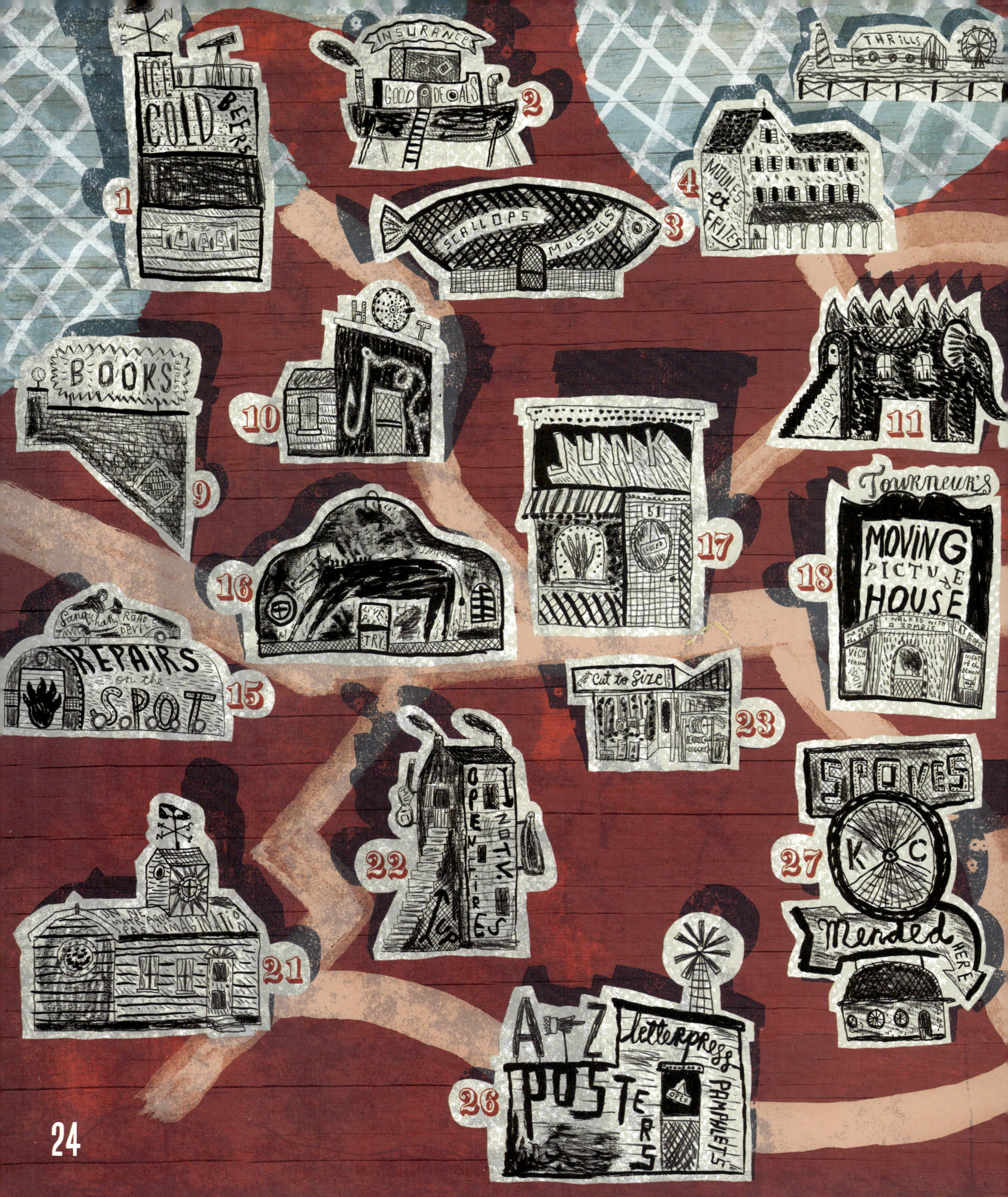
ICE COLD BEERS
1
INSURANCE
GOOD DEALS
2
THRILLS
MOULES et FRIES
4
SCALLOPS
MUSSELS
3
HOT
BOOKS
10
9
11
JUNK
51
CLOSED
17
16
TRY
Tourneur's
MOVING PICTURE HOUSE
I WALKED WITH A ZOMBIE
18
REPAIRS on the SPOT
15
Cut to Size
23
SPOKES
K C
Mended HERE
27
OPEN FIRES
22
21
A–Z
letterpress
POSTERS
PAMPHLETS
OPEN
26

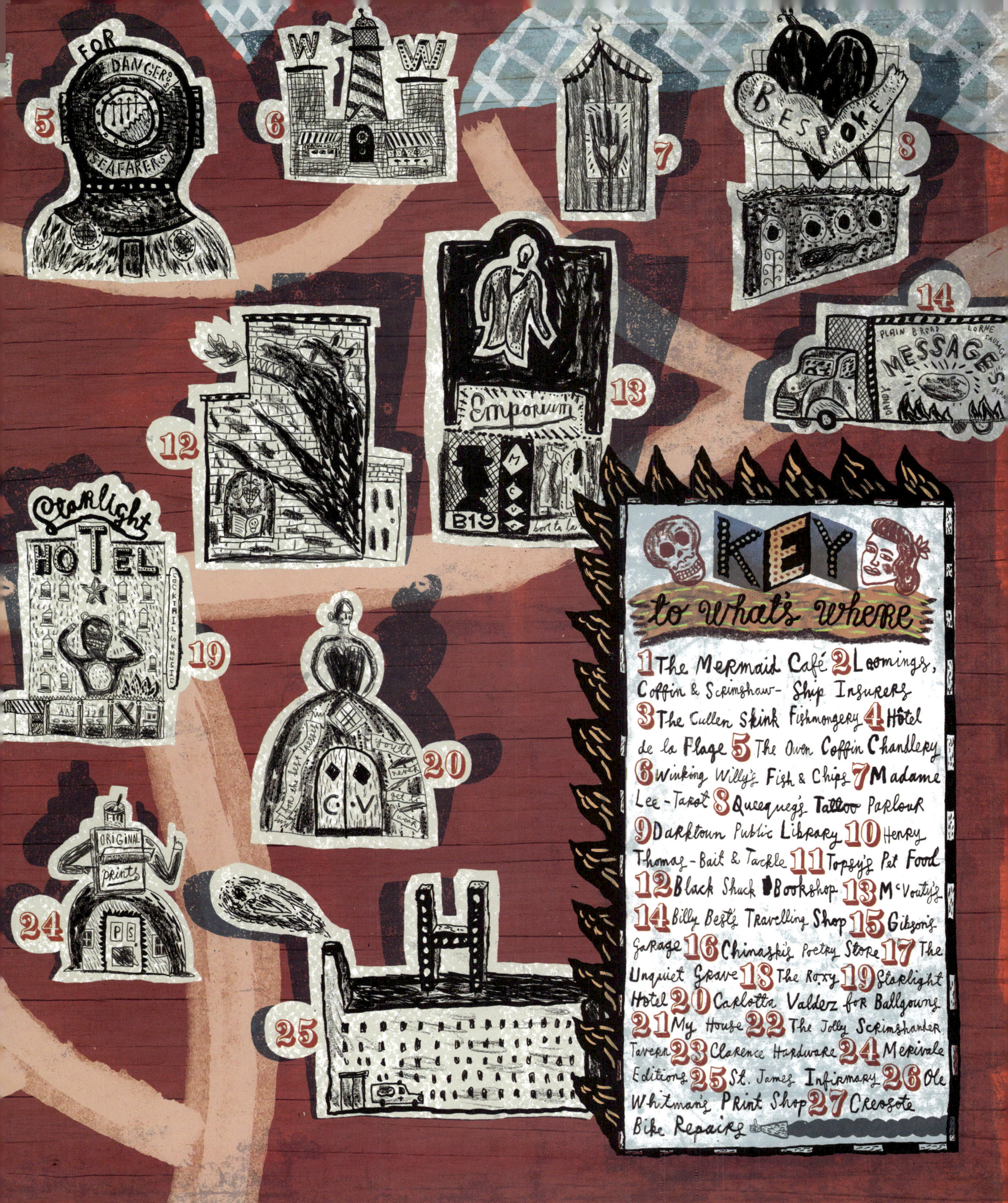

FOR DANGERS SEAFARERS
5
W W
6
7
BESPOKE
8
14
PLAIN BREAD
LORNE SAUSAGE
MESSAGES
DANDY
13
Emporium
B19
12
Starlight HOTEL
19
20
C V
ORIGINAL prints
PS
24
25
KEY
to what's where
1 The Mermaid Café
2 Loomings, Coffin & Scrimshaw - Ship Insurers
3 The Cullen Skink Fishmongery
4 Hôtel de la Plage
5 The Owen Coffin Chandlery
6 Winking Willy's Fish & Chips
7 Madame Lee - Tarot
8 Queequeg's Tattoo Parlour
9 Darktown Public Library
10 Henry Thomas - Bait & Tackle
11 Topsy's Pet Food
12 Black Shuck Bookshop
13 McVouty's
14 Billy Best's Travelling Shop
15 Gibson's Garage
16 Chinaski's Poetry Store
17 The Unquiet Grave
18 The Roxy
19 Starlight Hotel
20 Carlotta Valdez for Ballgowns
21 My House
22 The Jolly Scrimshander Tavern
23 Clarence Hardware
24 Merivale Editions
25 St. James Infirmary
26 Ole Whitman's Print Shop
27 Creosote Bike Repairs

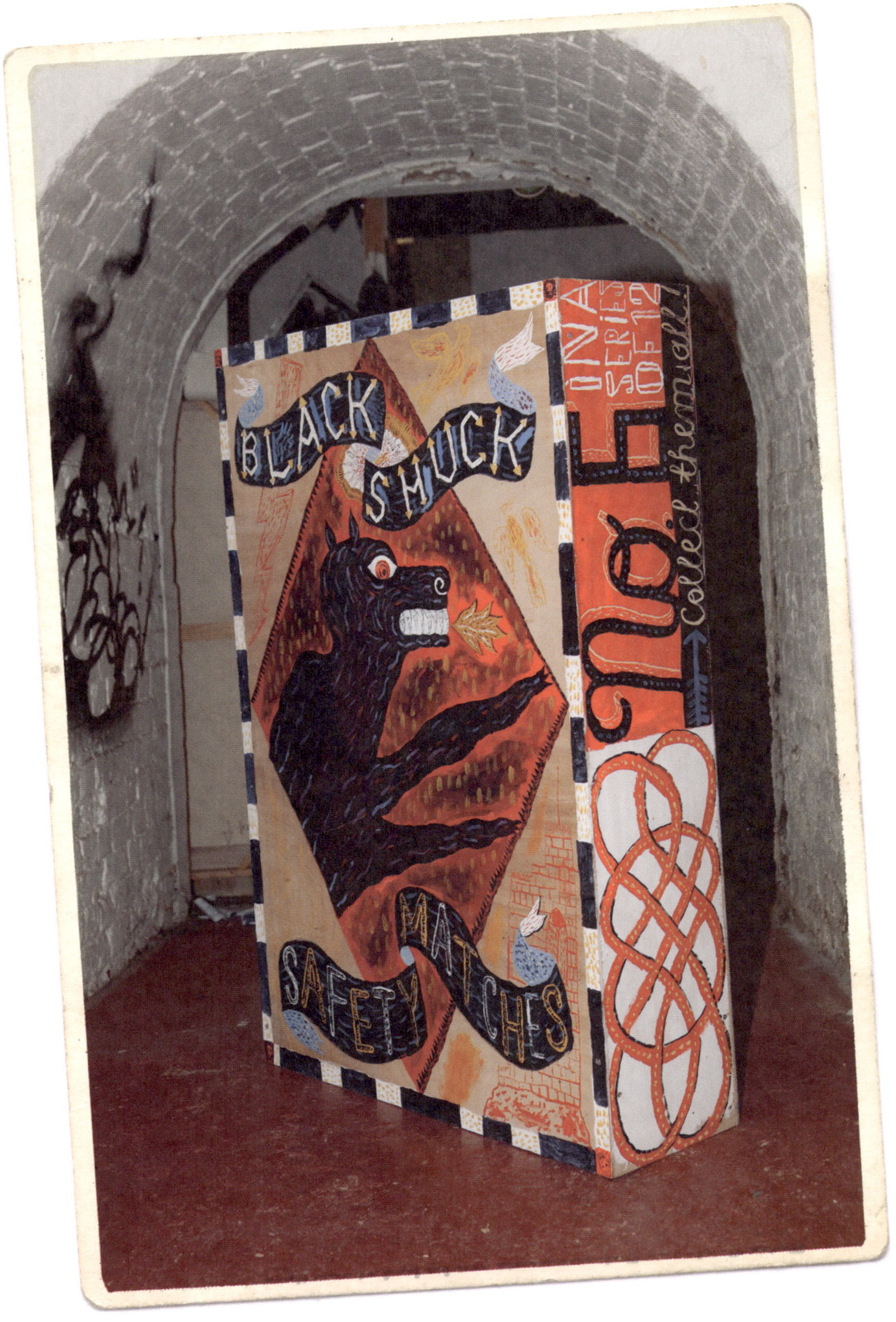


To commemorate the umpteenth anniversary of Darktown's existence, the local White Horse Matchbox Company produced twelve larger-than-life matchboxes – this being the Black Shuck one – often seen around the town.

GABBA-GABBA-HEY!
Music Car
Music Car
All Stars
CENTURY BUS
8
Miss Kay BRUCE for
TIN TOYS
DUNFERMLINE, FIFE
ACTION
MYSTERY

## The Mermaid Café

The Mermaid Café was inspired by a Joni Mitchell song, 'Carey'. It originally opened in Coney Island, not too far from Woody Guthrie's house on Mermaid Avenue, but moved to Darktown when the Brooklyn rates became too high. These linocuts were created over a number of years, from 2008 to 2011.

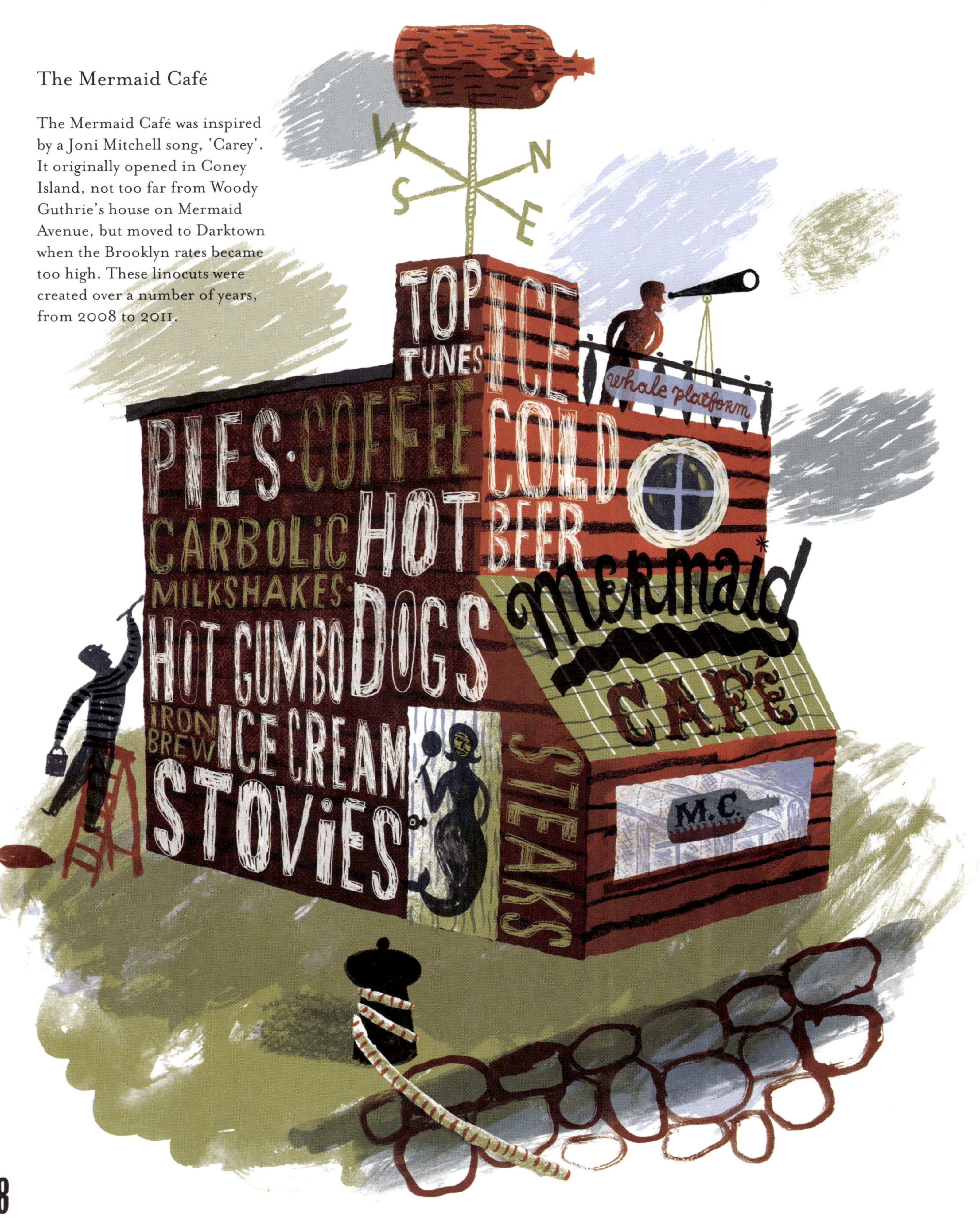

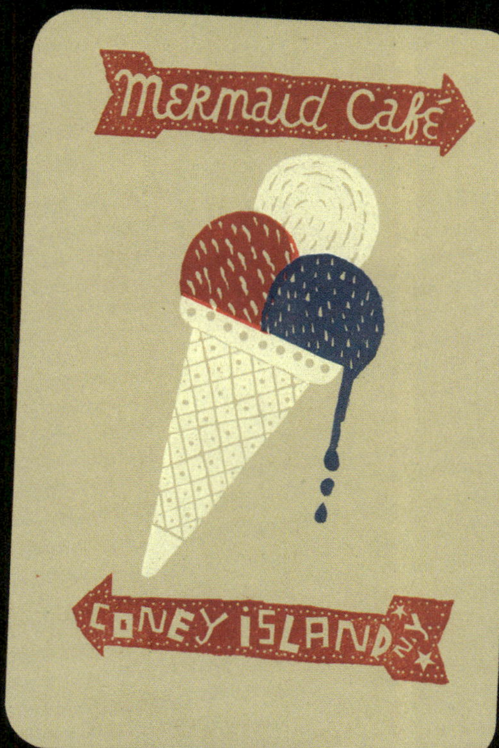
Mermaid Café
Coney Island

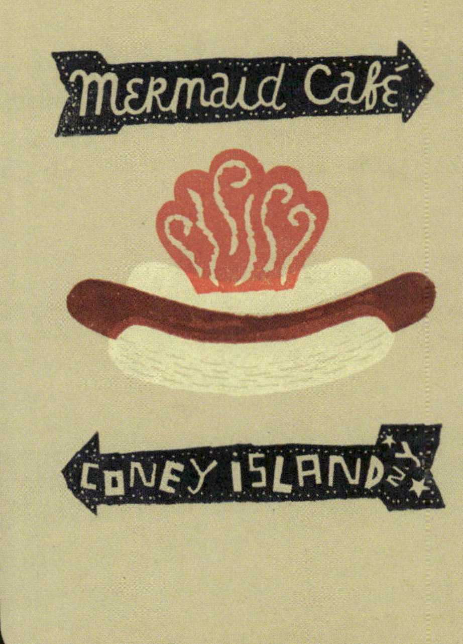
Mermaid Café
Coney Island

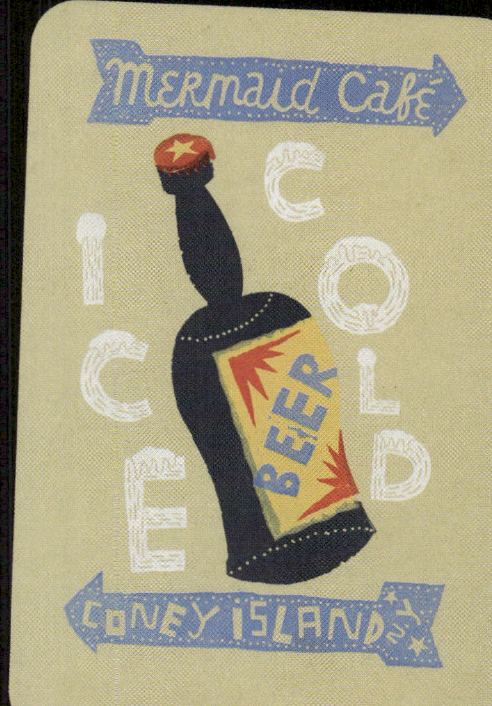
Mermaid Café
ICE COLD
BEER
Coney Island

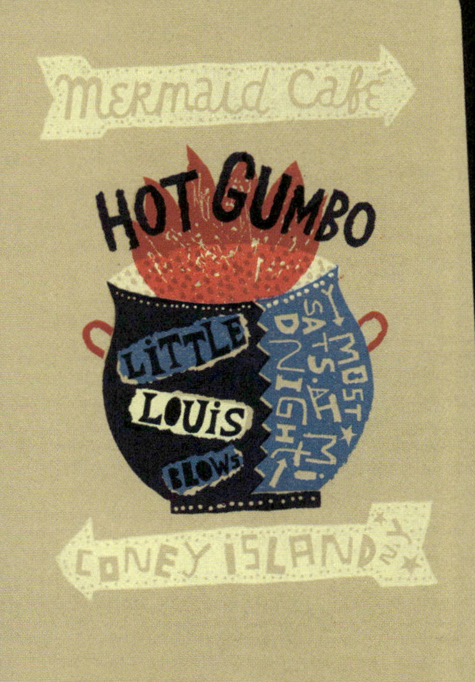
Mermaid Café
HOT GUMBO
LITTLE
LOUIS
BLOWS
Coney Island

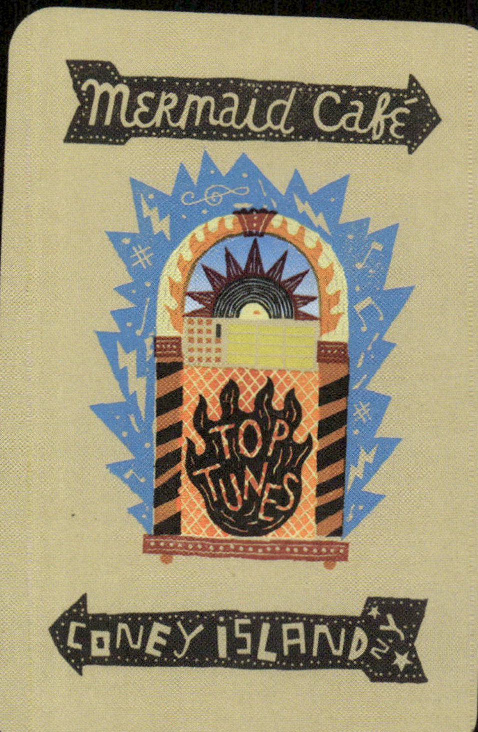
Mermaid Café
TOP TUNES
Coney Island

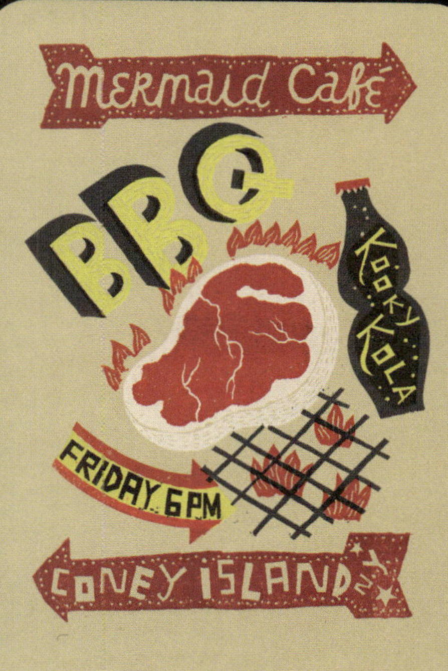
Mermaid Café
BBQ
KOOKY KOLA
FRIDAY 6PM
Coney Island

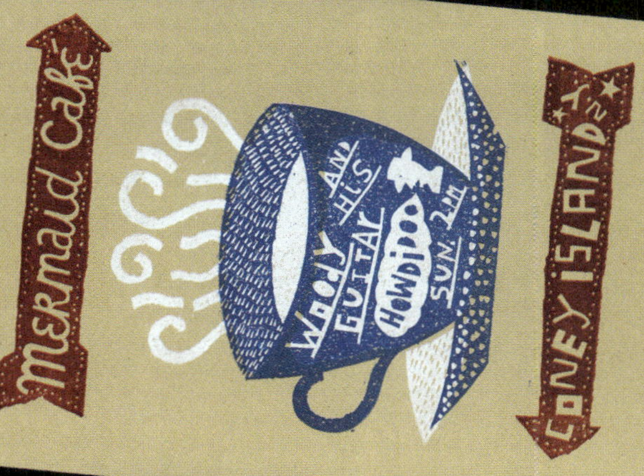
Mermaid Café
WOODY AND HIS GUITAR
Coney Island

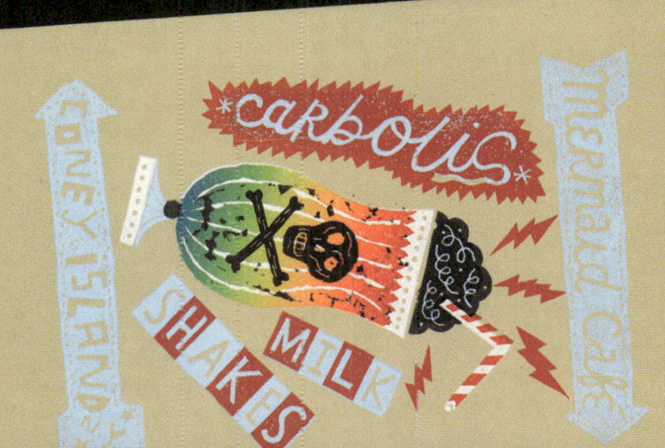
carbolic
MILK
SHAKES
Coney Island
Mermaid Café

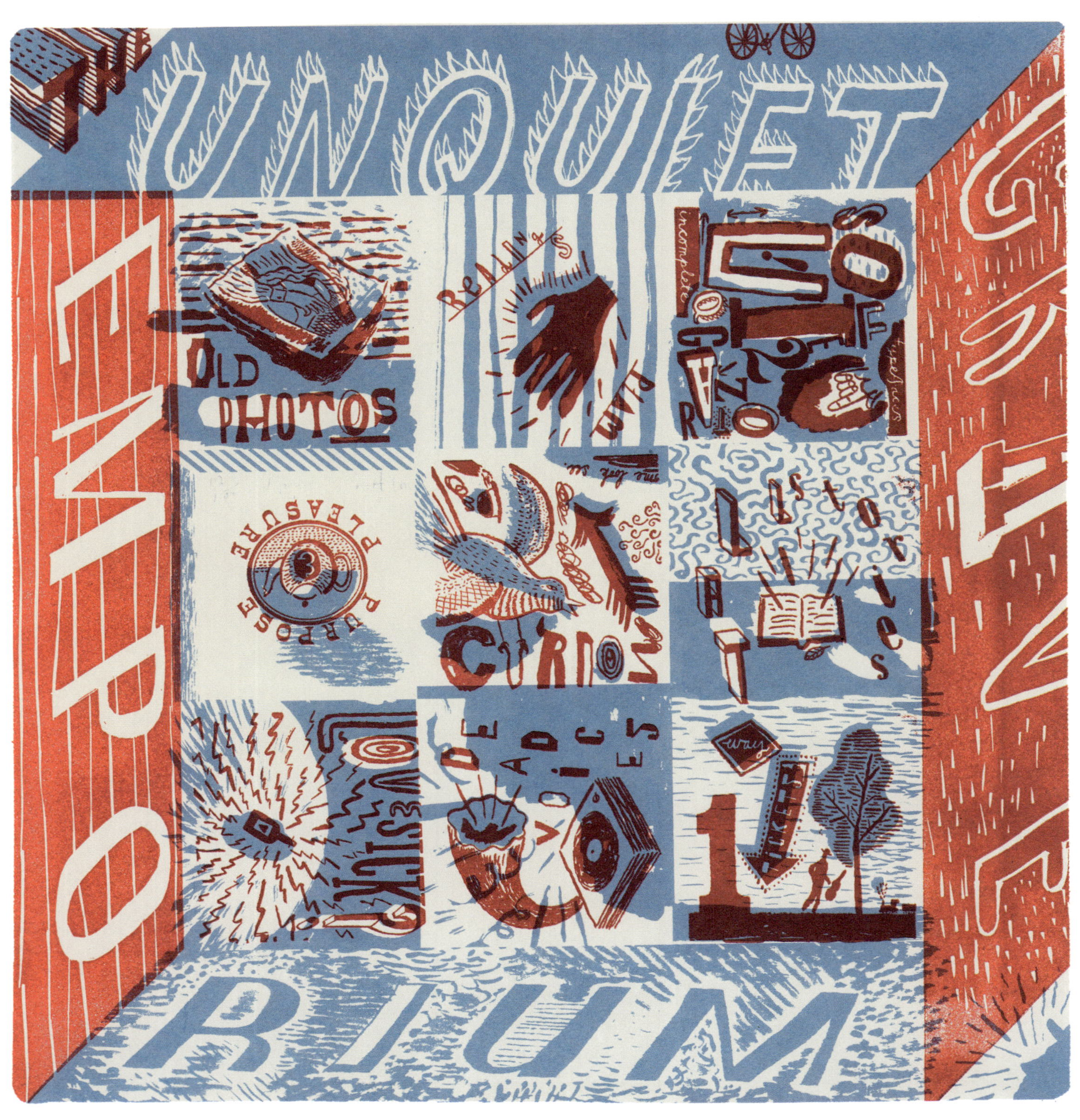

THE
UNQUIET
EMPO
RIUM
OLD
PHOTOS
PLEASURE
PURPOSE
incomplete

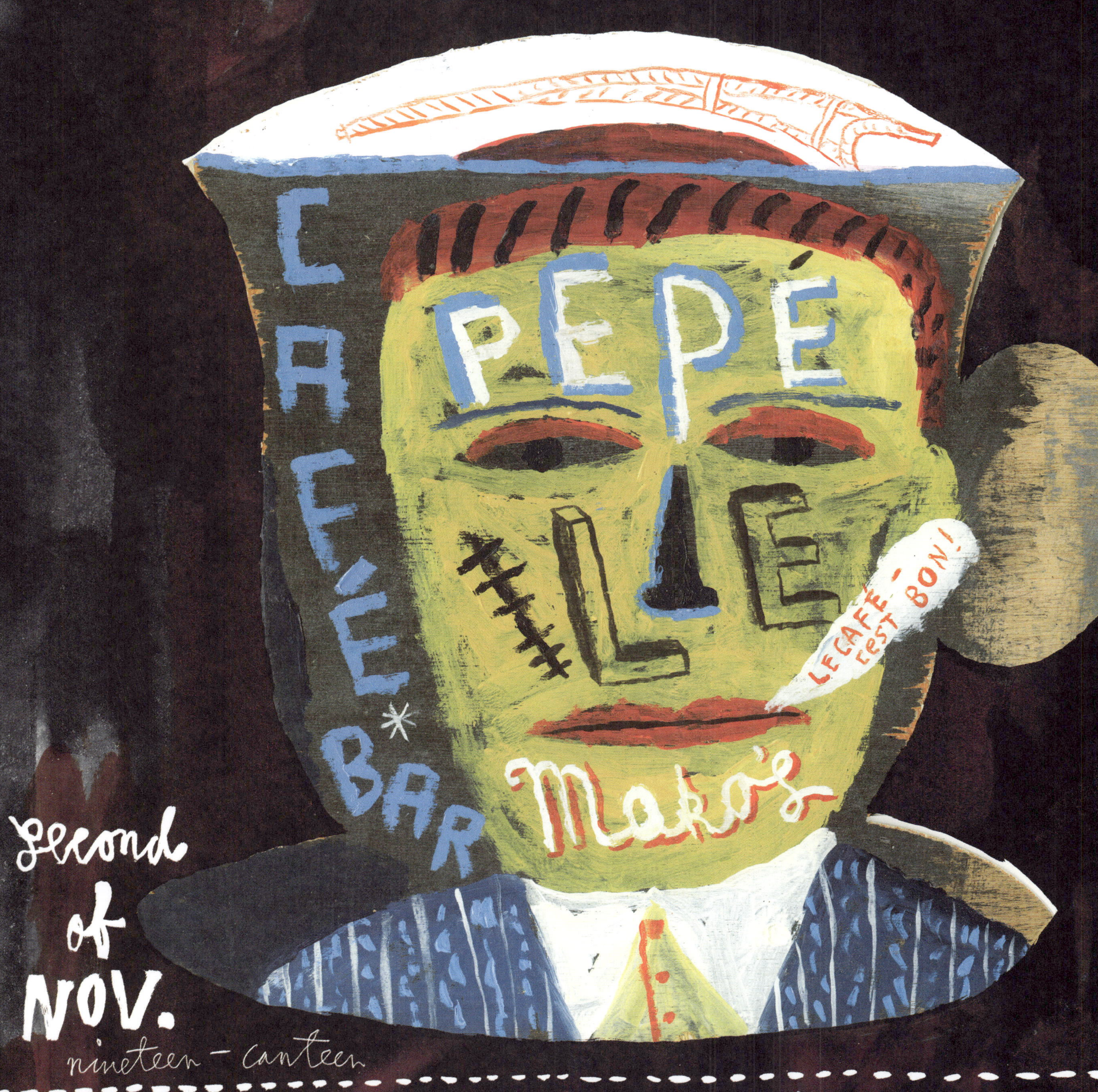


Second of NOV.

nineteen – canteen

With A grave Heart I write, dear diary, THAT THE Coffee WARS are about TO begin. Pépé Le Moko is soon to open his Algerian gangster-style coffee house. AND rumour has it, he only uses fresh grounds from the Auld Nick Coffee Bean Co. That's right, folks, the devil, through Americanos & Espressos, is about to walk the EARTH. Perhaps John Laurie was right all those years ago... 'WE'RE doomed!'...

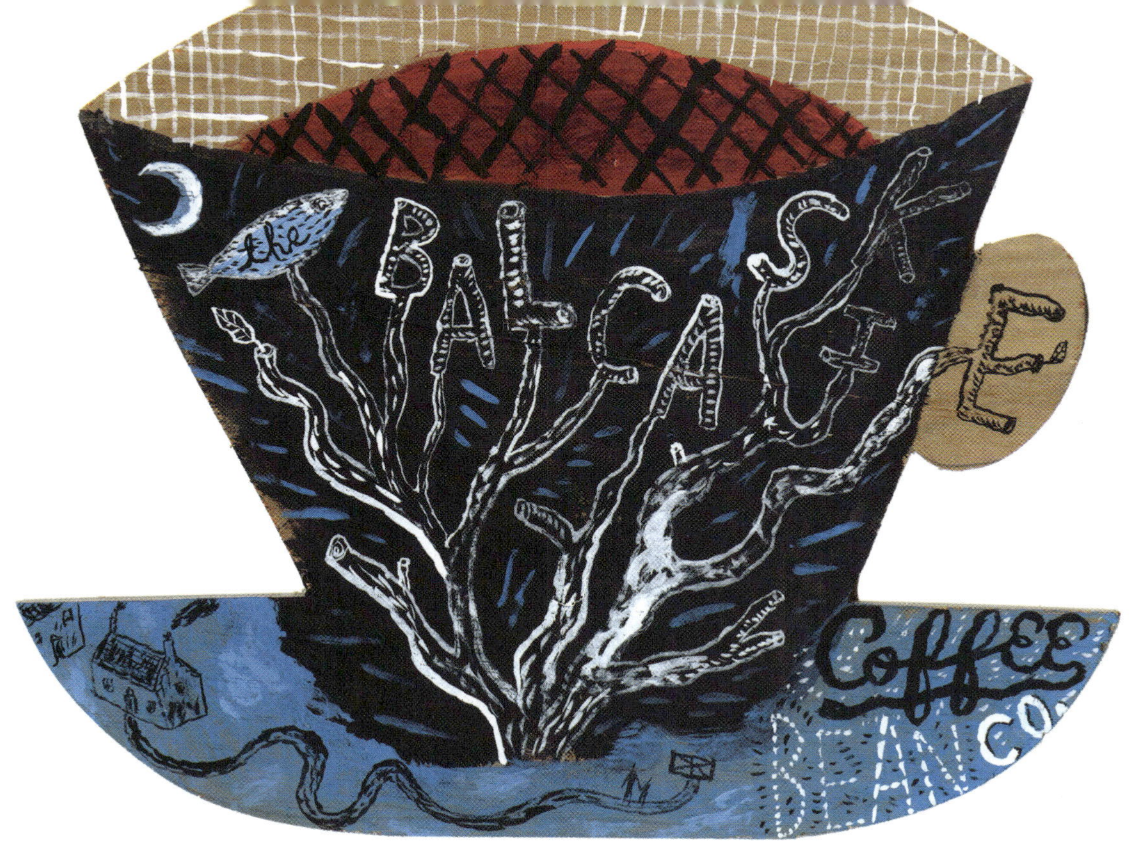
the
BALCASKIE
Coffee
BEAN CO

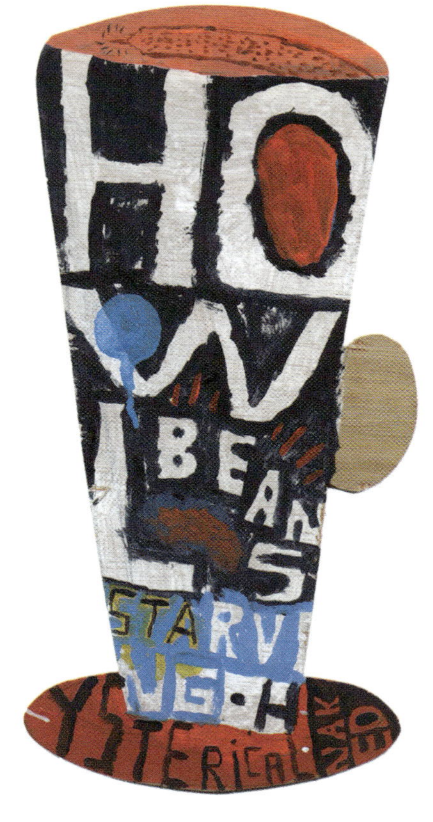
HOWL
BEANS
STARVING·H
YSTERICAL

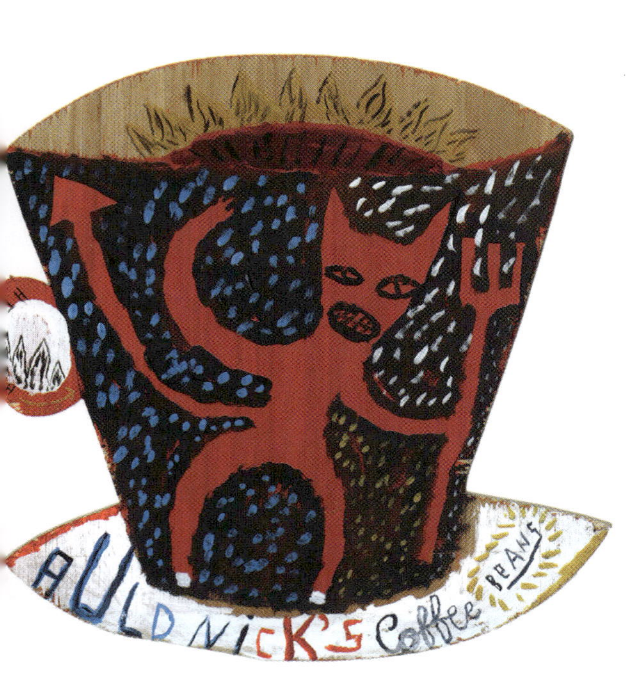
AULD NICK'S Coffee
BEANS

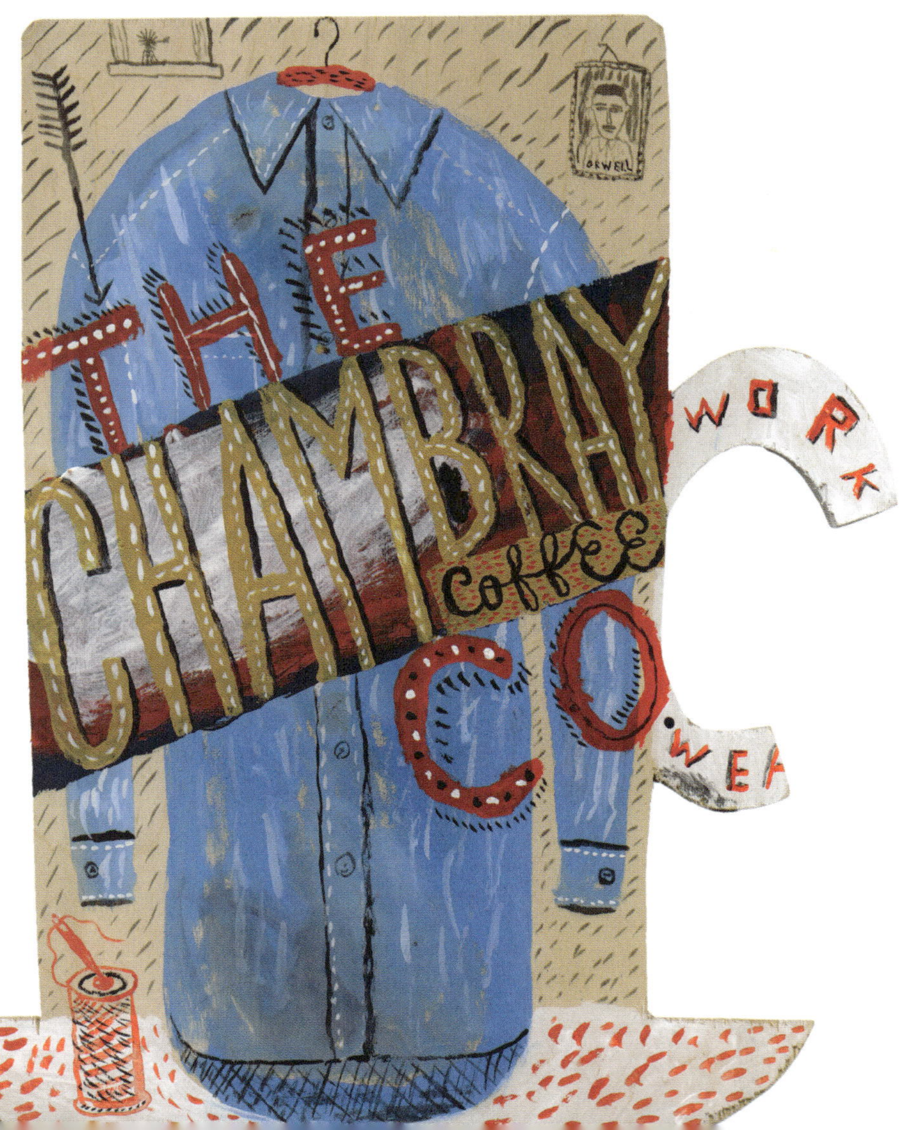
ORWELL
THE
CHAMBRAY
Coffee
CO
WORK
WEA

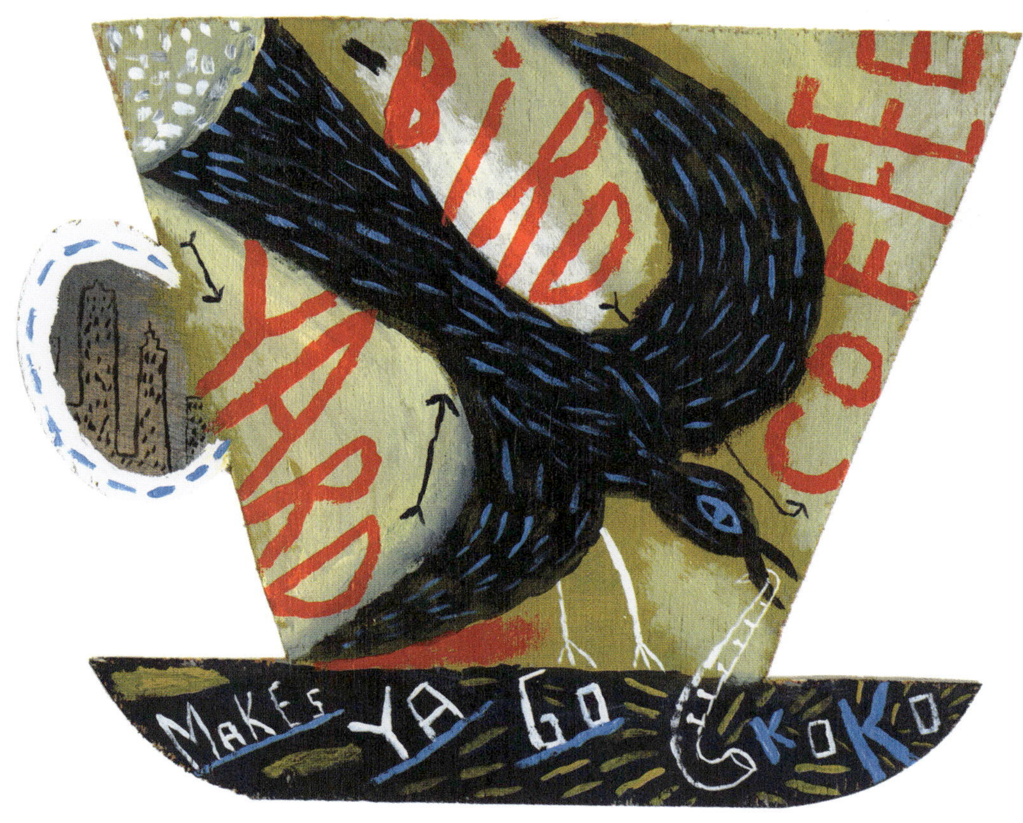
BIRD YARD COFFEE
MAKES YA GO KOKO

Bold & Coffee
DEVILISHLY GOOD.

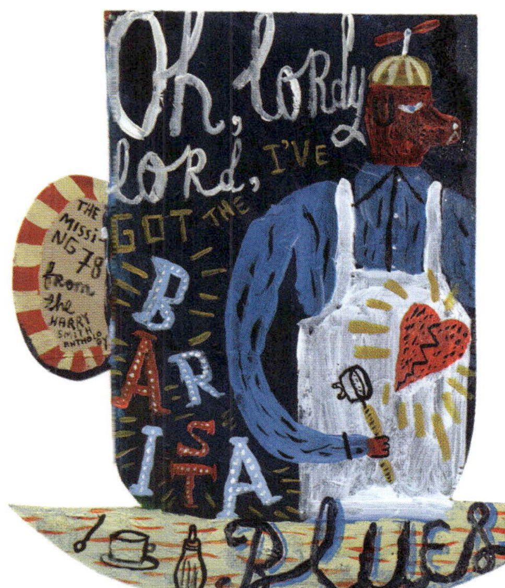
Oh, lordy lord, I've GOT THE BARISTA BLUES
THE MISSING 78 from the HARRY SMITH ANTHOLOGY

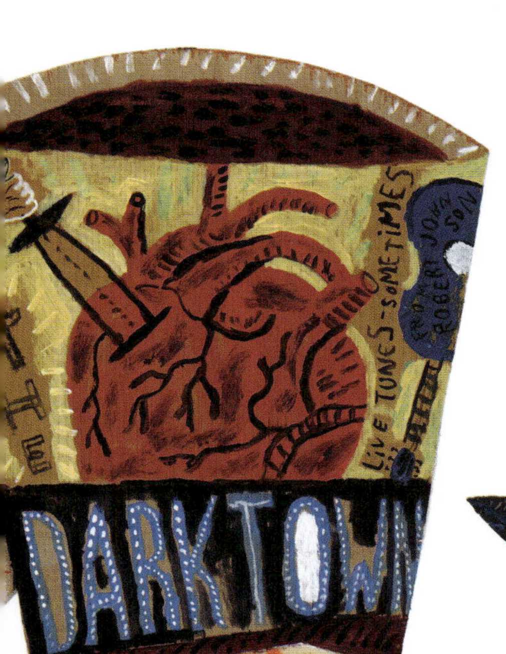
LIVE TUNES - SOMETIMES
ROBERT JOHNSON
DARKTOWN
COFFEE SHOP
COME ON IN MY KITCHEN

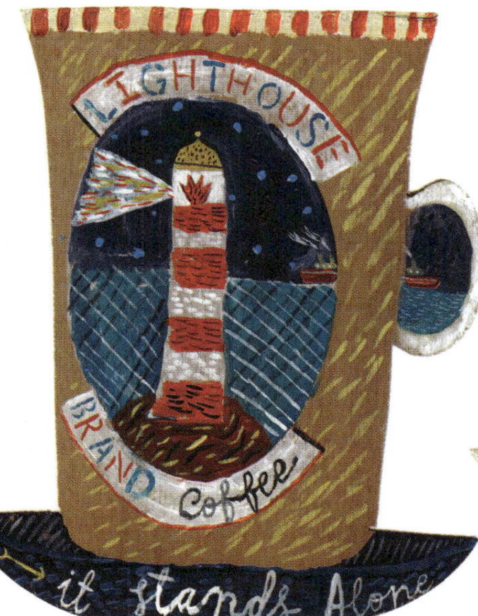
LIGHTHOUSE
BRAND Coffee
it stands Alone

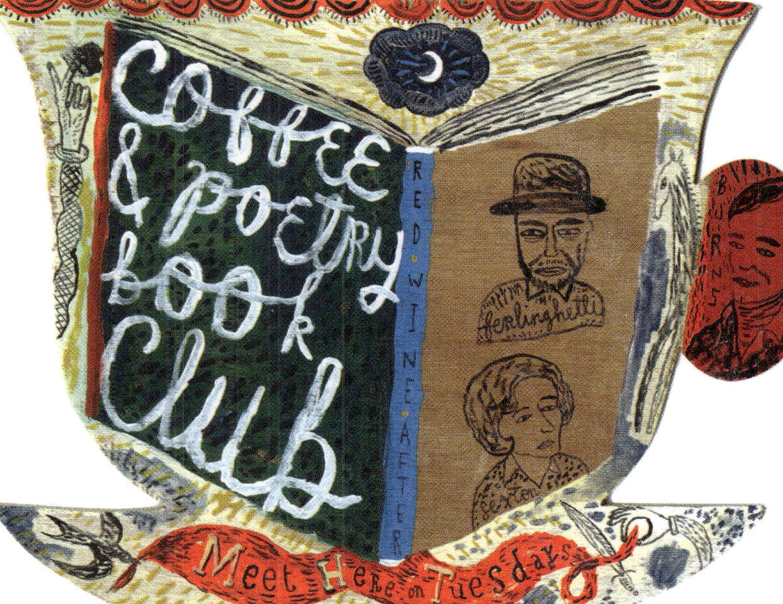
Coffee & poetry book club
RED WINE AFTER
ferlinghetti
Sexton
Meet Here on Tuesdays

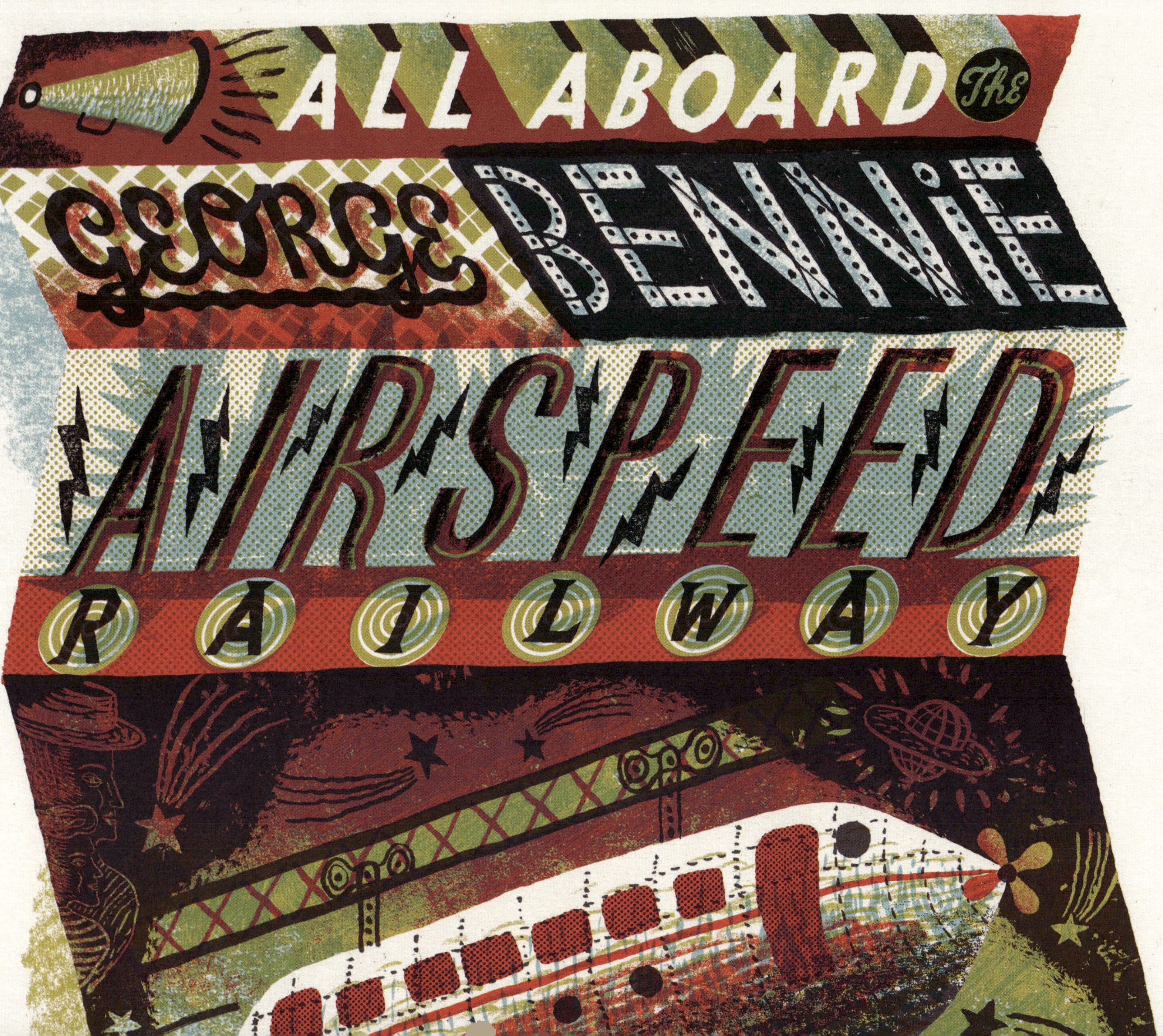
ALL ABOARD The
GEORGE BENNIE
AIRSPEED
RAILWAY

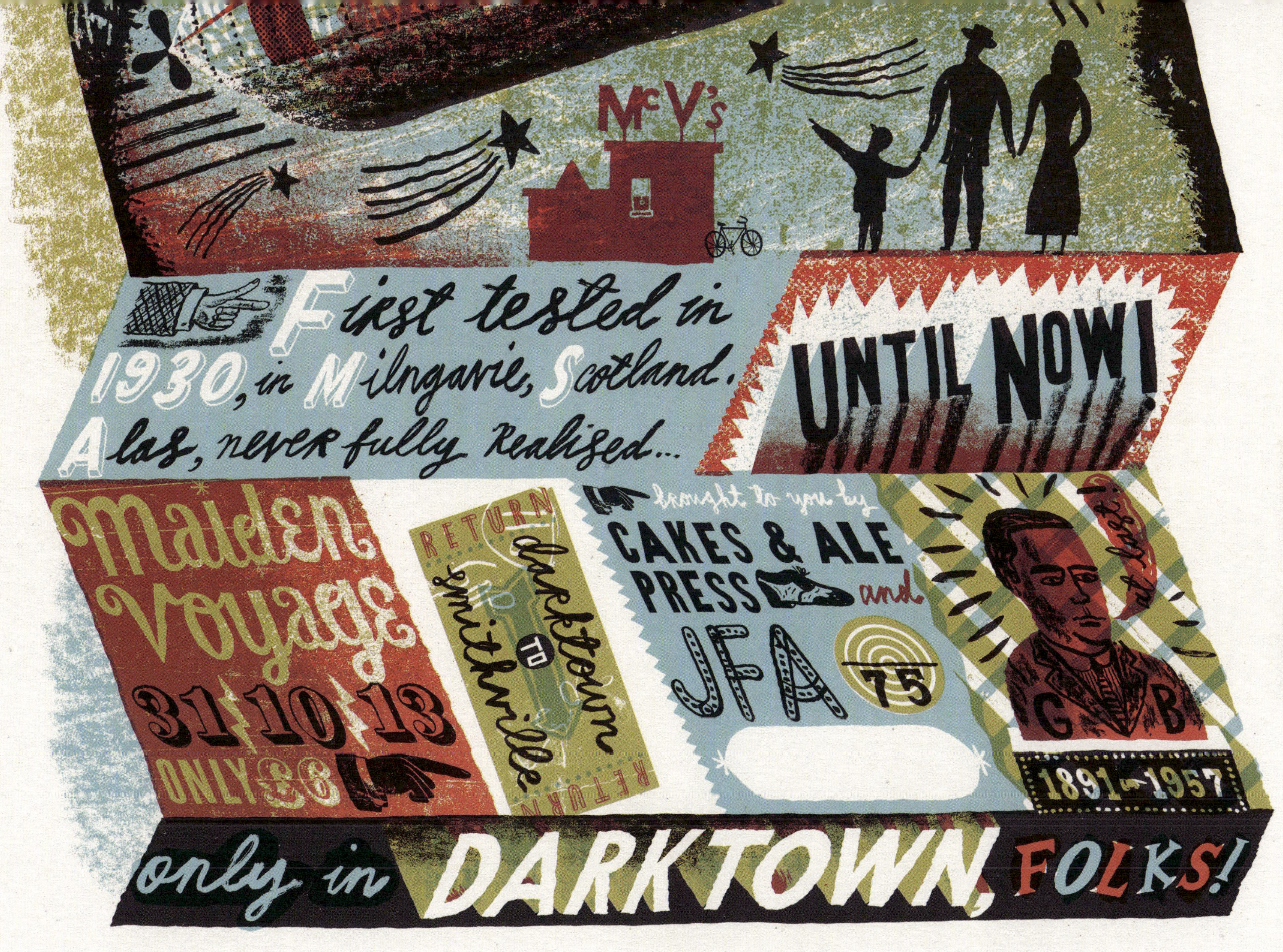


*The George Bennie Airspeed Railway*
2013

This screen print, a homage to a man before his time, was inspired by a trip to the Kelvingrove Art Gallery and Museum in Glasgow with the illustrator Marc Baines, who first alerted me to this remarkable Scot and his story. We agreed it would be a race to see who could get the Bennie monorail into our artwork first. The print was co-published with Neil Jennings at Jennings Fine Art.

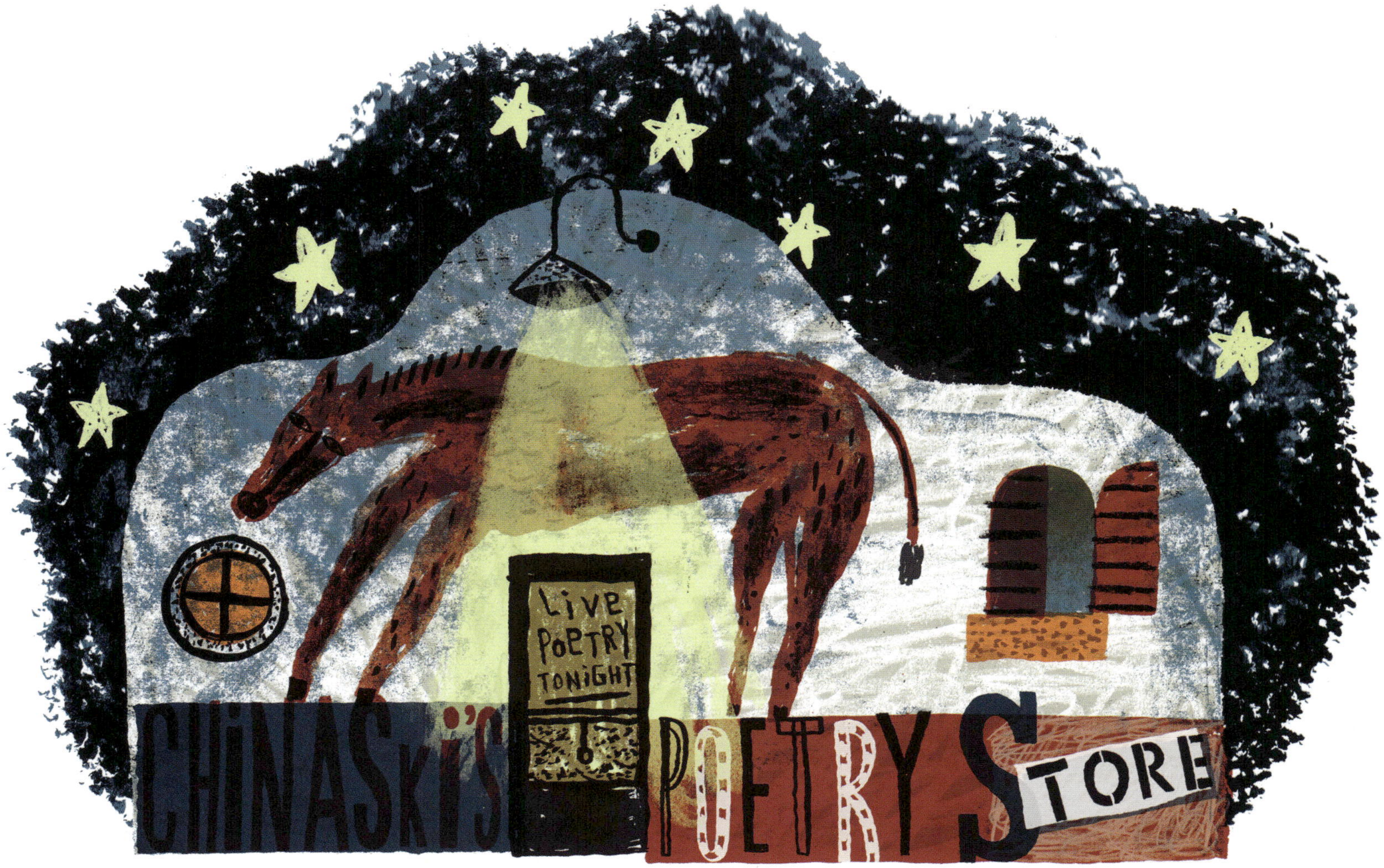

LIVE POETRY TONIGHT

CHINASKI'S POETRY STORE

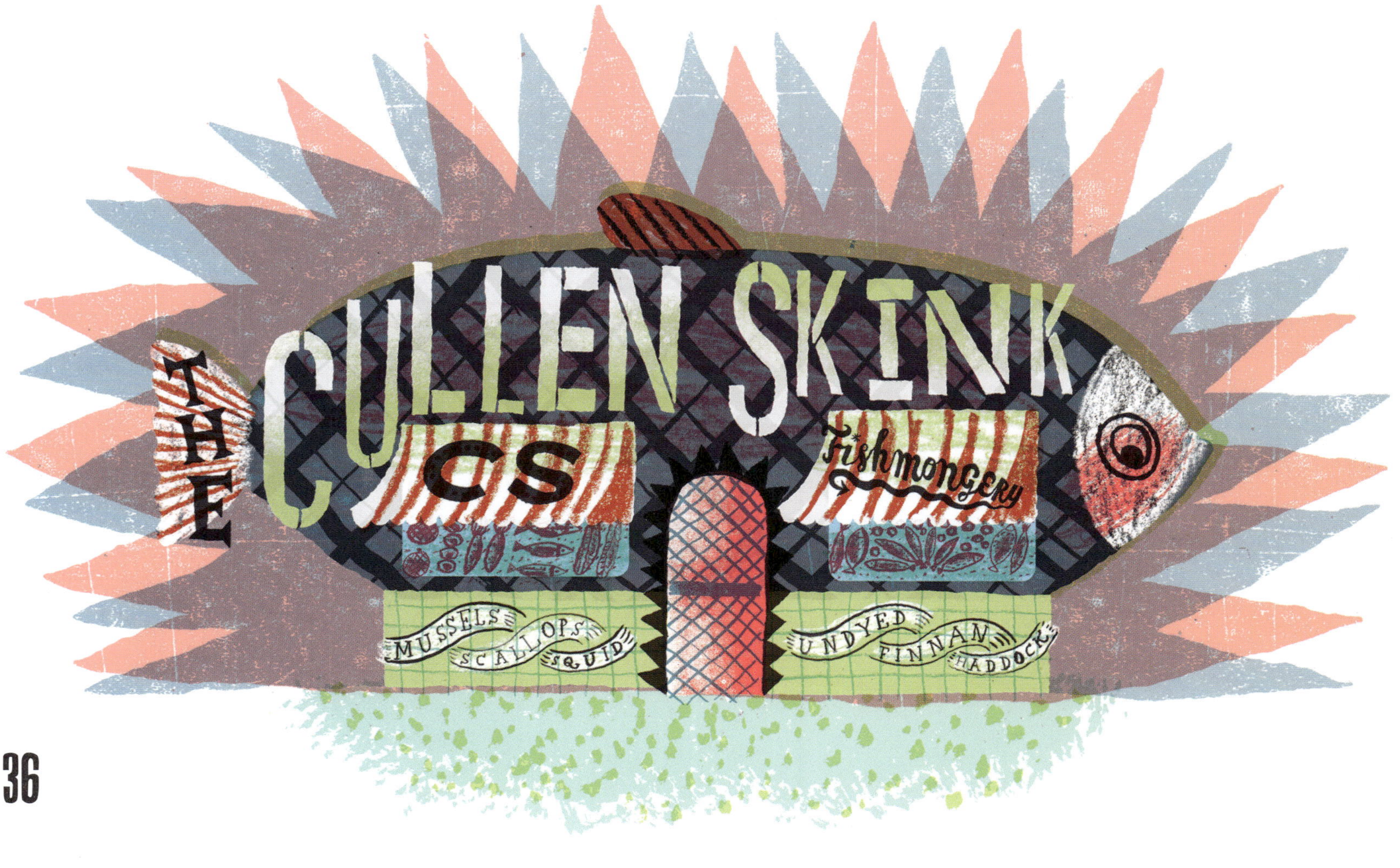

THE CULLEN SKINK

CS

Fishmongery

MUSSELS SCALLOPS SQUID

UNDYED FINNAN HADDOCK

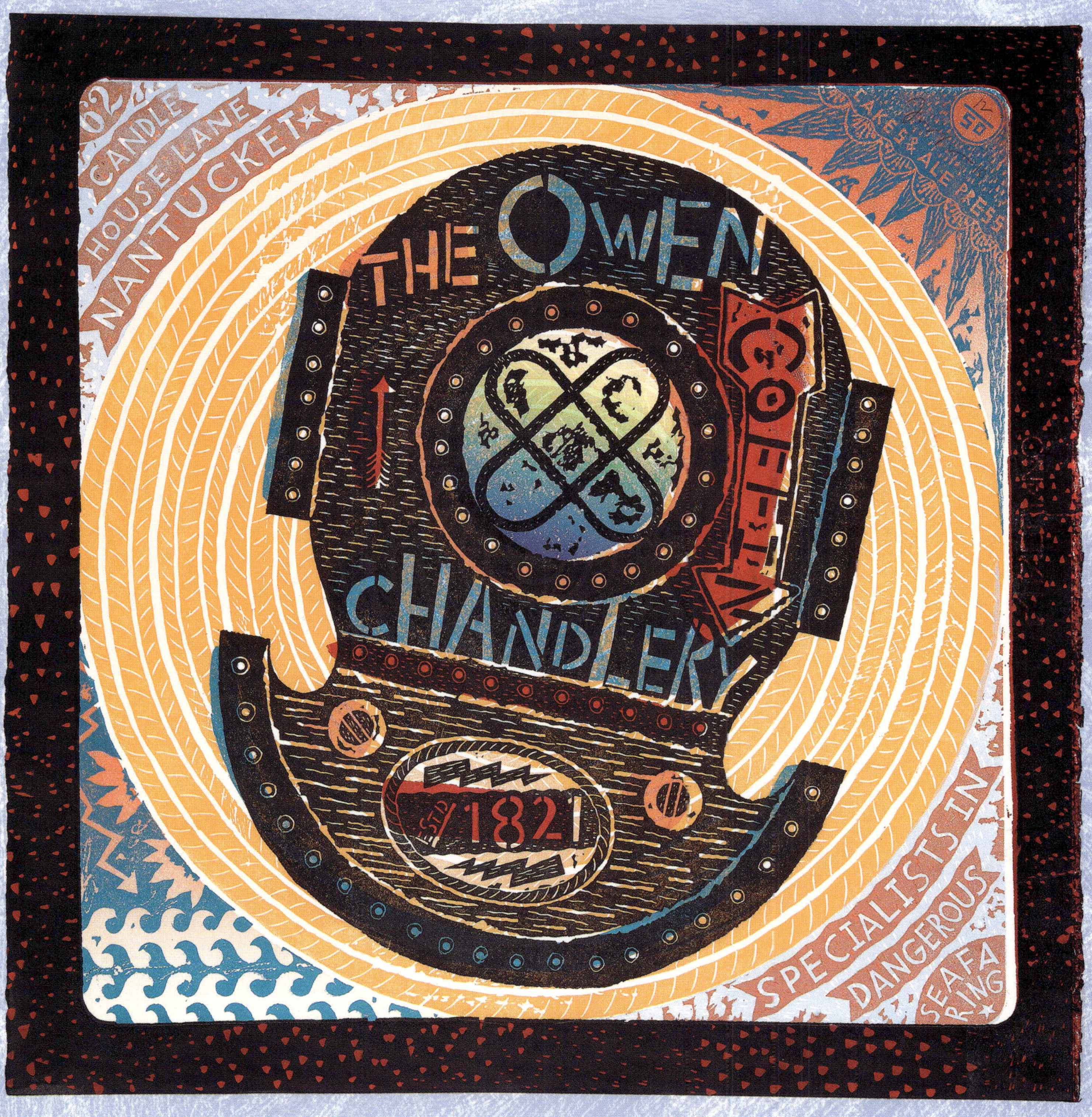


In 1819 a whaler called the *Essex* left Nantucket, but sadly never made it back. In the middle of the Pacific Ocean, a whale took umbrage and stove the ship in. The *Essex* quickly sank. The crew set sail in small boats and, some months later, only a few of them made it back to land. Owen Coffin, the captain's teenaged cousin, drew the short straw, all at sea, in the middle of nowhere. He was shot and then eaten by the remaining crew so that some of them could survive. The story made its way to Herman Melville, who sat down one day and wrote, 'Call me Ishmael.' This chandlery, which has its original branch in Nantucket, opened its doors in Darktown to the fanfare of Mountain's 'Nantucket Sleighride'. It does good business.

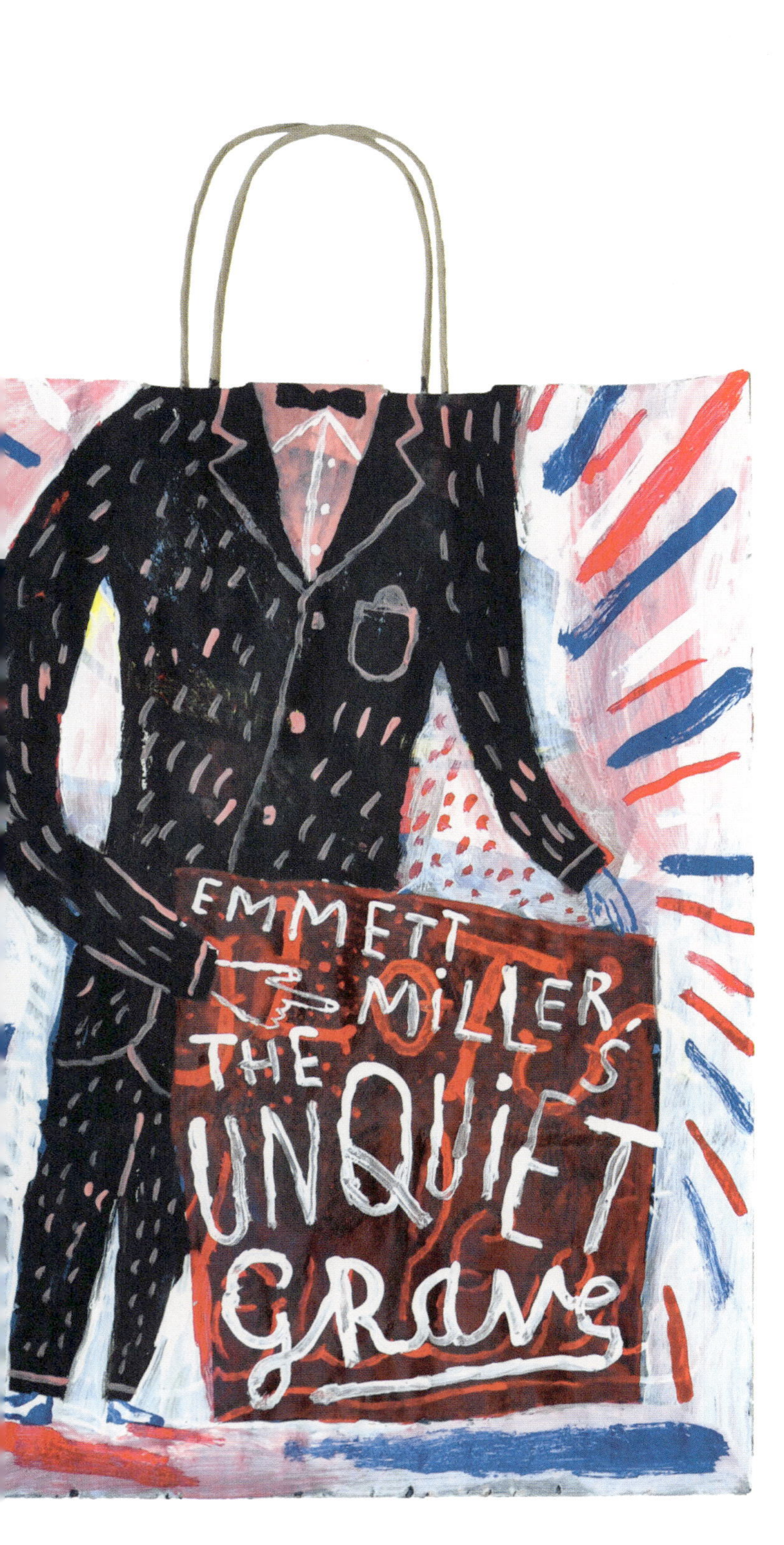
EMMETT MILLER'S
THE UNQUIET grave

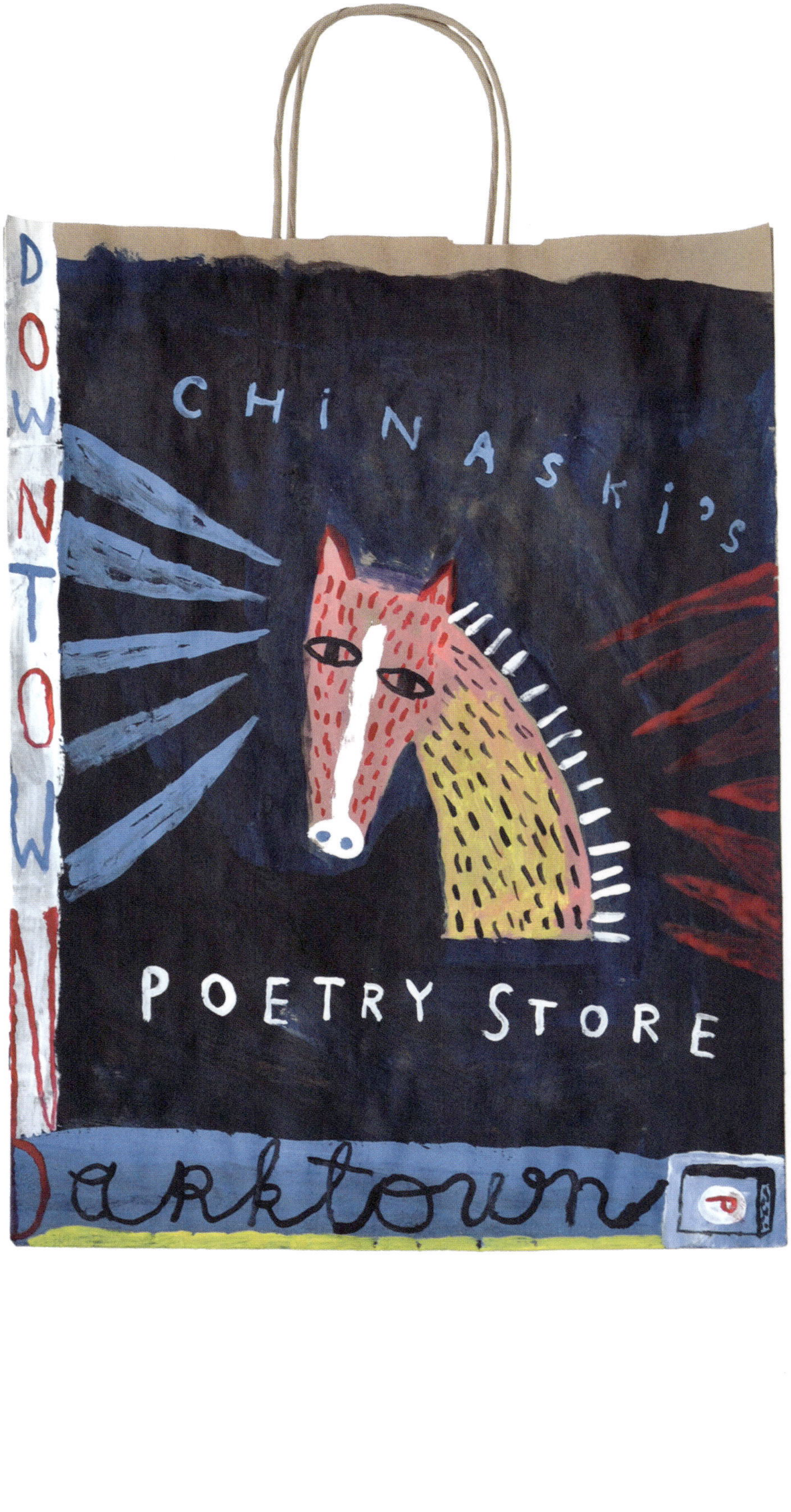

DOWNTOWN
CHINASKi'S
POETRY STORE
Darktown

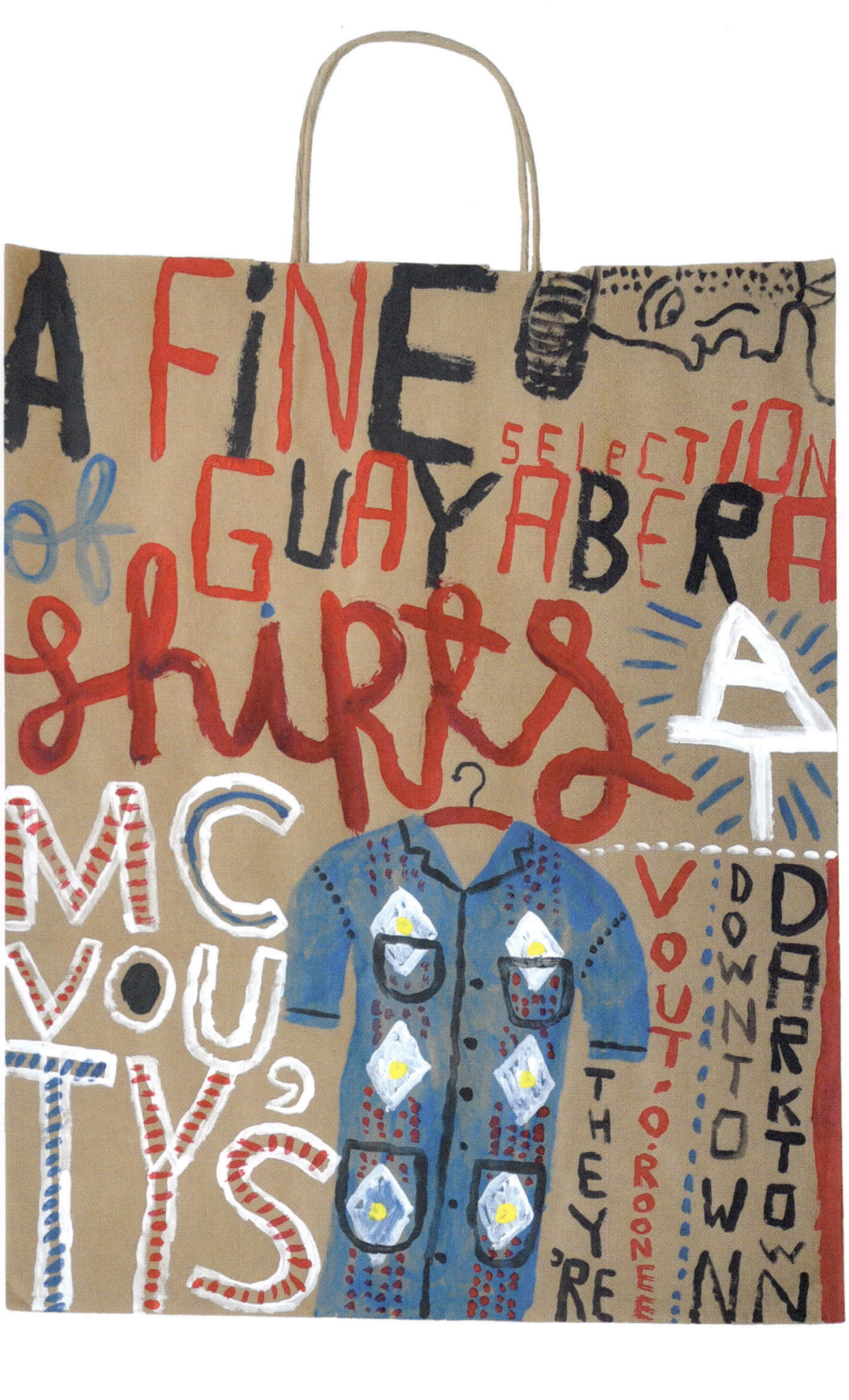

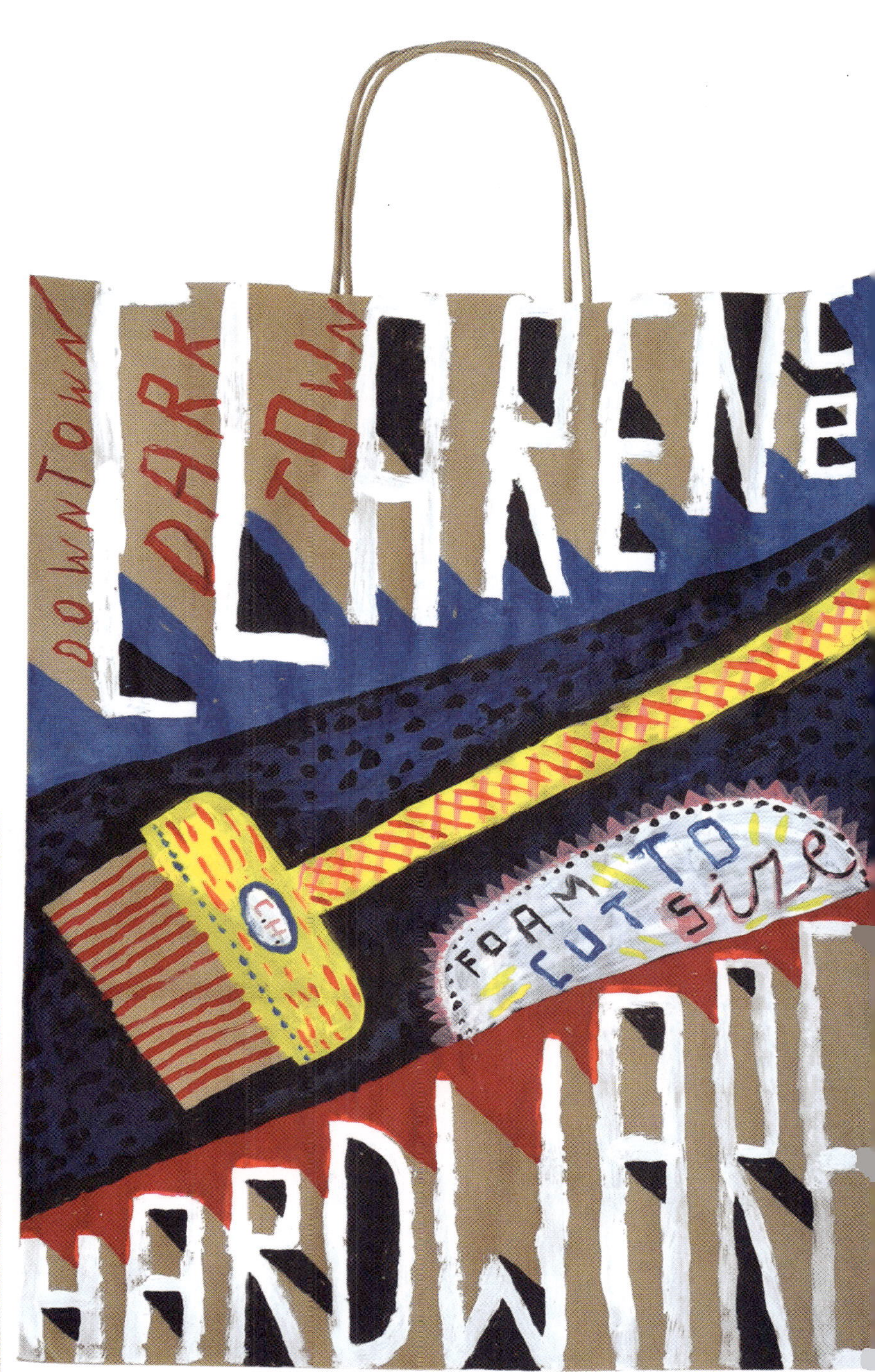
DOWNTOWN
DARKTOWN
FOAM CUT TO size
HARDWARE

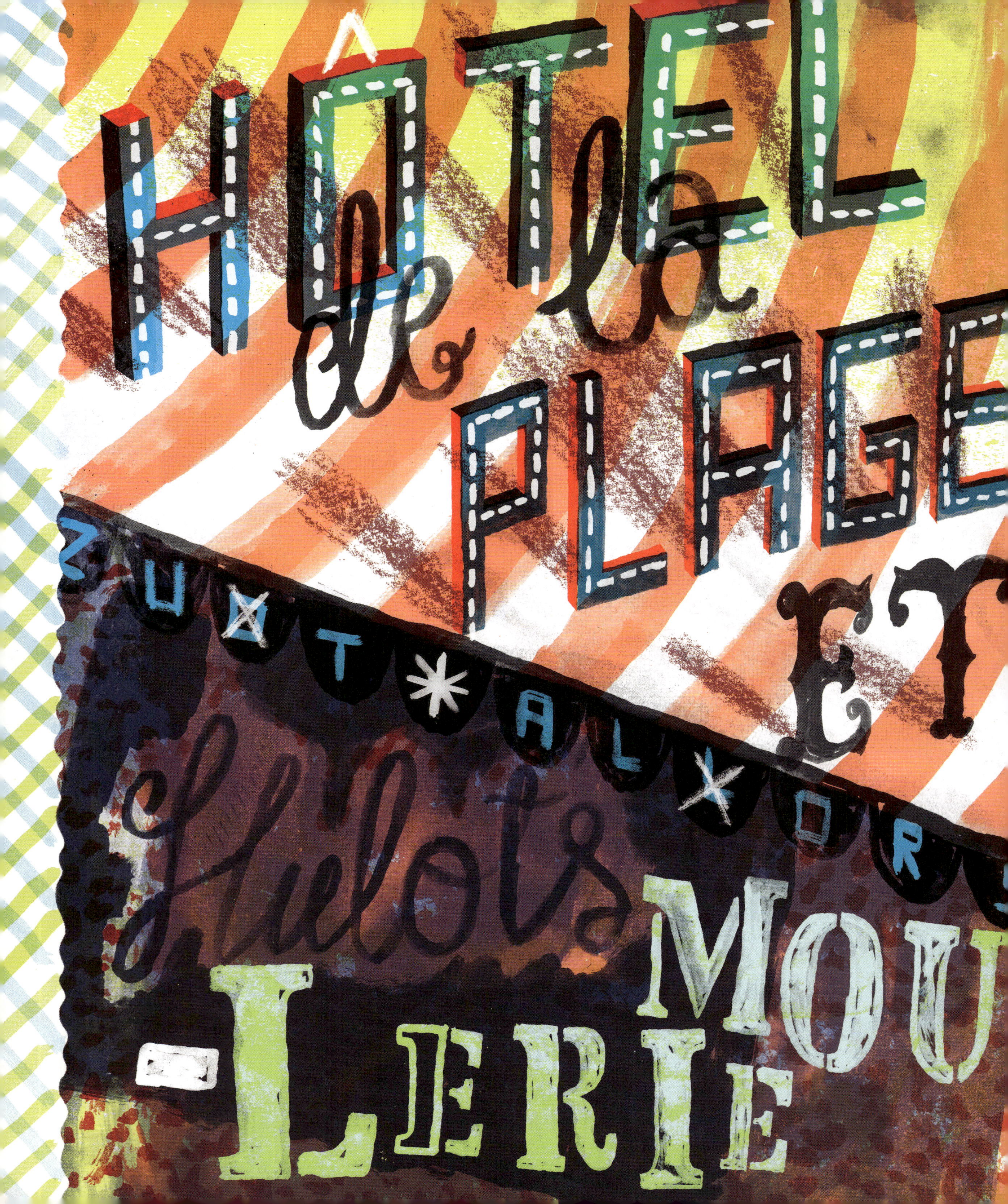

HÔTEL
de la
PLAGE
ET
ZUT ALORS
Hulots
MOU
-LERIE

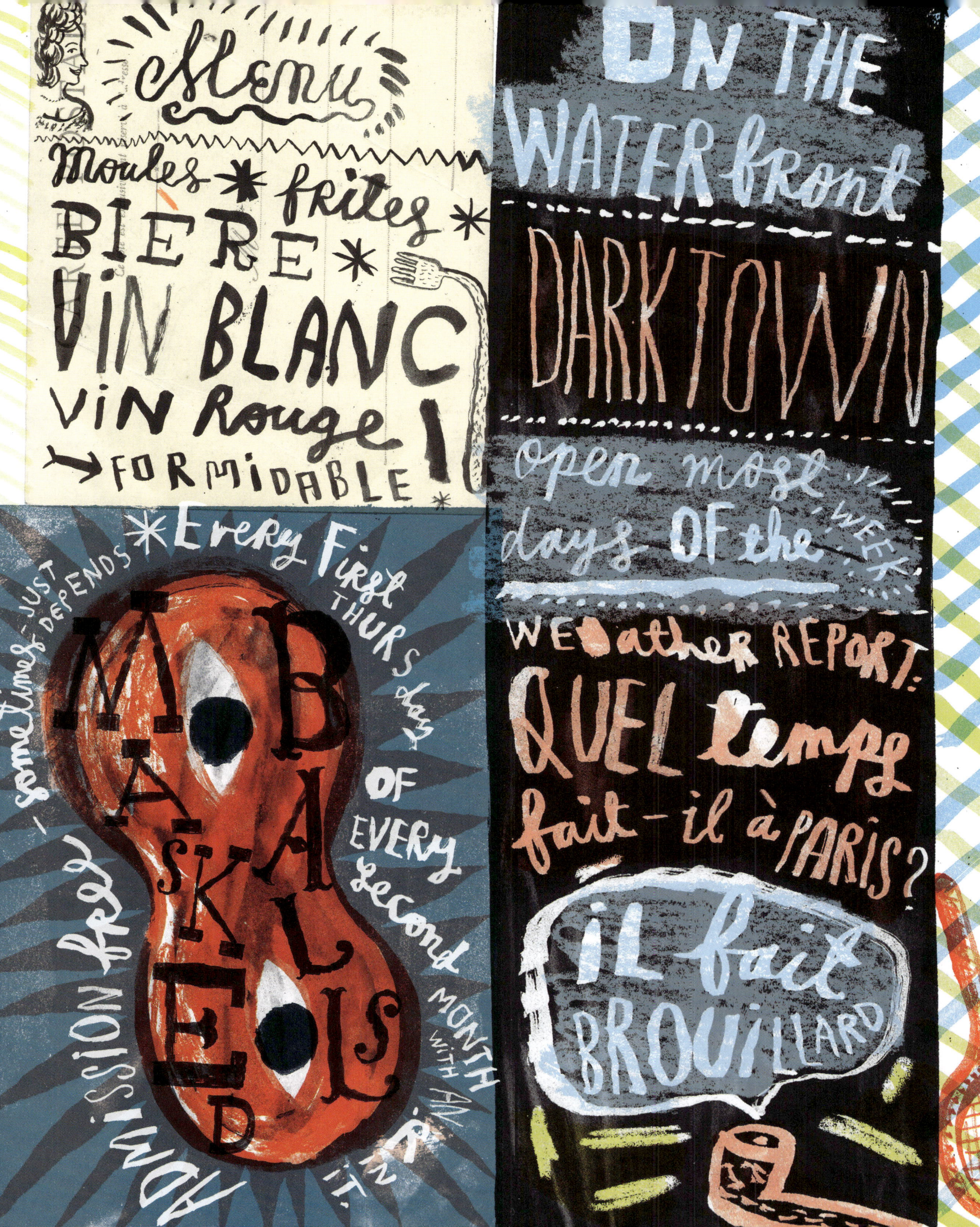
Menu
Moules * frites *
BIÈRE *
VIN BLANC
VIN Rouge
→ FORMIDABLE!
ON THE WATERfront
DARKTOWN
open most days OF the WEEK
WEather REPORT:
QUEL temps fait-il à PARIS?
iL fait BROUILLARD
*Every First THURSday OF EVERY second MONTH WITH AN R IN IT.
sometimes - JUST DEPENDS
ADMISSION free
MASKED BALLS

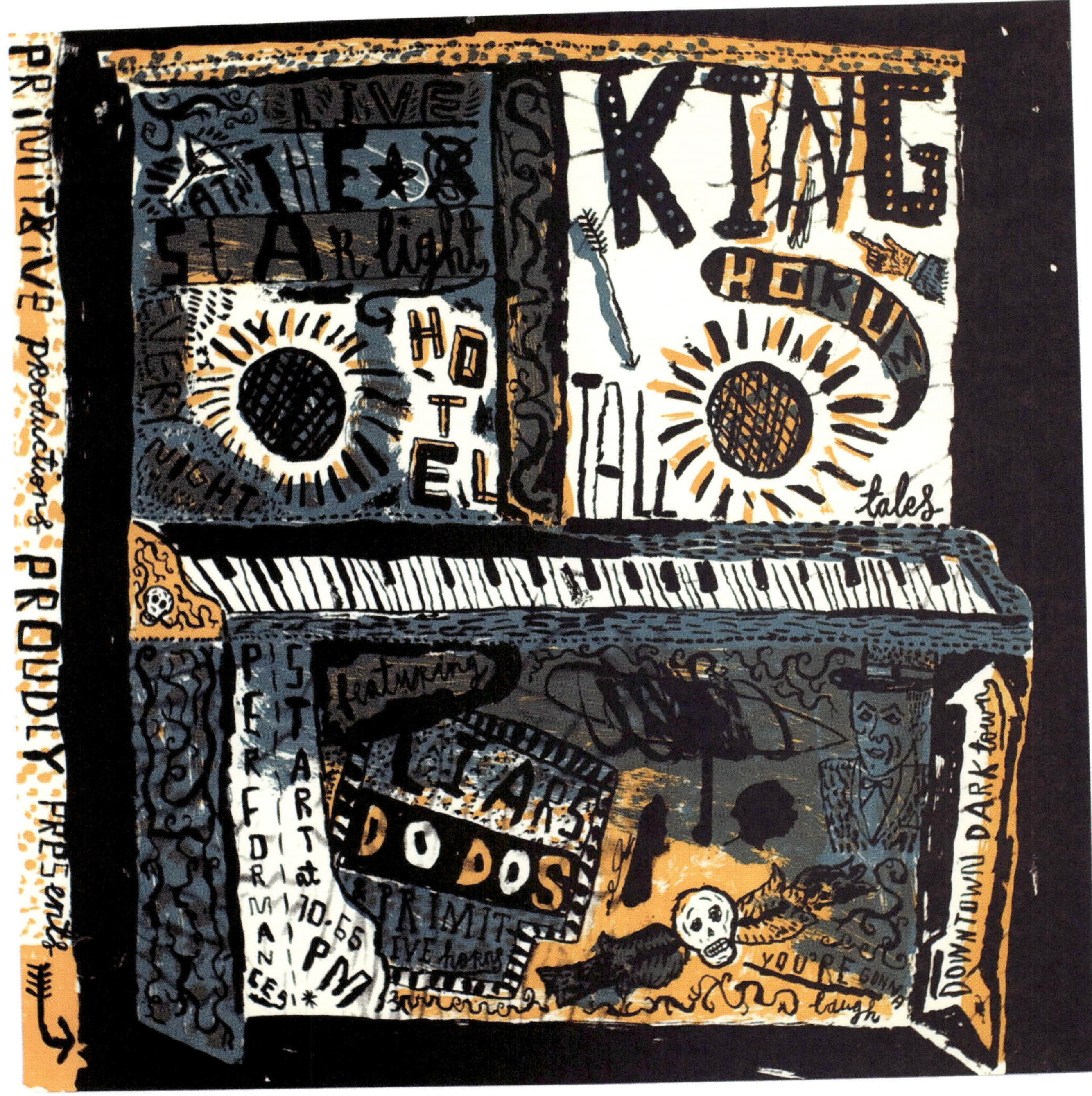


When Don Smith lent me a copy of an album by C.W. Stoneking, everything seemed to click. All the scrag-ends of wreckage of years and years came colliding together as this young Australian – sounding more like an old Blues musician from Alabama – sang. It was as if Dock Boggs, Emmett Miller and Uncle Bunt Stephens were all having a picnic at Hanging Rock, with voodoo charms, jungle river trips, Sunday clothes and Christmas treats thrown in. There were cautionary tales, too: 'Don't Go Dancin' Down the Darktown Strutter's Ball' – in complete contradiction to Fats Waller's advice all those years ago. Mr Stoneking now lives in Bristol, and I had the pleasure of designing a T-shirt for him, as an offshoot from my *Darktown Hokum Blues, Volume One*, a box set of screen prints (above). I finally gave him a set, but have yet to meet the great King Hokum in person. Willie, allow me to buy you a drink in the Starlight Hotel sometime.

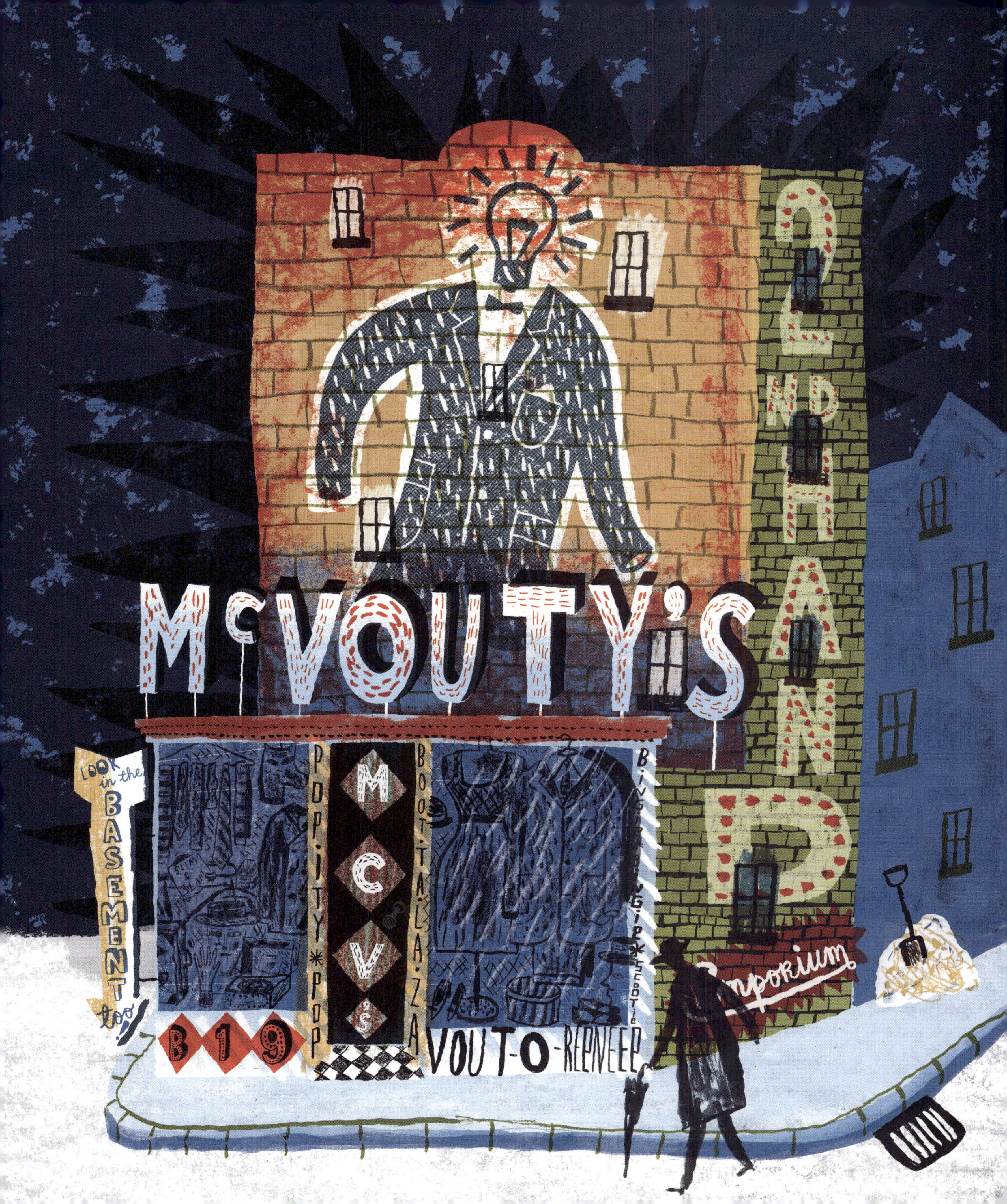

McVOUTY's
2ND HAND
Emporium
LOOK in the BASEMENT too!
POP-ITY*POP
M C V S
BOOT-TA-LA-ZA
BiNGie*BiNGie*SCOOTie
B 1 9
VOUT-O-REENEE

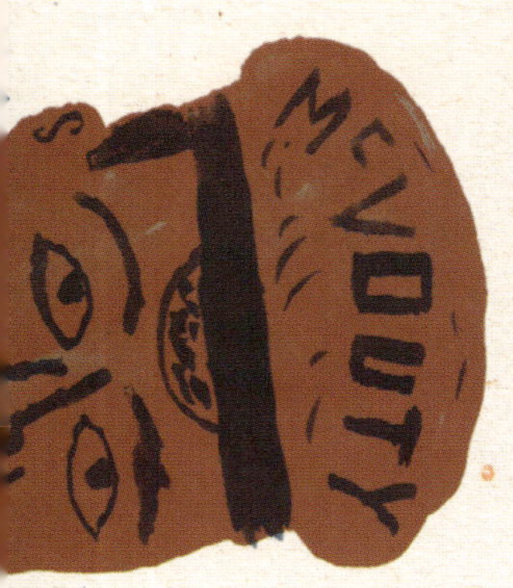


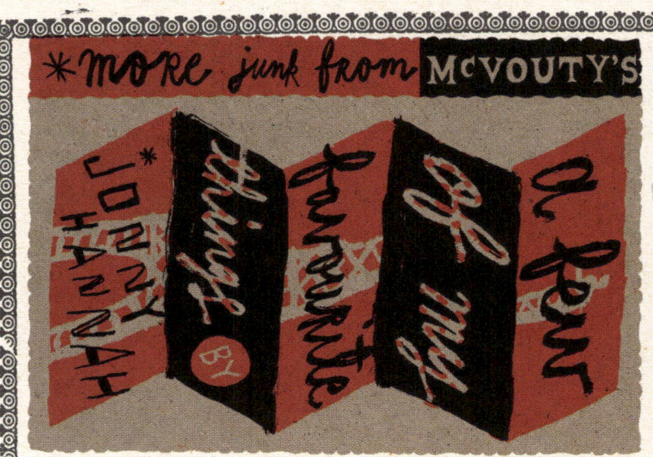

McVOUTY'S

I have, or had, a recurring dream. I find myself in the best vintage clothes shop in the world. It's all there: high-waist trousers, gabardine shirts and those flecked jackets. But as I look through the racks of wonderful garments, desperate to try this and that on, I soon realize that nothing fits. The jackets are like tents, the trousers far too small. I begin to panic. Surely to God, something must be the right size …

Then, in a recurring daydream, along came McVouty's second-hand emporium, an establishment of leviathan proportions. Four storeys high, with a basement too. You could spend a week in there and still be only halfway through the flannel shirts and French postman's workwear. But more importantly, everything fits. Like a glove. This is my shop, where dreams come true and only happy days are ahead. Step inside, take your time, and you'll leave looking like Mingus, Mulligan or even Monk.

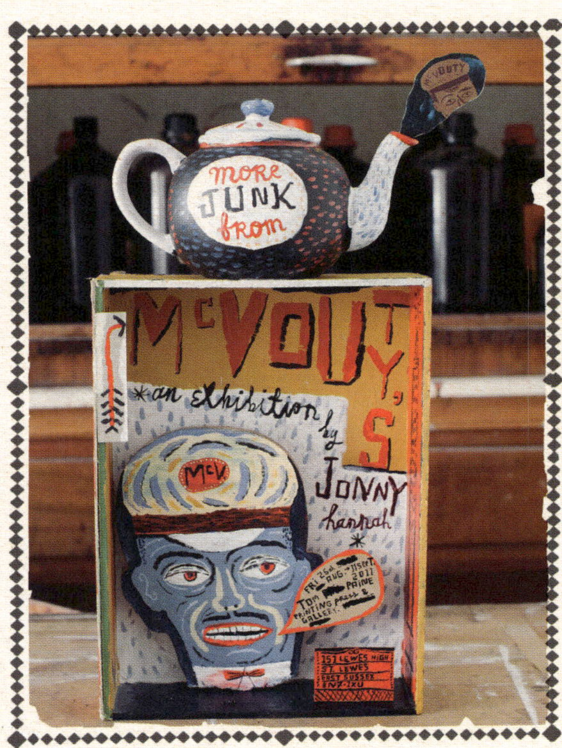


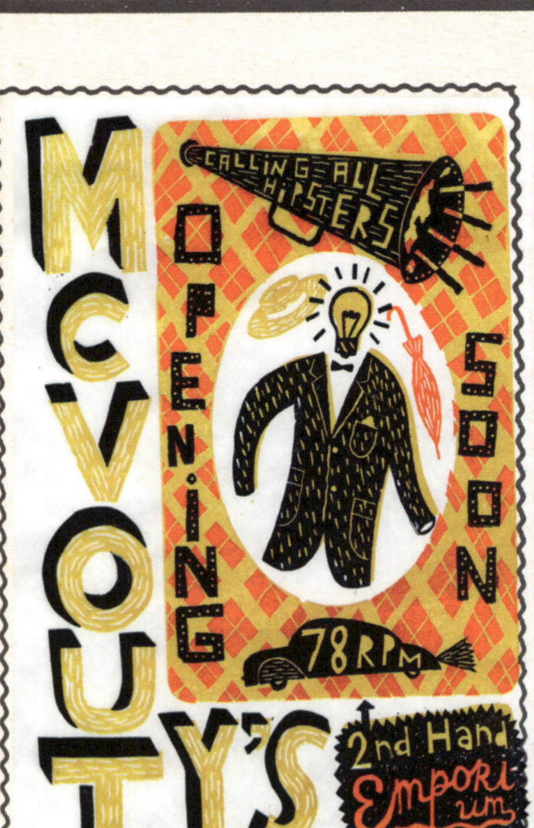


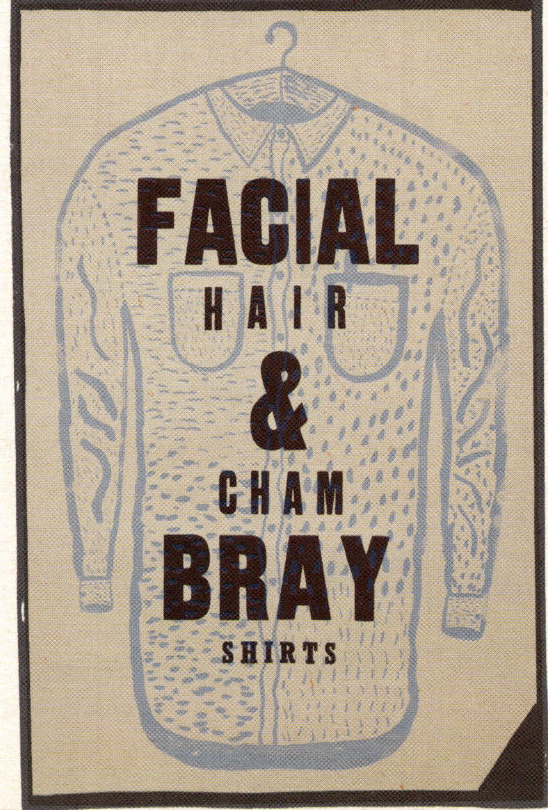


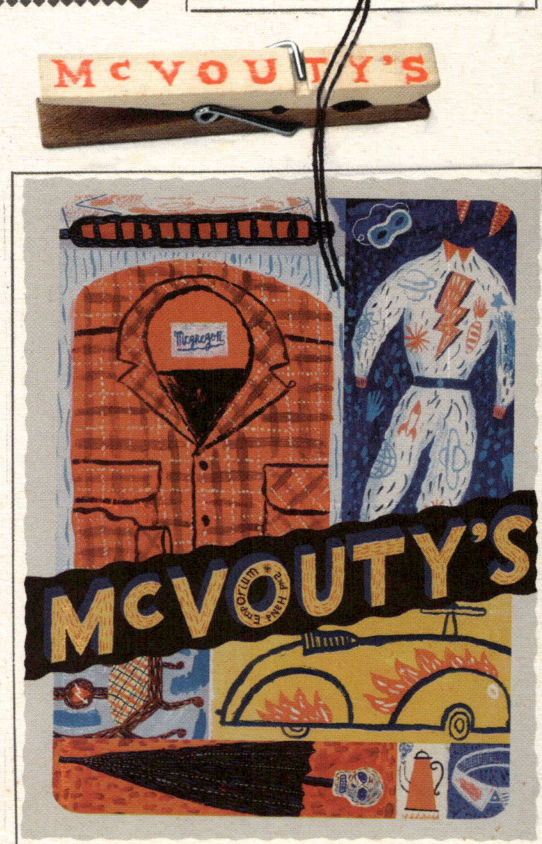

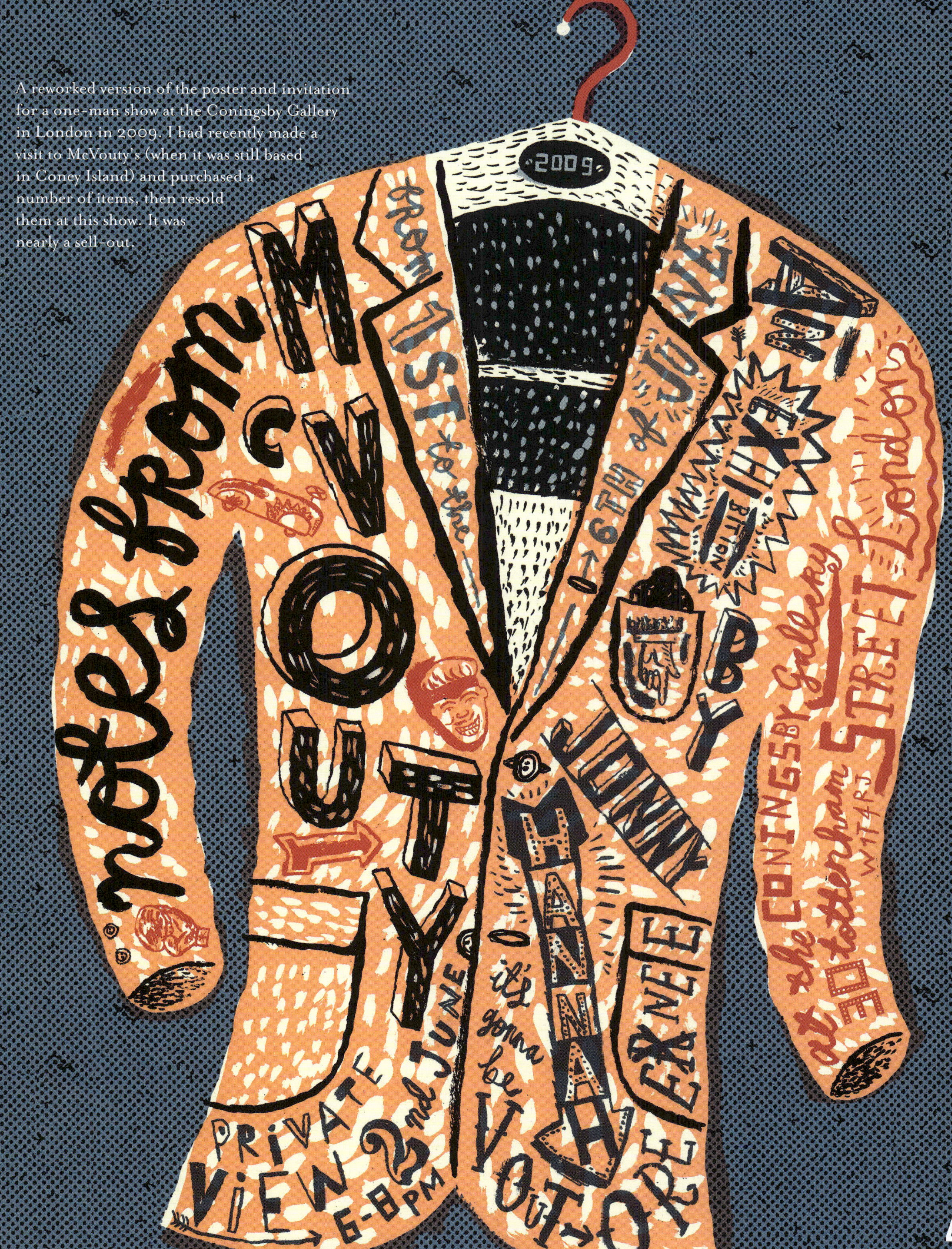


A reworked version of the poster and invitation for a one-man show at the Coningsby Gallery in London in 2009. I had recently made a visit to McVouty's (when it was still based in Coney Island) and purchased a number of items, then resold them at this show. It was nearly a sell-out.

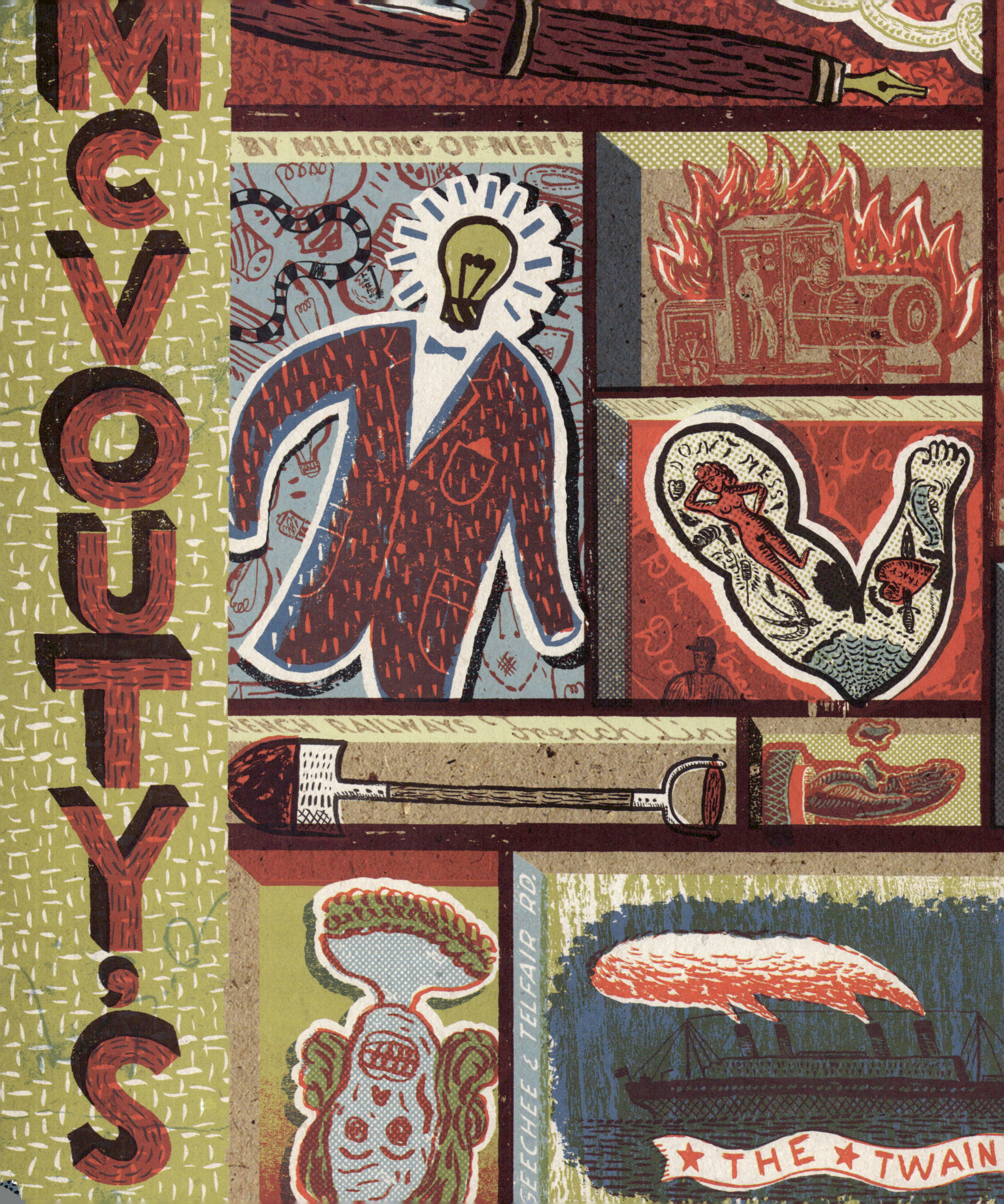
MCVOUTY'S
BY MILLIONS OF MEN!
DON'T MESS
GEECHEE & TELFAIR RD.
THE TWAIN

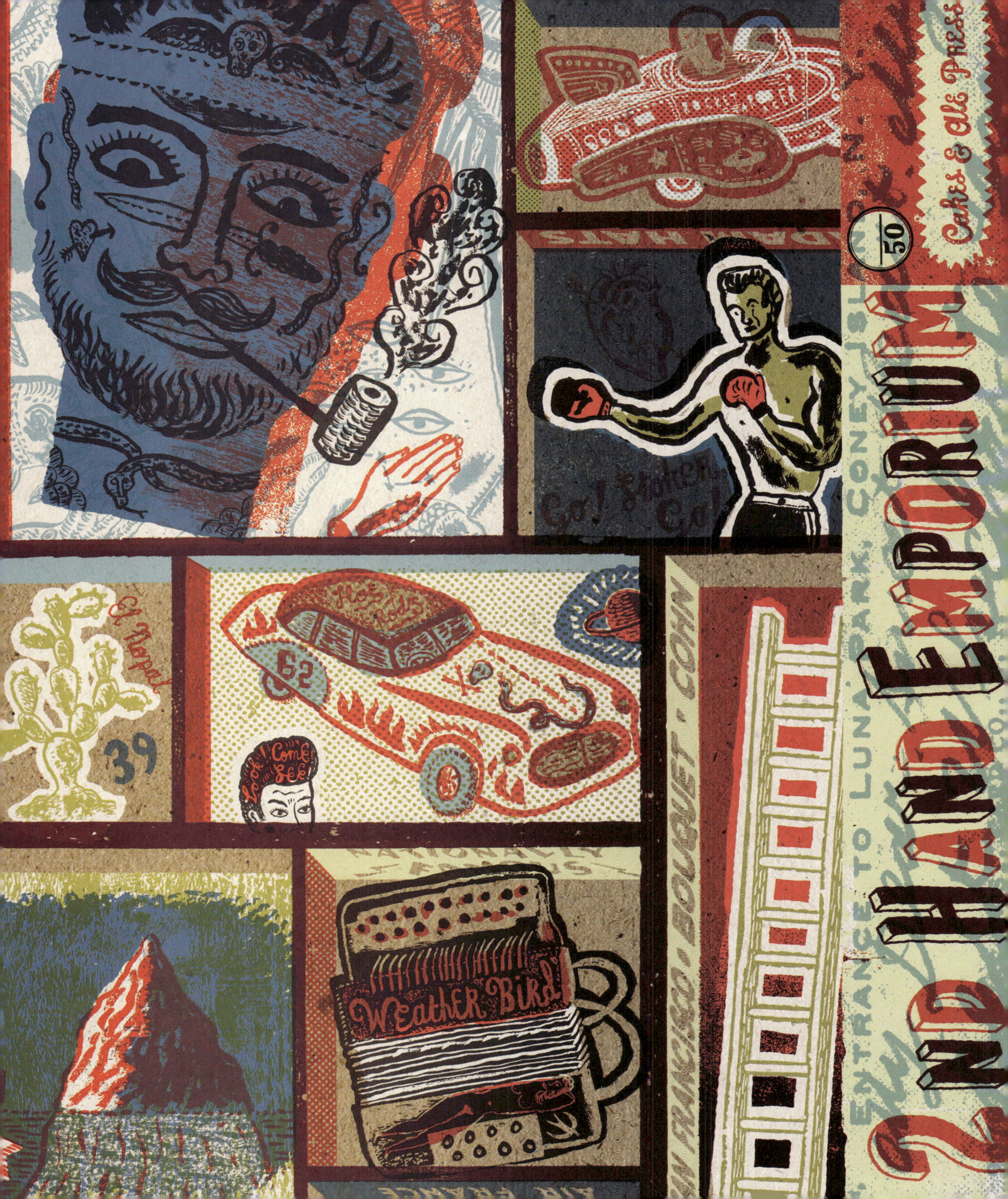

2ND HAND EMPORIUM
ENTRANCE TO LUNA PARK, CONEY ISL
Cakes & Ale Press
50
El Nopal
39
62
Weather Bird
NATIONALLY FAMOUS
FRANCISCO · BOUQUET · COHN

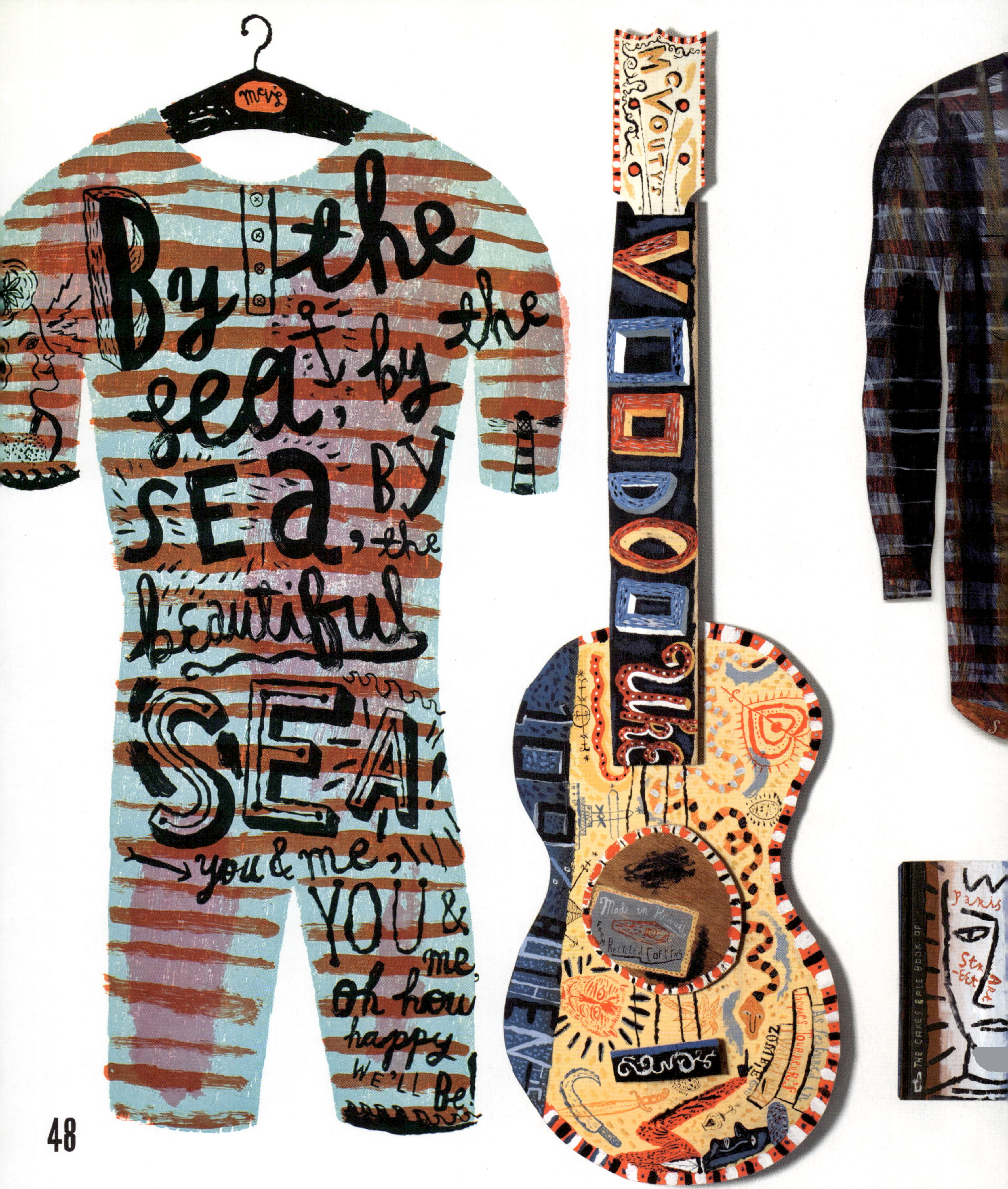
By the sea, by the sea, BY the beautiful SEA!
you & me, YOU & me,
oh how happy WE'LL Be!
MCVOUTY'S
VOODOO
Made in Hawaii
FROM RECYCLED COFFINS
ZOMBIE
THE CAKES & ALE BOOK OF
Paris
Street Art

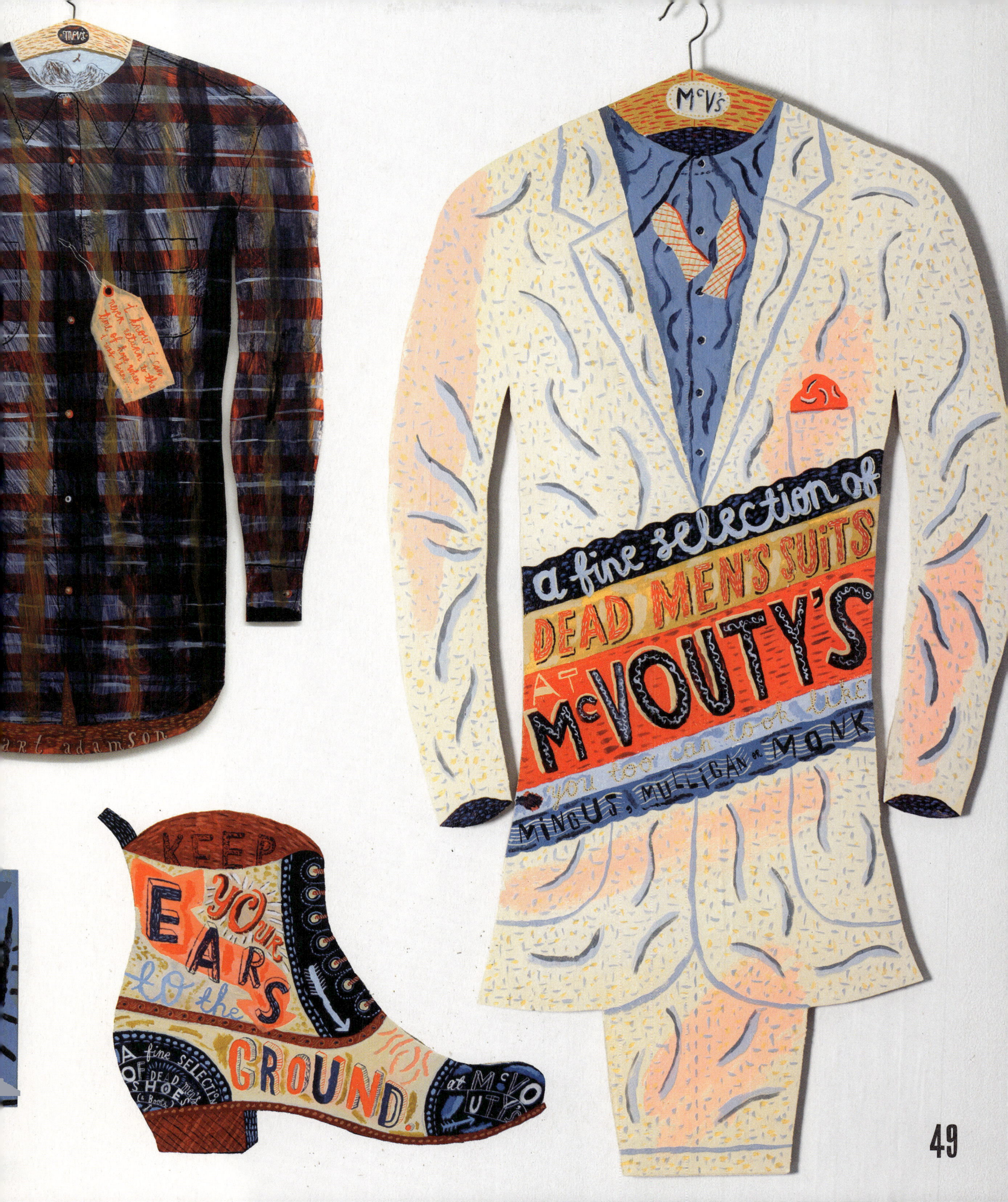
McV's
art adamson
McV's
a fine selection of
DEAD MEN'S SUITS
AT
McVOUTY'S
you too can look like
MINGUS, MULLIGAN or MONK
KEEP
YOUR
EARS
to the
GROUND.
A fine selection OF DEAD men's SHOES & Boots
at McVOUTY'S

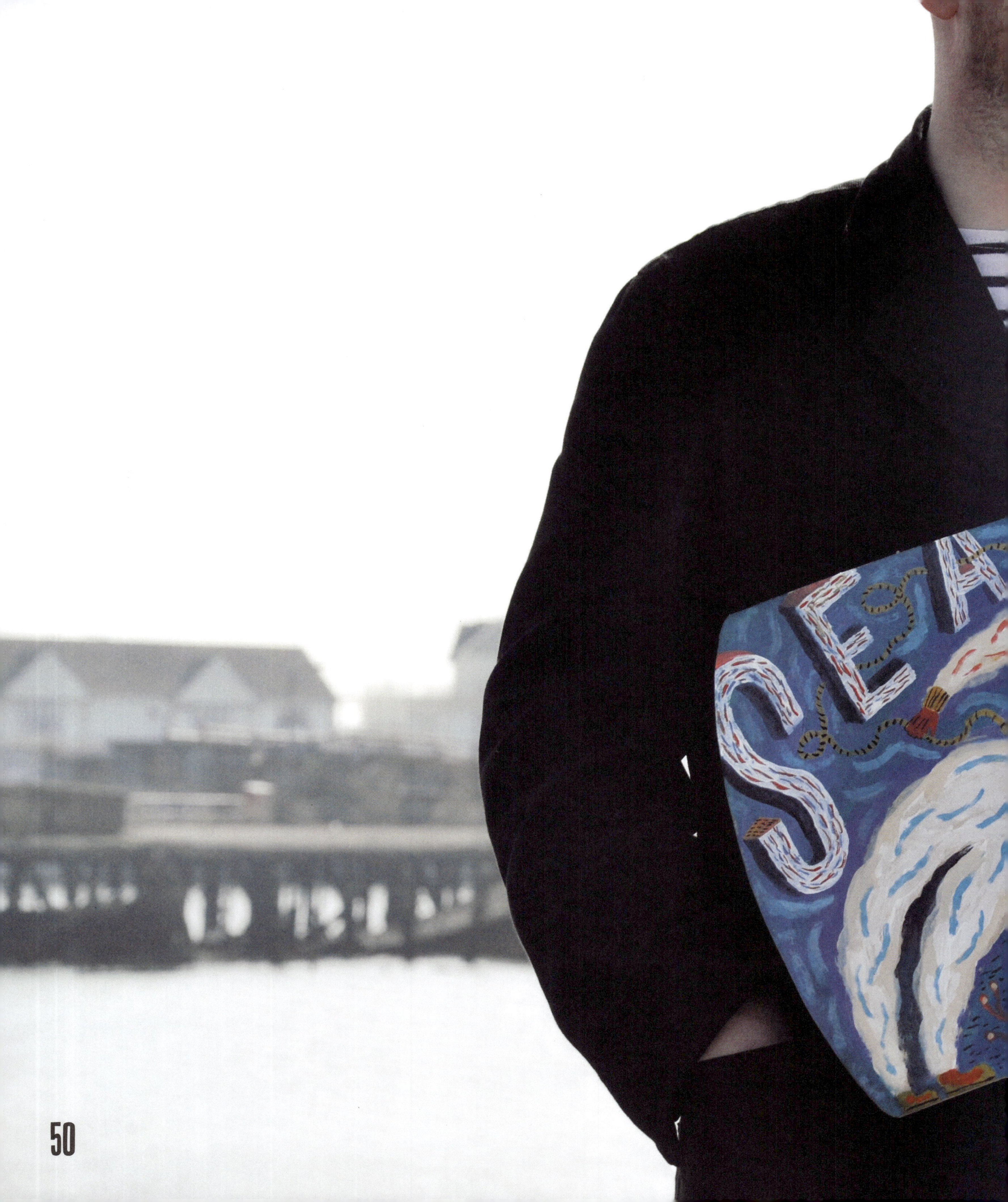

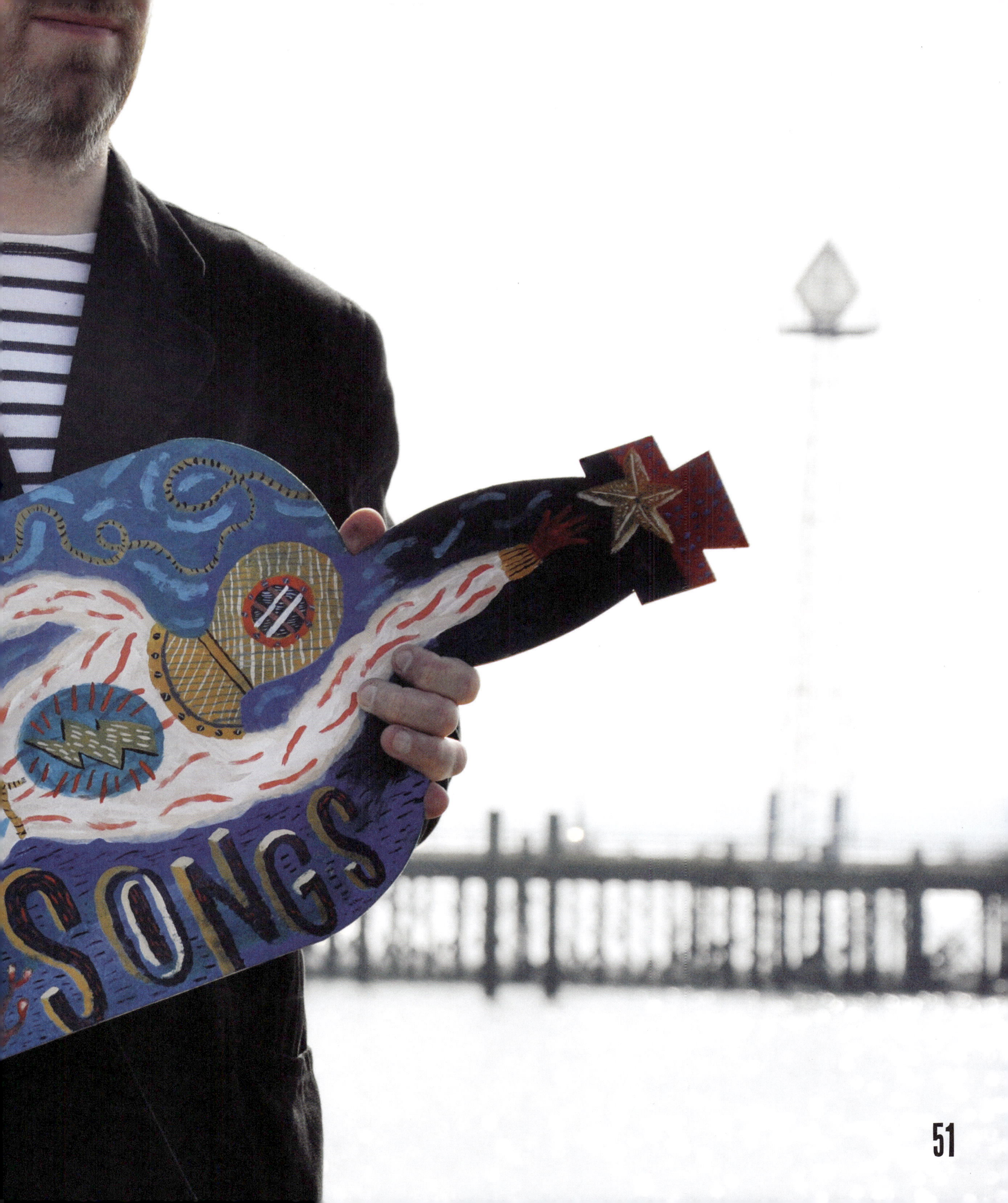
SONGS

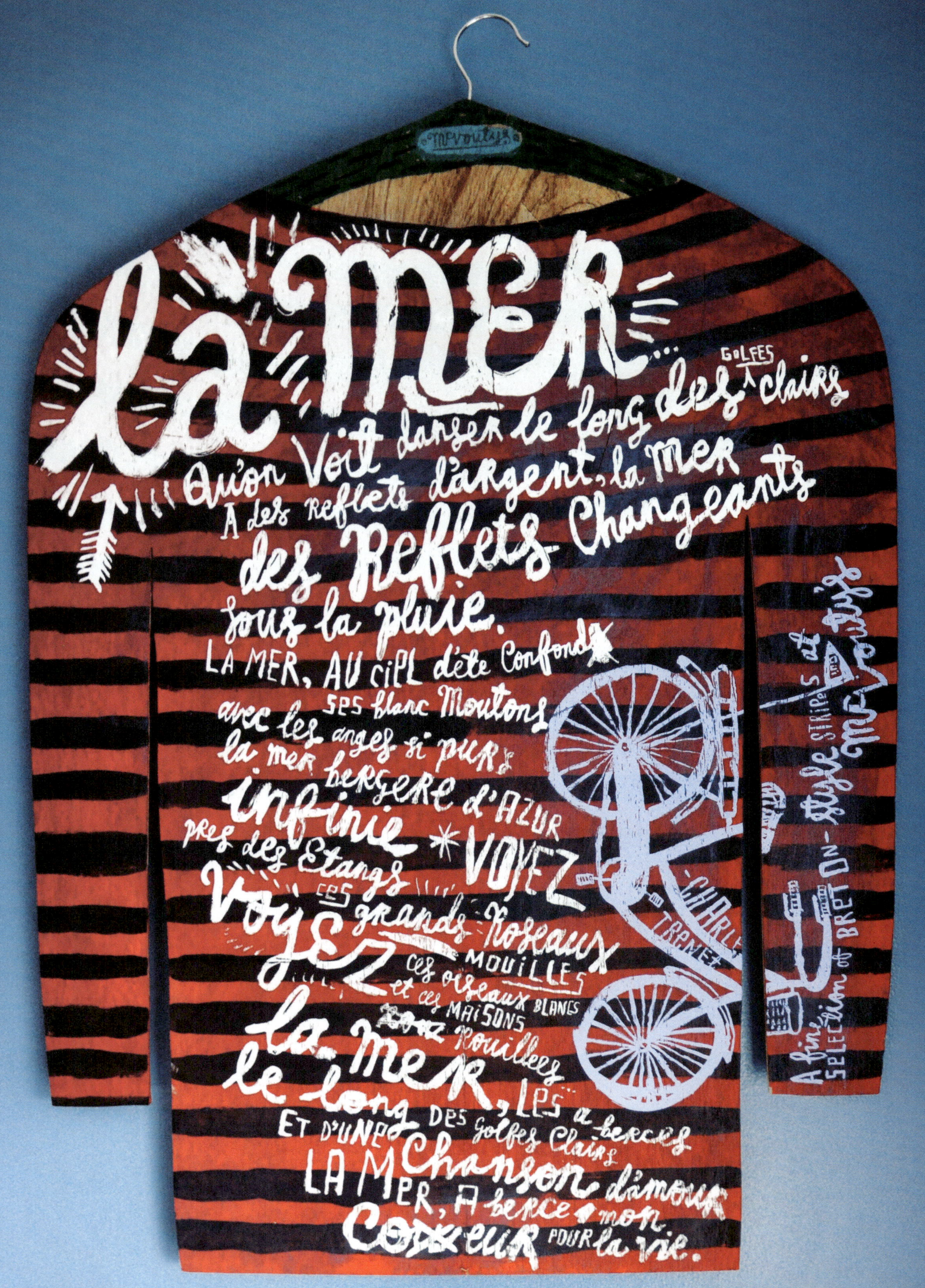

la Mer...
Golfes
Qu'on Voit danser le long des clairs
A des reflets d'argent, la Mer
des Reflets Changeants
sous la pluie.
LA MER, AU CIEL d'été Confond
ses blanc Moutons
avec les anges si purs
la mer bergère d'azur
infinie
près des Etangs
* VOYEZ
Voyez ces grands roseaux
MOUILLÉS
ces oiseaux blancs
et ces MAISONS
rouillées
la mer, les a bercés
le long des golfes clairs
ET D'UNE Chanson d'amour
LA MER, A bercé mon
cœur pour la vie.
CHARLES TRENET
A fine selection of BRETON-style STRIPES at

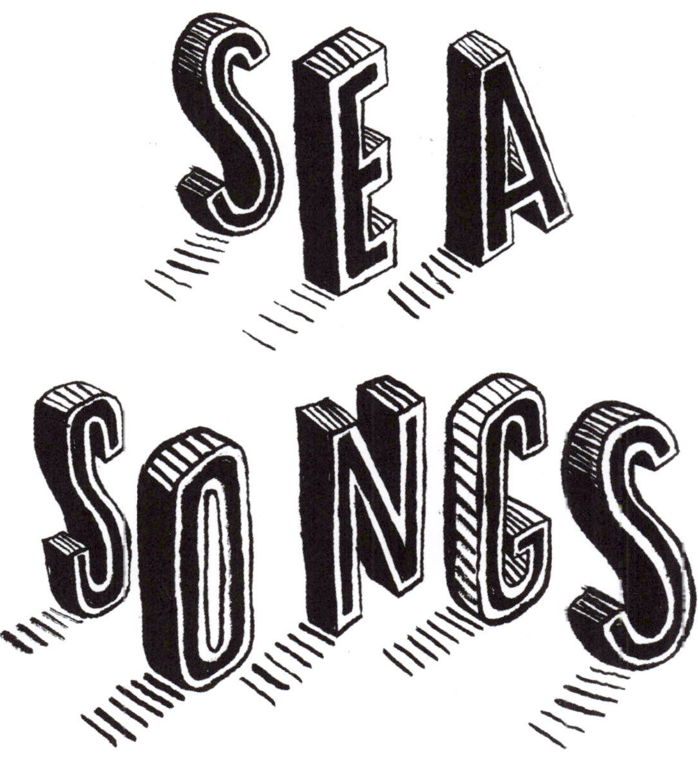


When I first arrived in Darktown, I flew into the Count Arthur Strong Airport. It wasn't exactly a pleasing experience, but, much to my joy, I discovered that Darktown is on the coast, and an overnight ferry from Pompey leaves every evening. So, ever since then, I've always got here by sea, which is so much more fun.

Having the sea near by is essential. I grew up close to the Firth of Forth, lived near the Mersey for some time and now look out over Southampton Water towards the Isle of Wight. So it made perfect sense to choose Darktown, surrounded by the Sea of Possibilities. As far as I'm concerned, the bigger the expanse of water, the better. It fascinates me, partly because I'm such an awful swimmer. If my feet can't touch the bottom, forget it. But books, poems and stories about the watery main have become an obsession.

Mighty leviathans, tall ships and stars to steer them by, mermaids and shanties are part of my everyday inspiration. The Handsome Cabin Boy isn't a boy, you know. The first edition of *Moby-Dick* didn't even come close to selling out, and the remaining copies were burned in a fire at the publisher's warehouse in New York. Charles Trenet supposedly wrote 'La Mer' on toilet paper while on a train. My idea of bliss is being set adrift with Alfred Wallis, Billy Budd and Tim Buckley's 'Song to the Siren'.

But the simplicities of an hour or two at the seaside are equally satisfying. If you time it right, you can stand amid the breakers, battered about to one's heart's content. You then feel reborn just in time for a walk along the pier and a whizz down the helter-skelter, which was condemned years ago, making it all the more fun. Then it's time to cycle along the seafront to Winking Willy's Fish and Chip Shop. It may not be the best, but it does the job and has a wee sit-in café where they even have Tennent's lager on draught.

Darktown's twin town, St Monans, has the motto 'Mare Vivimus'. Grip fast, good people, grip fast.

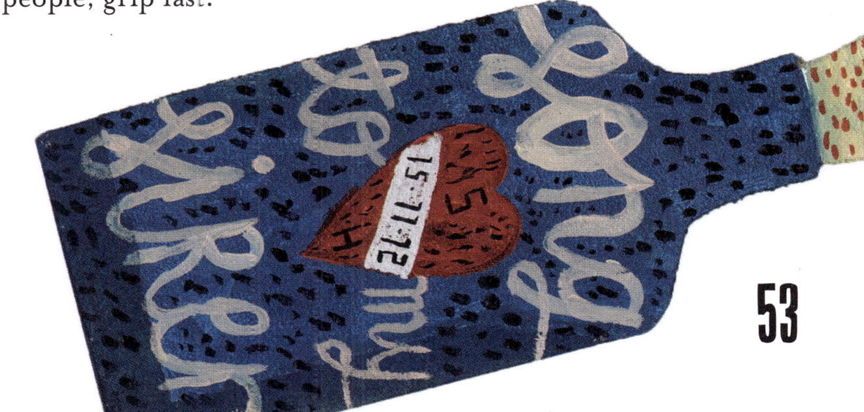

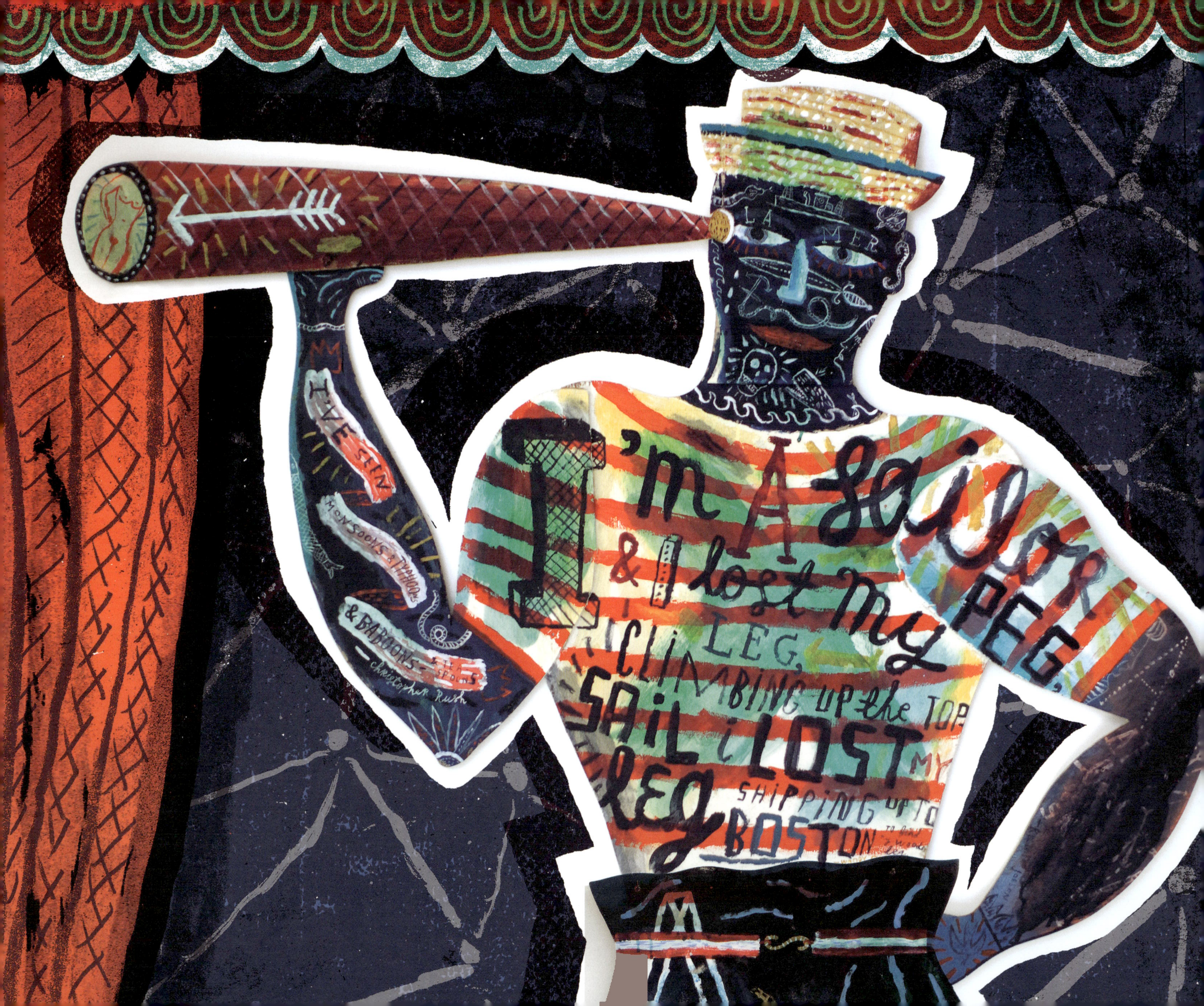
I'm A Sailor
& I lost my PEG,
LEG,
CLIMBING UP the TOP
SAIL i LOST MY
leg
SHIPPING UP TO
BOSTON
I'VE SEEN
MONSOONS & TYPHOONS
& BABOONS
LA MER
christopher Rush

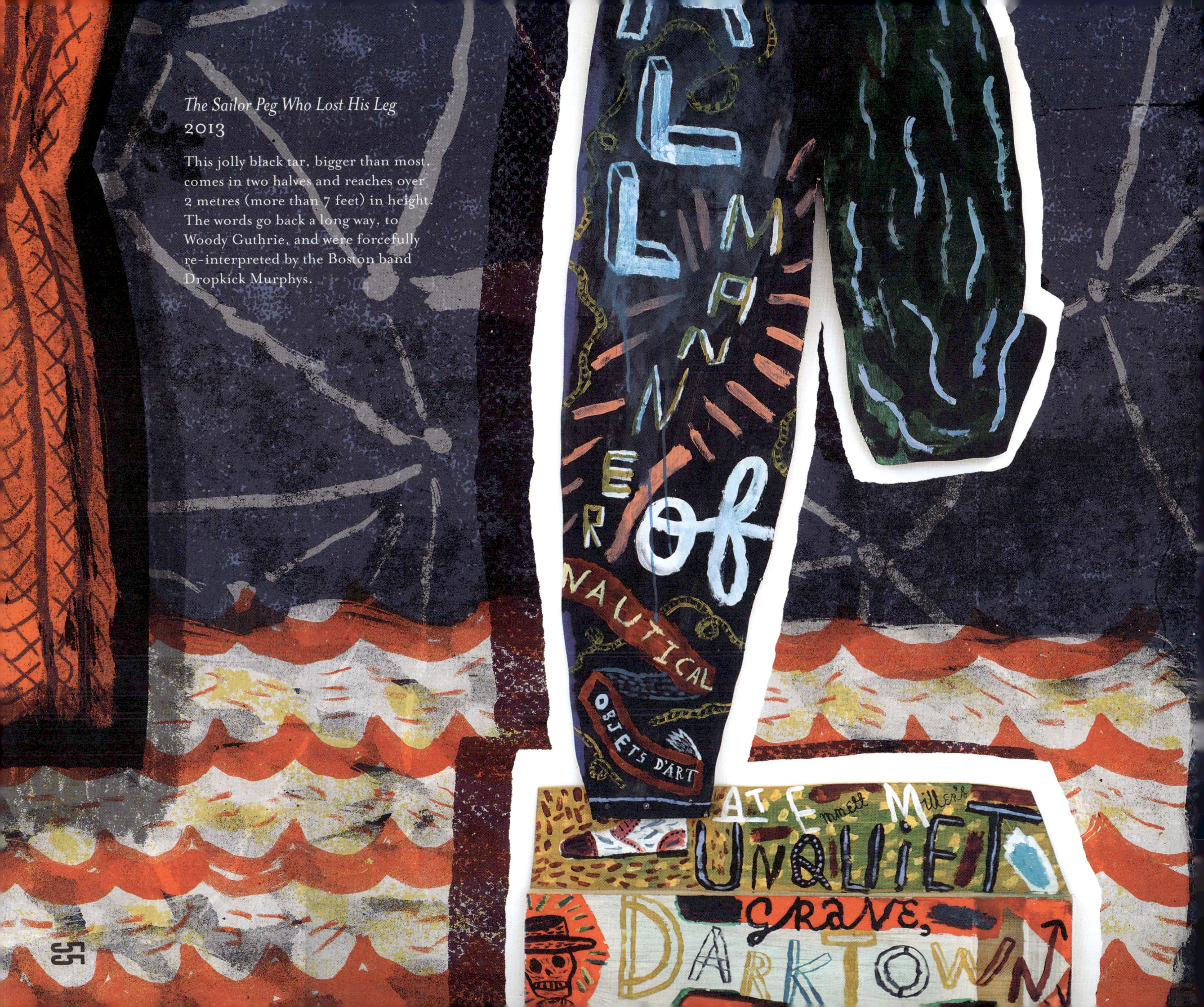


*The Sailor Peg Who Lost His Leg*
2013

This jolly black tar, bigger than most, comes in two halves and reaches over 2 metres (more than 7 feet) in height. The words go back a long way, to Woody Guthrie, and were forcefully re-interpreted by the Boston band Dropkick Murphys.

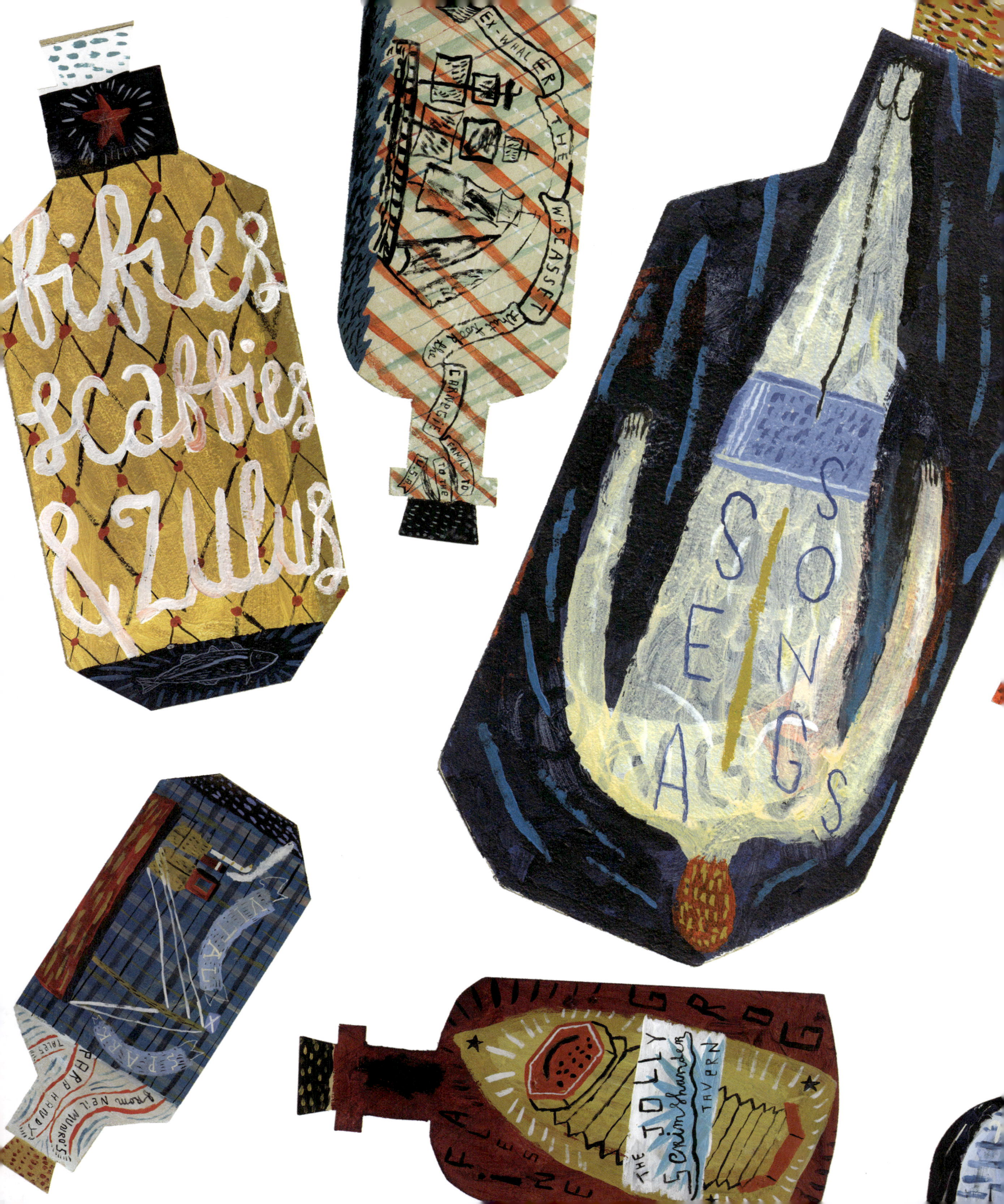
fifies scaffies & Zulus
SEA SONGS
THE JOLLY Scrimshander TAVERN
From NEIL MUNRO'S PARA HANDY TALES
EX-WHALER

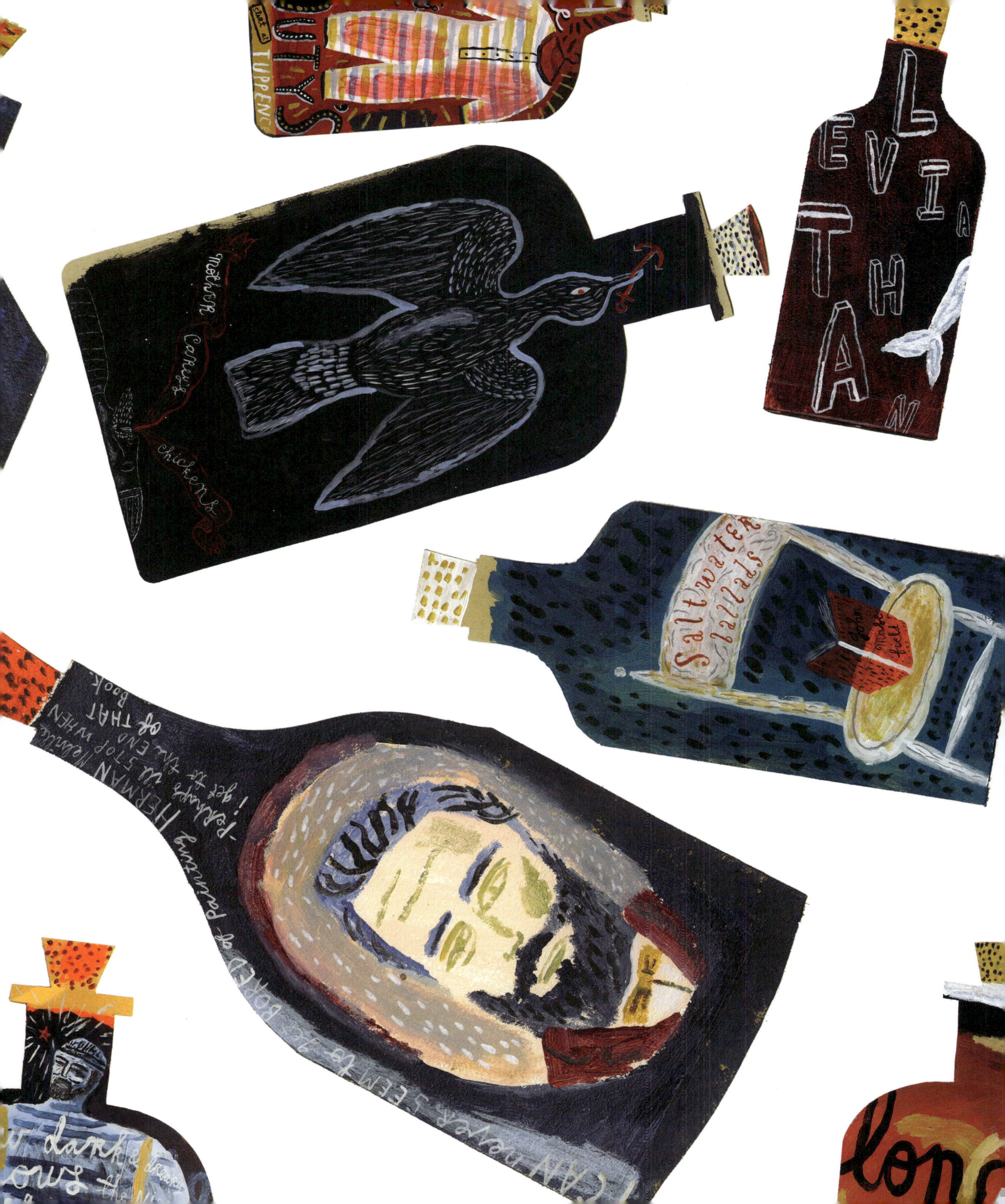
LEVIATHAN
mother Carey's chickens
Saltwater ballads
John Masefield

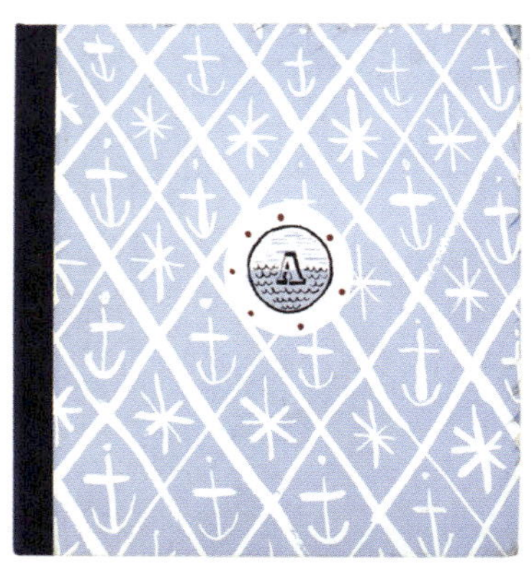

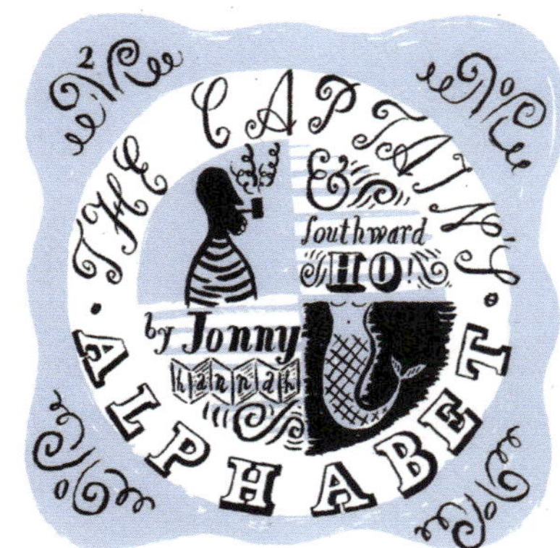


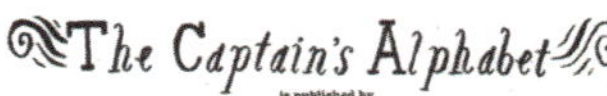

The Captain's Alphabet

is published by

Merivale Editions

14 Merivale Road, London SW15 2NW

and

Cakes & Ale Press

21 Goldsmid Road, Hove, East Sussex BN3 1QA

Screenprinted at XXY Press

Fifty sets have been hand-printed on 280 gsm paper by the artist Jonny Hannah, who also hand-printed the paper sides of the book-form boxes made by Smith Settle of Ottley, Yorkshire.

Twenty-six sets lettered A to Z numbered & signed on this page by Jonny Hannah

Twelve *special* sets numbered I to XII with an extra print & an original drawing

Seven sets numbered 1 to 7 available as individual prints

There are five sets of Artist's Proofs

This is set No.

COMPLETE

UNEXPURGATED

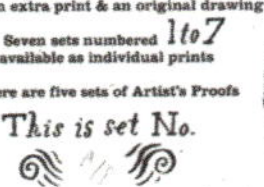

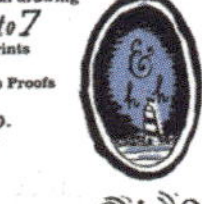

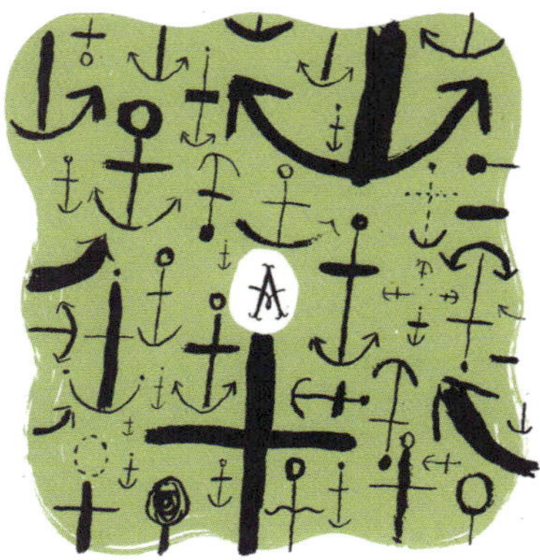

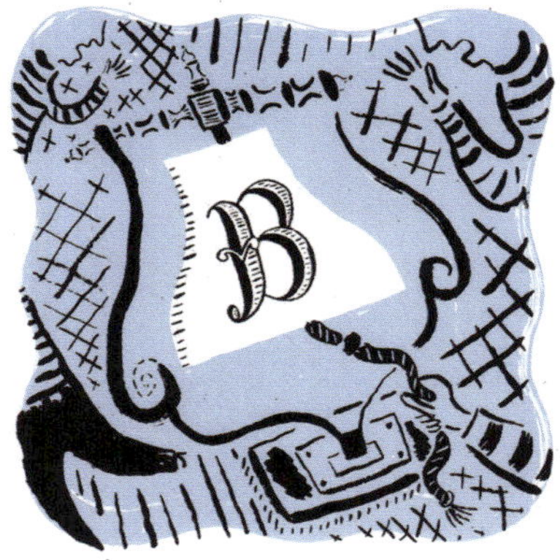

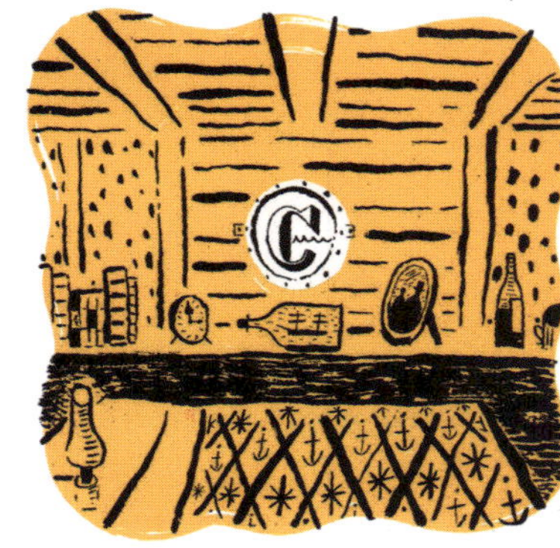

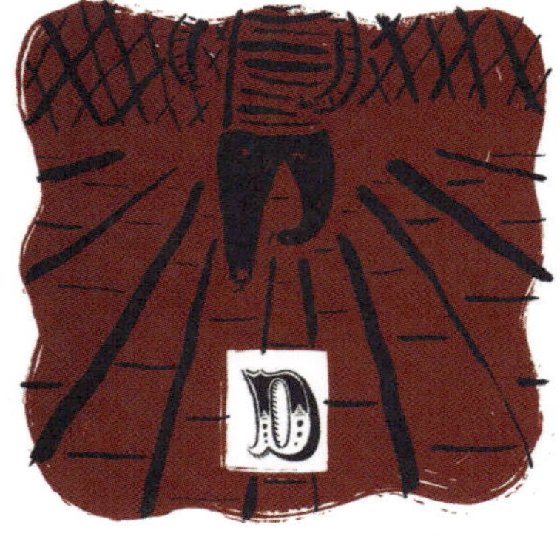

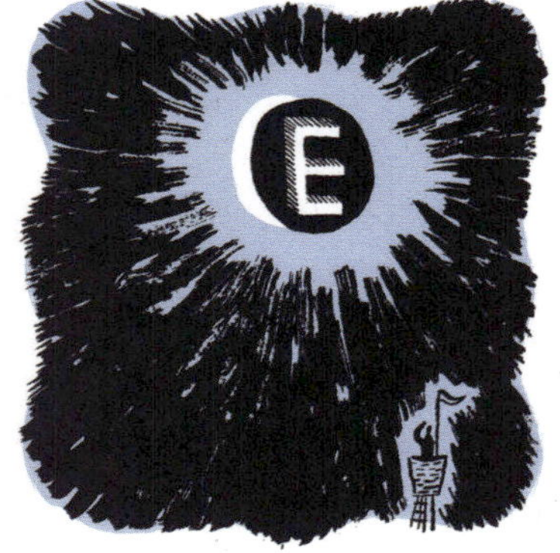

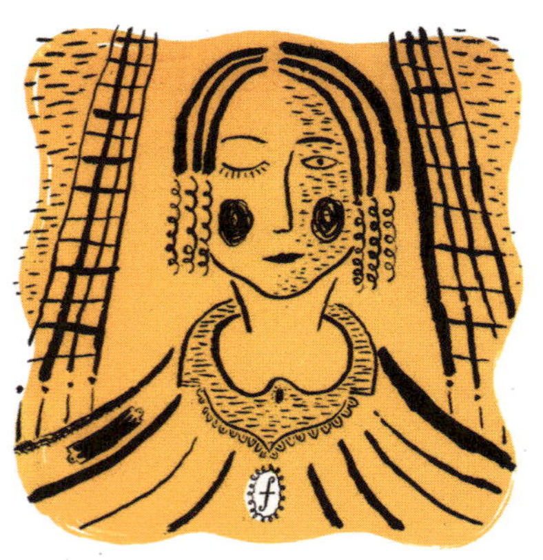

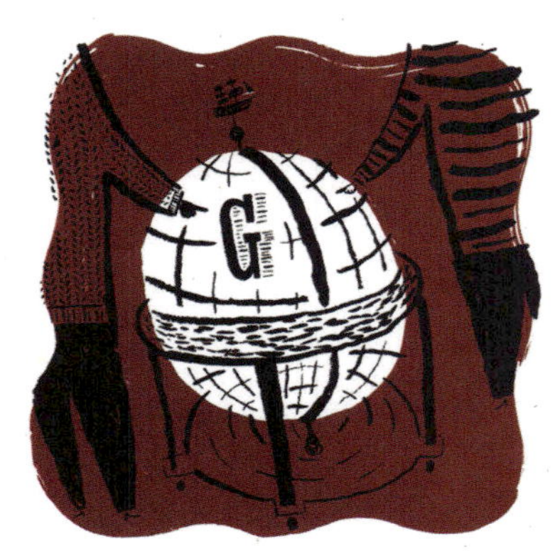

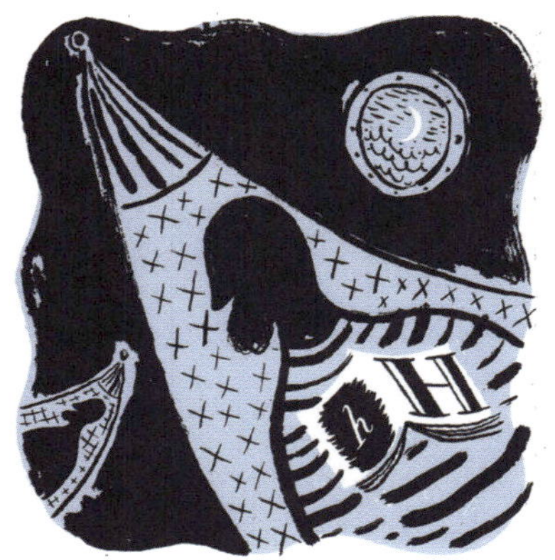

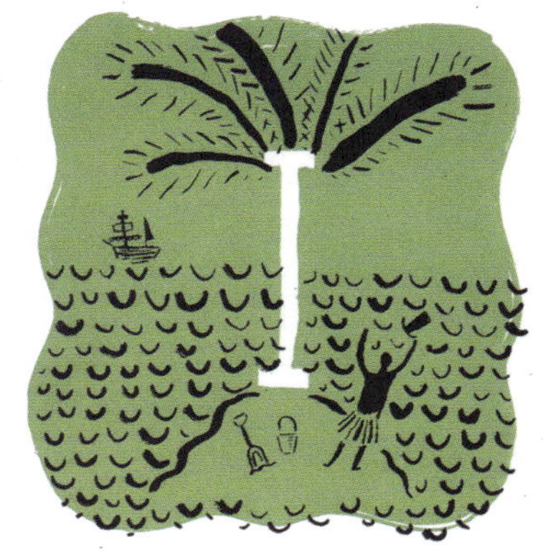

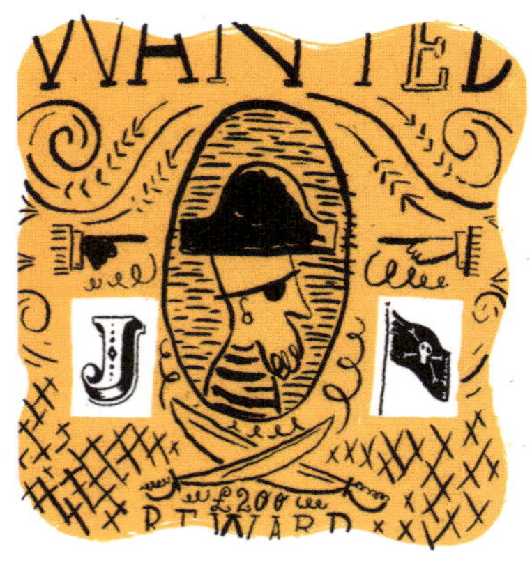


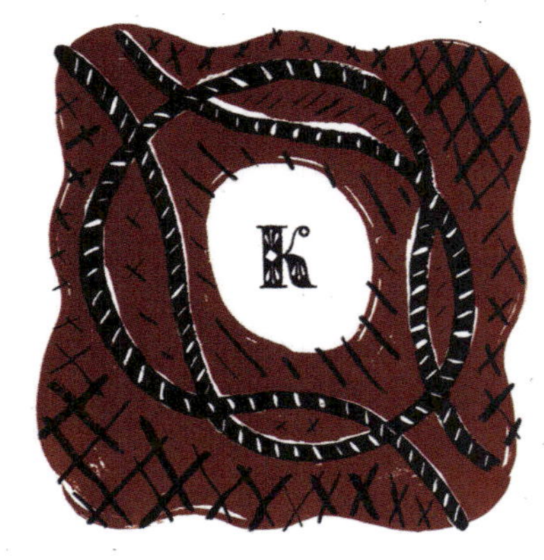

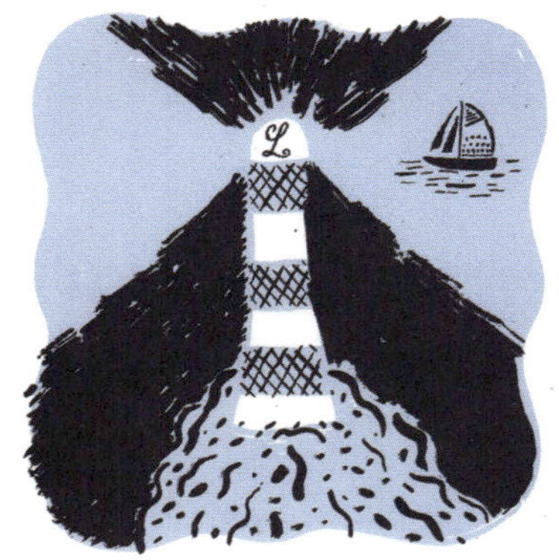

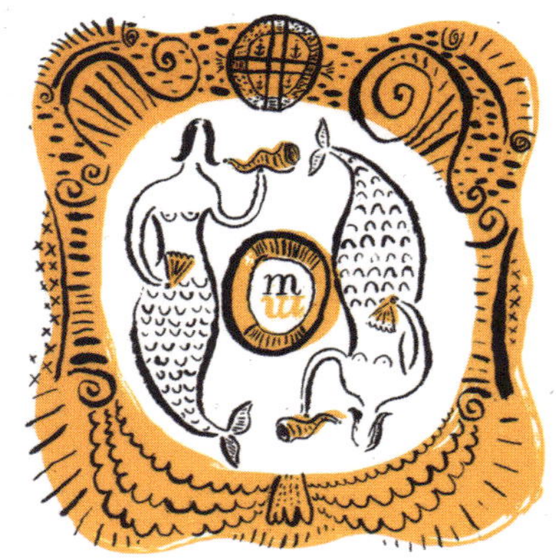

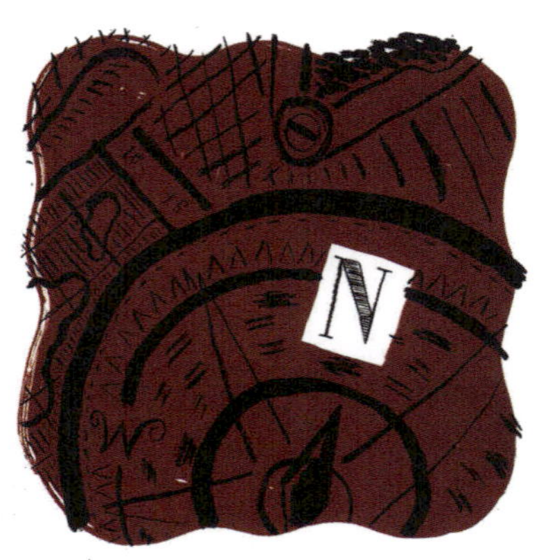

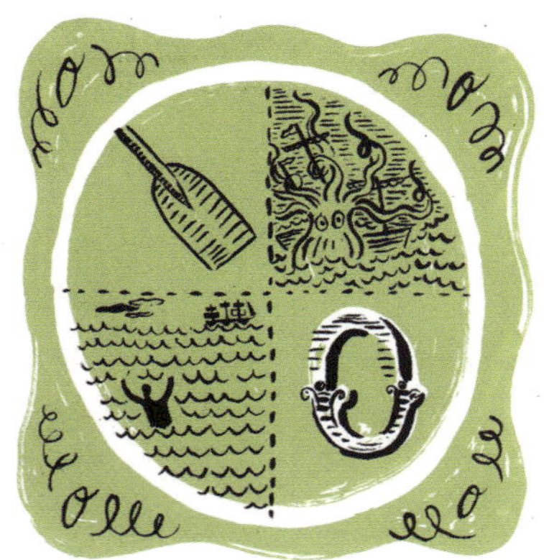

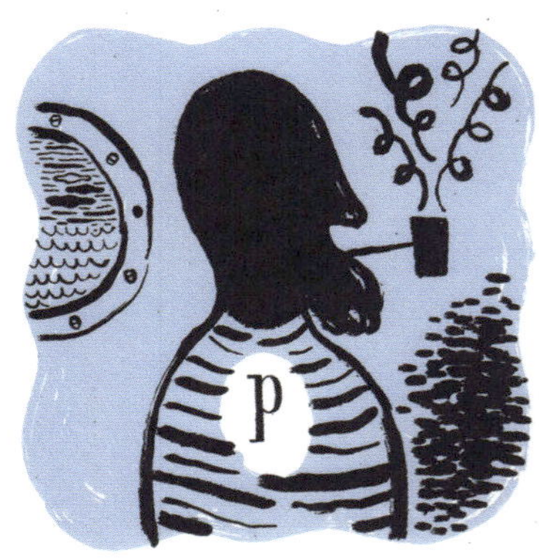

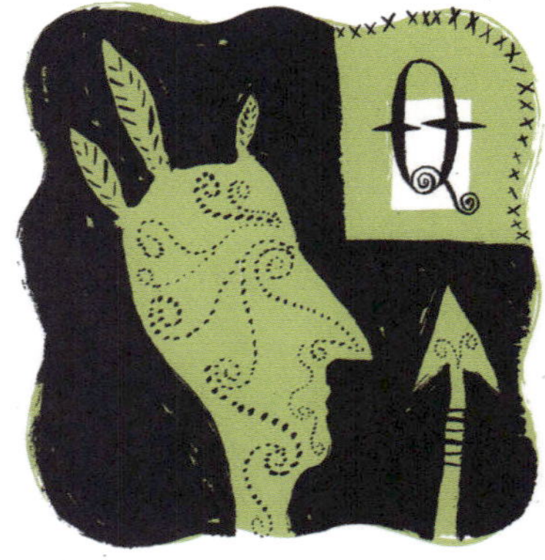

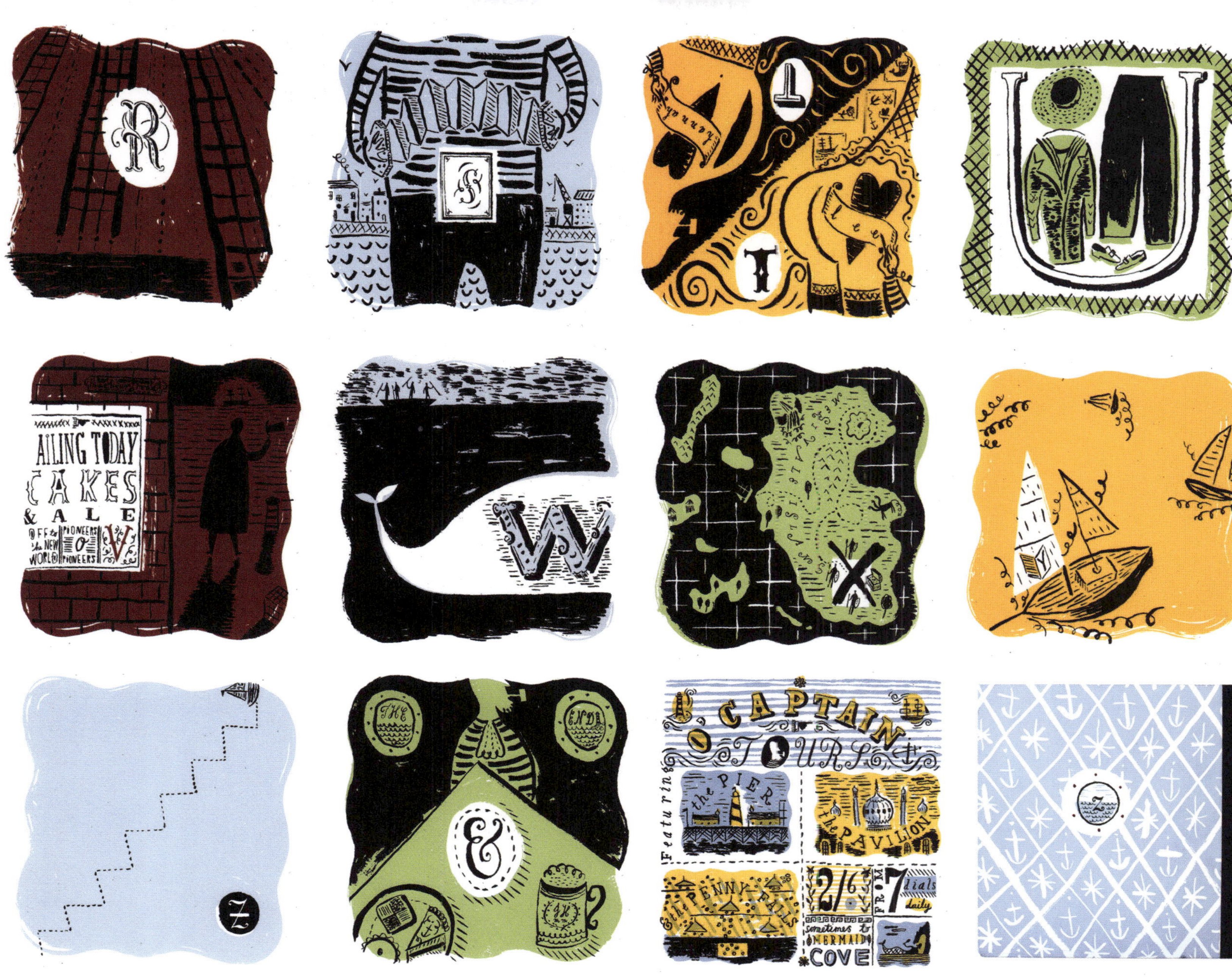


# The Captain's Alphabet

'I Have No One to Love Me (But the Sailor on the Deep Blue Sea)' is a song by the hillbilly trio the Carter Family. It's a simple enough tale about a maiden who waits for her true love to return. When he doesn't show up, she asks, 'O Captain, can you tell me, can you tell me where he may be?' The idea of the Captain, nameless but knowing, captured my imagination. And so began 'The Captain's Alphabet', my nautical A to Z. I was fortunate to meet Peter Sampson through my old tutor Christopher Brown. Peter ran Merivale Editions, rather like my own Cakes & Ale Press – only he was much better organized than me and made a living from it. And Peter was interested in my work. On reflection, he is much to blame for where I am today, for he had a confidence and faith in me that were much needed, as – like the sailor on the deep-blue sea – I was somewhat adrift back then; all at sea, struggling to find a comfortable spot at the Royal College of Art. When I left there, Peter agreed to publish my box set of sea-inspired prints. They were printed in a shed in Bermondsey and put together over a period of a year, during which Sharon and I moved to Brighton and had our first son. It was a key period and Peter Sampson was a key part of it, for which I shall be always grateful. Plain and simple, he was a very nice man, someone to admire. The prints quickly sold out (or did they?), and I worked with Peter again, always involving pizza and good wine. He died rather suddenly in 2012. Considering that I saw him only once or twice a year, he's sorely missed.

To answer the question: the sailor, it turned out, 'drownded in the deep blue sea'. But the Captain knows all. Go on, ask him anything you want; he'll tell you.

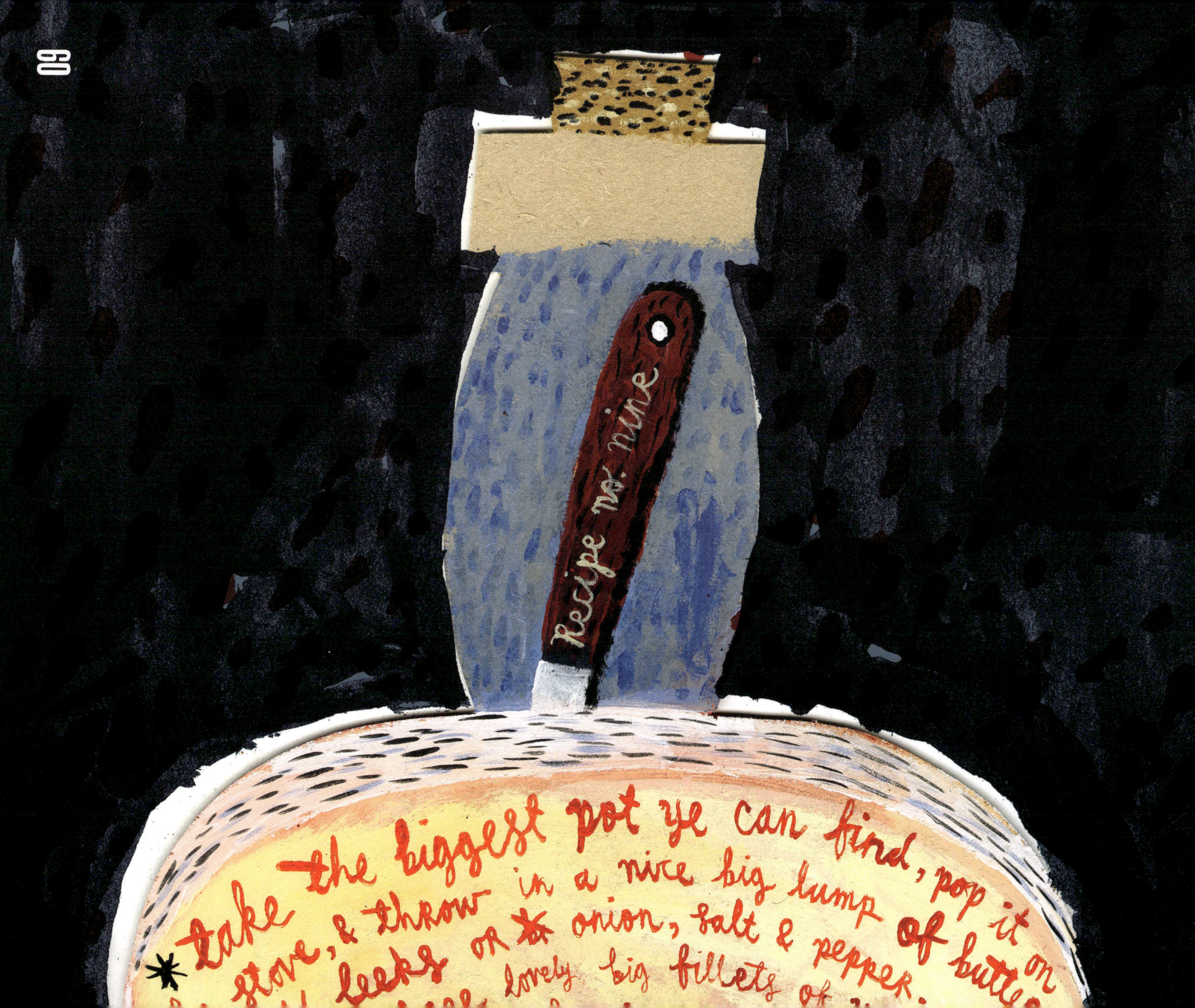
Recipe no. nine
take the biggest pot ye can find, pop it on
stove, & throw in a nice big lump of
leeks or * onion, salt & pepper.
lovely big fillets of

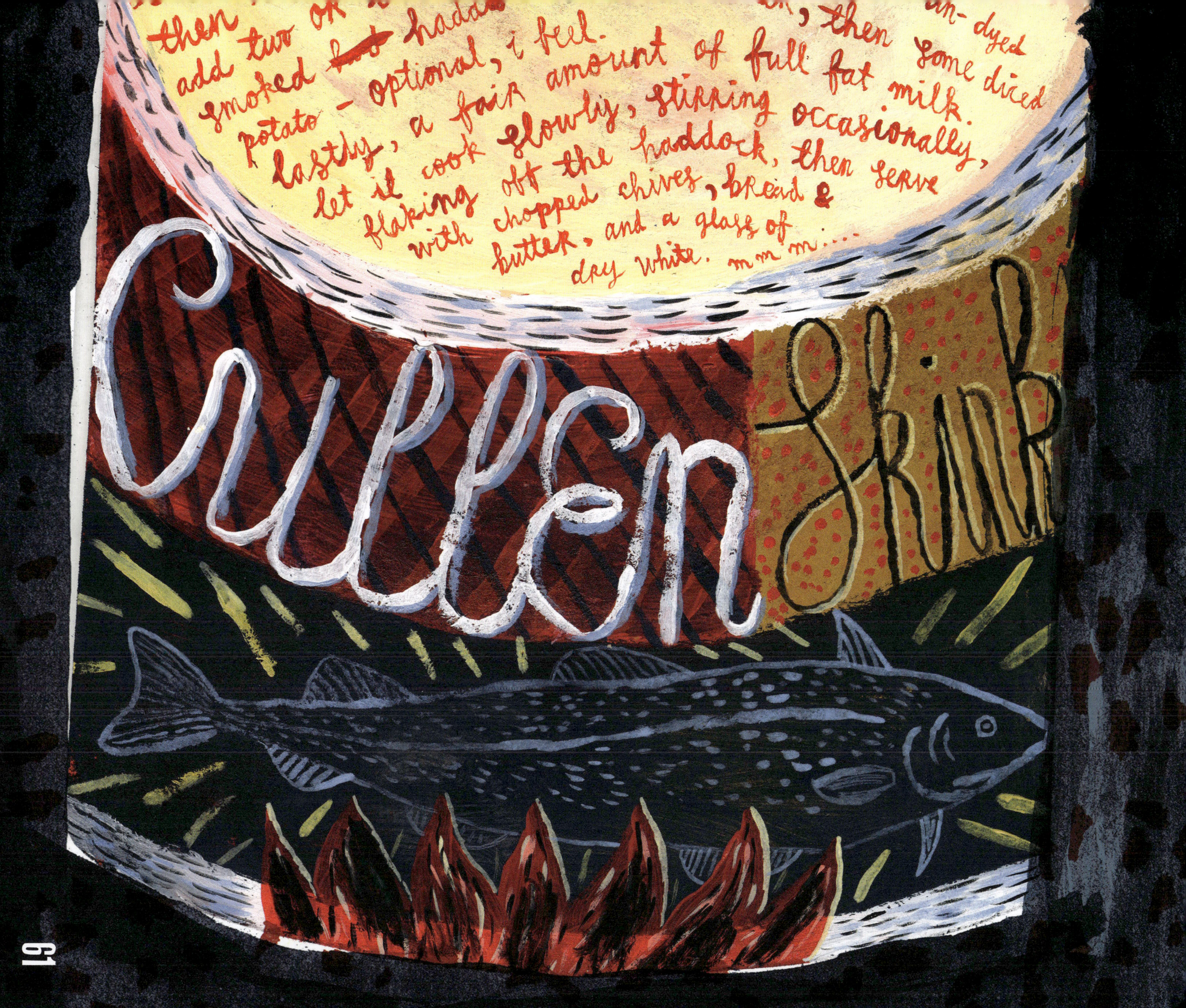
then two or
, then un-dyed
add two ~~lots~~ hadd
smoked haddock, then some diced
potato - optional, i feel.
lastly, a fair amount of full fat milk.
let it cook slowly, stirring occasionally,
flaking off the haddock, then serve
with chopped chives, bread &
butter, and a glass of
dry white. mmm....
Cullen
Skink

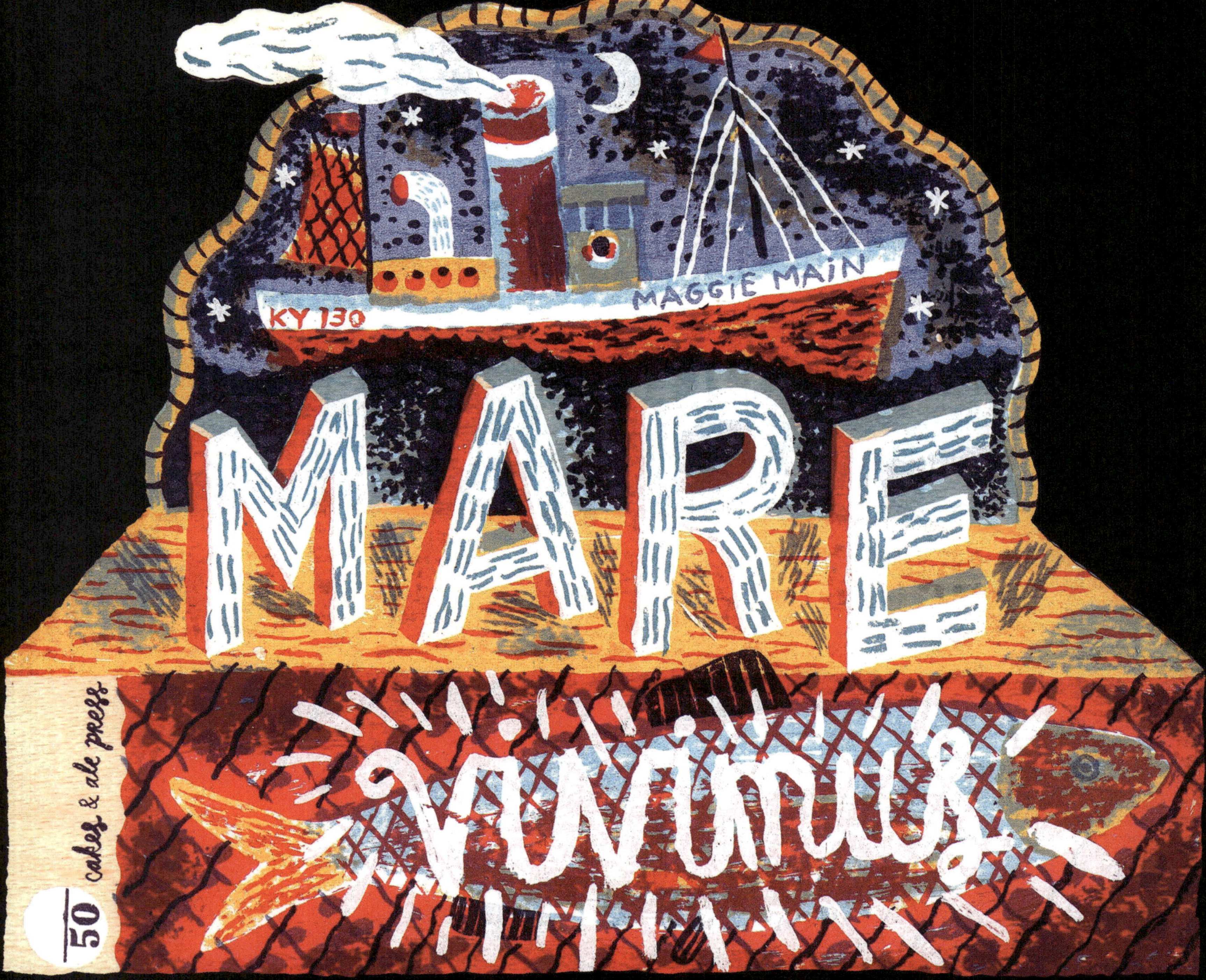

MAGGIE MAIN
KY 130
MARE
vivimus
cakes & ale press
50

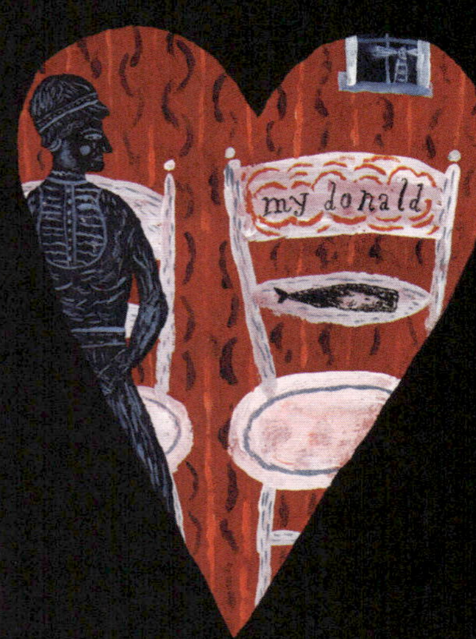


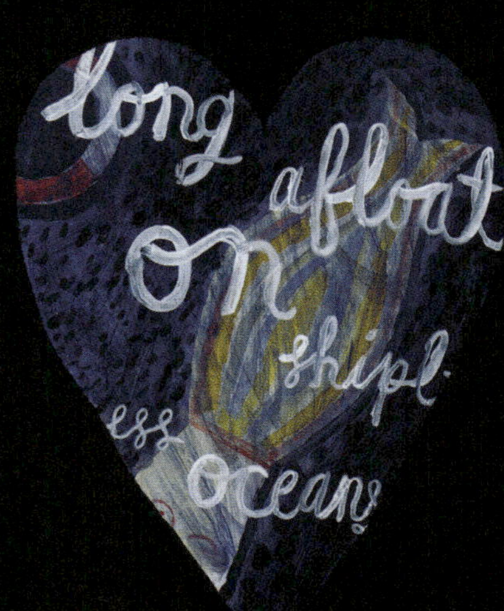


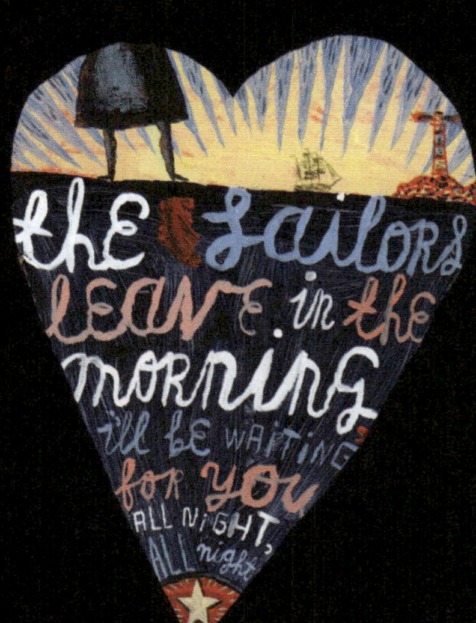

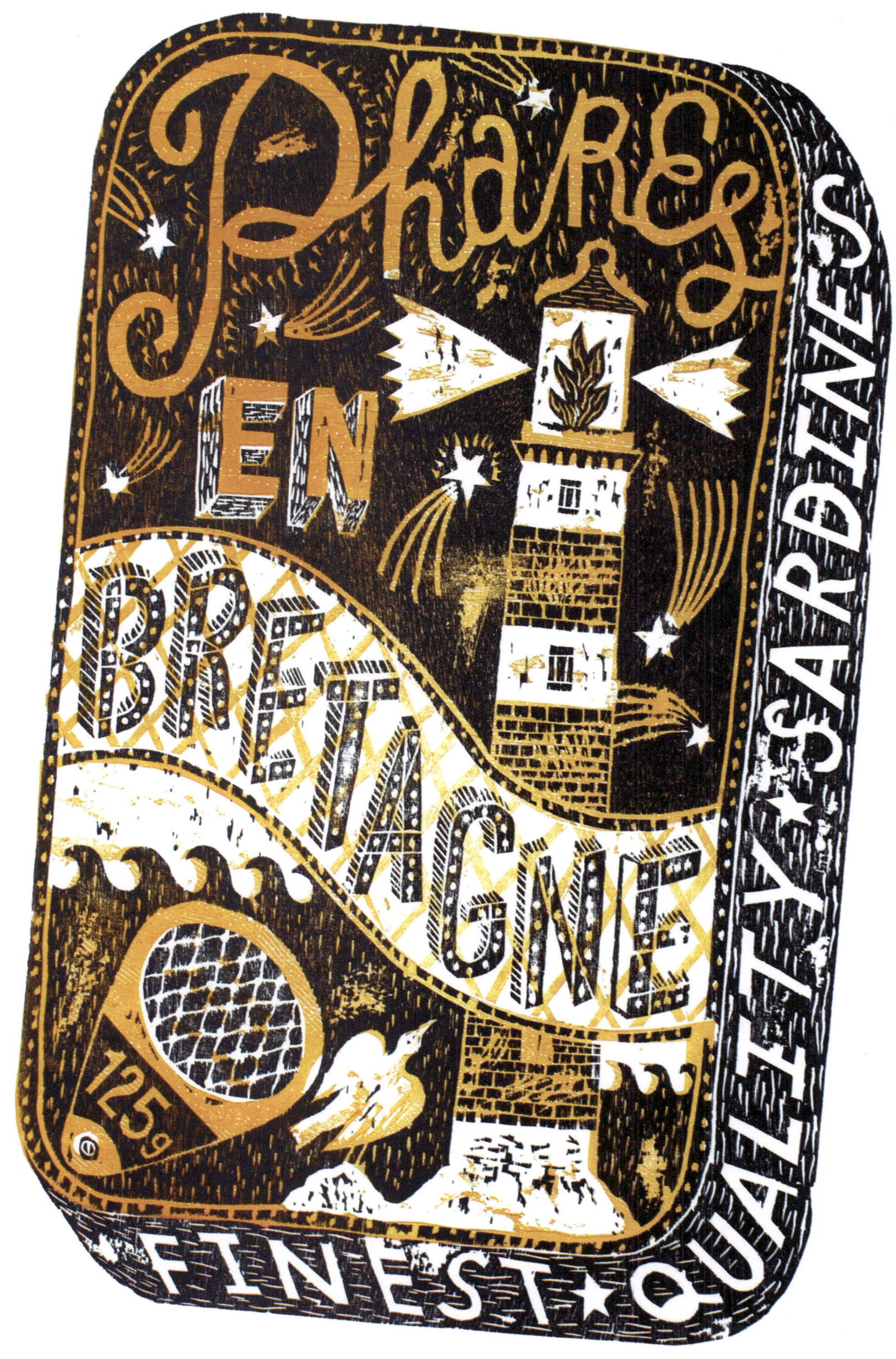
Phares
EN
BRETAGNE
125g
FINEST ★ QUALITY ★ SARDINES

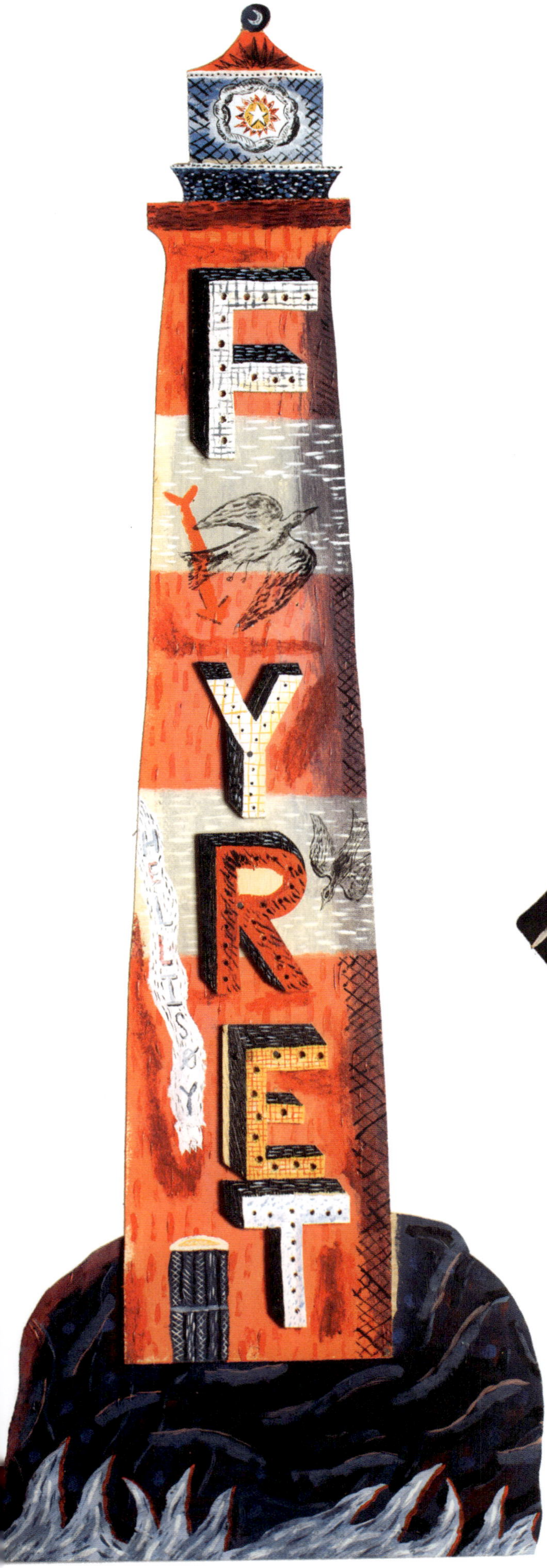

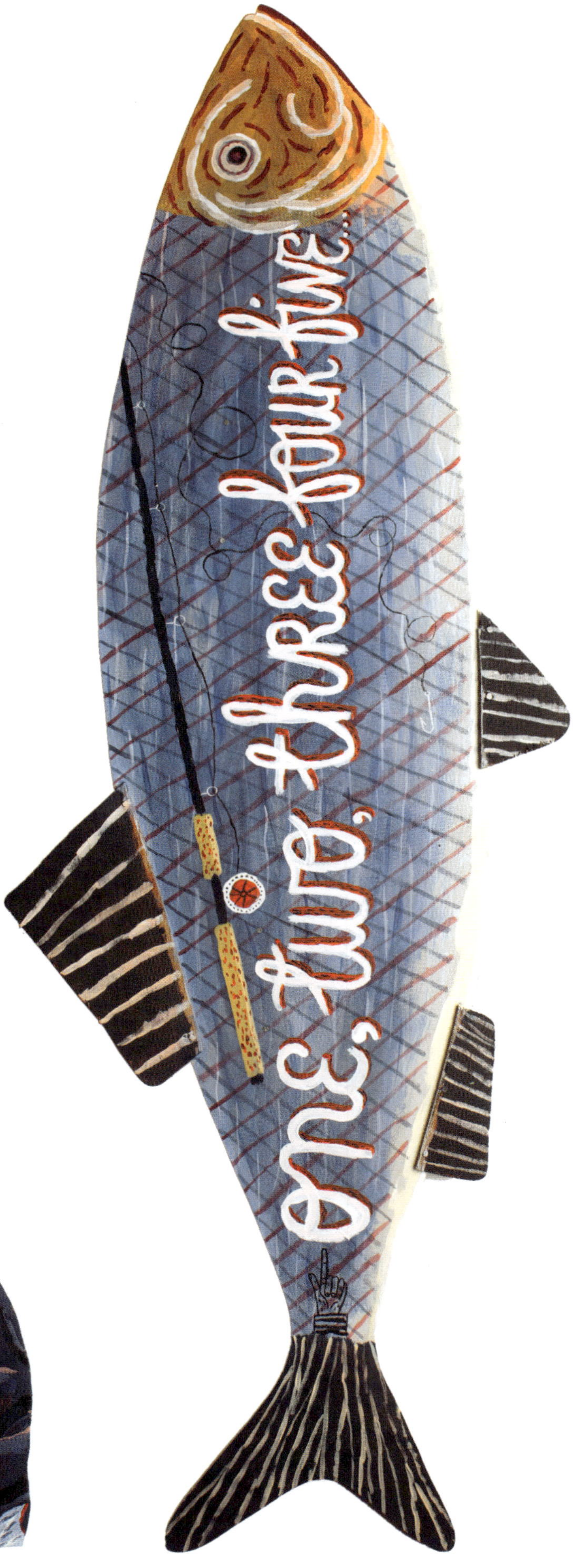

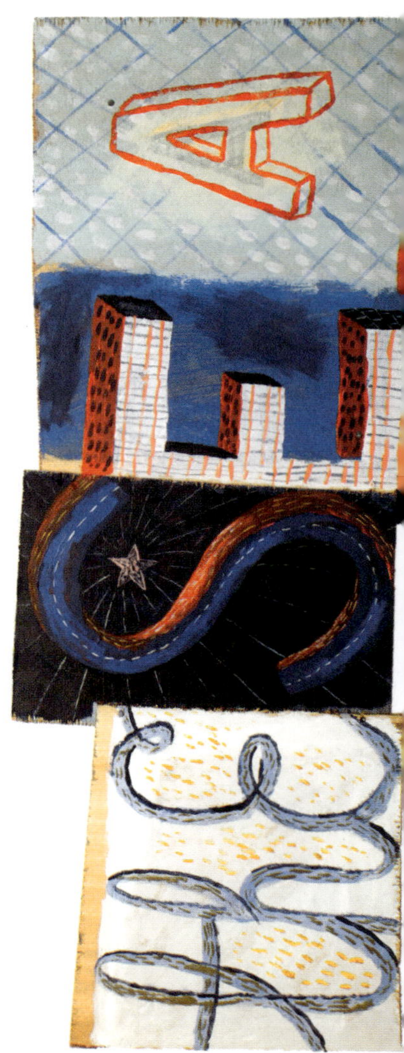

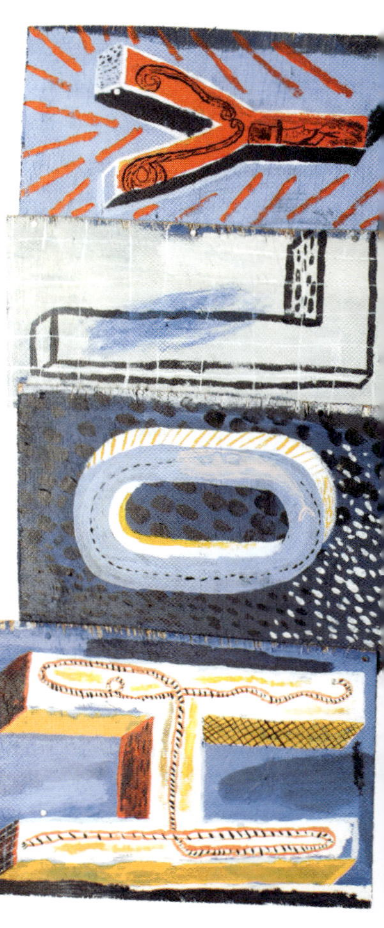

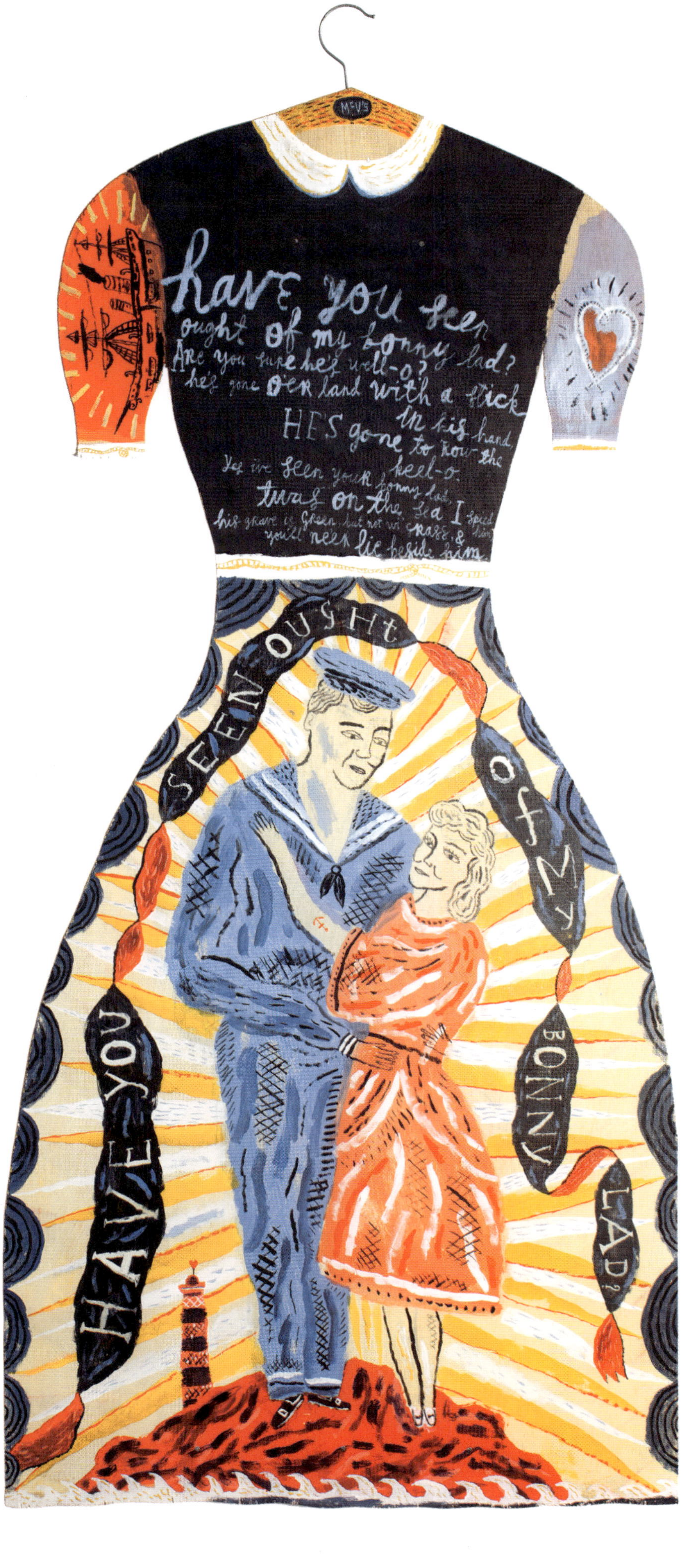

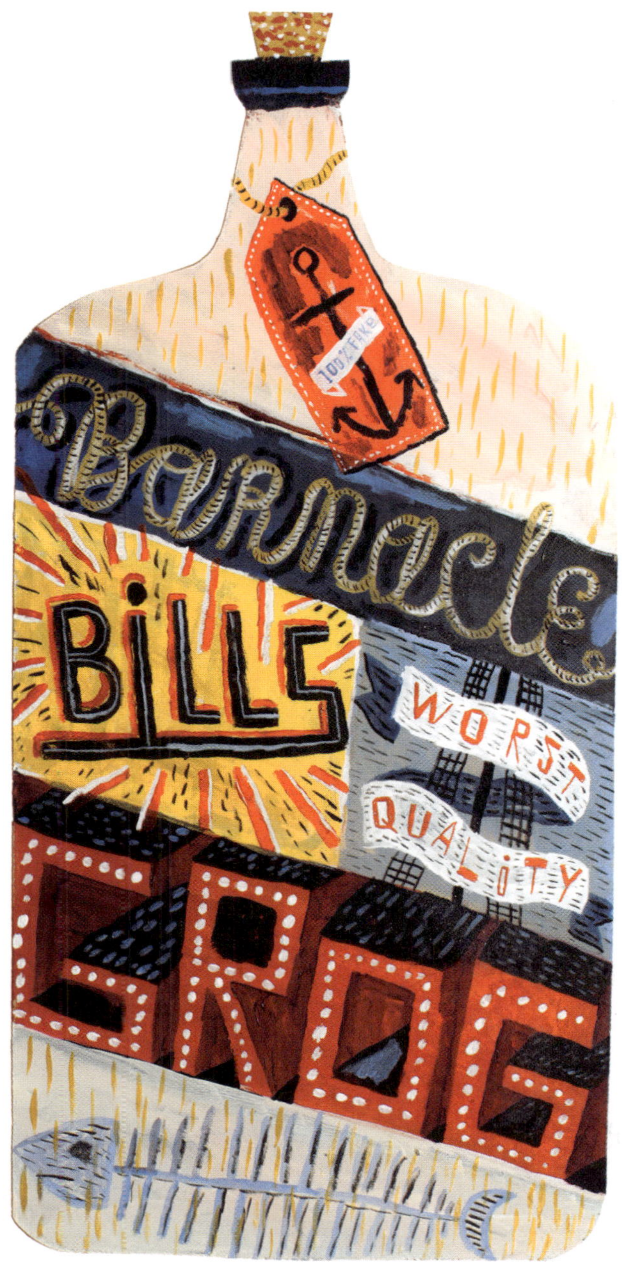
Barnacle
BiLLS
WORST QUALiTY
GROG

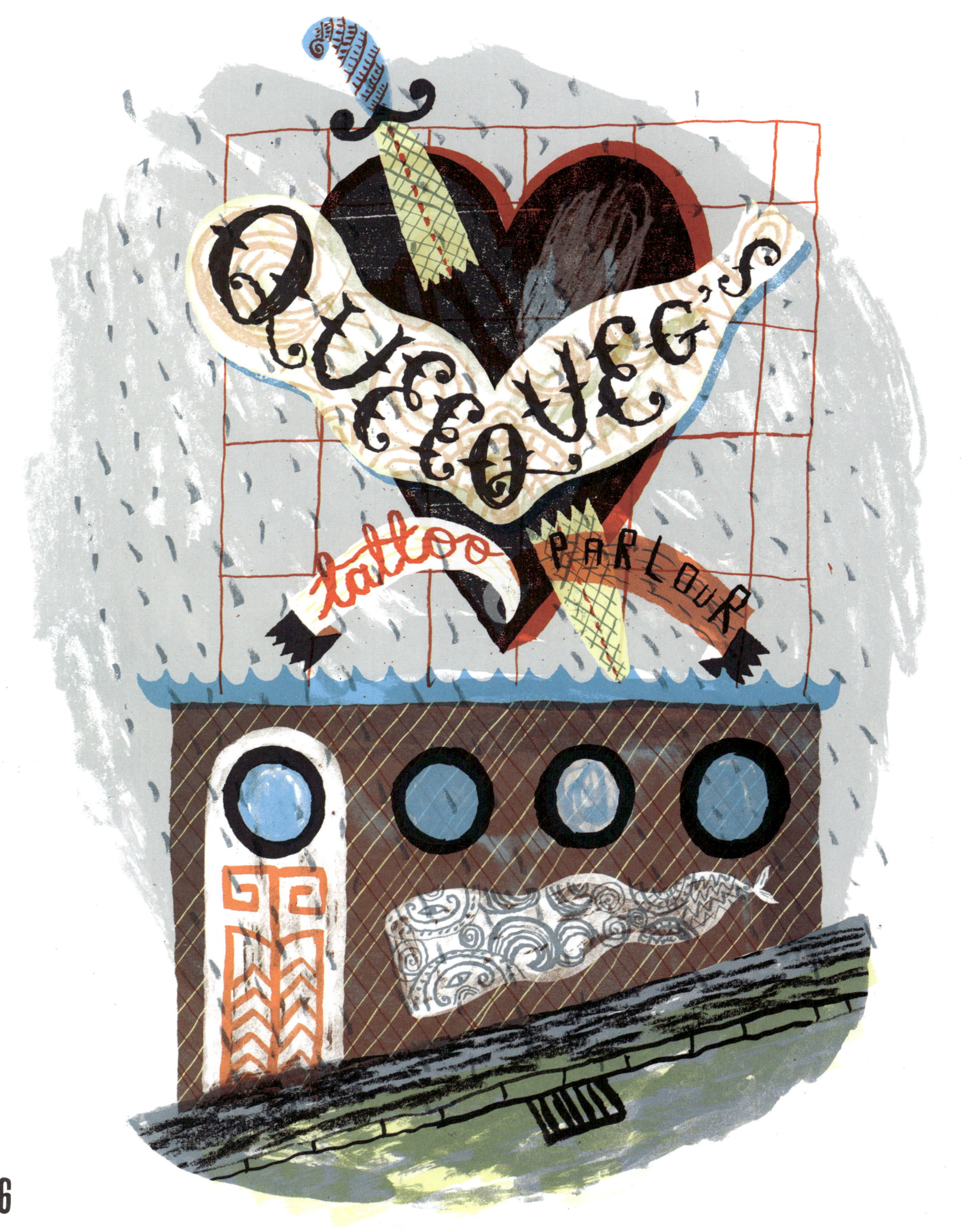
QUEEQUEG'S
tattoo
PARLOUR

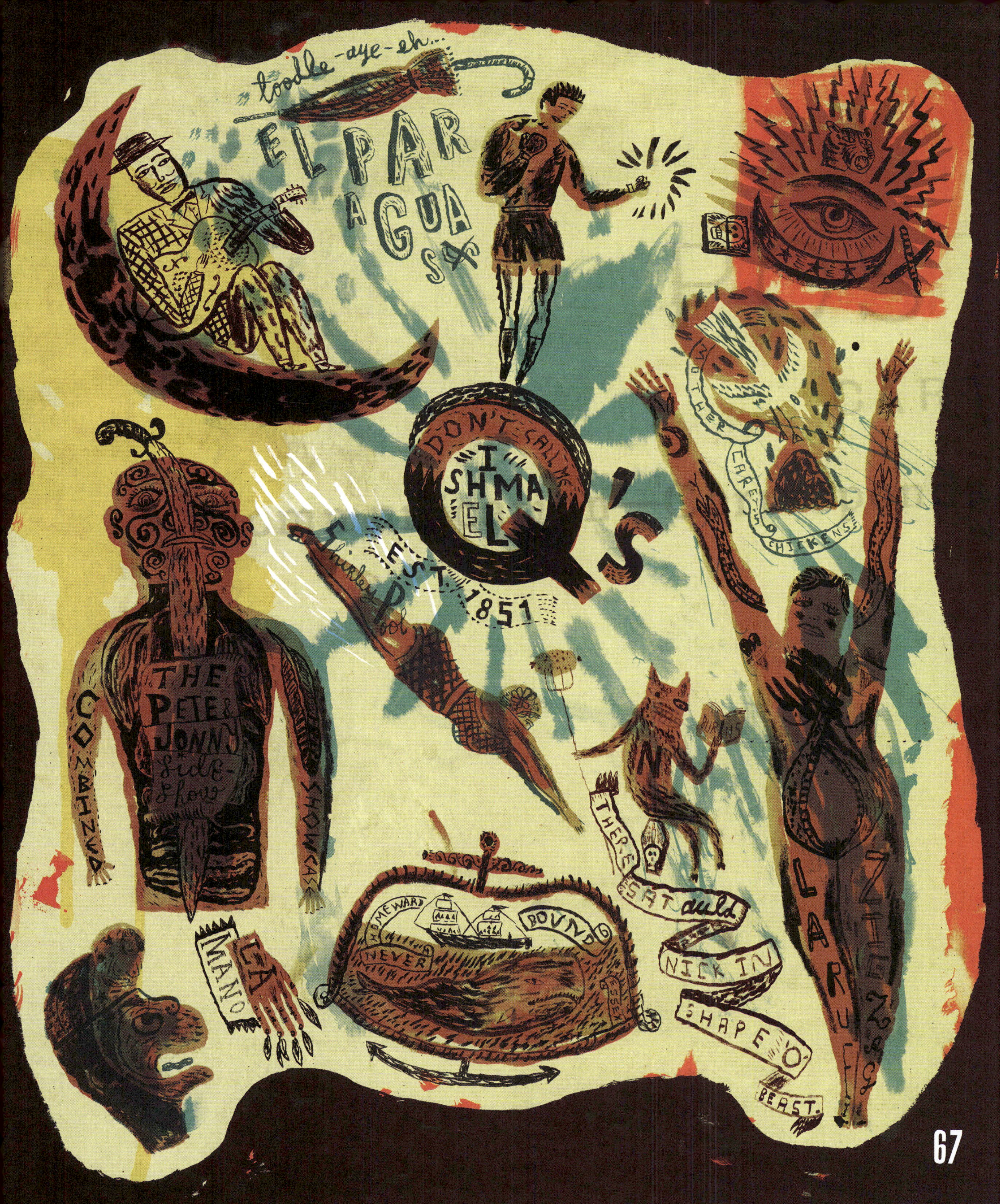

toodle-aye-eh...
EL PARAGUAS
DON'T CALL ME
ISHMAEL
Q'S
EST 1851
MOTHER CAREY'S CHICKENS
THE PETE & JONNY Side-show
COMBINED
LA MANO
HOMEWARD BOUND
NEVER
ESSEX
THERE SAT auld
NICK IN
SHAPE O'
BEAST.
BURNS

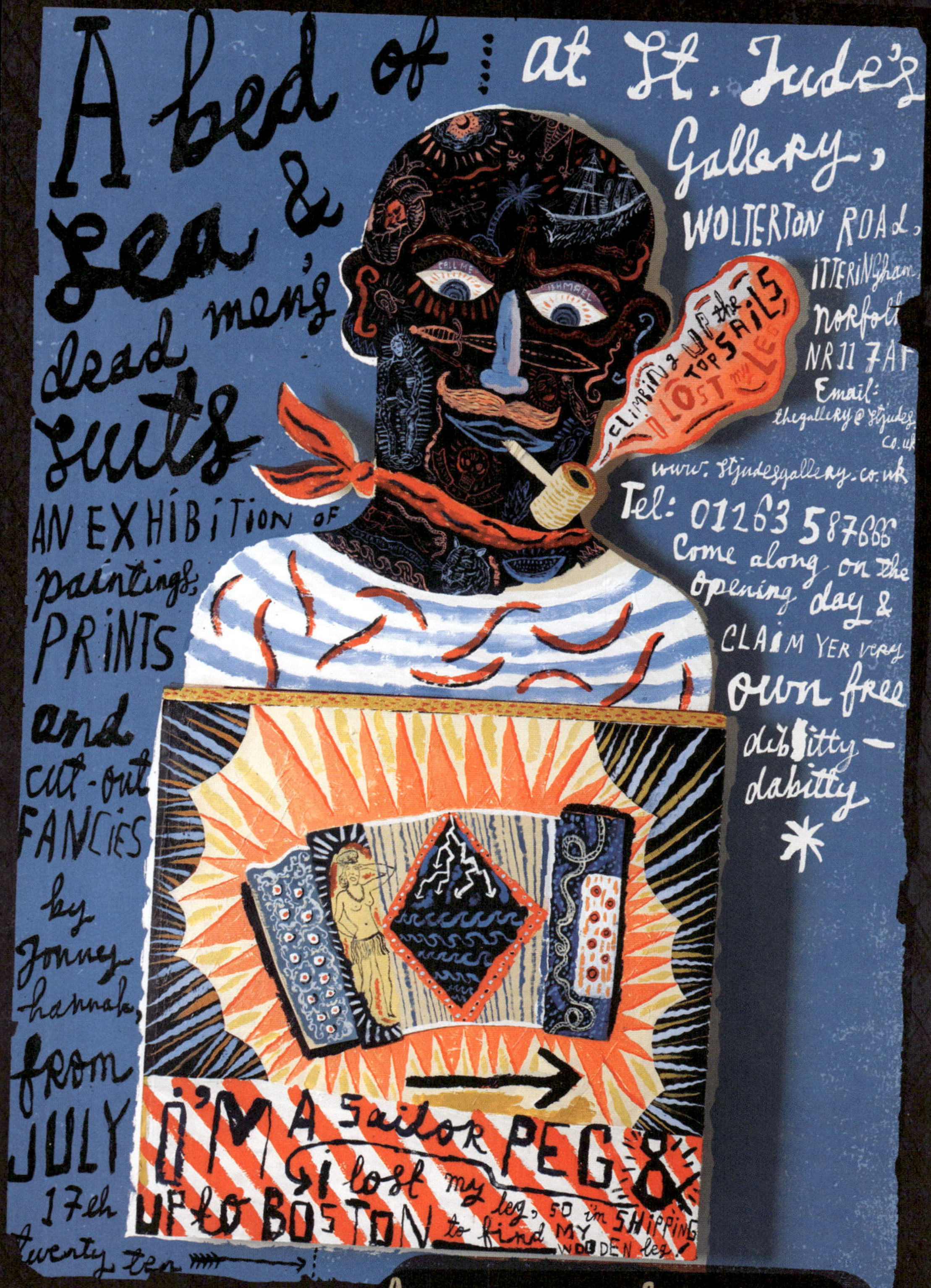

A bed of sea & dead men's suits

at St. Jude's Gallery, Wolterton Road, Itteringham, Norfolk NR11 7AF
Email: thegallery@stjudes.co.uk
www.stjudesgallery.co.uk
Tel: 01263 587666

An exhibition of paintings, prints and cut-out fancies by Jonny Hannah, from July 17th twenty ten

Come along on the opening day & claim yer very own free dibbity-dabbity

Climbing up the top sails I lost my leg

I'm a sailor Peg & I lost my leg up to Boston, so I'm shipping to find my wooden leg.

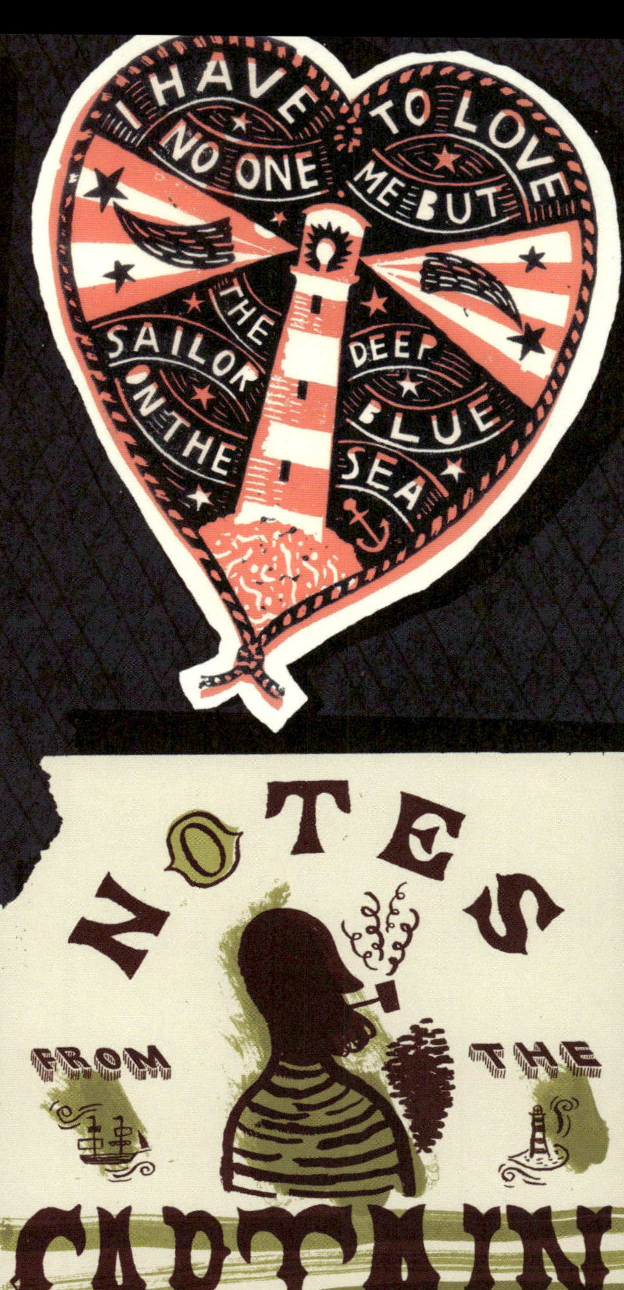


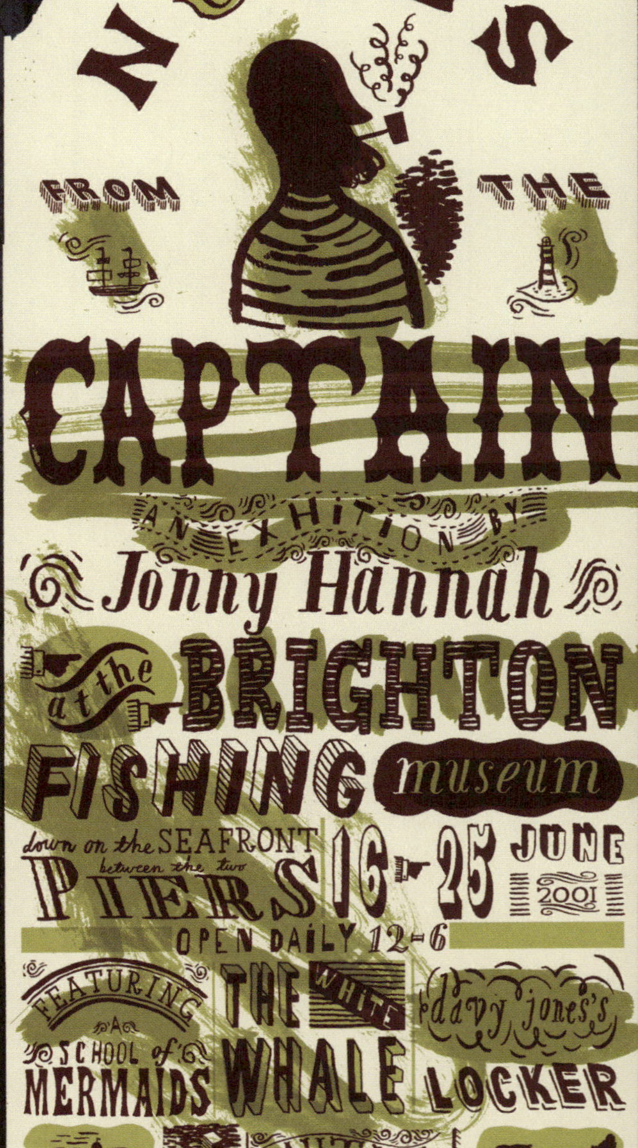

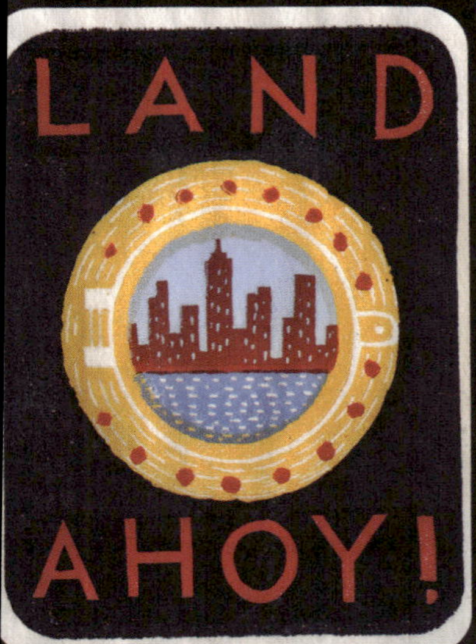

Land Ahoy!

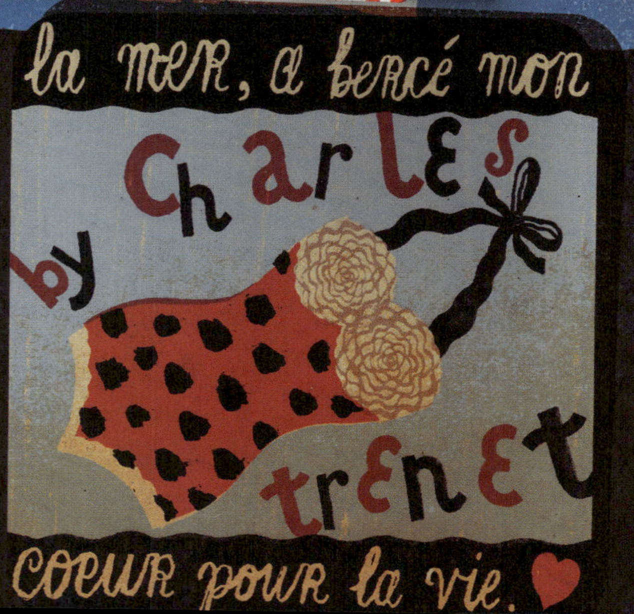

la mer, a bercé mon coeur pour la vie.
by Charles Trenet

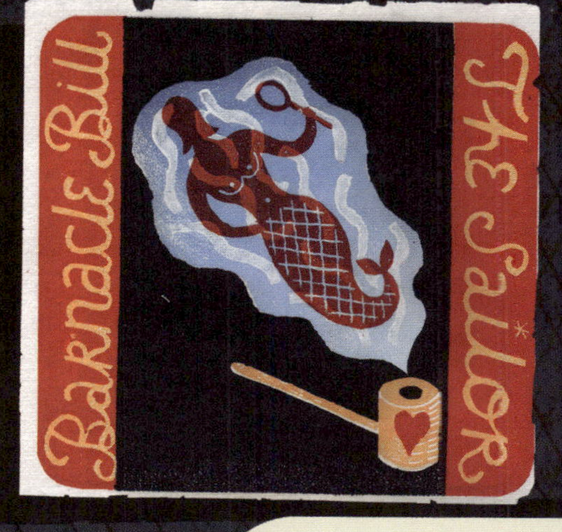


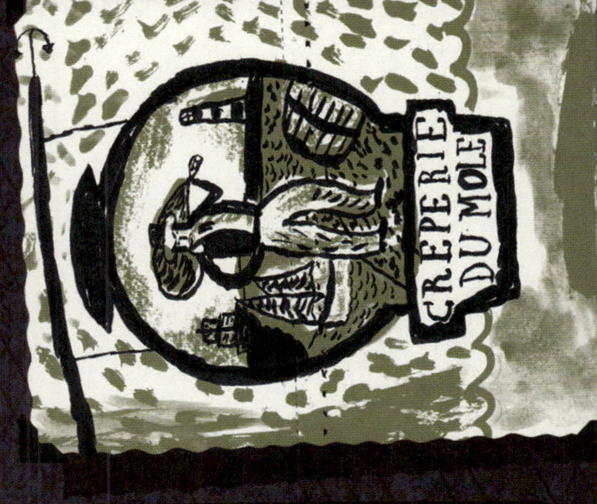


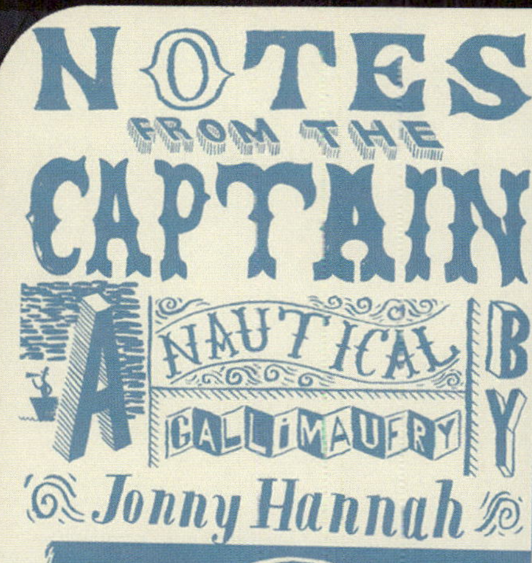


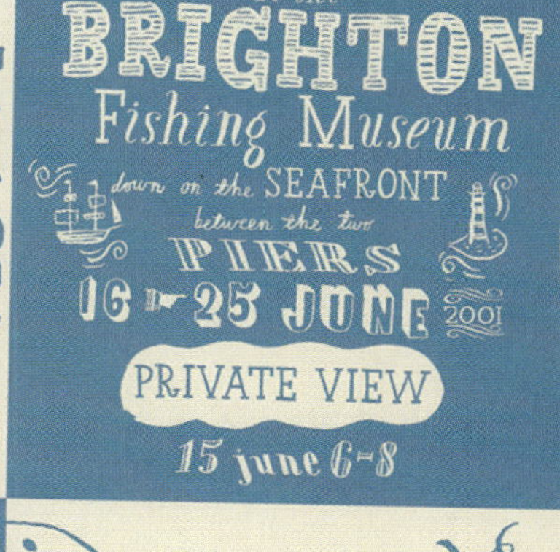


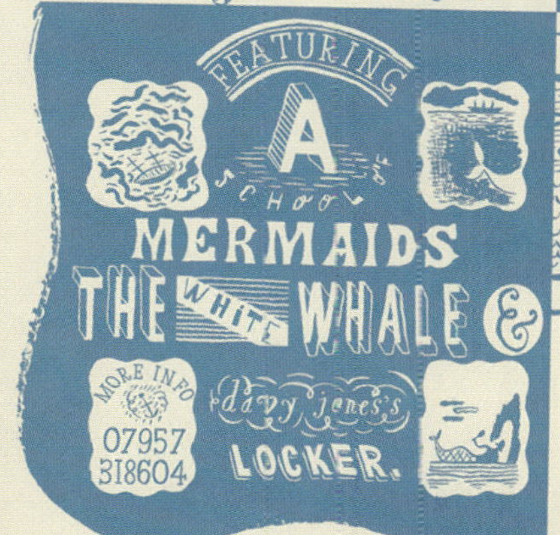


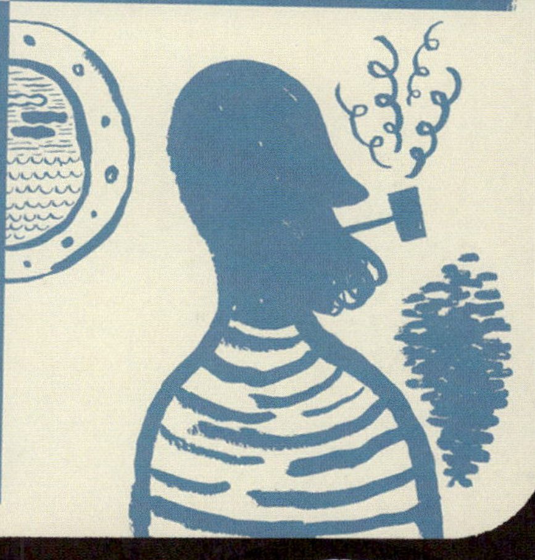

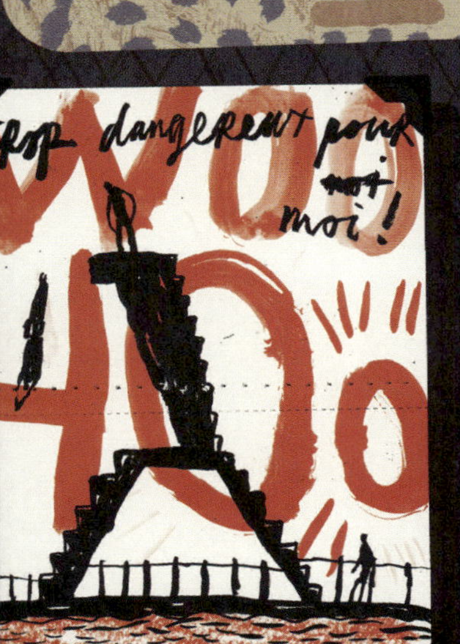


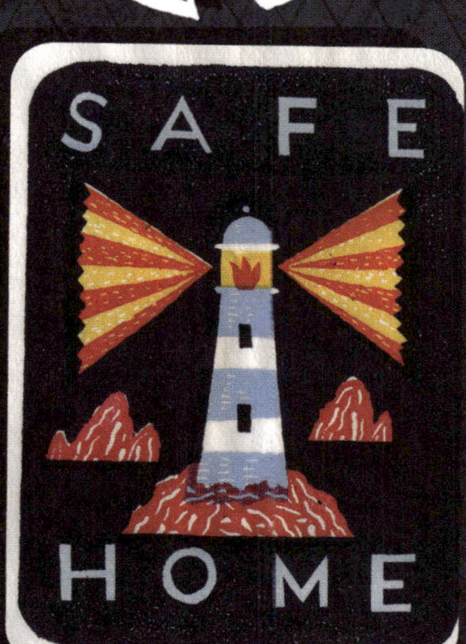


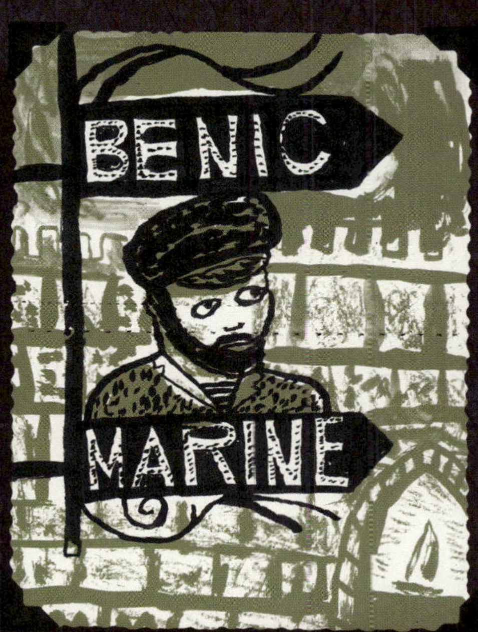


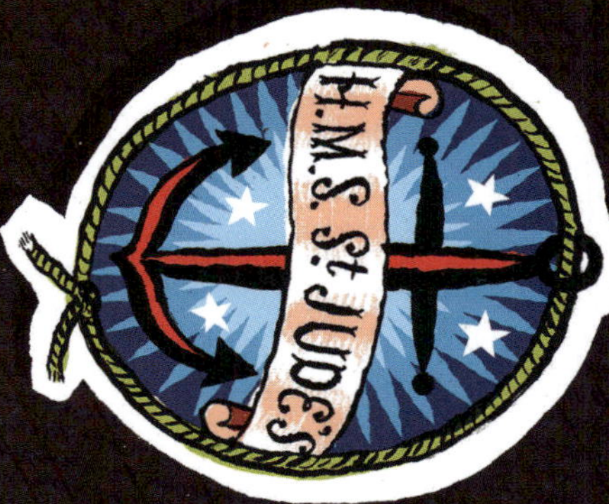


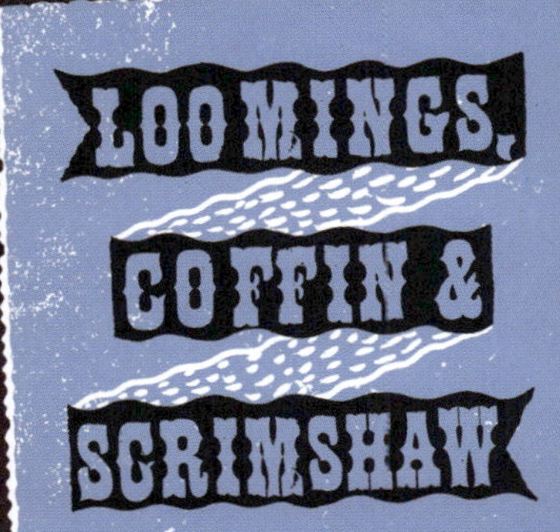


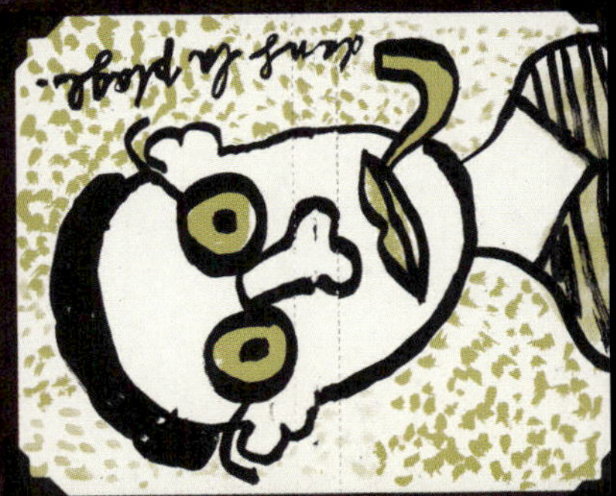

A variety – nay, gallimaufry – of nautical bits and bobs, including a couple of exhibition posters, for the Brighton Fishing Museum and St Jude's Gallery, then based in Norfolk. The rest are linocuts and screen prints, all executed during my years at sea.

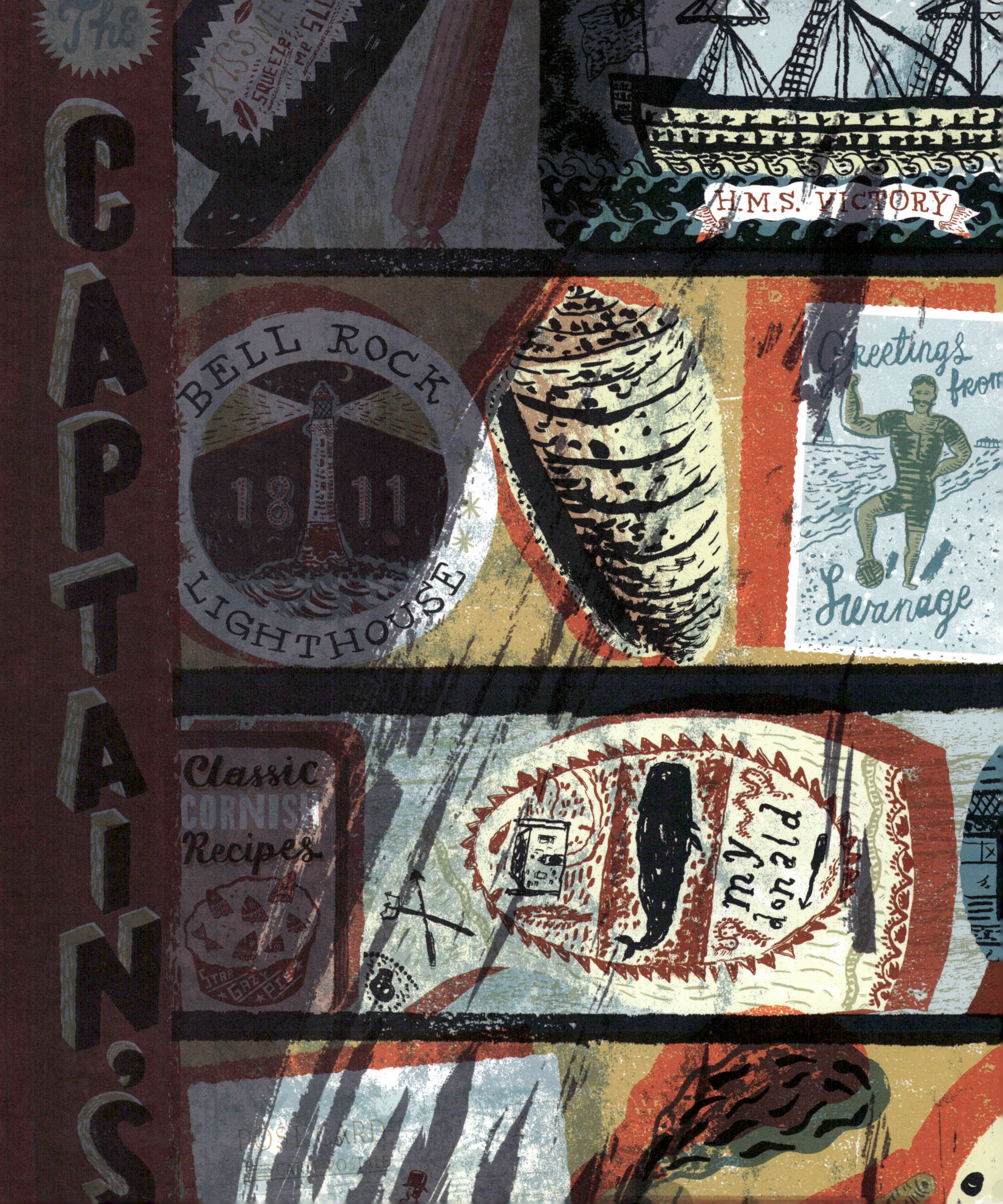

The
CAPTAIN'S
H.M.S. VICTORY
BELL ROCK LIGHTHOUSE
1811
Greetings from Swanage
Classic
CORNIS
Recipes
my donald

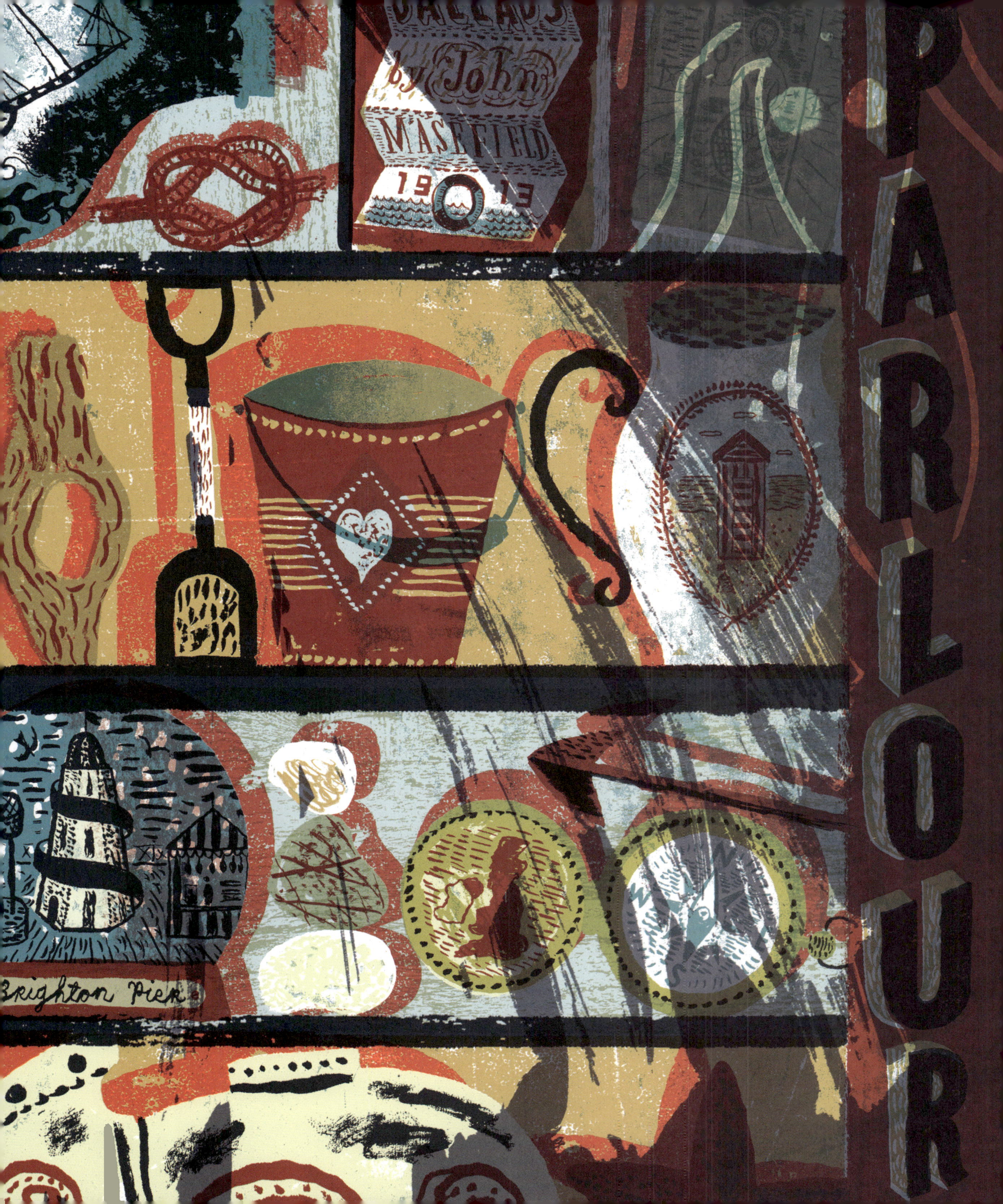
by John
MASEFIELD
19 13
Brighton Pier
PARLOUR

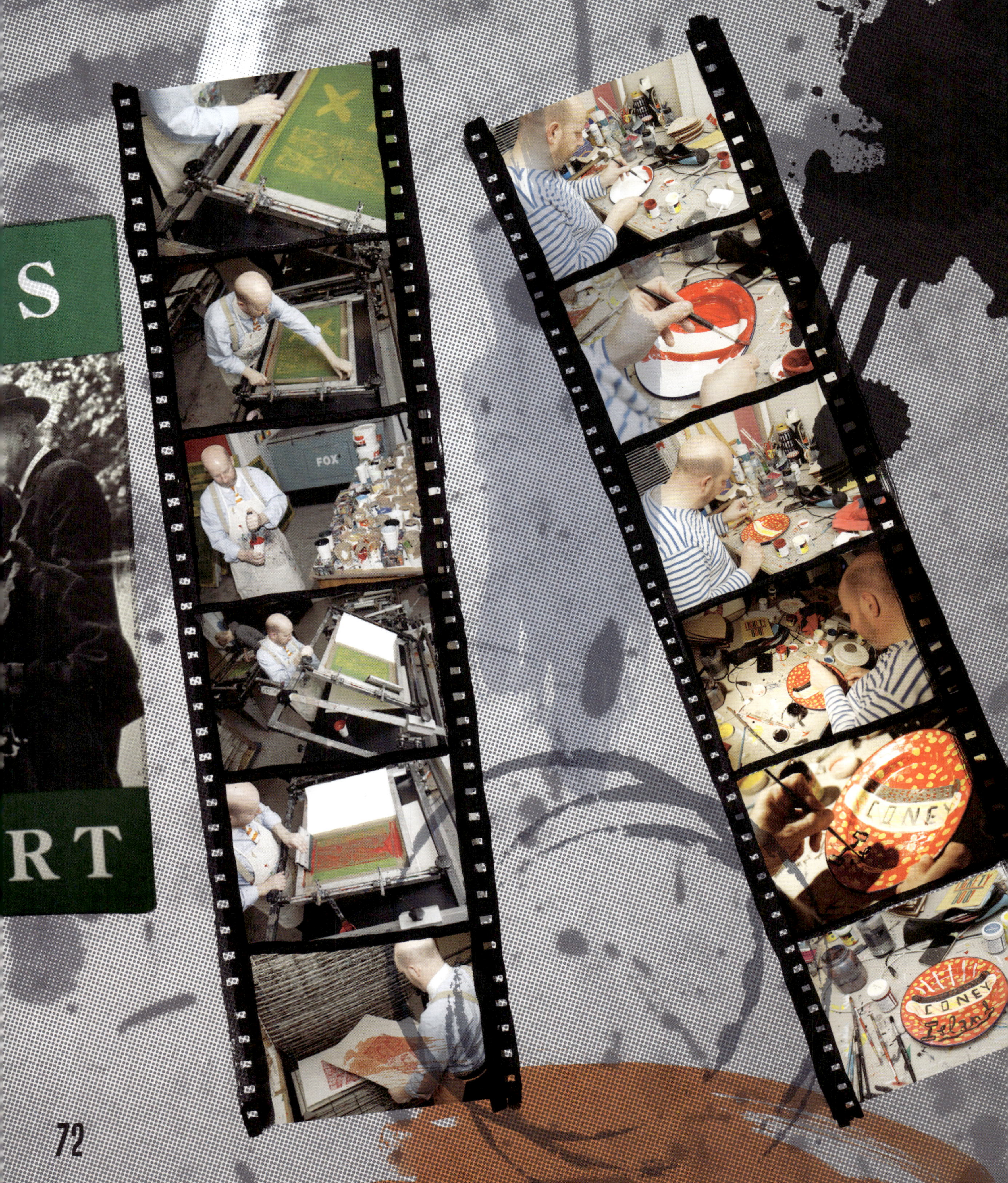
S
RT
FOX
CONEY
CONEY

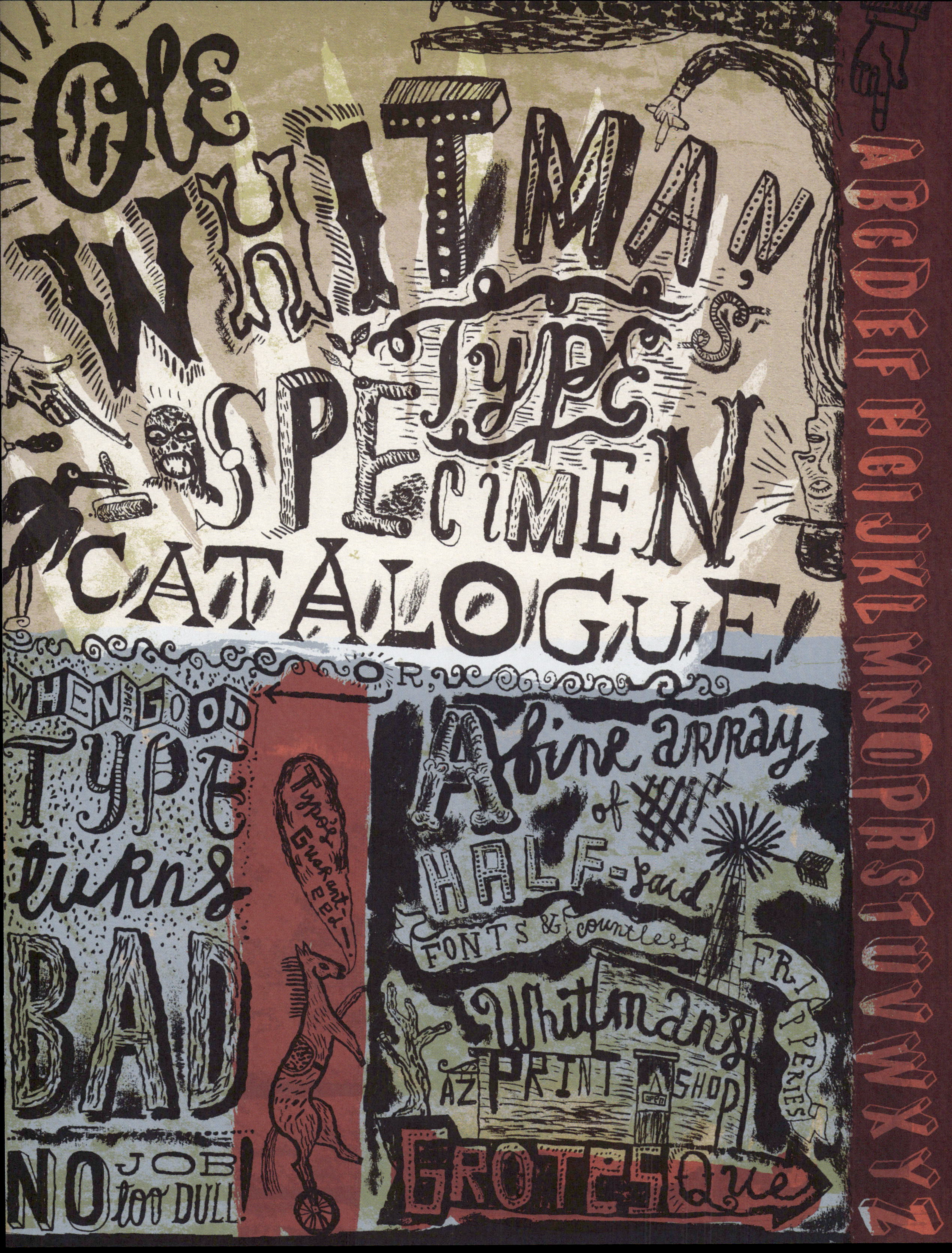

Ole Whitman's
Type Specimen Catalogue
or,
When good type turns bad
Typos Guaranteed
A fine array of
Half-said fonts & countless fripperies
Whitman's
AZ Print Shop
Grotesque
No job too dull!
ABCDEFHGIJKLMNOPRSTUVWXYZ

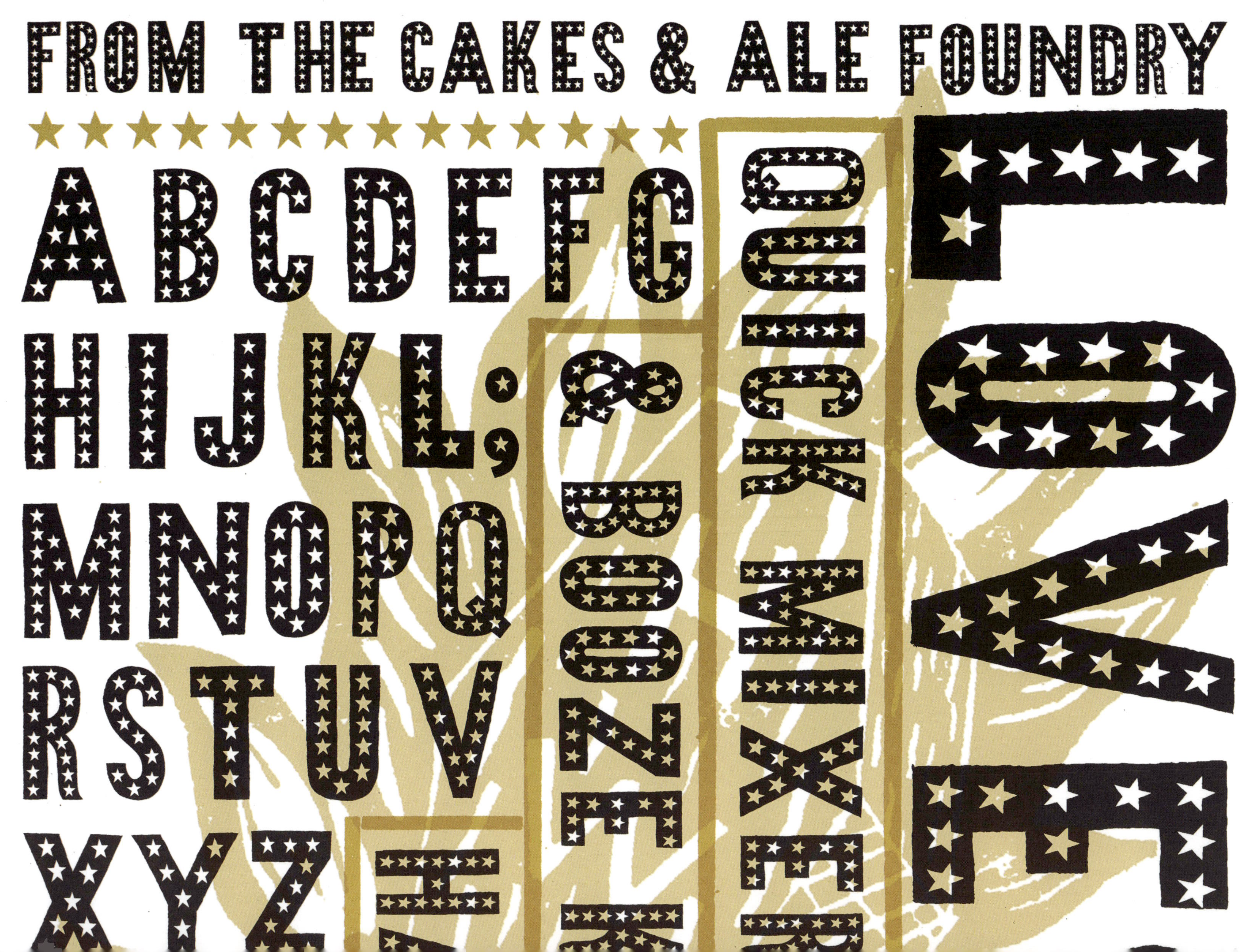
FROM THE CAKES & ALE FOUNDRY
ABCDEFG
HIJKL;
MNOPQ
RSTUV
XYZ
LOVE
QUICK MIXER
& BOOZE K
HA

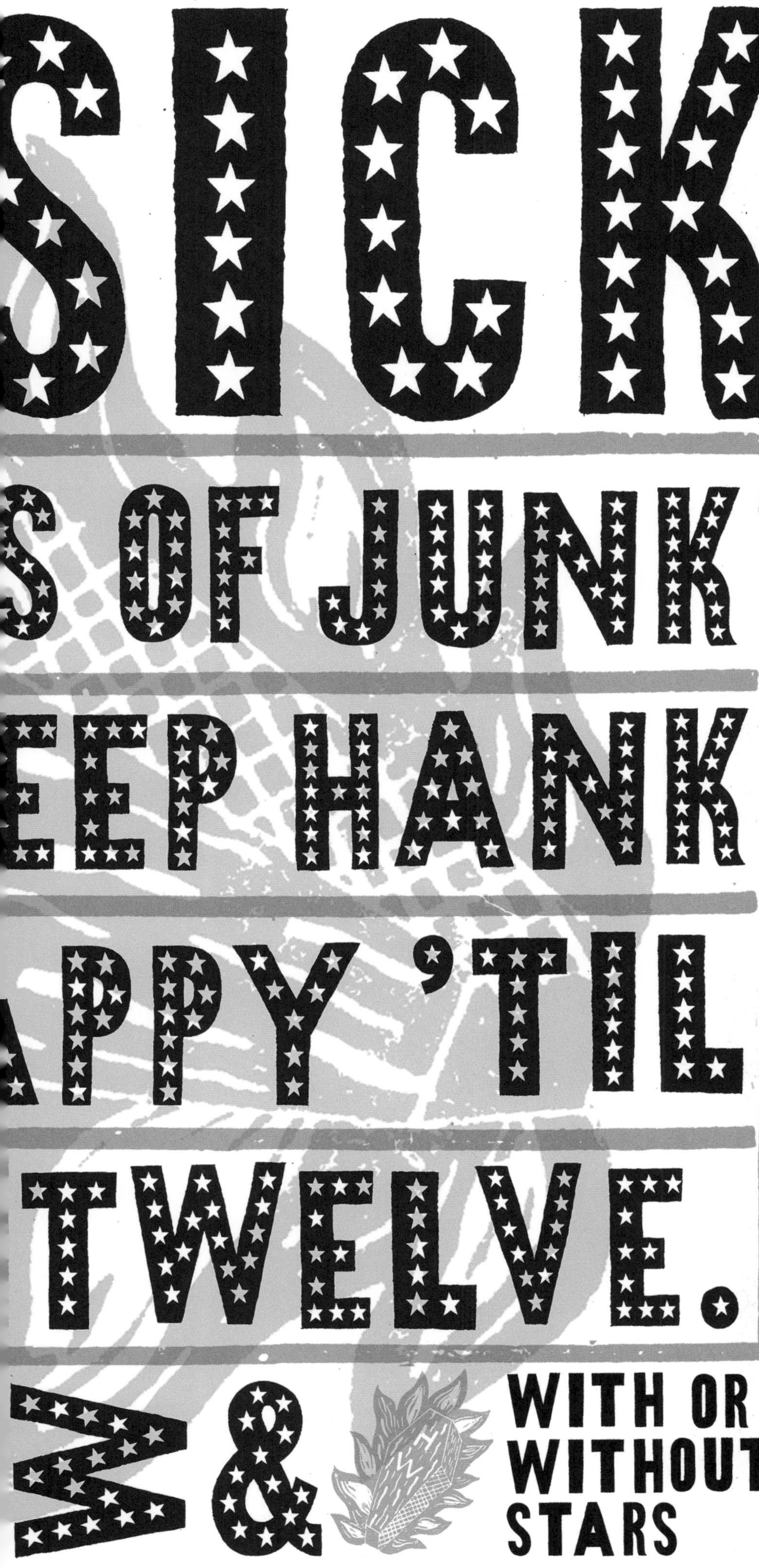


2 ☞ 3 LOVESICK 4 A POEM IS A CITY

5 RUSKIN 5 MISTAKE 6 BODY & SOUL 7 CUT

8 ☞ 9 ALLOTMENT 11 MCVOUTY 14 FRENCH CAFE BAR

14 EKOW 14 KALI MIRCHI 14 COWBOYS & INJUNS 15 REAL HOXTON

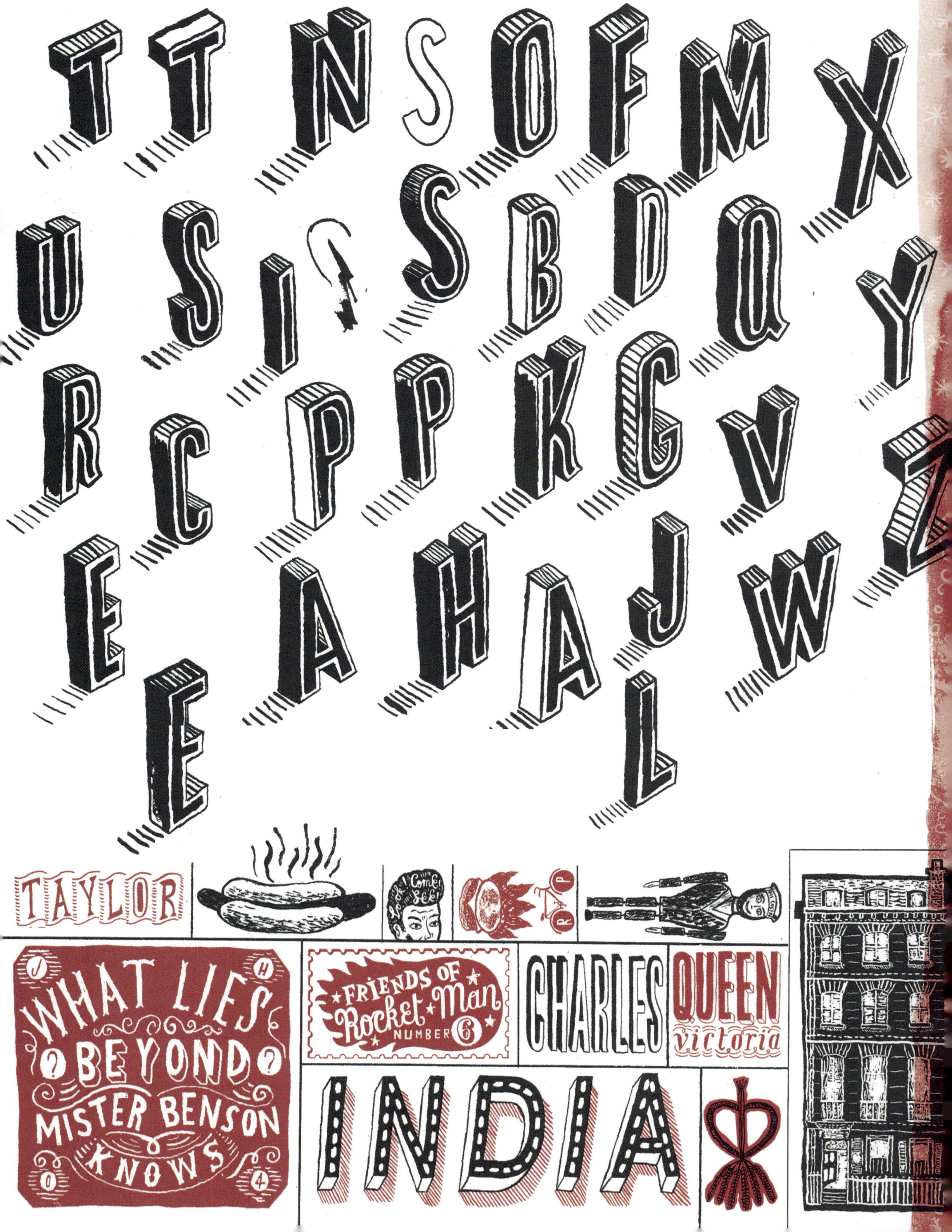

TAYLOR
Look! Come! See!
R P

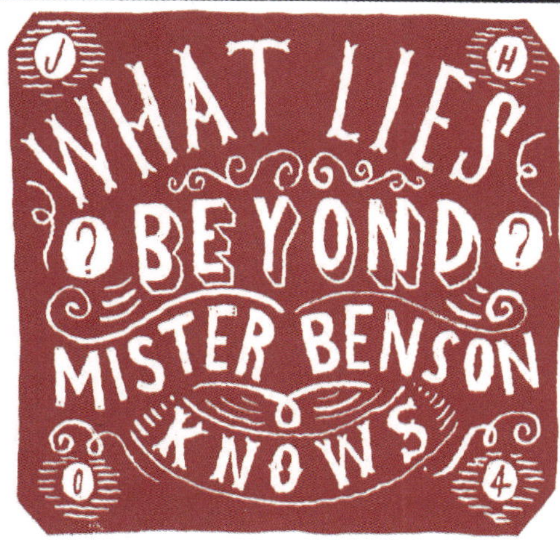
J
H
WHAT LIES
?
BEYOND
?
MISTER BENSON
KNOWS
0
4

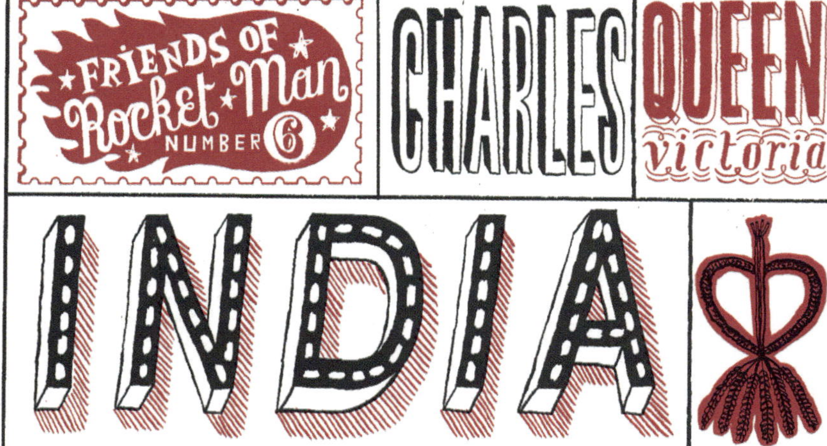
FRIENDS OF
Rocket Man
NUMBER 6
CHARLES
QUEEN
victoria
INDIA

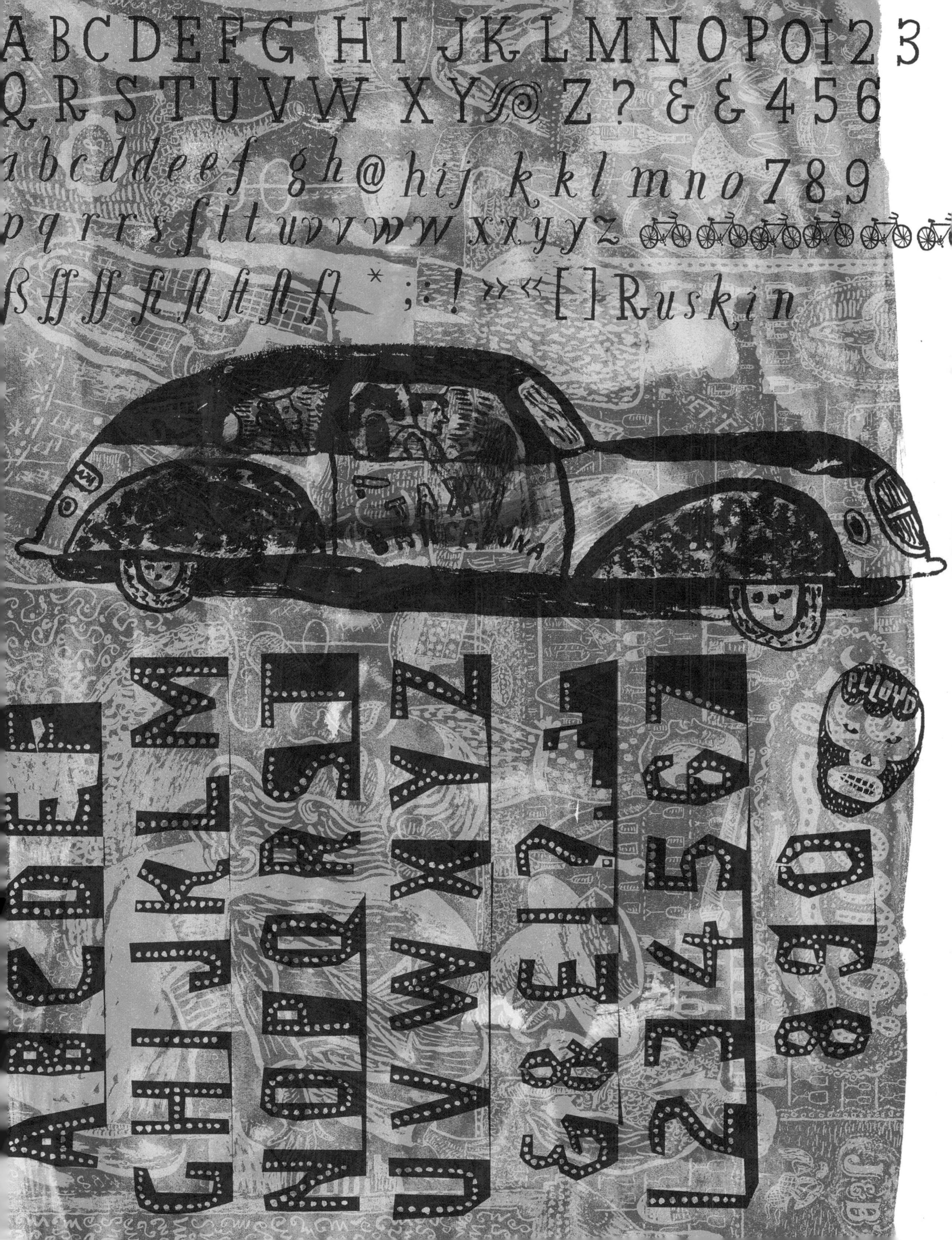
A B C D E F G H I J K L M N O P O I 2 3
Q R S T U V W X Y Z ? & & 4 5 6
a b c d d e e f g h @ h i j k k l m n o 7 8 9
p q r r s ſ t t u v v w w x x y y z
* ; : ! [ ] Ruskin

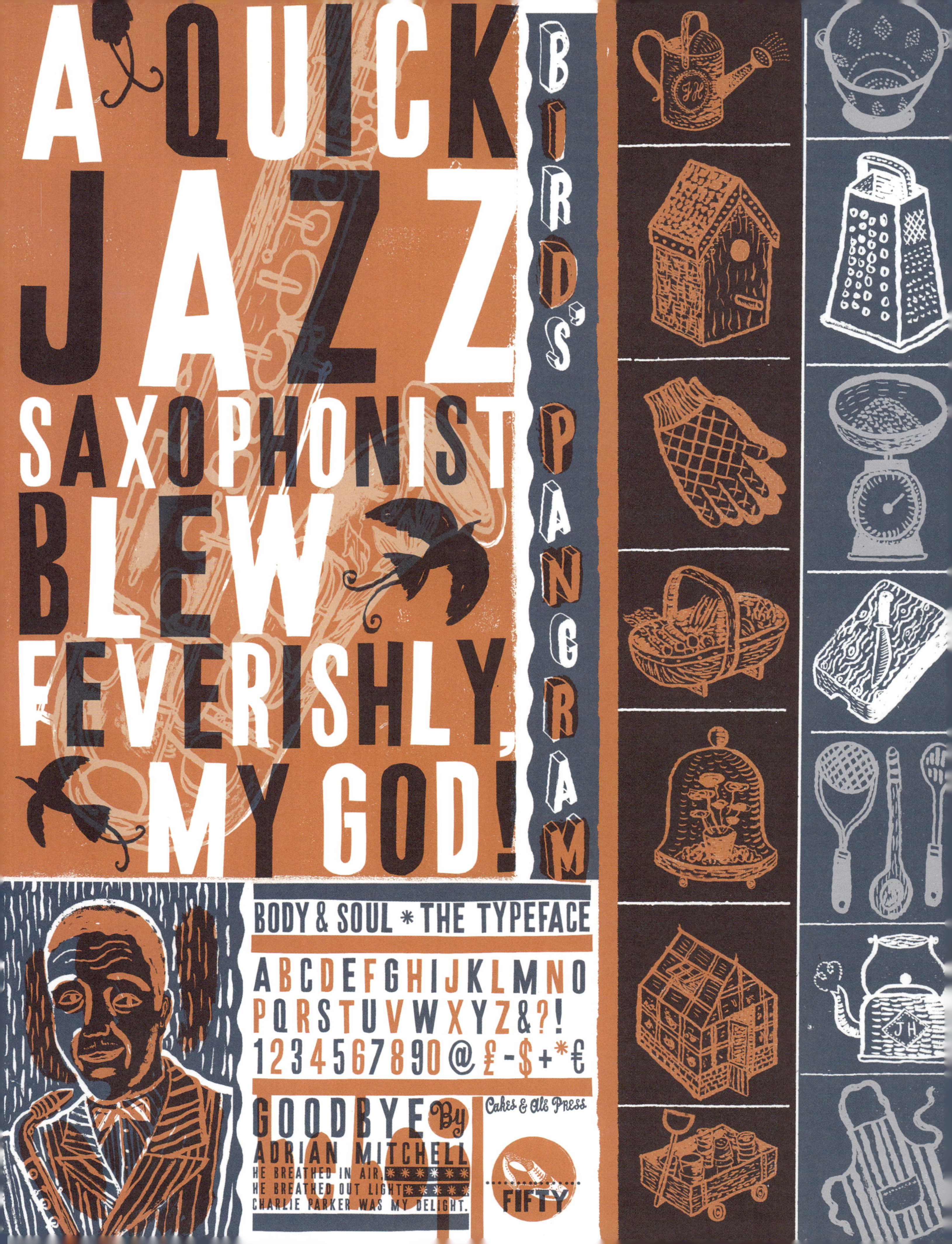

# A QUICK JAZZ SAXOPHONIST BLEW FEVERISHLY, MY GOD!

BIRD'S PANGRAM

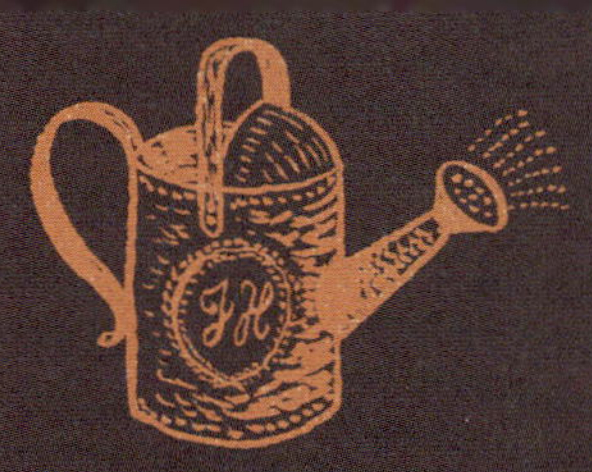
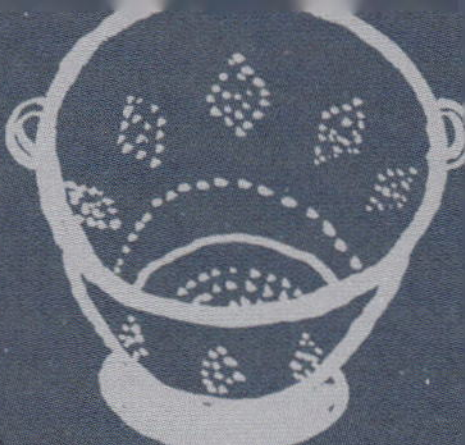

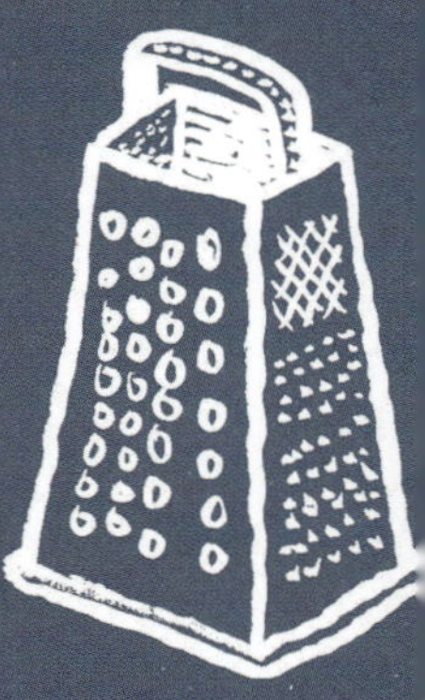
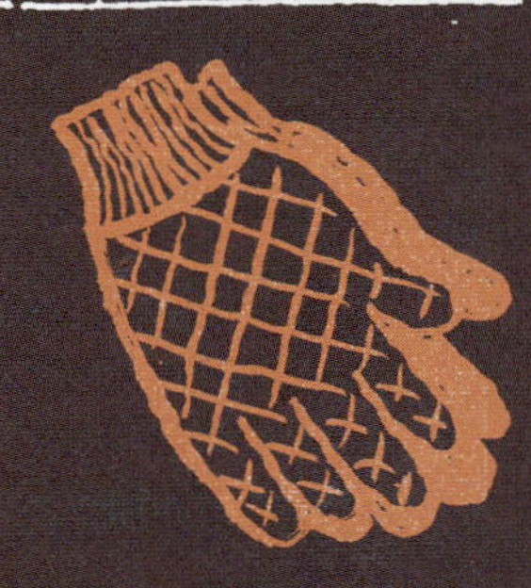
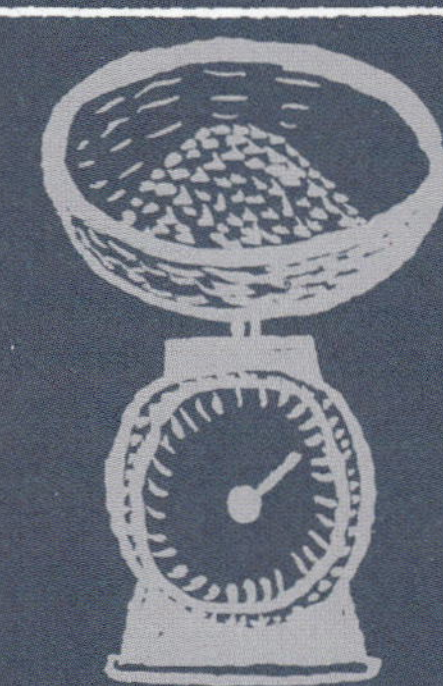
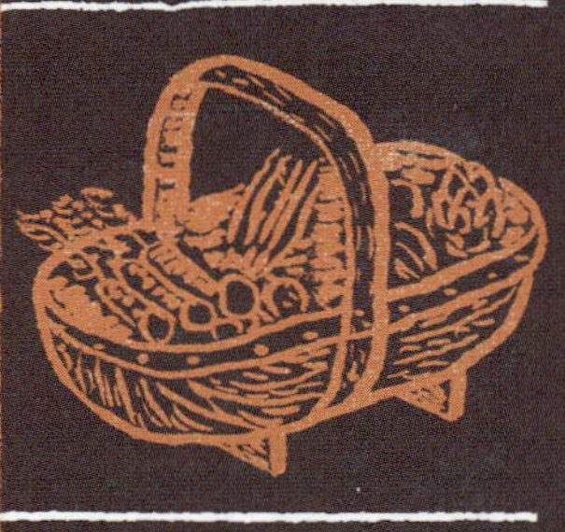
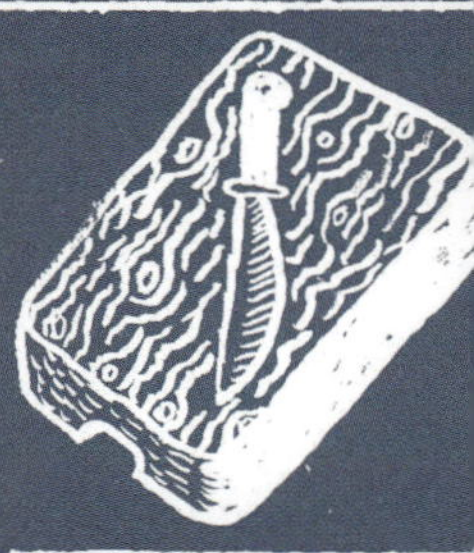
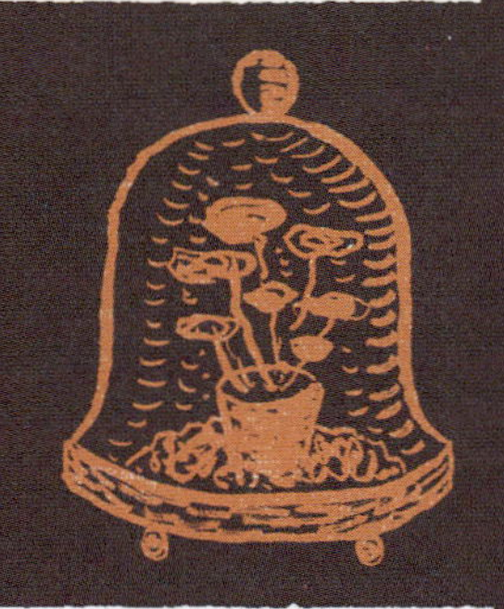
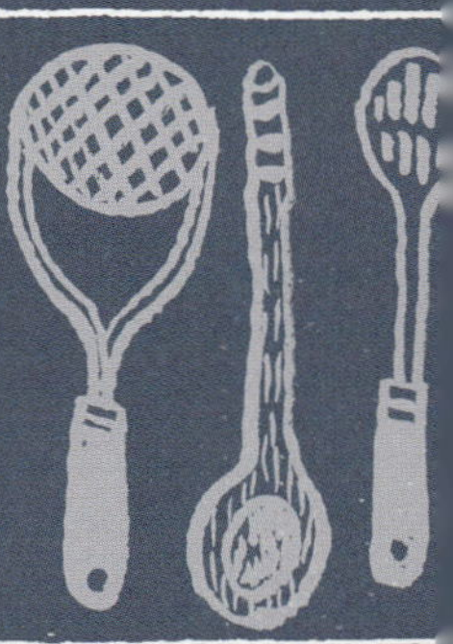
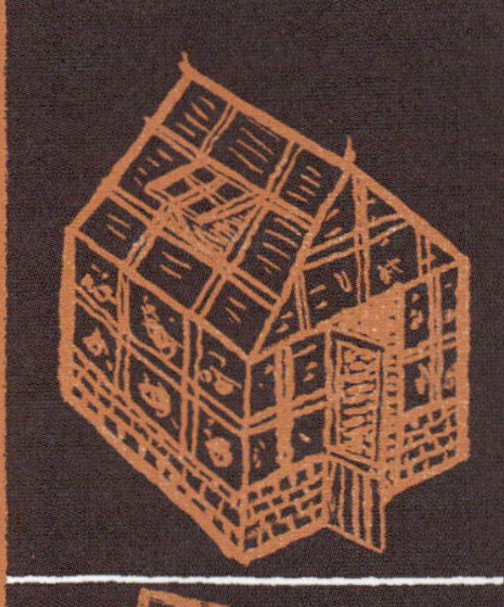
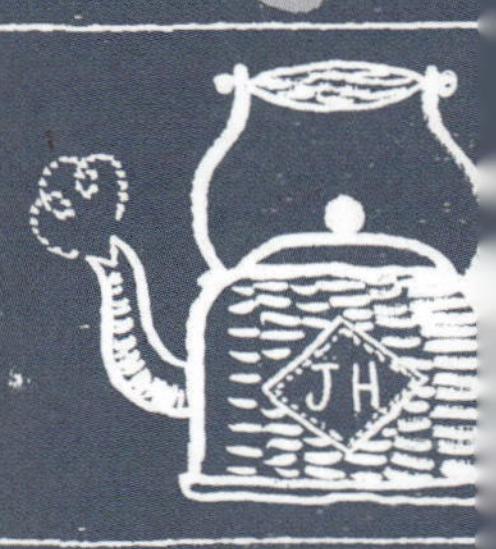
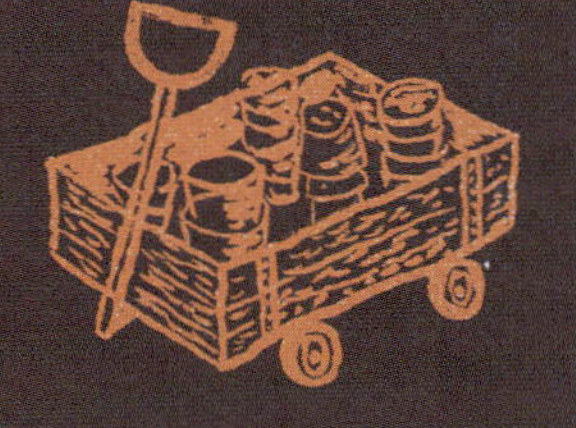

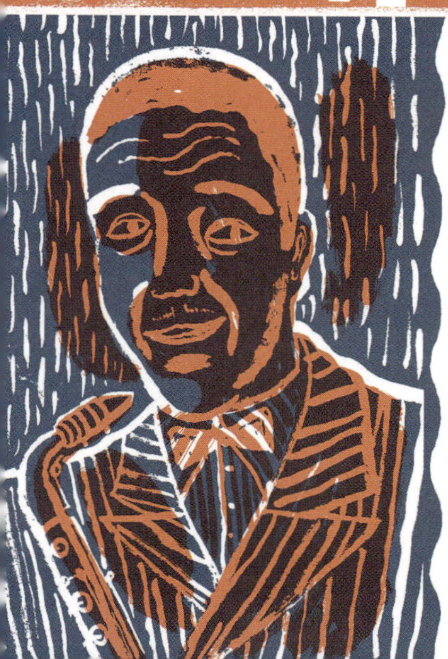

BODY & SOUL * THE TYPEFACE

ABCDEFGHIJKLMNO
PQRSTUVWXYZ&?!
1234567890@£-$+*€

Cakes & Ale Press

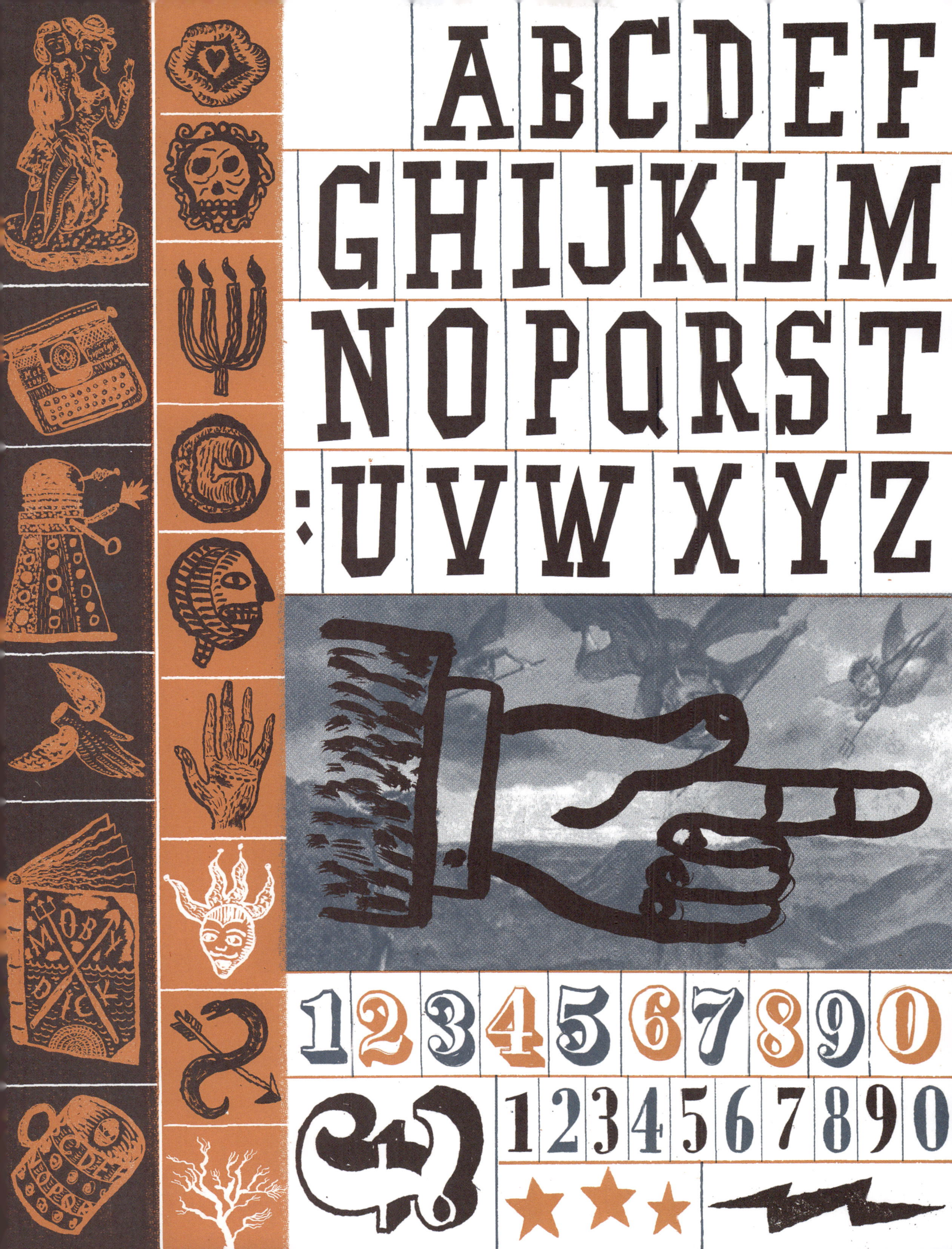
ABCDEF
GHIJKLM
NOPQRST
UVWXYZ
1234567890
1234567890

# OFF THE PAGE: JONNY HANNAH'S TYPEFACE DESIGNS

## BY DR. SHEENA CALVERT

> *Imagine that you have before you a flagon of wine. ... You have two goblets before you. One is of solid gold, wrought in the most exquisite patterns. The other is of crystal-clear glass, thin as a bubble, and as transparent. Pour and drink; and according to your choice of goblet, I shall know whether or not you are a connoisseur of wine. For if you have no feelings about wine one way or the other, you will want the sensation of drinking the stuff out of a vessel that may have cost thousands of pounds; but if you are a member of that vanishing tribe, the amateurs of fine vintages, you will choose the crystal, because everything about it is calculated to reveal rather than hide the beautiful thing which it was meant to contain.*
>
> Beatrice Warde, 'The Crystal Goblet, or Printing Should Be Invisible', 1955

The print historian Beatrice Warde famously stated that typography should relate to content, as a crystal goblet relates to wine; that is, it should be clear, transparent and concerned with providing a lucid, non-intrusive and humble window on to content. Any kind of wine glass, or typography, that would seek to draw attention to itself was an aberration – a wilful misappropriation of the 'canon' of typography, and a statement of the wrong priorities for wine. Warde continues: 'There are a thousand mannerisms in typography that are as impudent and arbitrary as putting port in tumblers of red or green glass!' Jonny Hannah's typography makes a gentle mockery of such prescriptives. His fonts and layouts *are* the gaudy, gold, exquisitely patterned goblet itself, in their celebration of the possibility that historically hybrid, anarchic, impatient, 'itchy', impure 'almost-fonts', which wobble, wave, shimmer, quiver and shimmy along with an impudent and arbitrary swagger, could better speak to the wonderful anarchy of language (and life) itself than Warde's somewhat austere and bloodless form of typography. Hannah puts the *fun* back into the *fun*ction of text, restoring the alchemical qualities of language as raw material by weaving fragments of typographic history into an irreverent and fierily undisciplined series of glyphic gestures. His fonts do not invoke Warde's 'front door of the science of typography', but rather a multiplicity of entrances, exits, detours and sometimes dead ends.

The 'beautiful thing' that is revealed is to be found precisely at that shimmering surface of material language, not despite it, as Warde would suggest. This surface suggests the impossibility of an abstracted 'scientific' ideal of language-as-communication, which Warde covets. The meaning of Hannah's typography is not to be found in the content, as through a window on to a world beyond, but at the surface, where text itself becomes content.

The typefaces that Hannah has designed for this purpose speak in a weird dialect of their/his own, with more than a touch of the absurd about them. Somewhere between a profligate circus vernacular and mischievous manuscripts, this cauldron of chaotic, unruly, undisciplined glyphs bounce irrepressibly off the page like a jazz ensemble. Hidden in these fonts is a collection of memories and stories, or half-broken narratives. They simply won't sit still. Like small children sitting impatiently on their hands, they excitedly tell endless stories and 'tall tales' about near and far history, industry, street signs, pop culture, Americana, Victoriana, ephemera, childhood utopias, music, performance, eclecticism, travels, other worlds, third dimensions, folk tales and oral stories, cultural memories and the everyday. These fonts are busy telling their own stories, in their own language, about themselves. Their conspicuous presence, their resolutely un-modernist performativity is not a distraction from, but a complement to, the art of storytelling itself, which similarly digresses, wanders, deals in half-truths and patches together random memories. By rebelling against their role as functional siblings to the image, Hannah's fonts become fully integrated into the field of imagery, which is energetically splayed across the extravagantly detailed pages (like modern-day, secular illuminated manuscripts). They are endless shaggy-dog stories with no punchline.

The brazen-faced non-conformity of these typographic gestures becomes, in the end, a homage to the 'true' origins of typography, one drawn through the history of the handwritten word, with all its imperfections, made by imperfect humans, and before the time when the invention of printing standardized the forms of written language, making possible the ideal of the 'crystal goblet'.

Warde is right in one sense: there *are* times when text should be invisible to content, but equally there are times when text should be a performer in its own right. In the case of Hannah's work, never mind the high modernist 'What must it do?' This type is all about 'How should it look?' In their suitably vulgar, bohemian and ostentatious displays of type as a metaphorical goblet with a big personality, Jonny Hannah's typefaces are theatrical virtuosos on the stage of both his imagination and typographic history. Impudent and arbitrary, anarchic and absurd, they are for the connoisseur of creativity itself.

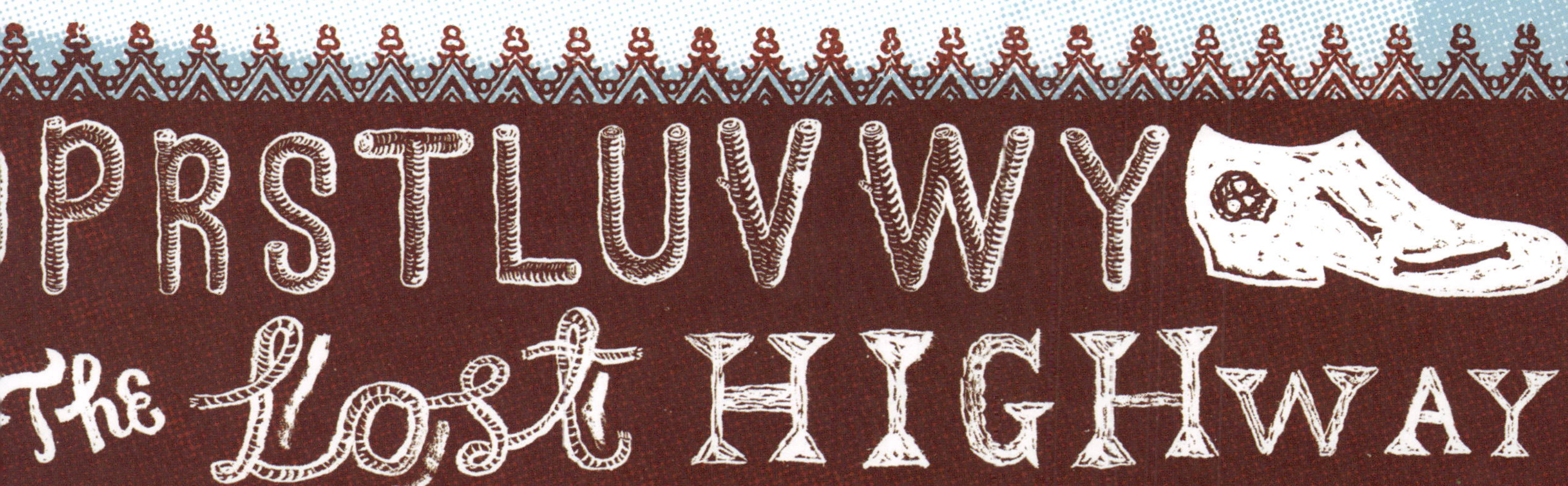

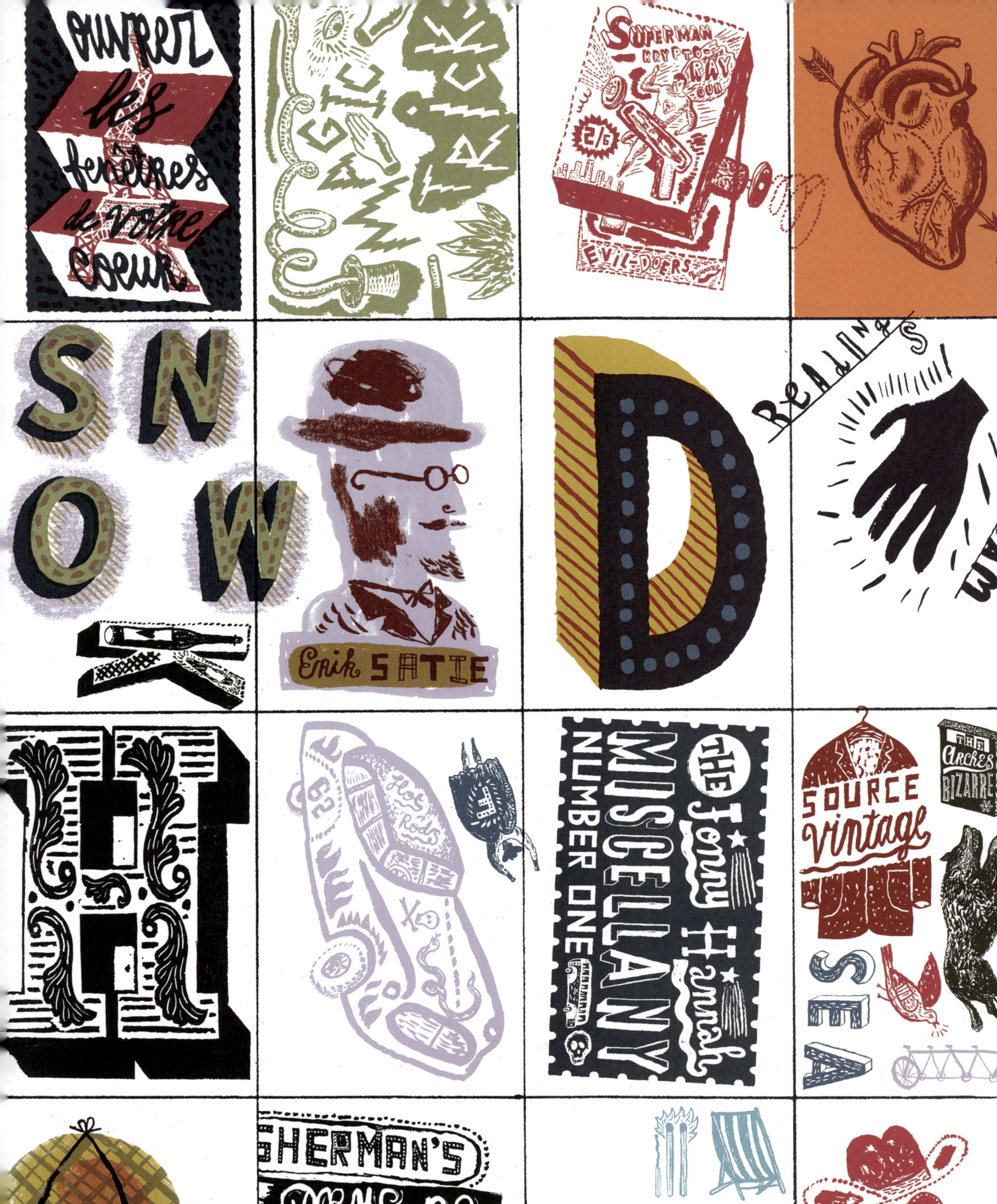
Ouvrez les fenêtres de votre coeur
SUPERMAN KRYPTO-RAY GUN
2/6
EVIL-DOERS
SNOW
Erik SATIE
D
Readings
H
Hot Rods
The Jonny Hannah
MISCELLANY
NUMBER ONE
Source Vintage
THE Arches BIZARRE
SEA
S.H.
SHERMAN'S
Drugstore
Open Late

# McVOUTY

ABCDE
FGHIJK
LMNOP
QRSTU
VWXY
Z&?!.,

A NEW TYPEFACE FROM THE CAKES & ALE PRESS, PUTTI PUTTI.

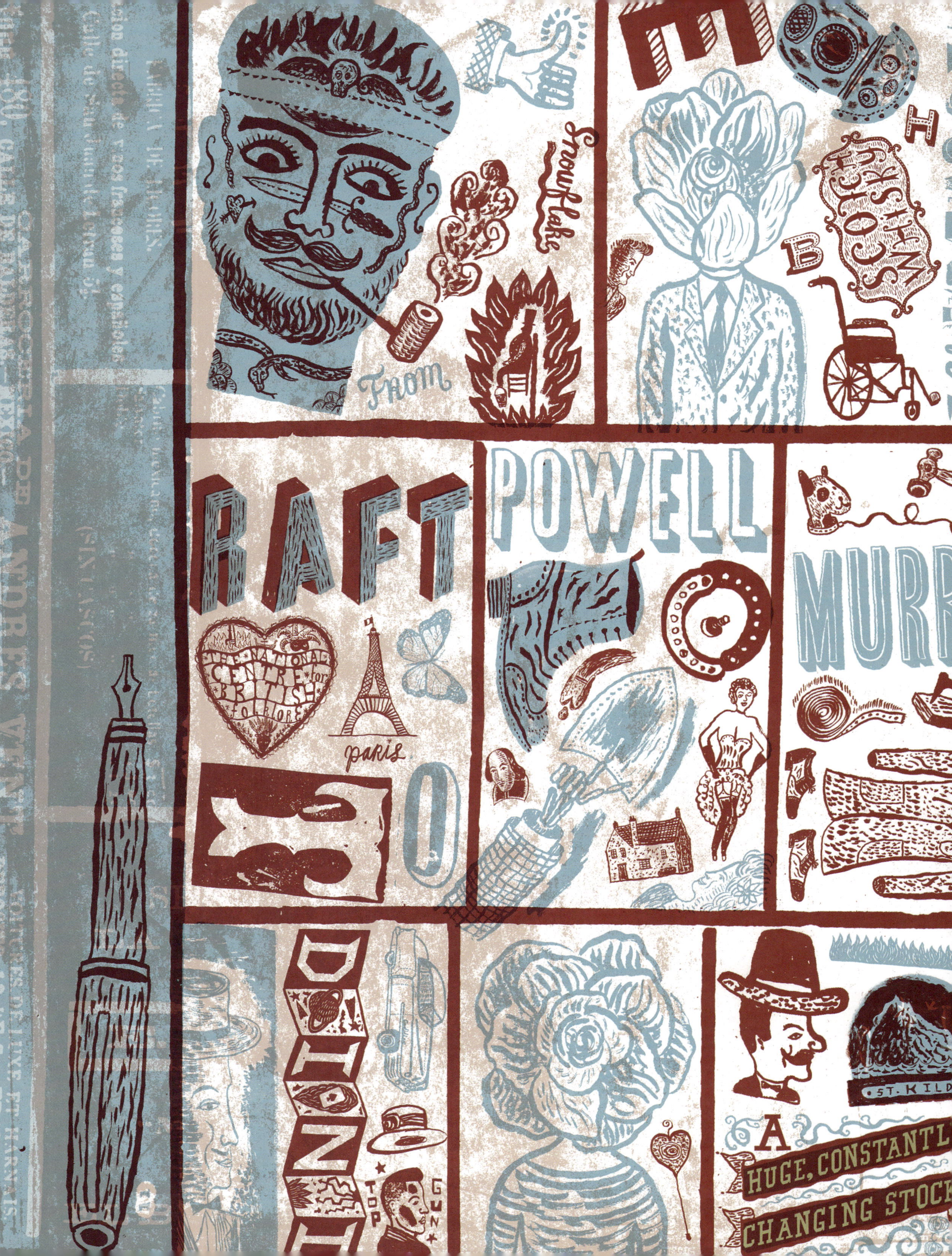

Snowflake
From
RAFT
paris
POWELL
MURR
ST. KILD
A
HUGE, CONSTANTL
CHANGING STOCK
TOP
GUN

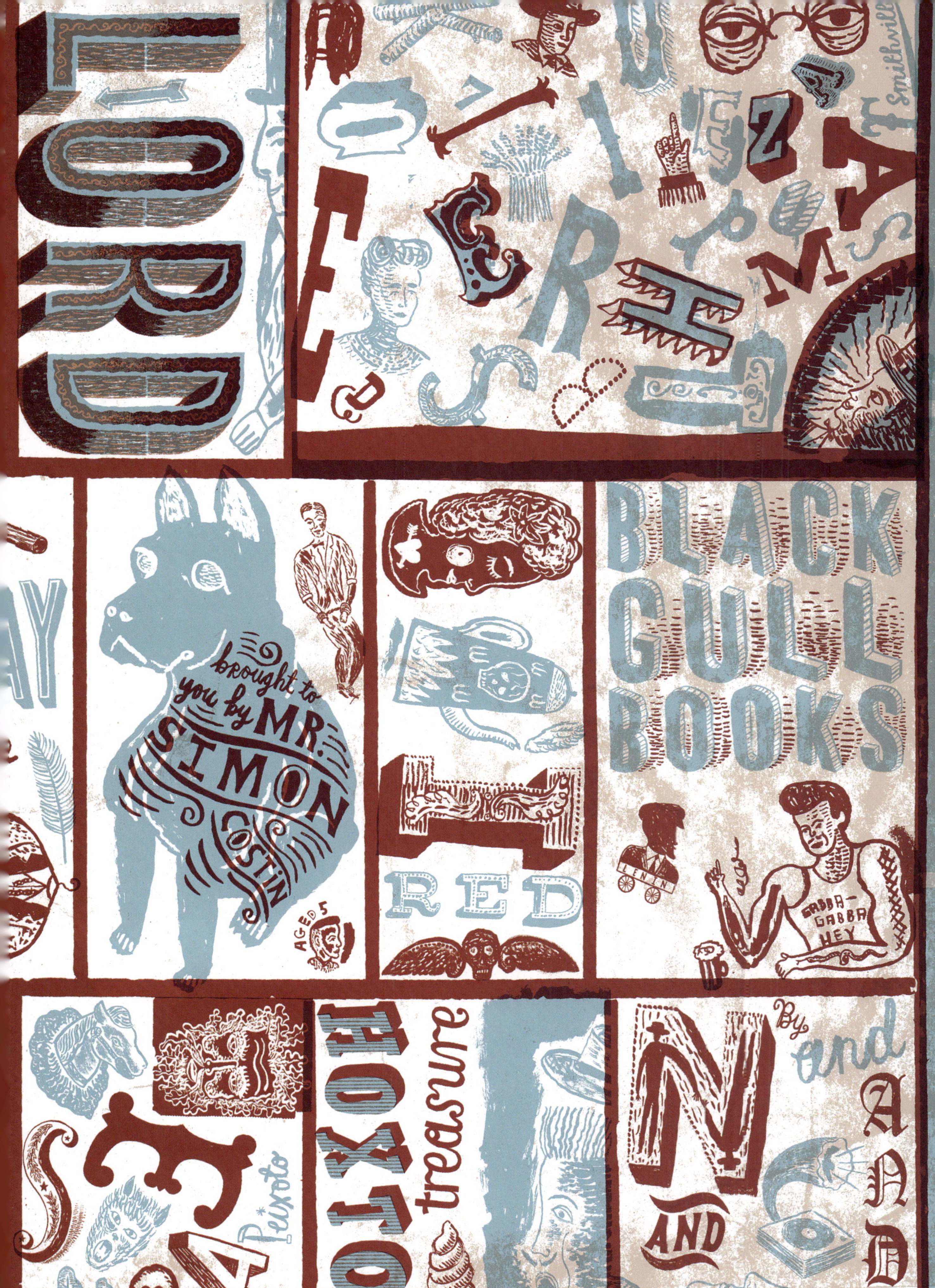

LORD
BLACK
GULL
BOOKS
brought to you by MR. SIMON COSTIN
AGED 5
RED
LENIN
GABBA-GABBA HEY
HOXTON
treasure
Peixoto
By
and
AND
AND
Smithville

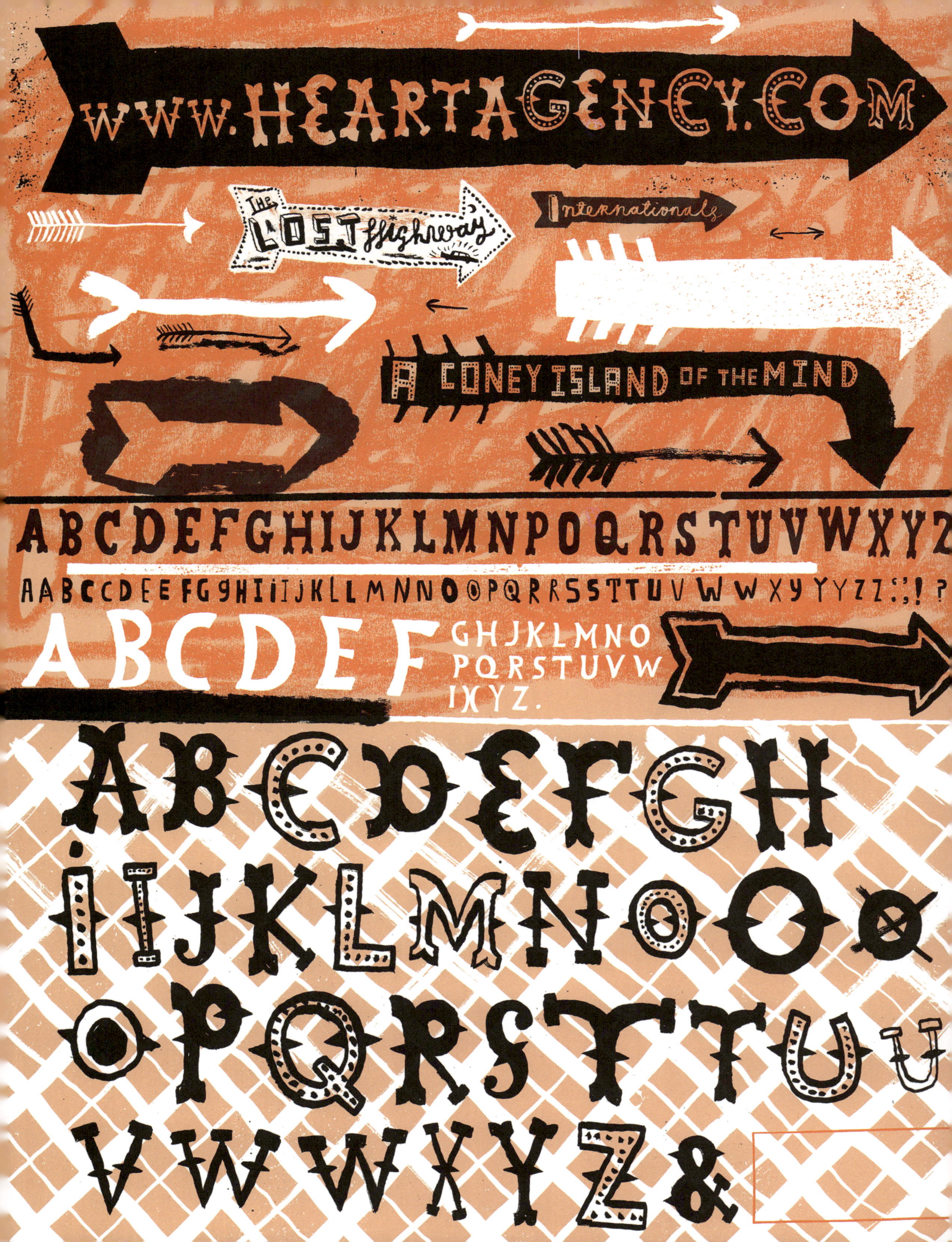
WWW.HEARTAGENCY.COM
The LOST Highway
Internationals
A CONEY ISLAND OF THE MIND
ABCDEF
GHJKLMNO
PQRSTUVW
XYZ.

ABCDEF

GHIJKLM

NOPQRST

UVWXYZ

&&£!?.,:-

1234567

890

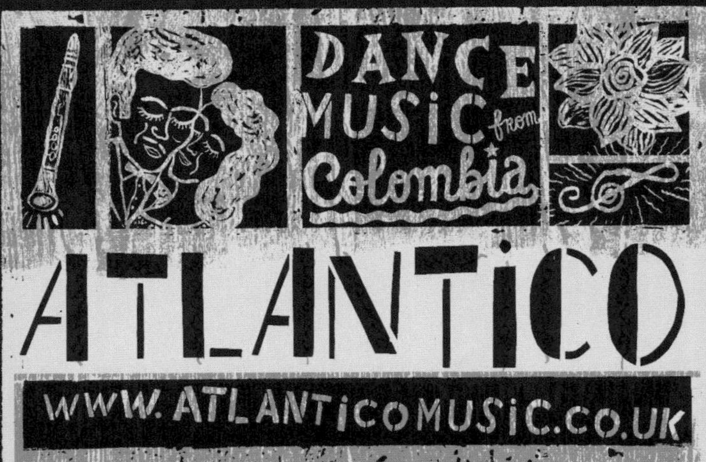




DRINK
LOWERS
COFFEE

HORNSEYS
THE GALLERY
WWW.HORNSEYS.COM

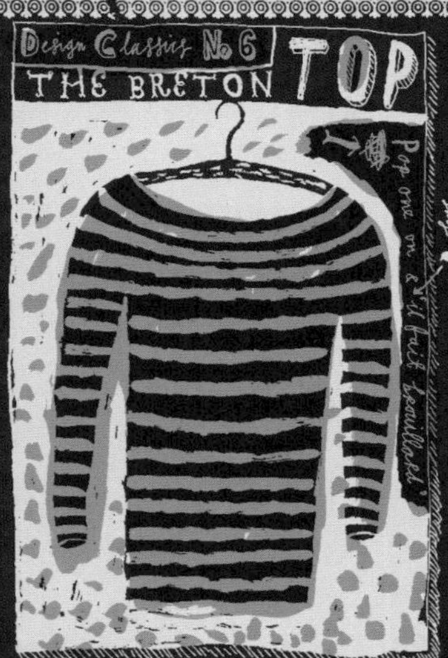


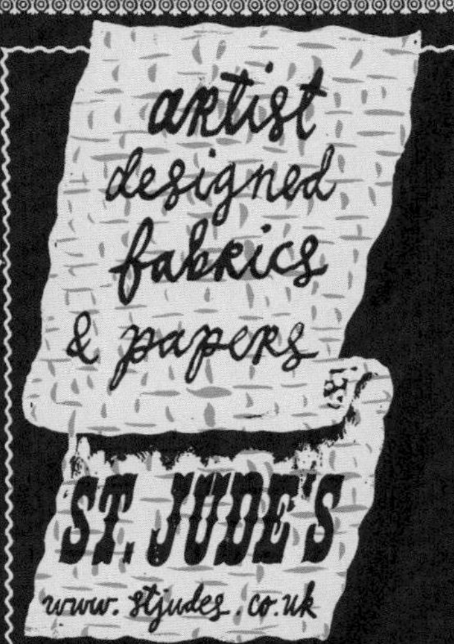


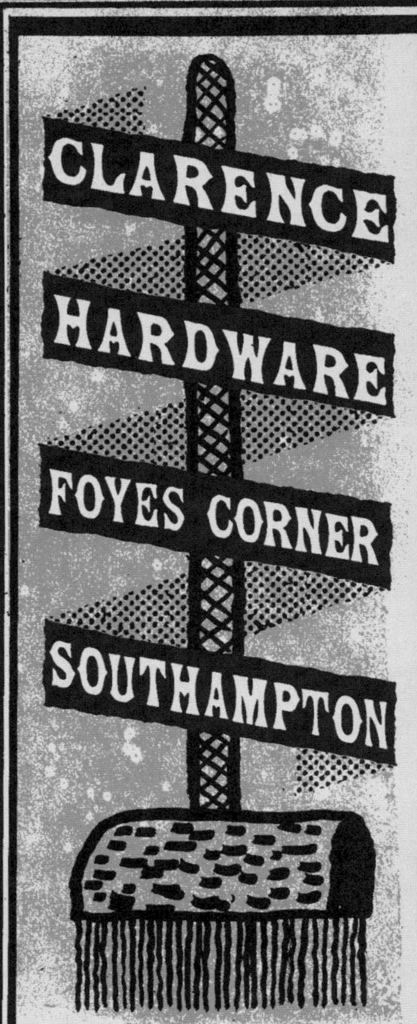


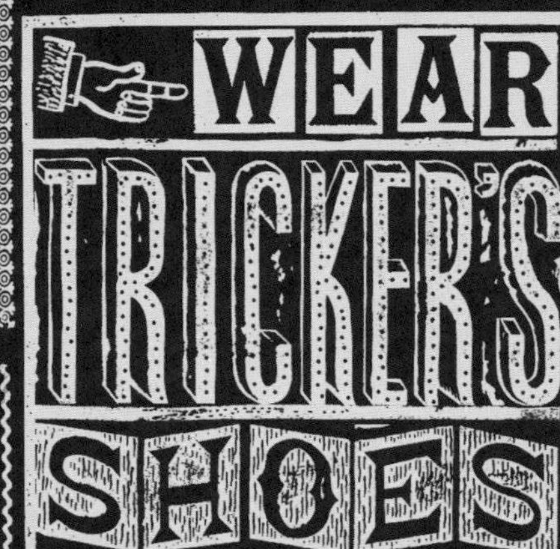


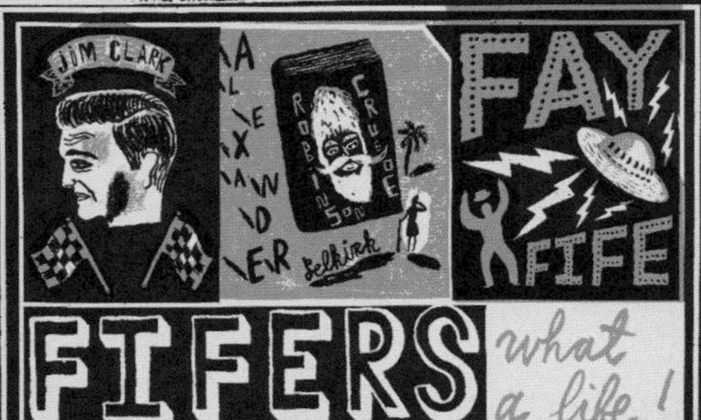


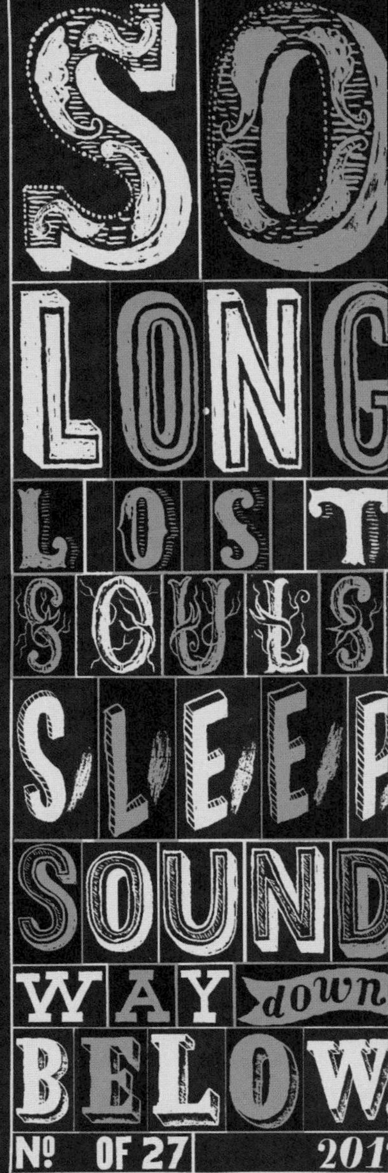


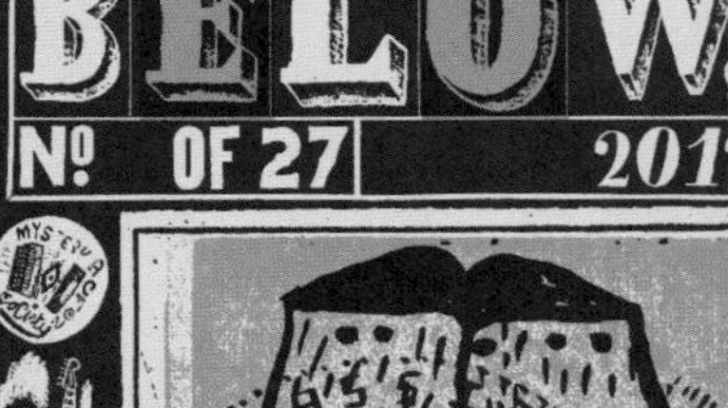


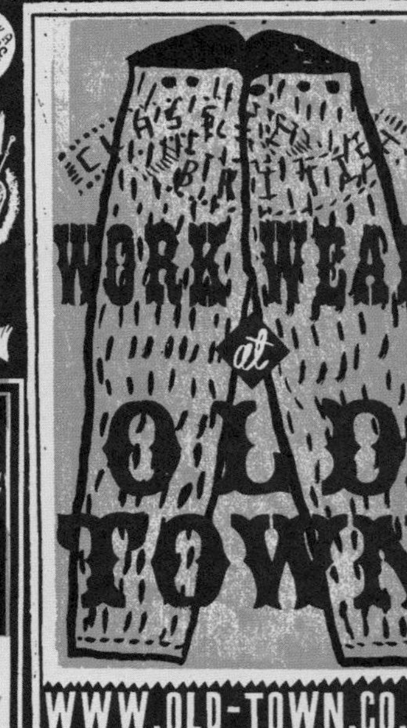

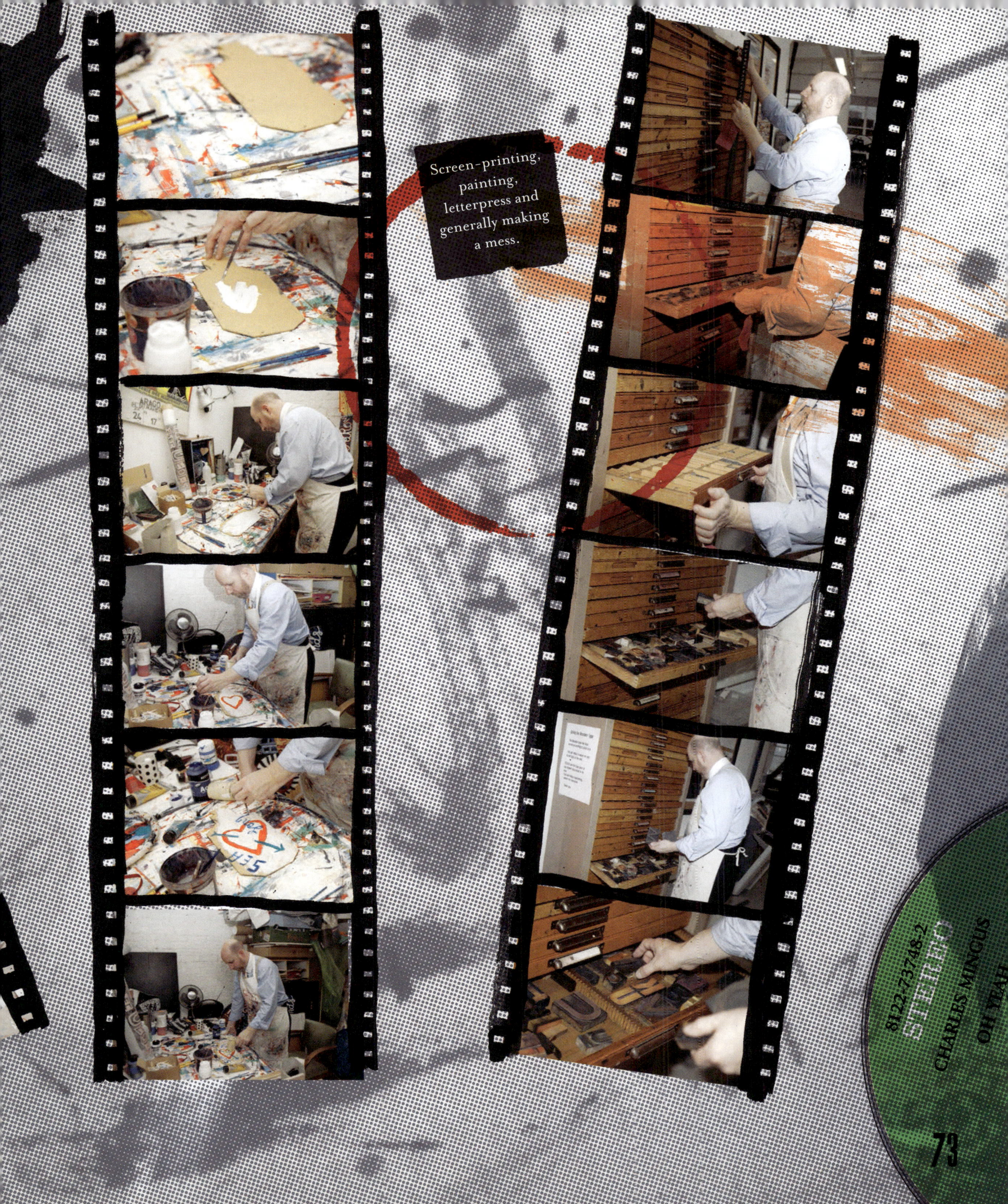

Screen-printing, painting, letterpress and generally making a mess.

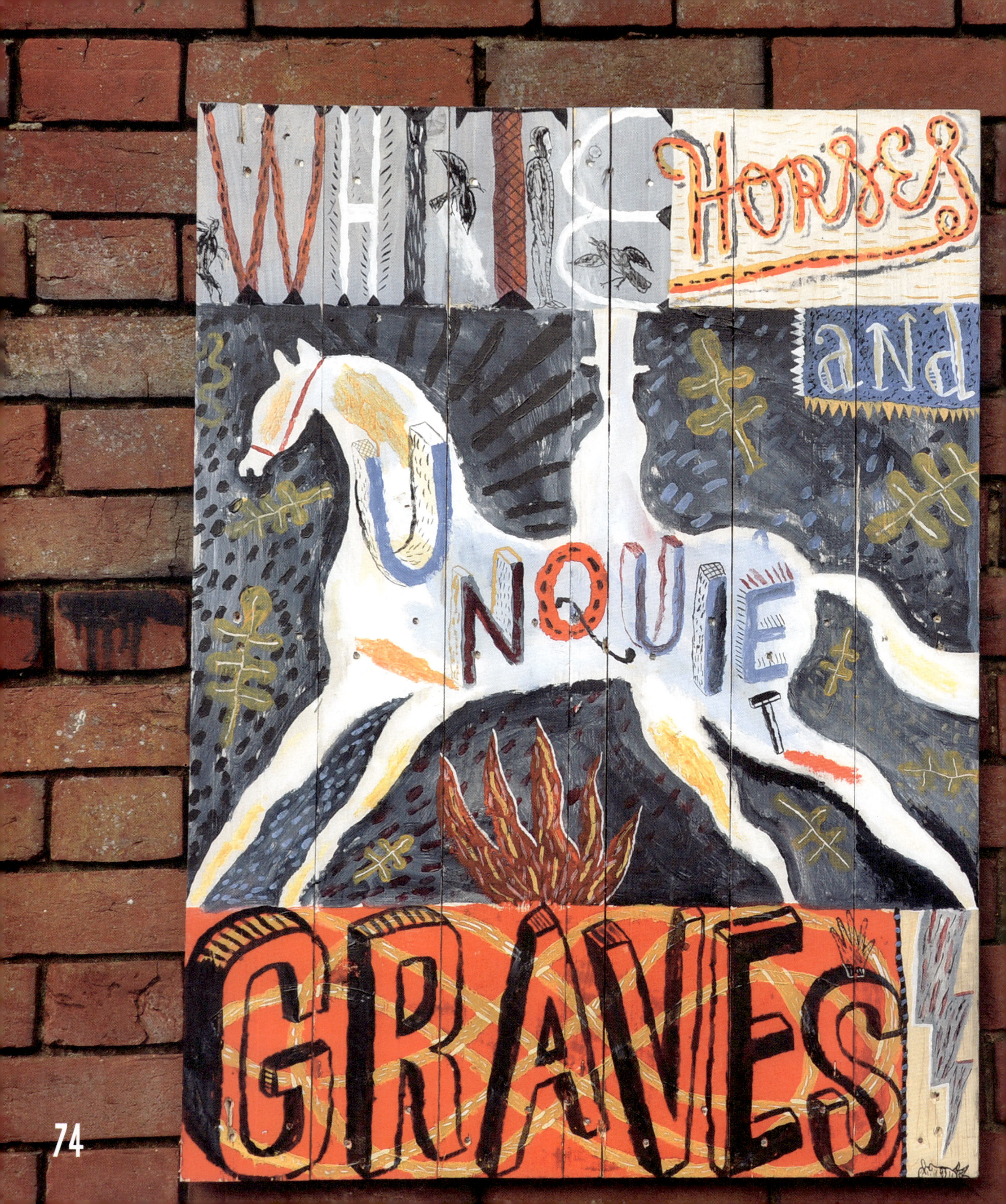
Horses
and
UNQUIET
GRAVES

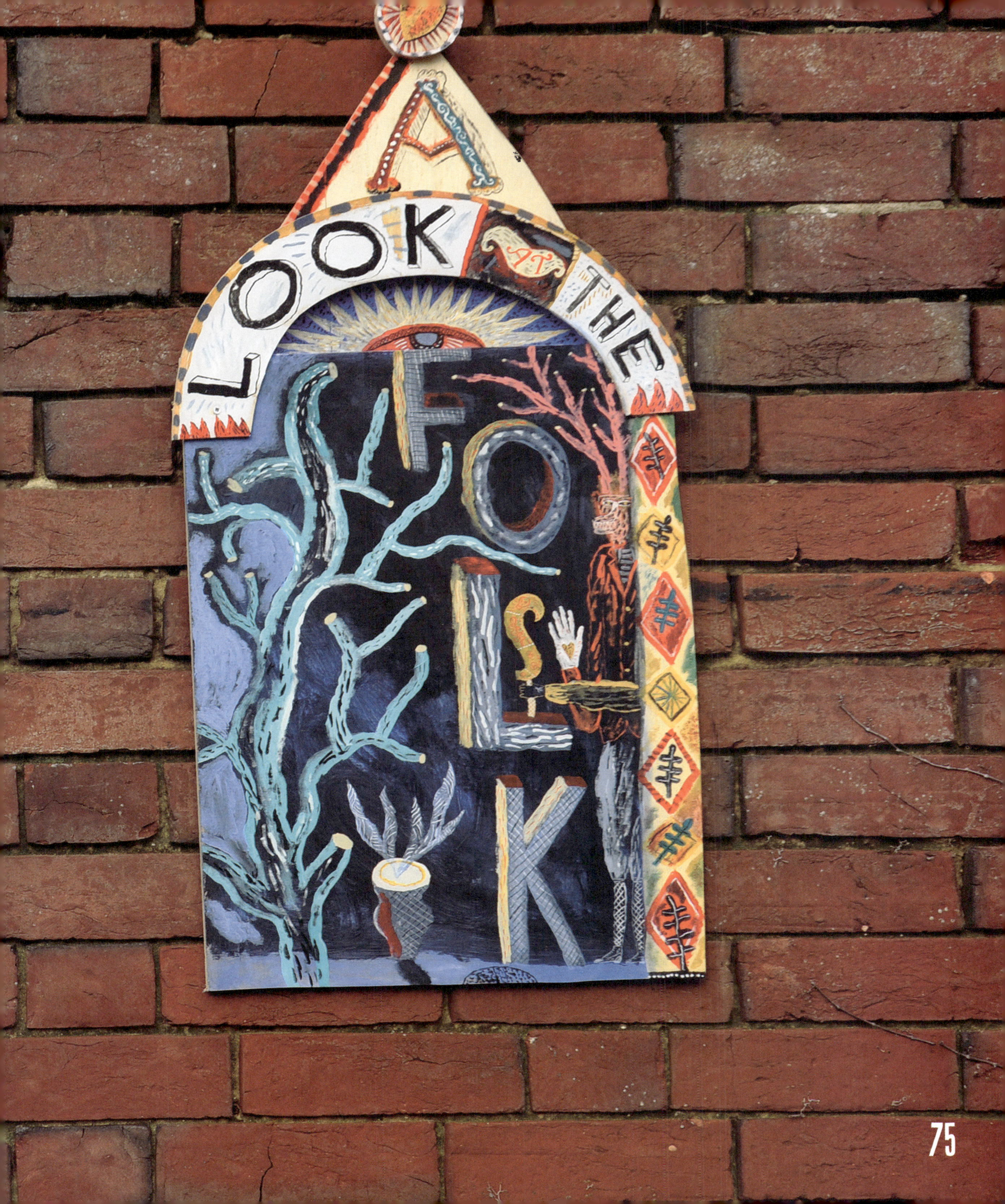
A
LOOK AT THE
FOLKS

# White Horses and Unquiet Graves: A Look at the F O L K

I like to think of myself as one of the folk. I come from the cheap Fife concrete of Arthur Street, from the mud of Headwell Park, bolstered by Lorne sausage from the back kitchen of auld Jeannie's council semi. And I like to think I've come a long way, but perhaps the 500 miles I've travelled are a splash in the ocean compared to the journey of others.

But the folk have always been with me. The small social stepladder I obtained years ago only ever got me so far. And it's hard to say where I feel most comfortable: back on the ground or halfway up? The very top step makes me giddy, so forget that.

Much of my inspiration comes from the ground up, however. The brown-dirt-soul of the everyday, even if it has been paved over. When I was growing up in Fife, being in a band was just what you were supposed to do. So I'd go for my Sunday guitar lessons with Rodney Relax, my cheap Spanish catalogue guitar wrapped up in a bin bag. My mum made it clear I'd get a case only if I were serious about it all. I didn't realize it then, but I was part of a rich heritage: Fay Fife from The Rezillos, Skids, Sir Patrick Spens. And decades later, as I listen to Sir Harry Lauder, I realize one thing for certain – it's all folk. Entertainment, done for all the right reasons, handed over to the masses: Jimmy Shand ('Muchty does me fine!'), Bascom Lamar Lunsford ('a railroad man, they'll ... drink up your blood like wine'), King Creosote ('how the Vauxhall bounced'), 'Monkey McGuire Meets Specky Potter Behind Lochore Institute' ('Whitdidyestoapfur?'). And, more exotically, The Mighty Sparrow (eating the mango vert).

And why do folk stories and tales persist to excite and entertain? Anyone seen Black Shuck lately? Sawney Bean and his cannibal clan gave birth to so many other bad men: Hannibal Lecter, Ed Gein and that big bloke from *The Texas Chainsaw Massacre*, among many others. Is there a more cautionary tale than 'Tam o' Shanter'? Don't drink too much, don't be seduced by scantily clad lassies and, most of all, don't shout out inappropriately, especially if you're viewing a witches' coven.

This level of direct simplicity has also been one reason why certain alternative minds have picked up brushes loaded with paint, to tell us other stories: Rev. Howard Finster, the secretive Henry Darger and the joyously

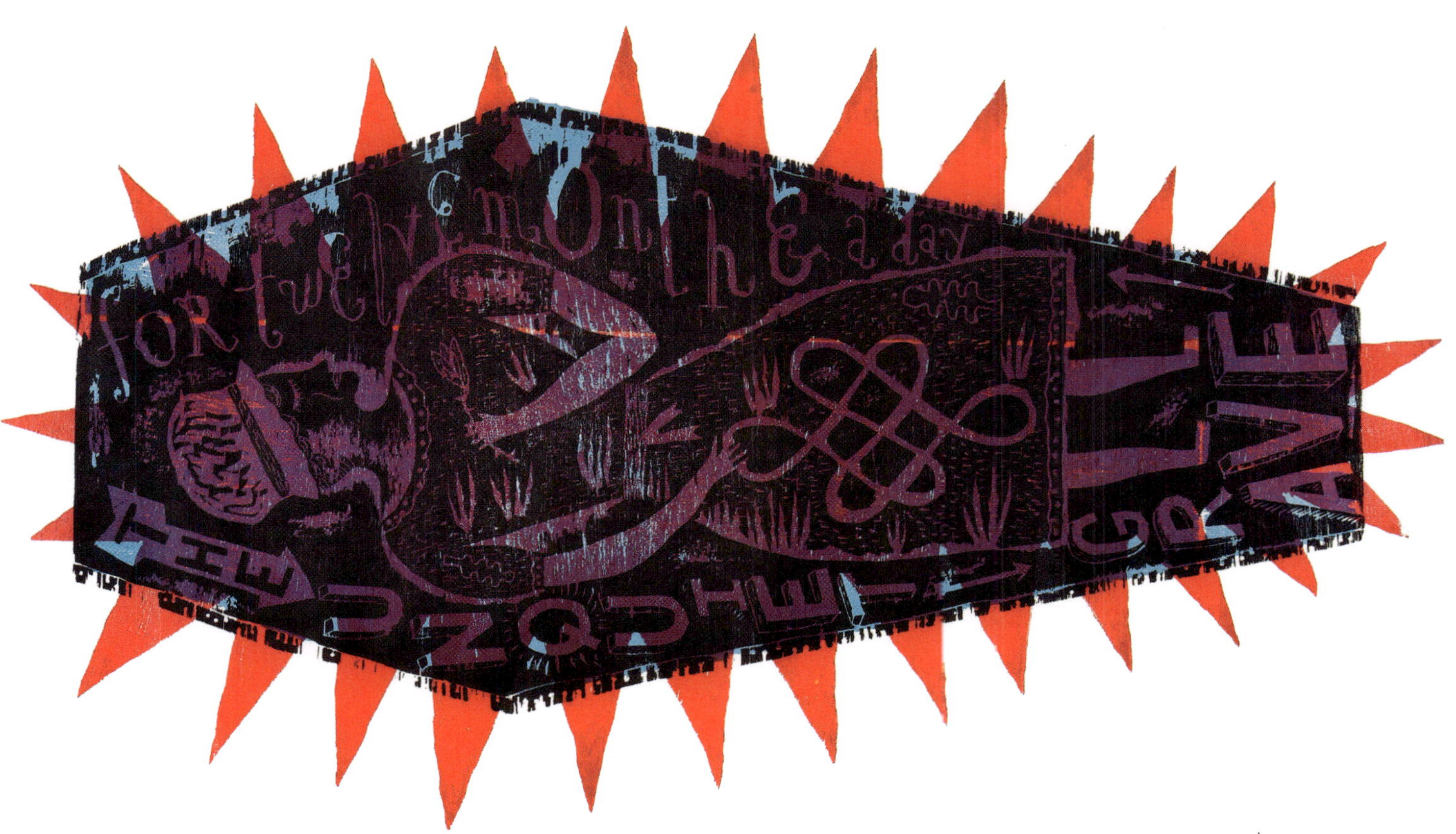


celebratory Ralph Fasanella. Their work points to a certain path forward that no Michelangelo, Reynolds or Hirst ever could do. It's a path that takes us around the houses, sometimes through galleries, and into a world of sublime beauty, littered with instinctive, brutal and abandoned marks that delight the eye in a truly unique way.

The twenty-first century gives us it all. News every minute of the day. Facts and figures from the internet that used to take weeks of research in Dunfermline Library. Weather reports on our phones. We can photograph anything we want, wherever we want, both good and bad. And that's exactly why folk is back on the agenda. These stories don't have conclusions, hard facts or clear outcomes. The songs aren't over-produced to the *n*th degree, but instead have a home-made feel; yet we have access to them through the internet. So modern technology is working well with antiquated notions, brightening up our potentially over-digitized century. It could so easily be a boring mass of X, Y and Z factors, veneered and polished so that we don't have to worry about what to choose to like. And this is partly why Simon Costin has decided to create a Museum of British Folklore (pages 80–83). The museum celebrates the past and offers us an alternative to the ultra-modern universe. It's something we're hankering after increasingly, as not all of us want to read blogs or tweet and trend.

I was delighted when Simon asked me to work with him on the museum project, partly from a design point of view, but also partly because it's just such an exciting, mysterious and historically important area. The caravan, home to the museum in its current state, is a treasure trove of goodies, old and new. And, best of all, it's home-made, in true folk style.

So, yes, Darktown has the internet, and you can watch whatever you want. But a night in the Jolly Scrimshander Tavern, with Kenny Anderson and an acoustic guitar, is a night to remember, completely unavailable anywhere else.

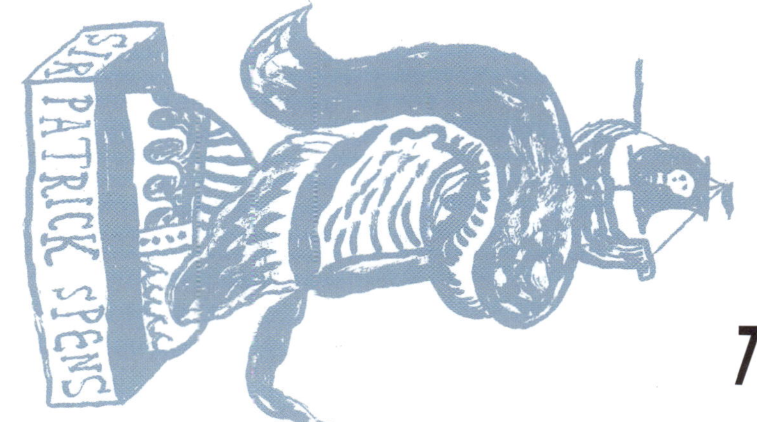

## Atlantico CD cover
2012

Atlantico are a Southampton-based band steeped in the heat and passion of Colombia. The percussionist, Rosy Maguire, asked me to decorate the cover of their recording *Cumbia Sabrosa*, so I cut several bits of plywood and started painting. I was paid in beautiful photographic prints and bottles of fine wine.

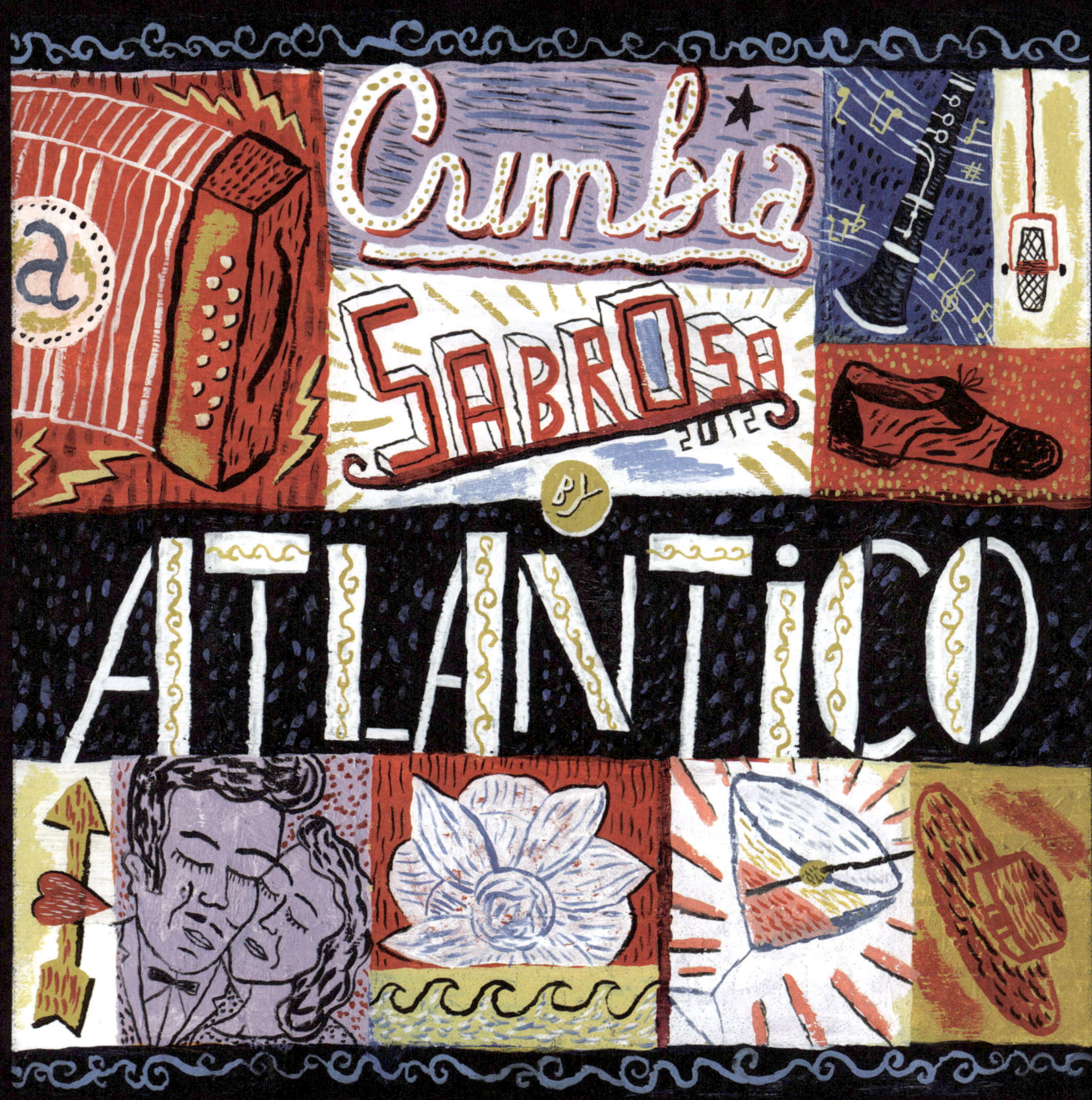

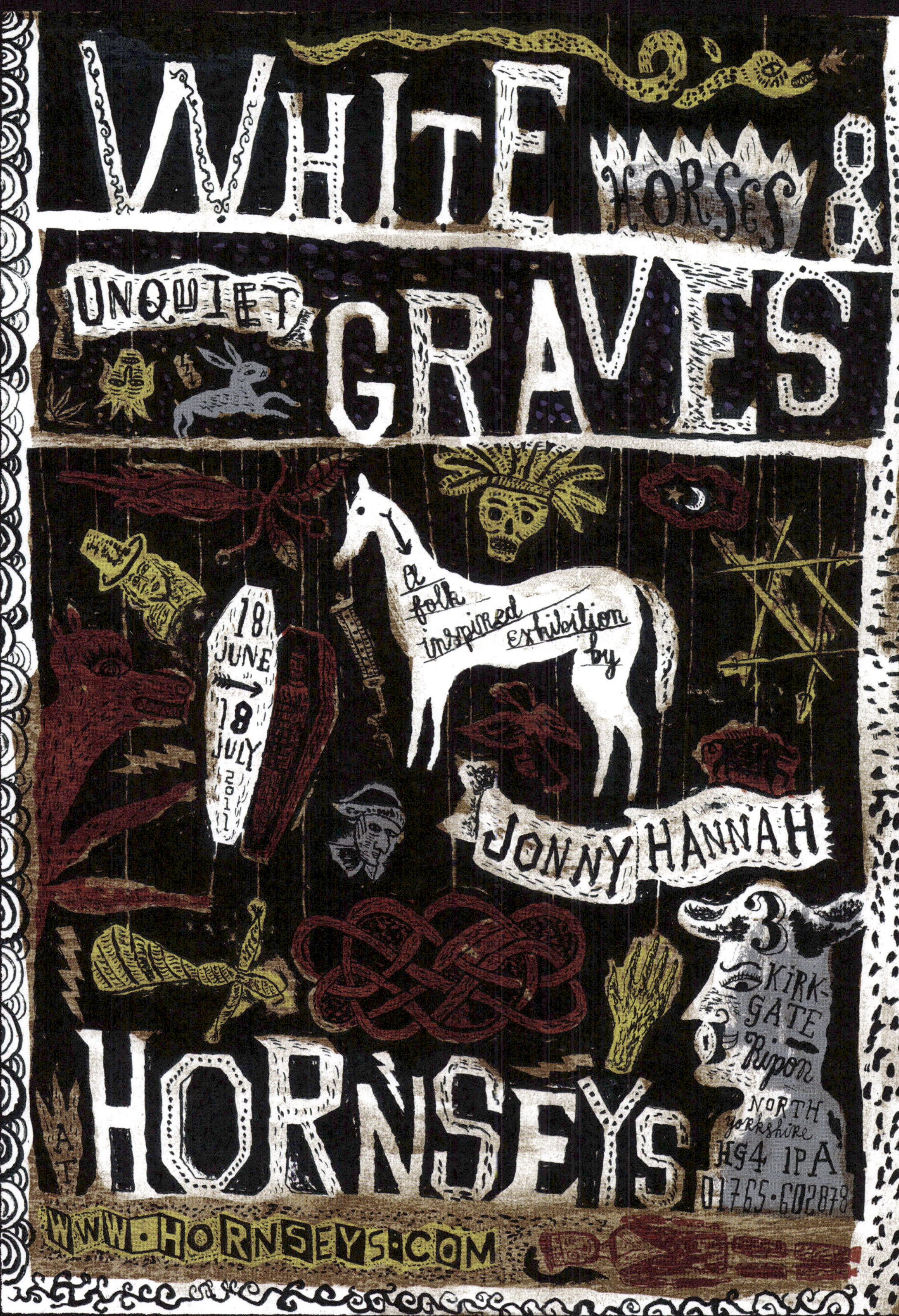


In 2011 Dan Hornsey asked me to stage an exhibition on British folklore at his excellent gallery in Ripon. I jumped at the chance and promised the clientele some entertainment at the private view, including Dr George Rhind reciting the whole of 'Tam o' Shanter' from memory. The following day, the artist Mark Hearld treated me to a visit to the nearby Kilburn White Horse.

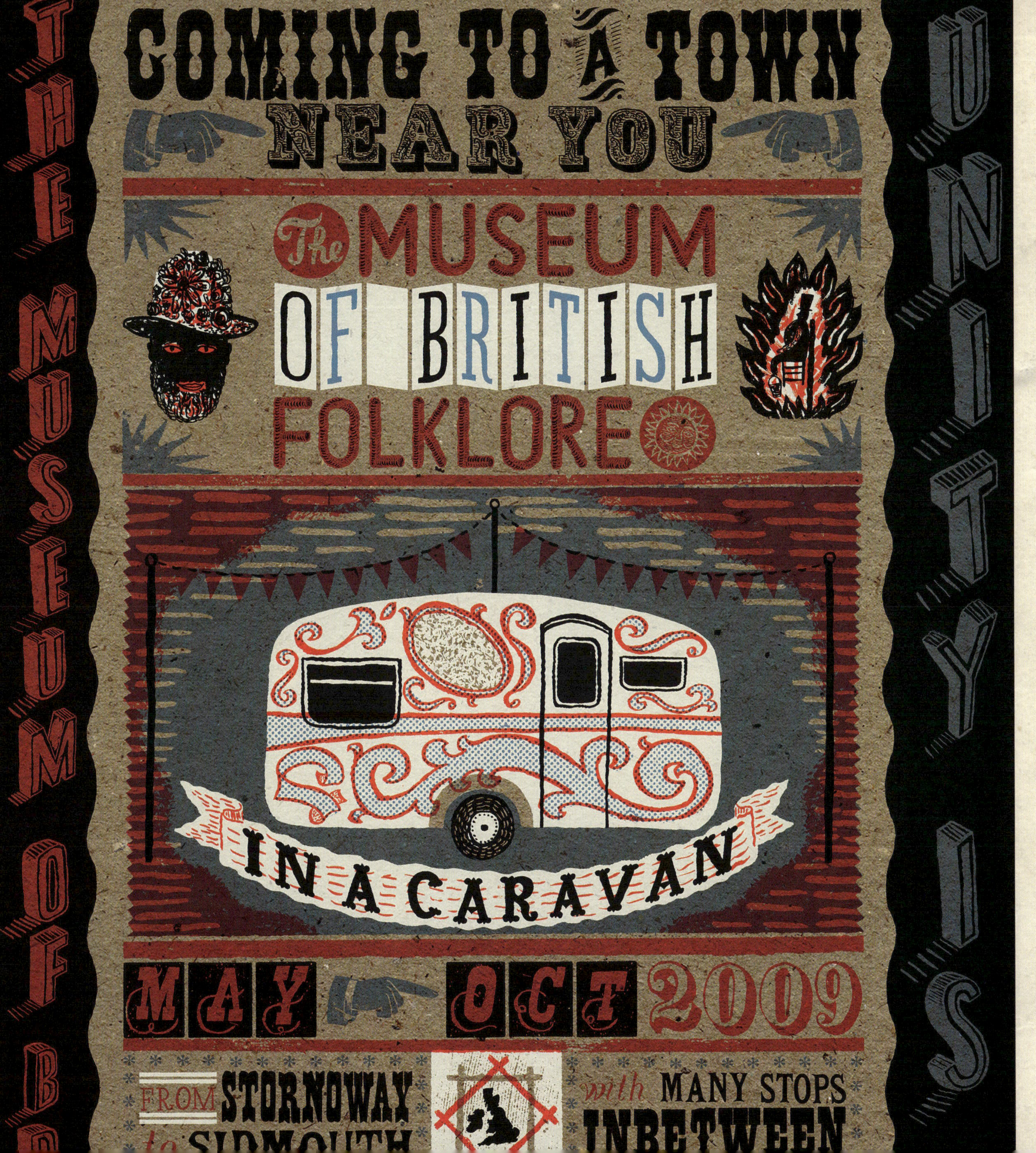
THE MUSEUM OF
COMING TO A TOWN
NEAR YOU
The MUSEUM
OF BRITISH
FOLKLORE
IN A CARAVAN
MAY OCT 2009
FROM STORNOWAY
with MANY STOPS
INBETWEEN
UNITY IS

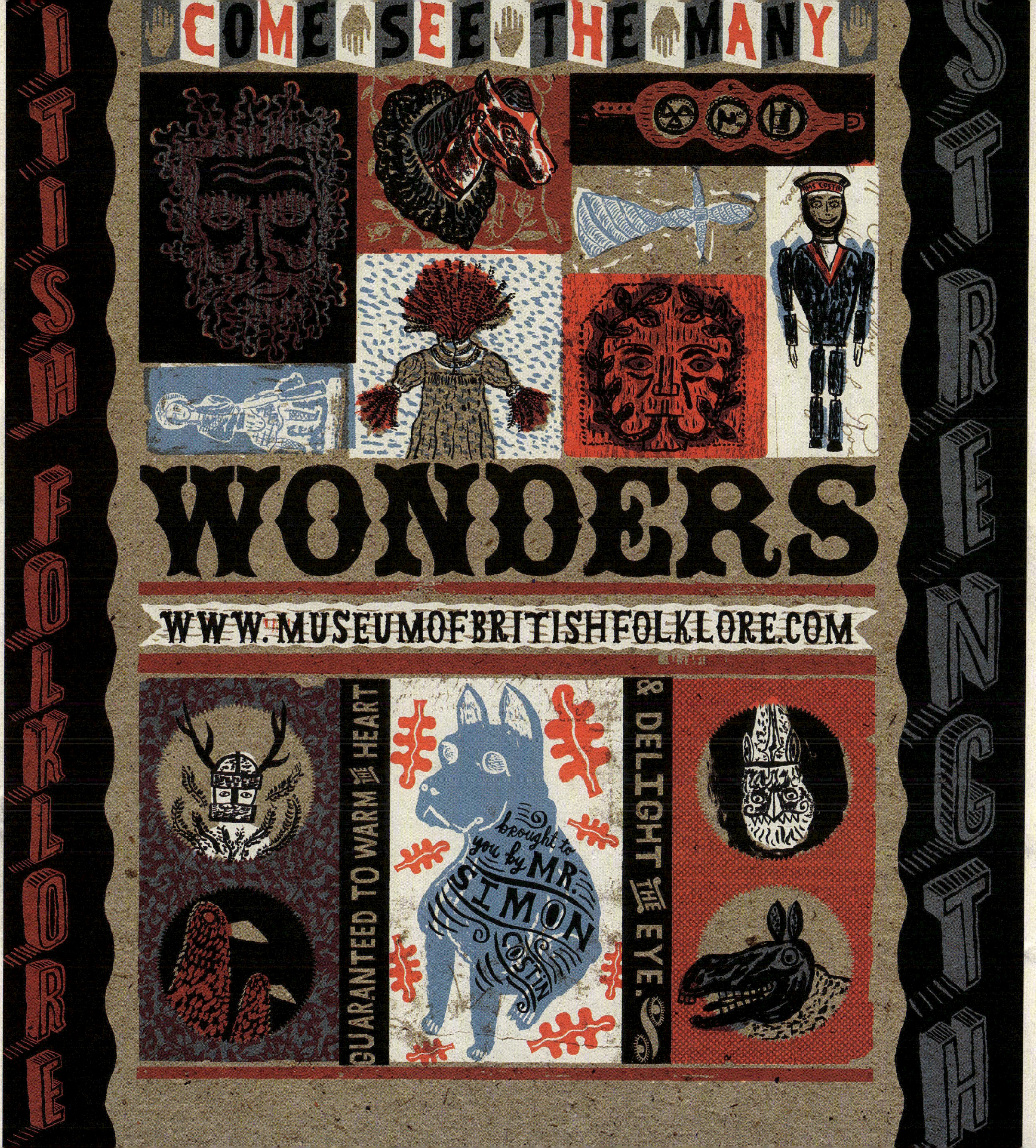
STRENGTH
COME SEE THE MANY
WONDERS
WWW.MUSEUMOFBRITISHFOLKLORE.COM
GUARANTEED TO WARM THE HEART
brought to you by MR. SIMON COSTIN
& DELIGHT THE EYE.
ITISH FOLKLORE

# The Museum of British Folklore

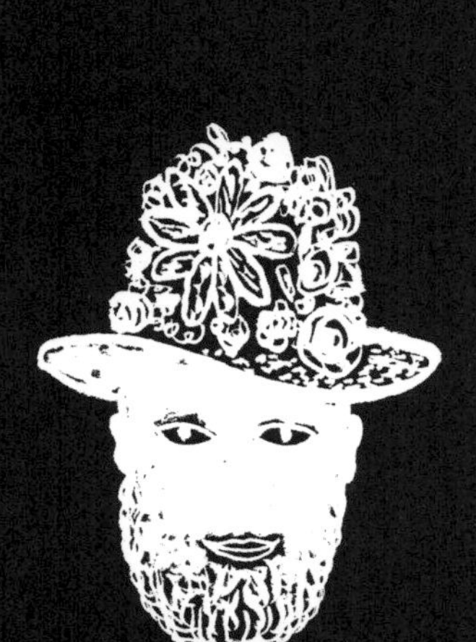

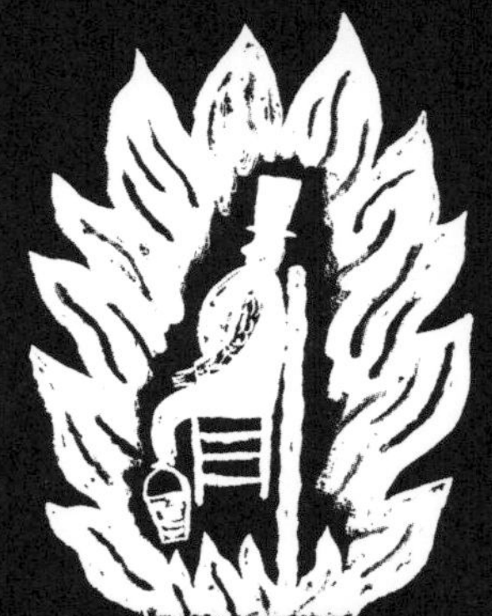

## by Simon Costin

British folklore: morris dancing and May Day revels? Yes, but folklore shows itself in many other ways, too. The 'ghost bike' chained to railings to memorialize the spot where a cyclist was killed, playground games, slang, urban legends, suburban houses festooned with thousands of Christmas lights – all are folkloric expressions. These things offer insights into who we are and the things we hold dear; they are about community identity and cultural heritage, linking the past to the present, and expressing our shared humanity.

Currently there exists no single museum or cultural institution in the United Kingdom that celebrates, charts and cherishes the rich diversity of folk practice in Britain today. For a long time, folklore has been overlooked or belittled by the greater museum fraternity, but we are now witnessing a renaissance, an upsurge of interest in folklore through music, art and dance, and a growing trend and desire for people to reconnect with their communities, their heritage and their environment at large.

The foundation of the Museum of British Folklore aims to address the yawning gap within the cultural landscape of Britain. We hope to establish a place that will not only impart knowledge and stimulate inquiry, but also will provide aesthetic experiences and kindle individual ambition by strengthening community ties and making visitors aware of the richness of our shared folk culture in all its manifold forms.

I'm the museum's director, and I was introduced to Jonny Hannah's work by a friend. I felt that Jonny's unique blend of playful and deceptive naivety suited what we were trying to achieve with the Museum of British Folklore. Here was something that, at first glance, seemed quite unrefined, spontaneous and uncomplicated, but on further inspection revealed a wealth of carefully considered detail and immense craftsmanship, along with a depth of historic references. Such a folk custom as morris dancing may superficially be seen as a quaint rural tradition but, once examined, contains many complex steps and movements drawn from a rich history. Jonny produced a number of works in support of the museum (pages 80–81), shown at an exhibition at Hornseys Gallery in Ripon, and he also designed the museum's logo.

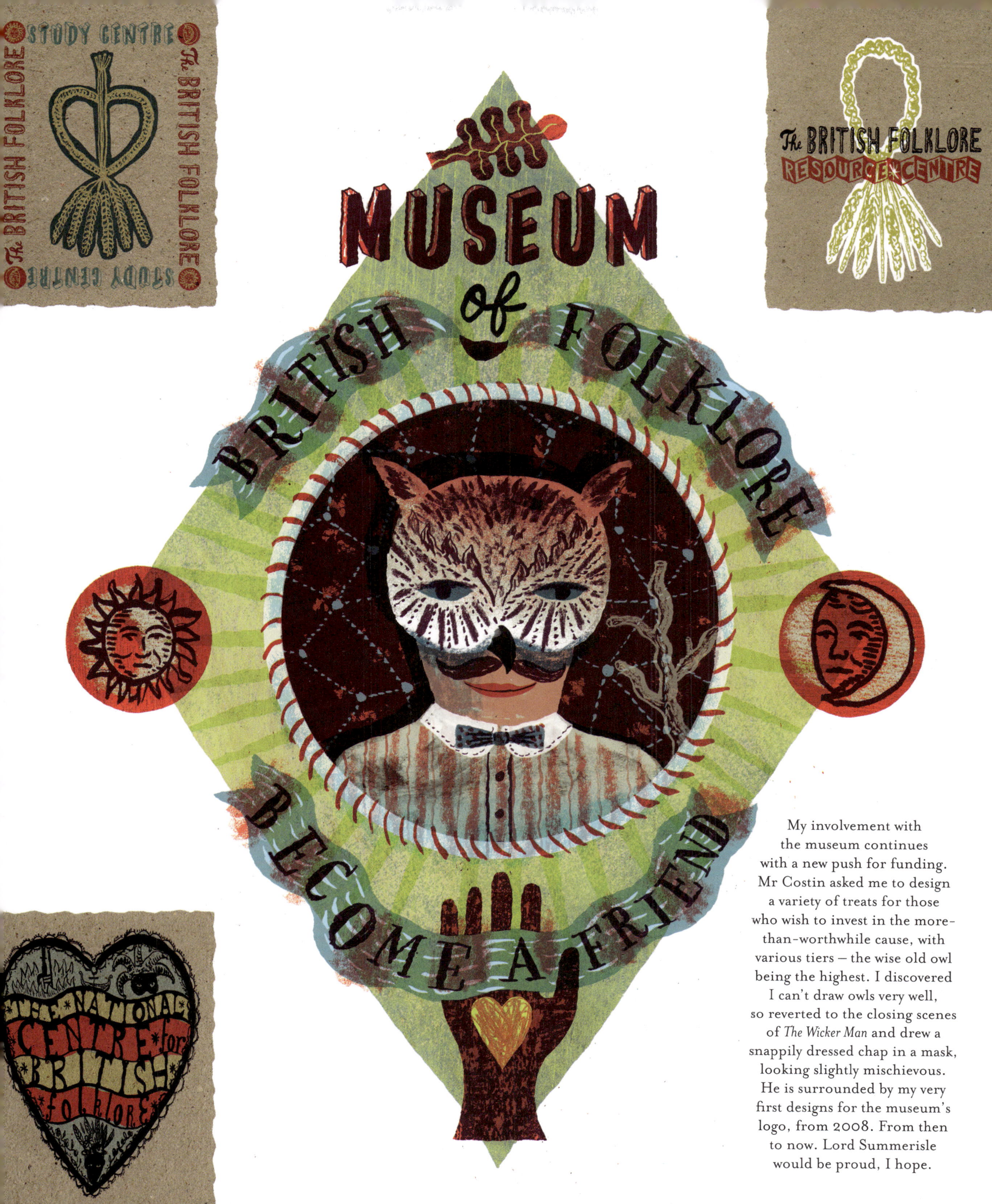


My involvement with the museum continues with a new push for funding. Mr Costin asked me to design a variety of treats for those who wish to invest in the more-than-worthwhile cause, with various tiers – the wise old owl being the highest. I discovered I can't draw owls very well, so reverted to the closing scenes of *The Wicker Man* and drew a snappily dressed chap in a mask, looking slightly mischievous. He is surrounded by my very first designs for the museum's logo, from 2008. From then to now. Lord Summerisle would be proud, I hope.

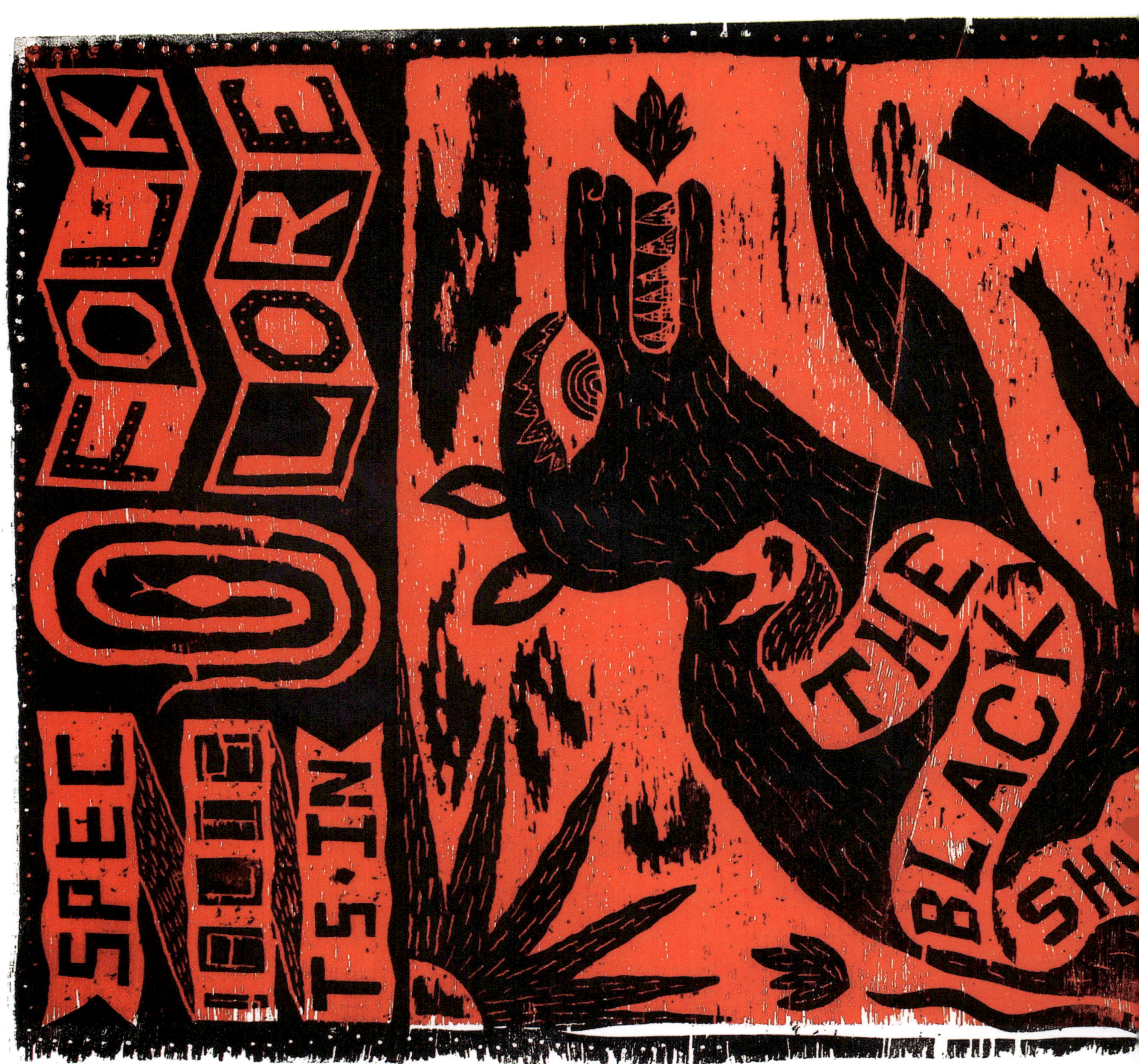
FOLK
LORE
THE
BLACK

*The Black Shuck Bookshop*
2010

This is my biggest print to date, hand-printed at Red Hot Press in Hampshire on a hot sunny day while I was getting ready for my *Bed of Sea & Dead Men's Suits* exhibition at St Jude's Gallery in Norfolk.

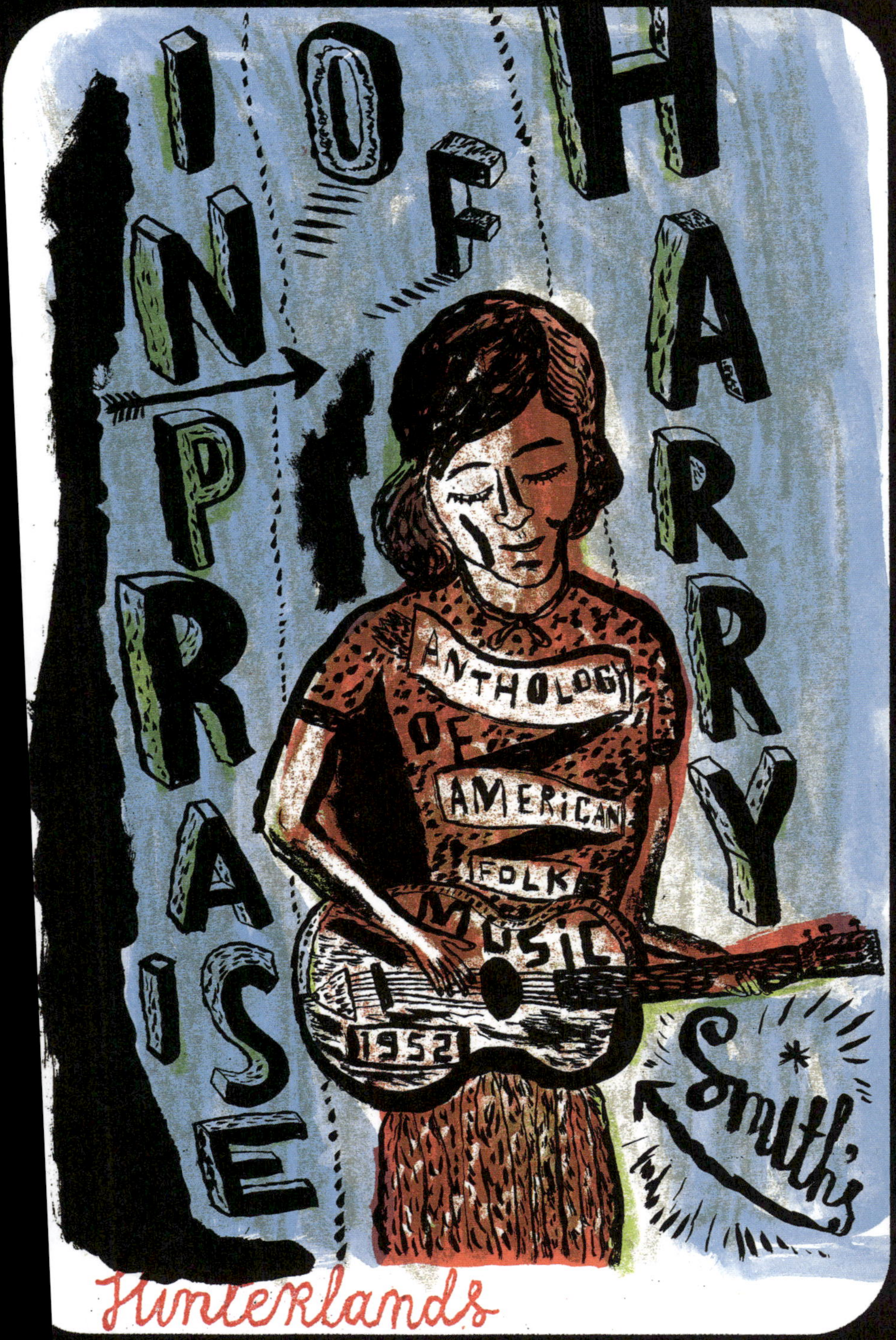

In Praise of Harry Smith's

Anthology of American Folk Music

1952

Hinterlands

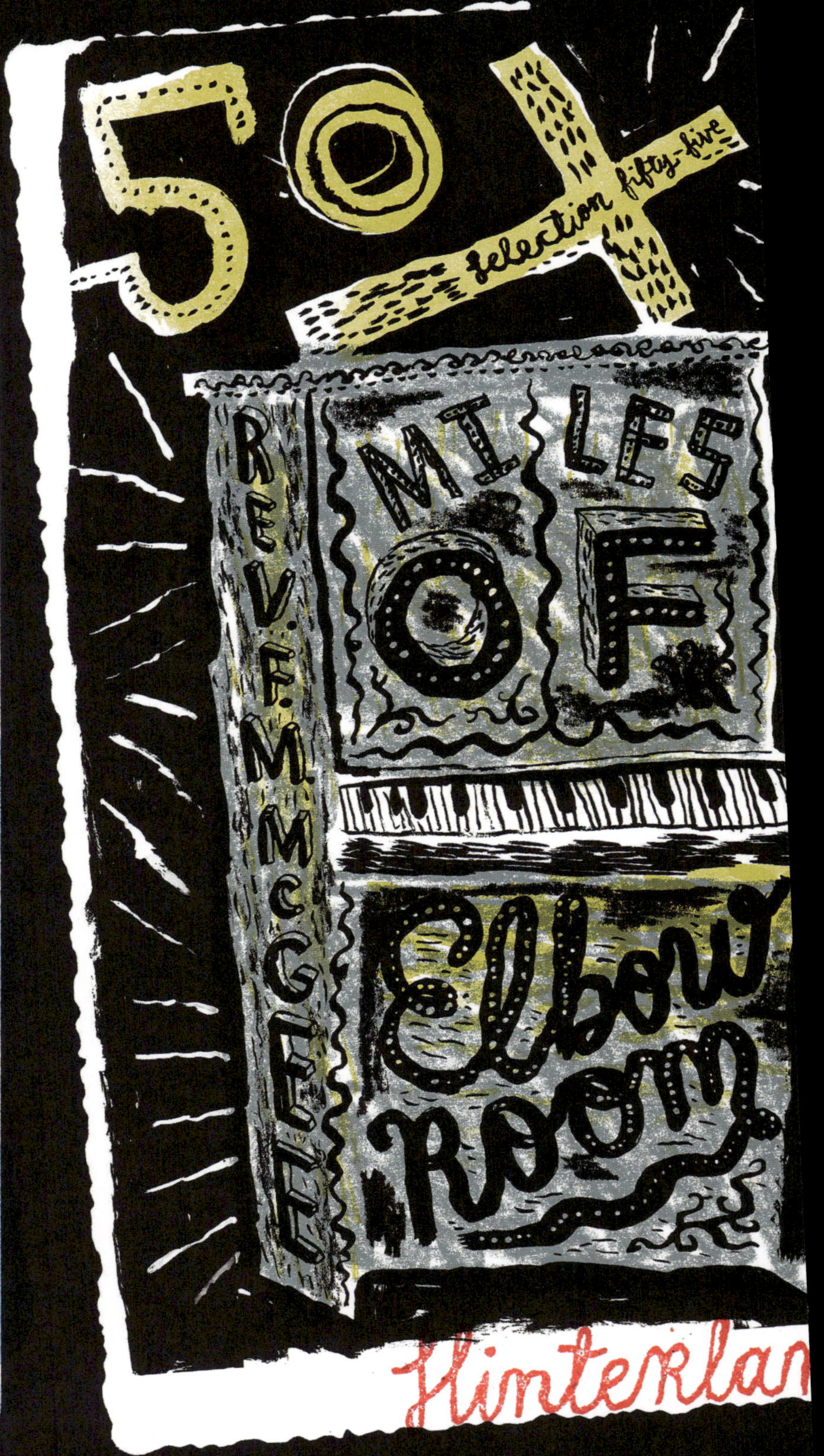

50 selection fifty-five

Rev. F. M. McGee

Miles of Elbow Room

Hinterlan

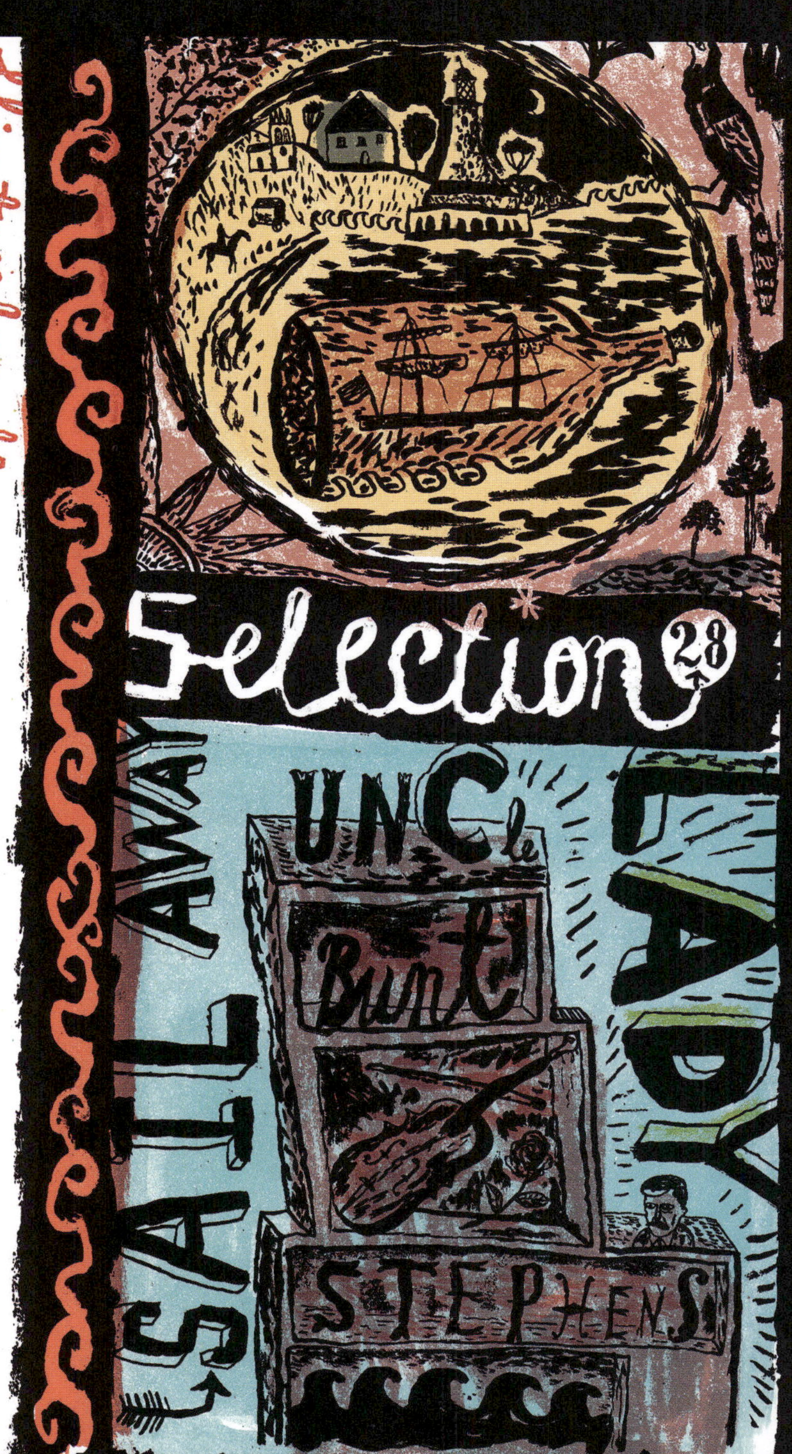


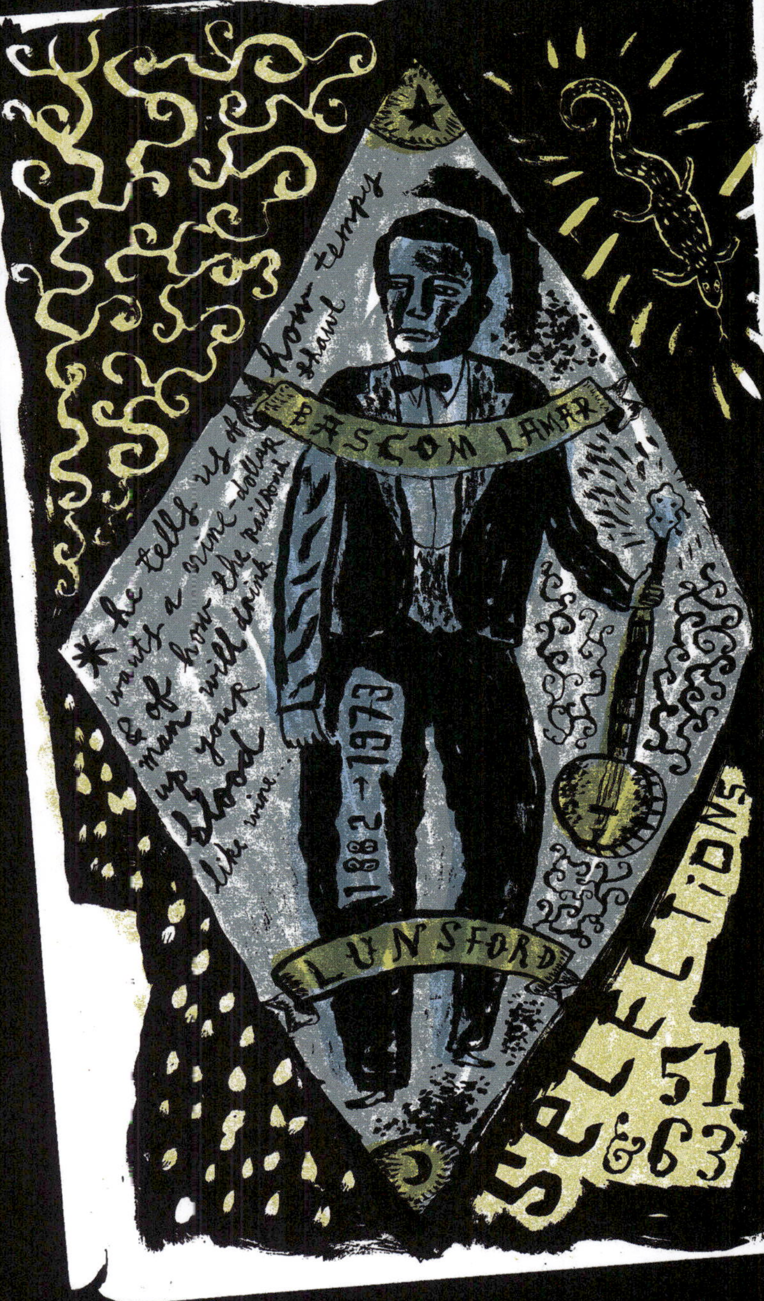


I was asked to make a contribution about folk to a small but perfectly formed publication called *The Ministry of Frogs*, edited by Desdemona McCannon, who now teaches in Manchester. I chose something that had long rumbled around in my head: *Anthology of American Folk Music*, first published in 1952 by legendary oddball Harry Smith. It was Martin Colyer at *Reader's Digest* who first mentioned this mythical set of recordings to me, and I became obsessed until I bought it as a thirtieth birthday present to myself. My life has never been the same since.

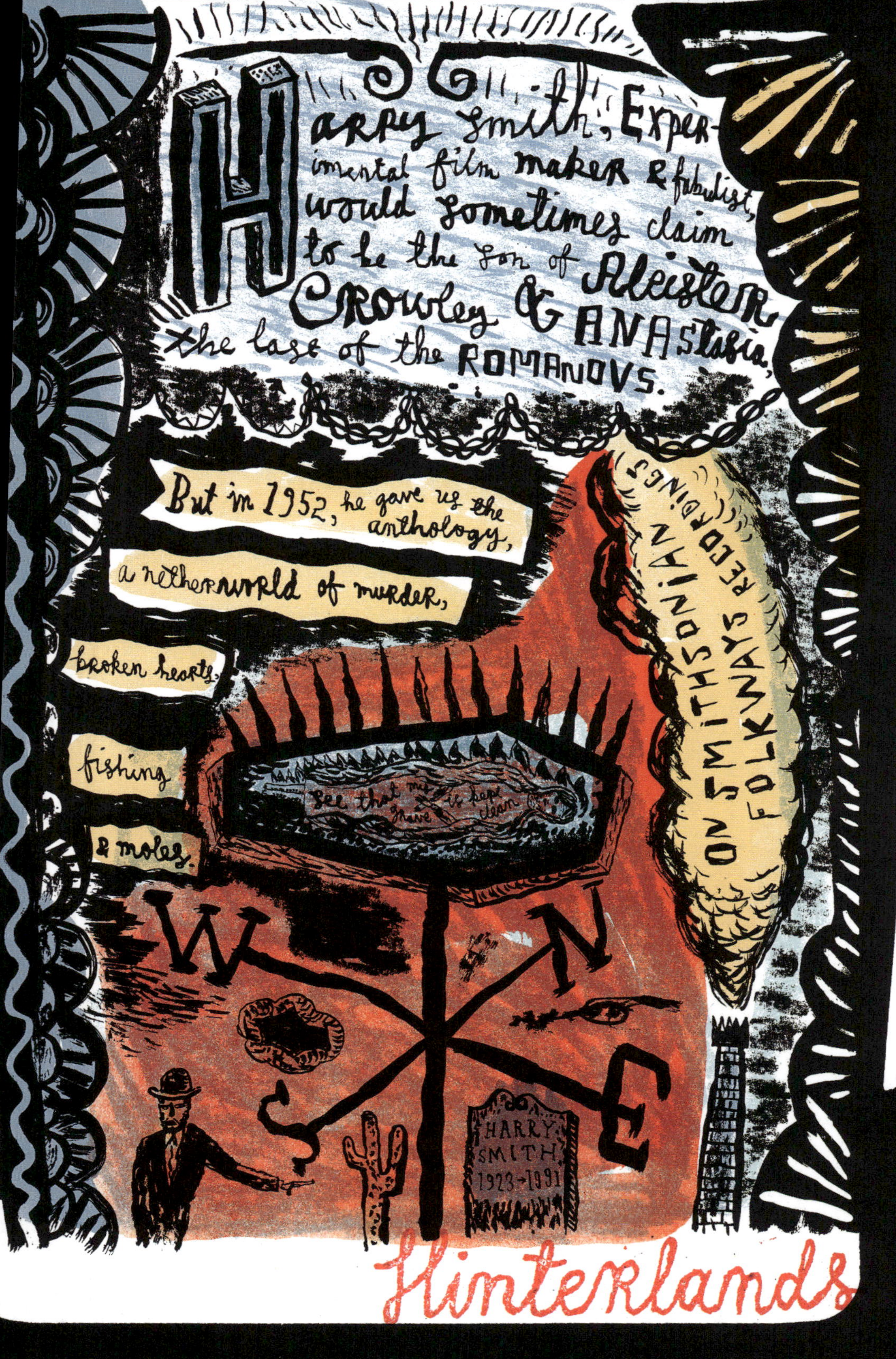


Hinterlands

* born blind & christened lemon, the handful of recordings for PARAmount Records are a haunting collection. His meagre existence as a blues-man was supported by his part-time WREstling. In selection 76 lemon's guitar becomes a death-bell, tolling. HE ... to death in ... CHIC... an abandoned tenement flat

BLIND LEMON JEFFERSON
1897–1929
SELECTIONS
*75*76*69*

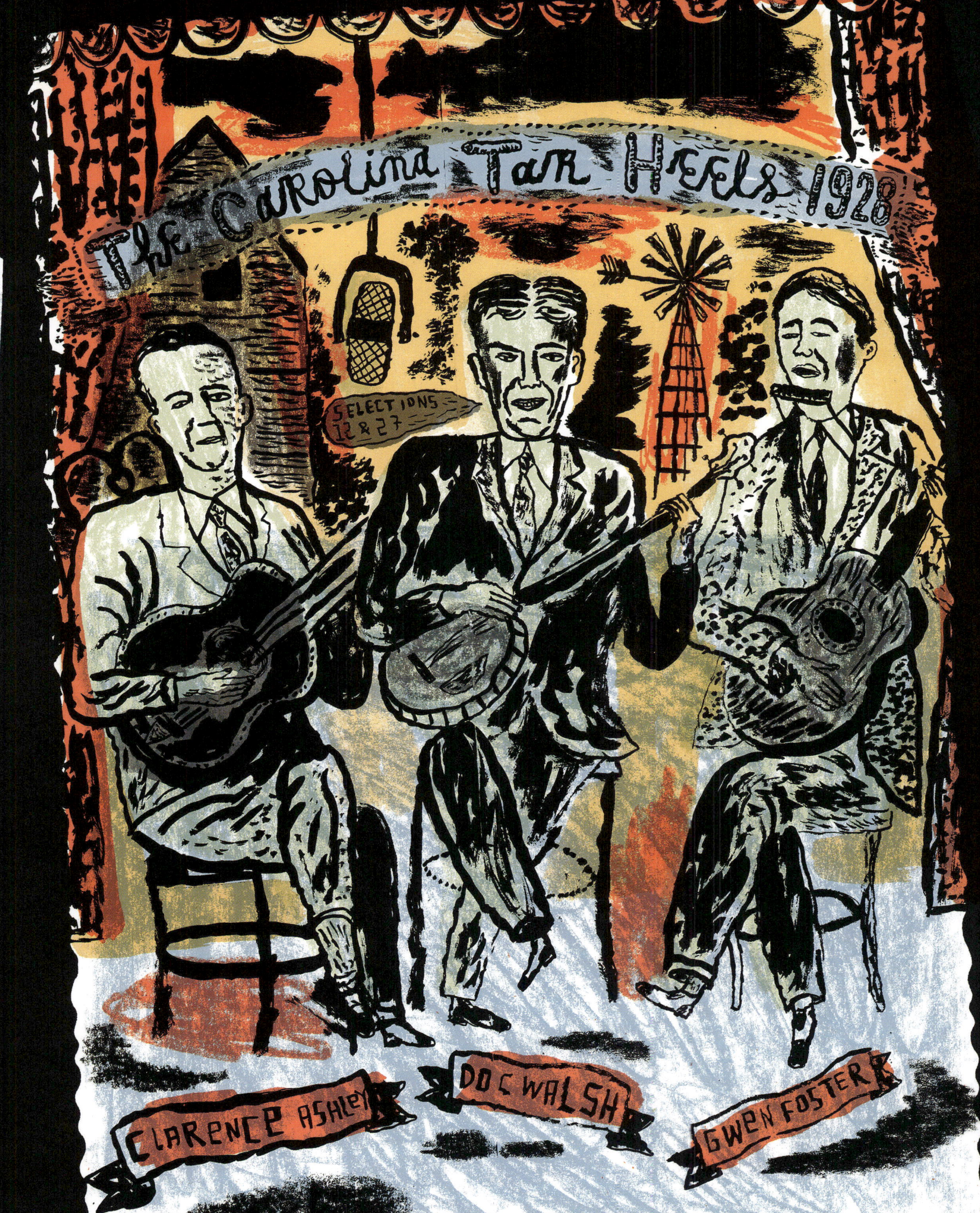
The Carolina Tar Heels 1928
SELECTIONS 72 & 27
CLARENCE ASHLEY
DOC WALSH
GWEN FOSTER

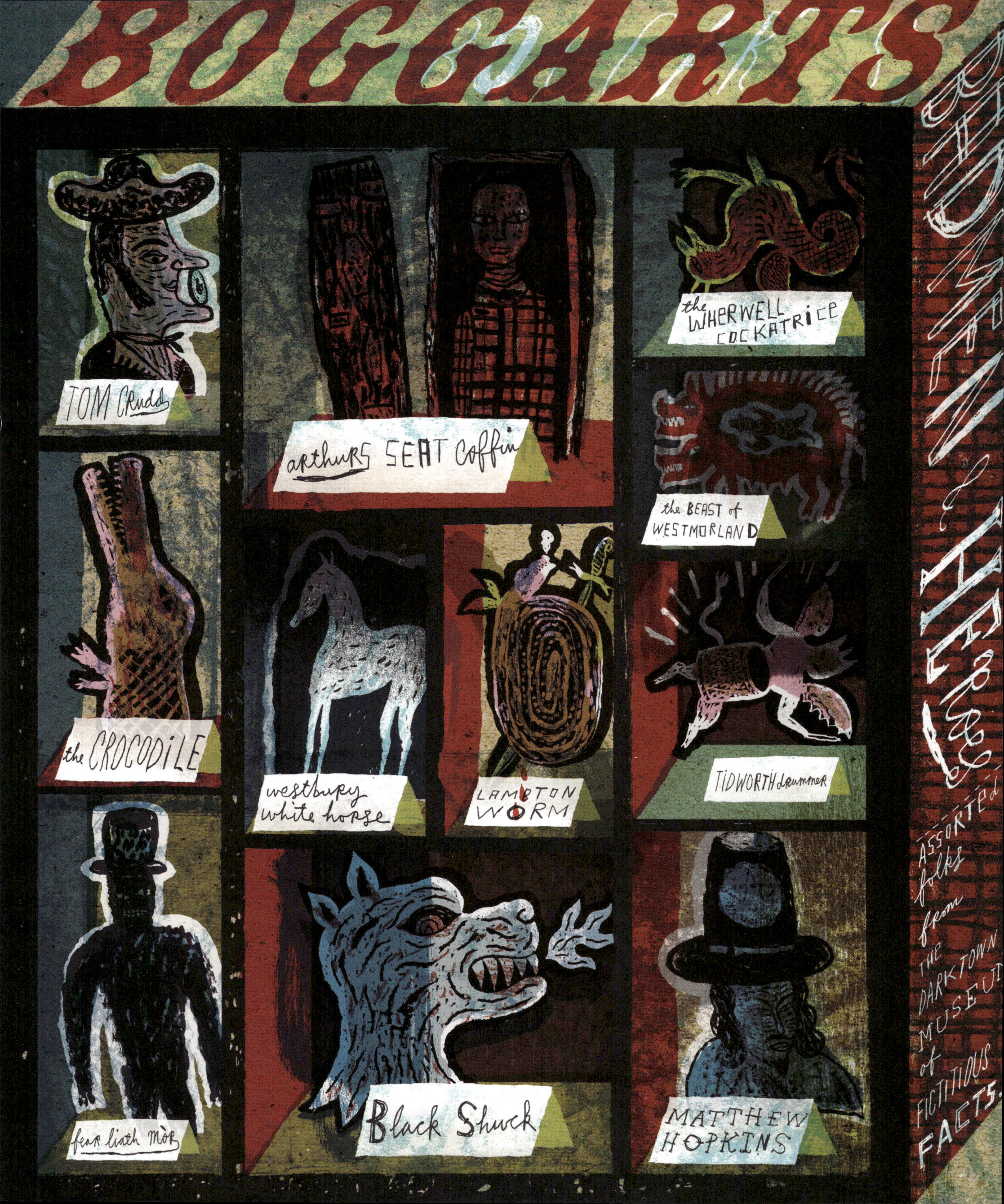

# BOGGARTS

TOM CRUDD

arthurs SEAT coffin

the WHERWELL COCKATRICE

the BEAST of WESTMORLAND

the CROCODILE

westbury white horse

LAMBTON WORM

TIDWORTH drummer

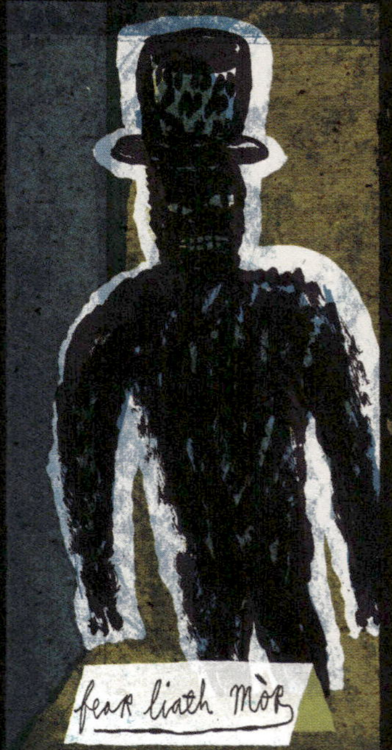


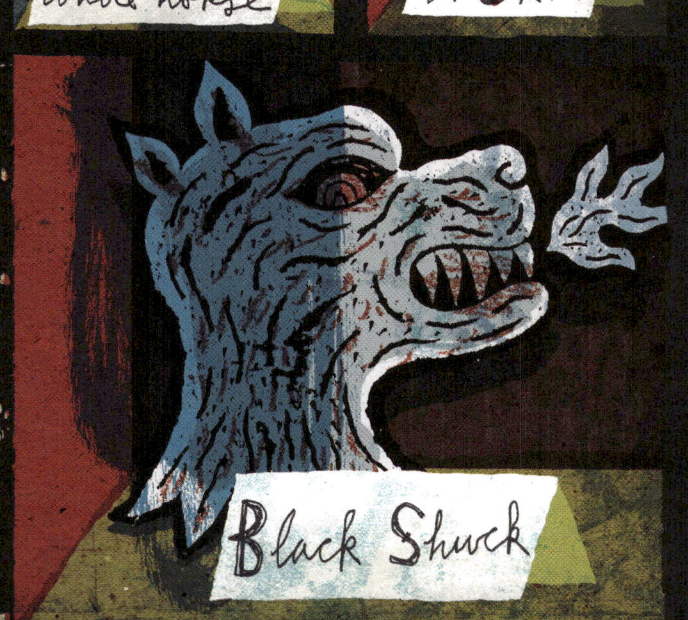


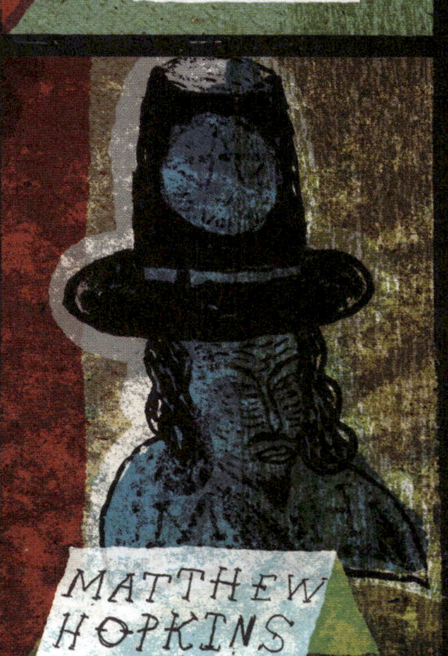


ASSORTED folks from THE DARKTOWN MUSEUM of FICTITIOUS FACTS.

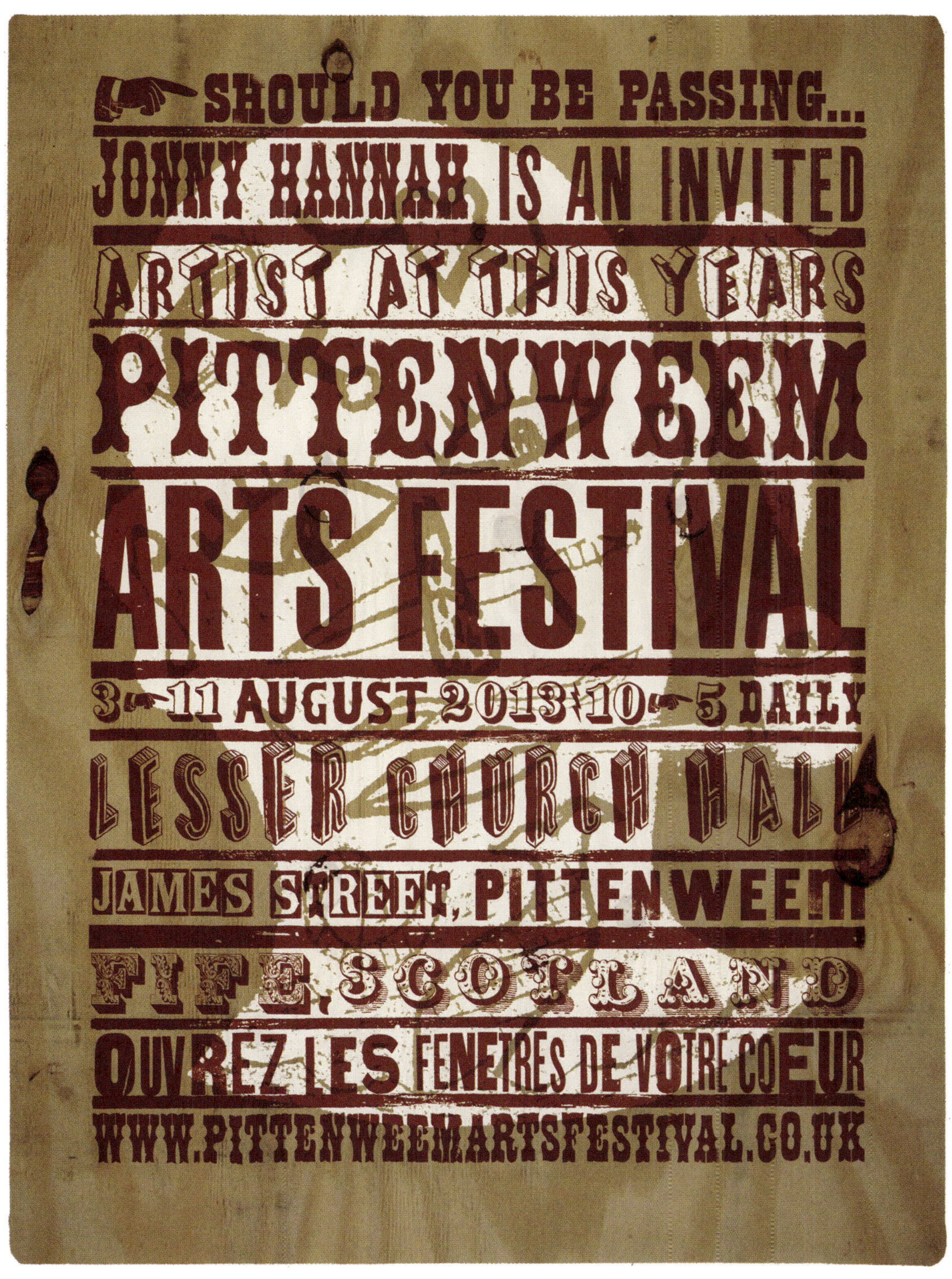


My poster and invitation to all and sundry for the Pittenweem Arts Festival in 2013, just in case they were passing a small fishing village in the East Neuk of Fife.

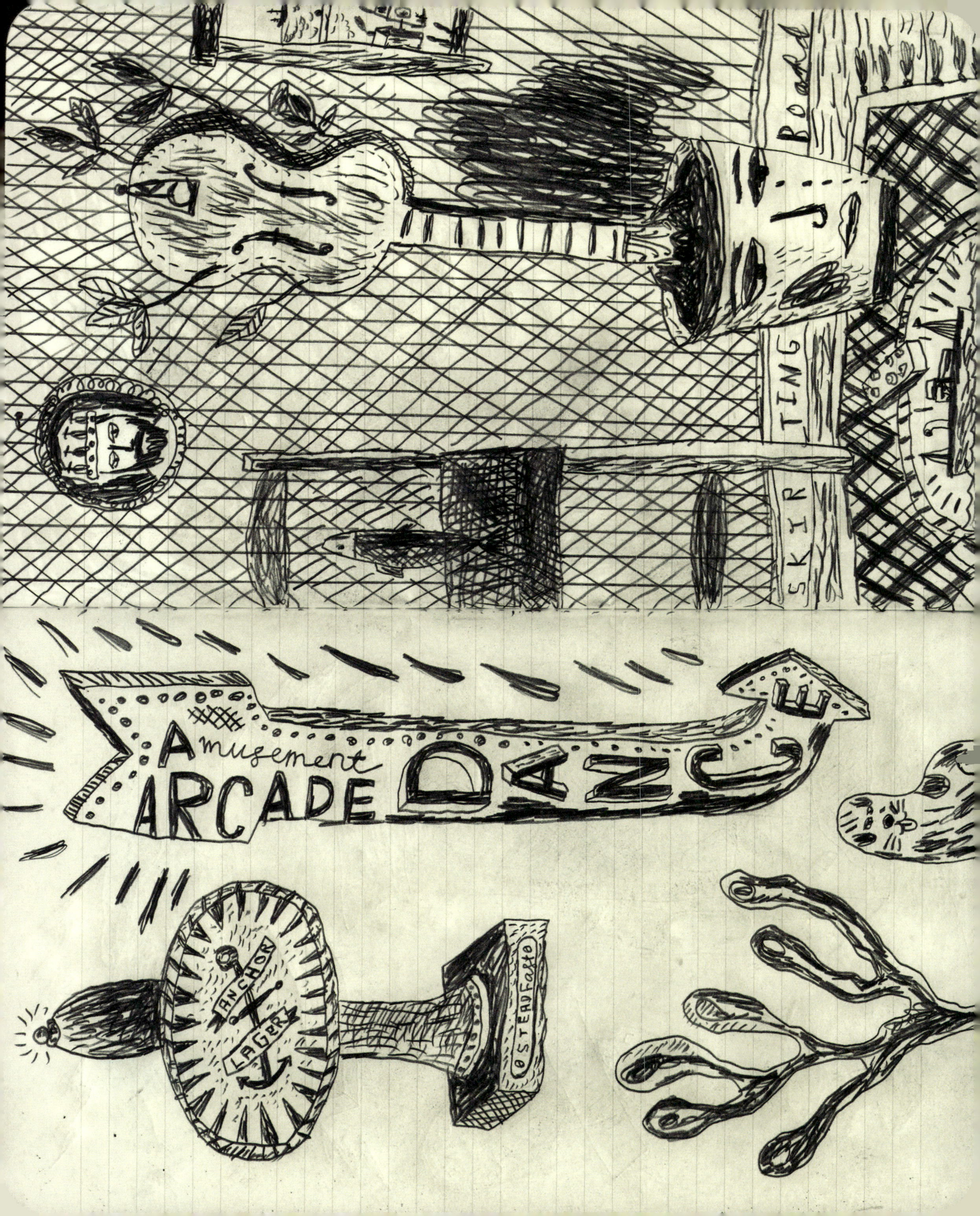
Amusement
ARCADE
DANCE
ANCHOR
LAGER
SKIRTING
Board

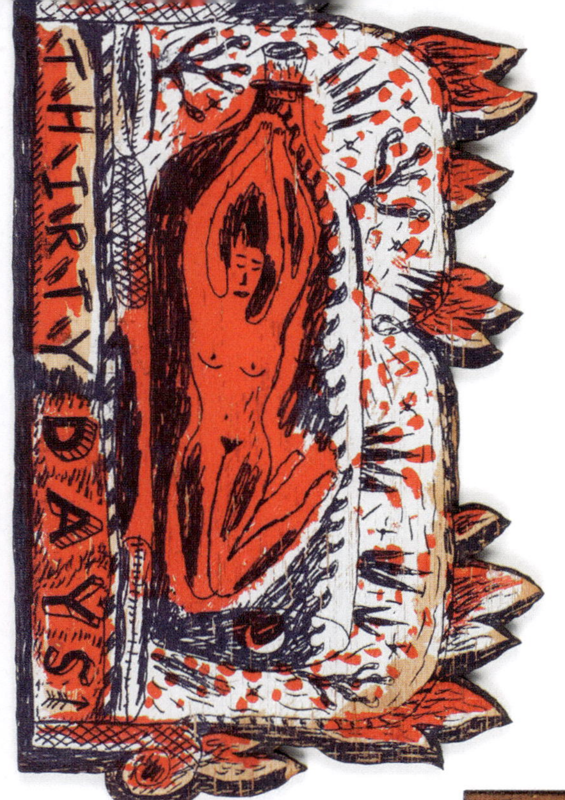


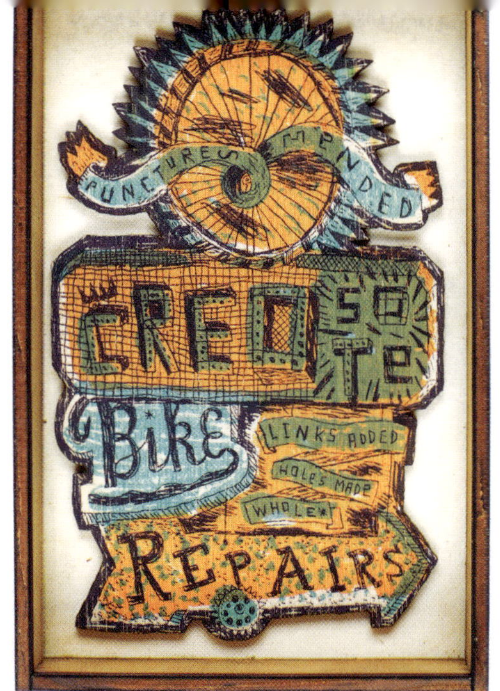


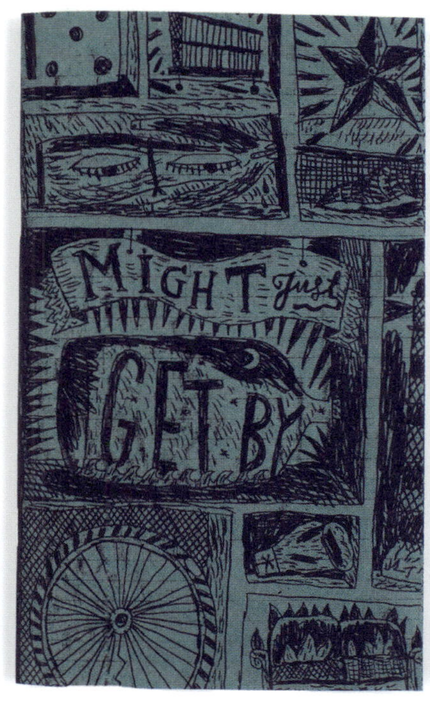


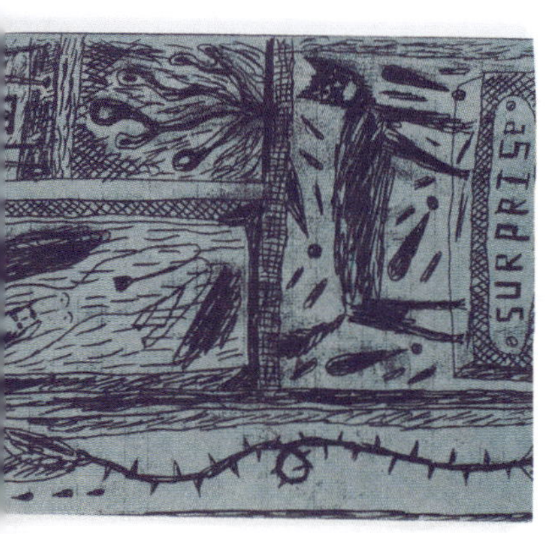


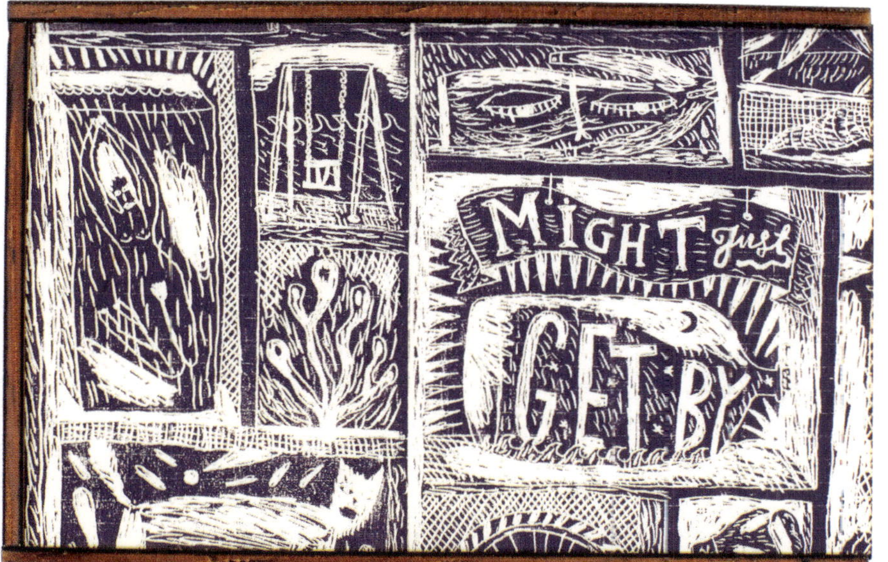


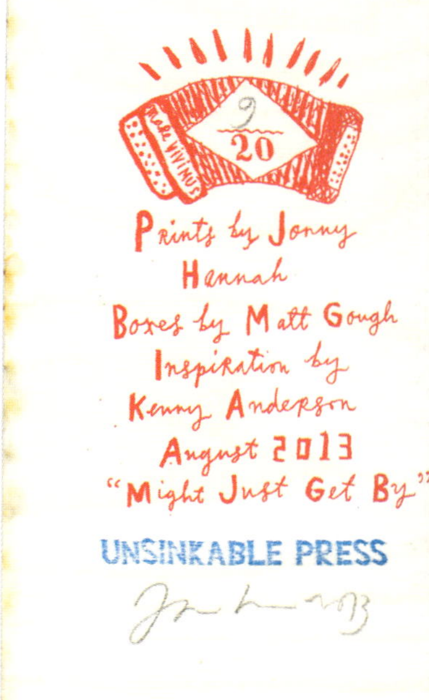


Inspired by the domino boxes of yesteryear, this container of goodies was my homage to the wonderful music of King Creosote. The edition was limited to only 20 copies.

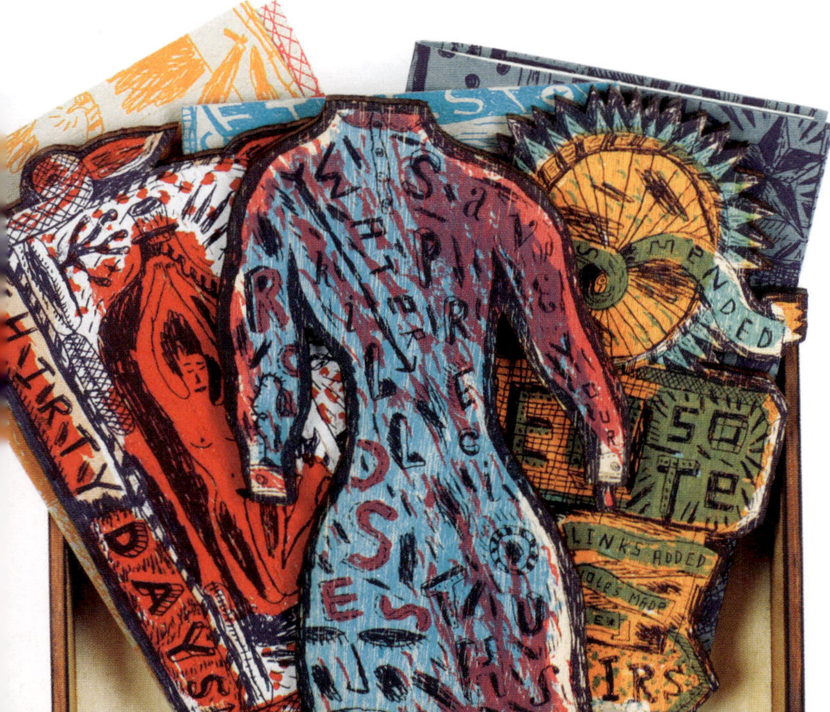


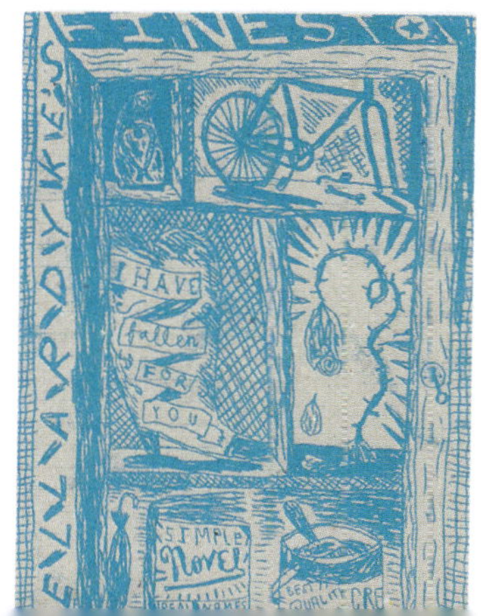


*the line from Kirkcaldy to Leuchars. And Hank Williams isn't too far away either. There must surely be a lost highway somewhere in the Neuk of Fife. And with the everyday comes humour, needless to say. Buffoonery sometimes too, like Naked Cat Jumping. A sprinkling of Harry Lauder? Monsieur Hulot? These tales act as short stories that W. Somerset Maugham would enjoy. Recollections from yesteryear, but incidents from the last half hour too.*

*And in the kingdom of King Creosote, there's a high street with a cluster of shops. That coffee shop that only gives out written receipts. A ship's chandlers for those who sail on The Reaper. And for John Taylor, of course. On one of the corners there has to be a bike repair shop. I'm not entirely sure why, but not all has to make sense in Creosoteville. Open, always ready to mend the odd puncture. Remove or add links in chains, to keep the repaired wheels turning. Fixing the brake cables, with frayed ends, leading to accidents when they snap altogether. The bikes are repaired best as they can be. But in some of the songs, you get the feeling that it's just as well to buy a new bike altogether, should the money be there. And if it isn't, Shank's Pony, or an old Vauxhall Chevette*

I was delighted to be asked to exhibit at the Pittenweem Arts Festival in 2013, so I began making new work, much of it based on the sea, yet again. But my other inspirations on the Road to the East Neuk of Fife were the book 'A Twelvemonth and a Day' by Christopher Rush, and the songs of King Creosote. I contacted the King and asked if he'd mind if I did a something or other based around his magical songs. He granted me permission, and I eventually made a set of plywood, laser-cut prints, along with a wee book – an appreciation, if you like. He loved it, and so sang a set of songs in my exhibition space. It was a night to remember, in more ways than one. Listen to King Creosote immediately, if you haven't already. He's best enjoyed on a Saturday evening while cooking the tea ('dinner' to some of you). Halfway through your second or third glass of wine, just as you're about to drop the trout in the frying pan, or cooking the mussels, you might find that the power of 'Bats in the Attic' or 'Honest Words' is enough to bring a tear to the eye – in a good way.

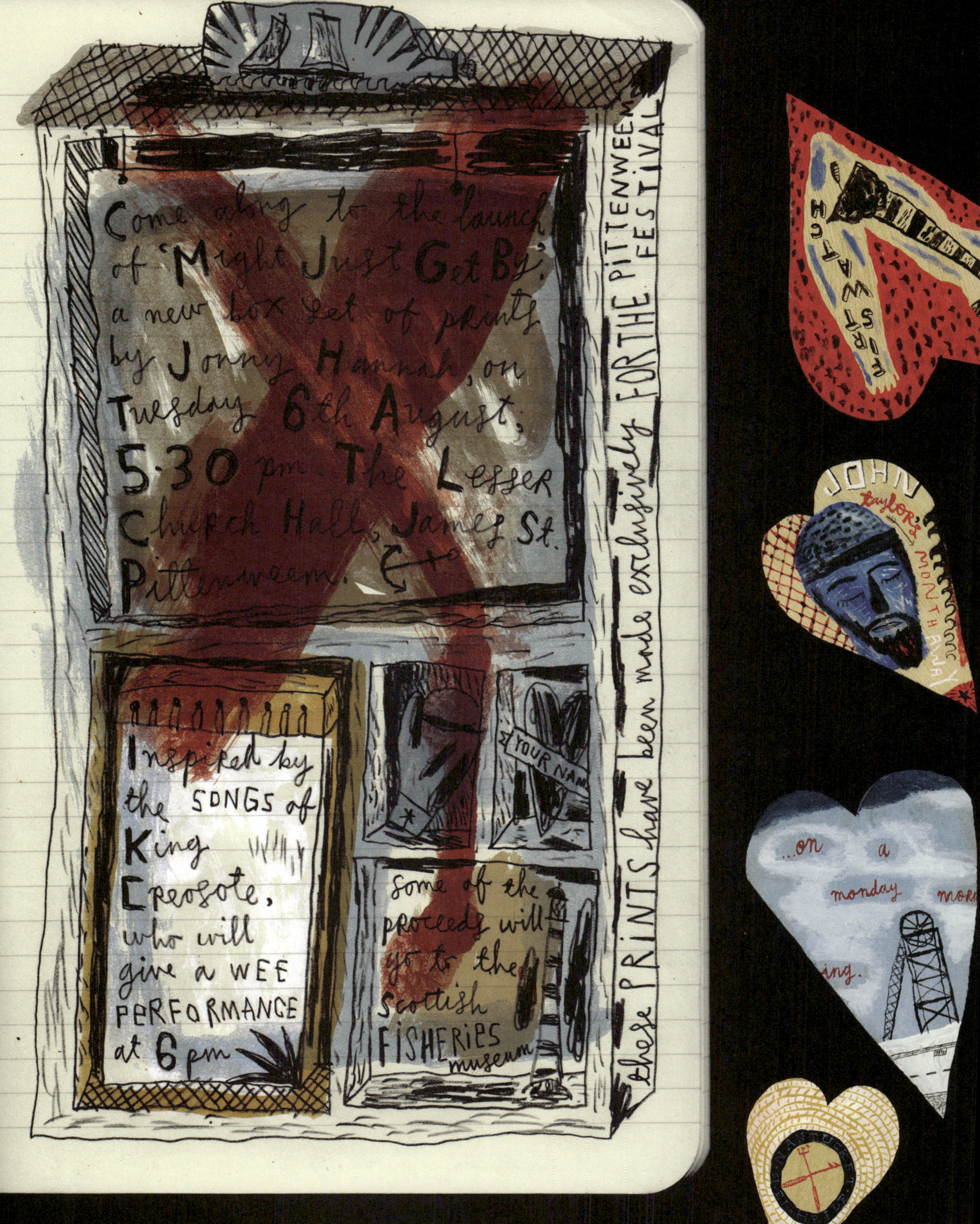
Come along to the launch of 'Might Just Get By': a new box set of prints by Jonny Hannah, on Tuesday 6th August, 5.30 pm. The Lesser Church Hall, James St. Pittenweem.
Inspired by the SONGS of King Creosote, who will give a WEE PERFORMANCE at 6pm
Some of the proceeds will go to the Scottish FISHERIES museum
YOUR NAM
these PRINTS have been made exclusively FOR THE PITTENWEEM FESTIVAL
JOHN
taylor's
...on a monday morn
ing.

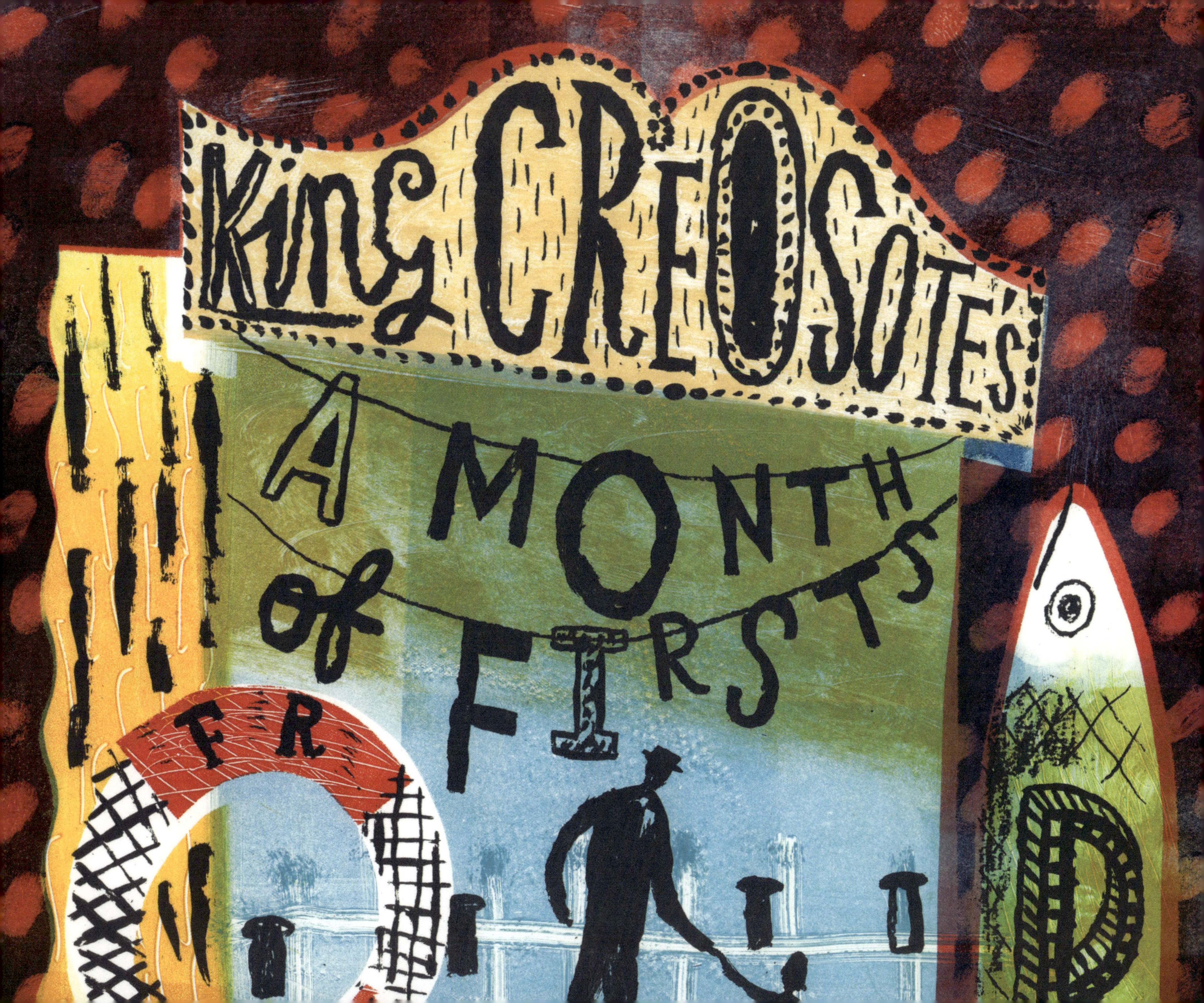
King Creosote's
A Month of Firsts

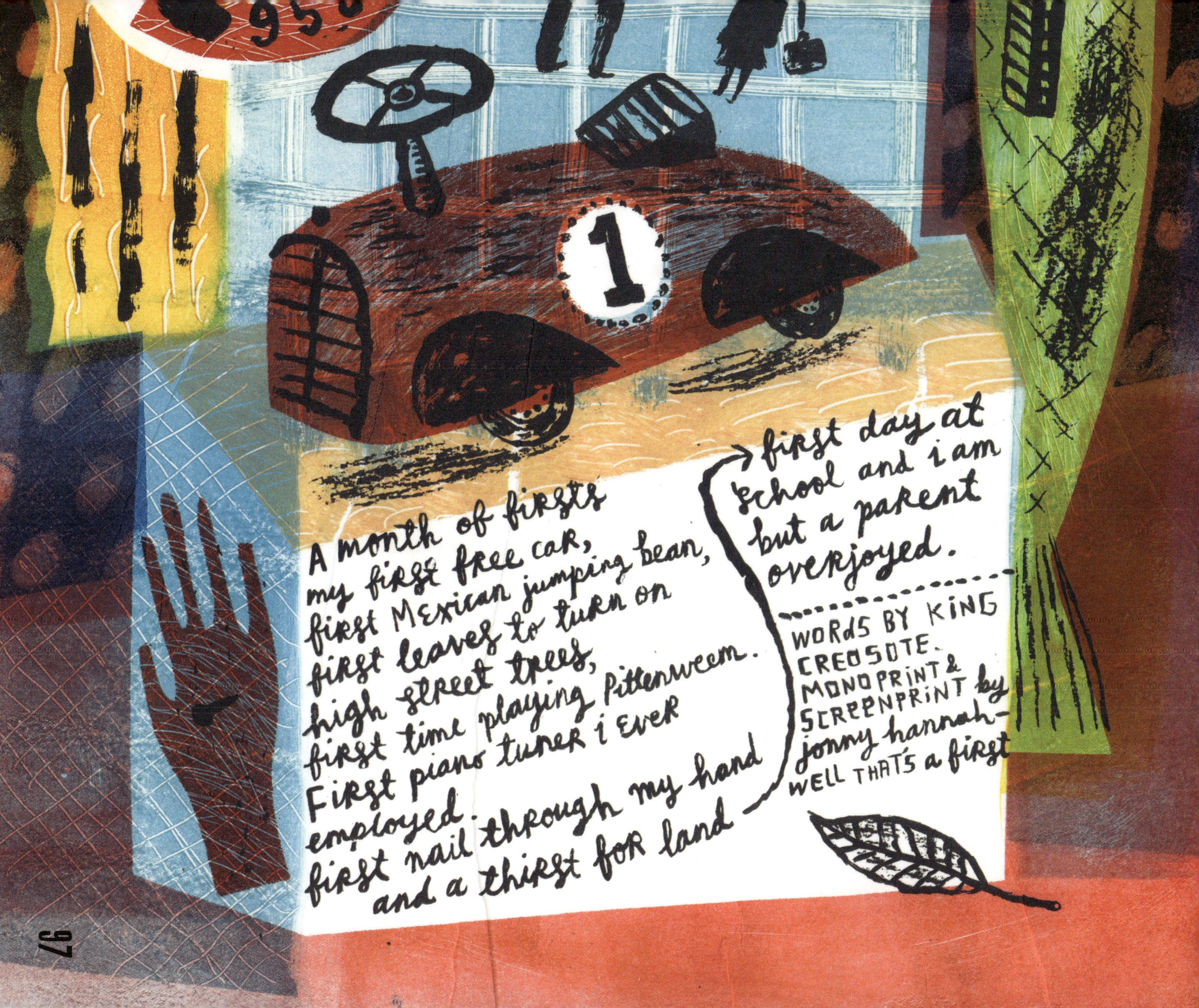
A month of firsts
my first free car,
first Mexican jumping bean,
first leaves to turn on
high street trees,
first time playing Pittenweem.
First piano tuner i ever
employed.
first nail through my hand
and a thirst for land
first day at
school and i am
but a parent
overjoyed.
WORDS BY KING
CREOSOTE.
MONOPRINT &
SCREENPRINT by
jonny hannah-
WELL THAT'S a first

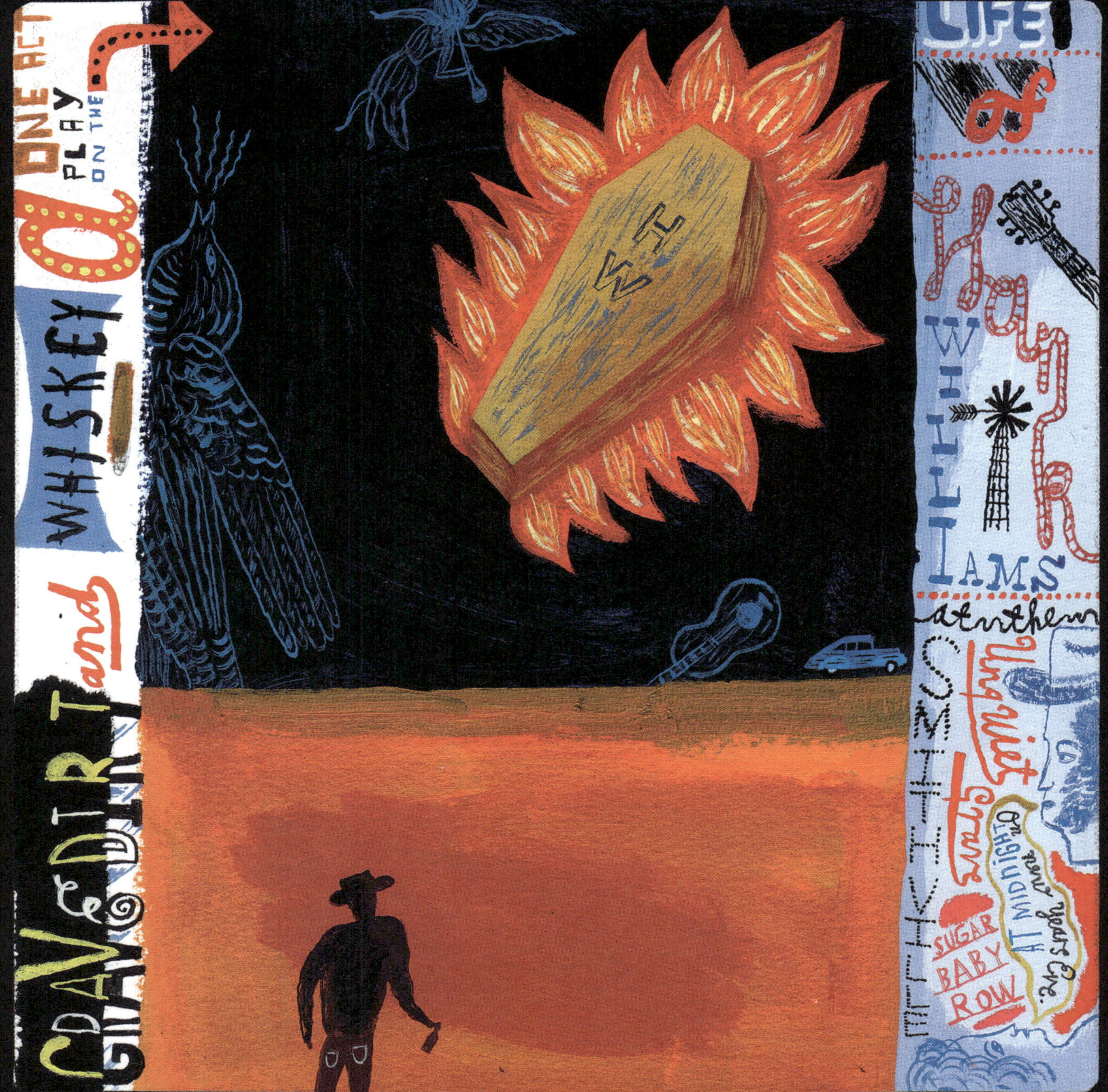


Perhaps the best musician of them all, the truest of the true, was Hank Williams. I'm not sure Hank ever found happiness, even when he was drinking. He and his wife, Audrey, were hardly a match made in heaven. But the art he left behind, when he died aged only twenty-nine, has to be the greatest collection of songs by any one person. The emotions never slip into sentimentality, much associated with post-Hank country music. The songs are a set of stories, both happy and dark, that reflected the lives and times of Hank's most important people, the listeners. This is quintessential love and death. Even now, many years later, Hank's songs speak volumes; they are a guiding star for whatever life may throw at us, and teach us how to avoid some of it – although some of it is drawn in the dirt from the get-go.

I like to think Hank will somehow exhume himself and end up in Darktown, perhaps still in the back of that Cadillac. But maybe he's best left, in peace, alone. I'd hate for him to be unhappy all over again …

Anyway, I didn't make it home that night. The thought of meandering back on the night bus seemed unbearable, so I stayed at Nik's, weird dreams and all. I made my way back south of the river at about eleven the next morning, Friday. My journey was broken, as it always is, at Victoria bus station, the sun blasting down on me and my hangover. I was in desperate need of a seat, something to quench my thirst – indeed, anything that could make me feel a little bit better. Seeking refuge from this horrible predicament, I staggered across the road to look in a bookshop window. It was one of those shops with all the books at knock-down prices, you know the kind – Penguin Classics for a pound and the odd picture book of The Beatles. But among all this there was one book I had to buy: *Hank Williams: The Biography* by Colin Escott. For some time I'd been listening to ol' Hank; nothing too serious, just flirting really. I knew that he died fairly young, and that he took a drink himself, but, staring at this book, I knew it was time to dig deeper. I searched my pockets and miraculously, after a night out, I found a fiver. The star-shaped price told me I was in luck. As soon as I had the book in my hand, the images came fast and furious. Not the wide open vistas of Aaron Copland, but the intimacy of people, people in love, people out of love, people up and down on their luck ...

From *Songs for Home Folks: Some Thoughts on Hank Williams*, the first proper Cakes & Ale Press publication, a limited-edition box set of screen, litho and letterpress prints, produced while I was still a student at the Royal College of Art, 1998.

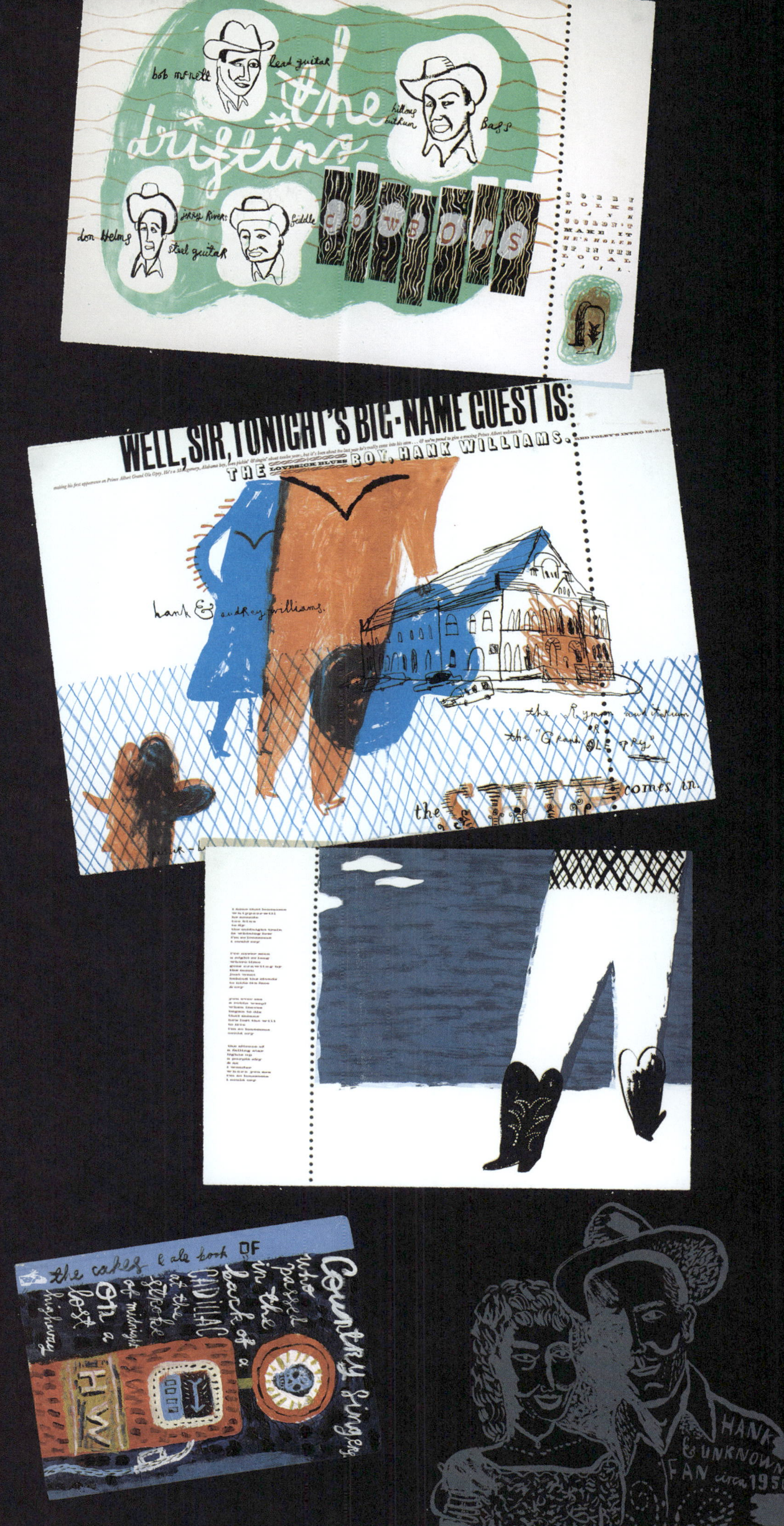

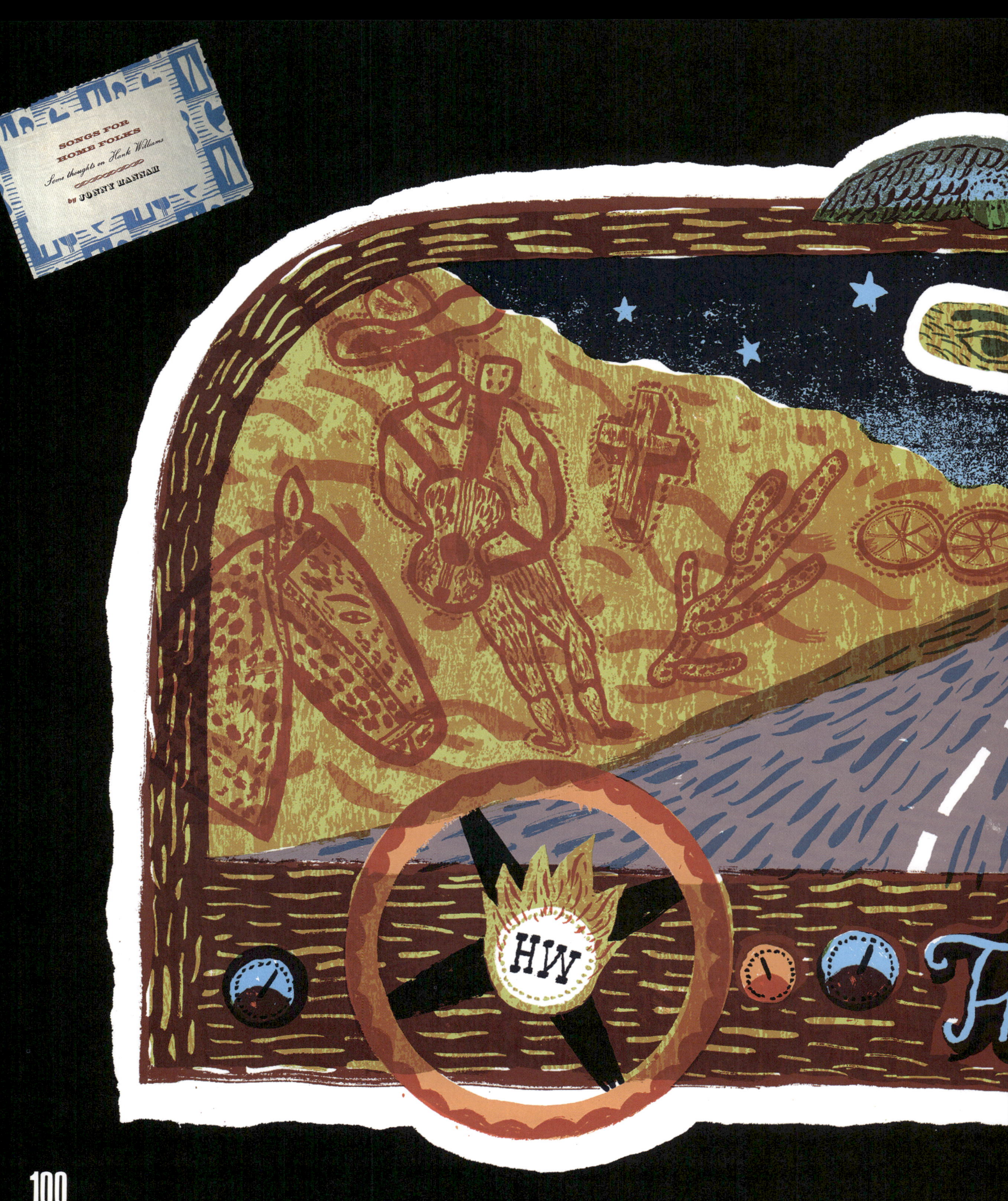
SONGS FOR
HOME FOLKS
Some thoughts on Hank Williams
by JONNY HANNAH
HW

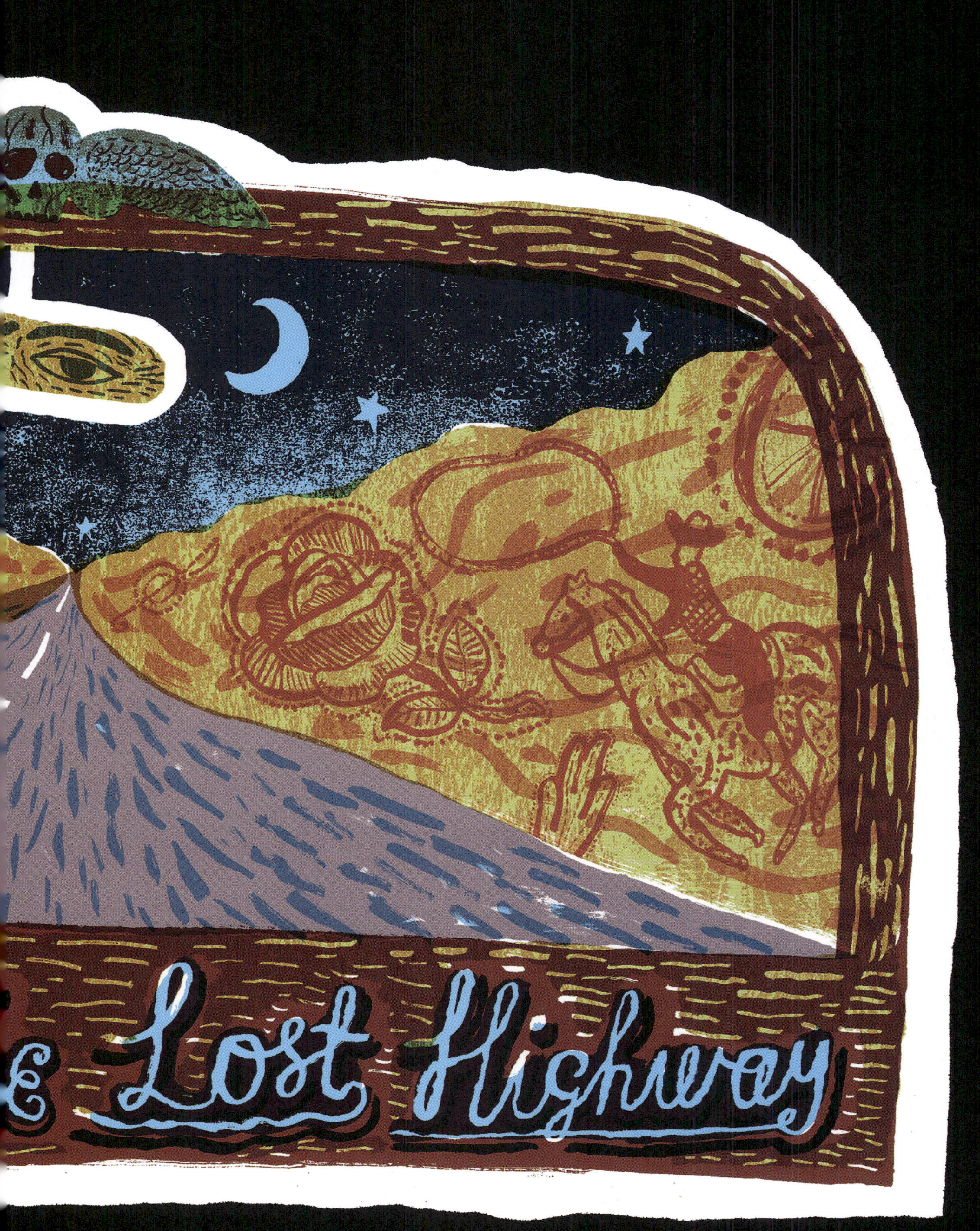
e Lost Highway

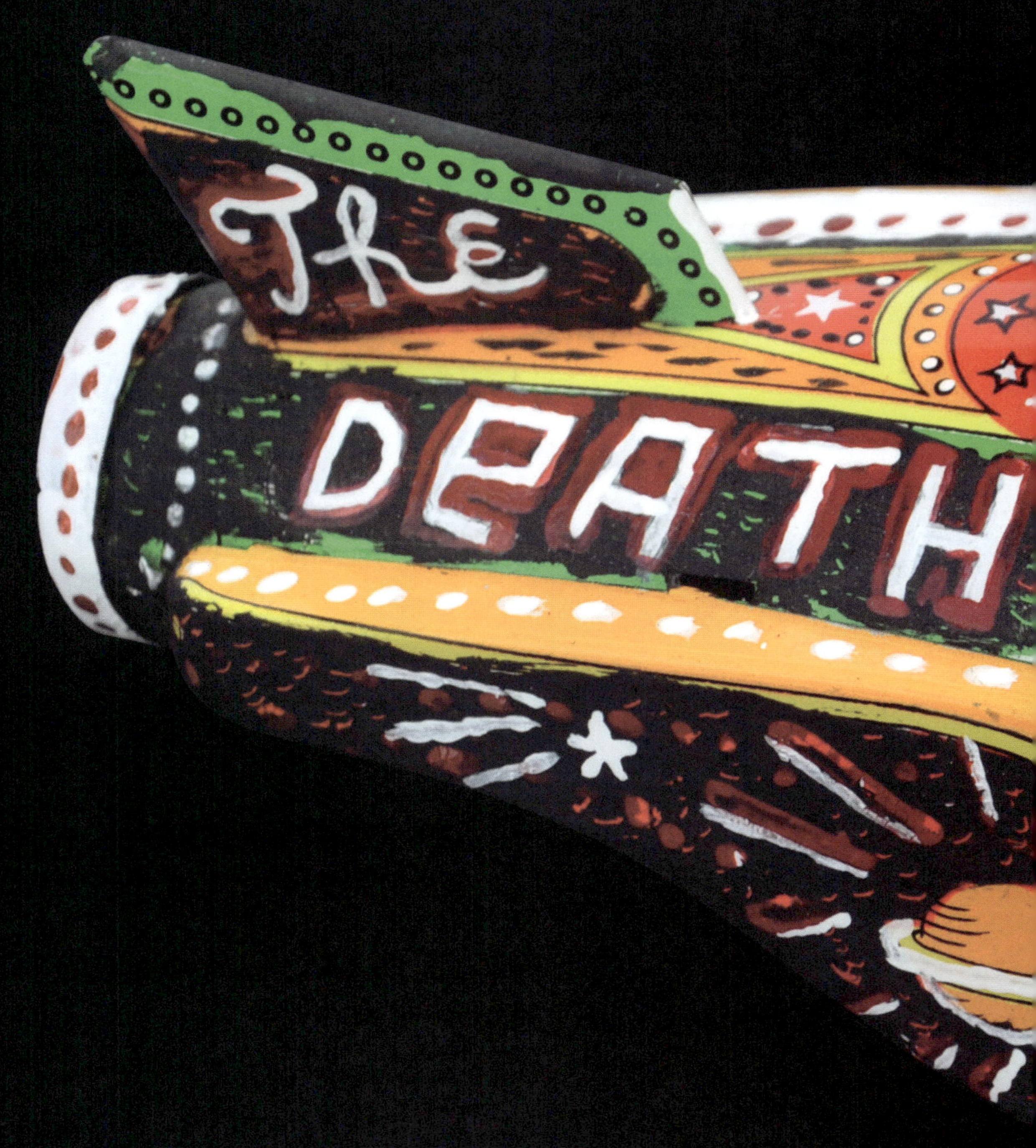
The
DEATH

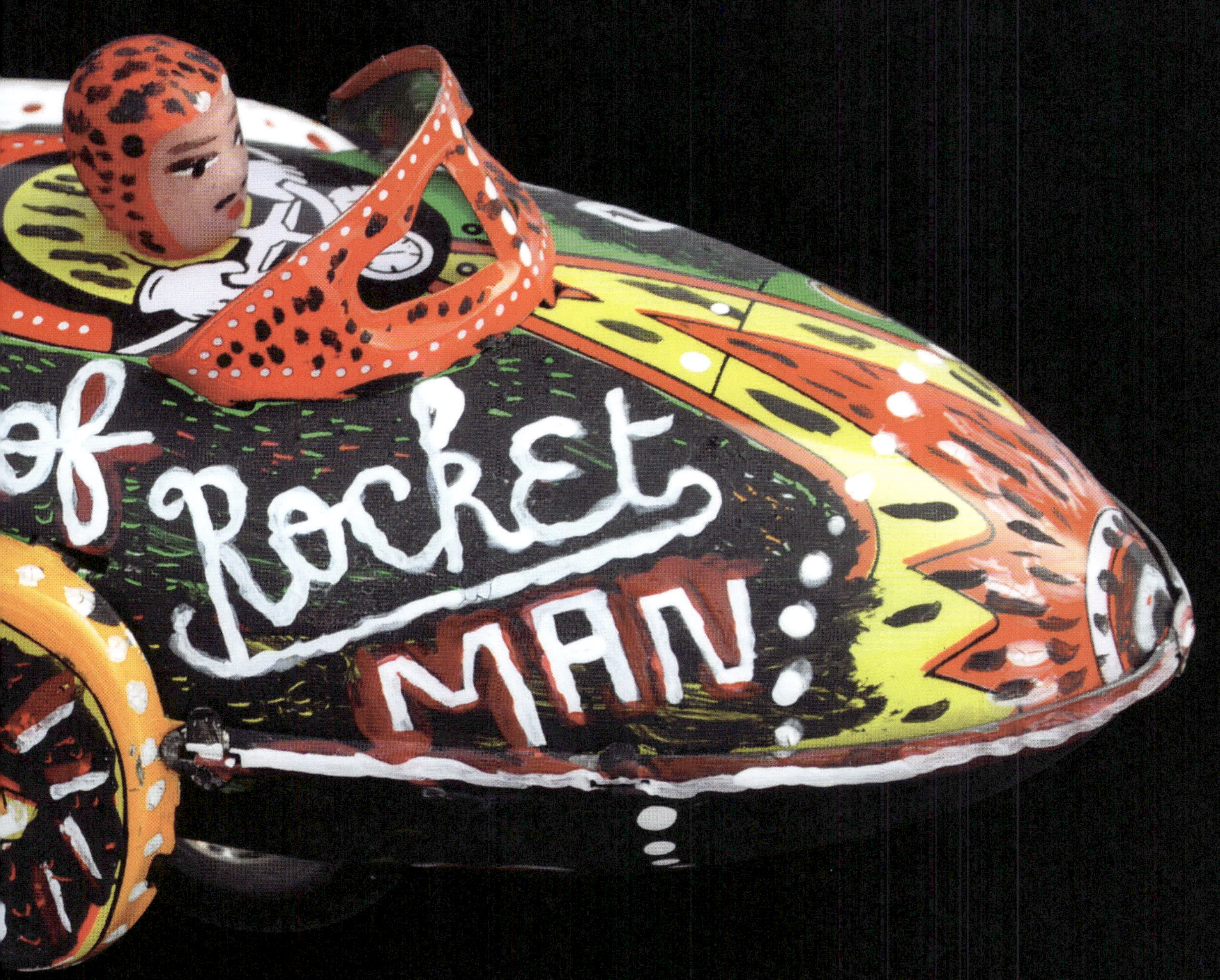
of Rocket
MAN

# THE DEATH OF ROCKET MAN!

I am not, nor have I ever been, a collector. I've dabbled, but ultimately there aren't enough hours in the day, and the semi-detached home I have in Darktown is too small. It's almost got to the stage that if I buy a book, I must then go through my bookshelf and get rid of one in order to make space.

But I do enjoy buying the odd wee treat. One such moment was when I bought the Rocket Racer in rainy Amsterdam as a present for Hamish, our eldest son. I secretly suspected that he wouldn't be bowled over by it, which meant I could then have it all for myself.

When that happened, I decided to draw it one night, with a big brush and a pot of black ink. I automatically wrote 'Go Rocket Man, go!' and began to wonder: where would this new alter ego of mine go? Who were his friends? What did he have for tea? Would he ever get that mortgage he so badly needed? There were so many questions that could be answered only by drawing and more drawing.

And so I discovered that Rocket Man had a love of cryptozoology, went to Coney Island now and again, and was close friends with Accattone, Jane Russell, Stoker Thompson and many others.

Rocket Man became a chance to vent spleen, to celebrate the darkest corners of pop culture, revive names from 'way back then', and to regurgitate little-known tall tales and present them to those who wanted to listen.

But Rocket Man has done his job. He's taken me out of the doldrums several times, and now must go free, into the great directionless home in the sky. So here, for your enjoyment, is the grand finale to the saga. Yes, folks, Rocket Man meets his maker. Stay tuned, dear reader, and enjoy ...

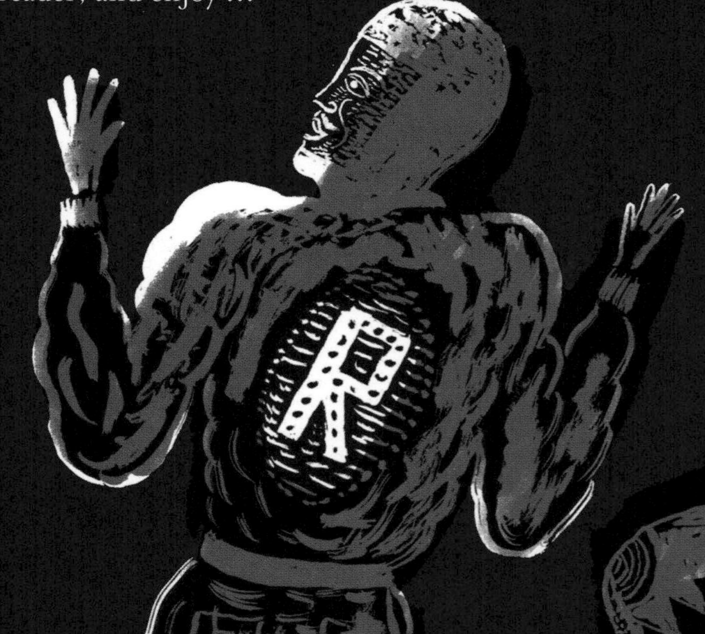

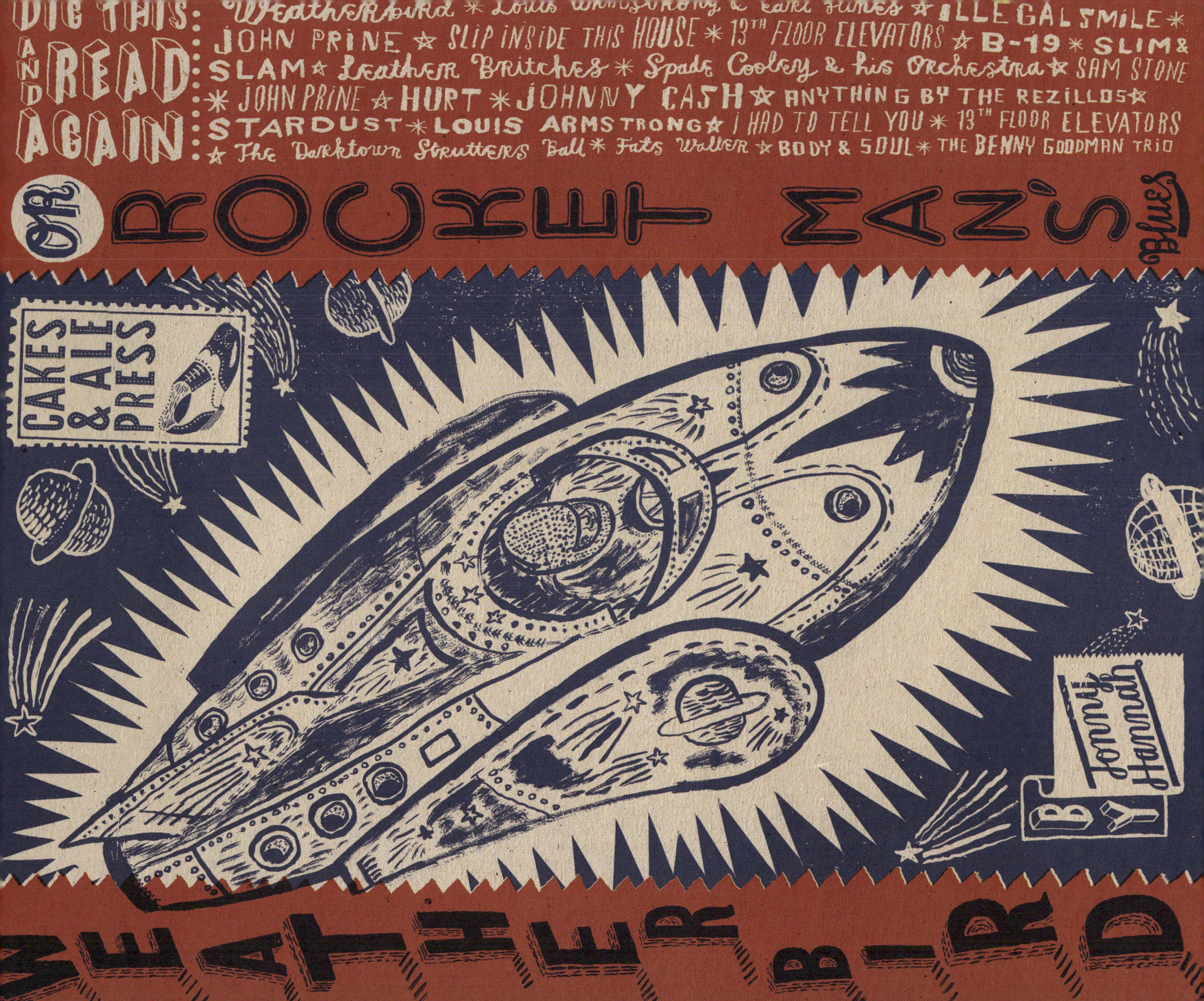
DIG THIS: AND READ AGAIN:
Weatherbird * Louis
ILLEGAL SMILE *
JOHN PRINE ☆ SLIP INSIDE THIS HOUSE * 13TH FLOOR ELEVATORS ☆ B-19 * SLIM & SLAM ☆ Leather Britches * Spade Cooley & his Orchestra ☆ SAM STONE * JOHN PRINE ☆ HURT * JOHNNY CASH ☆ ANYTHING BY THE REZILLOS ☆ STARDUST * LOUIS ARMSTRONG ☆ I HAD TO TELL YOU * 13TH FLOOR ELEVATORS ☆ The Darktown Strutters Ball * Fats Waller ☆ BODY & SOUL * THE BENNY GOODMAN TRIO
OR ROCKET MAN'S Blues
CAKES & ALE PRESS
BY Jonny Hannah
WEATHER BIRD

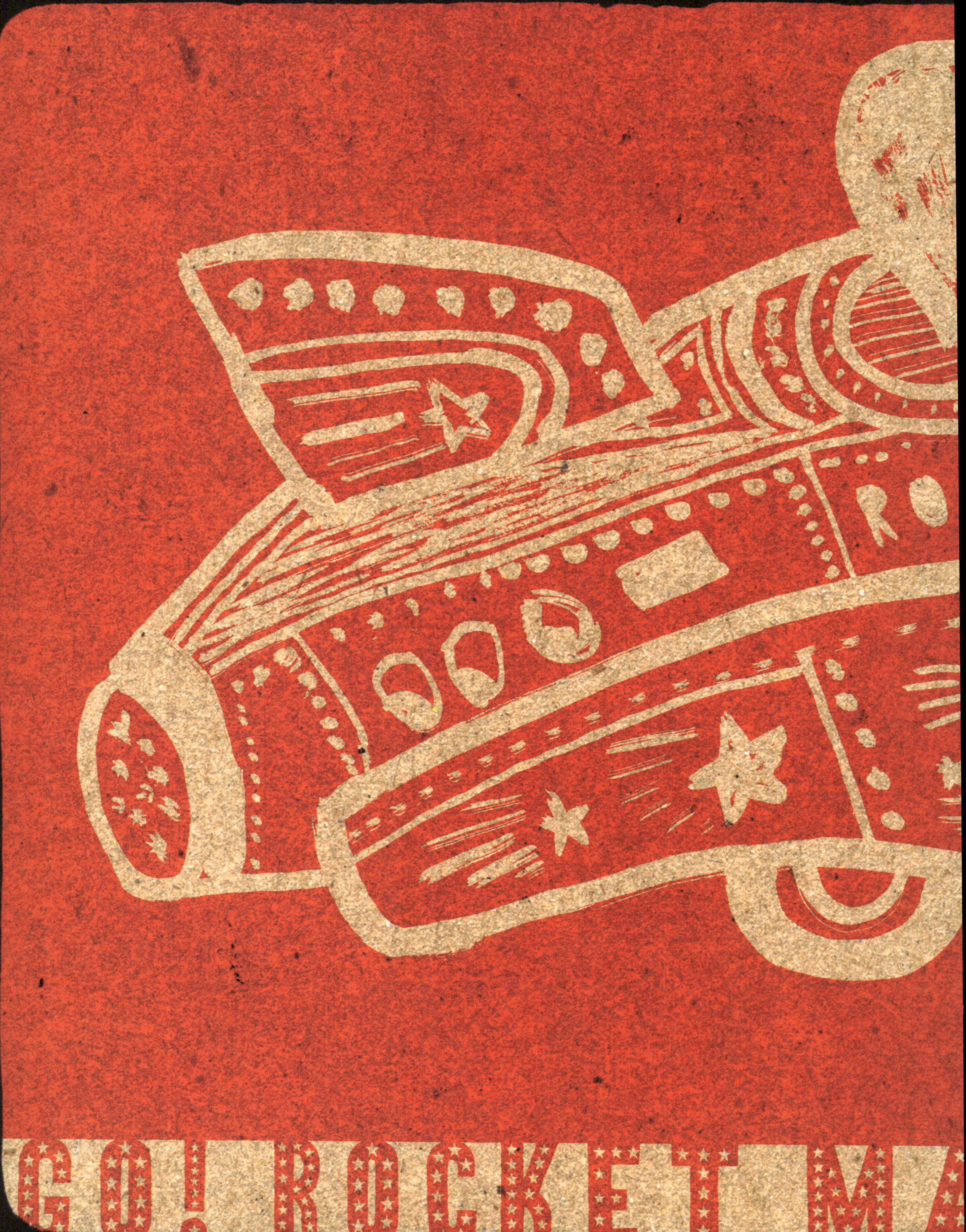
RO
GO! ROCKET MA

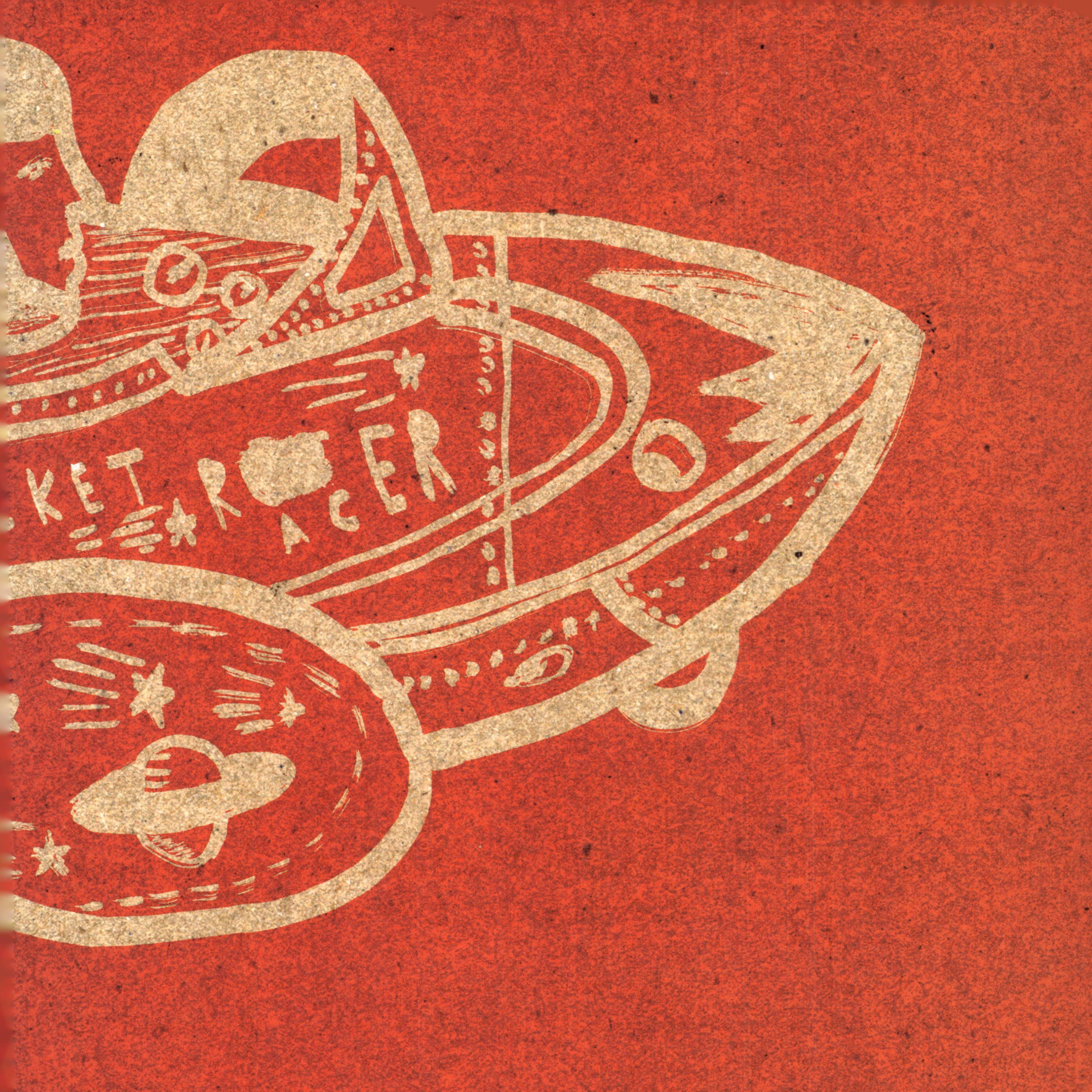

N, GO!NO. OF FIFTY

CAKES & ALE PRESS

03

Two pages from *Weather Bird*, a screen-printed book from the Cakes & Ale Press in 2006, at the height of my Rocket Man obsession – an unfulfilled dream and a nightmare.

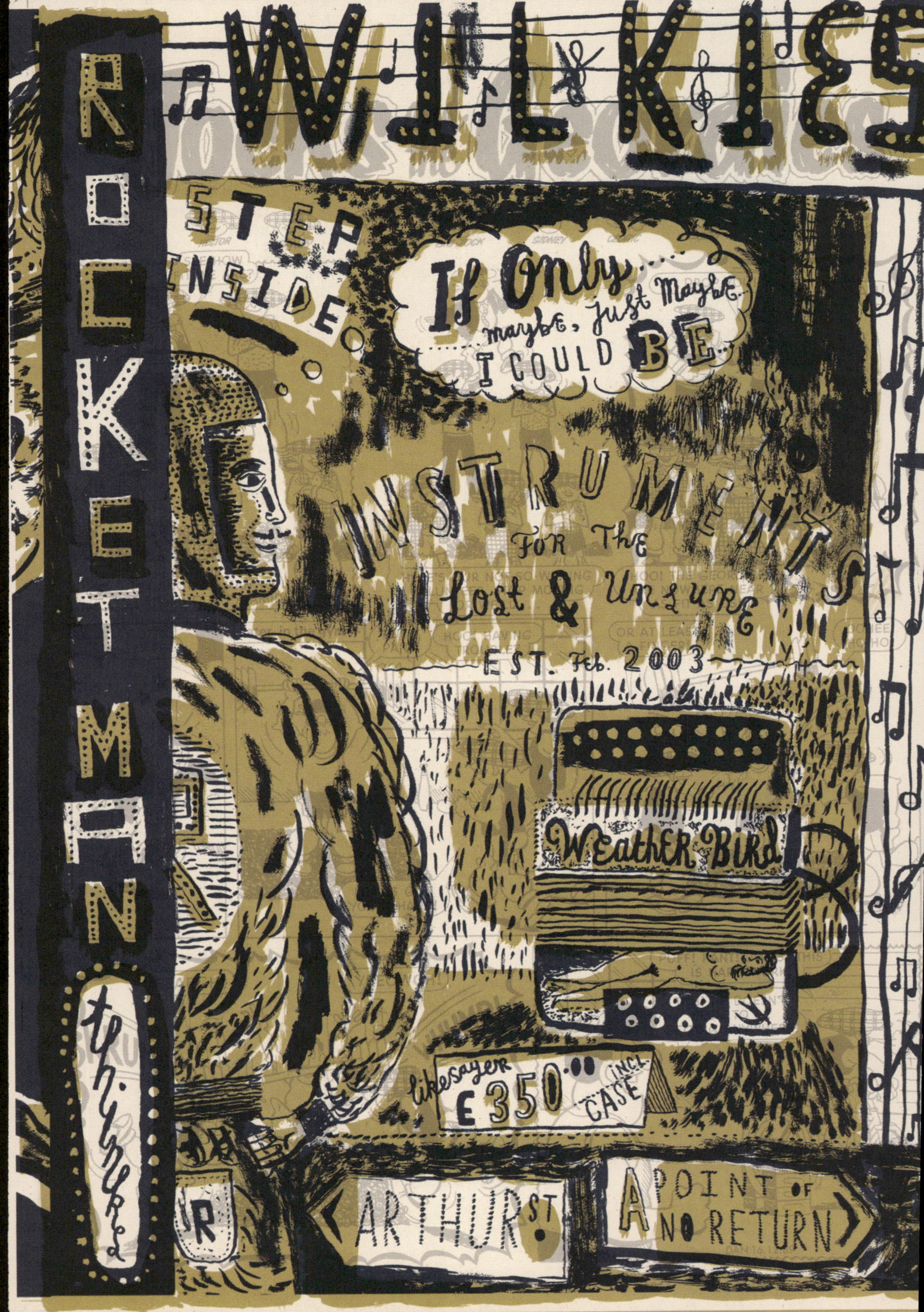

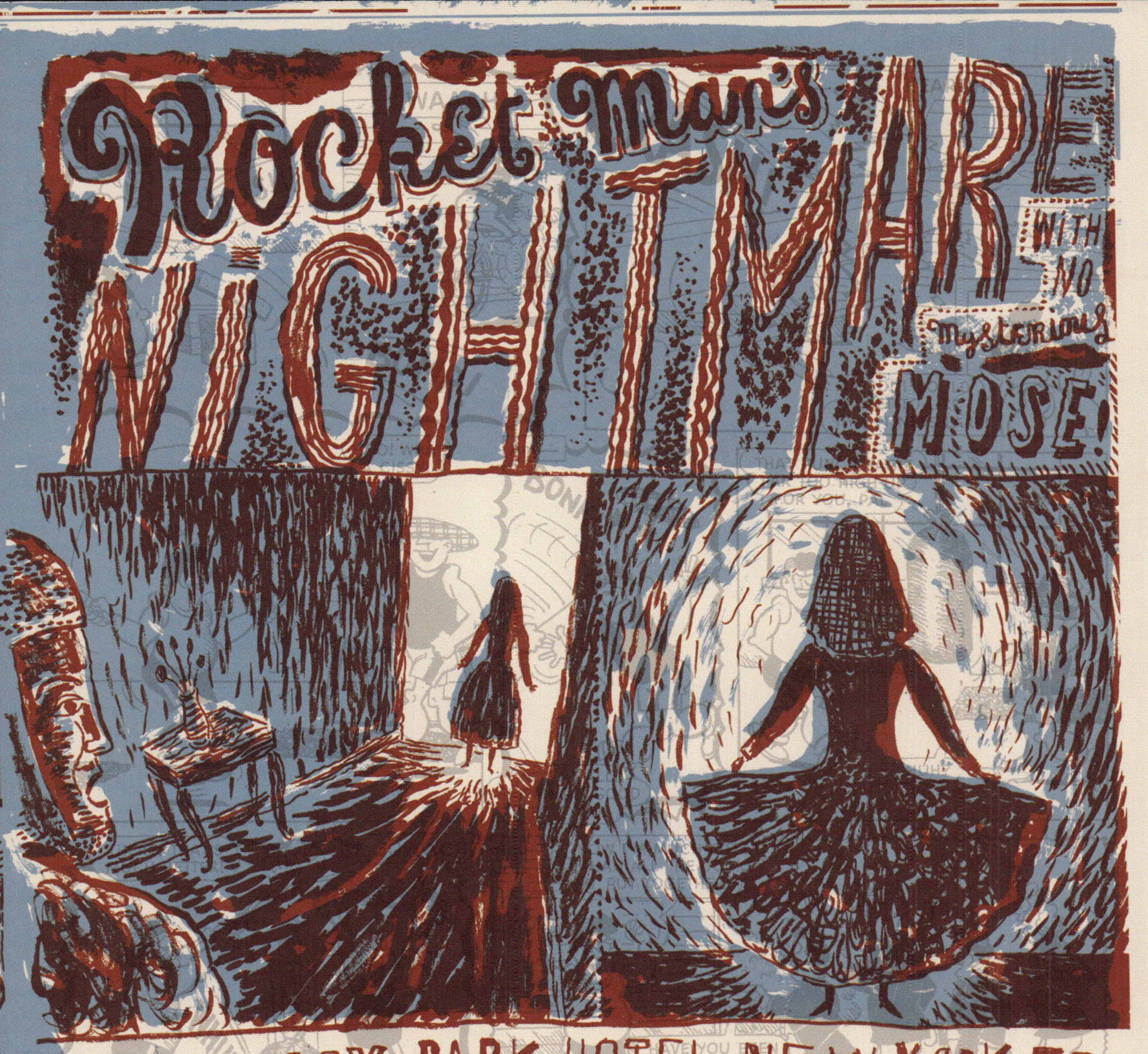


GRAMMERCY PARK HOTEL NEW YORK. SEEN BETTER DAYS. DECADENT. A WOMAN IN black. WITH BLACK VEIL, WAITS FOR ME. SHE HOLDS OPEN HER VICTORIAN DRESS. THE angel of death spreading her wings? PERHAPS. BUT NOT FOR ME. SO MUCH TO DO. SO MANY BOOKS TO READ. MUST TRY MOBY DICK AGAIN. another stab at JOURNEY TO THE END of NIGHT. I RUN THE OTHER WAY & WAKE UP SWEATING. I REALISE THREE MONTHS LATER WHO she has come for........

Rocket Man's
Tea-Time
Companion to the
Bonkers
World of Crypto-
Zoology.
By Jonny Hannah

### THE NAMELESS THING OF BERKELEY SQUARE, LONDON

Supposedly residing at no. 50, in the fourth floor flat, this monster has almost no description to speak of. It famously killed a drunken sailor in 1943, leaving behind his dismembered corpse, & leaving a London plod scratching his chin. Oh, nameless creature, step forward & be counted, or at least photographed. It hasn't been seen or heard of for ages, & is suspected to be lurking in Bazalgette's labyrinthine sewers. What you see below is strictly an artist's impression.

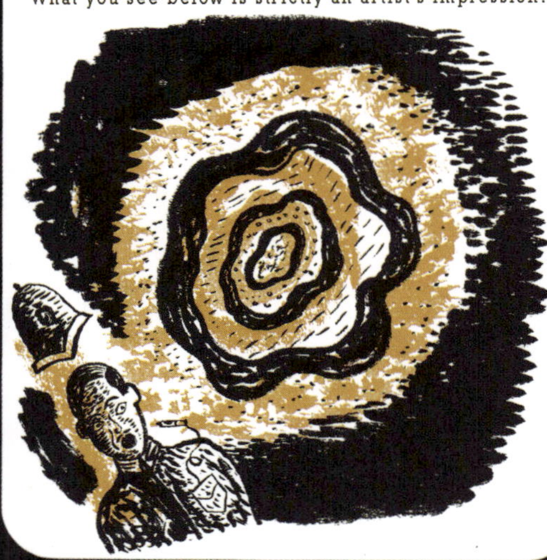

### WANDA THE WEREWOLF, NEW YORK

A regular at the Lycanthropes Hot Rodders dinner & dance events, Wanda is the sweetest of girls. She has no taste for human flesh whatsoever. It is a common myth to think that all werewolves crave a bit of you & me. Some do, some don't. Funiculi, funicula. By day she works in the Strand Bookstore. Go see her in the beat poetry section. Hooooowl!

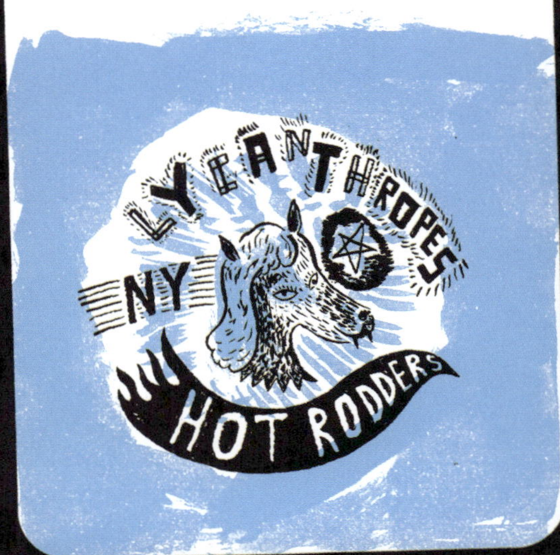


### BIG BIRD OF TEXAS

Appearing in the Rio Grande Valley in 1976, this 5ft. tall monkey-faced bird was by all accounts, really rather scary. It would lift prize cattle clean off the ground, & once decapitated a local rummy, flying off into the distance with the poor drunkard's head. A local entrepreneur immortalised the incident as a particularly potent brew. Since then, thankfully, there has been peace in the valley, for thee, oh lord.

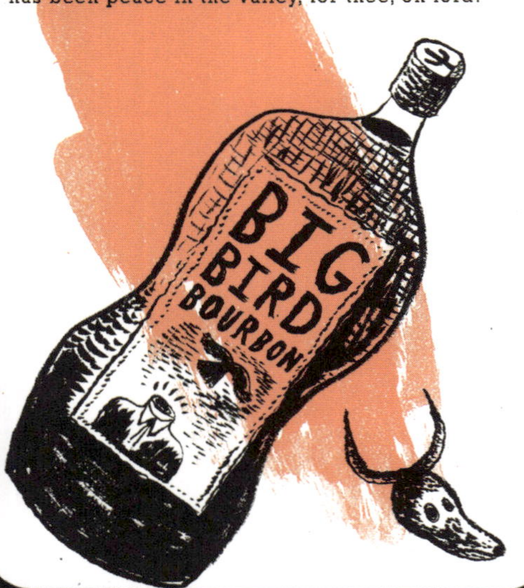


### THE WEST WEMYSS LEVIATHAN, NEUK OF FIFE

Washed up on the desperate shores of eastern Scotland in 1916, this strange sea-creature is still talked about today. This whopper measured 80ft in length. But before a cryptozoologist could make it to the scene, the locals, hard up at the time, cut it up for some well needed meat, to go with their meagre neeps & tatties. Its carcass was then boiled in cottages all along the coast for a poor man's cullen skink. It kept the hungry locals going for months. Some say it tasted awful.

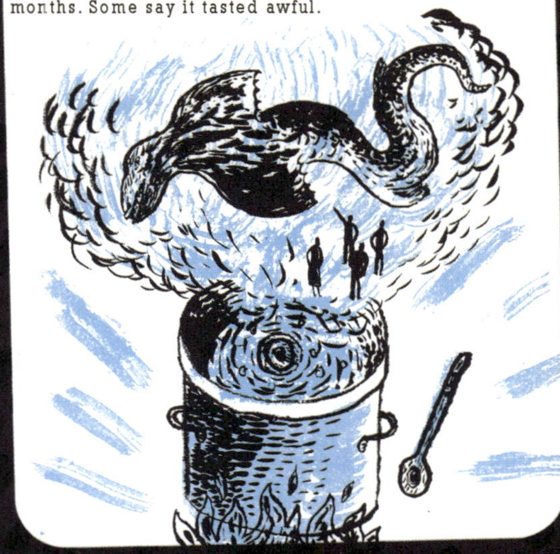

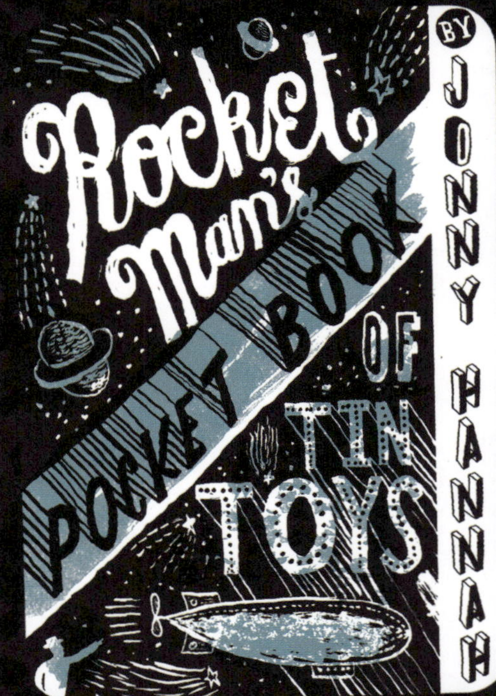


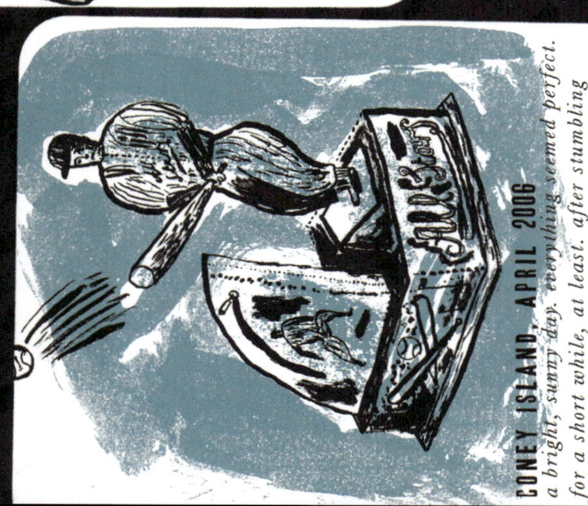


### CONEY ISLAND, APRIL 2006

*a bright, sunny day. everything seemed perfect. for a short while, at least. after stumbling across this old dodger, i went down to the seafront. only a handful of people around. so i even took off my boots & dipped my toes in the atlantic. the benny goodman trio kept me company. for you, dear, only...*

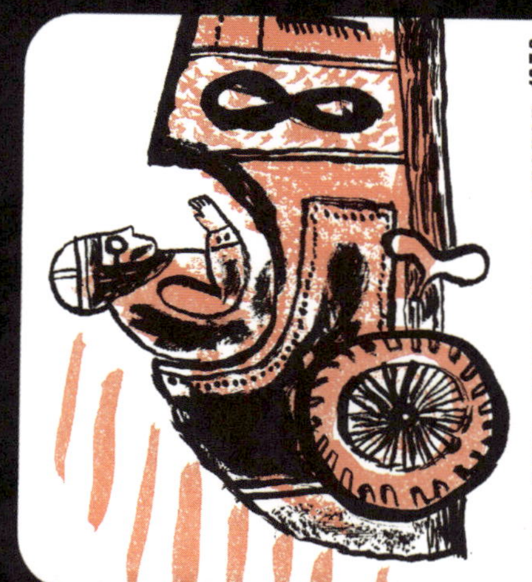


### EAST PORT, DUNFERMLINE, AUGUST 1978

*kay bruce's toy shop. what a treasure trove. never understood how she kept in business. until one day it was all gone. still, picked up this fellow there. whoosh! he can move. just turn the key & watch'im go. and just look at that face. always goin' through a tight wind, i reckon. some say miss bruce moved to new jersey...*

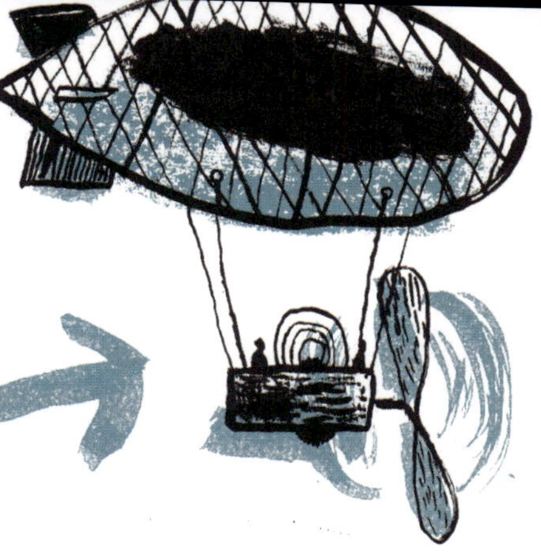

**SMITHVILLE, JANUARY 1ST 1953**
*bought this at old emmett miller's place, the unquiet grave. surprised to see he was open on new year's day. he had one hell of a hangover. we both sobered up though when the news came through from canton, ohio, about old hank. emmett got the whiskey out & we both took a good hit. then another. then another...*

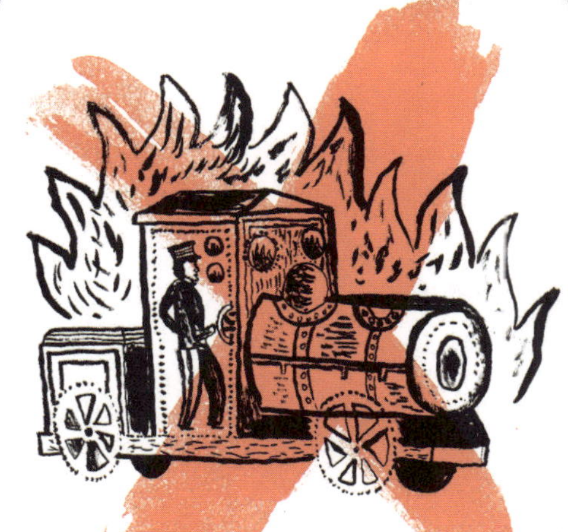

**KINROSS MARKET, FEBRUARY 2004**
*fairly certain this is old '97. it's probably bursting into flames just before impact. you can see steve, trying his best to keep control. the black, greasy fireman is to his right, just out of shot. in under a minute, the above engineer will be scalded to death. poor boy.*

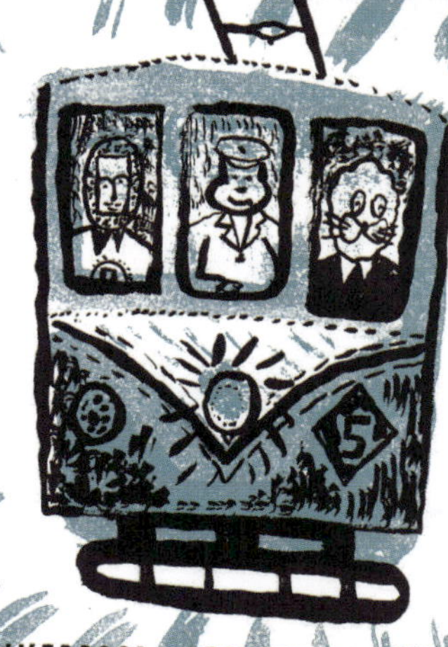

**69A, LIVERPOOL, SEPTEMBER 1993**
*i was writing my name in the dusty junk shop window when this streetcar caught my eye. i like to think it's a storyville streetcar. jelly roll would've caught this tram. several times. all the while learning his craft. there was a blank window next to the driver, so i carefully painted my good self. whadcha think?*

Many years ago, Barnacle Bill the Sailor was betrothed to a sweet young girl who was going places. But he'd just signed up, & his ship set sail soon after. When he returned he was covered in ornate decorations. From the four corners of the globe his glistening torso told many stories. Needless to say, young Mae was shocked, but it didn't put her off. Her bedtime reading is still to this day, never the same twice.
And he still can't swim a bloody stroke.

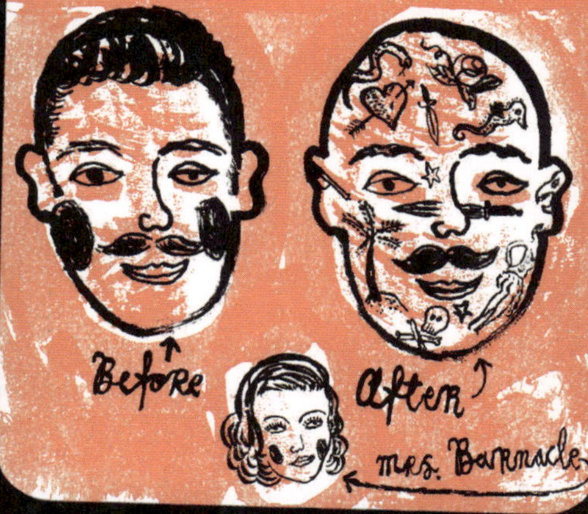


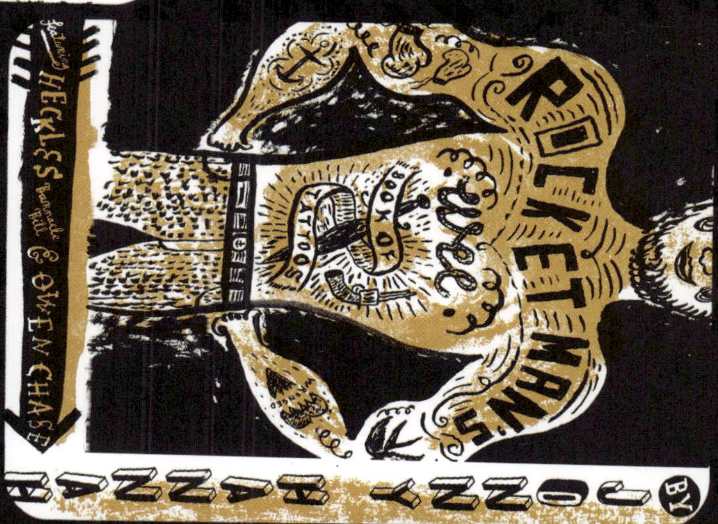


Davy Heckles. A man's man. A bit like Robert Ryan, only dumpier. Love & Hate on his knuckles. Just like Robert Mitchum. Only more psycho. I owe so much to Heckles. Much of the style comes from him. And a twinge in my left eye after that punch up with the valley boys in Chinese John's, at the top of Bruce Street, waiting for our chips & curry sauce. Oh, happy days. But of his many tattoos, one really took the biscuit. But I can't show you that one, as it's far too dirty. Instead, here's his right arm.

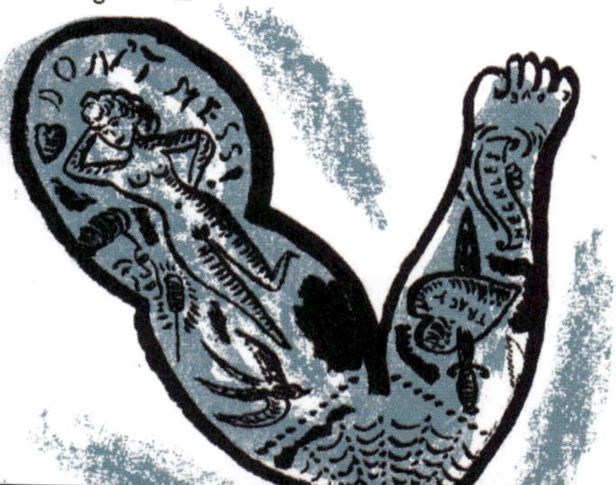


This is an East Fife criminal tattoo. Its encrypted code informs us that if you drink seven or more pints of the sub-standard Special in the Bruce Tavern, you might just meet your maker. These tattoos were especially popular in the Lochgelly & Auchtermuchty mafia underworld. Keep clear of the worse-than-death characters who sport such body art, but it could be beneficial to heed the warning about the 70 shilling.

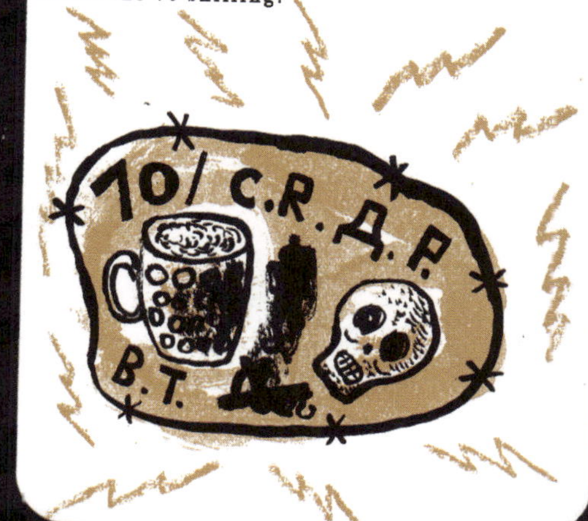


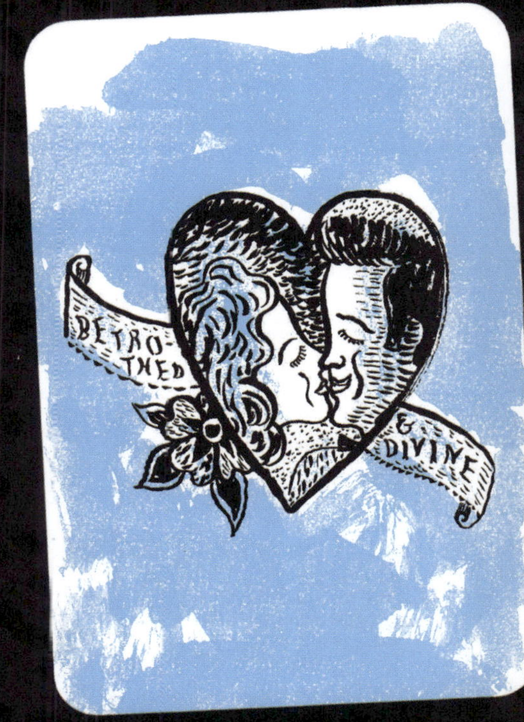

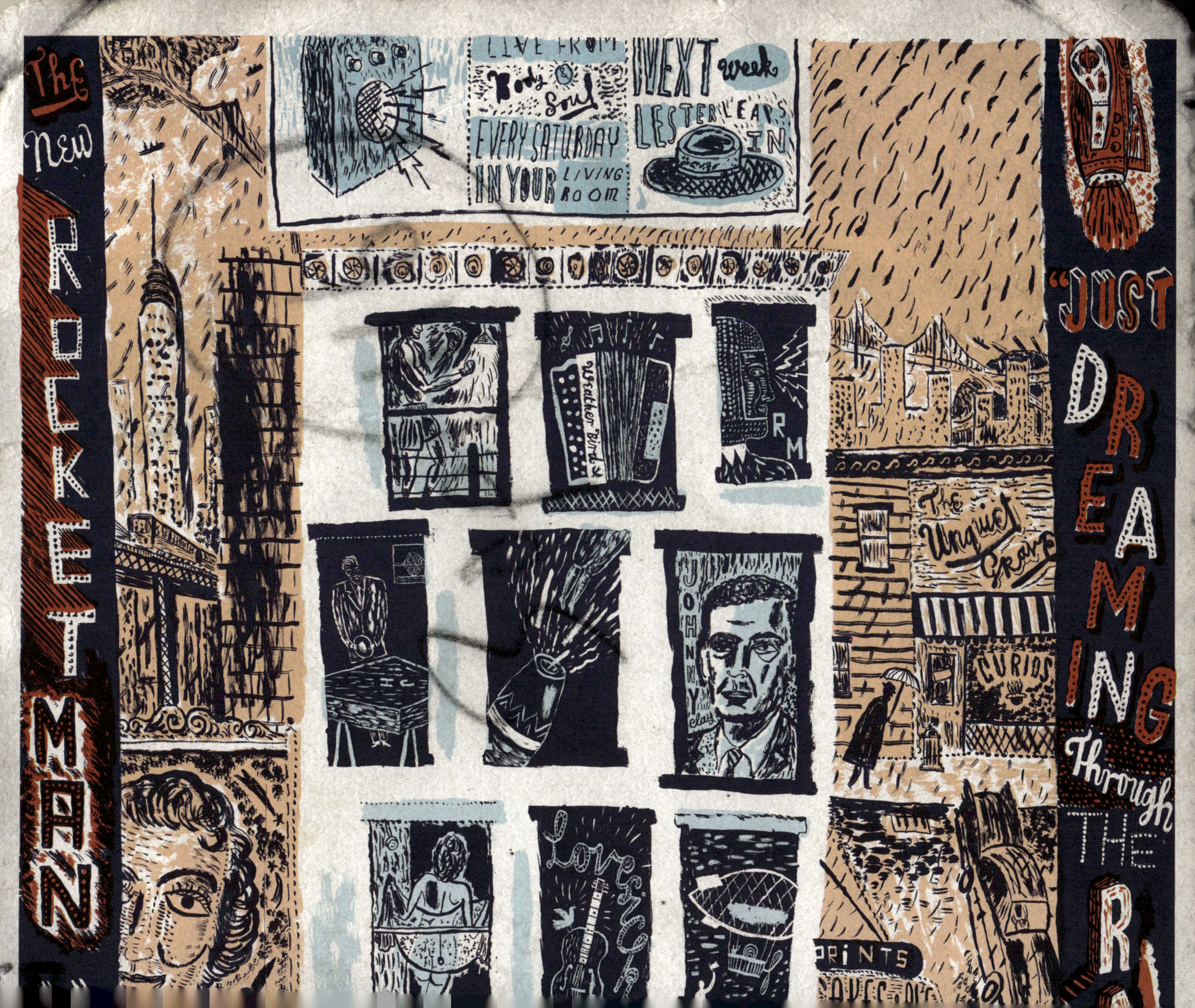

The new ROCKET MAN
LIVE FROM Body & Soul
EVERY SATURDAY IN YOUR LIVING ROOM
NEXT week LESTER LEAPS IN
Weather Bird
RM
JOHNNY
"JUST DREAMING through THE
The Unquiet Grave
CURIOS
PRINTS

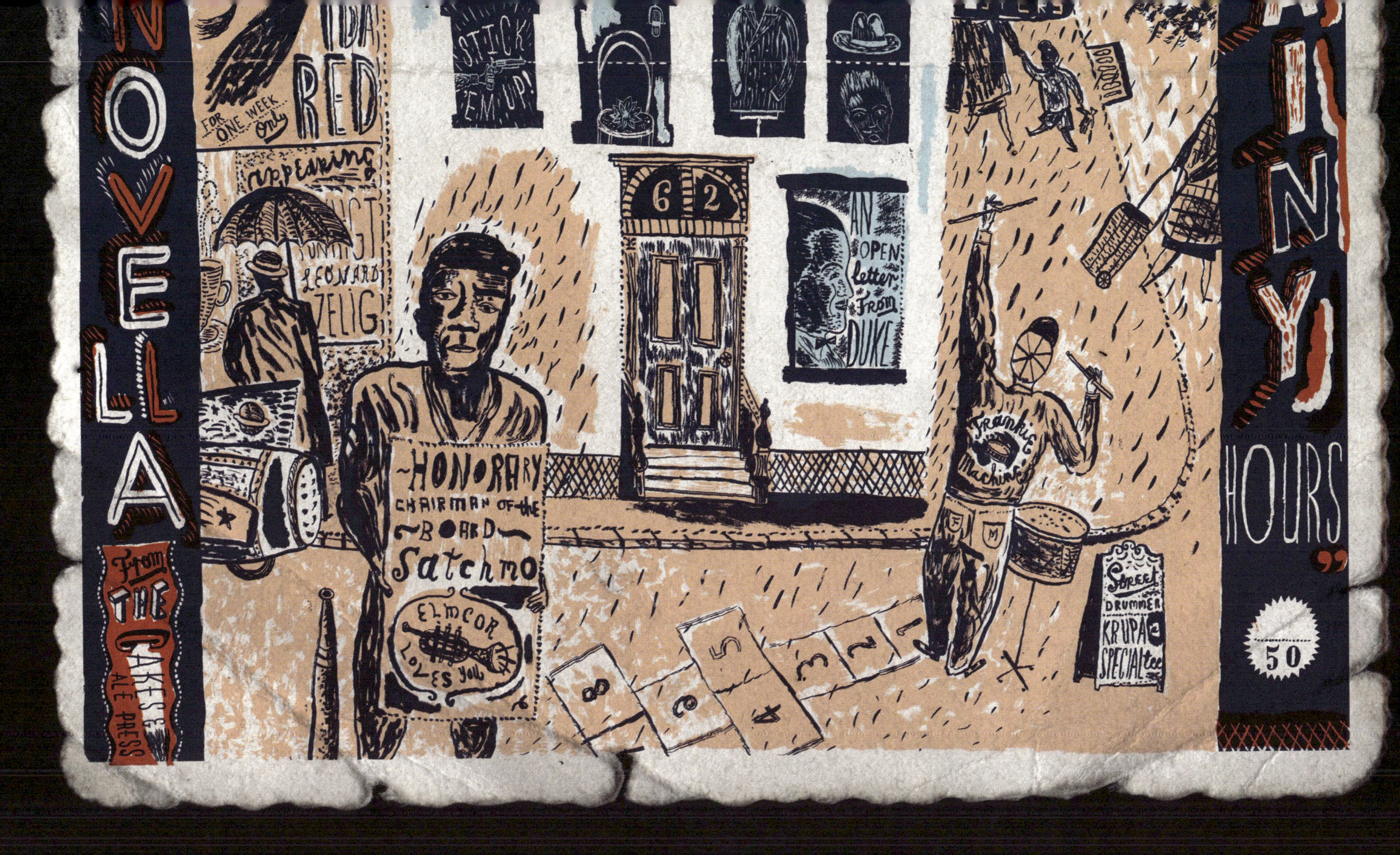


In the WINDOWS from top left: Stoker Thompson, practising * an accordian I'll never own, from WILKIES in Perth. * Pocket Man, thinking * My dad's coffin, waiting * Emanuel Zacchini Sr. the Human Cannonball * Sterling Hayden as Johnny Clay * Jane Russell just out of the bath – OOH-LA-LA * A lonesome whip-poor-will * A life-size tin toy on its maiden voyage * A HEIST * lady day about to Record A Prelude to a Kiss * My tailor-made suit * A Near death * MR. Ellington *

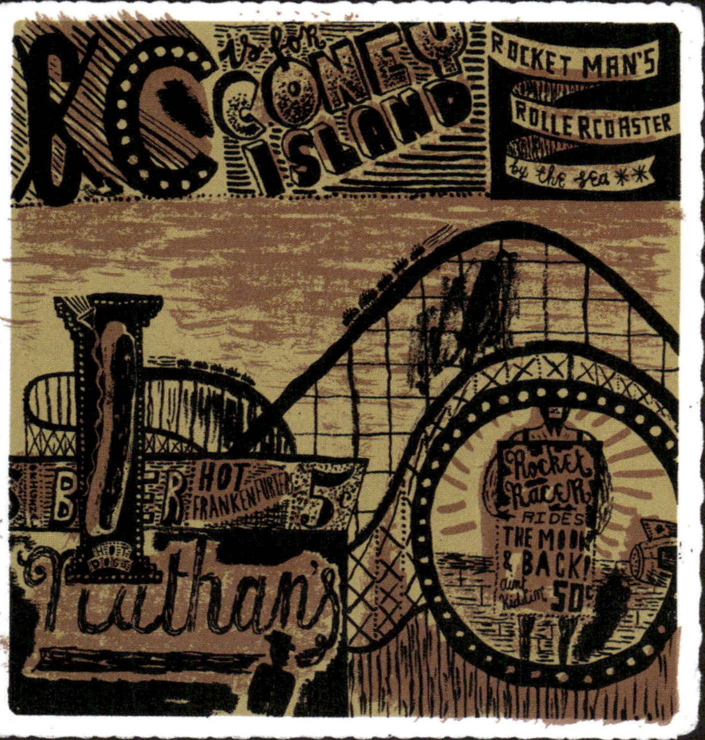


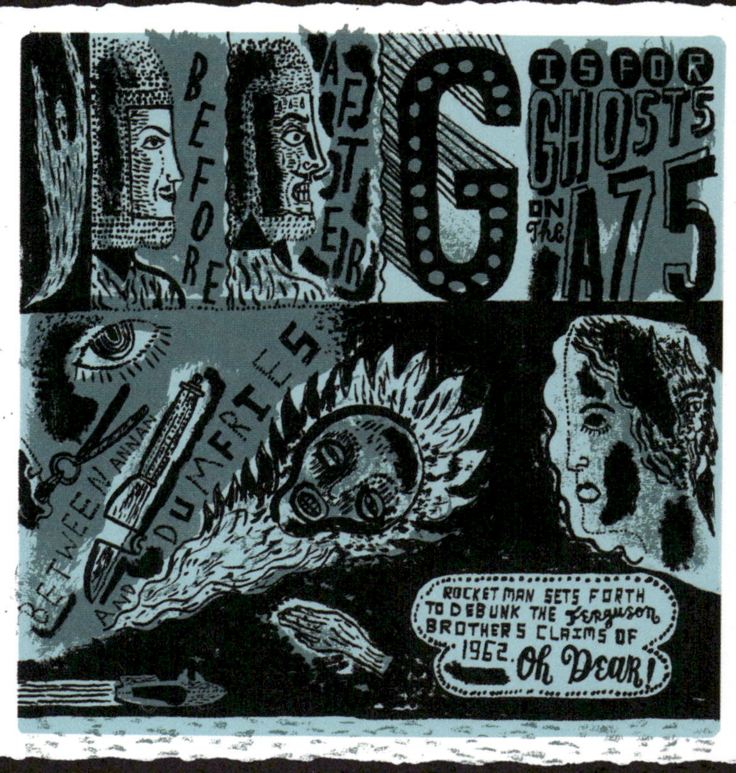


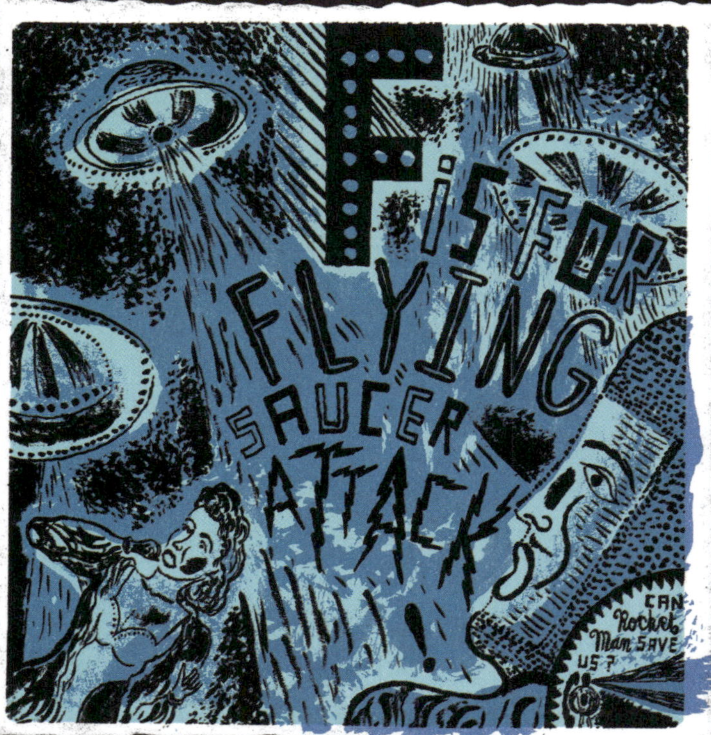


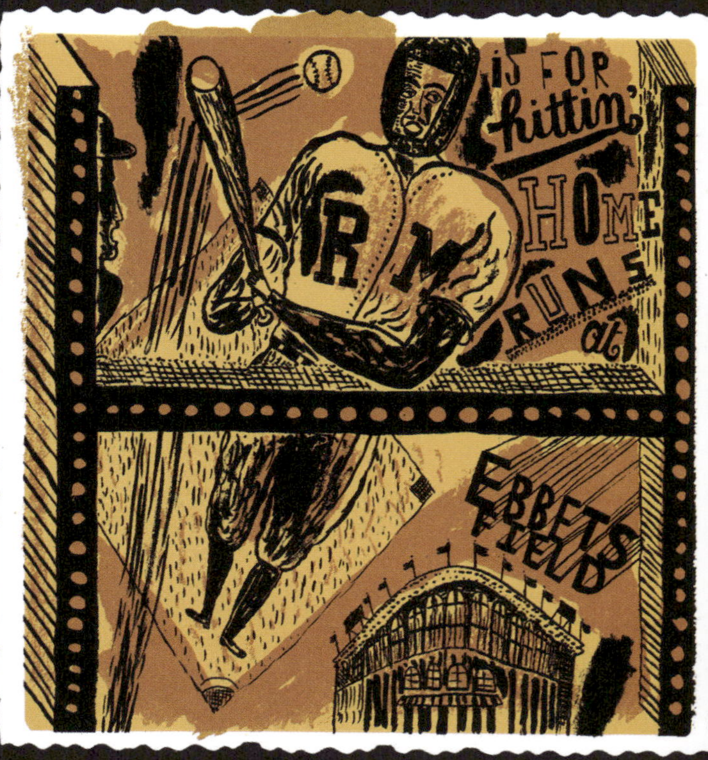


Rocket Man's far-from-complete A to Z, 2005. I think I did eight, then ran out of things to say.

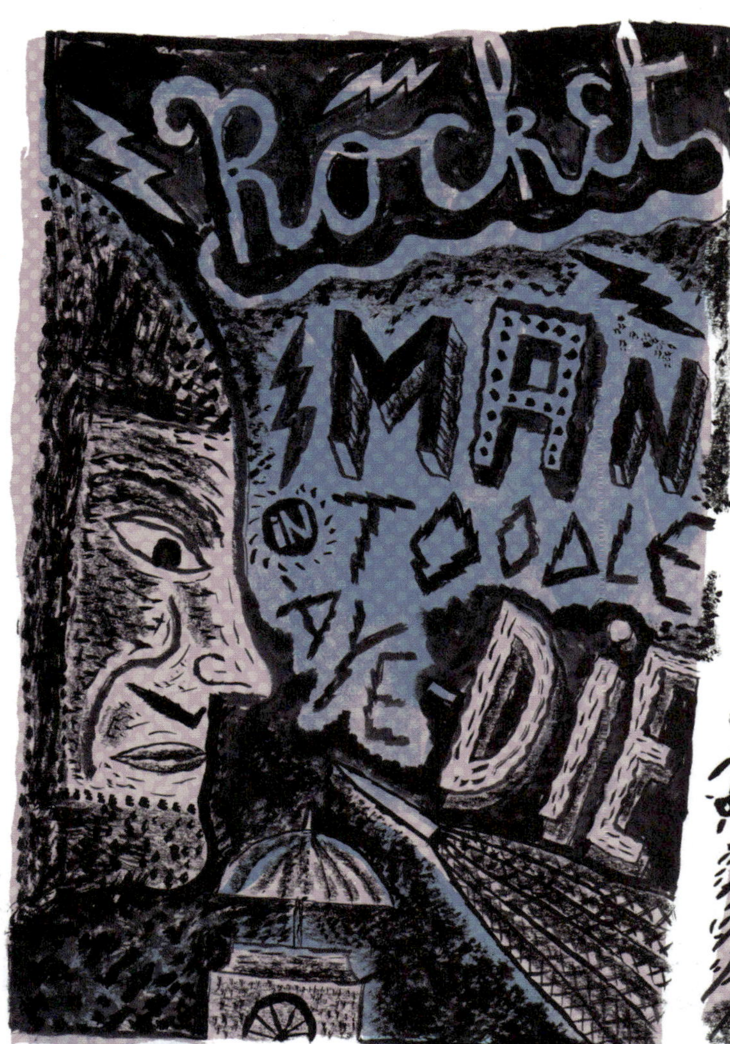


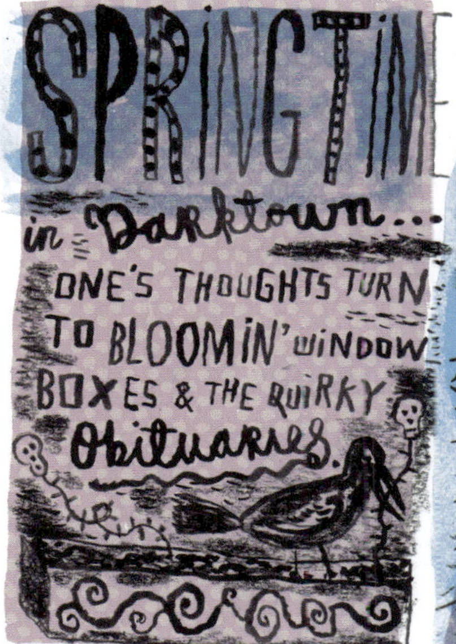


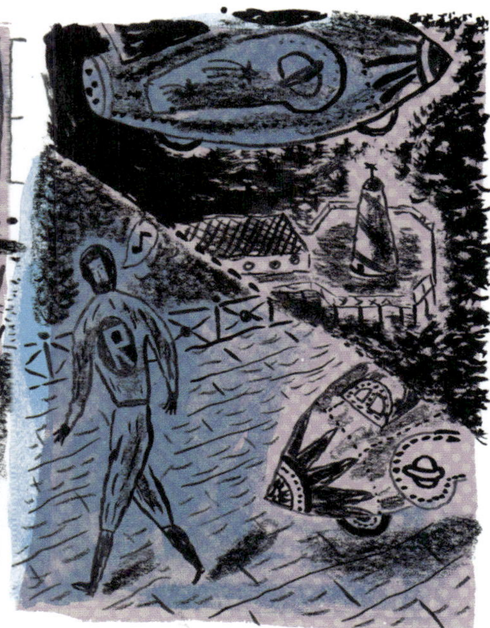

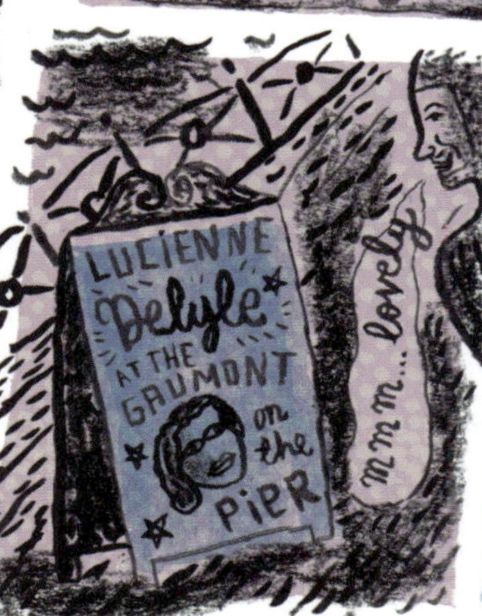


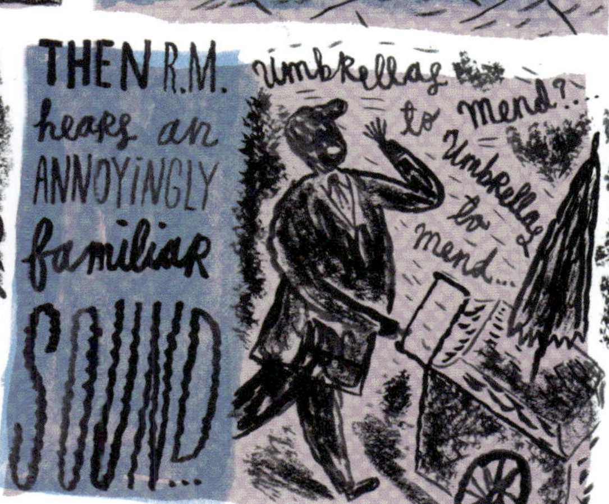


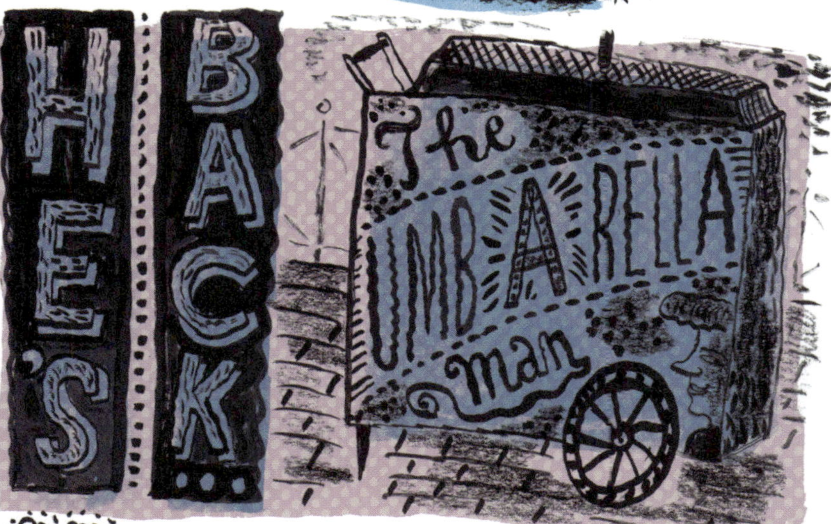


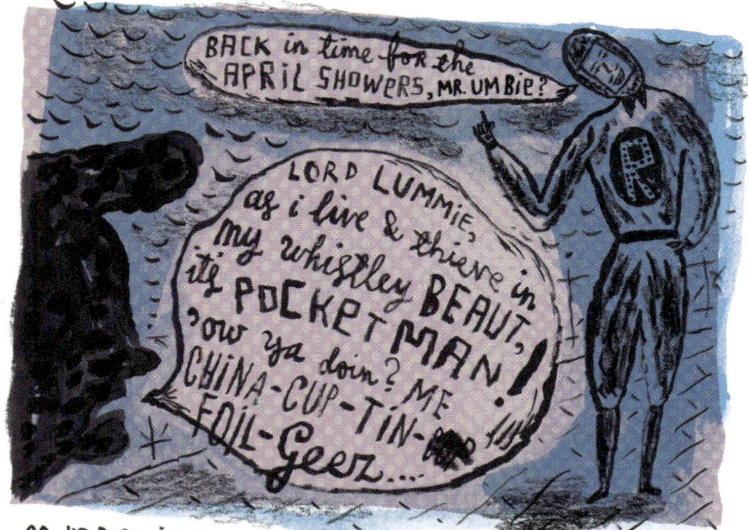


R.M. can never think of anything devilishly witty in these situations, so walks away, visibly miffed......
WHAT EVEN IS A TIN-FOIL-GEEZ anyway?....

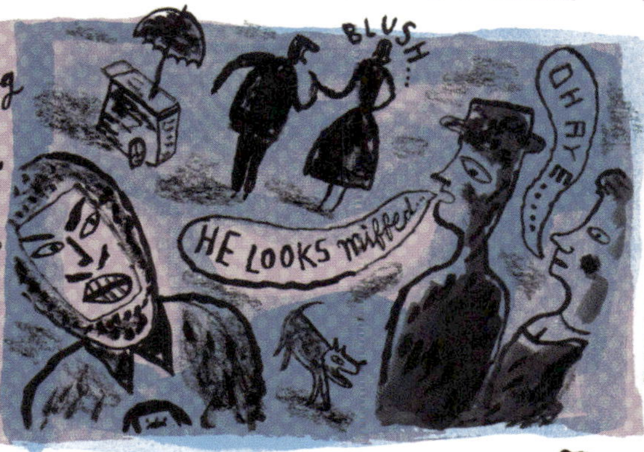


SO, HE POPS INTO THE JOLLY SCRIMSHANDER. God, he loves that place.

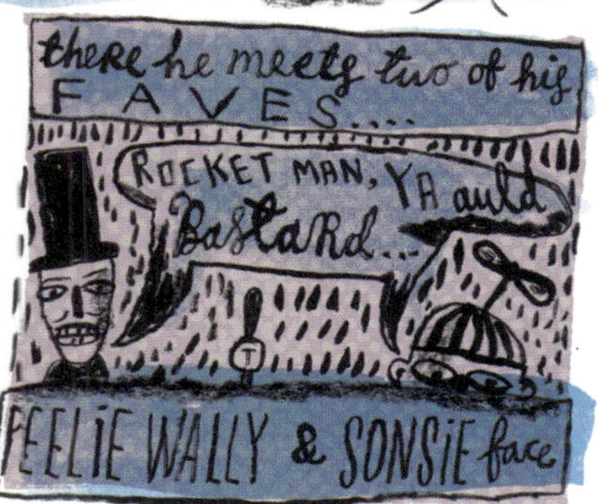

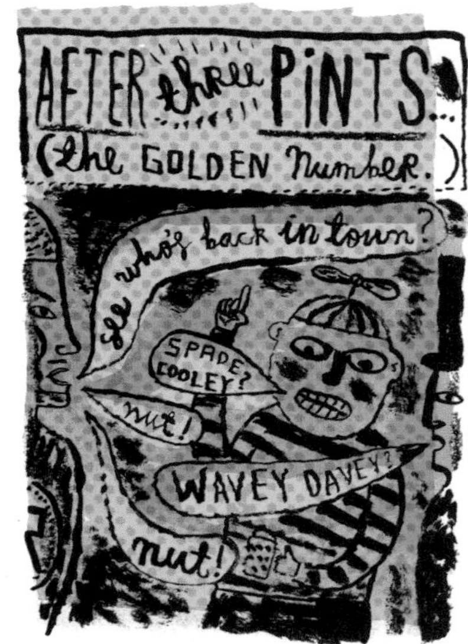

AFTER three PINTS...
(the GOLDEN number.)
see who's back in town?
SPADE COOLEY?
nut!
WAVEY DAVEY?
nut!


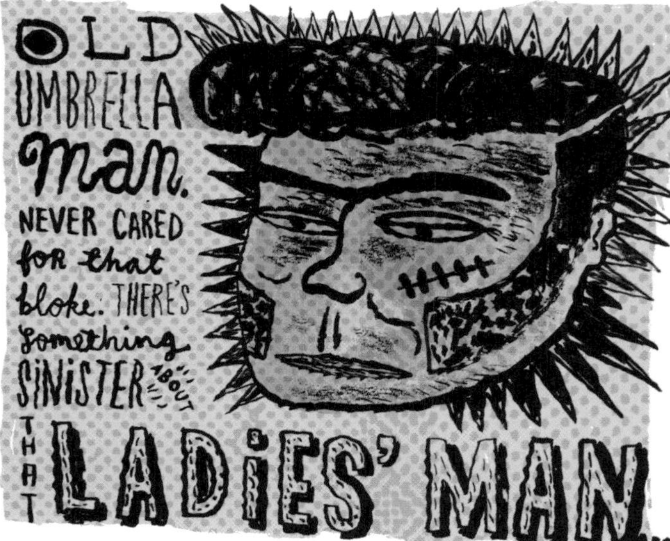

OLD UMBRELLA man.
NEVER CARED for that bloke. THERE'S something SINISTER ABOUT THAT LADIES' MAN...


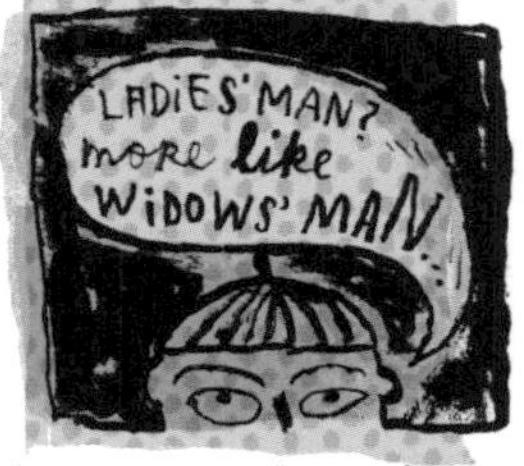

LADIES' MAN? more like WIDOWS' MAN.


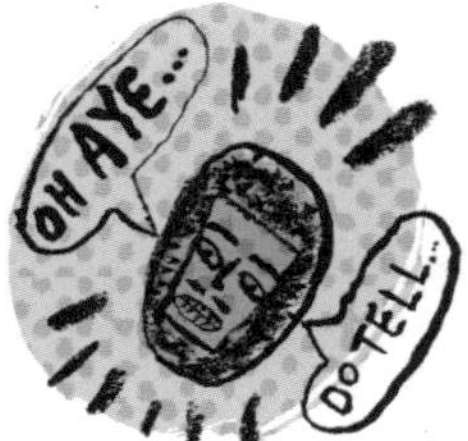

OH AYE...
DO TELL...


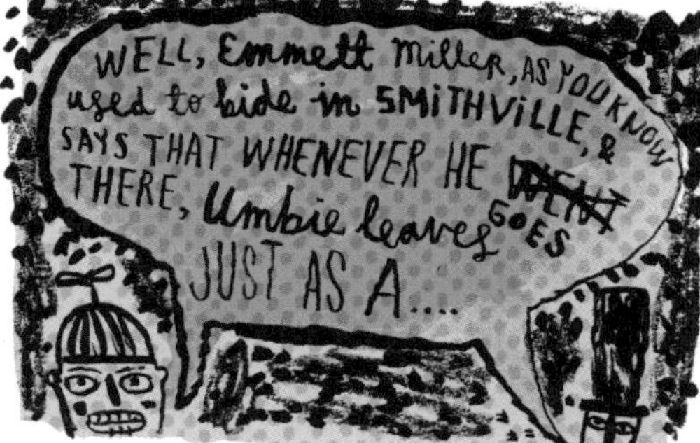

WELL, Emmett Miller, AS YOU KNOW used to bide in SMITHVILLE, & SAYS THAT WHENEVER HE GOES THERE, Umbie leaves JUST AS A....


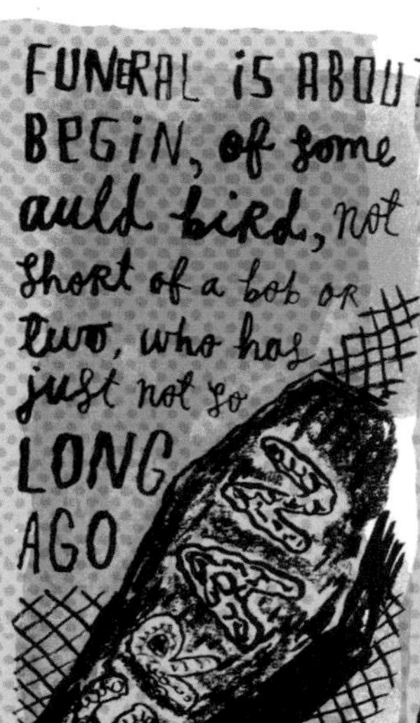

FUNERAL IS ABOUT BEGIN, of some auld bird, not short of a bob or two, who has just not so LONG AGO
CHANGED her WILL in guess WHO'S favour...


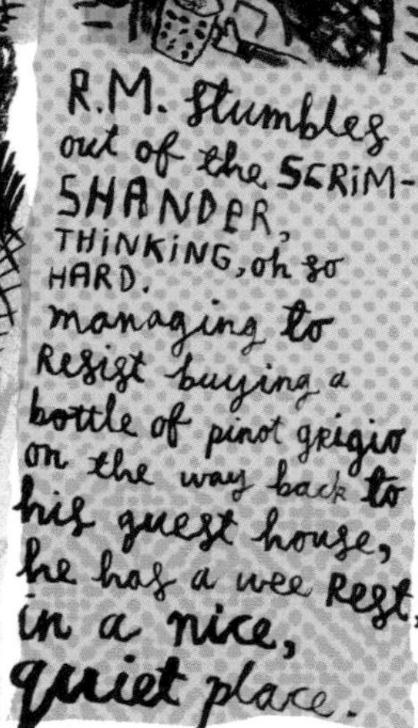

TUMMEL the WILKIES.
R.M. stumbles out of the SCRIMSHANDER, THINKING, oh so HARD. managing to resist buying a bottle of pinot grigio on the way back to his guest house, he has a wee rest, in a nice, quiet place.


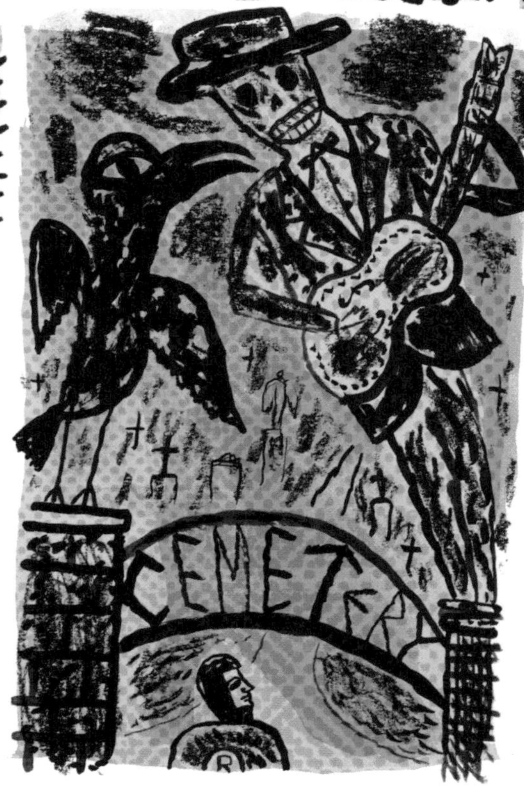

CEMETERY


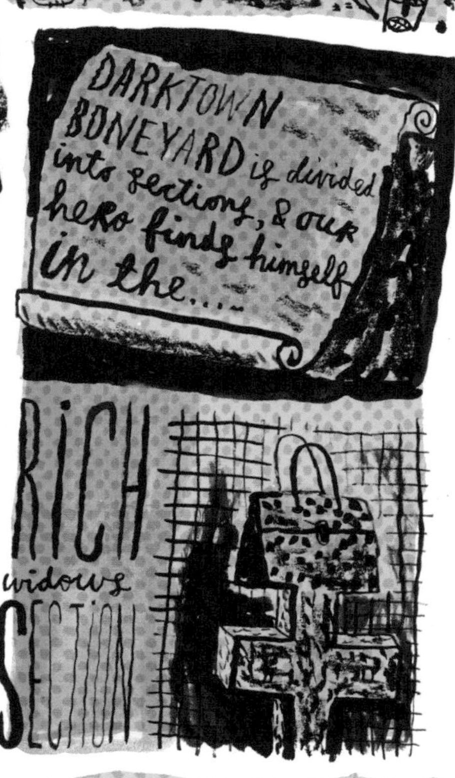

DARKTOWN BONEYARD is divided into sections, & our hero finds himself in the....
RICH widows SECTION


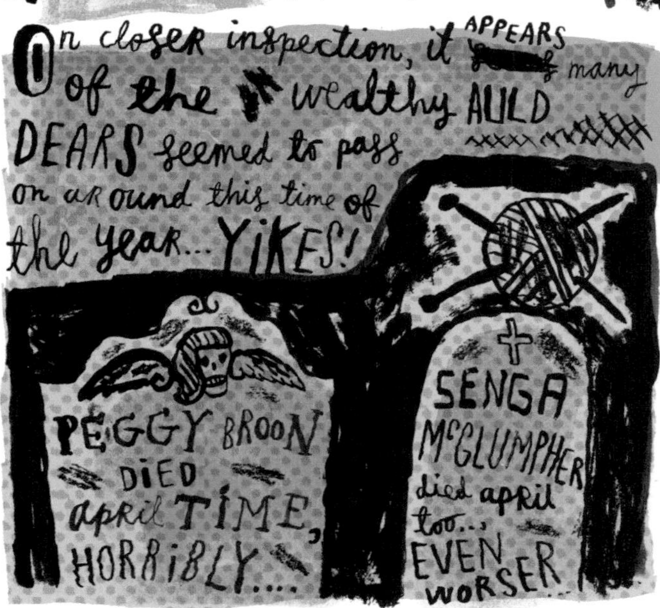

On closer inspection, it APPEARS many of the wealthy AULD DEARS seemed to pass on around this time of the year... YIKES!
PEGGY BROON DIED april TIME, HORRIBLY....
SENGA McGLUMPHER died april too... EVEN WORSER


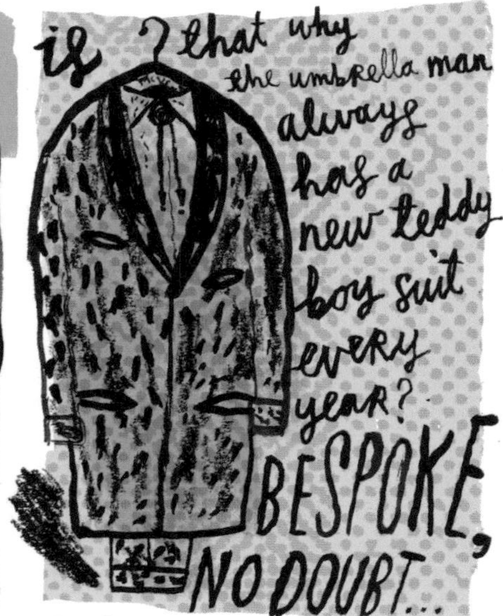

is that why the umbrella man always has a new teddy boy suit every year?
BESPOKE, NO DOUBT...


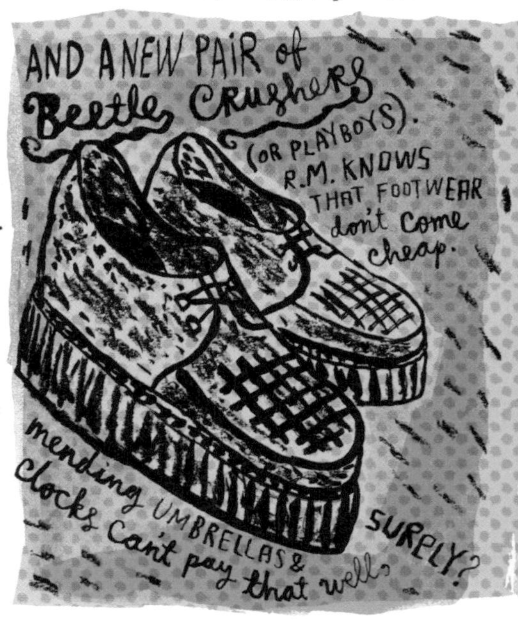

AND A NEW PAIR of Beetle Crushers (OR PLAYBOYS).
R.M. KNOWS THAT FOOTWEAR don't come cheap.
mending UMBRELLAS & clocks can't pay that well, SURELY?

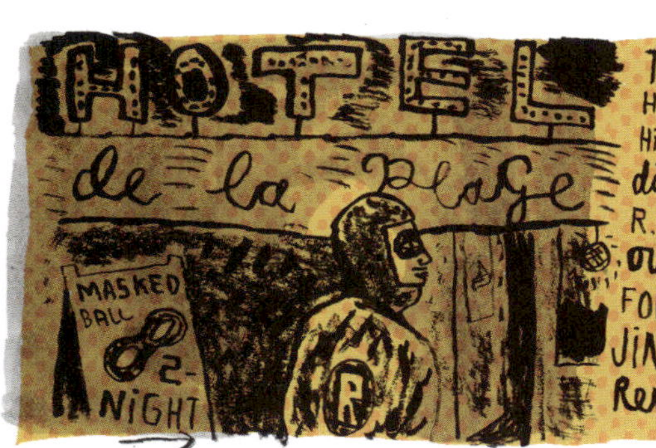

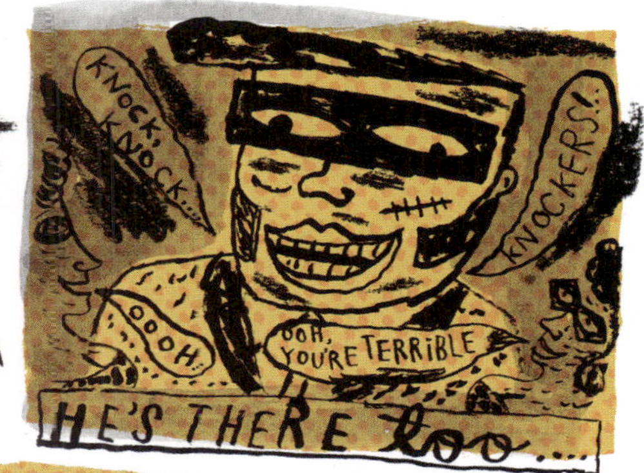


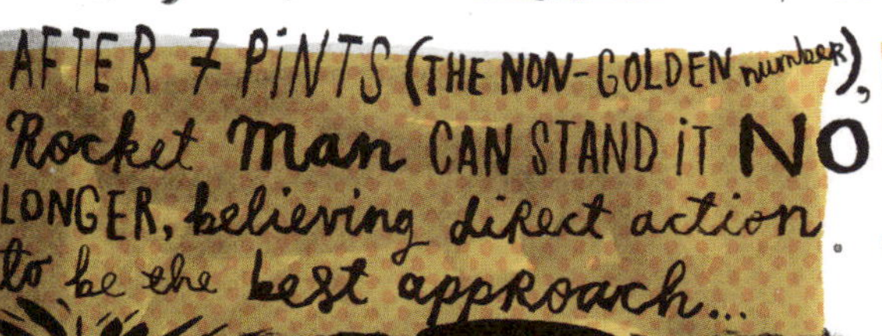

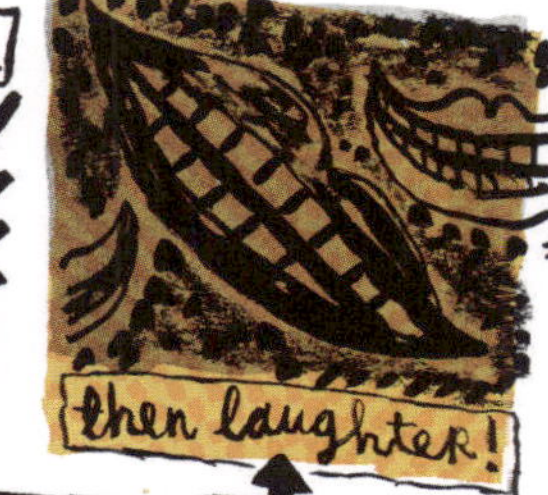


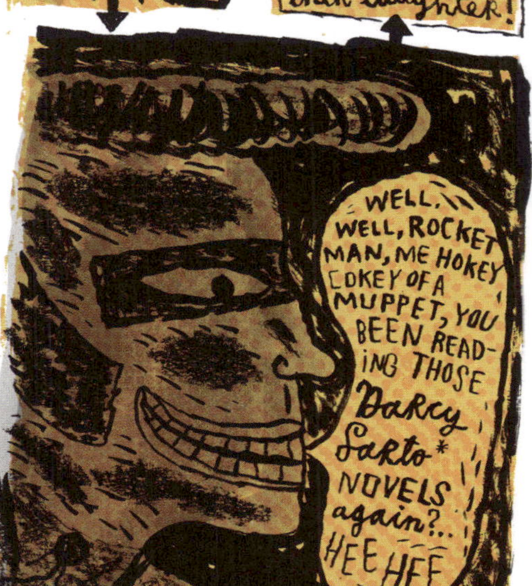


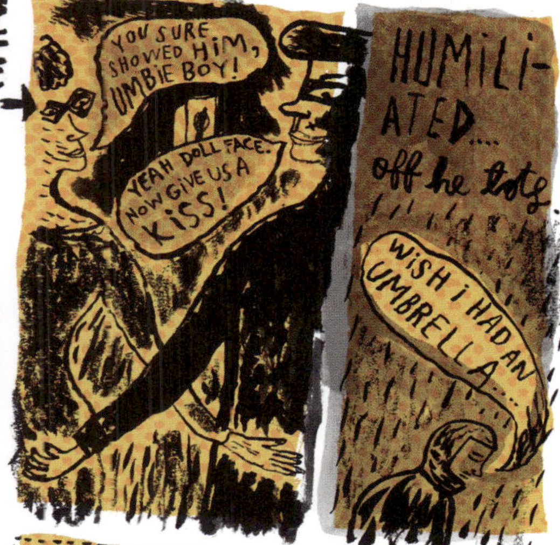


the following day, R.M. decides the trip is over, & puts the guitars in the cases & the covers on the drums IN OTHER WORDS... TIME TO GO Home...

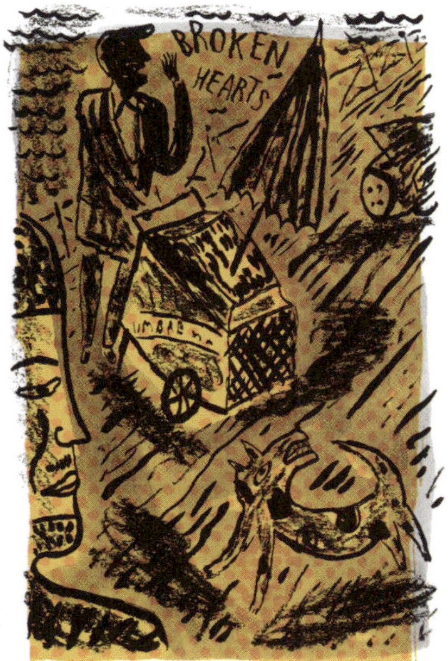


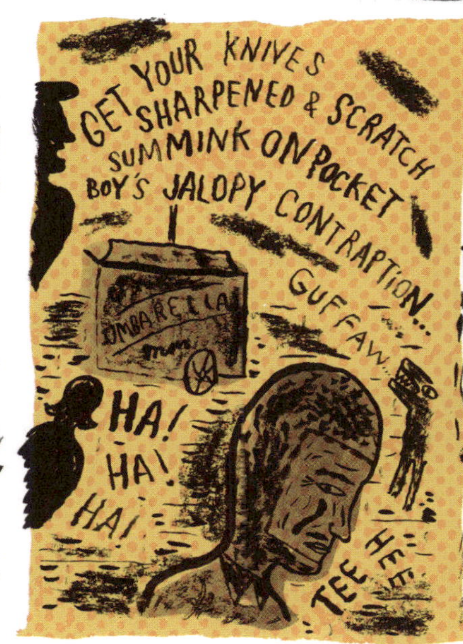


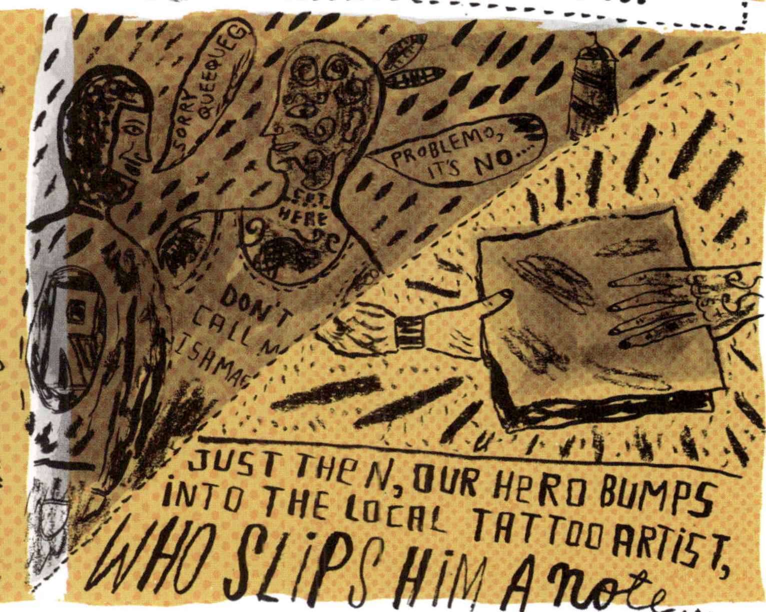


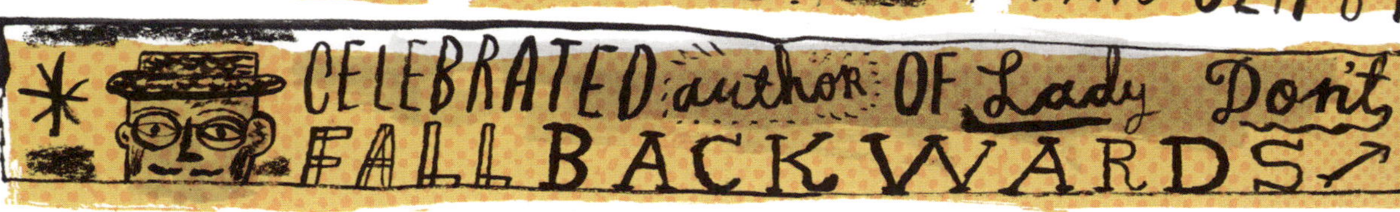

LOOK
AT HIS
CHEST.
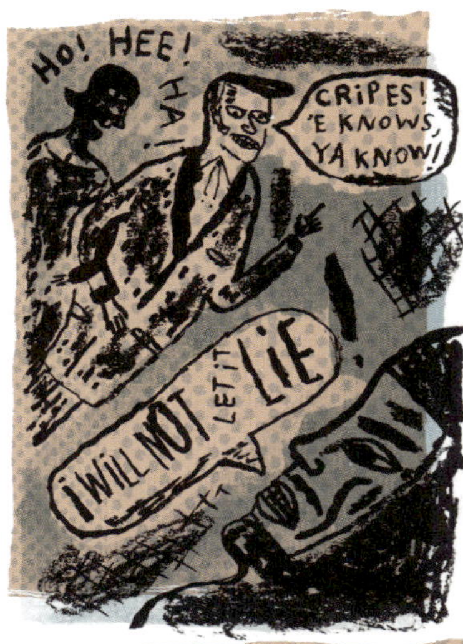
HO! HEE! HA
CRIPES! 'E KNOWS, YA KNOW!
I WILL NOT LET IT LIE
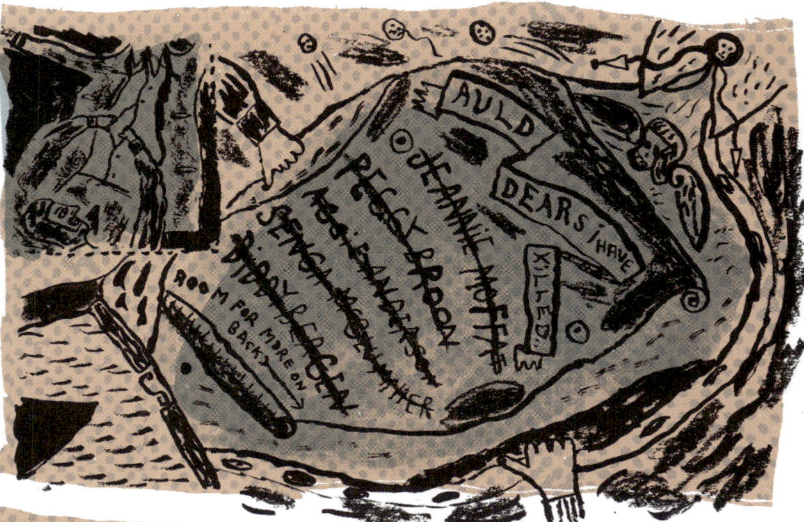
AULD DEARS HAVE EXITED
ROOM FOR MORE ON BATS

IT'S TRUE!!!
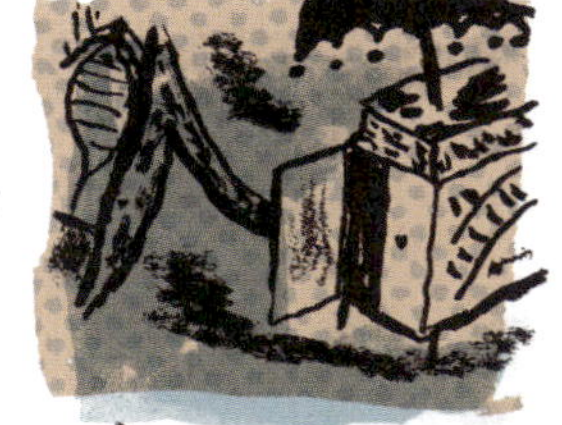
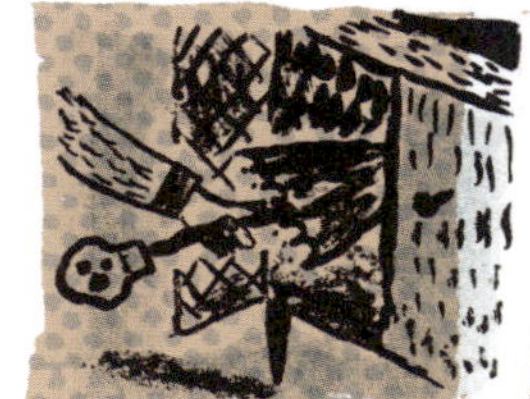
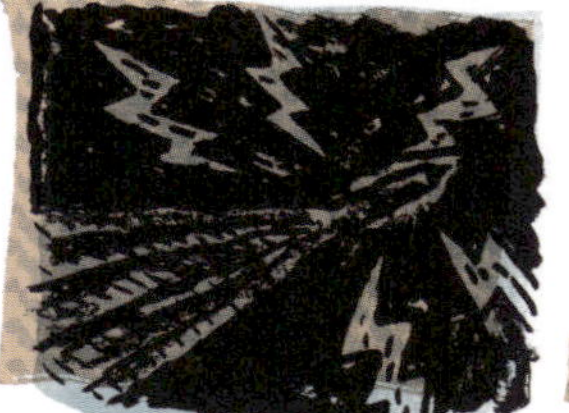

IT PIERCES the SKIN
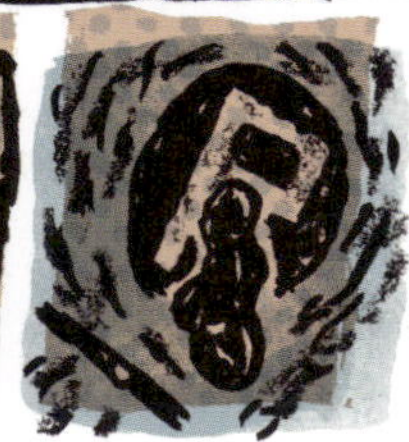
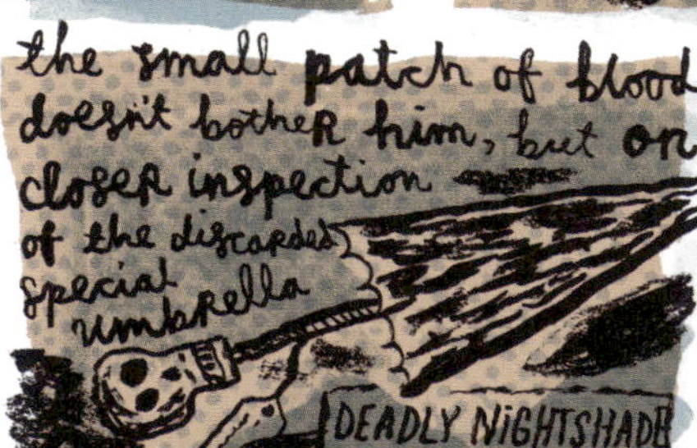
the small patch of blood doesn't bother him, but on closer inspection of the discarded special umbrella
DEADLY NIGHTSHADE 3 MINUTES LEFT, if that......
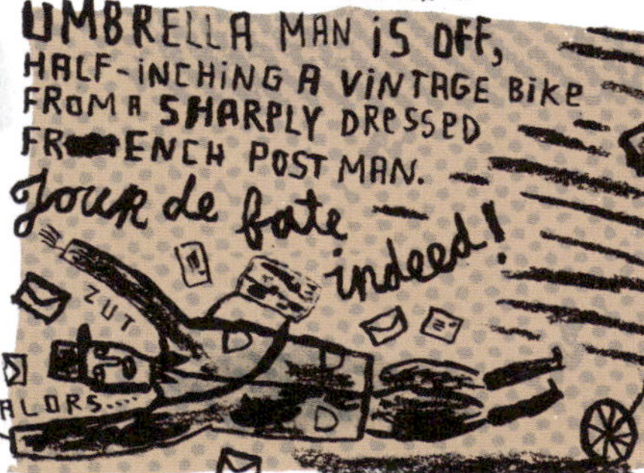
UMBRELLA MAN IS OFF, HALF-INCHING A VINTAGE BIKE FROM A SHARPLY DRESSED FRENCH POST MAN.
Tour de fate indeed!
ZUT
ALORS....
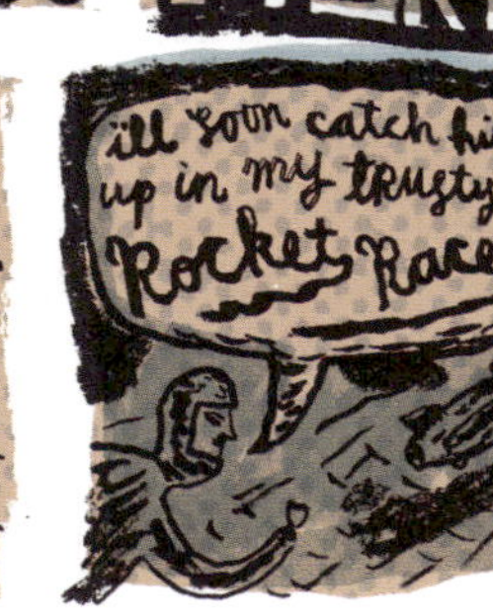
ill soon catch him up in my trusty Rocket Racer
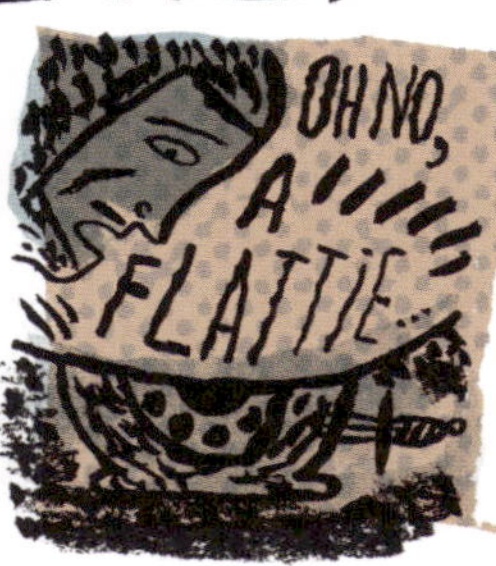
OH NO, A FLATTIE
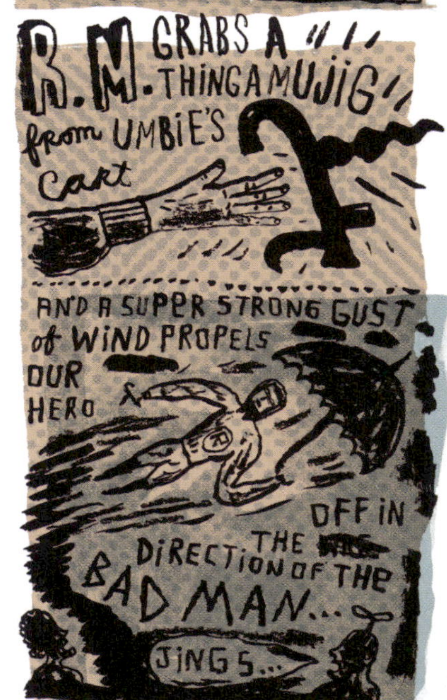
R.M. GRABS A THINGAMUJIG from UMBIE'S cart
AND A SUPER STRONG GUST of WIND PROPELS OUR HERO
OFF IN THE DIRECTION OF THE BAD MAN...
JINGS...
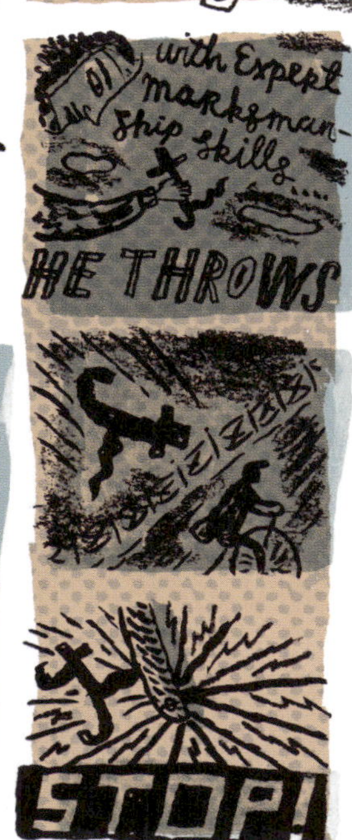
with Expert marksmanship skills...
HE THROWS
STOP!
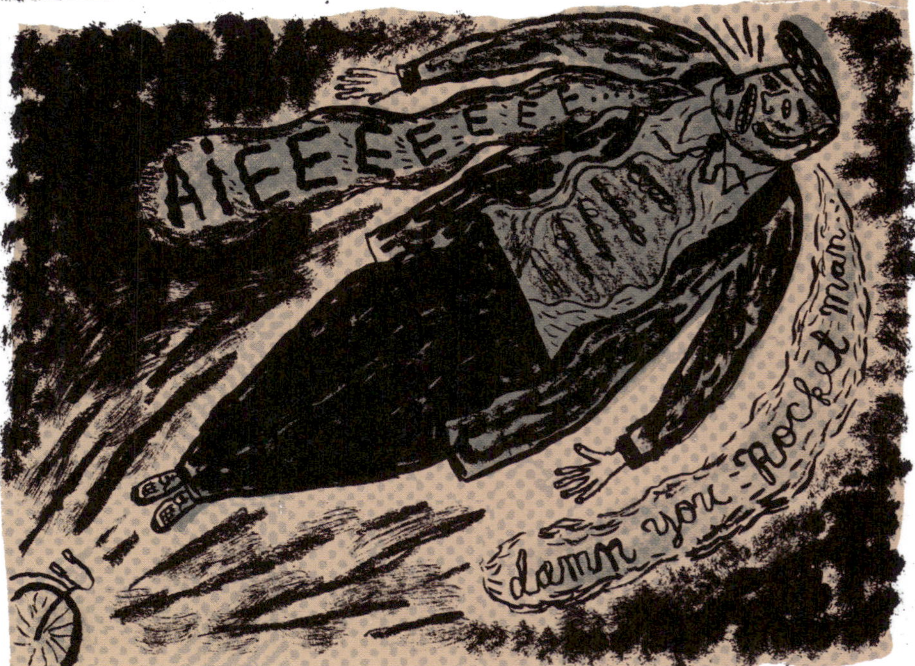
AiEEEEEEEE
damn you rocket man

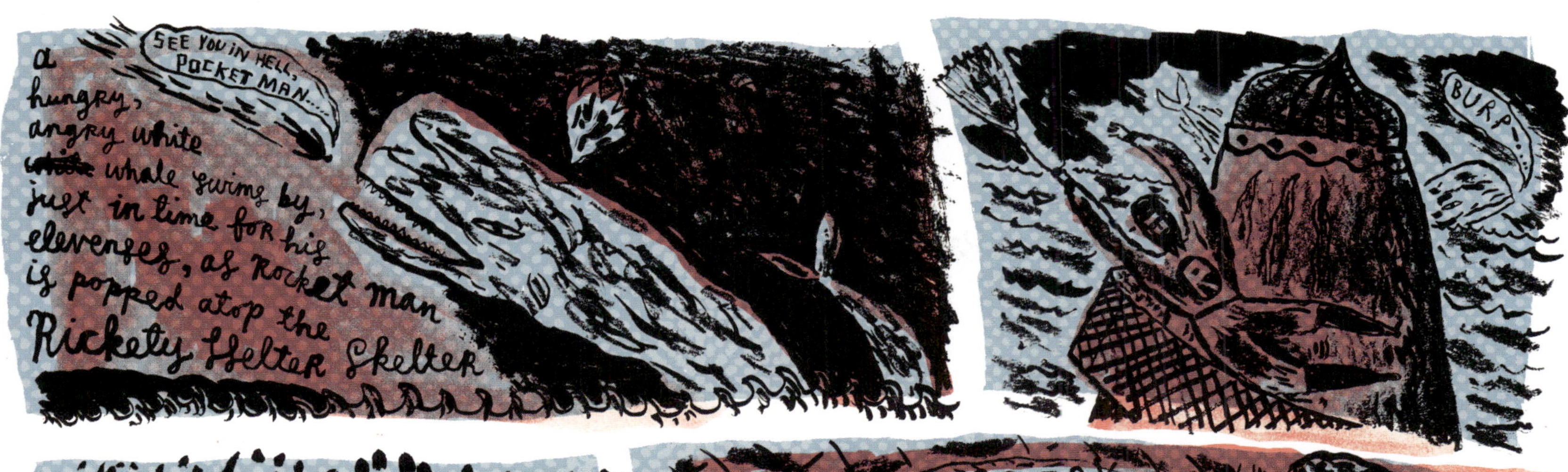


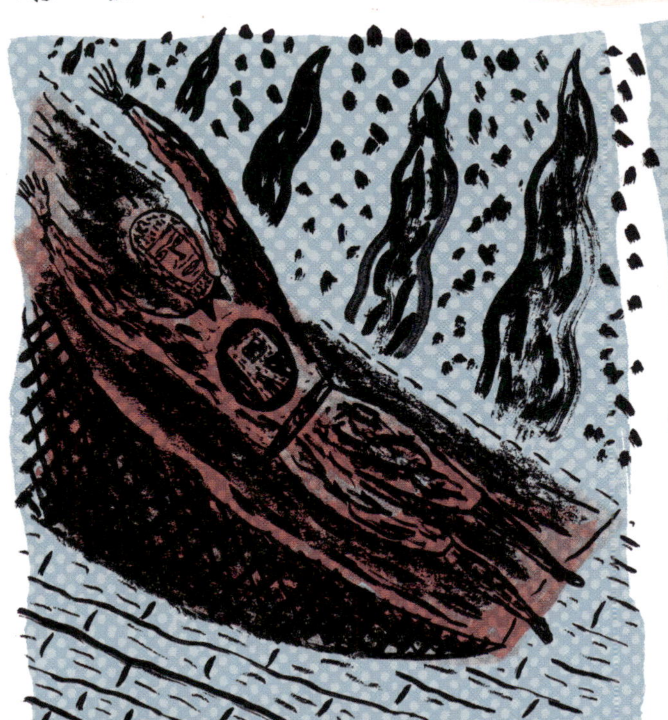

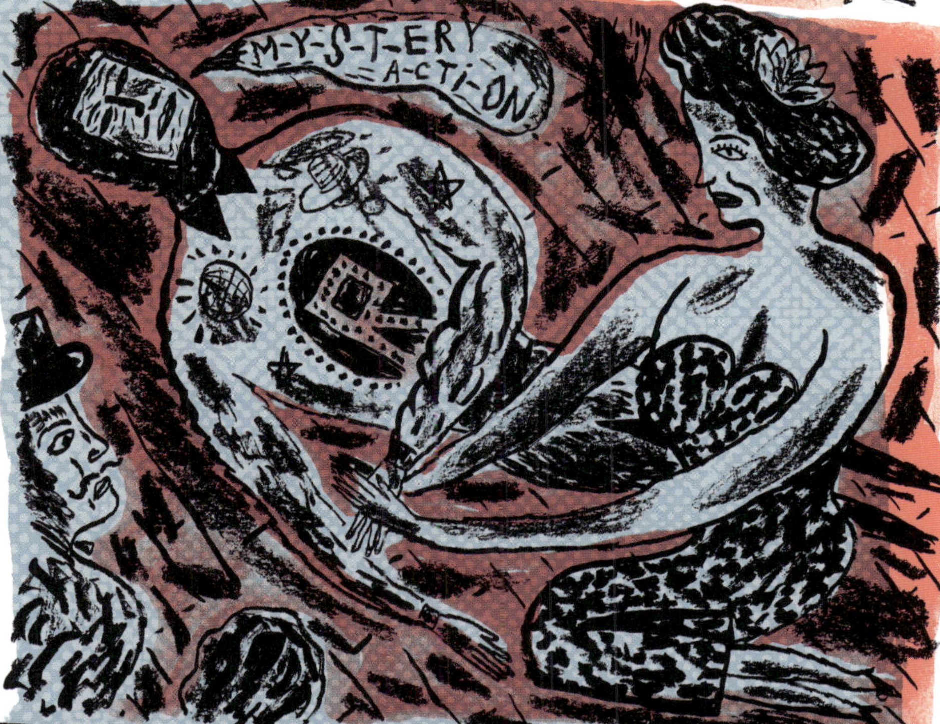


WITH SECONDS TO GO, a passing Jane Russell GENTLY HOLDS HIS HAND AND KISSES Rocket MAN au revoir...

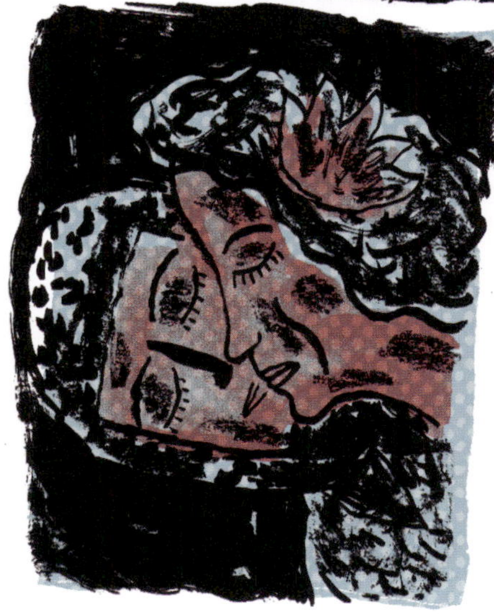

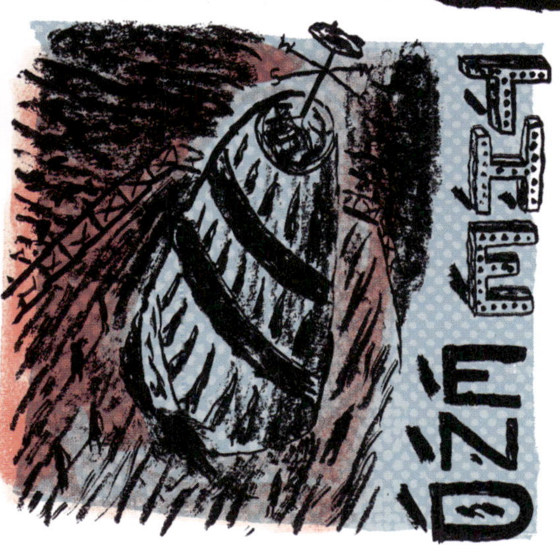


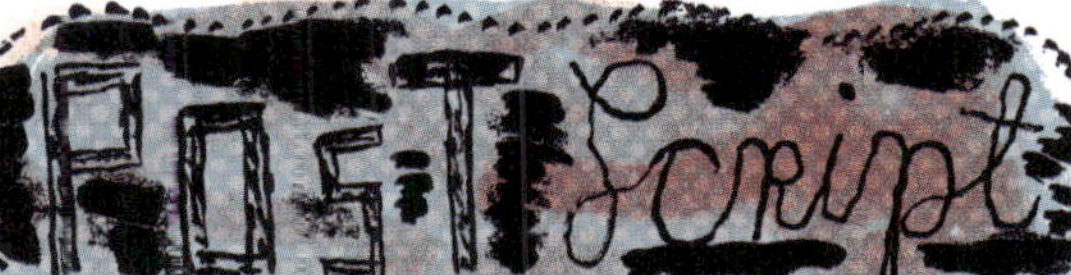


Rocket Man, our hero, someone to admire, was in fact in the middle stages of PANCREATIC CANCER. YOUNG, TOO YOUNG AT only SIXTY-EIGHT, HE GAVE HIS doomed life so that the well-heeled ageing wifeys of DARKTOWN COULD SLEEP EASY ALL NIGHT, EVEN IN THE DARKEST HOUR JUST BEFORE dawn....

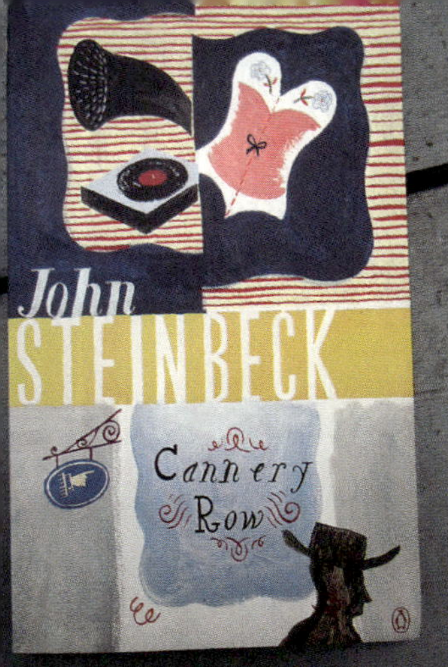


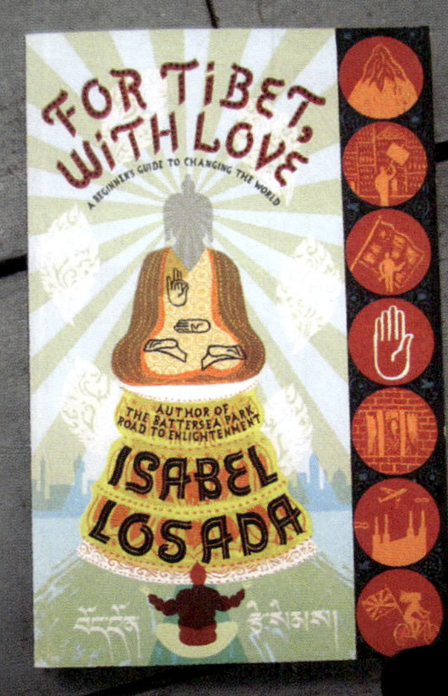


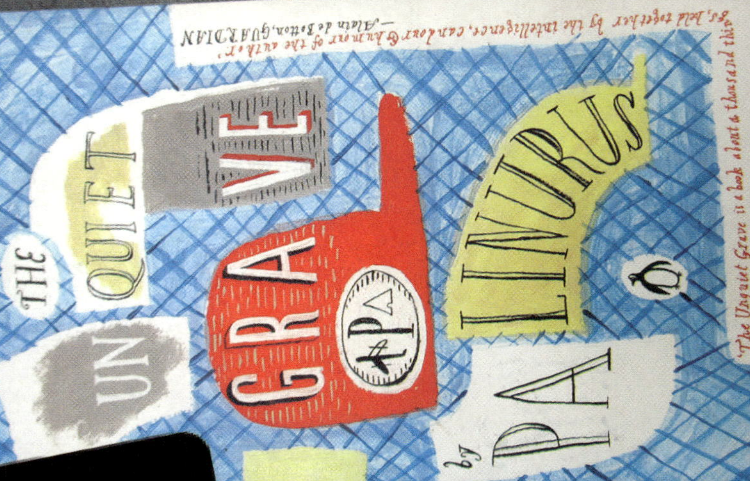


A variety of book covers, dating from 1999 to 2010. Kind commissioners have included Penguin, Bloomsbury, Random House and Tindal Street Press.

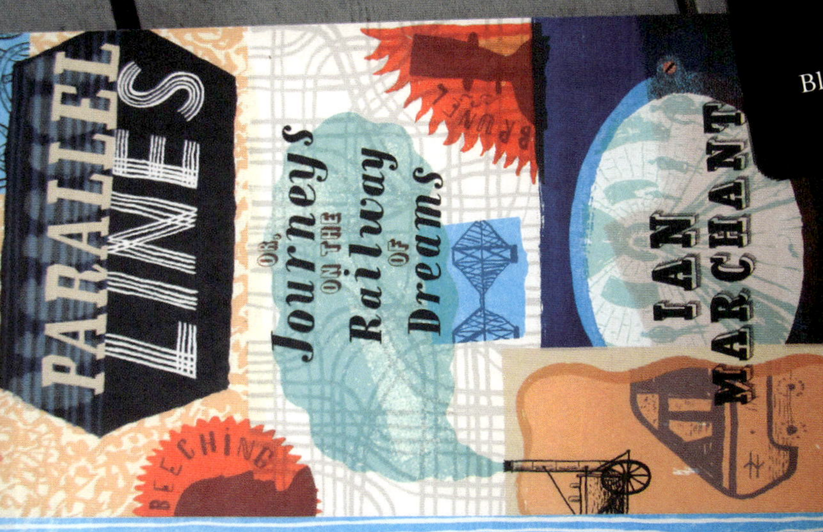


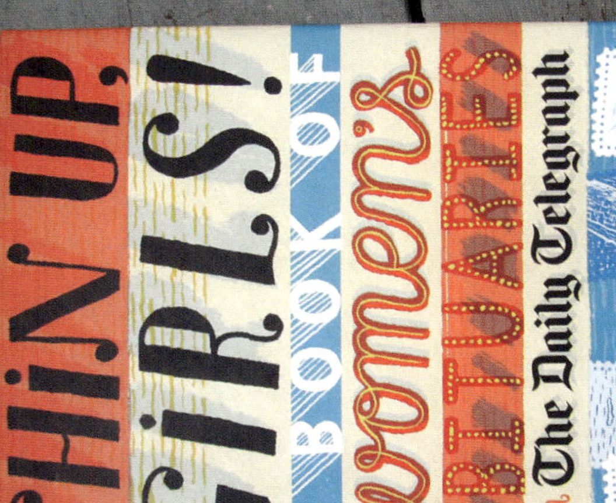


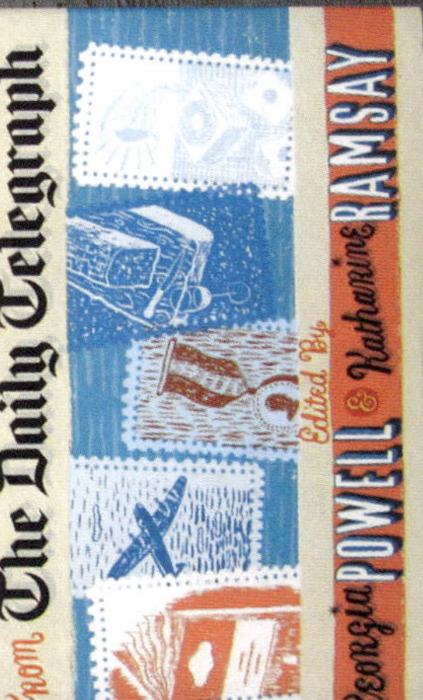


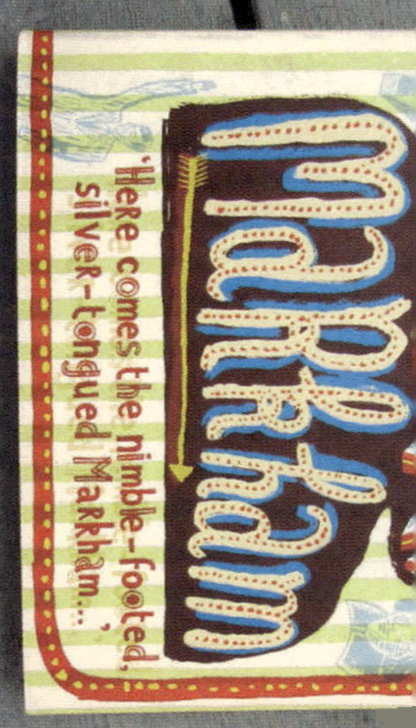

horse AND THE SAD girl AND THE village UNDER THE SEA MARK HADDON

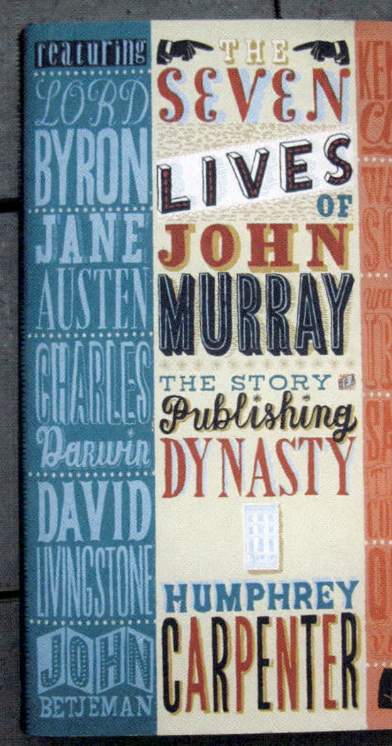


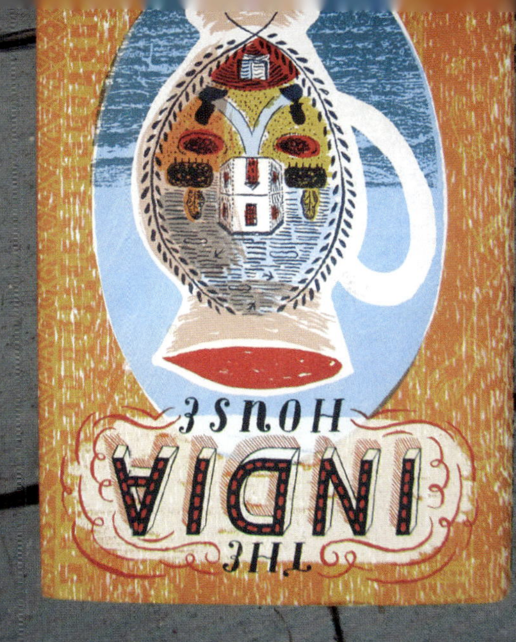


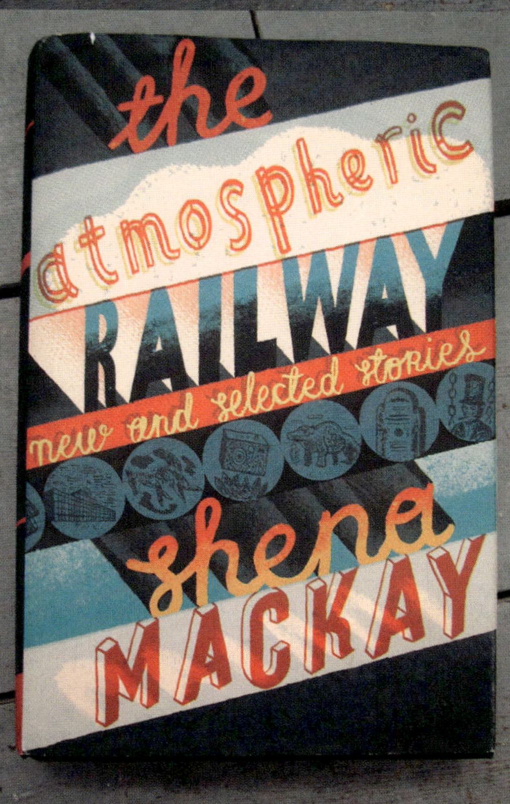


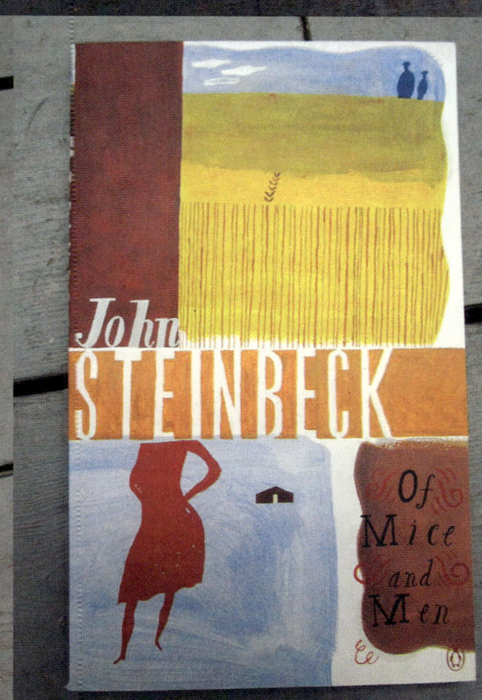


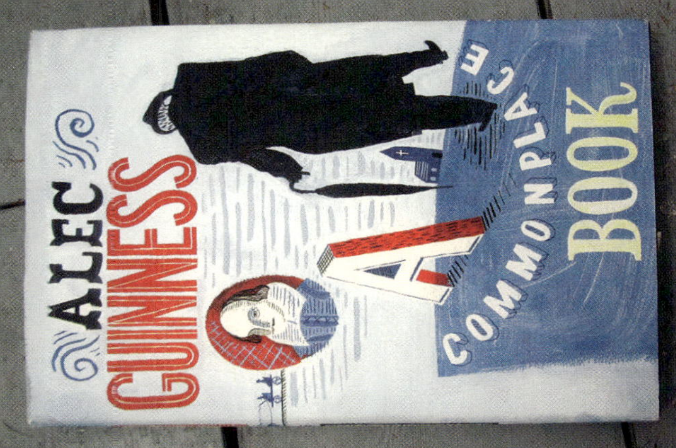


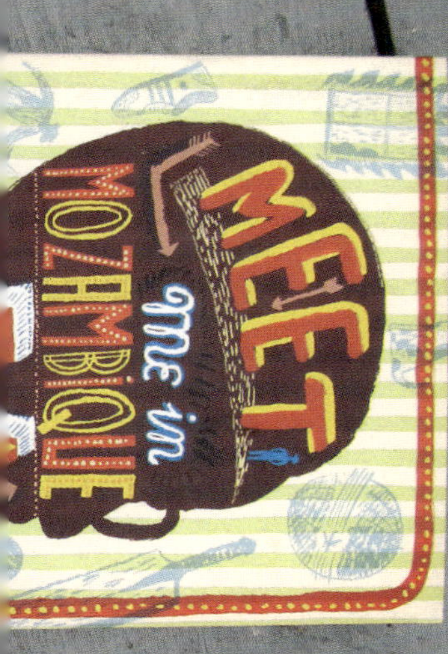


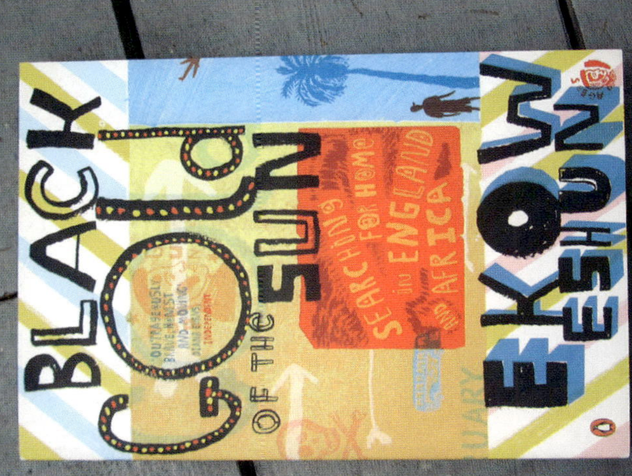


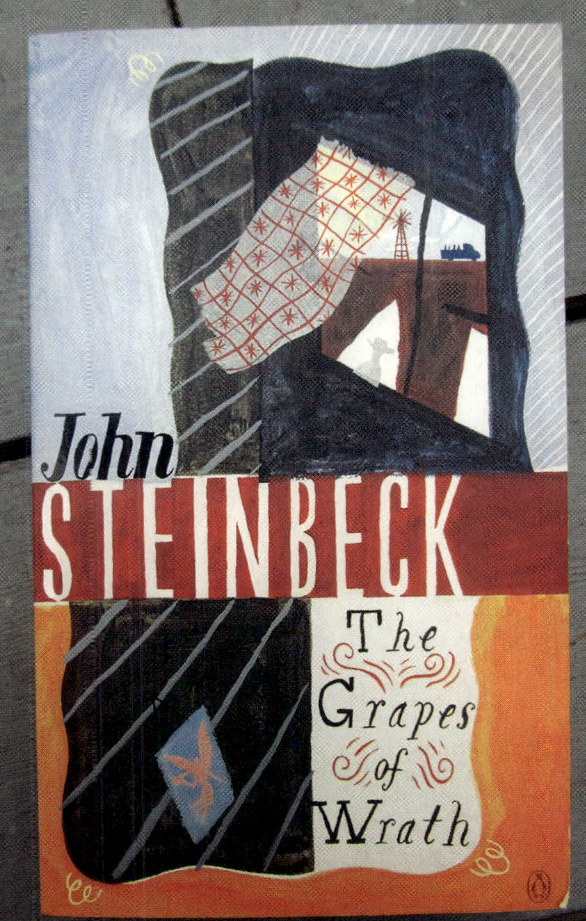

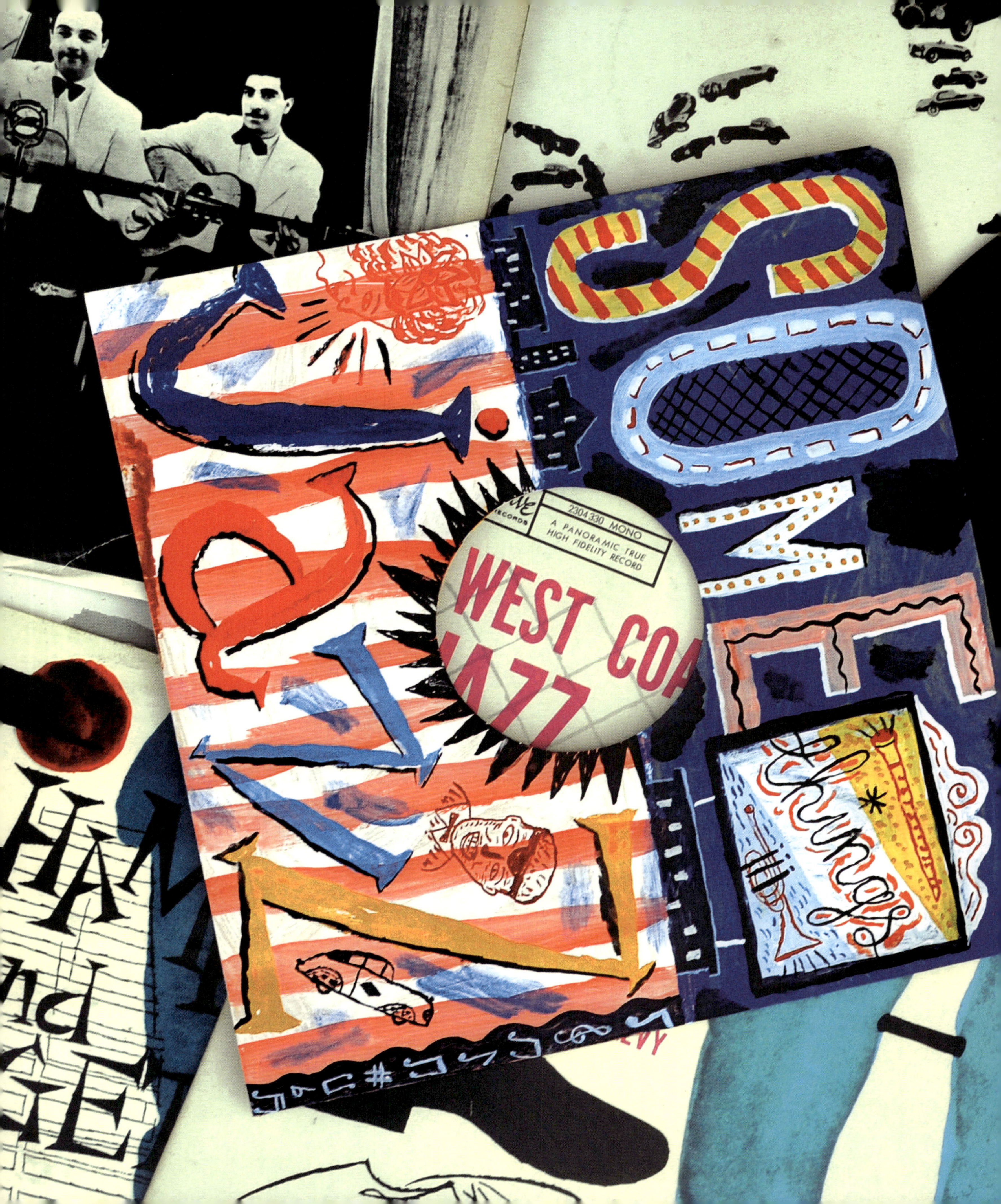

2304 330 MONO
A PANORAMIC TRUE
HIGH FIDELITY RECORD
WEST COA

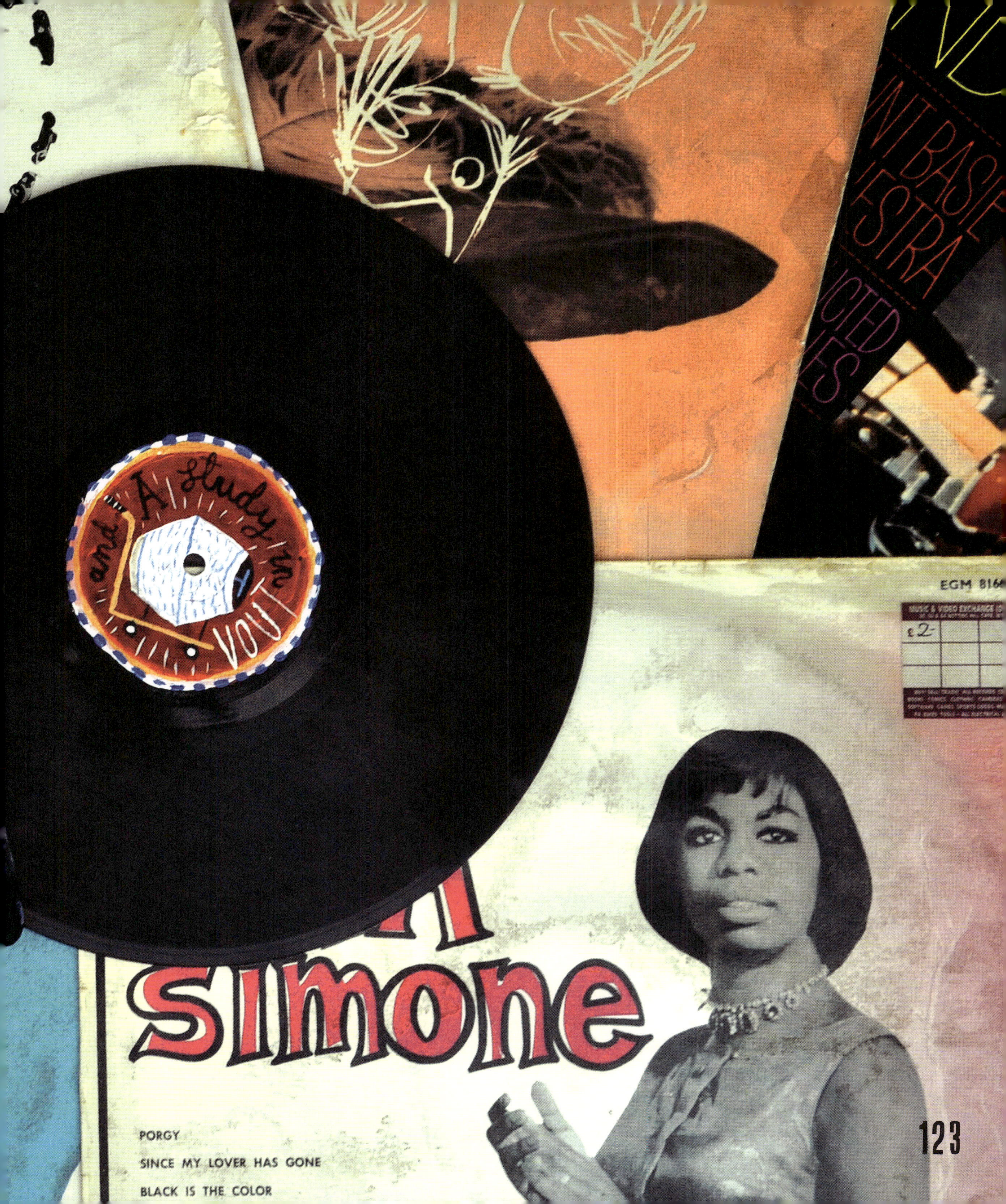
A Study in
VOUT
and
EGM 816
£2-
Simone
PORGY
SINCE MY LOVER HAS GONE
BLACK IS THE COLOR

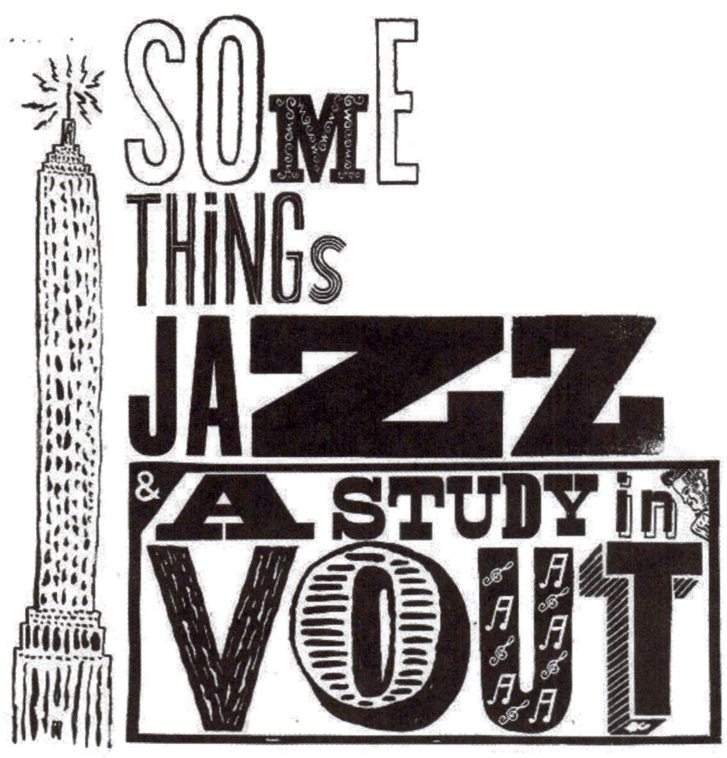


When Louis Armstrong put his lips to his trumpet and blew the introductory notes to 'West End Blues', the world was a brighter place. And when Deirdre McDermott and David Lloyd at Walker Books asked me to do a children's picture book on jazz, my world became a brighter place. I immersed myself in the hot, swinging tunes, going further back than I had ever before. Jelly Roll Morton's 'Wild Man Blues'; Duke Ellington's 'Caravan'; sing, sing, singing with Benny Goodman and Gene Krupa. Every day uncovered new songs, new artists, different genres within a genre. I ended up at bebop and rediscovered Charlie 'Bird' Parker. How could someone blow so many notes in such a short space of time and with such clarity? And how could he have a short, sad time on this planet, yet still make some of the most celebratory tunes you'll ever hear? The book, *Hot Jazz Special*, published in 2005, won an award and was appreciated by a small, dedicated group of cats and squares, including the delightfully colourful George Melly. Walker Books treated me very well, giving me the chance to have different endpapers (opposite and pages 130–31) and even a dustjacket that unfolded into a poster. It was a special project, working with very special people who afforded me huge artistic freedom. And now jazz is a full-blown addiction. I've even dragged myself into the meandering world of modern jazz, dabbling with Coltrane and painting regularly to the genius of Mingus. Oh yeah …

However, my love of jazz stems from those Hot Five and Hot Seven recordings, made nearly a century ago. Little Louis gave birth to so much of what we now consider to be pop culture. Suddenly, the personal take was essential, and improvisation was the only way forward. This approach was carried through all styles of jazz and all instruments, even the voice, with Billie Holiday being my firm favourite. The discovery of such albums as *Music for Torching* added more dimensions to my life than I could have imagined. They also reinforced my romantic notion that hard lives make great art. I hope to go through life with relative ease, but Billie wasn't so lucky. I revived my admiration for David Stone Martin, the master of limited colour, whose record sleeves for Lady Day are exquisite, sensitively drawn homages, capturing the subtle essence of the music in a way that no other graphic artist has come close to matching.

My jazz obsession has never stopped growing as I plunge in deeper and discover new people to admire, whether young or old, dead or alive. There are more artistes to welcome to Darktown, to be played on the Mermaid Café jukebox, even making guest appearances at the Starlight Hotel. Bird has moved there, tenor sax in hand. And Anita O'Day can be heard singing 'Quel Temps fait-il à Paris?' from her bedroom window at Hulot's seaside establishment. Fine and Mellow, geeks and groovers, with No Room for Squares …

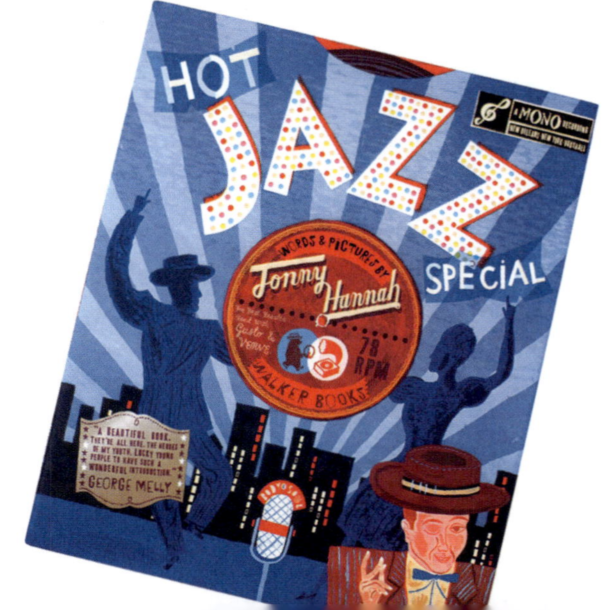

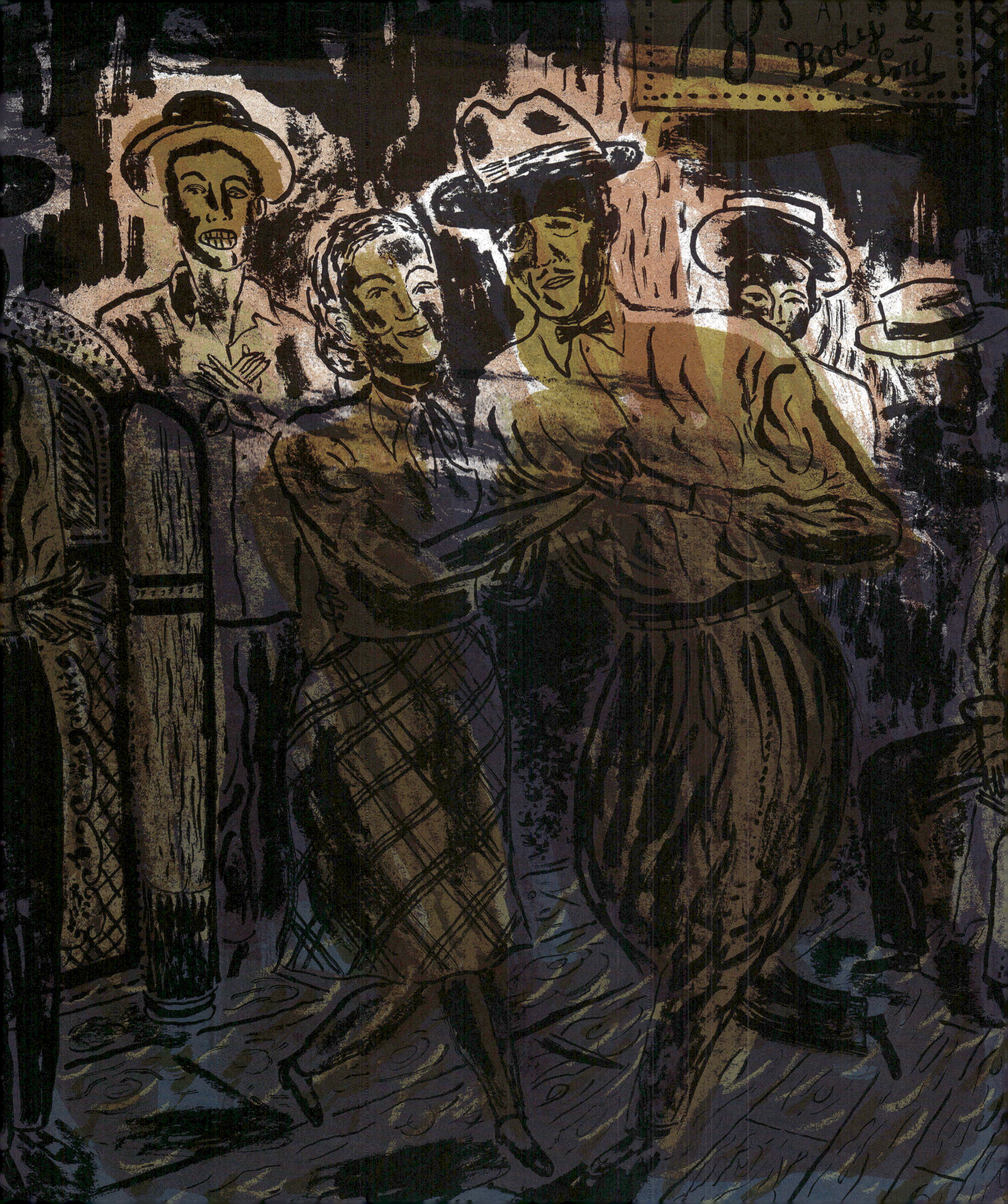
Body & Soul

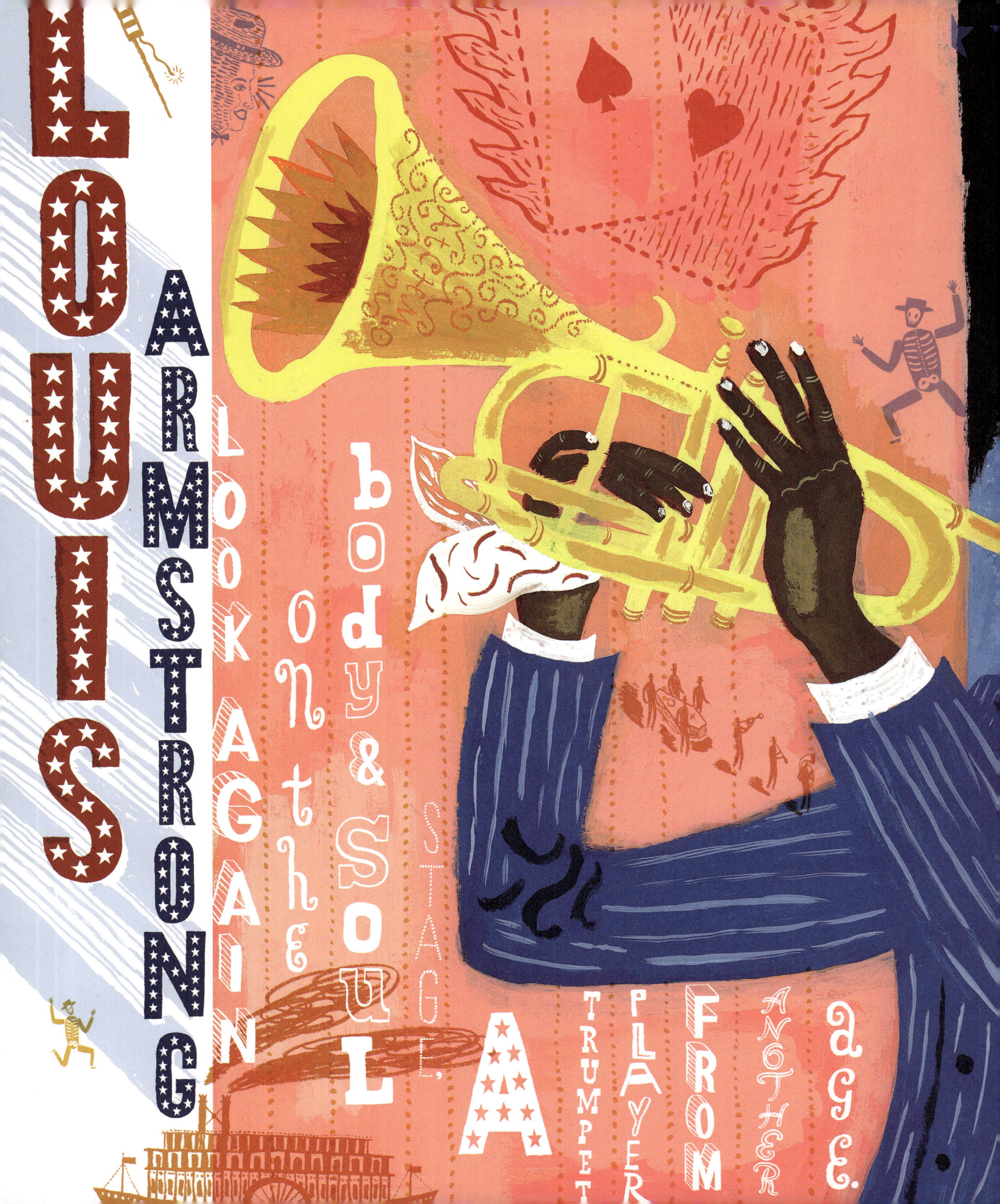
LOUIS
ARMSTRONG
LOOK AGAIN
on the
body & SOUL
STAGE,
A
TRUMPET
PLAYER
FROM
ANOTHER
age.

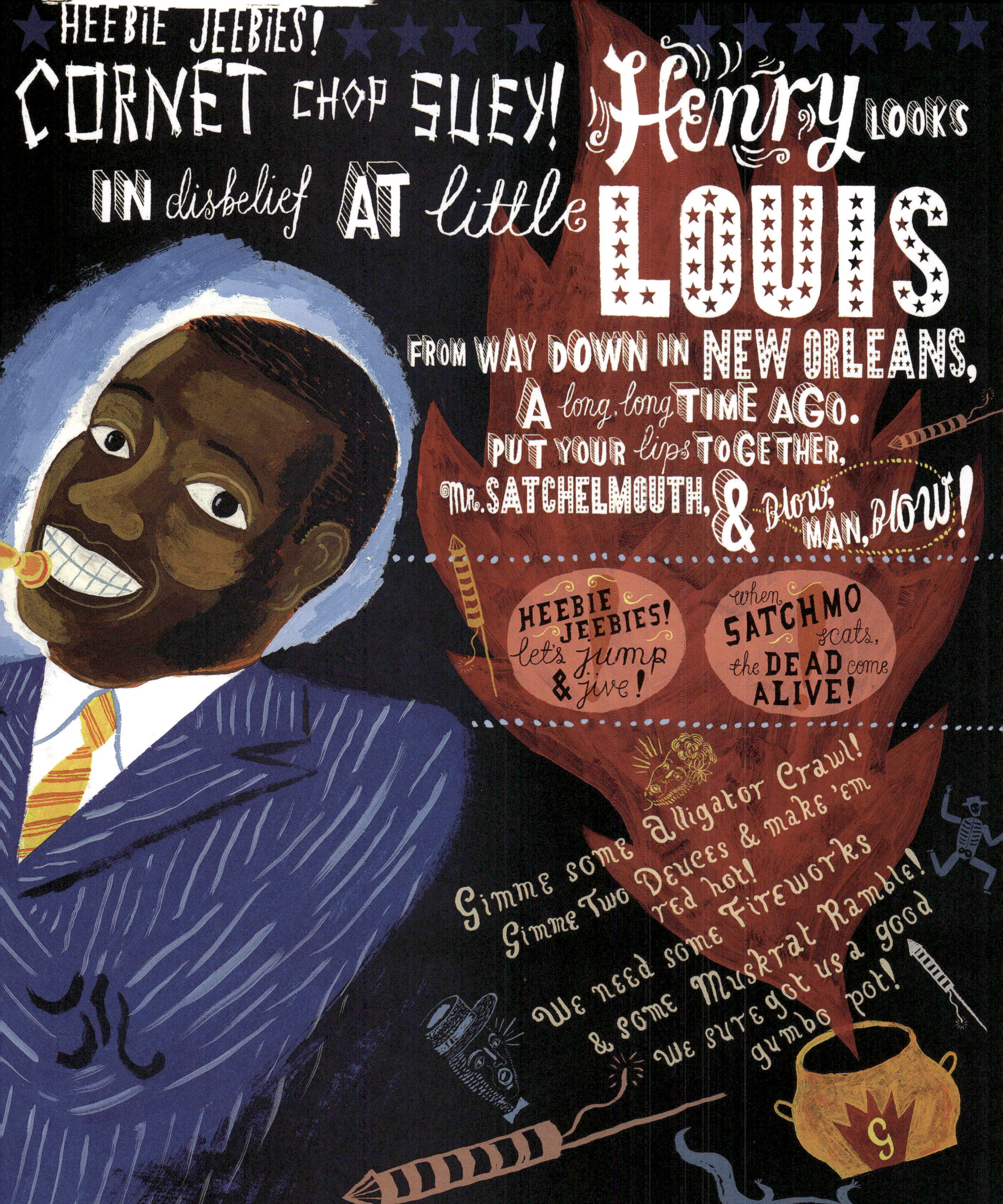
HEEBIE JEEBIES!
CORNET CHOP SUEY! Henry LOOKS IN disbelief AT little LOUIS FROM WAY DOWN IN NEW ORLEANS, A long, long TIME AGO.
PUT YOUR lips TOGETHER, Mr. SATCHELMOUTH, & blow, MAN, blow!
HEEBIE JEEBIES! let's jump & jive!
when SATCHMO scats, the DEAD come ALIVE!
Gimme some Alligator Crawl!
Gimme Two Deuces & make 'em red hot!
We need some Fireworks & some Muskrat Ramble!
We sure got us a good gumbo pot!

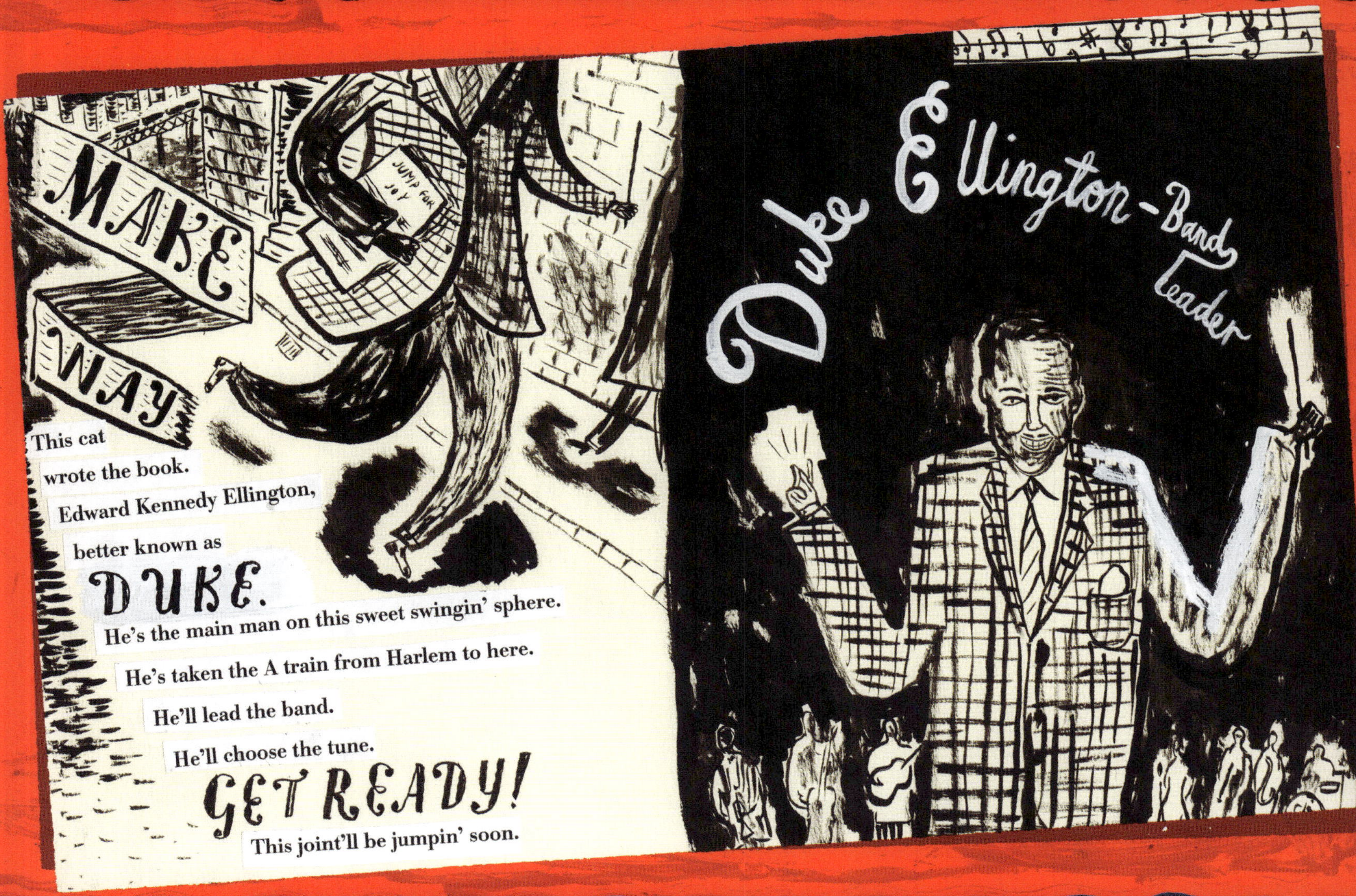

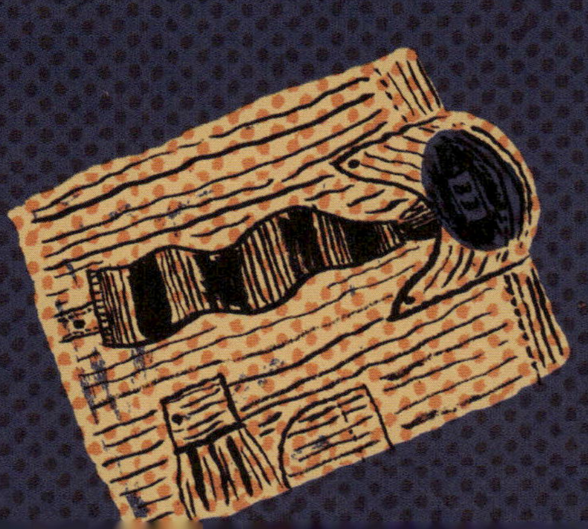

MAKE WAY

This cat
wrote the book.
Edward Kennedy Ellington,
better known as
DUKE.
He's the main man on this sweet swingin' sphere.
He's taken the A train from Harlem to here.
He'll lead the band.
He'll choose the tune.
GET READY!
This joint'll be jumpin' soon.

Duke Ellington - Band Leader

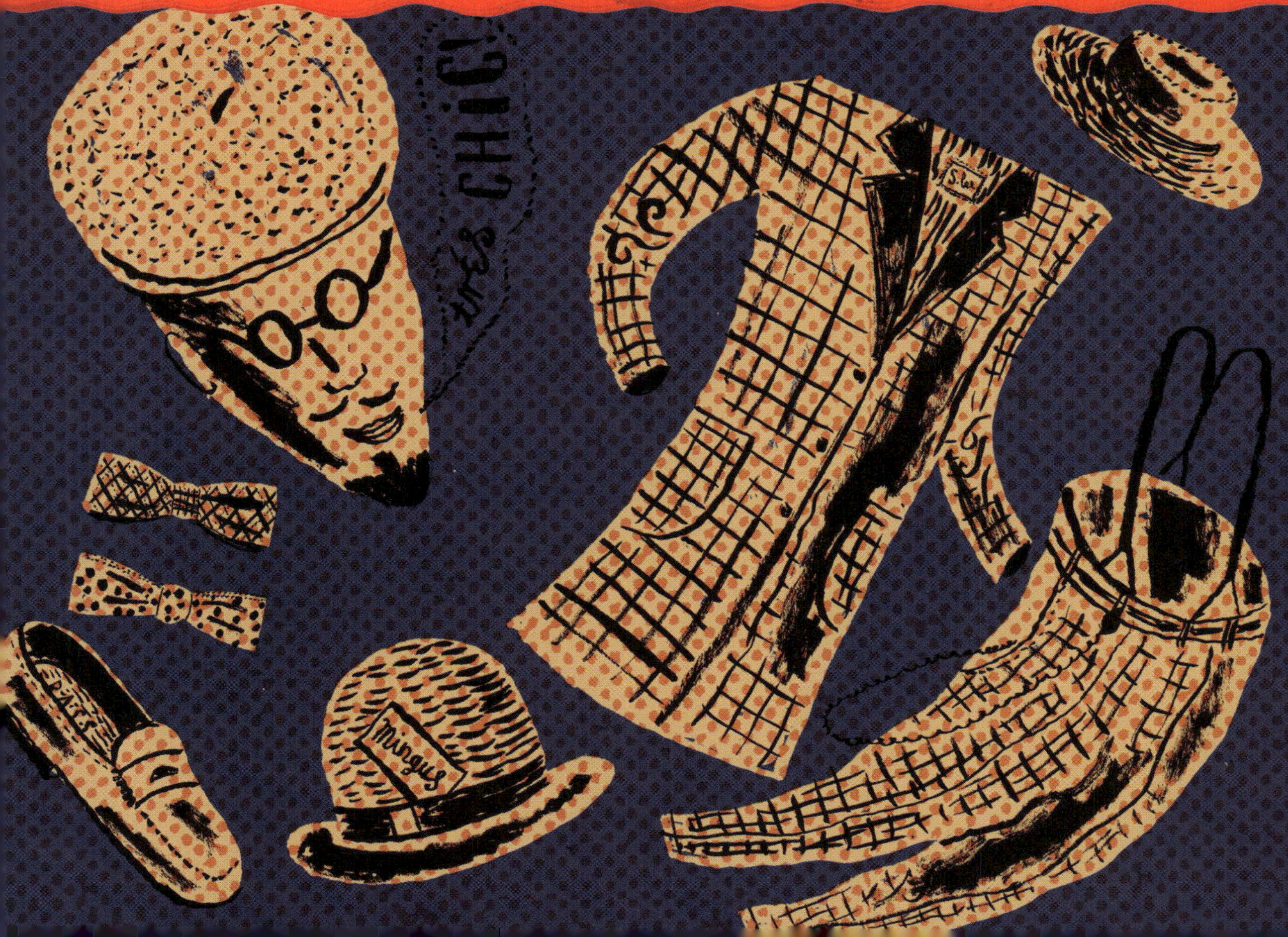

très CHIC!

Some of the earlier drawings I did of all my jazz heroes. They never made it into the book, but were such fun to do. And a page from one of the many dummy books I made on my journey to the Body & Soul Café.

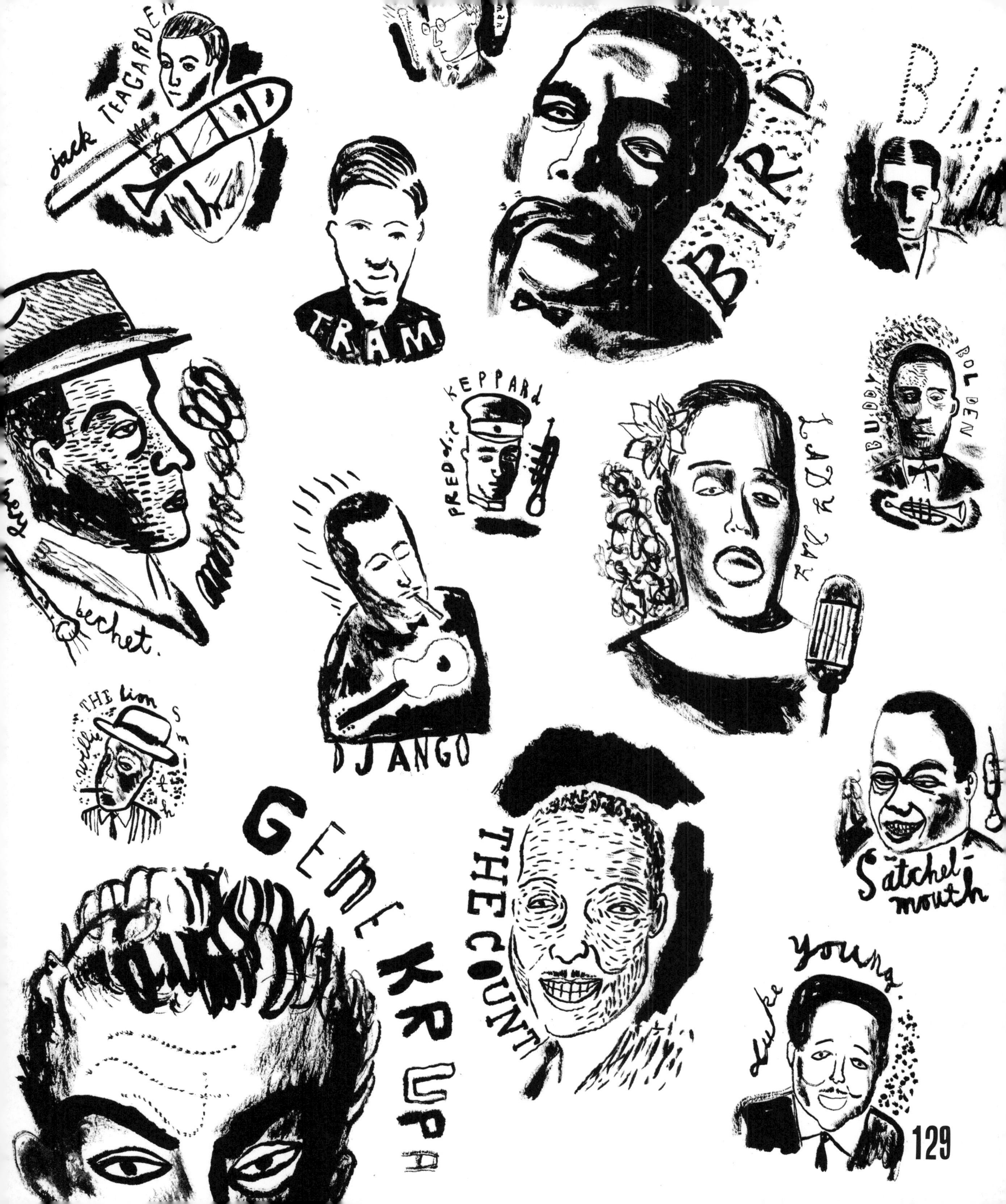
jack TEAGARDEN
TRAM
BIRD
KEPPARd
BUDDY BOLDEN
LADY DAY
bechet.
DJANGO
THE lion
willie
GENE KRUPA
THE COUNT
Satchel-mouth
young

DUKE ELLINGTON
and his FAMOUS ORCHEST RA
JUAN TIZOL
JOE "TRICKY SAM" NANTON
CHARLES "COOTIE" WILLIAMS
ARTHUR WHETSOL
FREDDIE

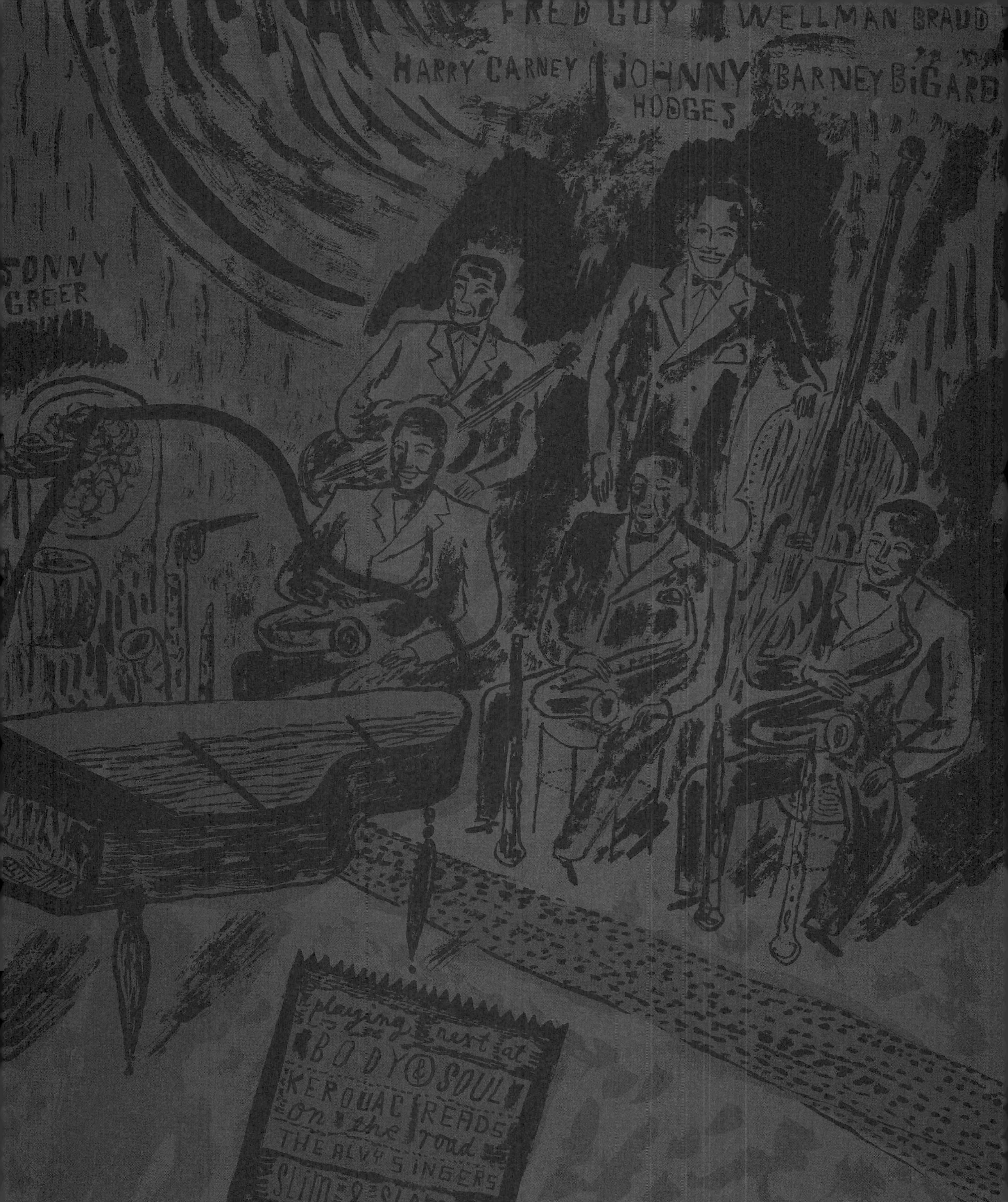
FRED GUY
WELLMAN BRAUD
HARRY CARNEY
JOHNNY HODGES
BARNEY BIGARD
SONNY GREER
playing next at
BODY & SOUL
KEROUAC READS
on the road
THE ALVY SINGERS

when i pressed play for the first time, on mingus AH UM, i had no idea of the world i was entering into, & unleashing into a semi-detached in Shirley, Southampton. Organised Chaos. & symphonic anarchy. Mingus, oh mingus, your times came along at just the right time. A homage to the past, & a great big pointy finger into a future. A future that would include Mingus Oh Yeah!

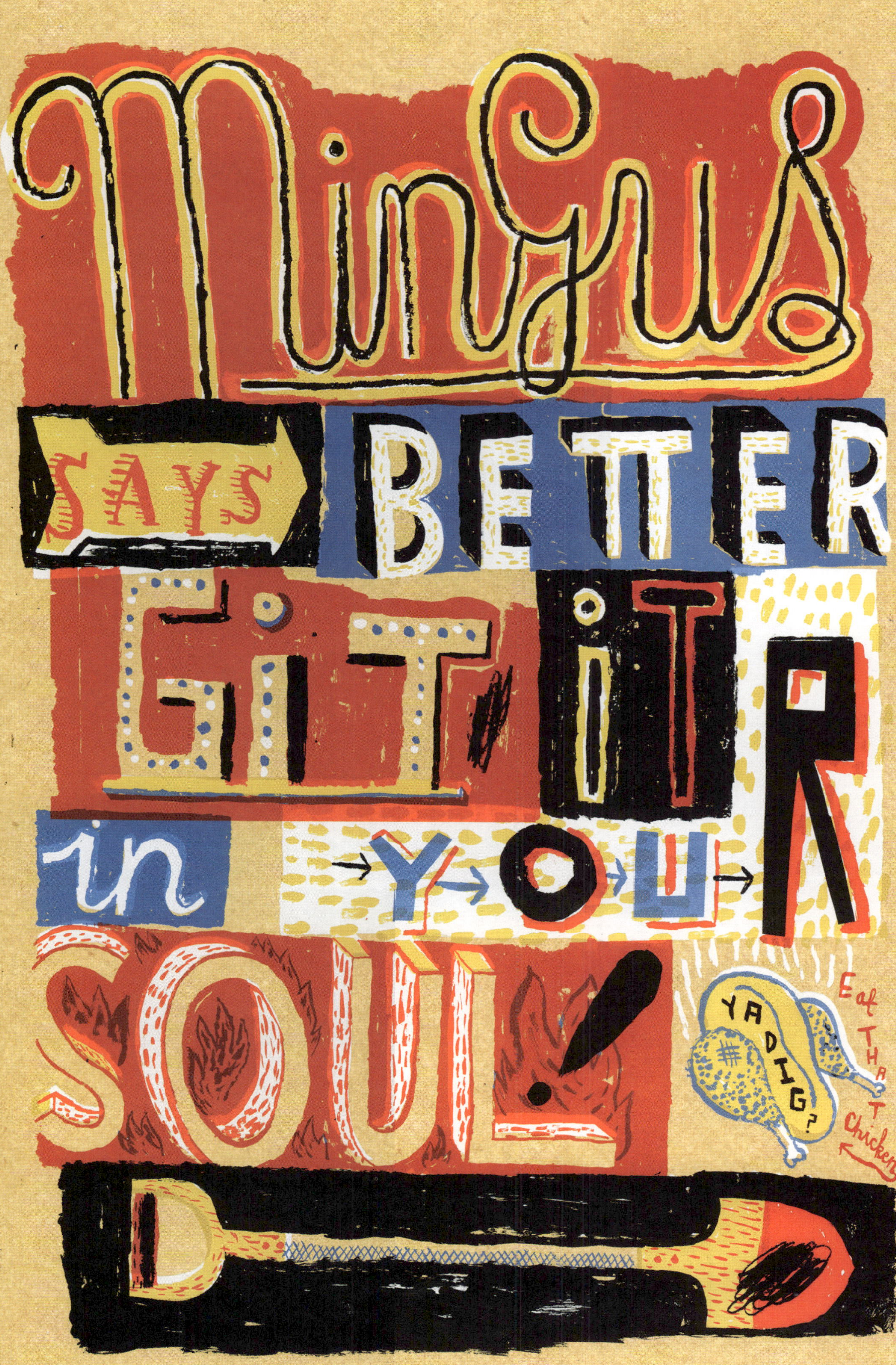


Oh yeah indeed! and i've been
Eating that Chicken ever since....

friday 27th march → double bill *
the Burns Project: Jazz in the
Scottish Dialect * the Euan Burton
Quartet with Phil Bancroft.
Saturday 28th march → double bill *
Ben Bryden Band *
John Randall Quintet *
Sunday 29th march *
* * John Lowrie
plus Paul
Towndrow
*

the 2nd Dumfries
2009
* the → JAZZ
CLAMJAMPHRIE
27th → 29th march

*
all events
are at So Below, 24 Castle Street,
Dumfries → Scotland * * *

www.dumfriesjazz.com ←

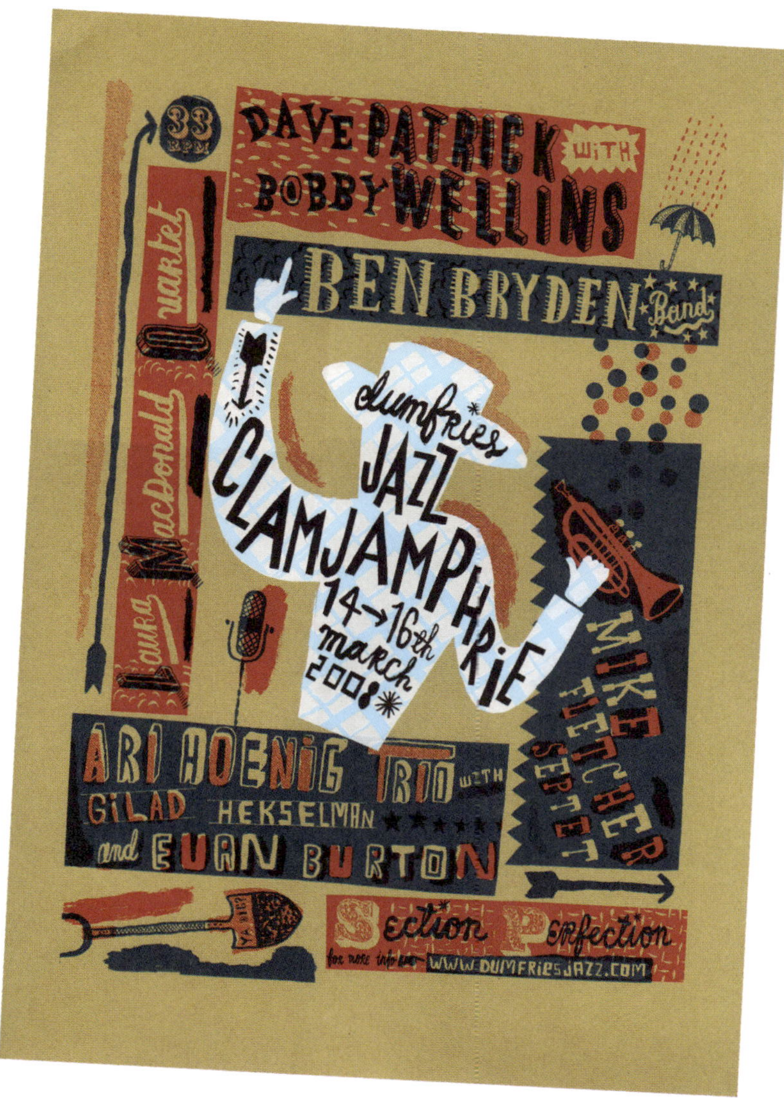


*Hot Jazz Special* led to several unpaid jobs, such as the publicity for the Birmingham International Jazz Festival in 2008, and several projects with the young saxophonist Ben Bryden. By the time I got to doing the cover of his *Bright Noise* CD in 2011, I was tired of drawing instruments, so instead recycled a photo I'd snapped of green circles on a wall at the old art school where I teach. Thanks to Ken Iizuka, who painted them.

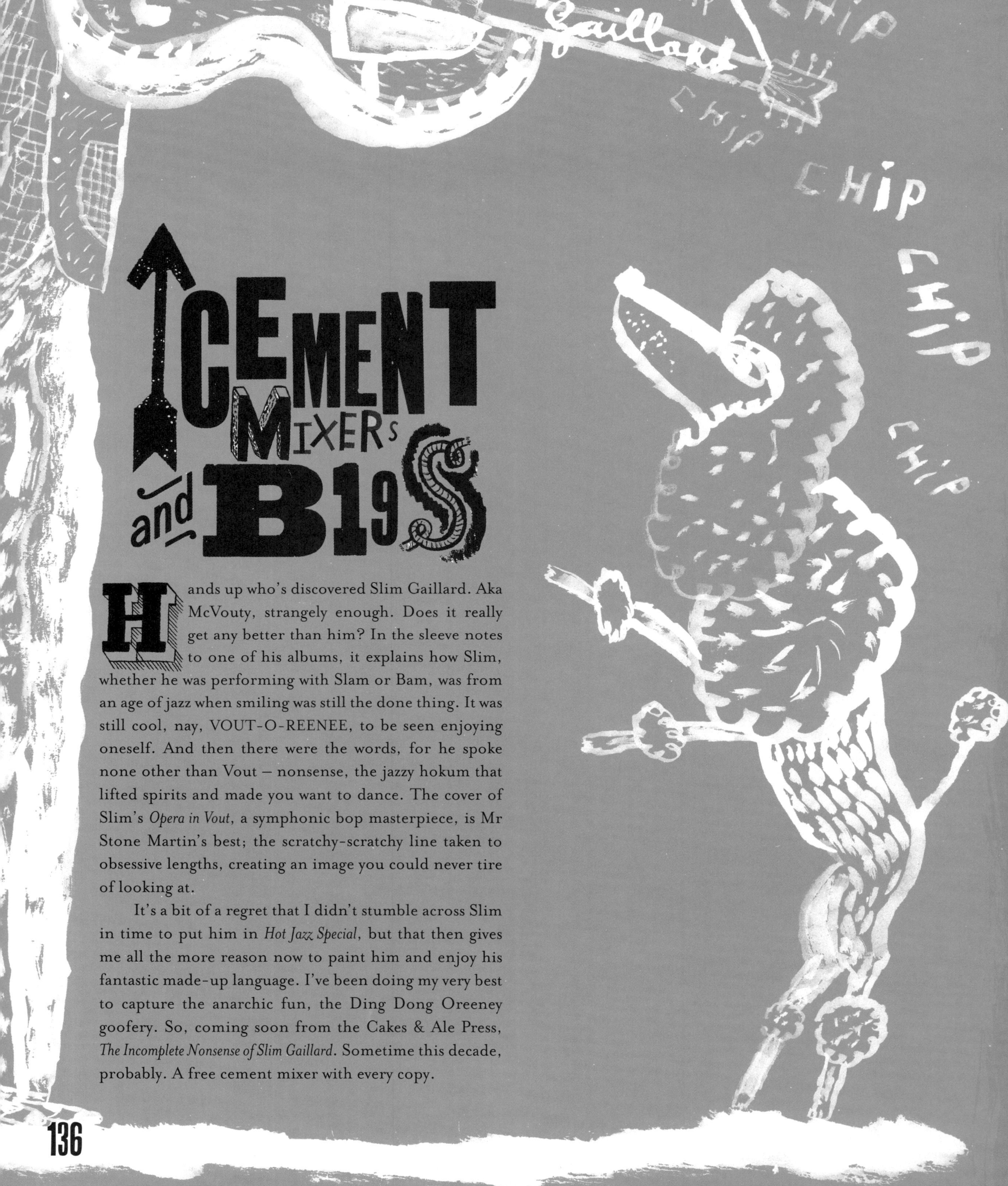


# CEMENT MIXERS and B19S

Hands up who's discovered Slim Gaillard. Aka McVouty, strangely enough. Does it really get any better than him? In the sleeve notes to one of his albums, it explains how Slim, whether he was performing with Slam or Bam, was from an age of jazz when smiling was still the done thing. It was still cool, nay, VOUT-O-REENEE, to be seen enjoying oneself. And then there were the words, for he spoke none other than Vout – nonsense, the jazzy hokum that lifted spirits and made you want to dance. The cover of Slim's *Opera in Vout*, a symphonic bop masterpiece, is Mr Stone Martin's best; the scratchy-scratchy line taken to obsessive lengths, creating an image you could never tire of looking at.

It's a bit of a regret that I didn't stumble across Slim in time to put him in *Hot Jazz Special*, but that then gives me all the more reason now to paint him and enjoy his fantastic made-up language. I've been doing my very best to capture the anarchic fun, the Ding Dong Oreeney goofery. So, coming soon from the Cakes & Ale Press, *The Incomplete Nonsense of Slim Gaillard*. Sometime this decade, probably. A free cement mixer with every copy.

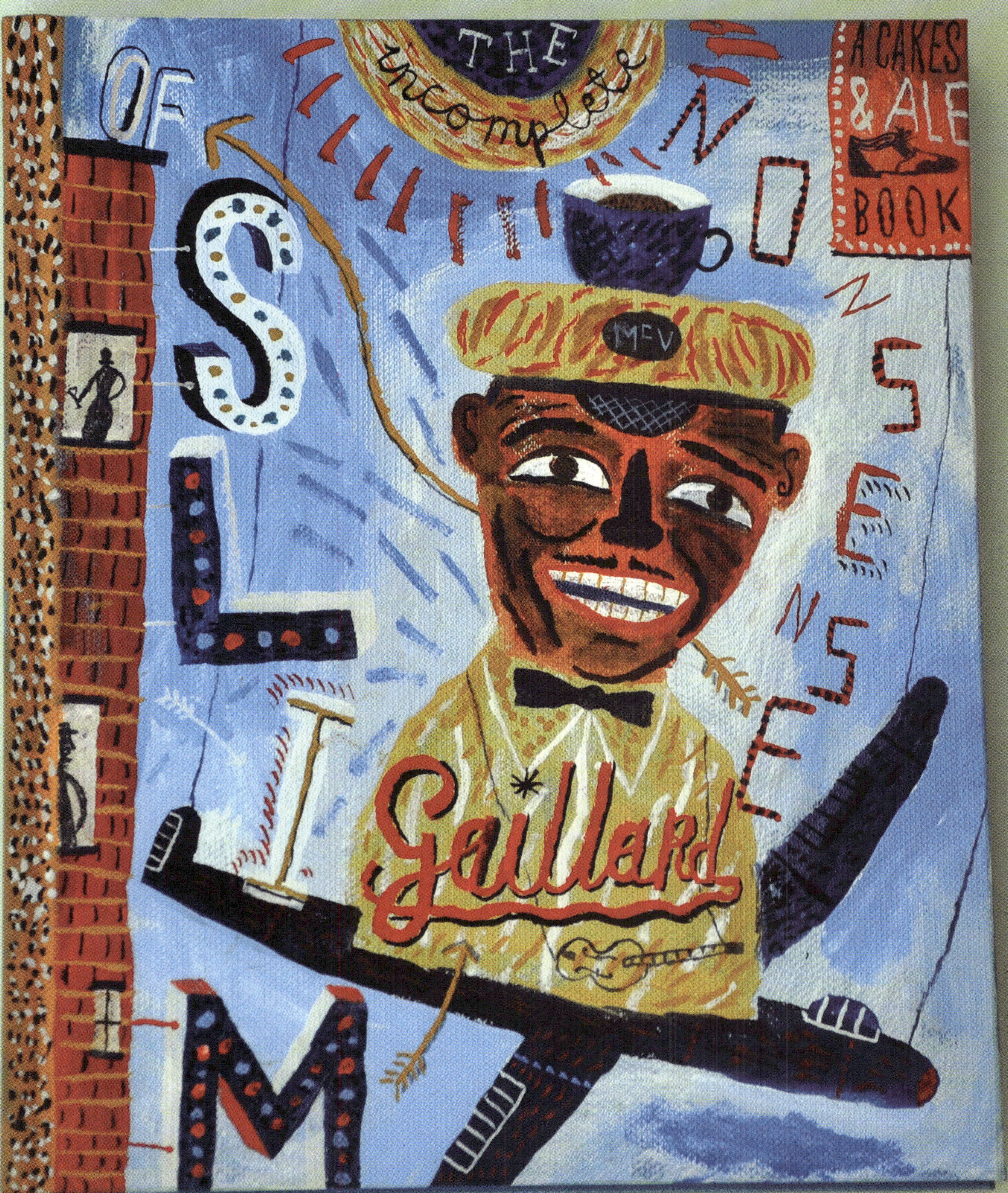
THE
incomplete
NONSENSE
OF
SLIM
Gaillard
A CAKES & ALE BOOK
McV

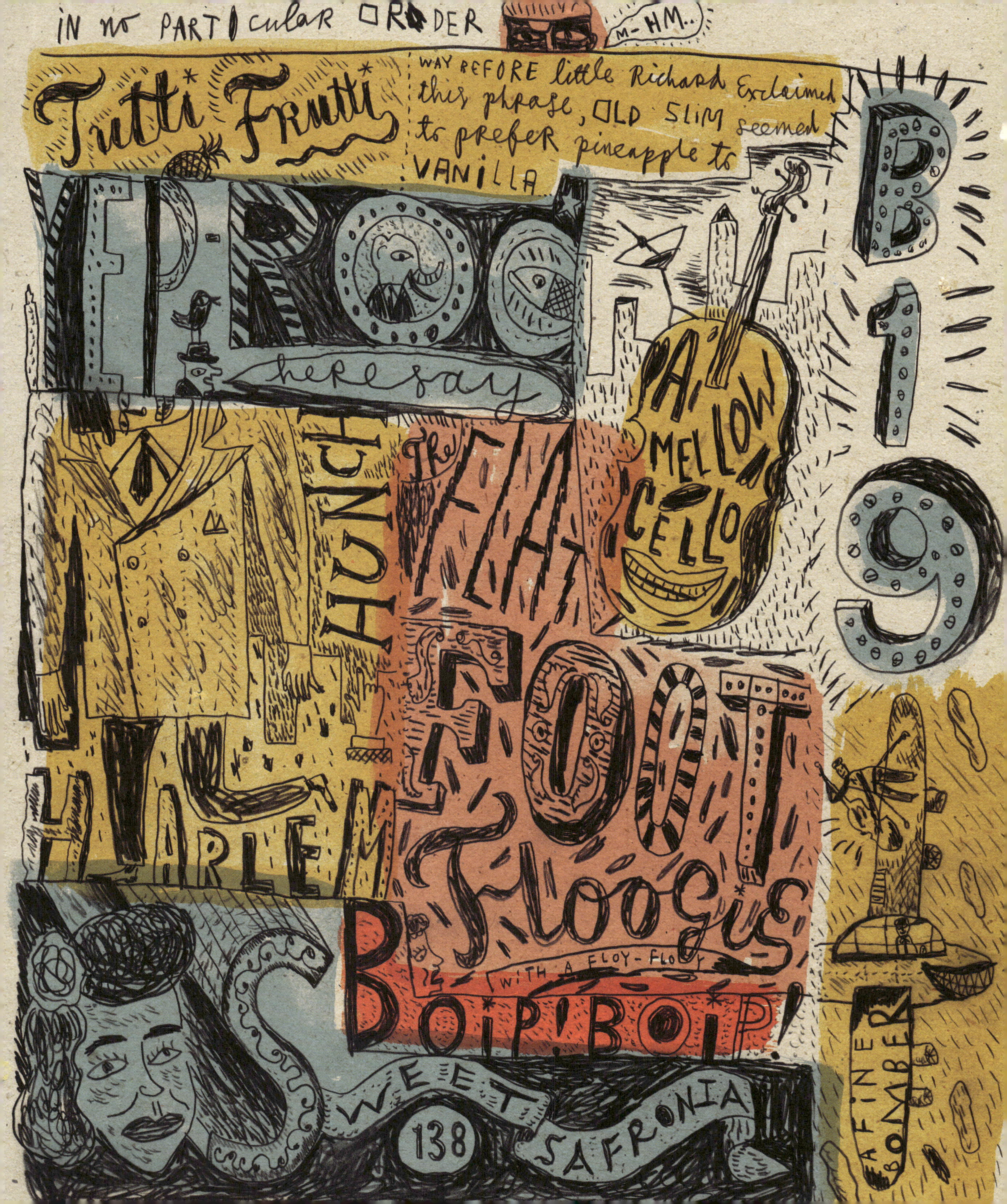
IN NO PARTICULAR ORDER
M-HM..
Tutti Frutti
WAY BEFORE little Richard Exclaimed this phrase, OLD SLIM seemed to prefer pineapple to VANILLA
B
1
9
heresay
A MELLOW CELLO
HUNCH
The FLAT FOOT Floogie
WITH A FLOY-FLOY
HARLEM
BOP! BOP!
SWEET SAFRONIA
138
A FINE BOMBER

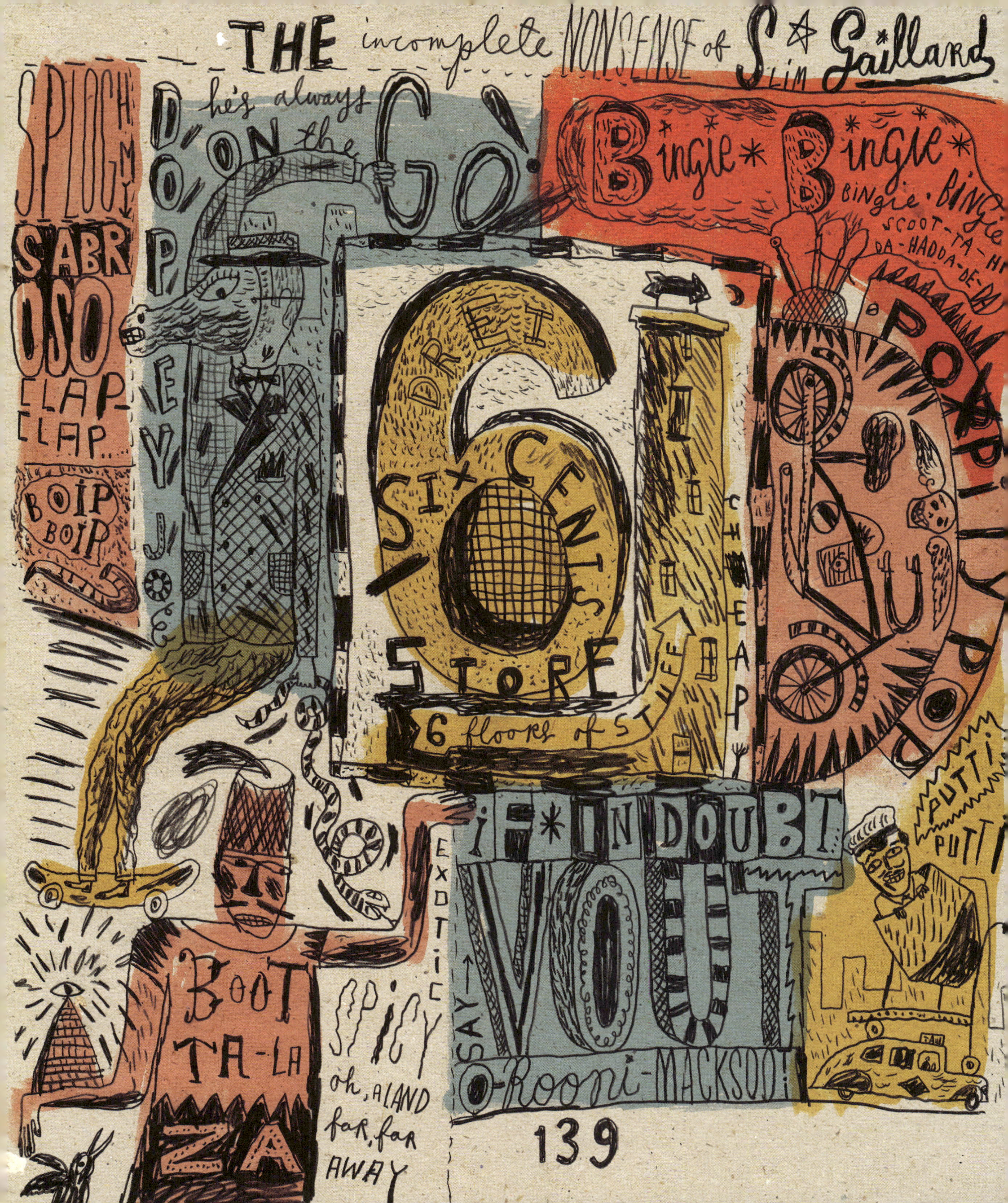
THE incomplete NONSENSE of Slim Gaillard
he's always ON the GO!
DOPEY JOE
SABROSO
CLAP-CLAP...
BOIP BOIP
Bingie*Bingie
Bingie·BINGie
SCOOT-TA-H
DA-HADDA-DE-DA
DREI
6
SIX CENTS STORE
6 floors of STUFF
CHEAP
iF*IN DOUBT
VOUT
SAY→
o-Rooni-MACKSOOT!
PUTTI PUTTI
BOOT TA-LA ZA
SPICY
EXOTIC
oh, ALAND far, far AWAY

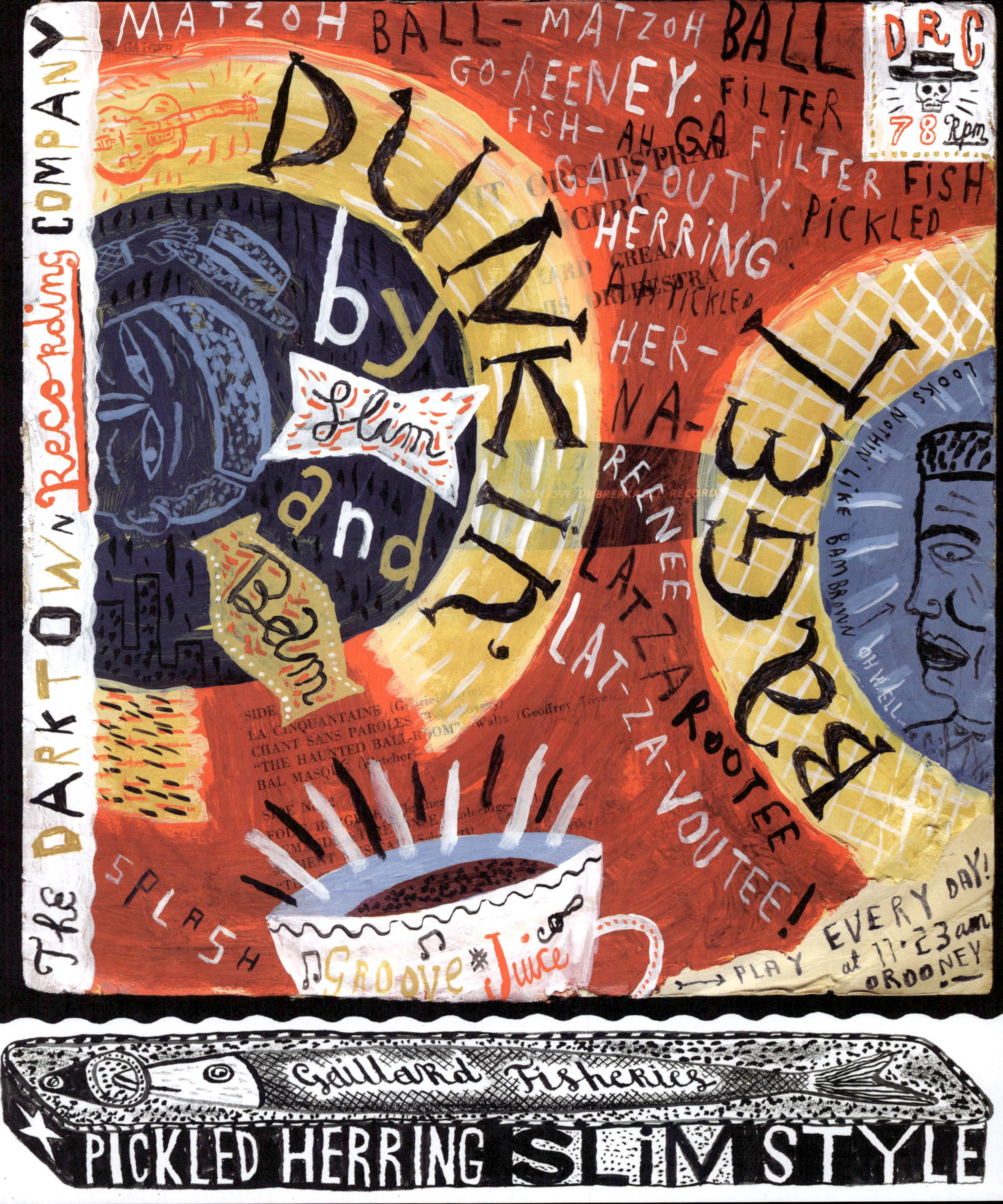

The DARKTOWN Recording COMPANY

DRC 78 Rpm

MATZOH BALL- MATZOH BALL
GO-REENEY. FILTER
FISH- AH GA FILTER FISH
GAVOUTY. PICKLED
HERRING.
PICKLED
HER-
NA-
REENEE
LAT-ZA-ROOTEE
LAT-ZA-VOUTEE!

DUNKIN' BAGEL

by Slim and Bam

LOOKS NOTHIN' LIKE BAM BROWN OH WELL...

SPLASH

Groove Juice

PLAY EVERY DAY! at 11:23 am
ROONEY

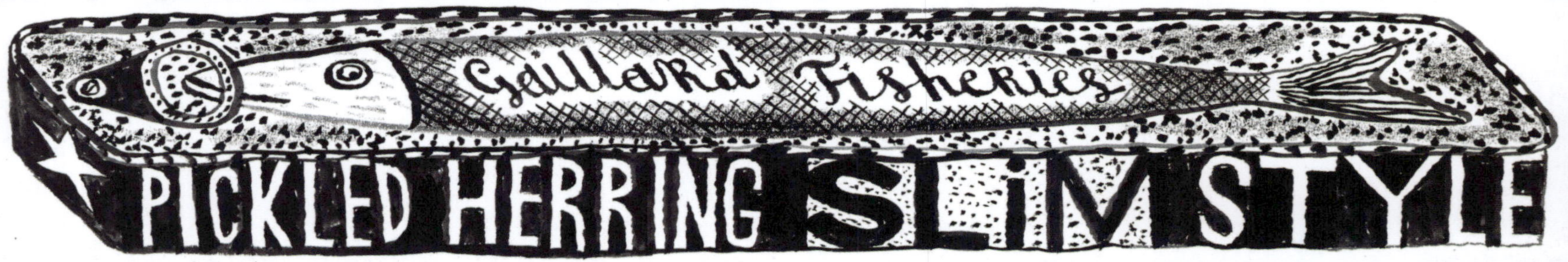

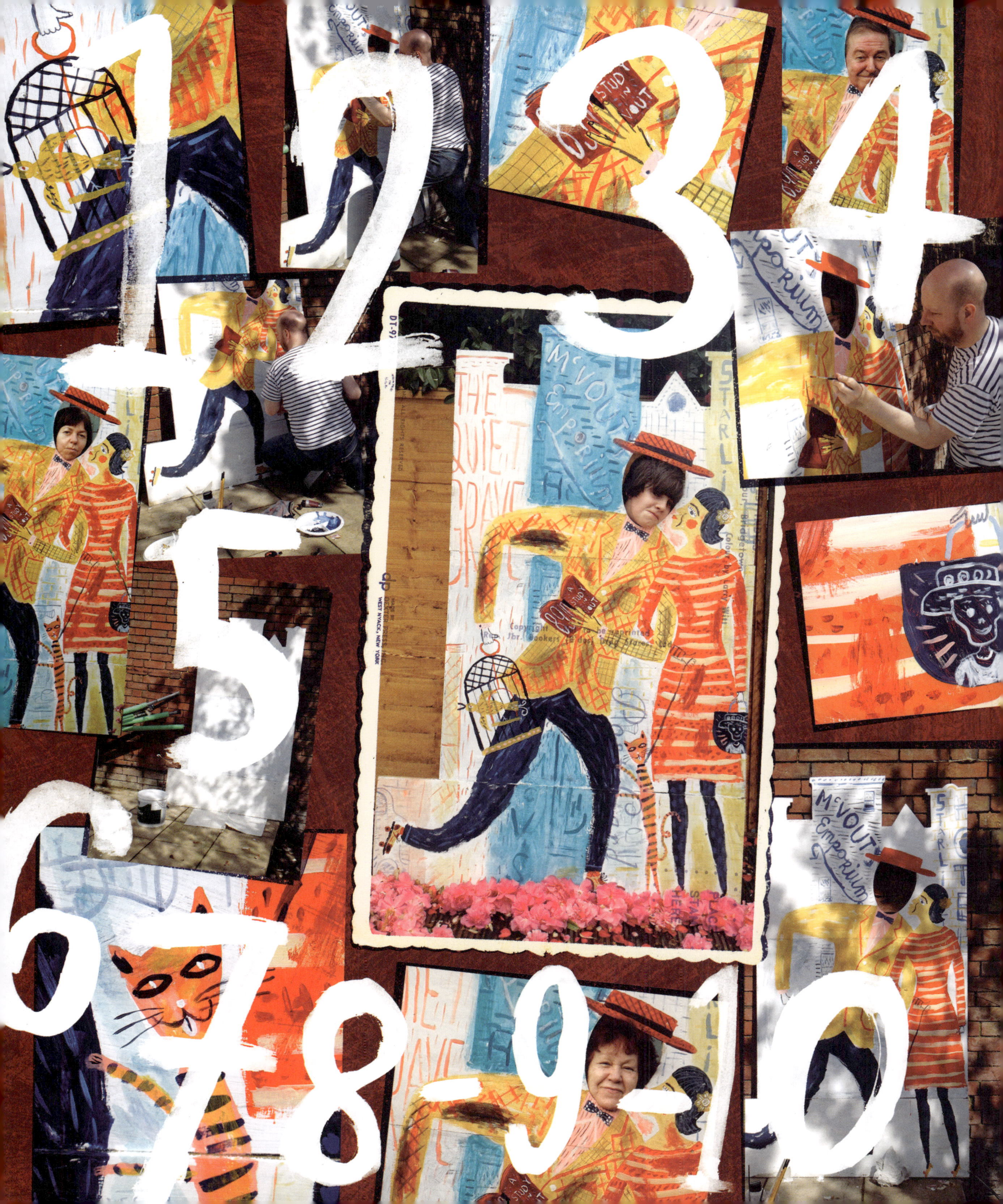

1 2 3 4
5
6 7 8-9-10
McVOUT Emporium
THE QUIET GRAVE
A STUDY IN VOUT

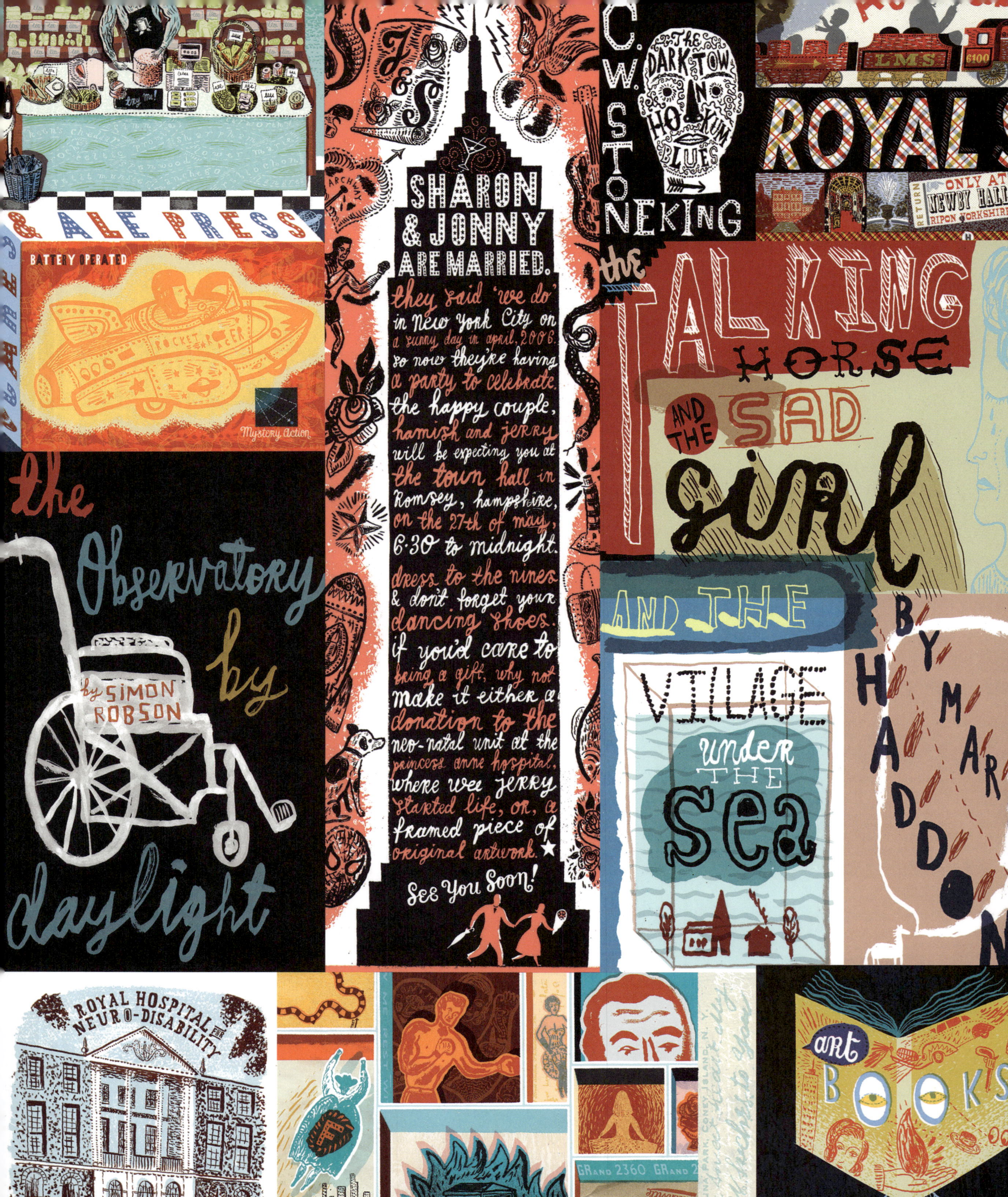

& ALE PRESS
BATTERY OPERATED
Mystery Action
the Observatory by daylight
by SIMON ROBSON
SHARON & JONNY ARE MARRIED.
they said 'we do' in New York City on a sunny day in april, 2006. so now they're having a party to celebrate the happy couple. hamish and jerry will be expecting you at the town hall in Romsey, hampshire, on the 27th of may, 6.30 to midnight.
dress to the nines & don't forget your dancing shoes. if you'd care to bring a gift, why not make it either a donation to the neo-natal unit at the princess anne hospital, where wee jerry started life, or, a framed piece of original artwork.
See You Soon!
C. W. STONEKING
THE DARKTOWN HOKUM BLUES
ROYAL
LMS
ONLY AT NEWBY HALL RIPON YORKSHIRE
RETURN
the TALKING HORSE AND THE SAD girl
AND THE VILLAGE under THE sea
BY MARK HADDON
ROYAL HOSPITAL FOR NEURO-DISABILITY
GRAND 2360 GRAND
art BOOKS

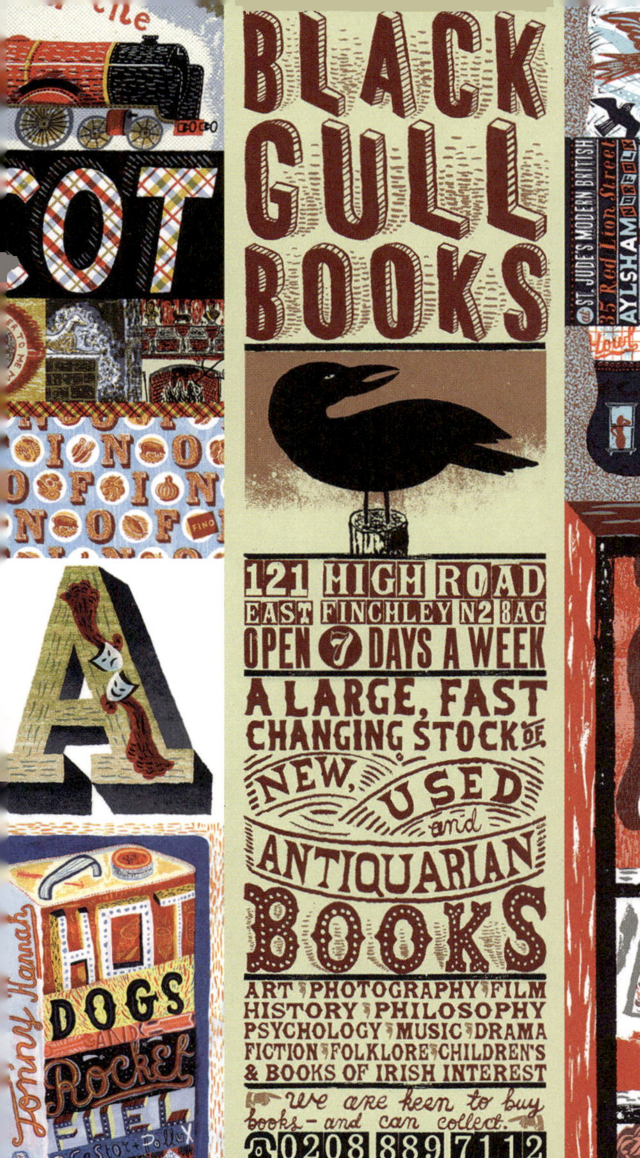


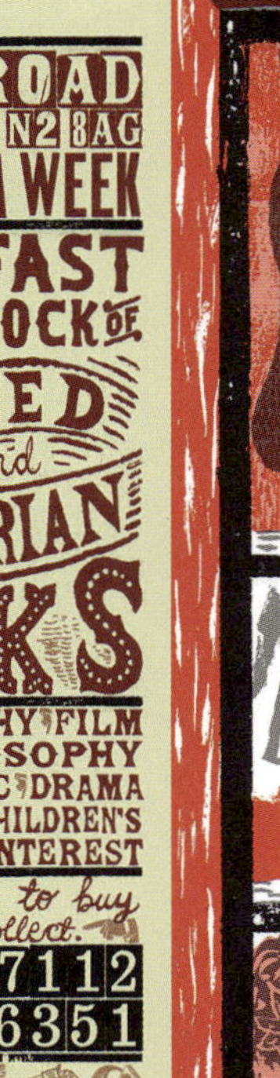

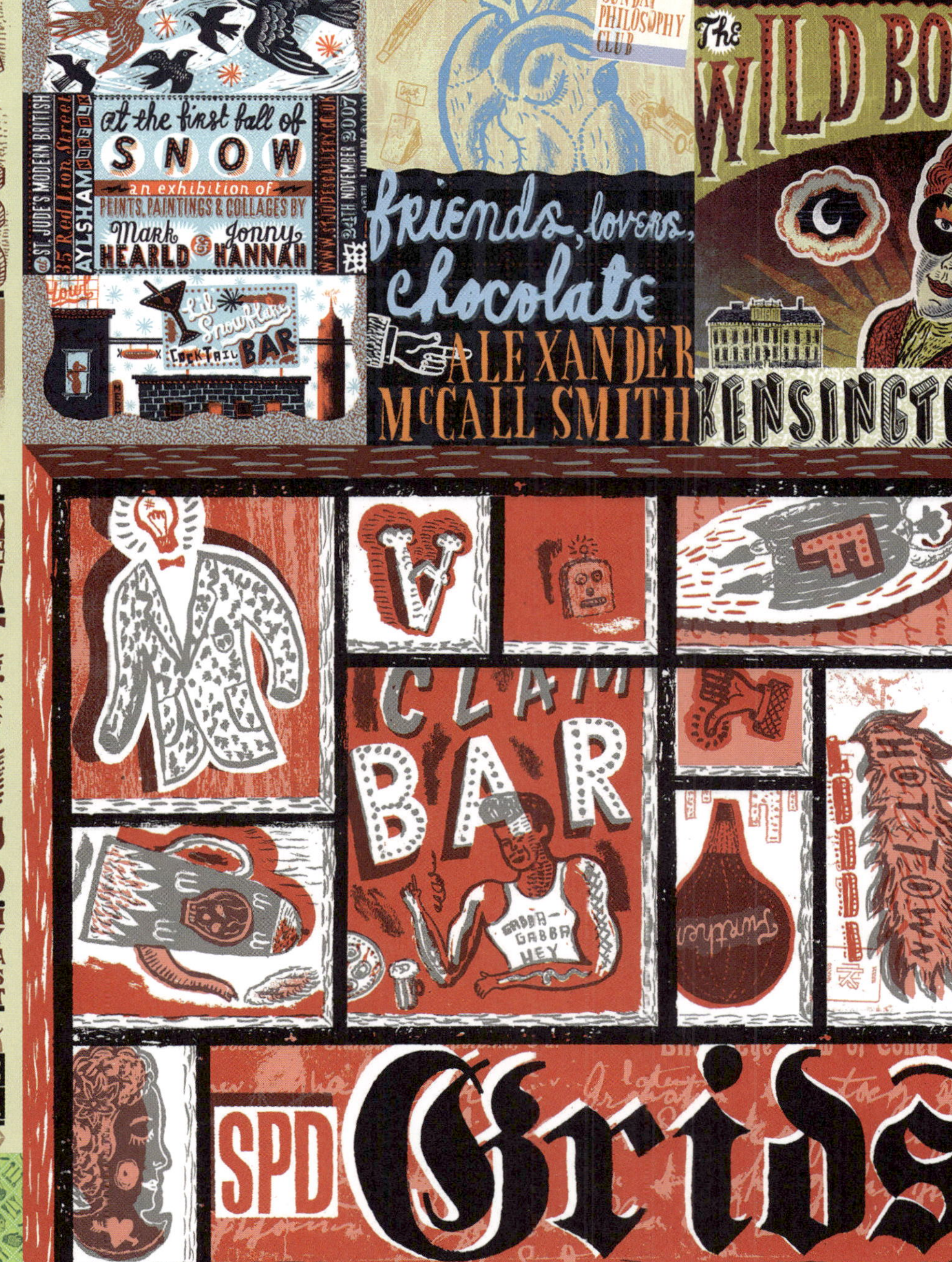


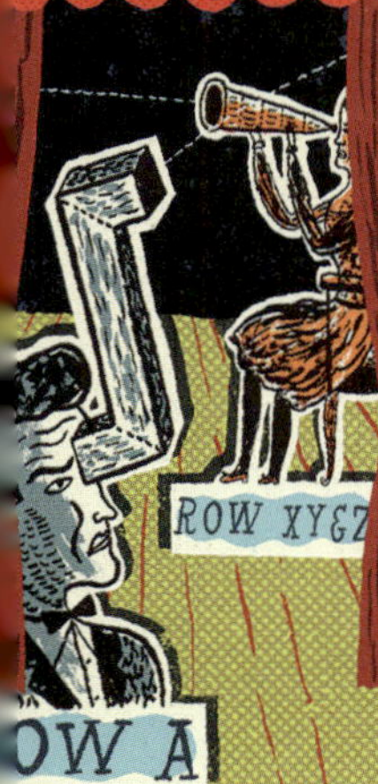



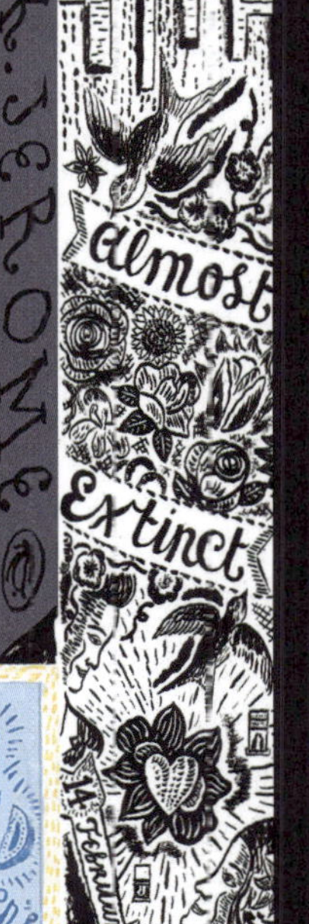


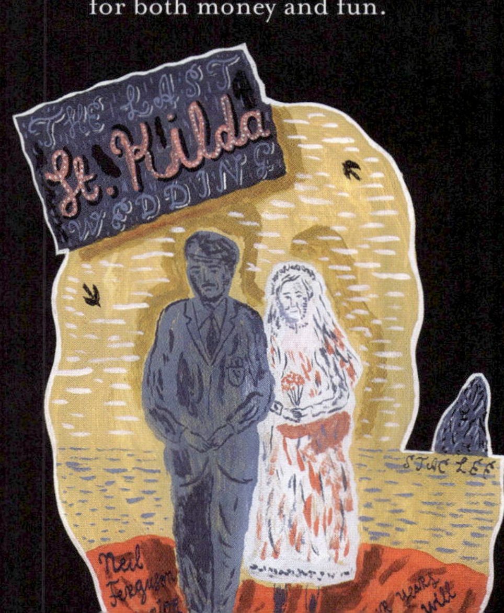


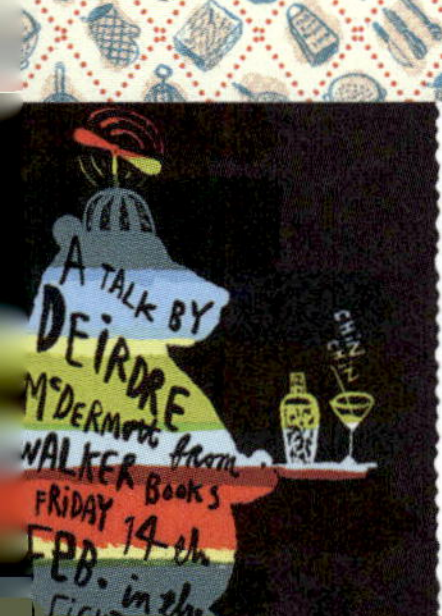


A miscellany of stuff, ranging from our wedding invitation to a poster for the Wild Boy's Ball – a fraction of my output as an illustrator, for both money and fun.

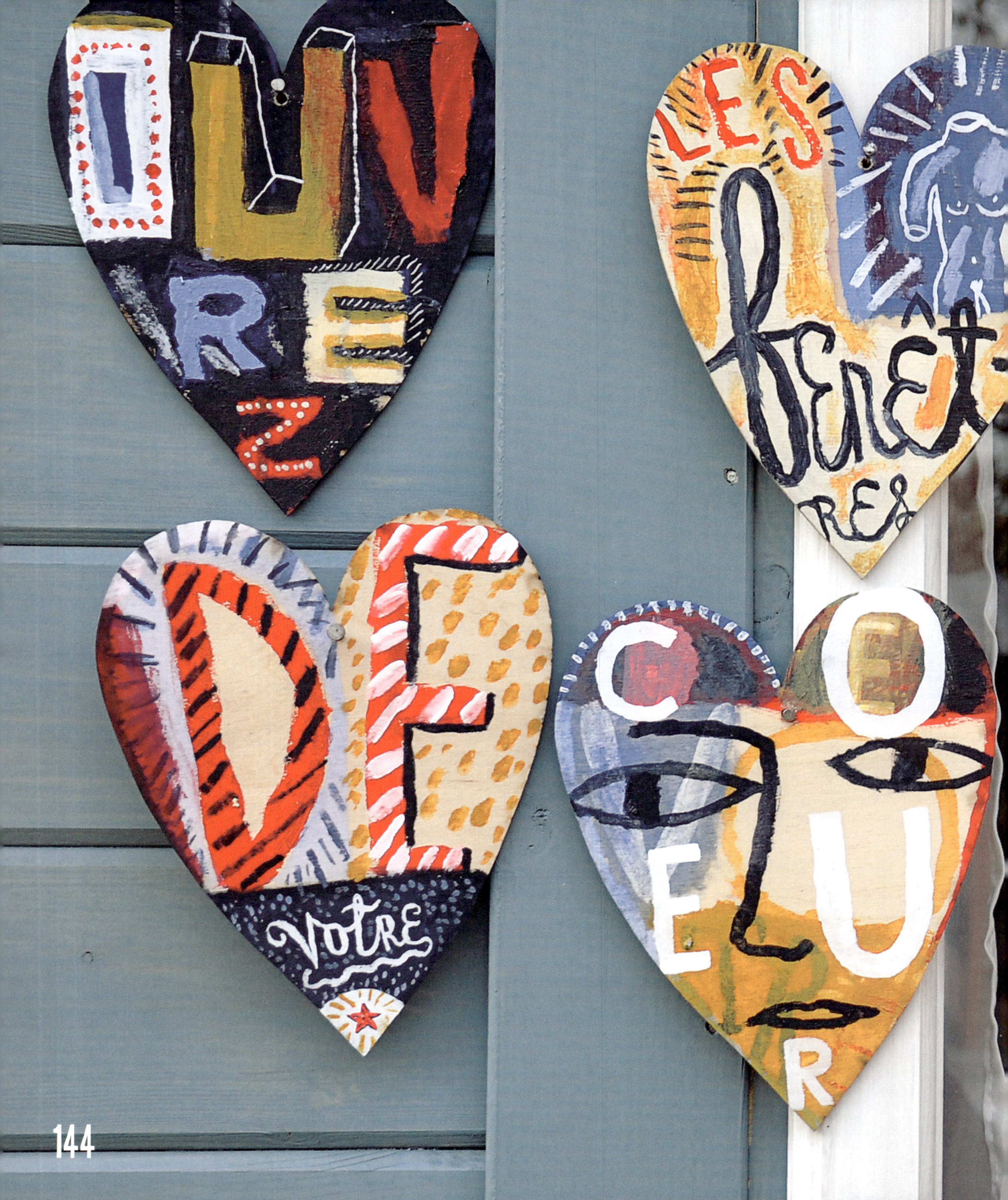
OUV
REZ
LES
fenêt-
RES
DE
votre
COEUR

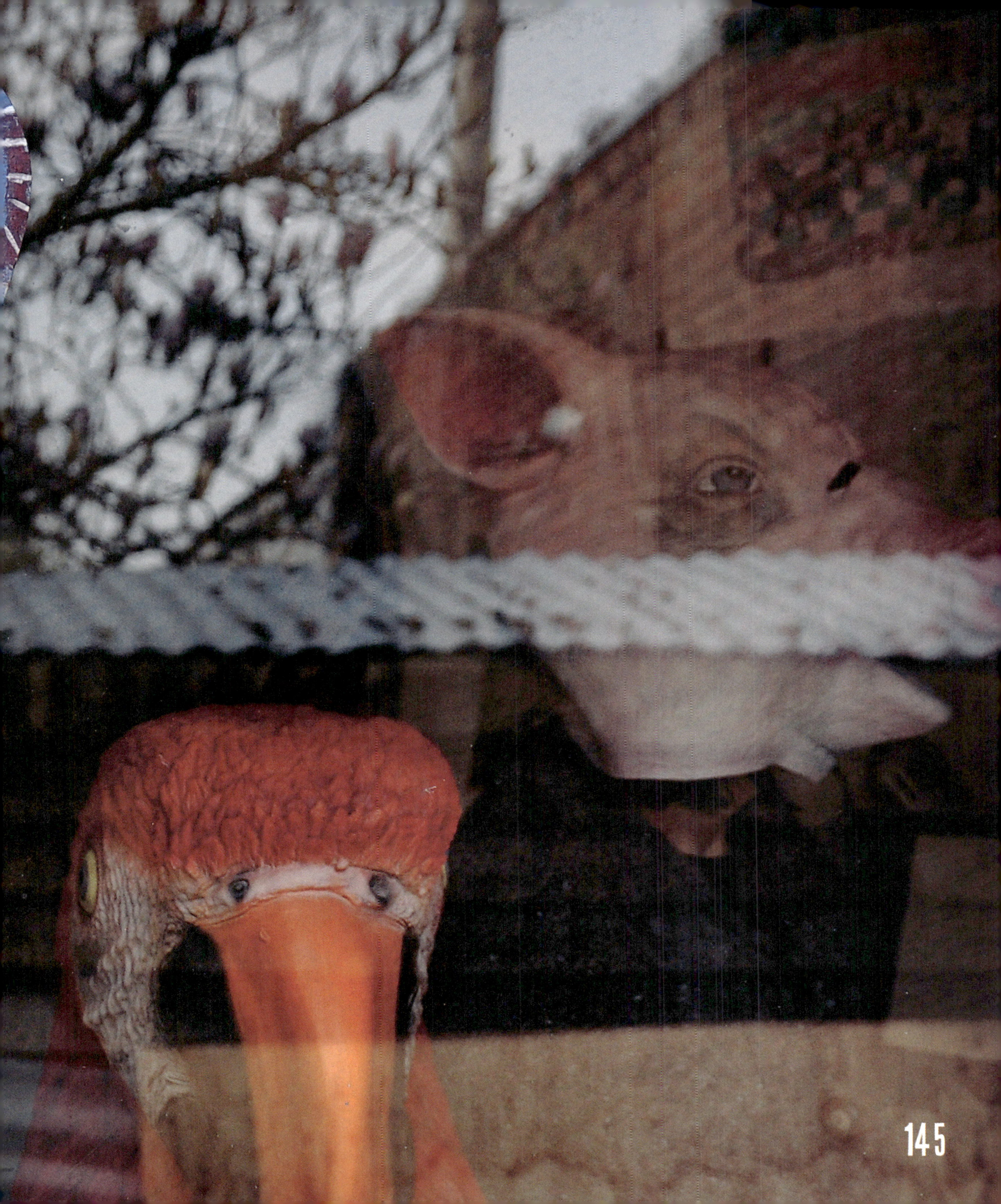

# Ouvrez les fenêtres de votre coeur

'Queequeg was a native of Kokovoko, an island far away to the West and South. It is not down in any map; true places never are.' I've always been fascinated by this paragraph. Partly because it's from one of the earlier chapters in *Moby-Dick*, so I have actually read it; but mainly because I still don't know what it means. If true places aren't down on any maps, then where on earth are we all right now? I don't have any dramatic or romantic stories of moving around or being displaced, but I have made several homes over the years. Mainly studies and work have led me here and there, always travelling south, nesting where it felt right.

I once had a fantasy of living in Brooklyn. I fell in love with Coney Island the minute I got off the subway at Surf Avenue. The Atlantic, the run-down rides and, of course, Nathan's hot dogs. It all clicked, and 'Body and Soul' (the Benny Goodman Trio version, naturally) became the theme tune that day, as I first dipped my toes in the sea.

Then Paris became the place for me, and it still is, I suppose. We rented a small apartment near the Sacré-Cœur and in the next few days trundled all over the city, even with Jerry and his chickenpox. We watched toy boats sail on the pond at the Jardin du Luxembourg; went up the Eiffel Tower on a chilly Sunday morning; and showed Hamish the *Mona Lisa*, which you couldn't help but find impressive. On my second visit, I discovered chic street art on the rue de Rivoli and popped into Shakespeare and Company to buy some Jacques Prévert poetry. And there it was, a volume with my name on it.

As I get older, however, I realize so well how much I love the British Isles. I am obsessed with anything that is remotely 'quintessentially English'. From chalk horses to larks ascending, if it has that romance of pots of tea and fine brogue shoes, then take me there and I'm happy. I loved the George Orwell essay about British cookery. Black pudding is a particularly guilty pleasure.

As a displaced Scotsman, I started celebrating Burns Night only after I'd moved to England. It soon struck me that my take on my home country was also becoming some daft, romantic notion, but I somehow managed to avoid kilts, thank God. I feel like a foreigner in the south of England and a tourist when I cross the border, but I enjoy this non-national status, as nationalism in most shapes and forms isn't for me. I've even stopped feeling any enjoyment when the England football team loses. It's a sign, I feel, of my maturity and sophistication towards my old and new homes. Hark at Mr La-di-da ...

In 2012 I had an exhibition in my home town. It felt liberating to walk around the streets of Dunfermline. I knew this place inside out, but was more than delighted to be a stranger, anonymous, outside of it all. I spent several hours in Andrew Carnegie's Pittencrieff Park, known as 'The Glen'. It was bliss. Venturing up slopes and down steps, I realized how lucky I was to grow up in a town with a public space that could rival Central Park in New York, even though it is a fraction of the size. The private view for the show was suitably busy, with the remnants of my old family and a smattering of old friends, but mostly new folks, pleased to see the work.

But I know I feel at home when travelling southward and reaching the Oxford area. I can enjoy being in the south once more. It's time then to get the Betjeman out and play some Vaughan Williams, and dream of a village green that I'll never live near. This feeling is rivalled only when the ferry pulls into the docks at Darktown. I've got to know most of the taxi drivers. And the friends I have here are often about, but not always, which makes for a great mix of happy and quiet times. It's like having a cake and eating it.

Perhaps it'll be in my Darktown house that one day I'll finish Melville's masterpiece. I'll complete my own *Journey to the End of the Night*, then maybe tackle Proust. There'll be time enough to listen to 'Sister Ray', all seventeen minutes of it, every day, just before I nip out for my morning coffee at the Mermaid Café. Perhaps one day I'll tire of it all. Grow up. But I don't think so. No matter how much council tax I have to pay, how much timetabling I have to do and how many unit reports I have to write, Darktown will always be there, waiting, with new residents and more shops just opening on the main street. There's still so much to explore. There's the chain walk, which I've yet to locate. And I've been promised a wee set-sail on the aged Fifie fishing boat *The Reaper*. And why, oh why, am I so reluctant to open up my very own Cakes & Ale Press shop? It's not as if the rents aren't reasonable enough. But having it all is never a good idea. If you have everything you want, what do you mull over when having a beer? King Creosote once said that he hoped he 'might just get by'. That's not a bad plan. Keep this in mind, open the windows of your heart, and take it from there.

But the ferry to Darktown is waiting for me. The return ticket is in my hand the sketchbooks are in my bag, and it won't be long before the bar opens. So think on, and all that other mother jazz. Au revoir.

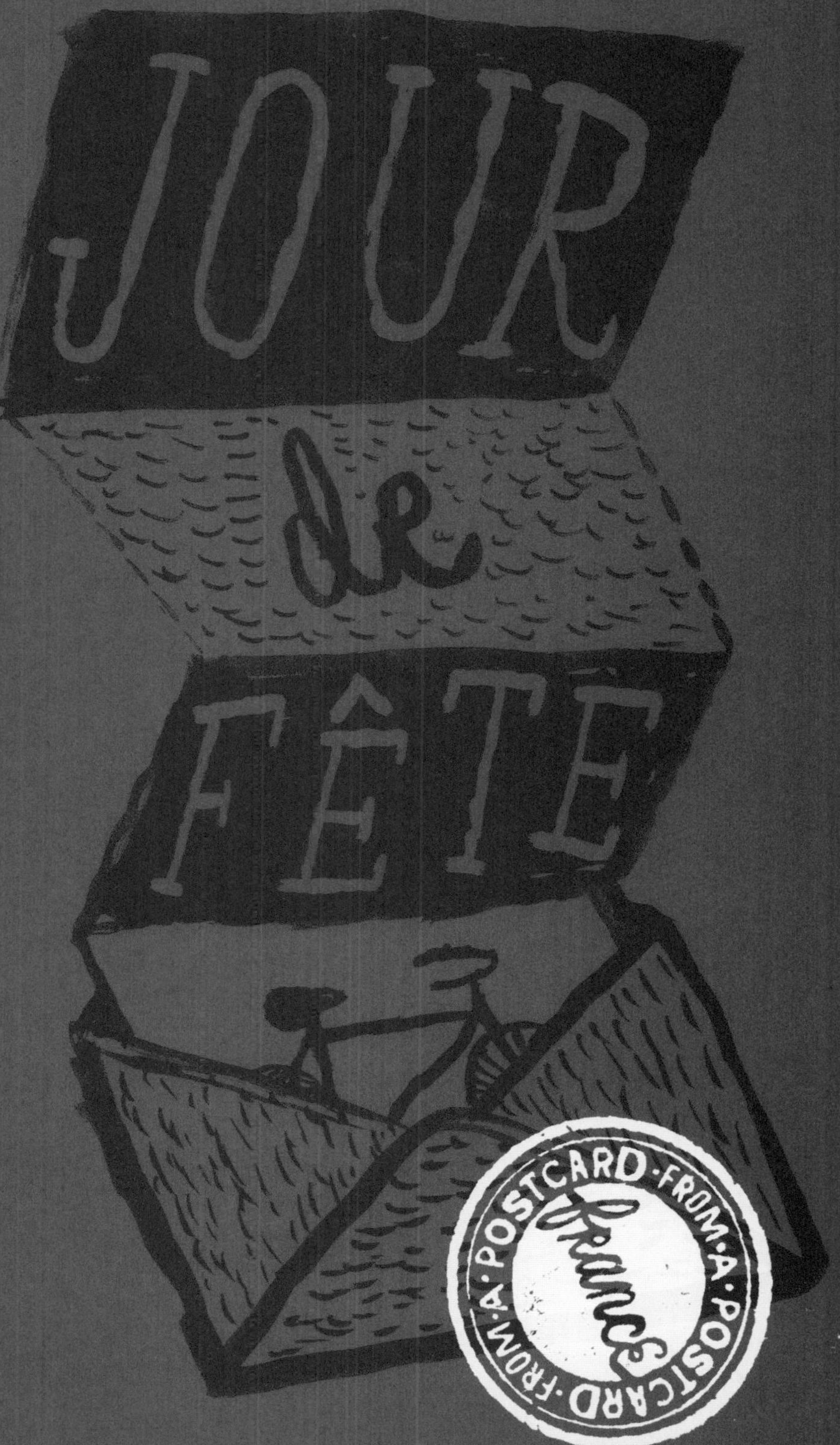

# ONE FOR THE ROAD

BY SHARON HANNAH

A hideaway town.
An aubergine, tan-leather and blue town,
Entrapped with the sea,
Taken past a daydream from me
And you or whoever you find or wanna be.
Everyone has a dark town,
Hidden in the corners of their mind,
And contrary to popular belief,
The sun can sometimes shine,
As Monsieur Hulot pulls his trolley,
Full of wine and cheese,
And people are so polite,
They always say 'please'.
The hills are a willow sage green,
Like faraway lands
In the books you've seen.
The emporiums have golden bells,
When you enter the carved oak doors,
And you must wipe your feet,
On the bristle-matted floors,
Tip your stetson and smile,
Read from your messages,
Don't rush, wait a while …
Go for a coffee in the Mermaid Café,
Walt Whitman's corpse is hanging there,
Decked out for the Old Town Cabaret,
Then on to the Darktown Strutters' Ball,
Follow the masked Pépé le Moko,
Listen for the Slim Gaillard call.
Down the knotted Ash Tree Street,
Search yellow ochre, broken pathways,
That eventually meet,
Leading you to the silvery sea.
The crescent moon is sure to be out,
What strange creatures must be free,
Perhaps they look quite normal,
Like you or me …
Fats Waller misbehavin',
Outside the Jolly Scrimshander Tavern,
Howlin' and a-shoutin',
For that distant flame-red car,
Through the night, moving on,
Travelling afar.
Bat wings, seagulls and fox cries,
Dog barks, doors banging
And cat sighs.
Don't forget the sound of the waves,
Rushing, gurgling, racing with the wind,
In cold frosty air,
That sends you in a trance,
As you paddle and stare.
What music beholds the next hour,
Listen if you dare,
Lady Day, Hank and The Ramones,
Bascom Lamar Lunsford,
Singing 'Dry Bones'.
Frank, Country, and Western Swing,
Bluegrass, Count Basie,
Big Maybelle and C.W. Stoneking.
It rises from the seashell pressed to your ear,
Makes you jive on the sand,
Or shed a smooth tear.
It ascends from Hôtel de la Plage,
A harmonious cacophony,
Rocket-fuel montage,
Of … piano, drum, trumpet and saxophone.
One for the road,
Before you set sail alone.
'D' marks the spot, on this heart-shaped space,
But maps have proved wrong,
Invincibly out of place,
Surrounded by the Sea of Possibilities,
Most try to understand and lead the way,
But the wise know, the only way there,
Is to be led astray.

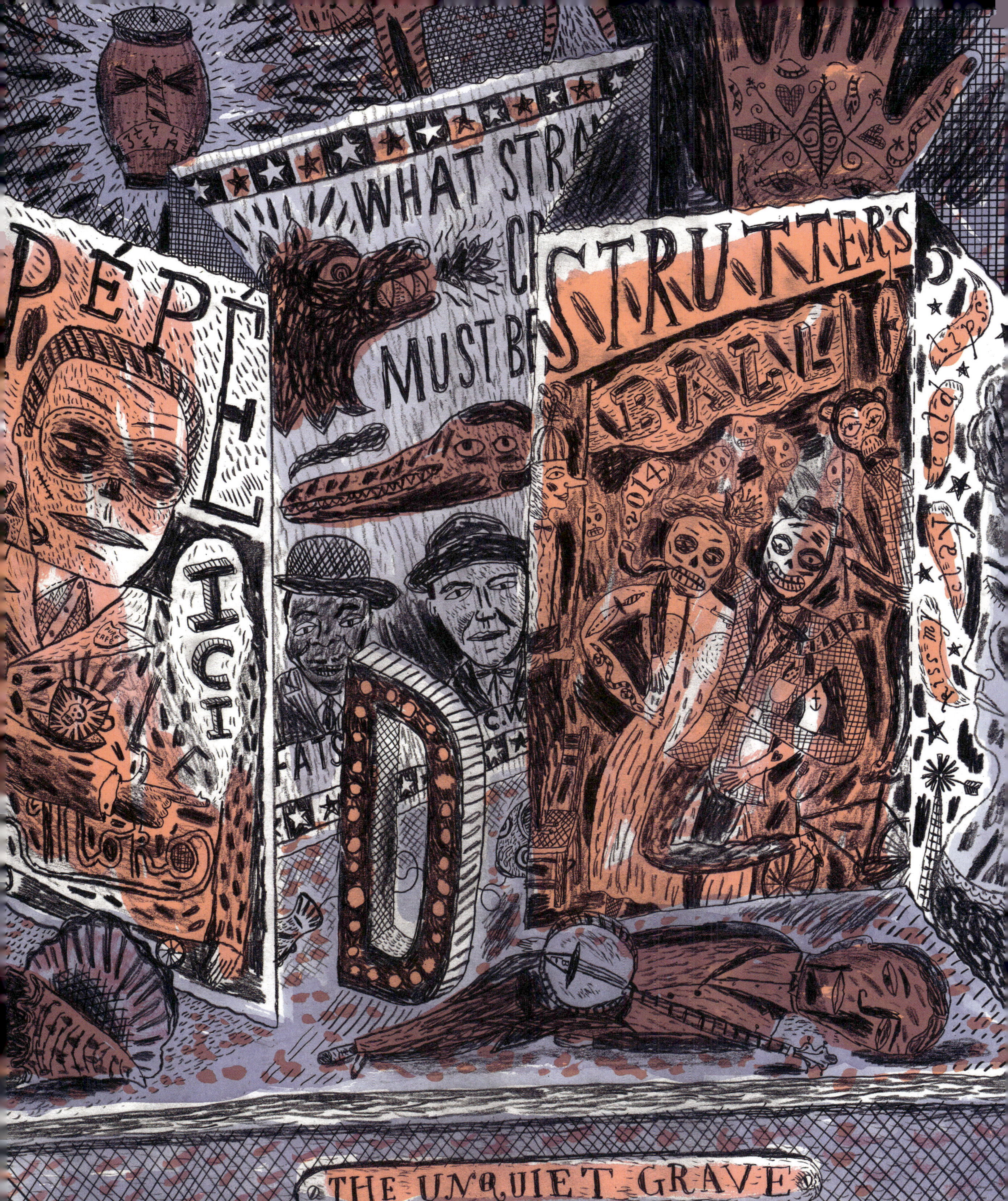
PÉPÉ
ICI
WHAT STRA
MUST BE
STRUTTER'S
BALL
2014
FATS
THE UNQUIET GRAVE

OLD STOKE & MISS JULIE Forever
VAUGHAN
williams
Rocket 54

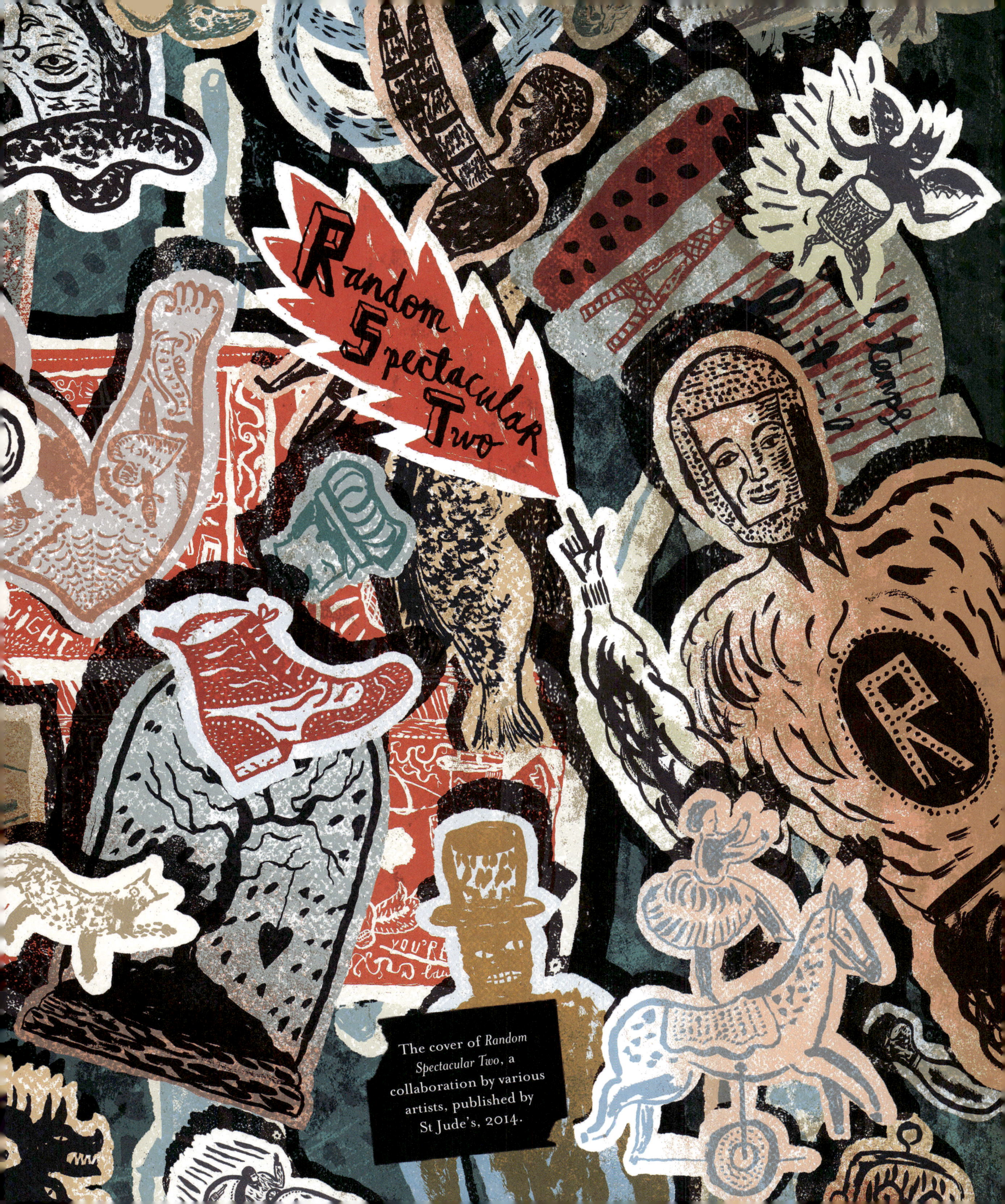


The cover of *Random Spectacular Two*, a collaboration by various artists, published by St Jude's, 2014.

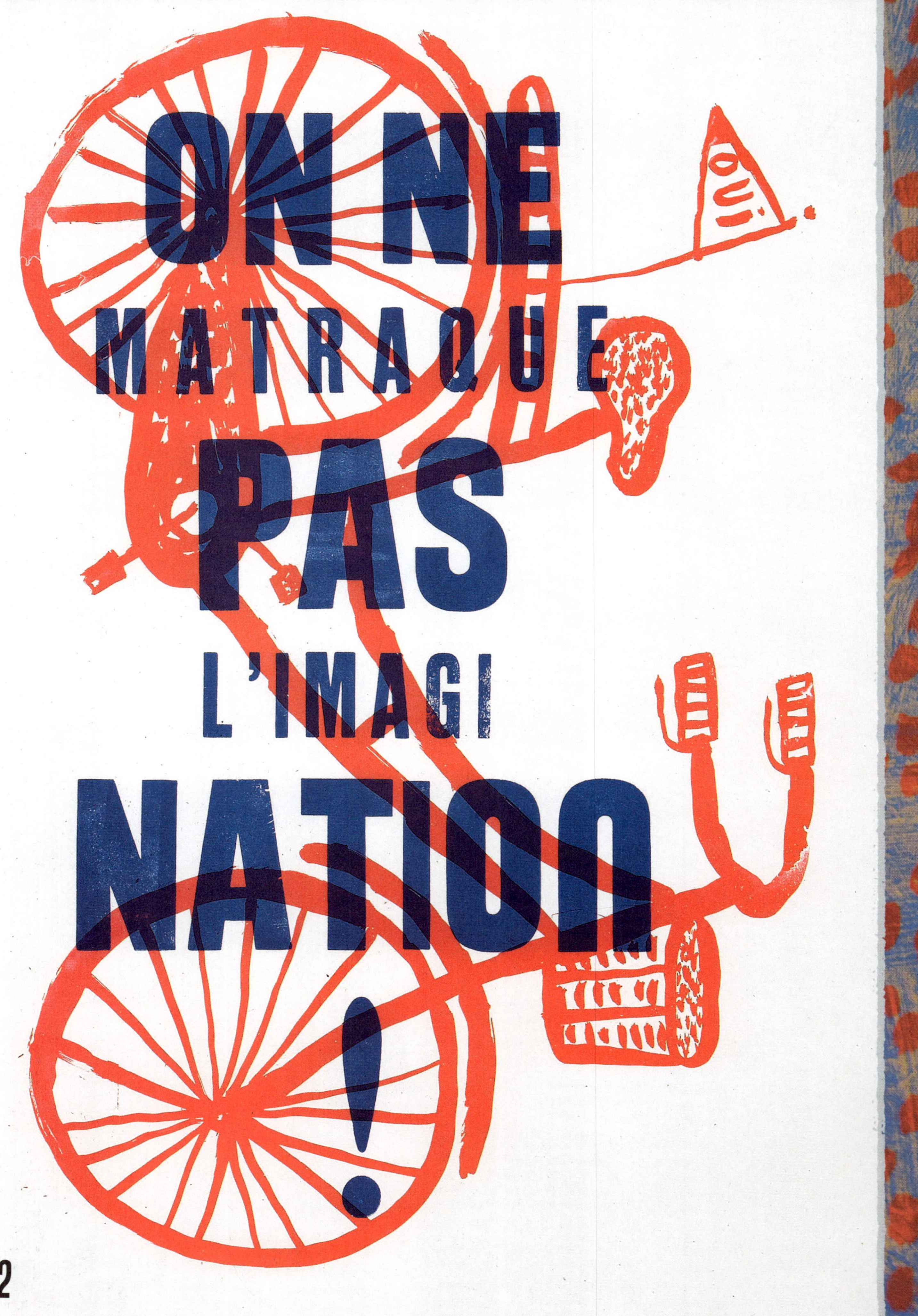
ON NE
MATRAQUE
PAS
L'IMAGI
NATION
!
OUI

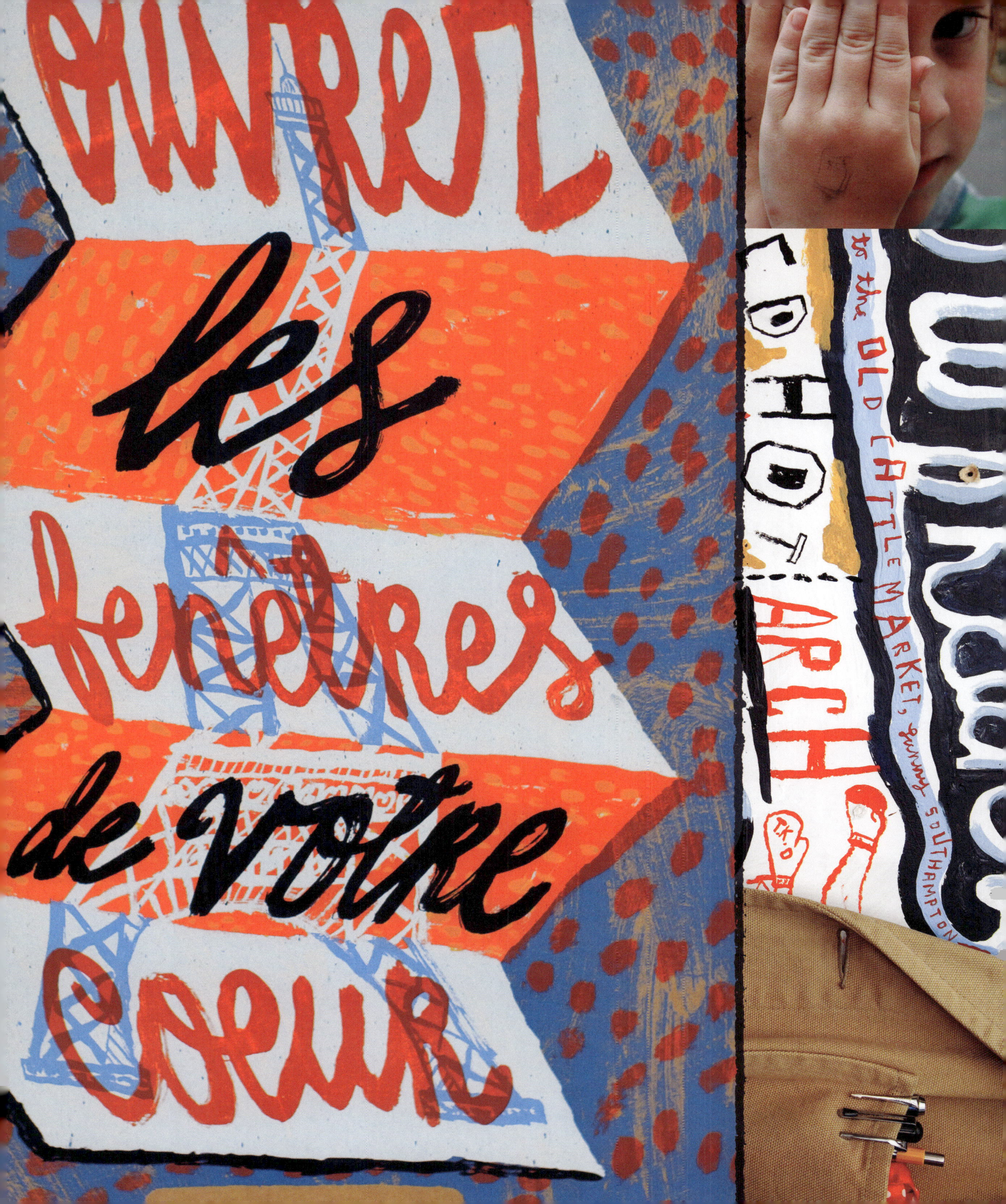
les
fenêtres
de votre
coeur
to the OLD CATTLE MARKET, Sunny SOUTHAMPTON
ARCH
T.K.O

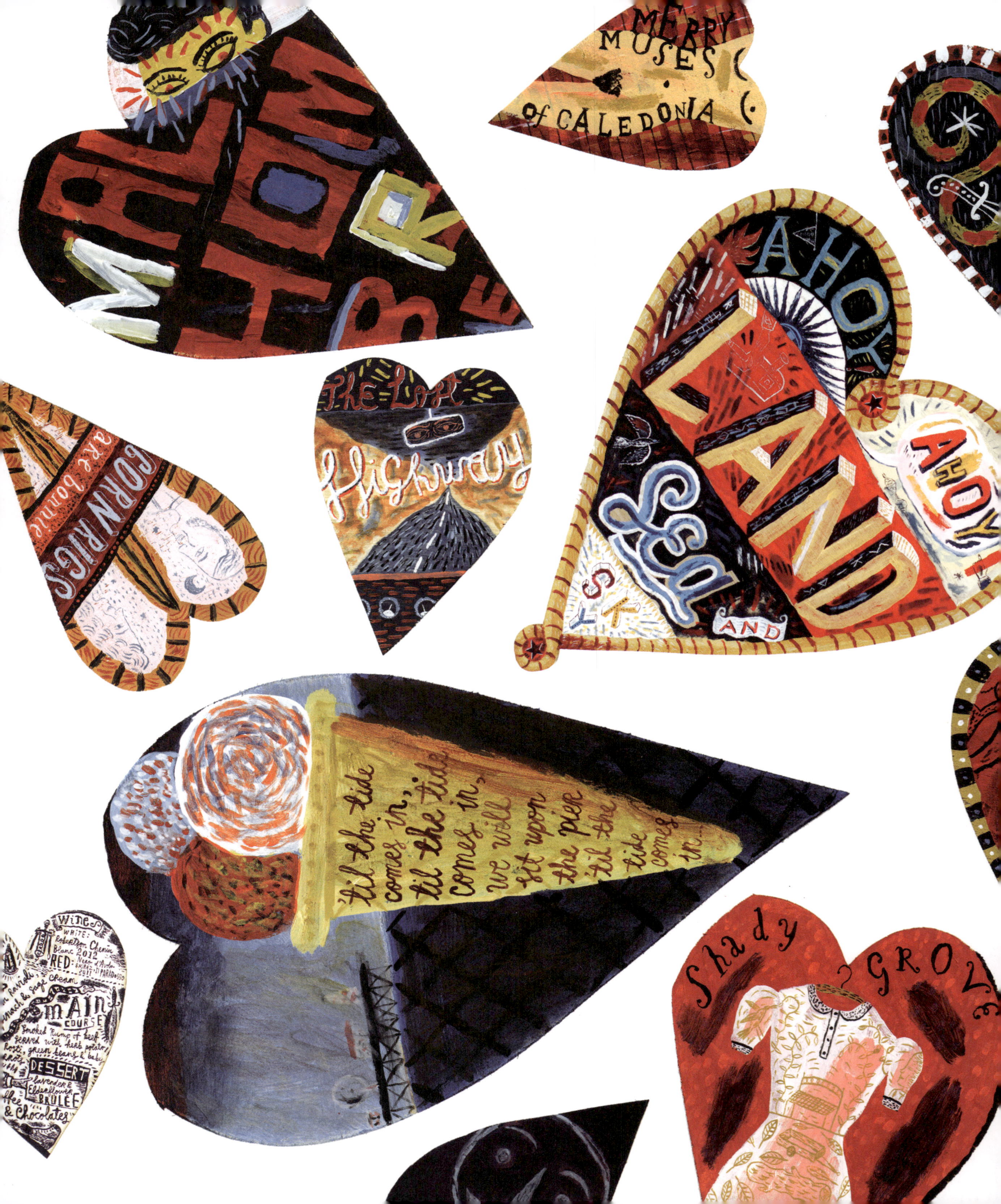
MERRY MUSES
of CALEDONIA
AHOY
LAND
SEA
AND
AHOY
The Lost
Highway
CORN RIGS
are bonnie
'til the tide comes in, 'til the tide comes in, we will sit upon the pier 'til the tide comes in.
Wine
WHITE:
Robertson Chenin Blanc 2012
RED:
MAIN COURSE
Smoked Rump of beef
served with herb potato
rosti, green beans & baby
DESSERT
Lavender &
Elderflower
BRULEE
& Chocolates
Shady GROVE

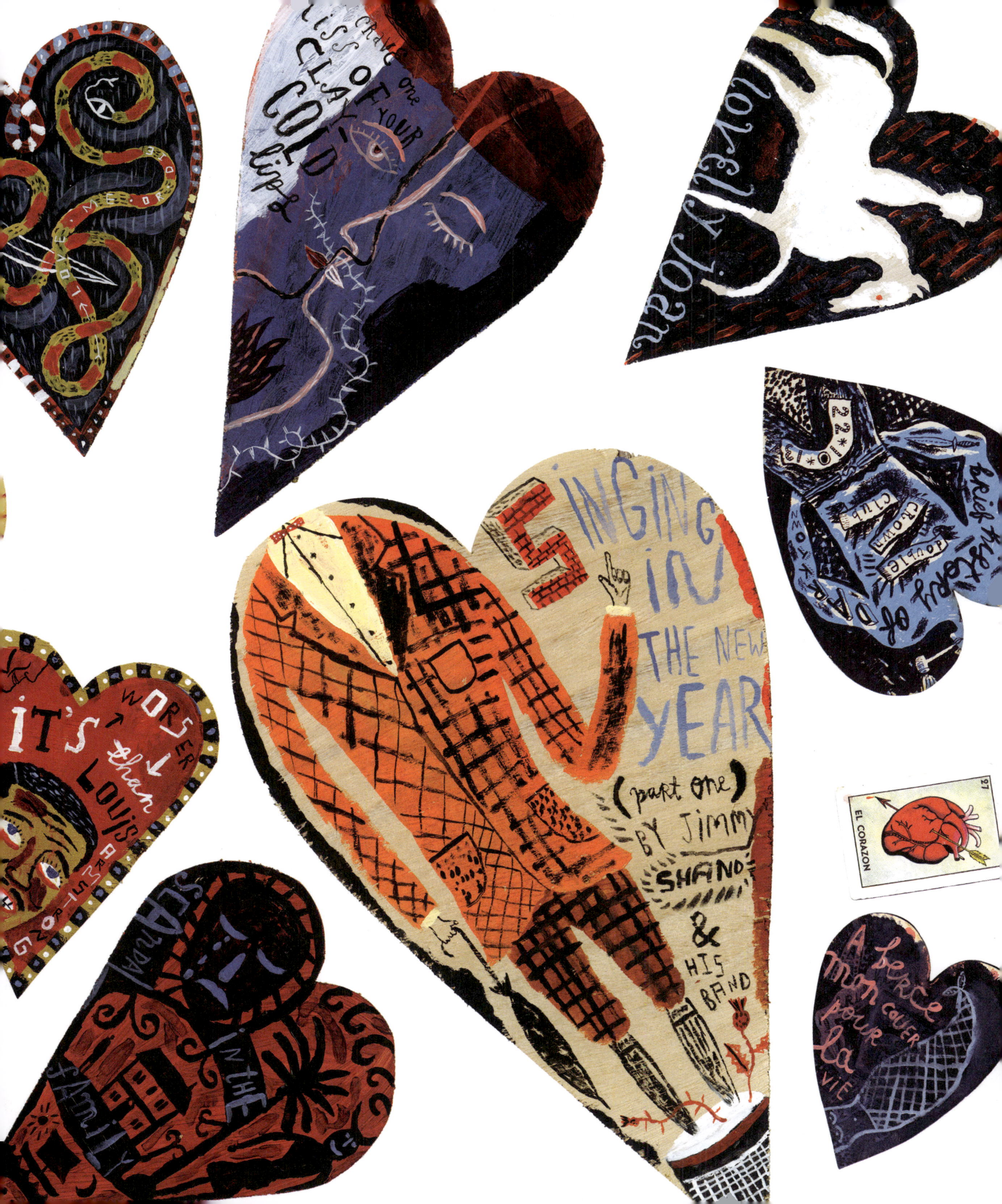

LOVE ME OR DIE
CRAVE one KISS OF YOUR CLAY COLD lips
lovely Joan
Crown Club
SINGING IN THE NEW YEAR
(part one)
BY JIMMY SHAND & HIS BAND
IT'S WORSER than LOUIS
SCANDAL IN THE FAMILY
EL CORAZON
27
A berce mon coeur pour la vie

# JONNY HANNAH'S CAST OF CHARACTERS BY PETER CHRISP

Walking along Brighton seafront on a sunny day in June 2001, my partner, Lisa, and I spotted a beautiful poster outside the Fishing Museum. It advertised *Notes from the Captain*, an exhibition by Jonny Hannah. The poster depicted the Captain, a bearded, pipe-smoking sea dog in a striped shirt, and described the show as a 'nautical gallimaufry'.

We went in and met the immaculately dressed Hannah, surrounded by his nautical screen prints featuring the Captain, a school of mermaids, tattooed sailors, Moby Dick and Davy Jones's locker. I fell instantly in love with Hannah's style, which reminded me of Edward Bawden, Eric Ravilious, the Mr Magoo cartoons of John Hubley, and David Stone Martin's great jazz album covers of the 1950s.

I bought Hannah's book *Southward Ho!* (2000), in which he explained that the Captain was a character from the Carter Family's song 'I Have No One to Love Me (But the Sailor on the Deep Blue Sea)'. In the song, a maiden, with no one to love her but the sailor, asks the Captain, 'Can you tell me where he may be?' His grim answer is, 'Oh yes, my little maiden, he is drownded in the deep blue sea.' In his book, Hannah writes that, when he heard the song, 'I suddenly had my central character. This man knew everything.' As the phrase 'central character' shows, Hannah creates a series of artworks as if he were making a film, casting characters and choosing locations.

The Carter Family song, like a lot of Hannah's source material, is dark, but his treatment is always colourful and witty. He is drawn to quirky detail, such as the lovely word 'drownded'.

I came to know Jonny properly thanks to my friends Chris Lord and Judy Stevens, who invited him to exhibit at the Artists Open Houses festival in Brighton, each May and Christmas, from 2002 to 2011. For the Open House, Hannah made vividly coloured, richly decorated acrylic paintings on cardboard cut-outs. He invented an emporium called The Unquiet Grave, named after another dark folk song in which a young man mourns his dead love so excessively that her ghost tells him to let her rest. Hannah located The Unquiet Grave in Smithville, Greil Marcus's name for the world of Harry Smith's *Anthology of American Folk Music* (1952), which Marcus summed up beautifully as 'the old, weird America'. The

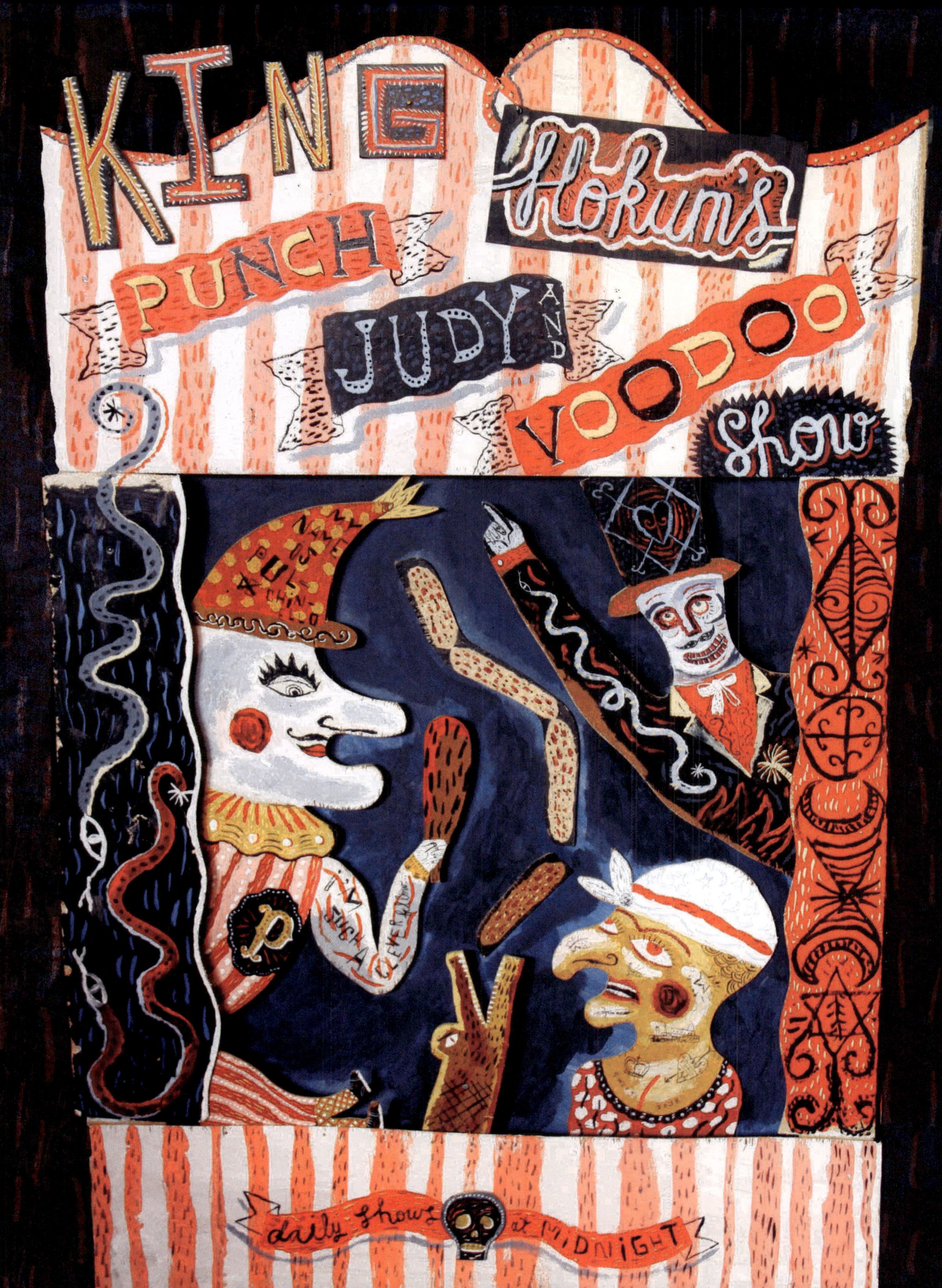
KING
Hokum's
PUNCH
JUDY
AND
VOODOO
Show
daily shows at MIDNIGHT

Unquiet Grave was also a theatre, with nightly showings of *Gravedirt and Whiskey*, the story of the doomed country singer Hank Williams.

Hannah's new cast of characters included the escapologist Harry Houdini; Henry Chinaski, alter ego of the writer Charles Bukowski; Barnacle Bill the Sailor, shown with black skin covered in tattoos; Ida Red, from the western song ('I'm a plumb fool 'bout Ida Red'); and Stoker Thompson, Robert Ryan's has-been boxer from the great film noir *The Set-Up* (1949).

The central figure was Rocket Man, inspired by a Chinese tin toy known as Rocket Racer. While the toy reveals only Rocket Man's helmet-covered head as he sits in his racer, Hannah imagined a white uniform for him, with a big letter 'R' on the back. He produced a series of pocket books, including *Rocket Man's Pocket Book of Tin Toys* and *Rocket Man's Tea-Time Companion to the Bonkers World of Cryptozoology* (pages 110–11). In *Rocket Man's Mortgage*, our hero, refused a mortgage on account of not having a proper job, gets in such a state that he defaces his beloved Rocket Racer. Rocket Man, a Scot who likes Hank Williams, whisky and stovies, is a sort of self-portrait.

In 2006 Jonny visited New York, where he married his sweetheart, Sharon. He also discovered Coney Island, with its crumbling fairground rides, hot dog stands and clam bars. These all appeared in Hannah's next Open House show, where the paintings, with numbered targets painted on them, were presented as a Coney Island shooting gallery.

A big new influence, in 2008, was C.W. Stoneking, an Australian who performs as a 1920s hokum blues singer. Stoneking, or 'King Hokum', could have stepped out of the Harry Smith *Anthology* or a Hannah painting. He's a dapper dresser, with a bow tie, white clothes (like Rocket Man!) and hand tattoos that might have been drawn by Jonny. Stoneking claims to have worked in a voodoo doctor's shop in New Orleans. This inspired Hannah to introduce a new character in his 'King Hokum' series: Baron Samedi, the top-hatted voodoo loa (spirit) of the dead. In voodoo ceremonies, each loa has its own decorative symbol, or vévé, drawn on the floor with ash as a beacon to attract the spirit. Vévés appeal to Hannah's love of decoration, and they often appear in his recent work.

Another key Hannah character is McVouty, or Slim Gaillard, the surreal jazz singer who invented his own nonsense language ('O'Voutie O'Rooney!'). In his 2009 exhibition, *Notes from McVouty*, at the Coningsby Gallery in London, Hannah imagined Gaillard retiring to Coney Island to run a second-hand emporium. For McVouty's Emporium, Hannah created his first three-dimensional works – junk transformed into beautiful artefacts. There was an old guitar, painted as a tribute to Hank Williams; a Slim Gaillard 'Dunkin' Bagels Coffee Pot'; and a 'Cakes & Ale Tool Box', which came with a decorated hammer 'to get you started'. Hannah had also bought lots of second-hand books, stuck the pages together and painted new covers, paying honour to his musical heroes.

Hannah's next move was to make his own assemblages by sawing up wood in his Southampton shed. This coincided with a new-found passion for Paris, and so Hannah began to refer to himself in his work as Monsieur Bricolage. The biggest bricolage work I've seen is *King Hokum's Punch, Judy and Voodoo Show* (2012; page 157), complete with Baron Samedi, vévés and a heavily tattooed Judy.

The Hannah cast of characters keeps growing. In 2012 he reconnected with his Fife roots, with an exhibition in Dunfermline of notable fellow Fifers, including Moira Shearer, star of *The Red Shoes* (1948), and the accordionist Jimmy Shand.

Hannah's work often reminds me of the advice that Peter Blake gave his student Ian Dury in 1961 at the Walthamstow School of Art: 'Paint the things that you like or that you are interested in.' Hannah has always done this, and because he has such wonderful and eclectic taste in music, books, films and clothes, his work is always an inspiration and an education. I'm looking forward to seeing what he does next!

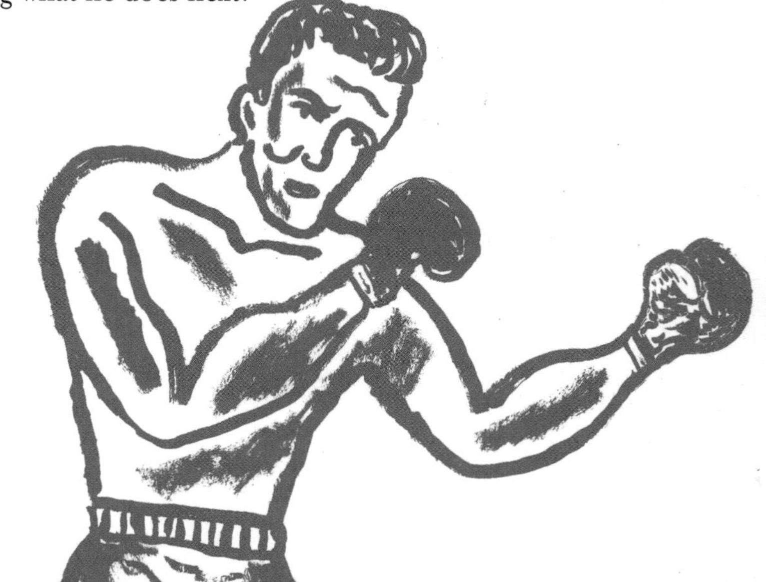

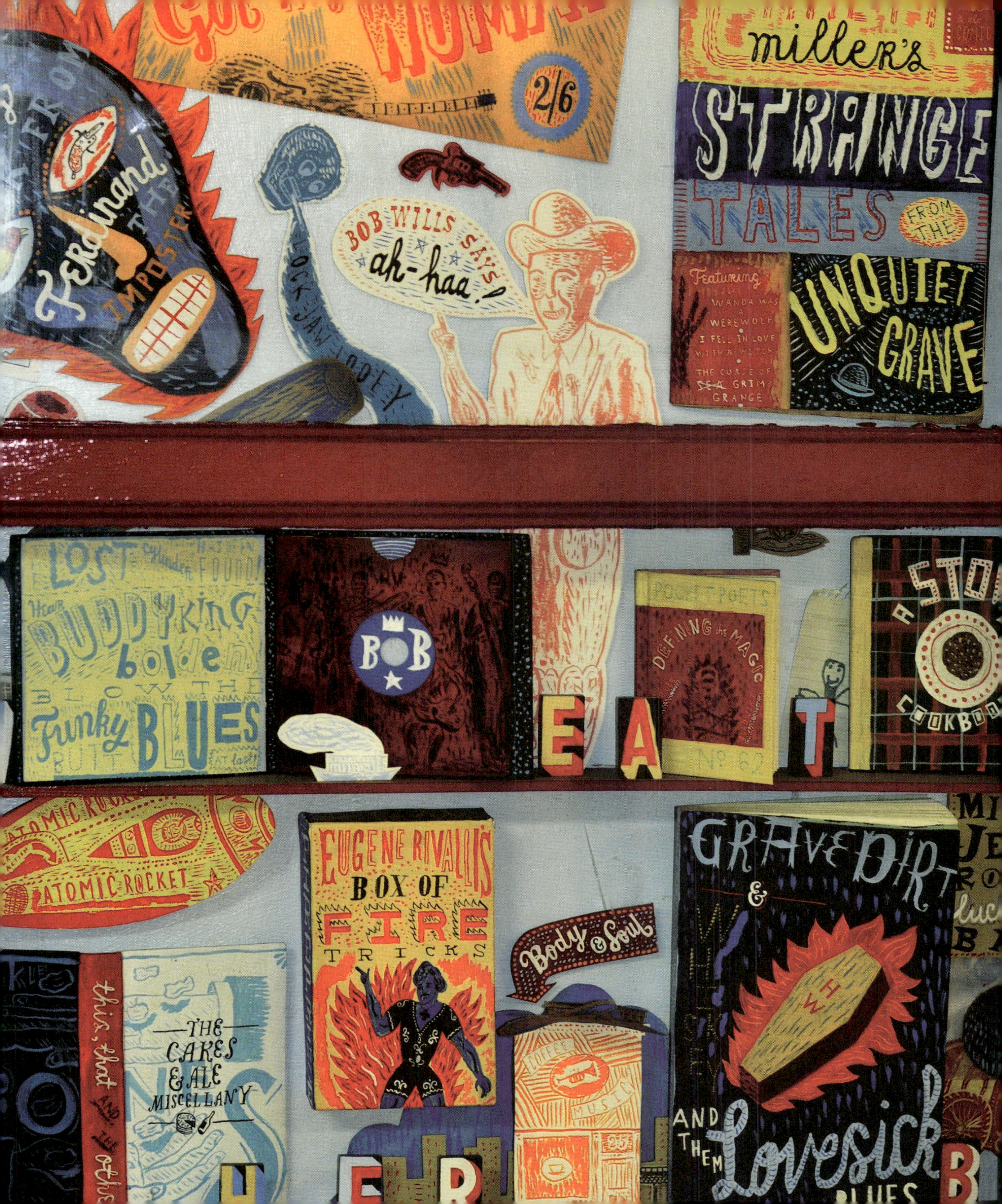

2/6
miller's
STRANGE
TALES
FROM THE
UNQUIET
GRAVE
Featuring
WANDA WAS A WEREWOLF
I FELL IN LOVE WITH A WITCH
THE CURSE OF SEA GRIM GRANGE
Ferdinand
THE IMPOSTER
LOCK JAW LOOEY
BOB WILLS SAYS!
ah-haa!
LOST cylinder HAS BEEN FOUND
Hear BUDDY KING bolden
BLOW THE Funky BLUES
AT last!
BOB
POCKET POETS
DEFINING the MAGIC
No 62
E A T
A STO
COOKBOO
ATOMIC ROCKET
EUGENE RIVALLI'S
BOX OF
FIRE
TRICKS
Body & Soul
COFFEE
MUSIC
GRAVEDIRT
&
AND THEM
Lovesick
BLUES
THE CAKES & ALE MISCELLANY
this, that AND THE other

# LOOMINGS, COFFIN & SCRIMSHAW

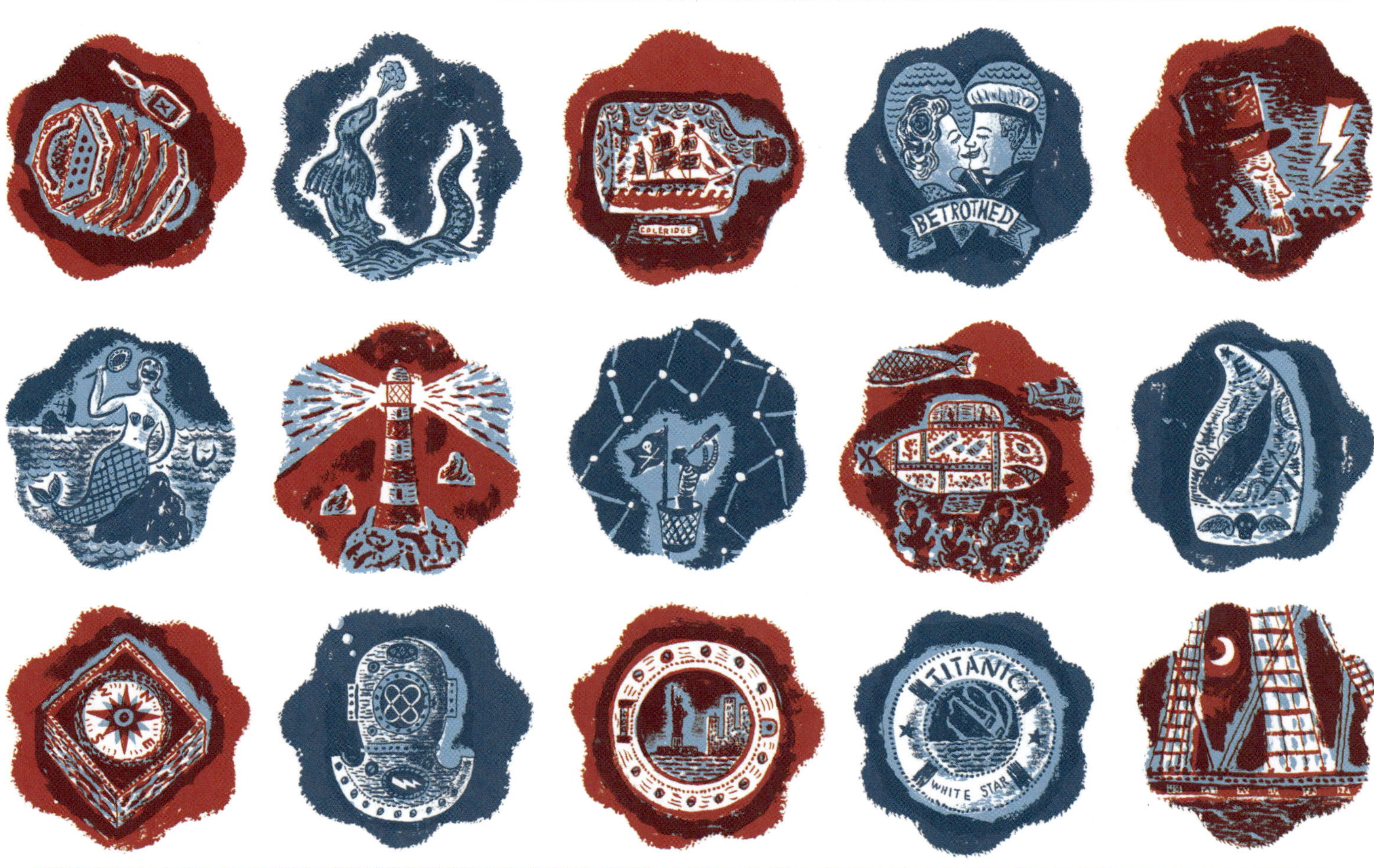


Simon and Angie Lewin at St Jude's are slowly showing us the way forward. The last recession meant great business for some cheaper high street stores, but it also taught some of us that another option is to buy home-grown, well-made products that last longer than five minutes. St Jude's fabrics and wallpapers are all printed in England, not sent abroad for a cheap, easy and quick turnaround. So when the Lewins asked me to design a fabric for them, I was delighted. For a theme, I went back to one of my favourites, the sea, and revived my anonymous hero 'The Captain', who first appeared all those years ago in his own alphabet (pages 58–59). Now – oh, at last – I could have cushion covers, pillowcases, almost anything, with my drawings on them. I'm not kidding: when my wife, Sharon, drew my 'Captain's Pattern' curtains for the first time, I sat there, in my dining room, with a glass of wine and kidded myself that I had arrived. St Jude's asked me back to design a wallpaper too, so overleaf is 'The Darktown Billets-Doux', half-opened letters of my objects of desire, odes to all I hold high. I've joked many a time that I'll ask Old Town, another home-grown diamond mine and close comrades of Simon and Angie, to make a suit out of my fabric. Oh, how heads would turn on Shirley High Street. And if only Old Town would open a branch in Darktown. But maybe the pilgrimage to deepest, darkest Norfolk is half the fun.

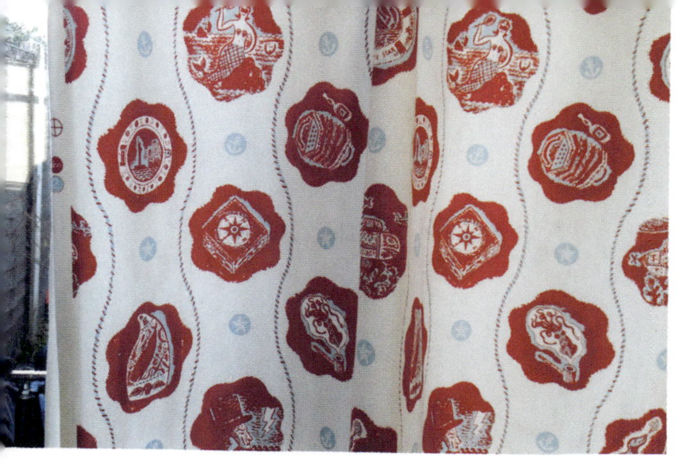

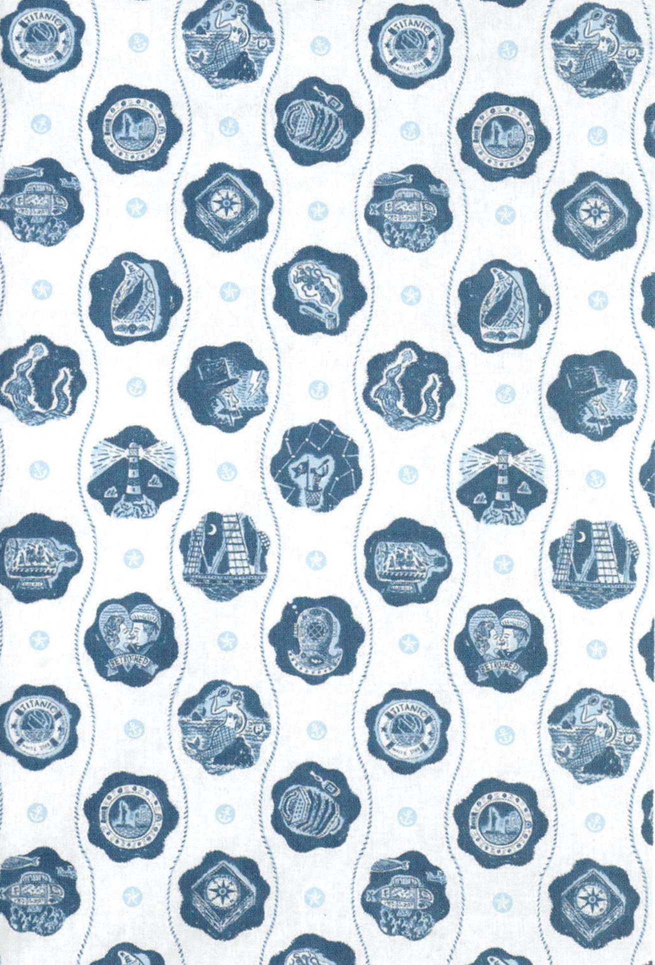

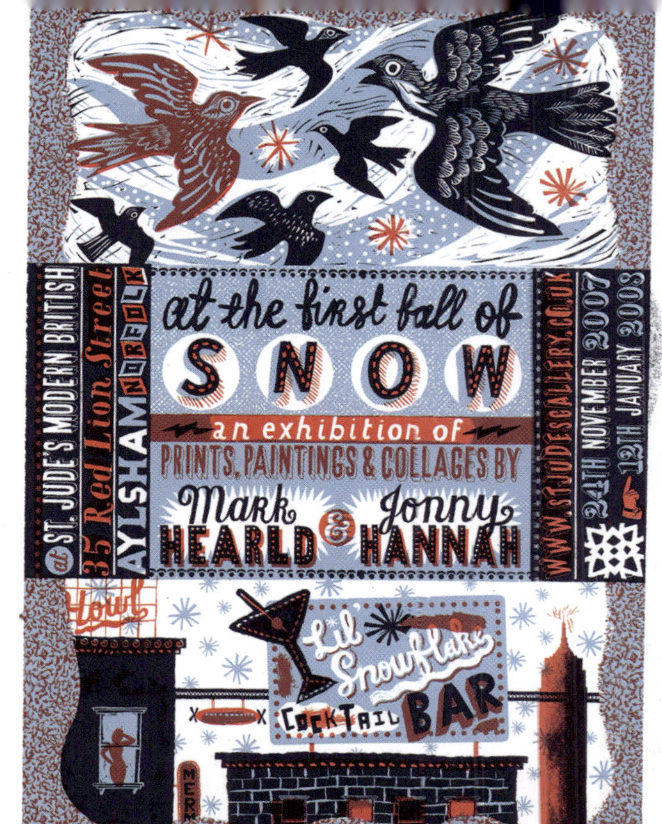
at St. Jude's Modern British
35 Red Lion Street
AYLSHAM NORFOLK
at the first fall of
SNOW
an exhibition of
PRINTS, PAINTINGS & COLLAGES BY
Mark HEARLD & Jonny HANNAH
WWW.STJUDESGALLERY.CO.UK
24TH NOVEMBER 2007
13TH JANUARY 2008
Lil Snowflake
COCKTAIL BAR

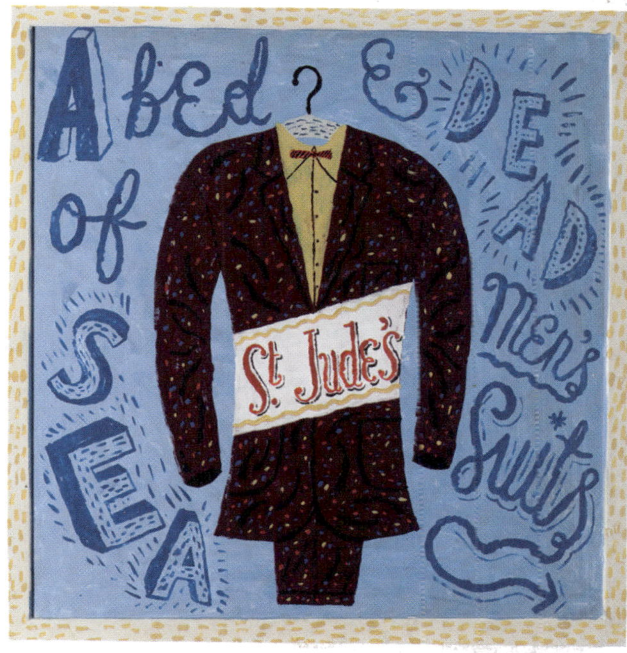
A bed of SEA
& DEAD men's suits
St Jude's

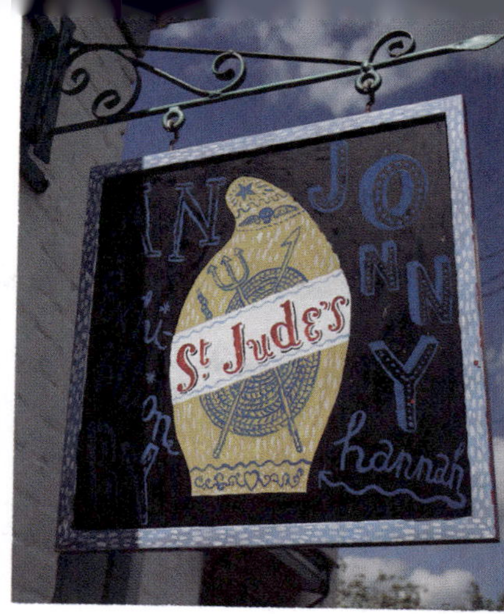
St Jude's
hannah

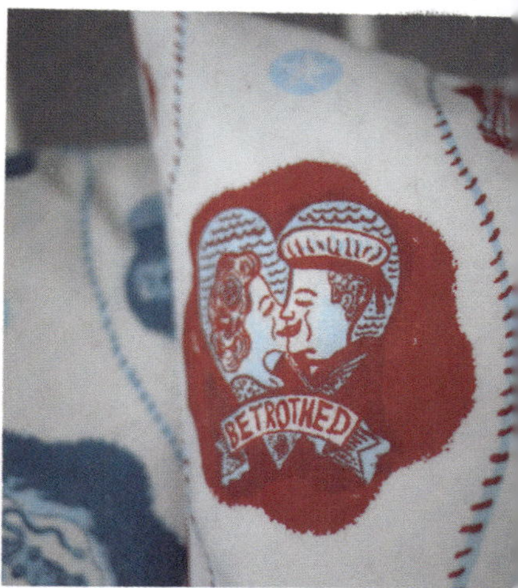
BETROTHED

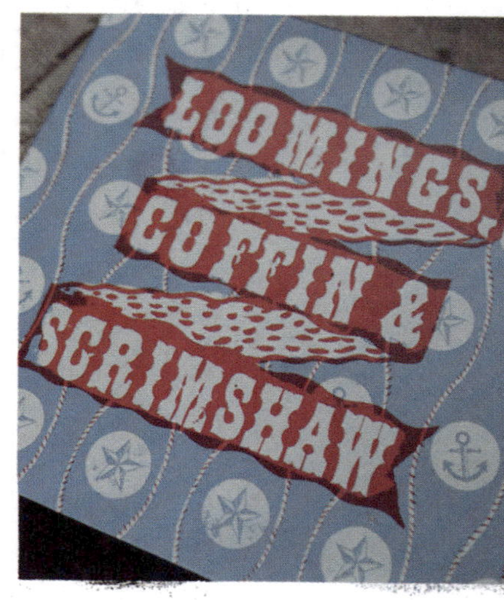
LOOMINGS,
COFFIN &
SCRIMSHAW

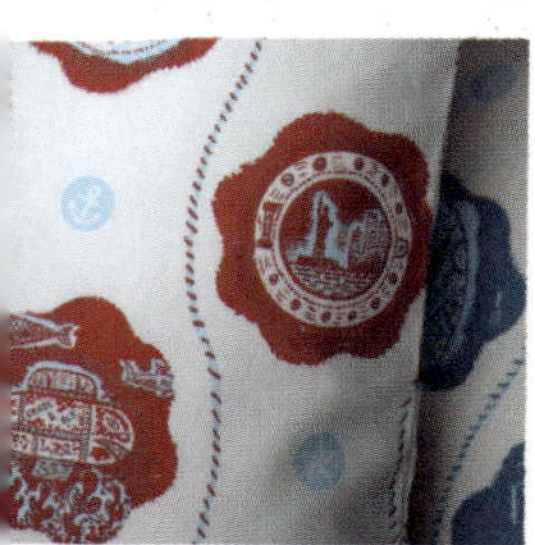

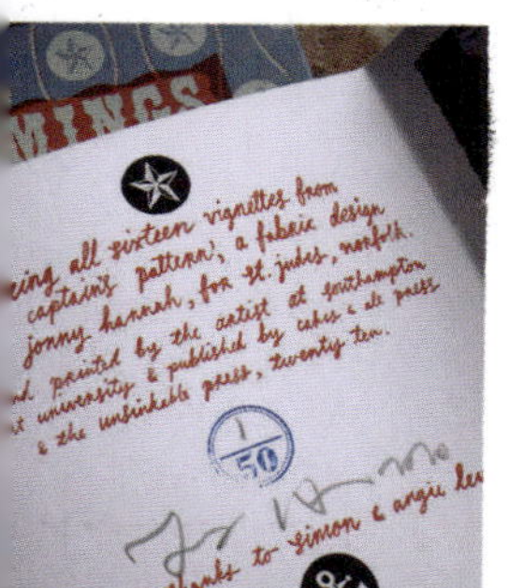

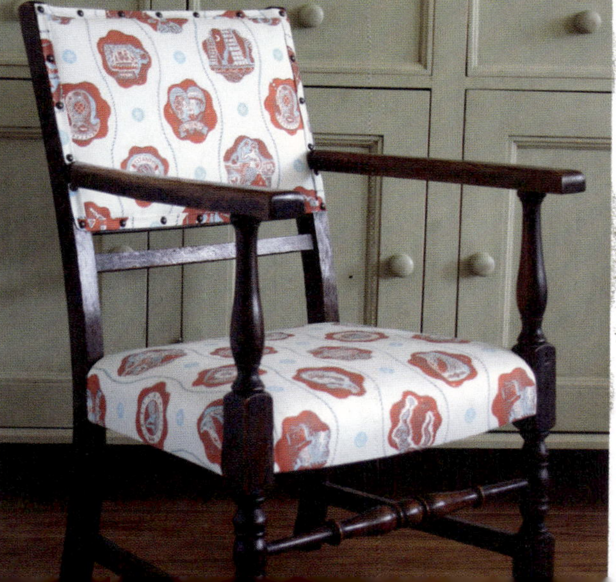

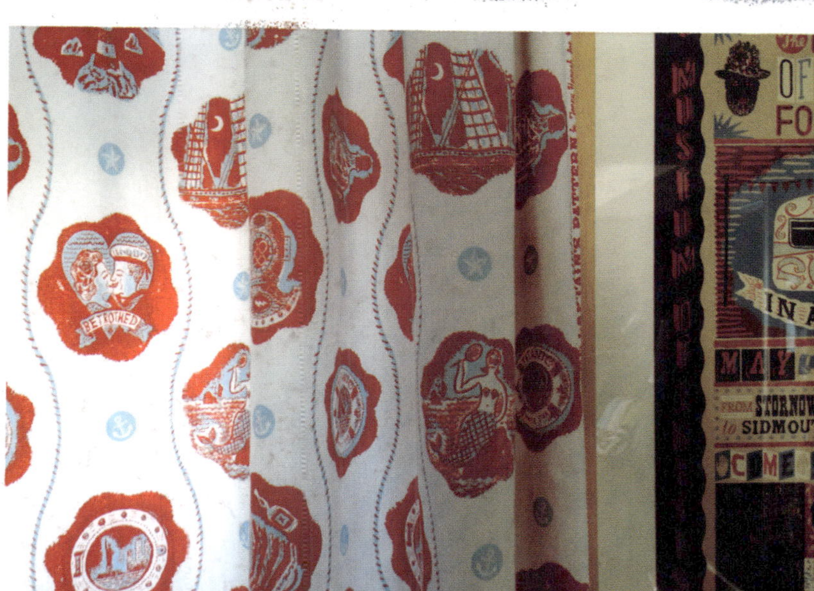
BETROTHED

The Darktown Billets-Doux — A WALLPAPER DESIGN BY JONNY HANNAH for ST. JUDE'S

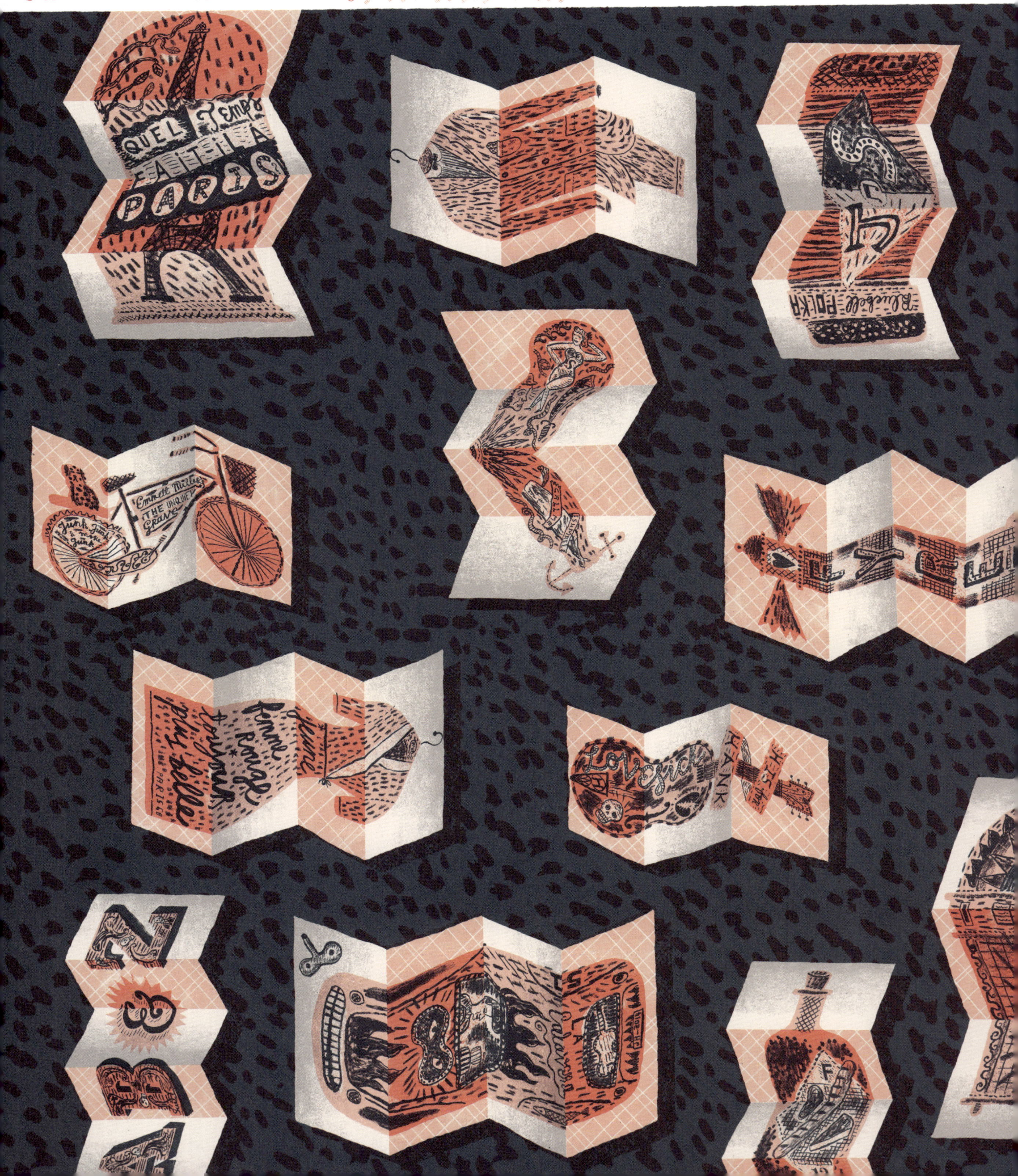

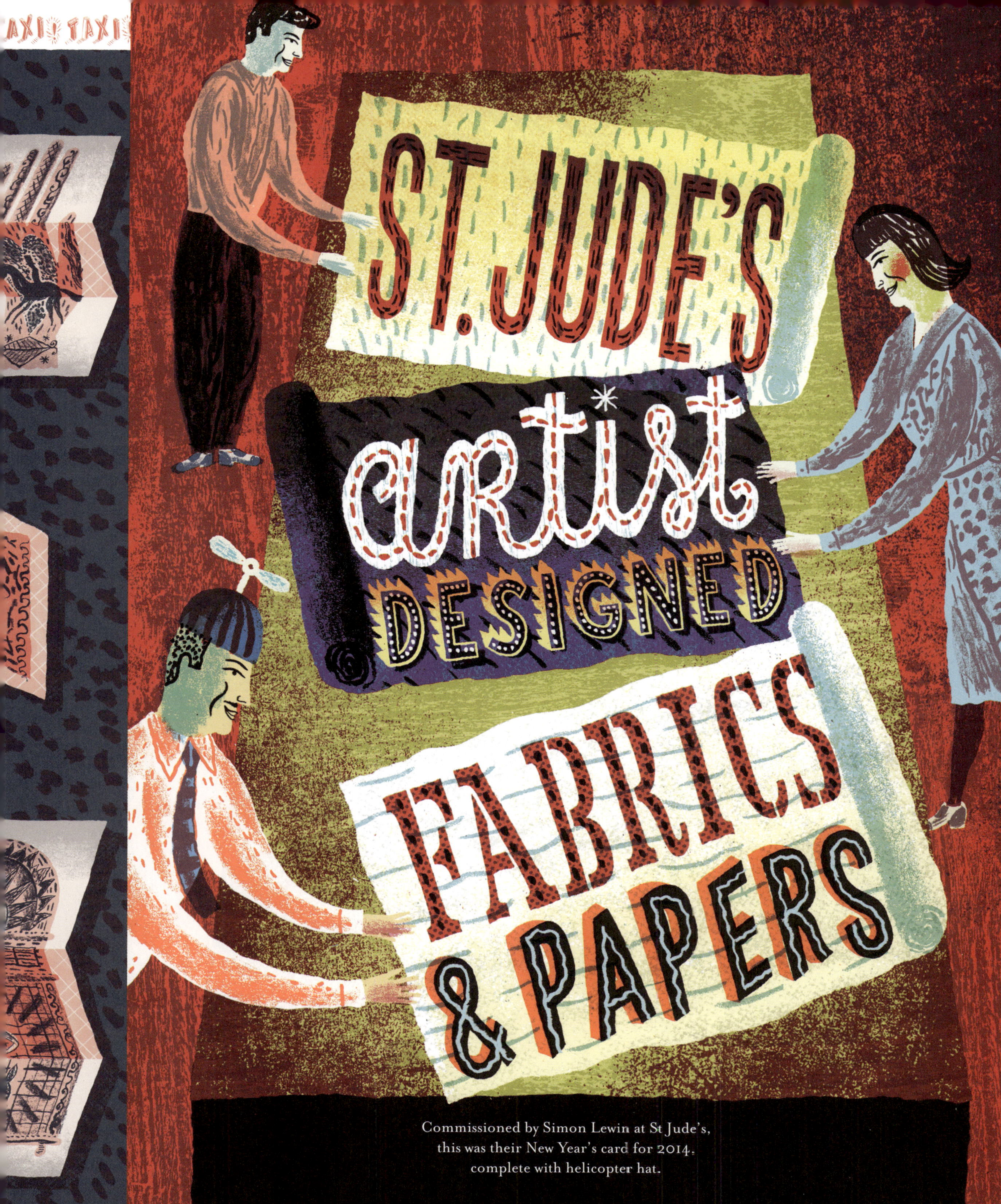


Commissioned by Simon Lewin at St Jude's, this was their New Year's card for 2014, complete with helicopter hat.

Meanwhile, In Downtown Darktown....

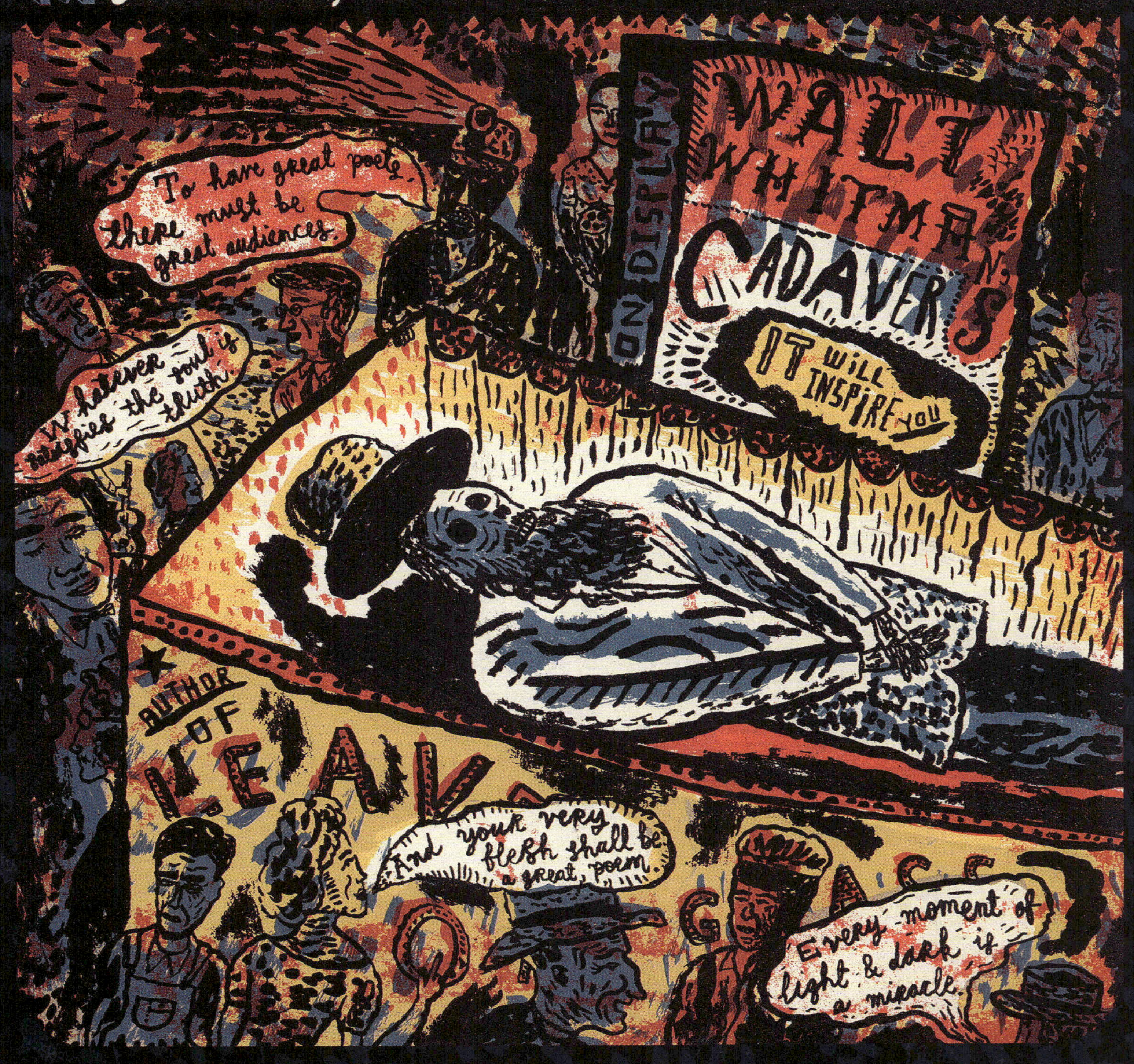

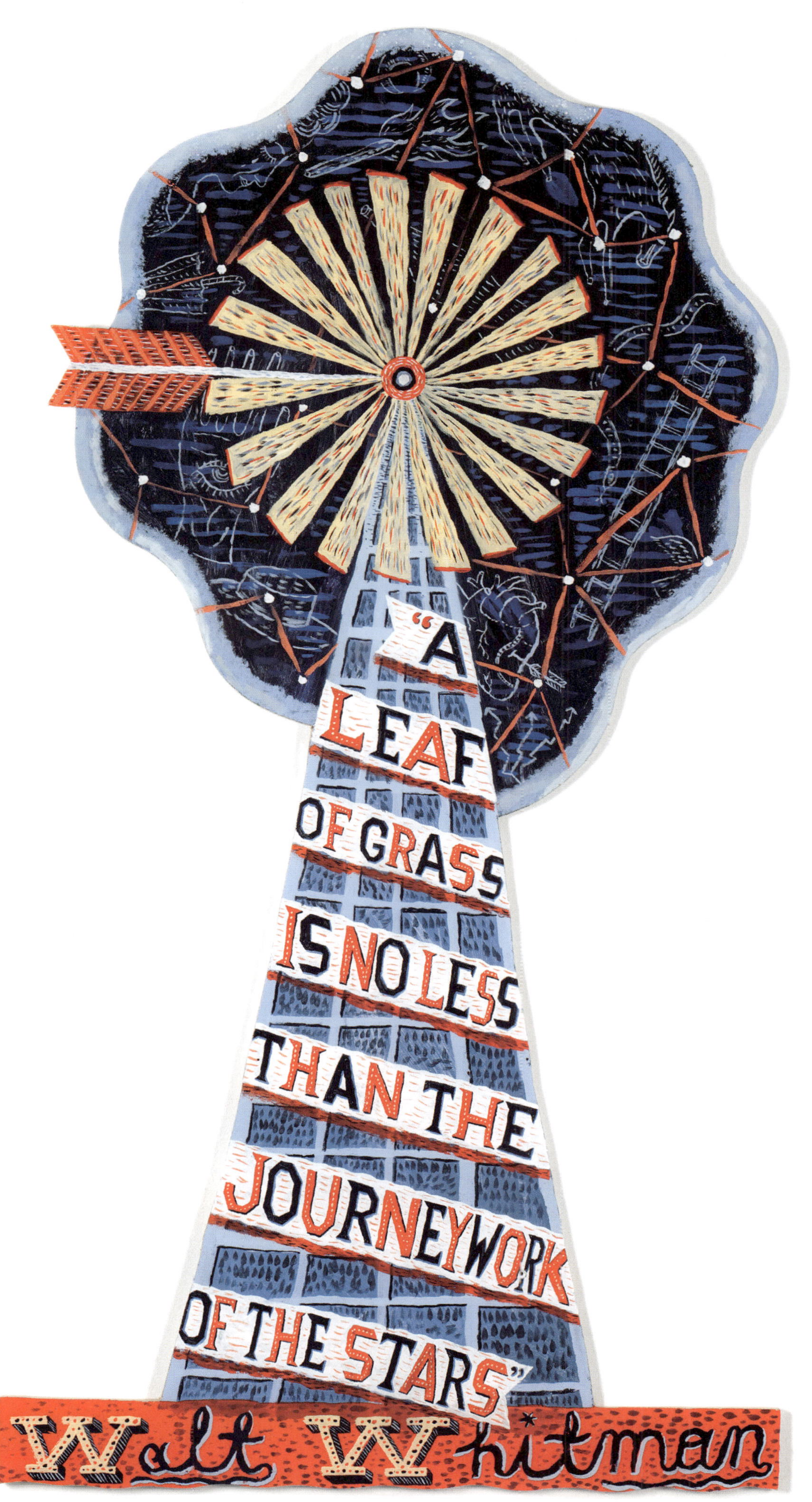
"A LEAF OF GRASS IS NO LESS THAN THE JOURNEYWORK OF THE STARS"
Walt Whitman

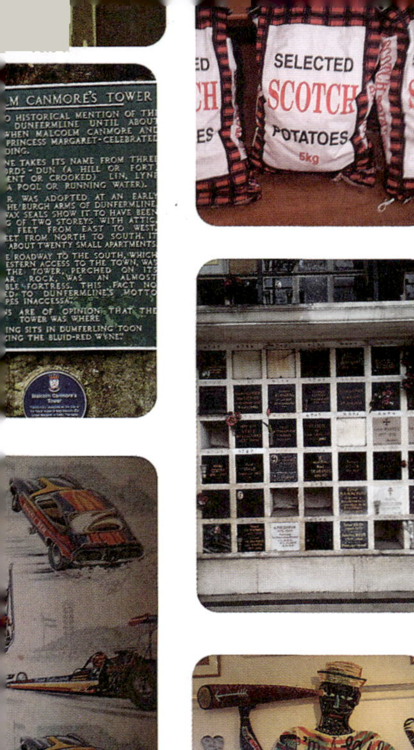
SELECTED
SCOTCH
POTATOES
5kg

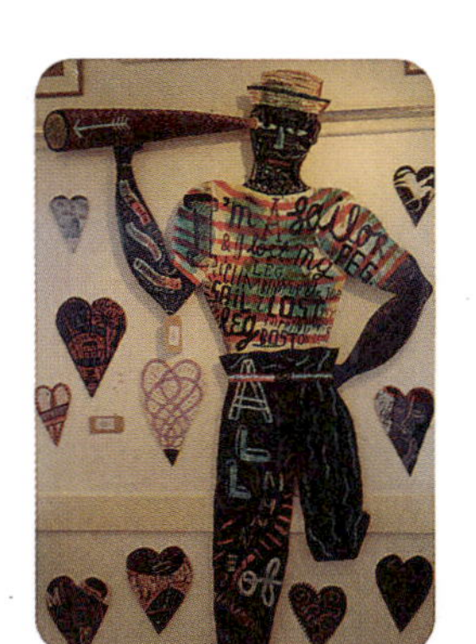

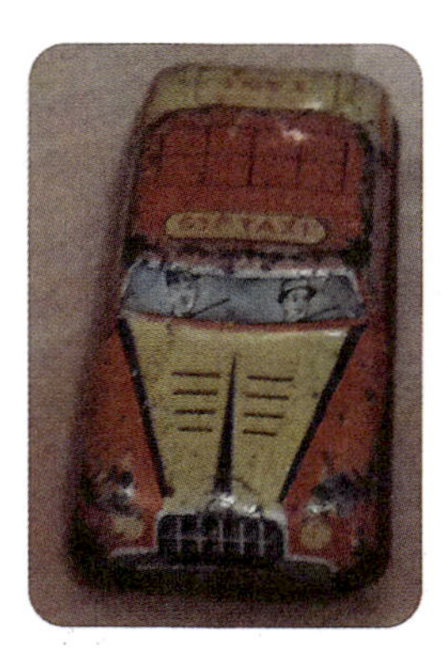

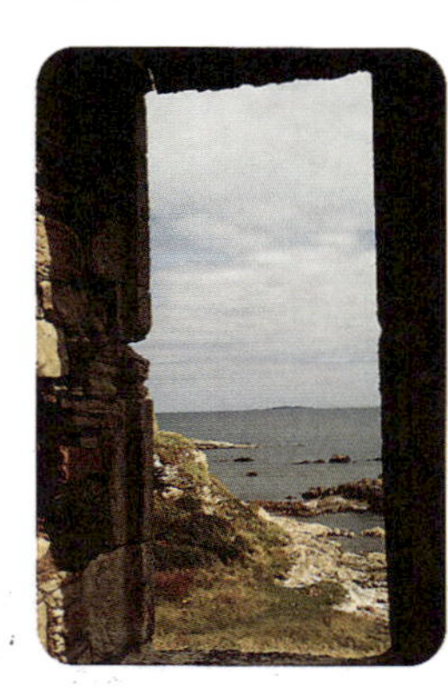

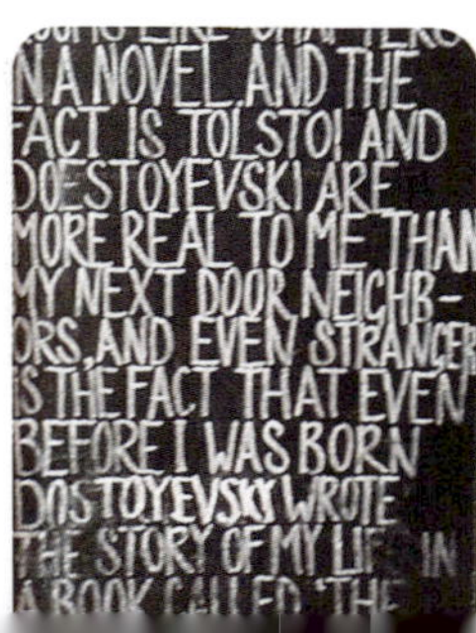
N A NOVEL AND THE FACT IS TOLSTOI AND DOESTOYEVSKI ARE MORE REAL TO ME THAN MY NEXT DOOR NEIGHB-ORS AND EVEN STRANGER IS THE FACT THAT EVEN BEFORE I WAS BORN DOSTOYEVSKI WROTE THE STORY OF MY LIFE IN A BOOK CALLED 'THE

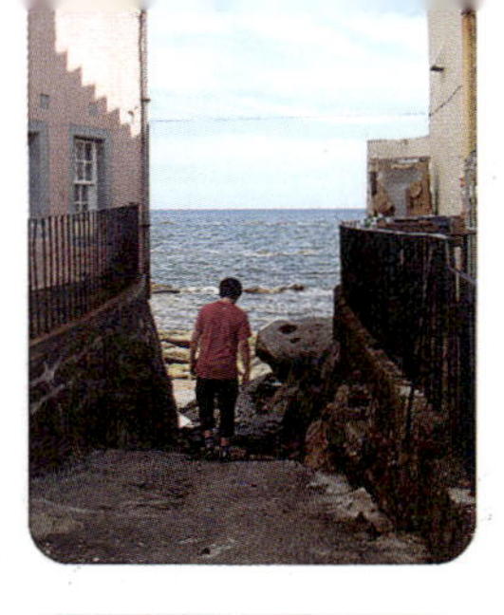

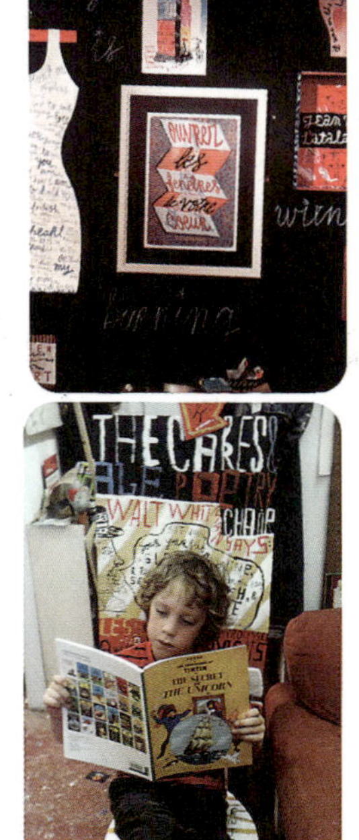

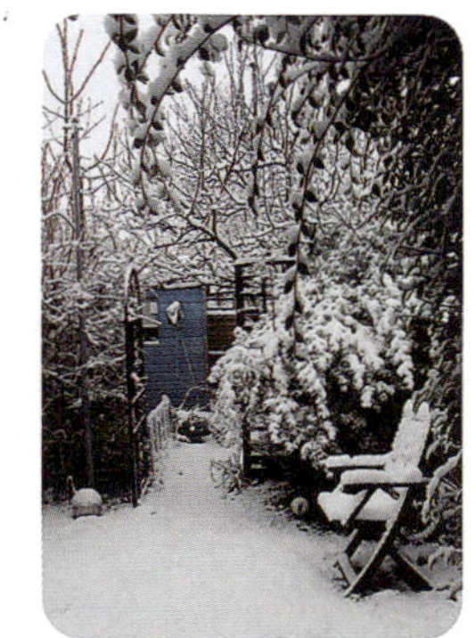

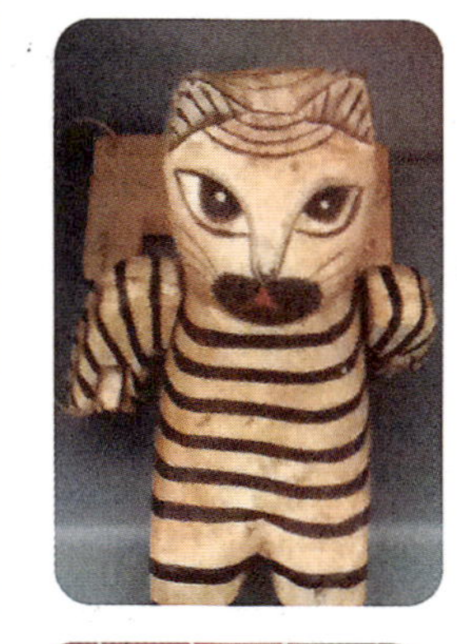

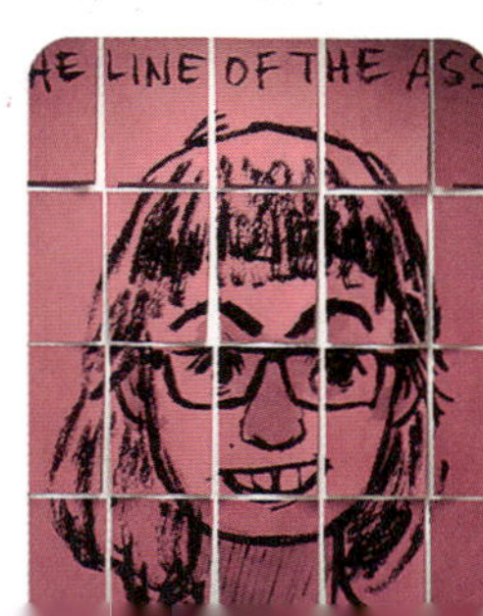
HE LINE OF THE ASS

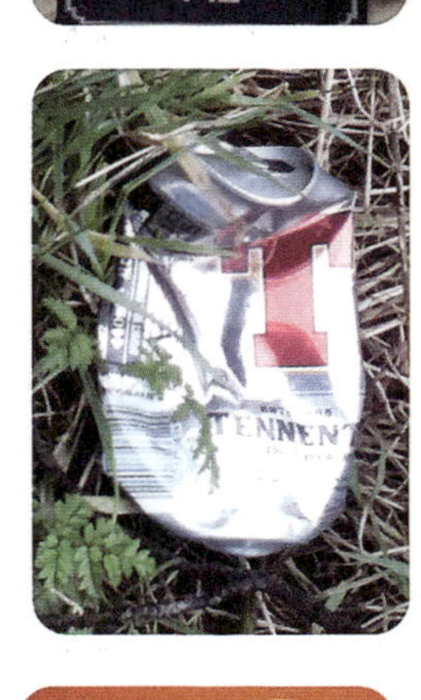
TENNENT

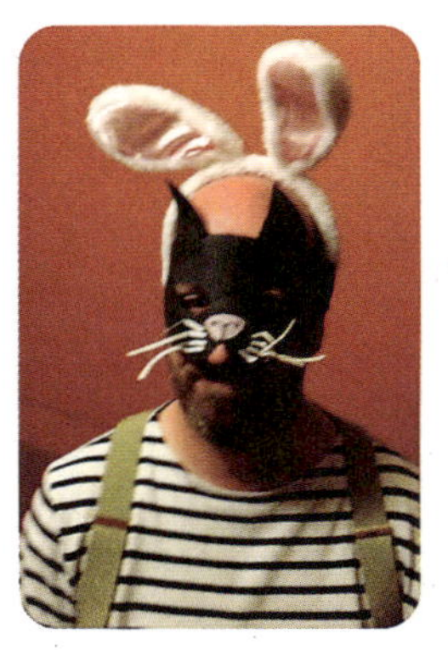

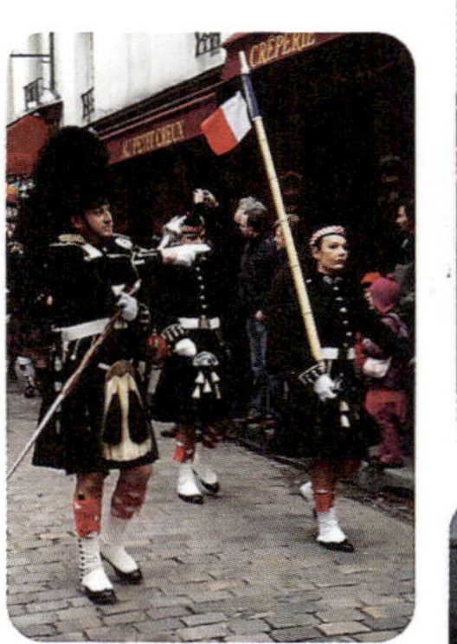

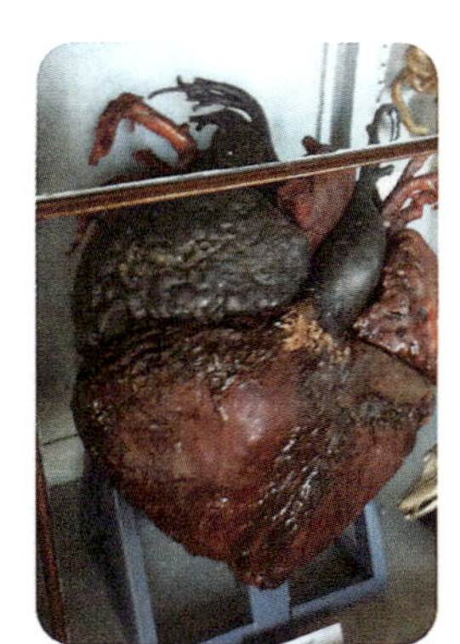

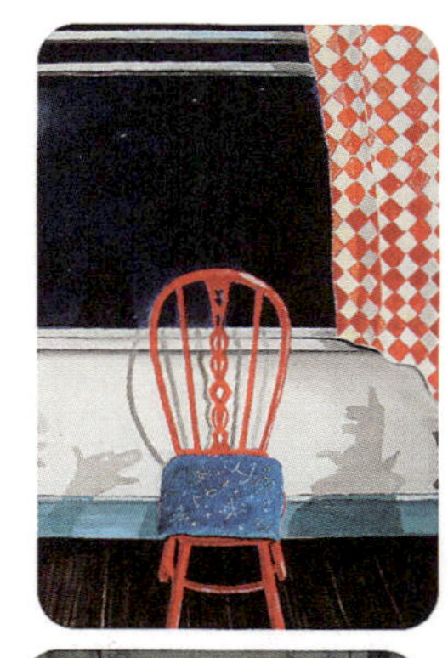

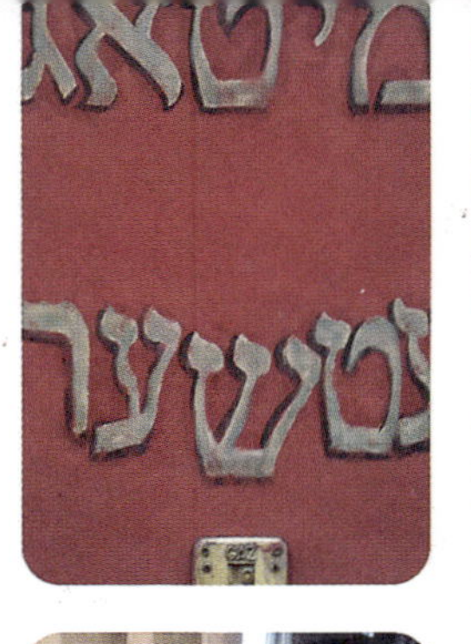

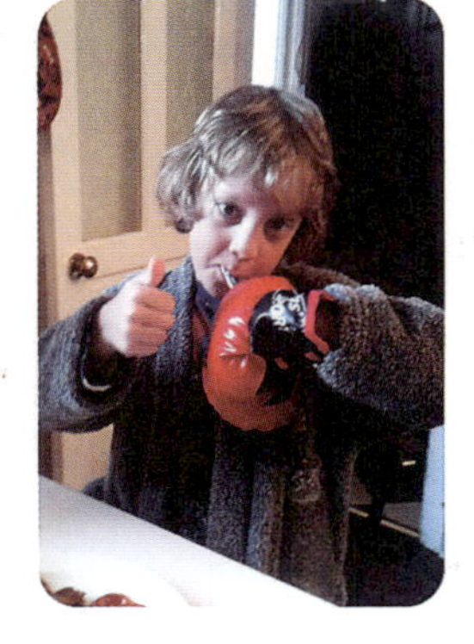

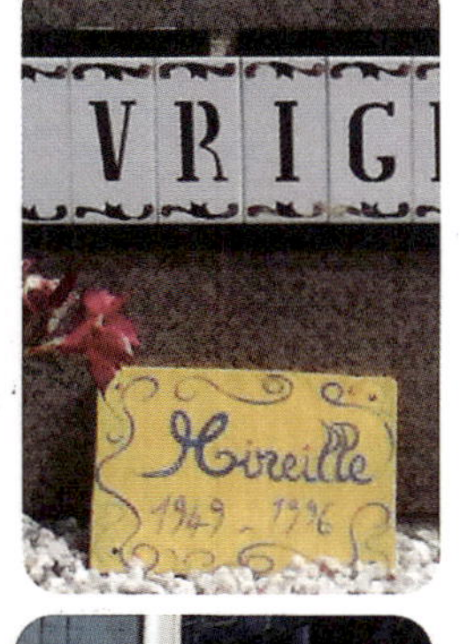
VRIG
Mireille
1949 – 1996

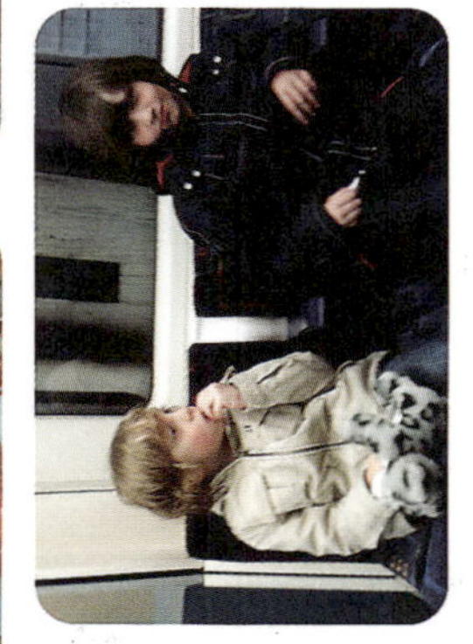

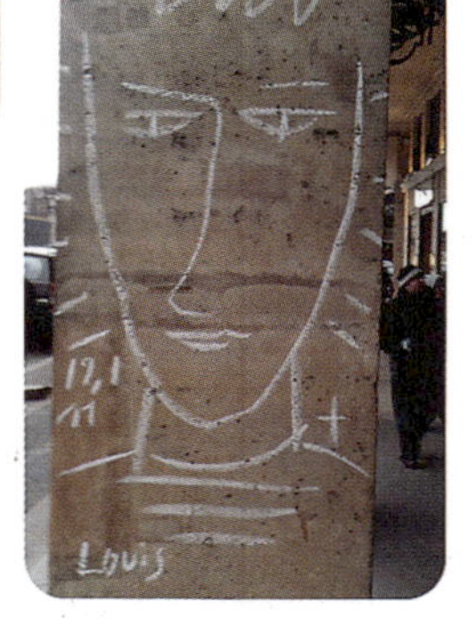
Louis

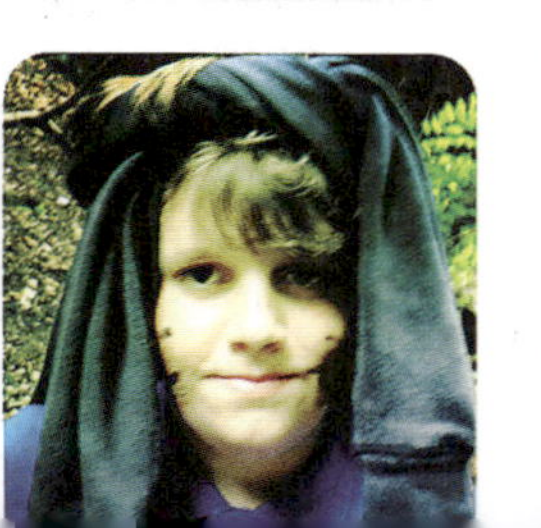

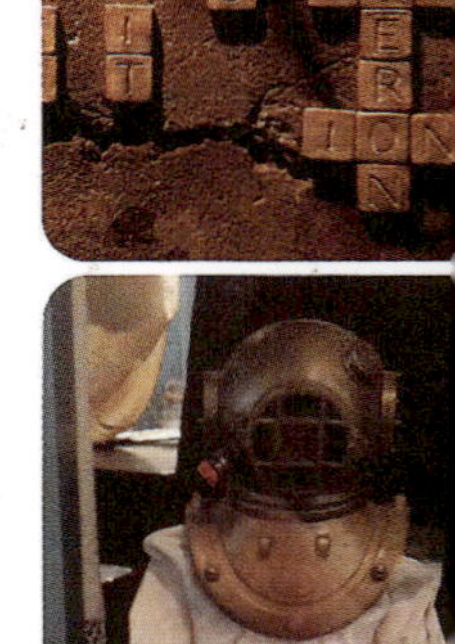

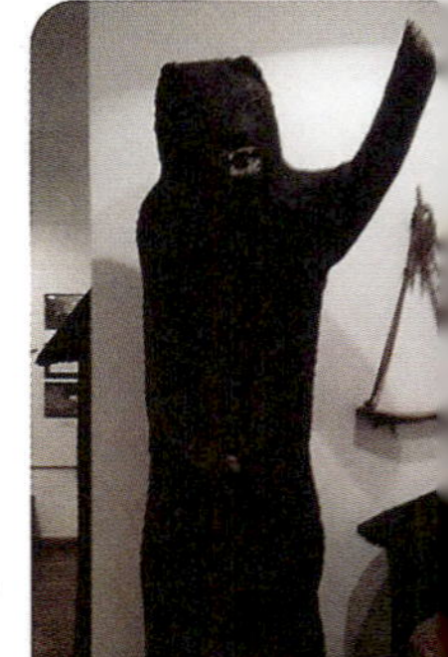

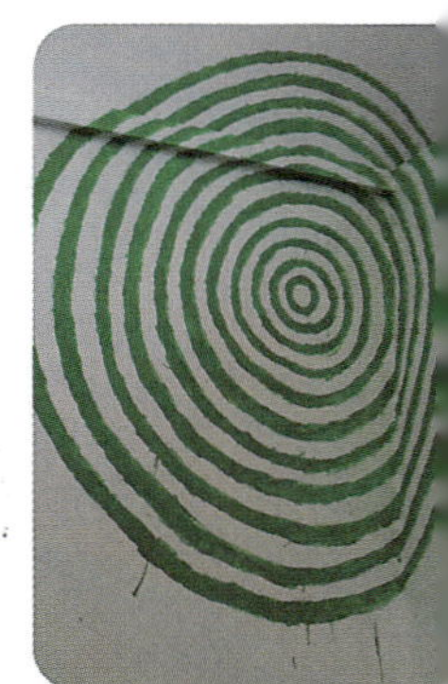

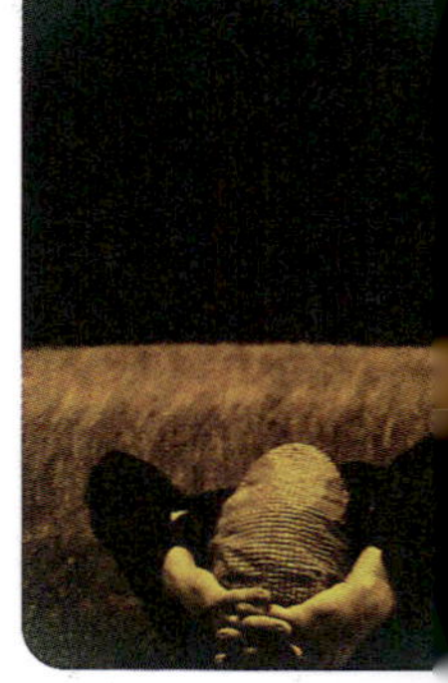

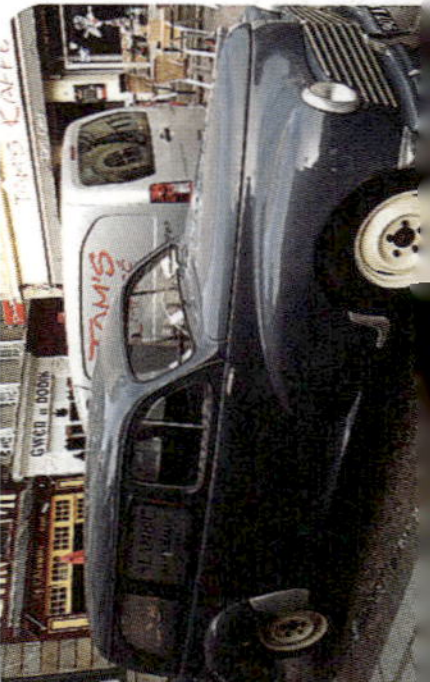

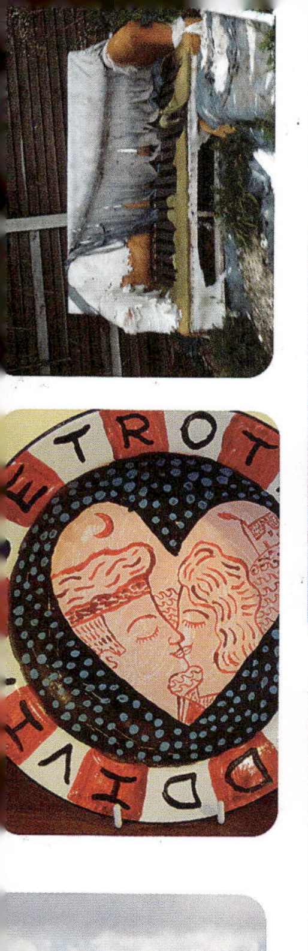
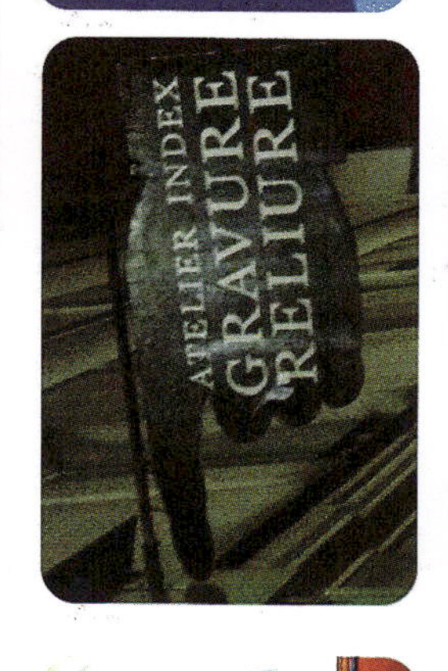
ATELIER INDEX
GRAVURE
RELIURE
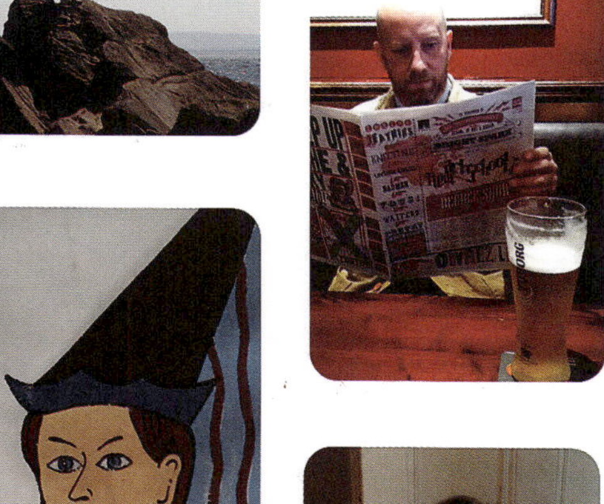
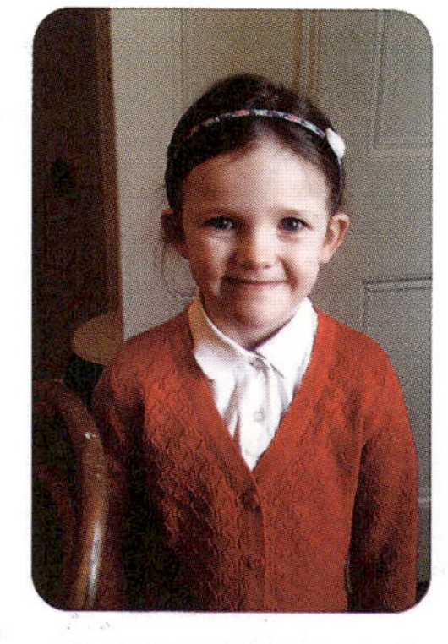
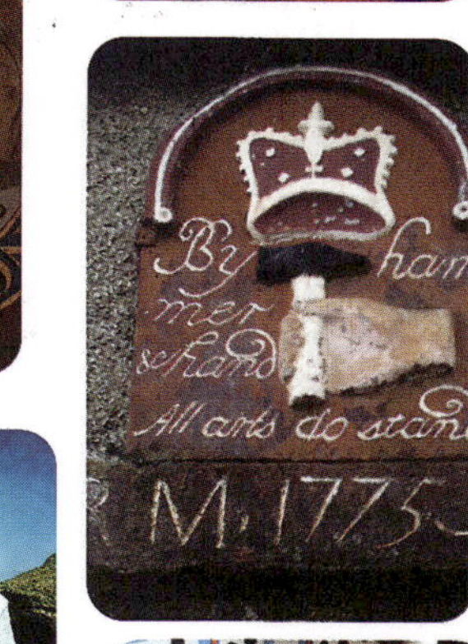
By hammer & hand
All arts do stand
M.1775
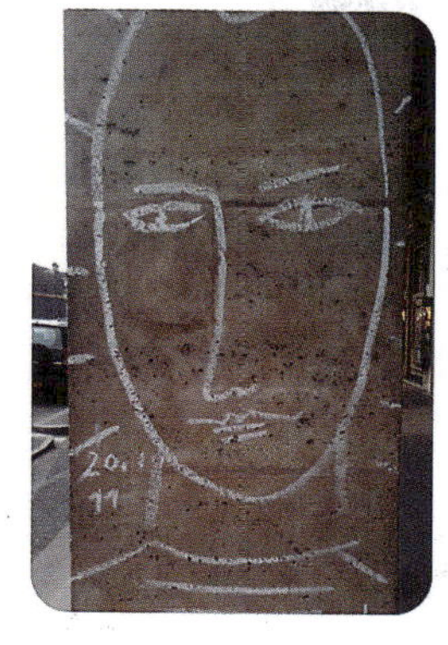
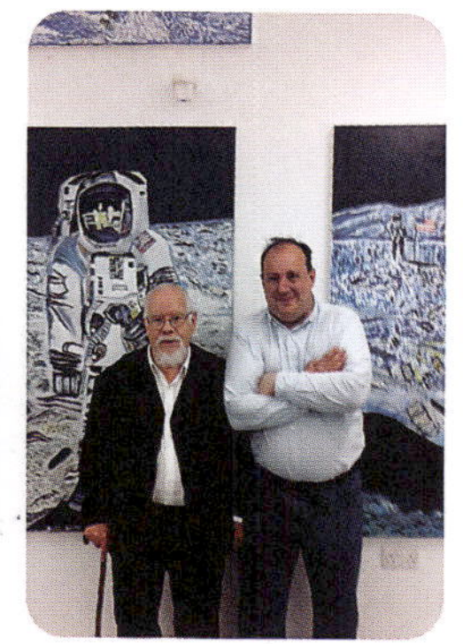
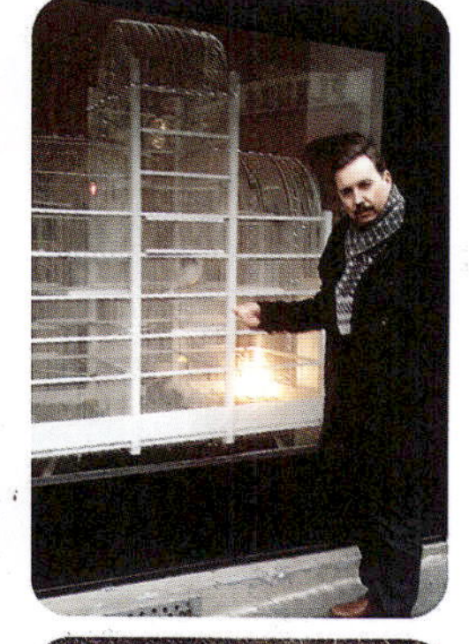
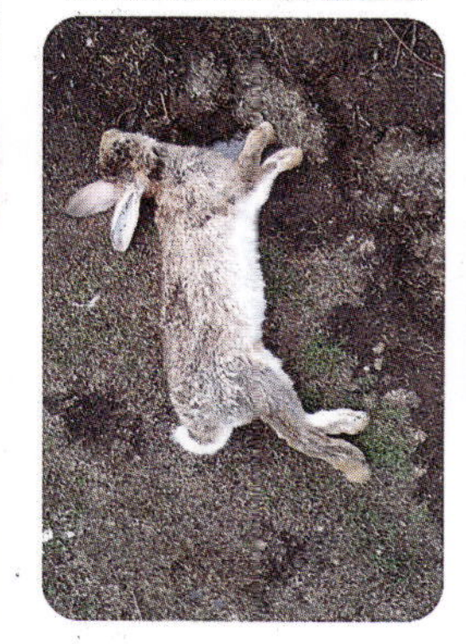
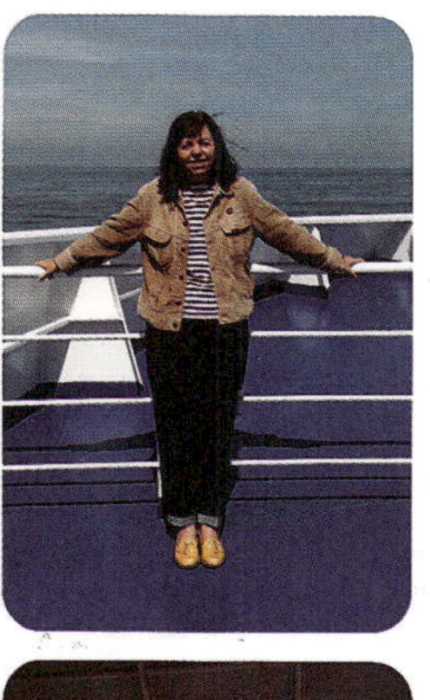
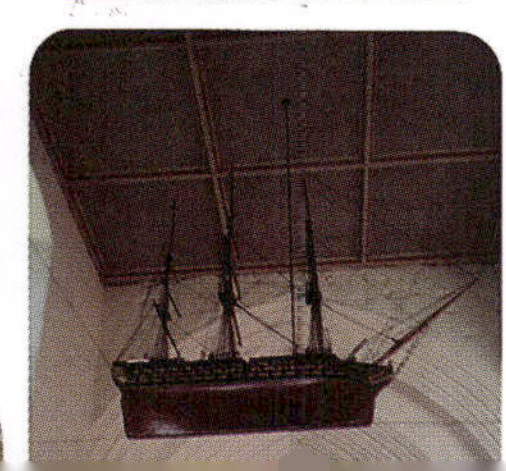
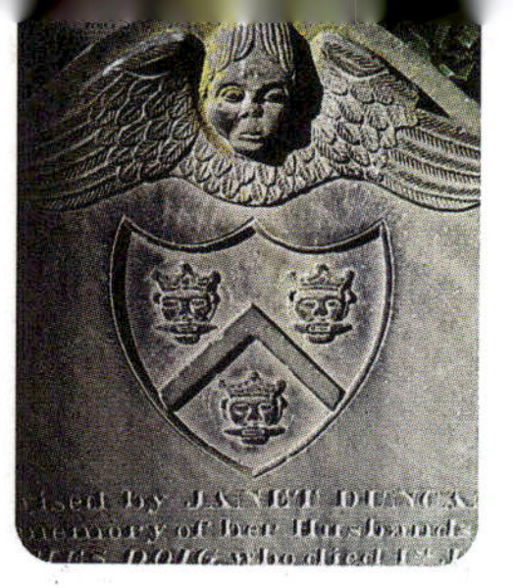
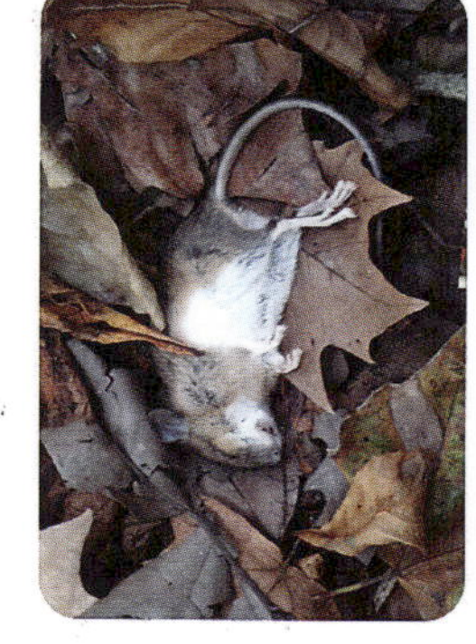
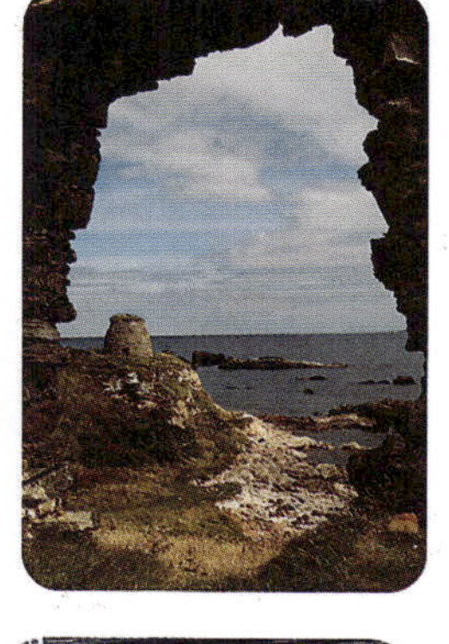
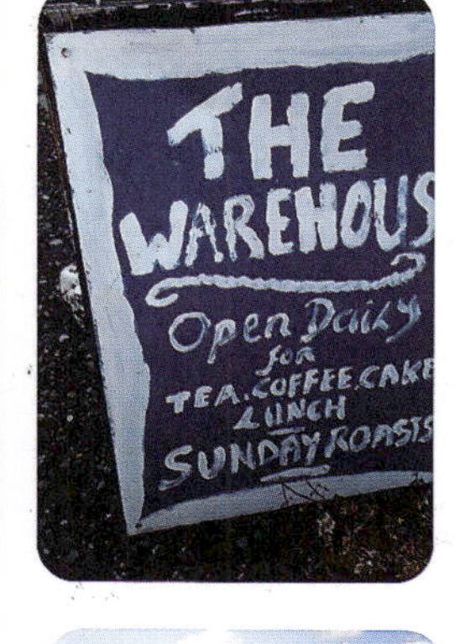
THE
WAREHOUS
Open Daily
for
TEA, COFFEE CAKE
LUNCH
SUNDAY ROASTS
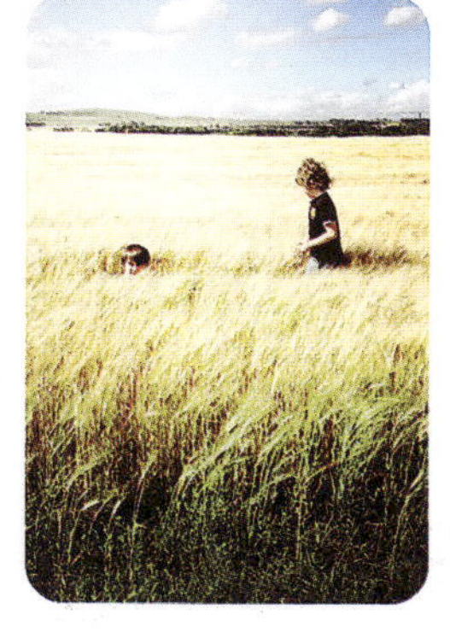
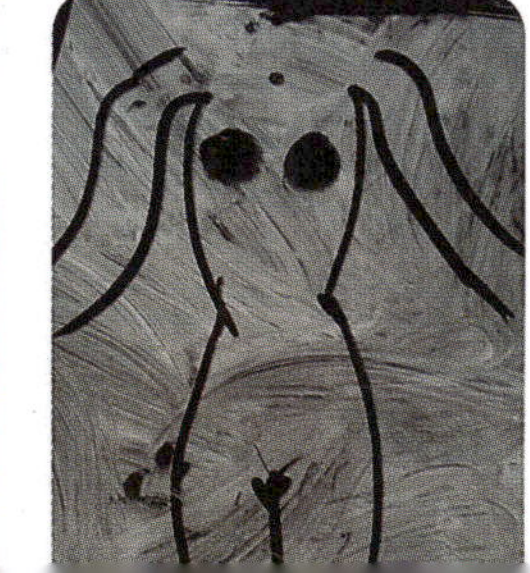
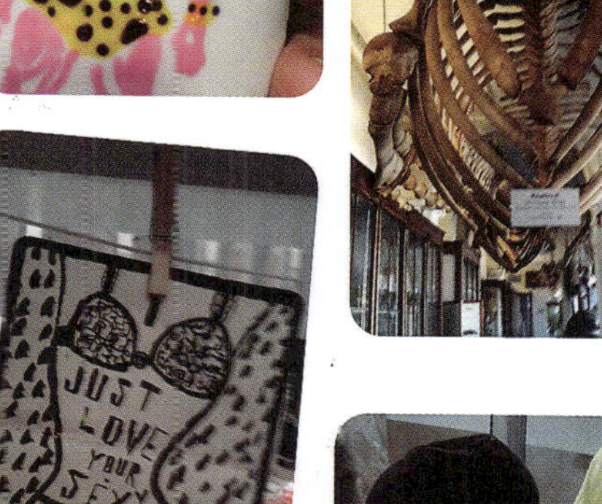
JUST LOVE YOUR SEXY
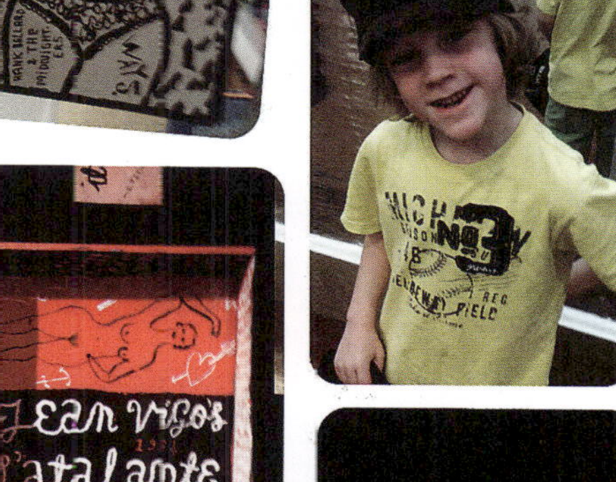
Jean Vigo's
Latalante
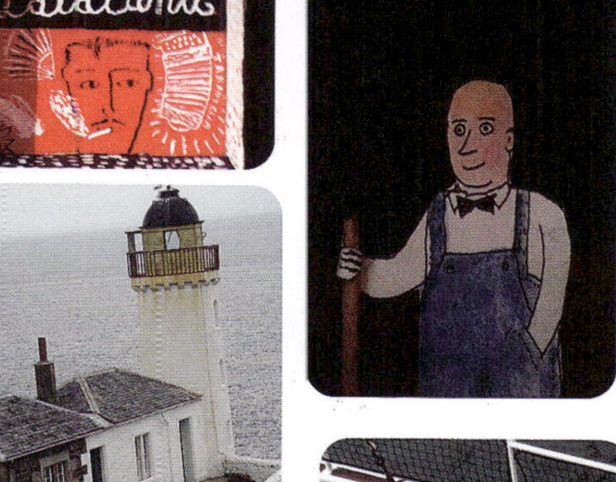
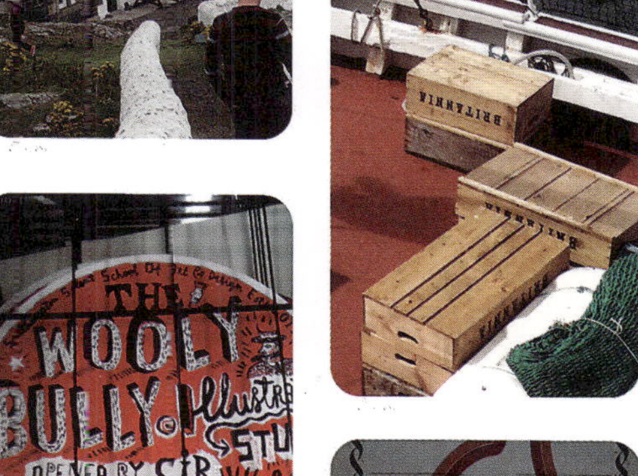
THE
WOOLY
BULLY
OPENED BY SIR
Peter Blake
JUNE
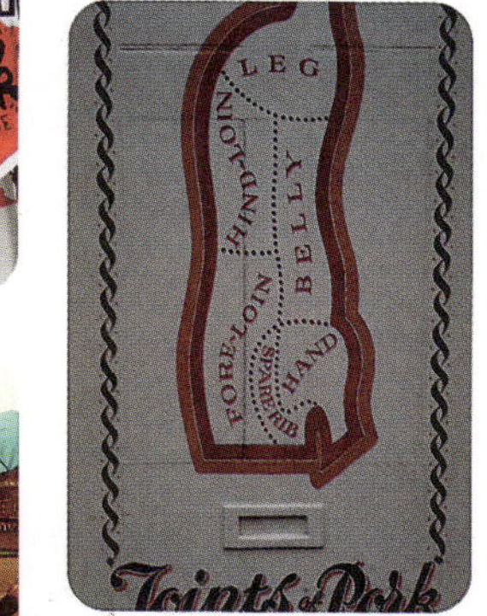
LEG
HINDLOIN
BELLY
FORE-LOIN
HAND
Joints & Pork
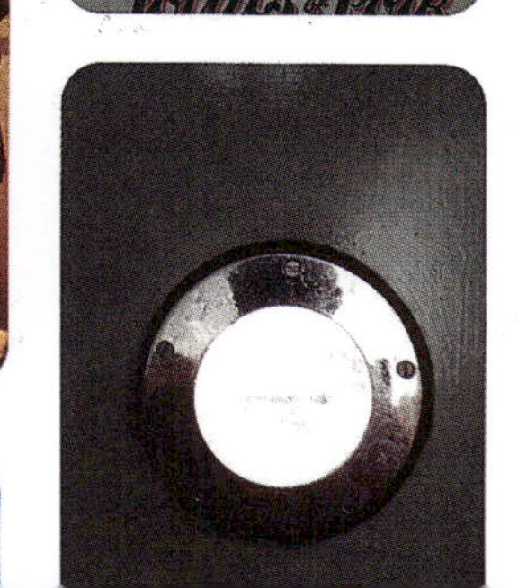
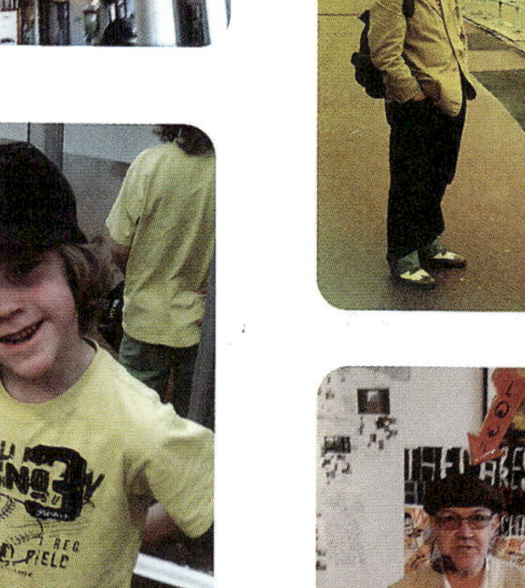
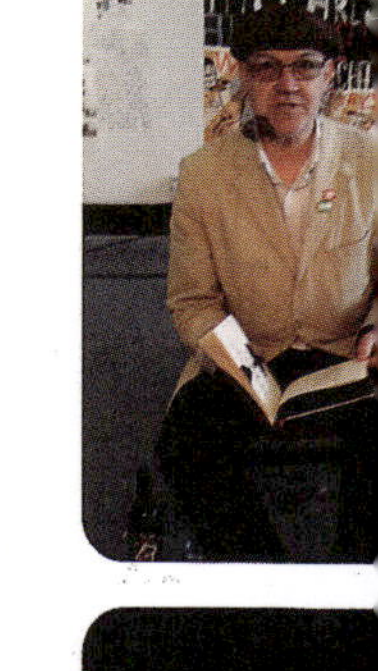
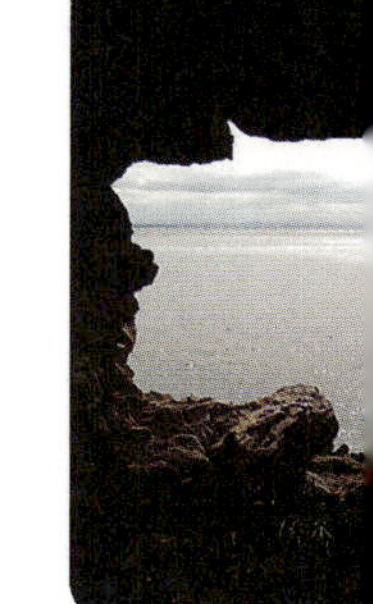
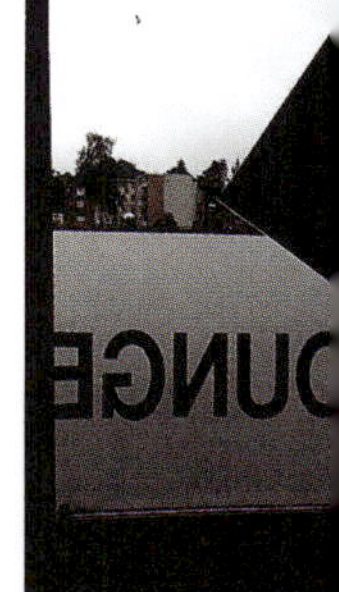
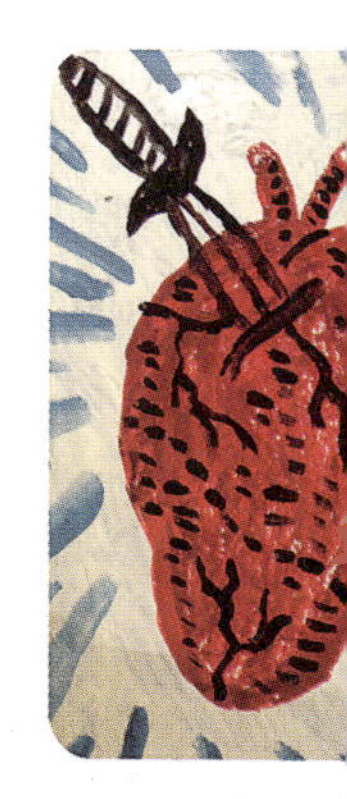
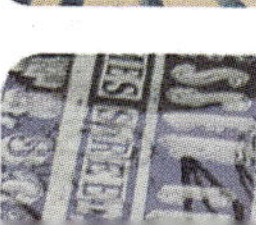

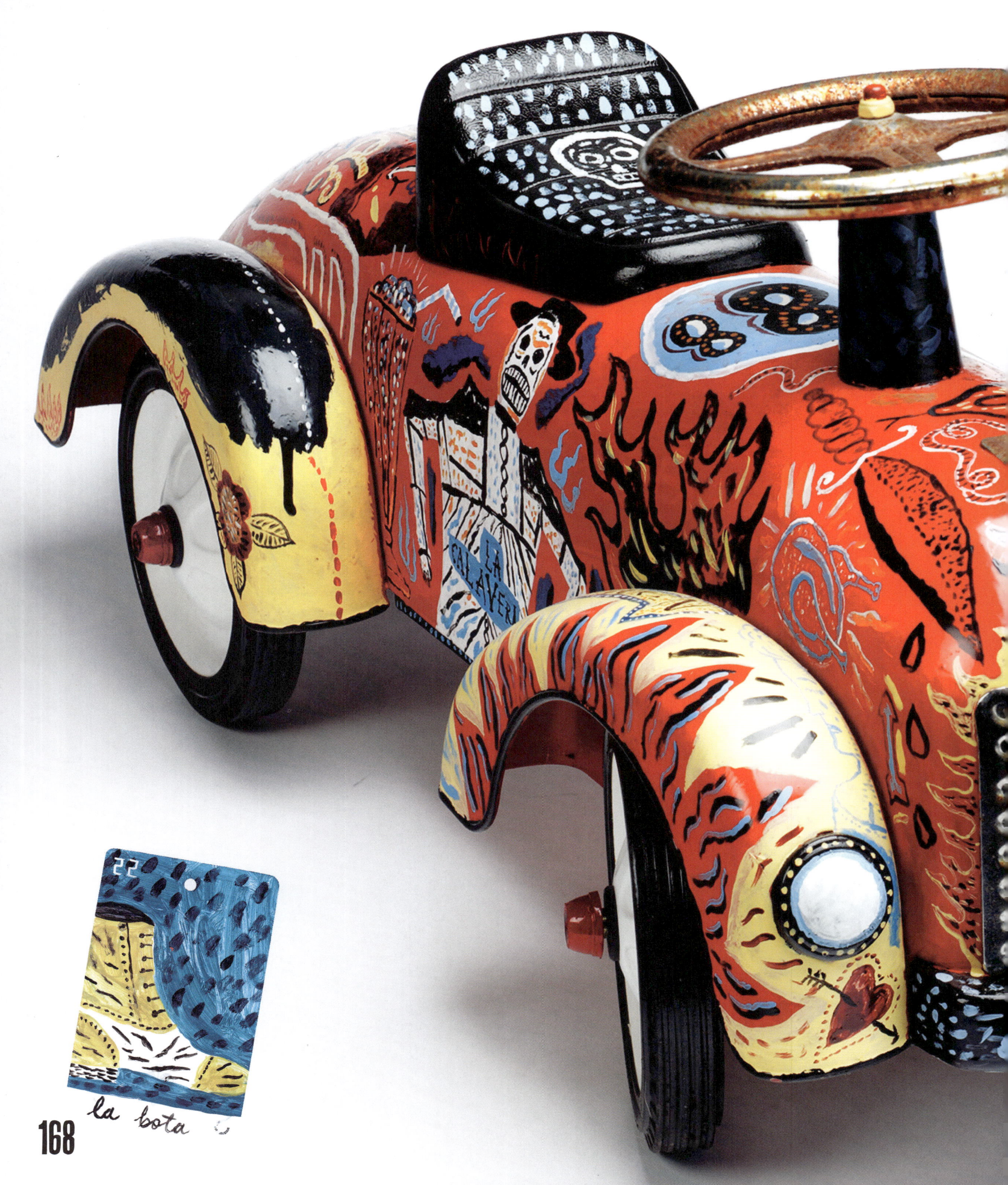
LA CALAVERA
22
la bota

*Wee Jerry's Red Motor*
2009

This car, a present to my youngest son from my sister, was in the garden rusting away until I pinched it and made my own hot rod. I have always craved a custom car, despite being unable to drive. So I had one for a short spell, until my agent bought it soon after, in 2009, at the *Notes from McVouty* exhibition.

And the Lotería cards, inspired by the Mexican game of the same name, are my homage to potent simplicity. Each card has hidden meanings. Choose a card. The future is written.

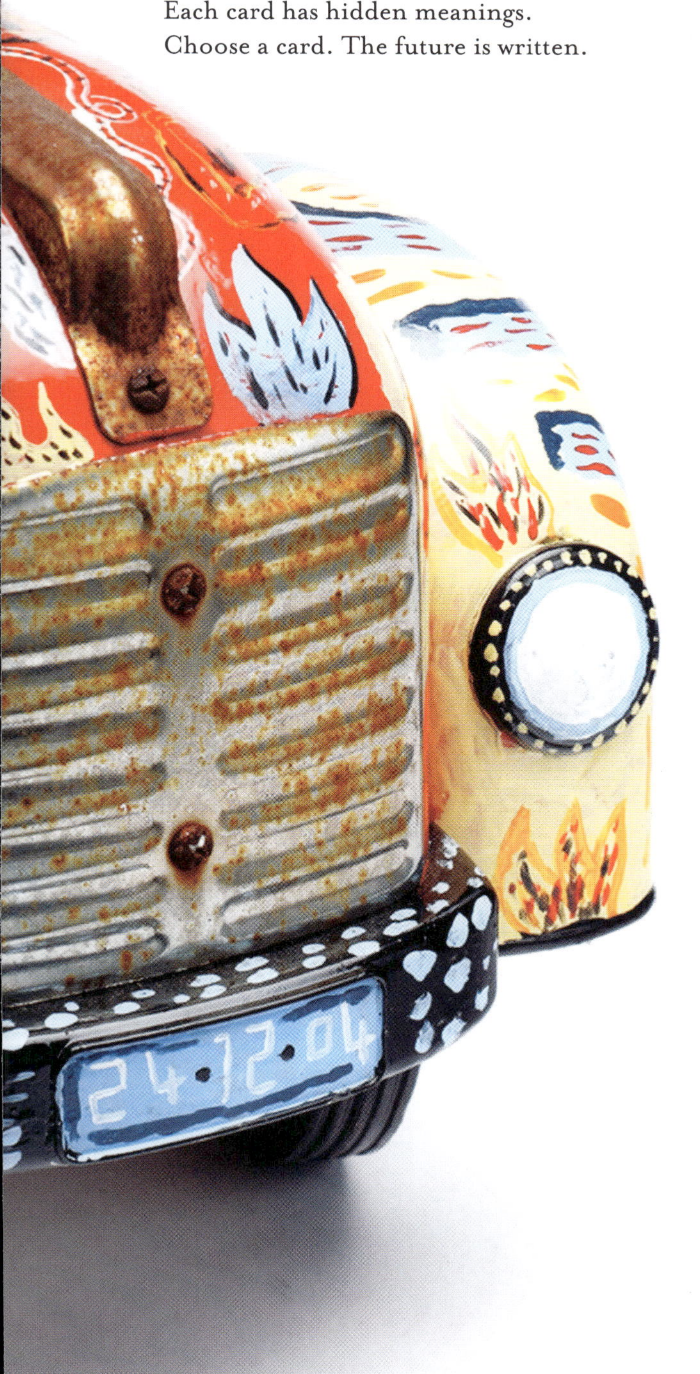

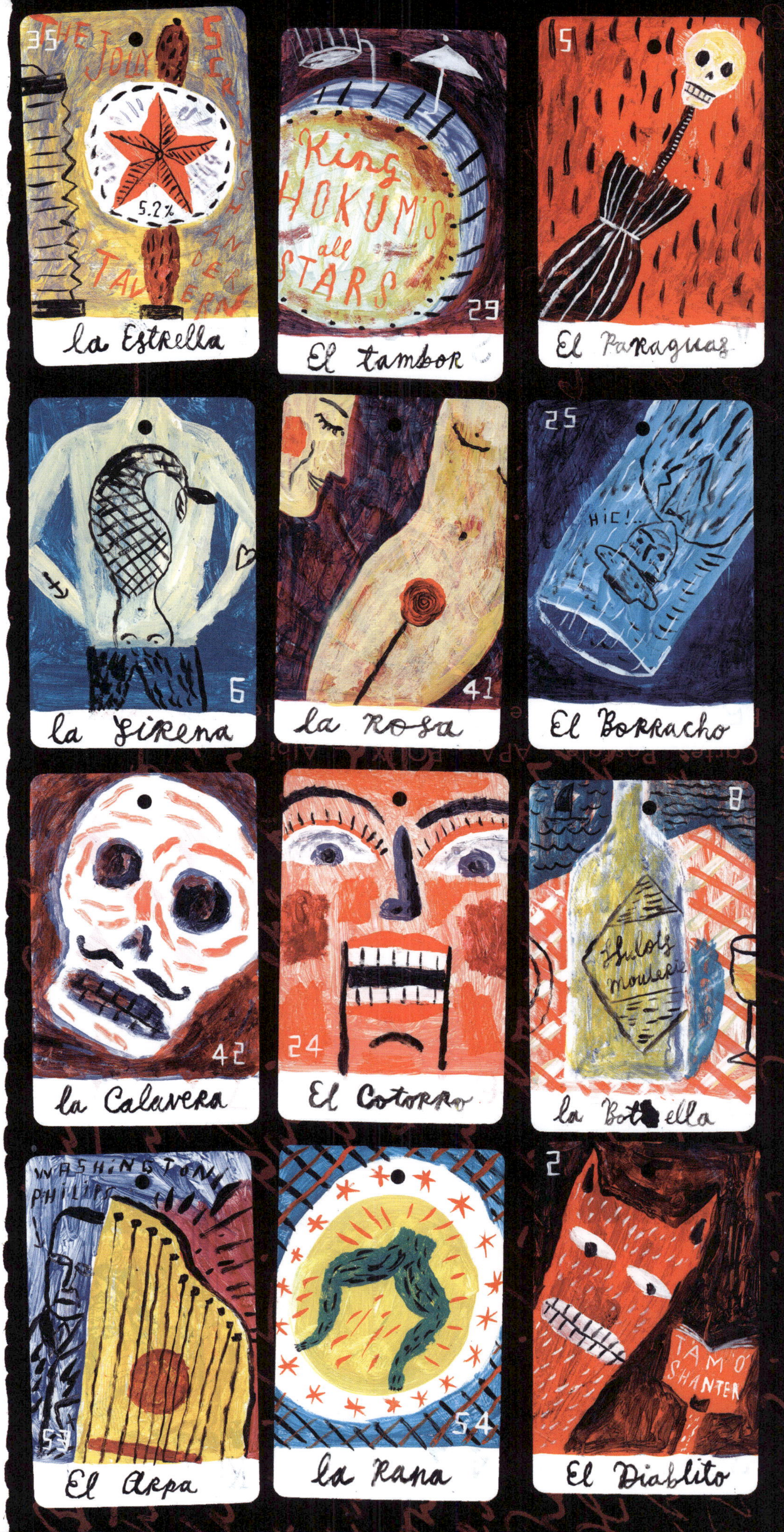

# READ

any poetry by CHARLES BUKOWSKI *
LEVIATHAN by PHILIP HOARE ♥ A CONEY ISLAND of the MIND by Lawrence FERLINGHETTI *
leaves of grass by WALT WHITMAN TAM O' SHANTER by Robert
BURNS * HOWL & OTHER POEMS by Allen Ginsberg ♥ Accordian Crimes by
E. ANNIE PROULX * Anything by CHRIS WARE * Billy Budd by Herman Melville
THE MOON & SIXPENCE & every short story by W. SOMERSET MAUGHAM * COUNTRY: THE twiste
ROOTS of ROCK 'N' ROLL by NICK TOSCHES THE WRECK of the WHALESHIP
ESSEX by OWEN CHASE * Anything by M.R. JAMES * AS I LAY DYING by
WILLIAM FAULKNER ♥ ANY POETRY by JACQUES PRÉVERT *

# STOVIES

WATCH * Anything by Jacques Tati * Everything by
Jean Vigo ♥ Pépé le Moko, starring Jean Gabin Whisky Galore! ♥
Basil Rathbone as Sherlock Holmes * OUT of the PAST, I walked with A ZOMBIE &
NIGHT of the DEMON by Jacques Tourneur The Red Shoes by MICHAEL POWELL
& Emeric Pressburger ♥ THE SET-UP by Robert Wise * ORPHÉE by JEAN COCTEAU
Jazz on a Summer's Day by Bert Stern * VERTIGO by Alfred Hitchcock
* Belleville Rendez-vous & The Illusionist by Sylvain Chomet WITCHFINDER
General, starring VINCENT PRICE ♥ Ratcatcher by Lynne Ramsay * UNE
femme EST UNE femme BY Jean-Luc GODARD LE BOUCHER by CLAUDE
CHABROL Les Diaboliques & The Wages of Fear by Henri-Georges Clouzot *
Force of Evil & Body & Soul, STARRING JOHN GARFIELD ♥ Trees Lounge
by Steve Buscemi * Fahrenheit 451 by François Truffaut LE
SAMOURAI, starring Alain Delon ♥ Les Enfants du Paradis by Marcel
Carné * ON THE TOWN, starring Gene Kelly LOCAL HERO by BILL FORSYTH

# LISTEN

DIAMOND MINE by King Creosote & Jon Hopkins ✱ THE LARK ASCENDING by Ralph Vaughan Williams ✱ the Lancashire Toreador by GEORGE FORMBY ✱ Every single song by HANK WILLIAMS ✱ LOUIS ARMSTRONG'S hot five & hot seven recordings ✱ the genius of Bud Powell ✱ Anything by Charlie Parker ✱ WEATHERBIRD by Satchmo & Earl Hines ✱ CONCERT by the SEA by ERROLL Garner ✱ the whole of CAN'T STAND the REZILLOS ✱ Harry Smith's Anthology of American Folk Music ✱ ROBERT CRUMB'S That's What I Call Sweet Music ✱ both Fleet Foxes albums ✱ MOST of the output of the SKIDS ✱ John Riley by the Byrds ✱ THE WEREWOLF by BARRY DRANSFIELD ✱ Sing, Sing, Sing by BENNY GOODMAN ✱ BODY & SOUL by the Benny Goodman TRIO ✱ Quel Temps fait-il à Paris? by Alain Romans, Gus Viseur & Lucienne Delyle ✱ SOMETHING THAT I SAID by THE RUTS ✱ Careless Love by LEADBELLY ✱ OUTDOOR Miner BY WIRE ✱ COLES CORNER by Richard Hawley ✱ SINATRA at the SANDS ✱ Anything by BOB WILLS & HIS Texas Playboys ✱ The Watson Family ✱ ANYthing BY ERIK SATIE

BANNED from THE ROXY by CRASS ✱ Anything by the Mighty Sparrow ✱ Day is Done by Nick DRAKE ✱ Fresh Fruit for Rotting Vegetables by Dead KENNEDYS ✱ Ruby, My Dear & IN WALKED BUD by Thelonius Monk ✱ WARRIOR IN WOOLWORTHS by X-RAY SPEX ✱ Jimmy Shand's Bluebell Polka ✱ VENEZUELAN LITTLE TUNE by Lionel Belasco ✱ What Did the Deep SEA SAY? by WOODY GUTHRIE ✱ Music for Torching by Billie Holiday ✱ anything by SLIM GAILLARD, but especially Dunkin' Bagel ✱ Milk & Honey by Jackson C. Frank ✱ Both FIRST AID KIT albums ✱ Blow the Wind Southerly by KATHLEEN Ferrier ✱ MAD DOGS & ENGLISHMEN by NOËL COWARD ✱ NOBODY BUT ME by the HUMAN BEINZ ✱ AH UM & OH YEAH by CHARLES MINGUS ✱ NO MORE HOT DOGS by Hasil Adkins ✱ HOT TOWN by Fess Williams & His Royal Flush ORCHESTRA ✱ by Django Reinhardt & Stéphane Grappelli ✱ My Sweet BY the CRAMPS ✱ PERPETUAL MOTION No 1 by FRANCIS POULENC ✱ LONESOME TOWN Shape of things TO COME by SLADE ✱ The St. Kilda Wedding by Fiddlin' Ian McCamy & His Celtic Reelers ✱ ALL of Elvis's SUN Recordings ✱ LANDED by BEN FOLDS ✱ TIME OUT by the DAVE Brubeck Quartet ✱ MY FAVOURITE THINGS by JOHN COLTRANE ✱ BOTH albums by C.W. Stoneking ✱ Devil Got my Woman by SKIP JAMES ✱ ONE LAST NIGHT ON THE TOWN by JONATHAN CAIRNEY

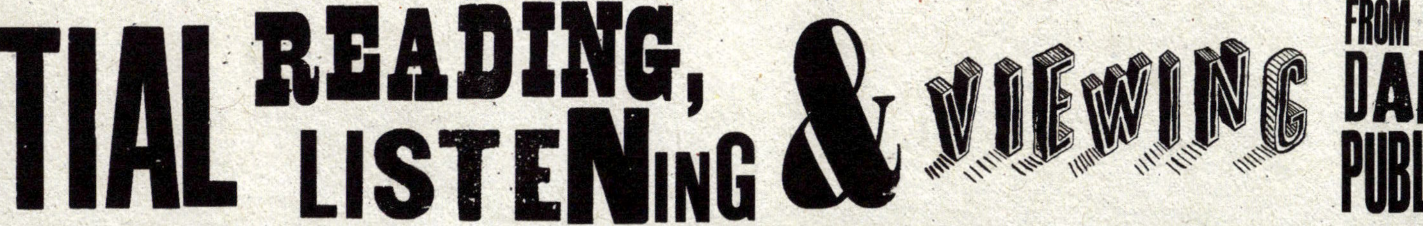

# ENJOY

THE WORK OF John Broadley, David Stone Martin, KEVIN BRADLEY'S Yee-haw Industries, MAIRA KALMAN, Ralph Fasanella, Bill Traylor, CHARLOTTE SALOMON, Peter Bailey, AND SO many others....

PRINTED EPHEMERA by John Lewis ✱ MOBY-DICK - oh, when will I finish Moby-Dick, by Herman Melville...

# ESSENTIAL READING, LISTENING & VIEWING FROM THE DARKTOWN PUBLIC LIBRARY

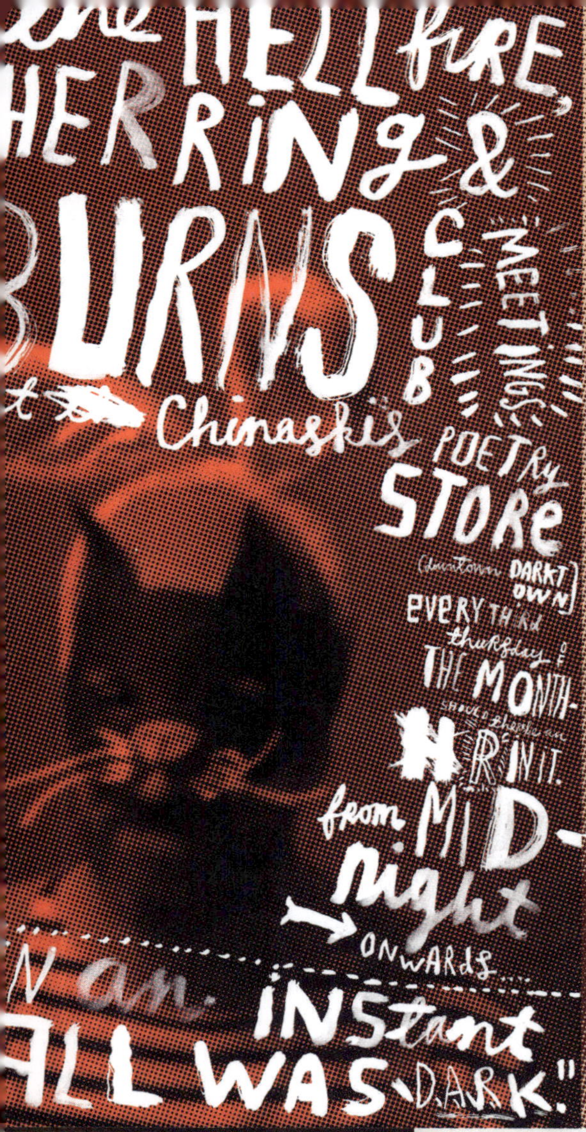

the HELLFIRE,
HERRING &
BURNS
CLUB
MEETINGS
at Chinaski's POETRY STORE
(downtown DARKTOWN)
EVERY THIRD thursday of THE MONTH
from MID-night ONWARDS
an instant ALL WAS DARK."
SEE BLACK SHUCK 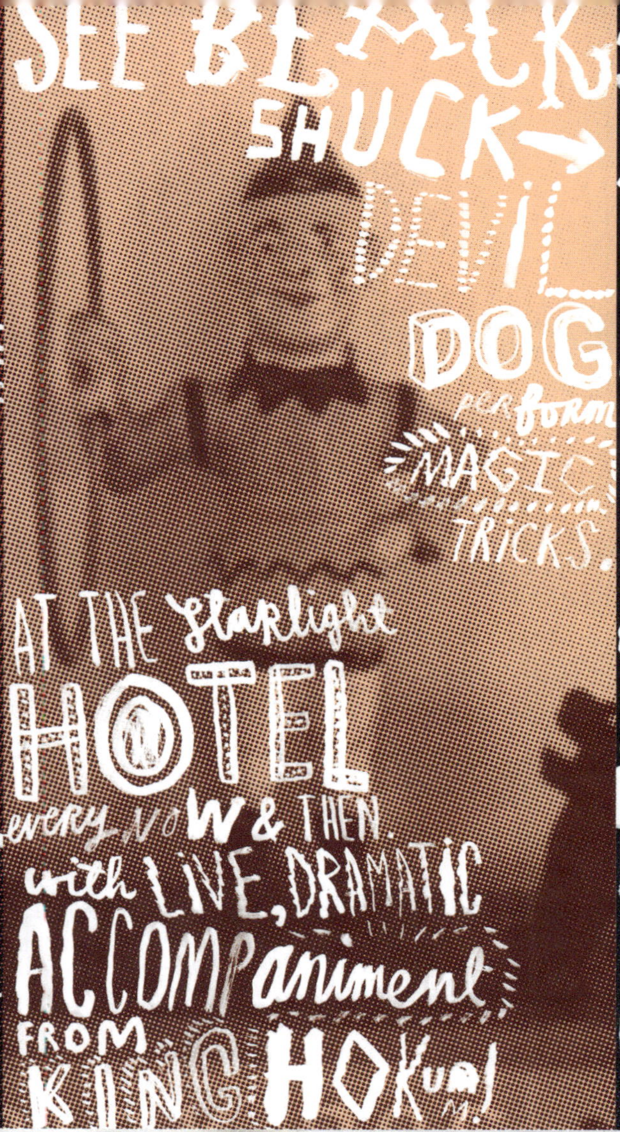
DEVIL DOG
perform MAGIC TRICKS.
AT THE starlight HOTEL
every NOW & THEN.
with LIVE, DRAMATIC ACCOMPaniment
FROM KING HOKum!
toodle-AYE 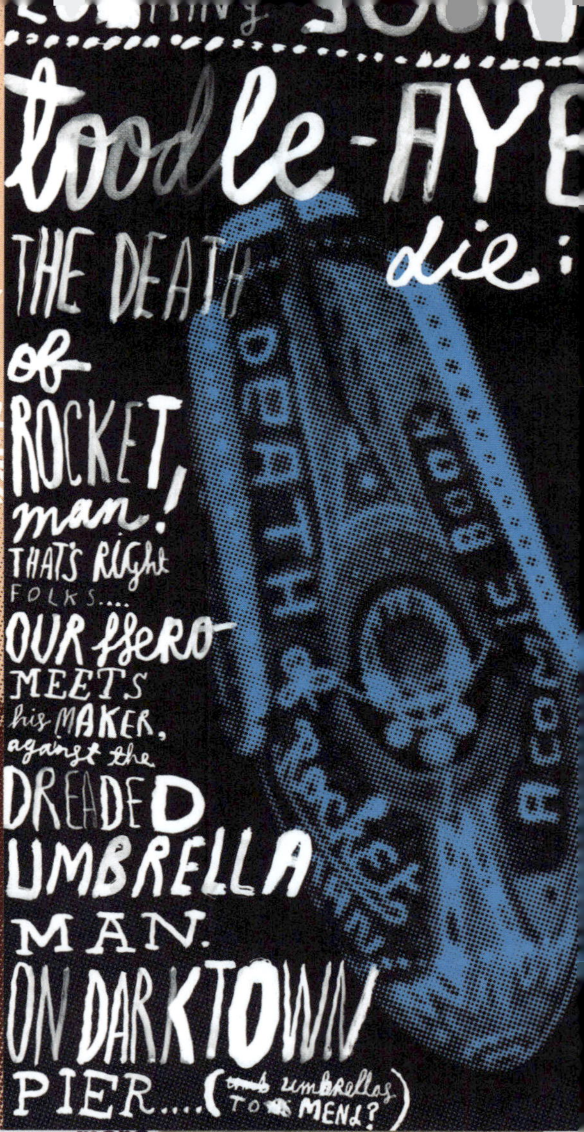
die:
THE DEATH of ROCKET, man!
THAT'S RIGHT FOLKS....
OUR HERO MEETS his MAKER,
against the DREADED UMBRELLA MAN.
ON DARKTOWN PIER....
THE ART OF THE FOLK-BLUES GUITAR
by Jerry Silverman
MOTOWN CHARTBUSTERS VOL.3 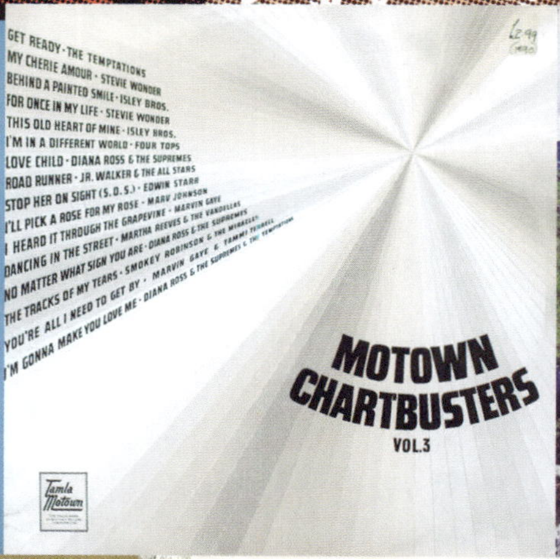
STEP WE GAILY • JIMMY SHAND 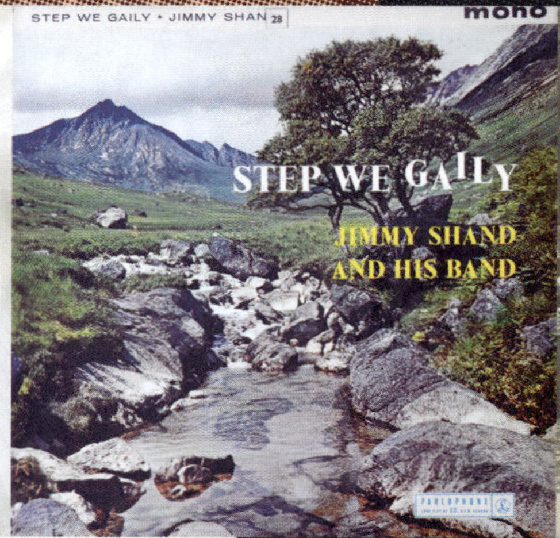
STEP WE GAILY
JIMMY SHAND AND HIS BAND
IAN DURY NEW BOOTS AND PANTIES 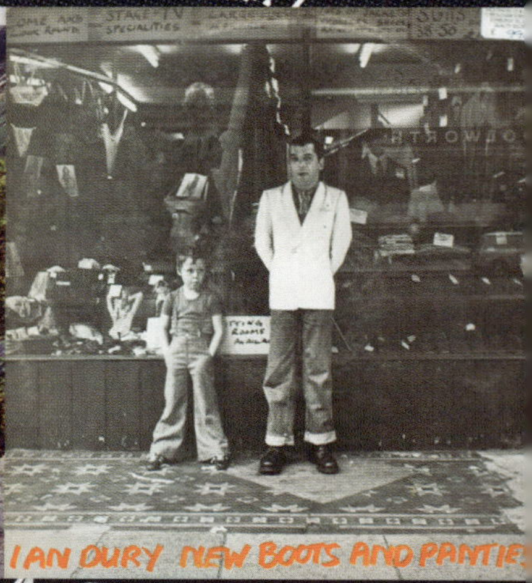

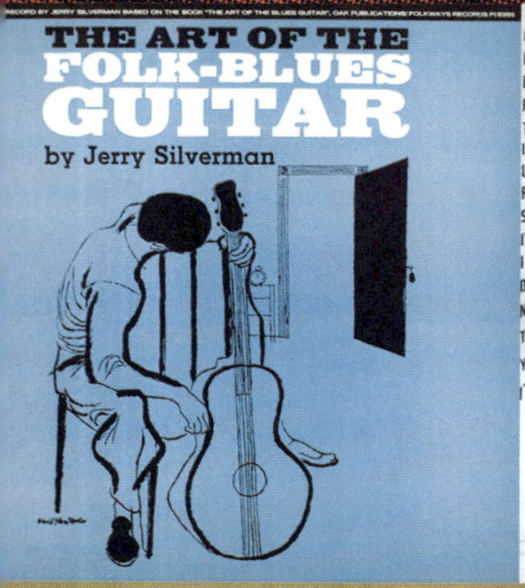

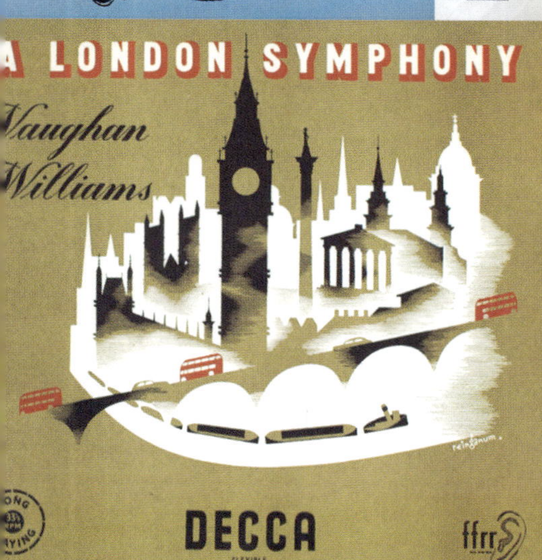
A LONDON SYMPHONY
Vaughan Williams
DECCA
ffrr

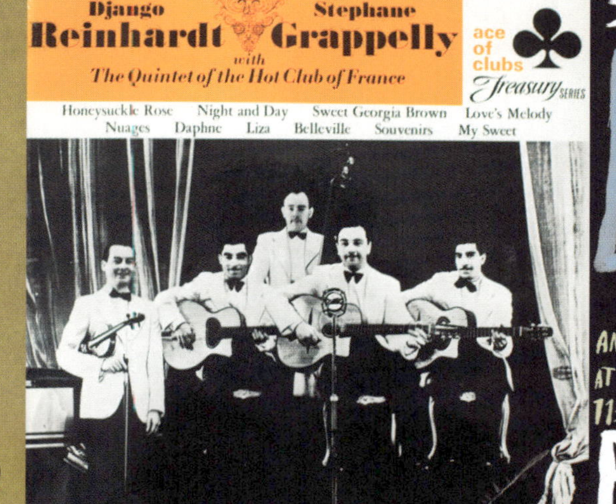
Django Reinhardt with Stephane Grappelly
The Quintet of the Hot Club of France
ace of clubs
Treasury SERIES
Honeysuckle Rose   Night and Day   Sweet Georgia Brown   Love's Melody
Nuages   Daphne   Liza   Belleville   Souvenirs   My Sweet

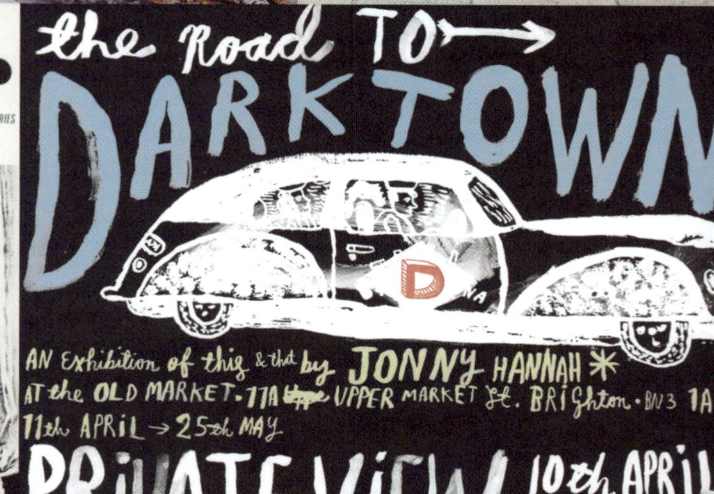
the Road TO
DARKTOWN
AN Exhibition of this & that by JONNY HANNAH *
at the OLD MARKET. 11A UPPER MARKET St. Brighton. BN3 1A
11th APRIL → 25th MAY
PRIVATE VIEW 10th APRIL

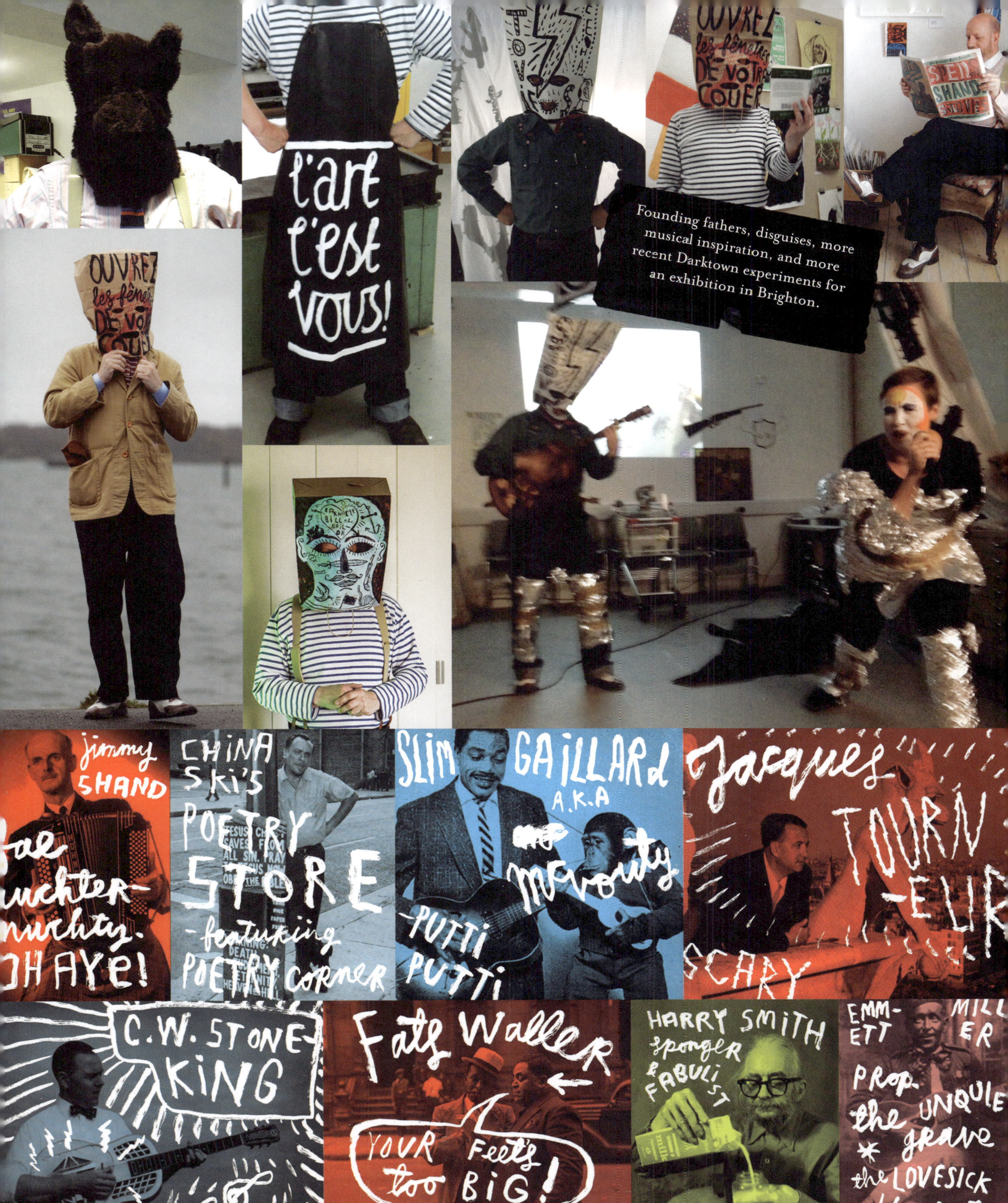


Founding fathers, disguises, more musical inspiration, and more recent Darktown experiments for an exhibition in Brighton.

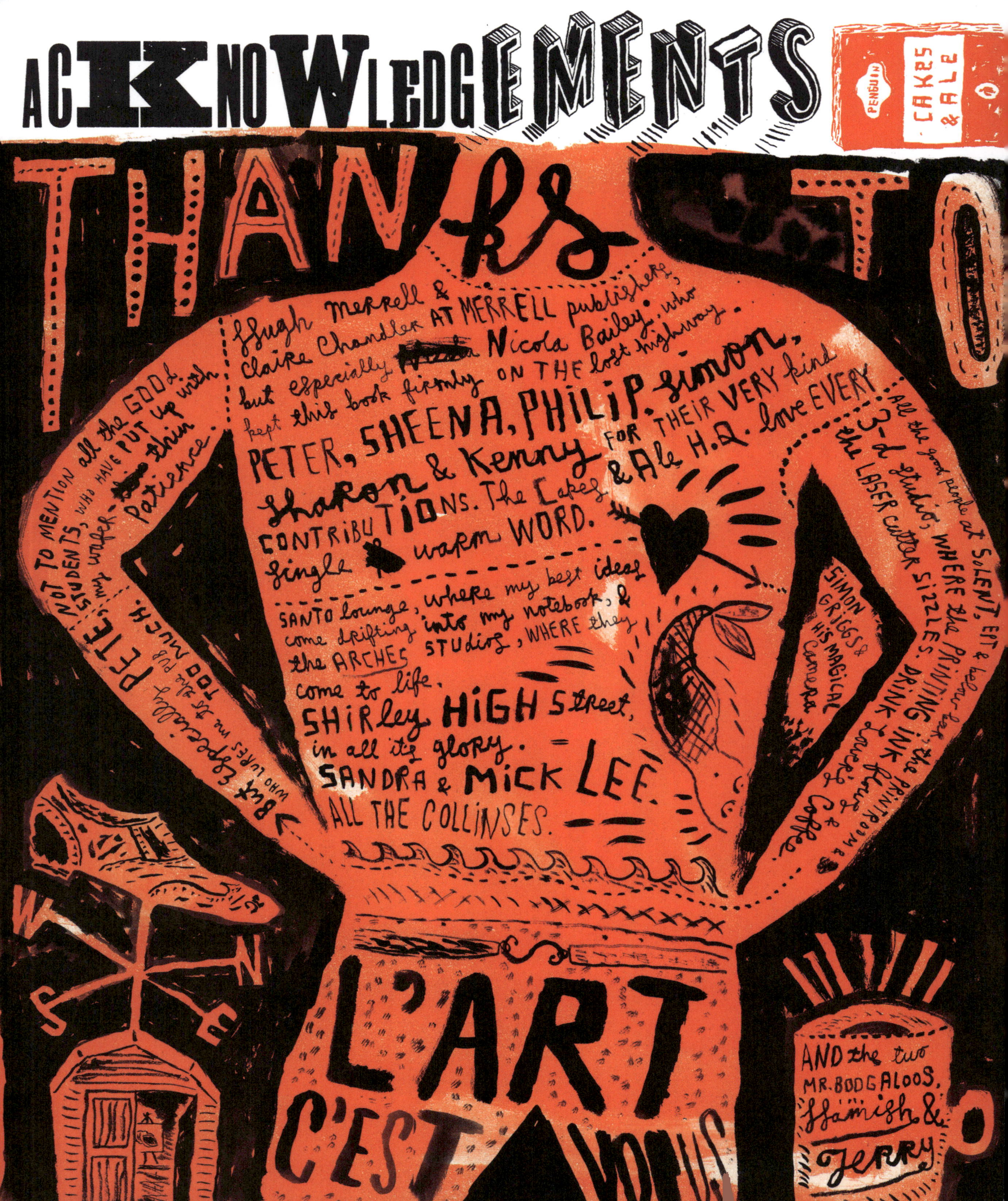

ACKNOWLEDGEMENTS
PENGUIN CAKES & ALE
THANKS TO
Hugh Merrell & Claire Chandler AT MERRELL publishers, but especially Nicola Bailey, who kept this book firmly ON THE lost highway.
PETER, SHEENA, PHILIP, Simon, Sharon & Kenny FOR THEIR VERY kind CONTRIBUTIONS. The Cakes & Ale H.Q. love EVERY single warm WORD.
SANTO lounge, where my best ideas come drifting into my notebook, & the ARCHES STUDIOS, WHERE they come to life.
SHIRley HIGH Street, in all its glory.
SANDRA & MICK LEE.
ALL THE COLLINSES.
NOT TO MENTION all the GOOD STUDENTS, WHO HAVE PUT UP with my waffle thin patience.
PETE, my TECH. But especially WHO LURES me to the PUB TOO MUCH.
All the good people at SOLENT, EPT & below, 3-d studio, WHERE the PRINTING INK the LASER cutter SIZZLES. DRINK lovely flour & coffee
SIMON GRIGGS & HIS MAGICAL camera
W N S E
L'ART C'EST VOUS
AND the two MR. BOOGALOOS, Hamish & Jerry

# THE AUTHOR AND CONTRIBUTORS

## JONNY HANNAH

studied at Liverpool School of Art and Design and the Royal College of Art, London. His illustrations have appeared in such publications as the *New York Times*, the *Sunday Telegraph* and the *St Kilda Courier*. His children's book *Hot Jazz Special* was published in 2005, and he produces screen-printed books, posters and prints for his own Cakes & Ale Press. He lives in Southampton, where he teaches at Southampton Solent School of Art and Design.

## DR SHEENA CALVERT

has more than twenty-five years' experience teaching critical theory, graphic design and typography at various institutions, including the University of Westminster, Central Saint Martins, the London College of Printing and Camberwell College of Arts. Her studio, the .918 press, is a fully equipped letterpress printing facility for the production of experimental typographic works.

## PETER CHRISP

is a writer and artist who has published more than eighty history books for children. He also writes 'From Swerve of Shore to Bend of Bay', a blog about James Joyce's *Finnegans Wake*. He lives in Brighton, where has exhibited his work as part of the Artists Open Houses festival.

## PHILIP HOARE

is a writer, broadcaster and cultural historian. His books include *Leviathan or, The Whale* (2008), which won the Samuel Johnson Prize for Non-fiction in 2009, and *The Sea Inside* (2013). He lives in Southampton.

First published 2014 by Merrell Publishers, London and New York

Merrell Publishers Limited
70 Cowcross Street
London EC1M 6EJ

merrellpublishers.com



British Library Cataloguing in Publication Data. A catalogue record for this book is available from the British Library.

ISBN 978-1-8589-4619-1

Produced by Merrell Publishers Limited
Designed by Nicola Bailey
Project-managed by Claire Chandler

Printed and bound in China

Picture Credits
Photographs by Simon Griggs, with the following exceptions: Nicola Bailey: back cover, pages 2–3, 12, 20–21, 23, 38–39, 50–51, 52, 74–75, 102–103, 122–23, 137, 159; Simon Costin: 157; Chris Hamer: 120–21; courtesy of Heart Artist's Agency: 168–69; Peter Jarvis/Simon Lewin: 161; Peter Lloyd: 8, 10, 153, 166–67, 172, 173, 176; Andreas Sprenger: 171

The extract from 'A Month of Firsts' on pages 96–97 appears with the kind permission of King Creosote.

Endpapers: From 'Tam o' Shanter' (1791) by Robert Burns (front); from *Orphée* (1950) by Jean Cocteau (end)

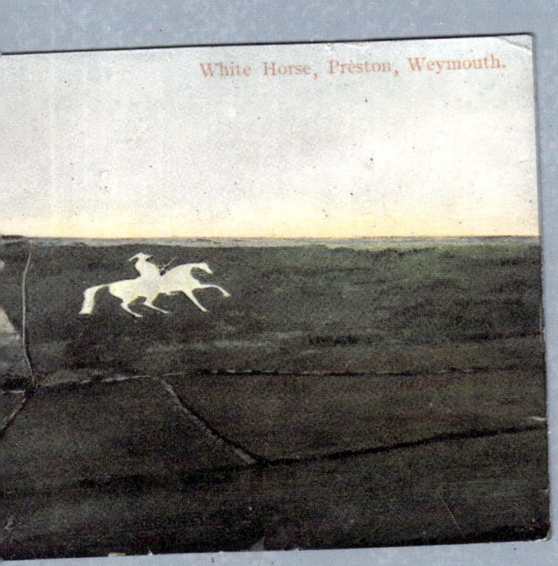


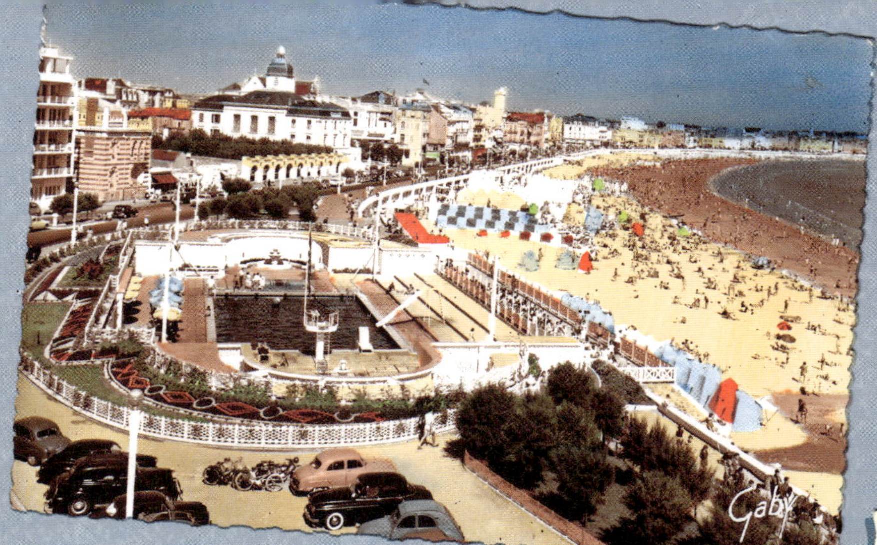


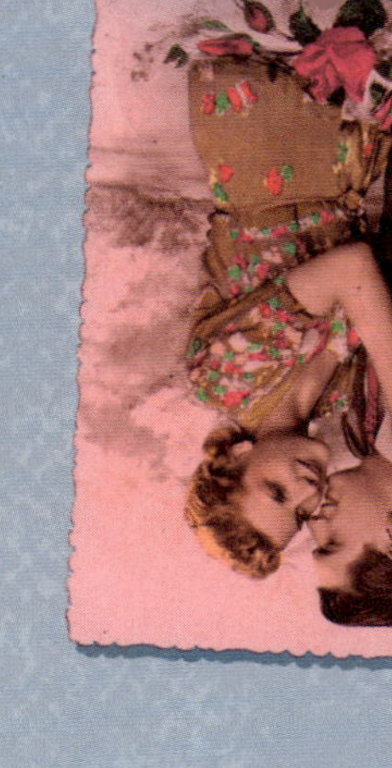

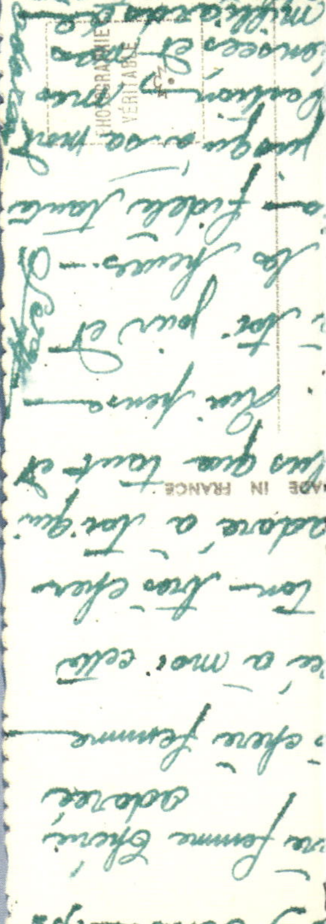

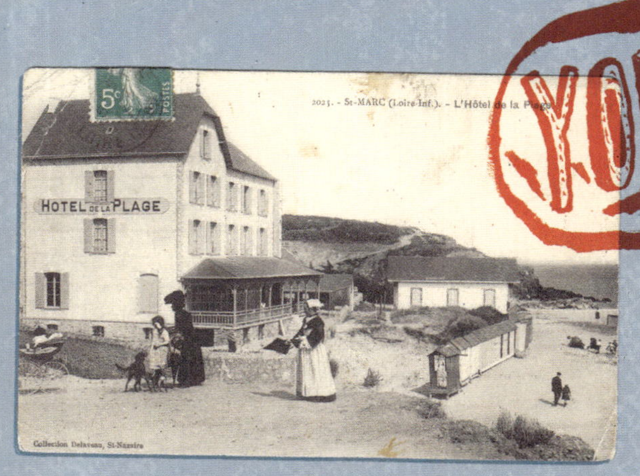


YOU are NOW leaving DARK town...

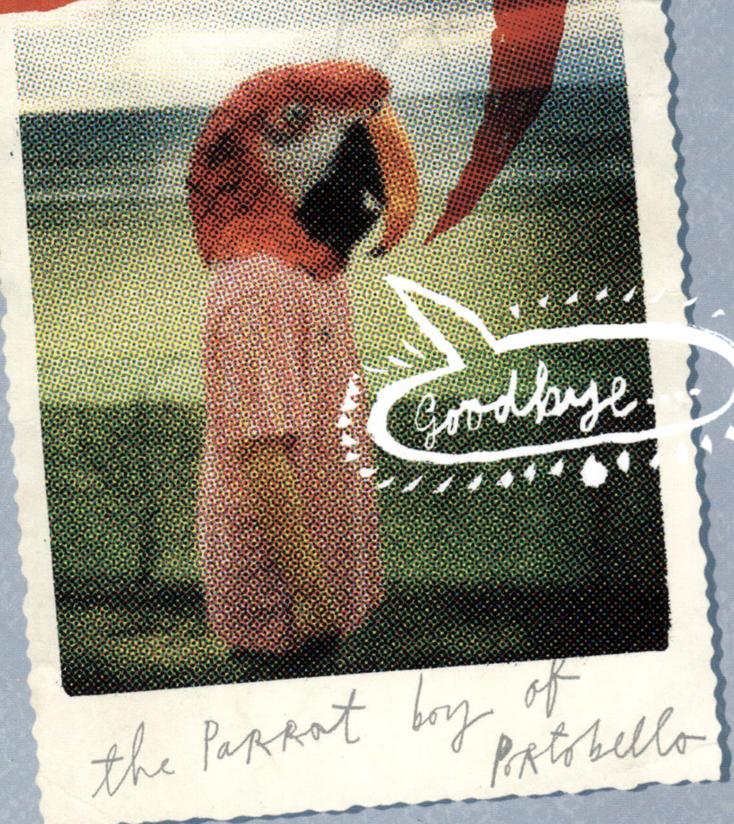


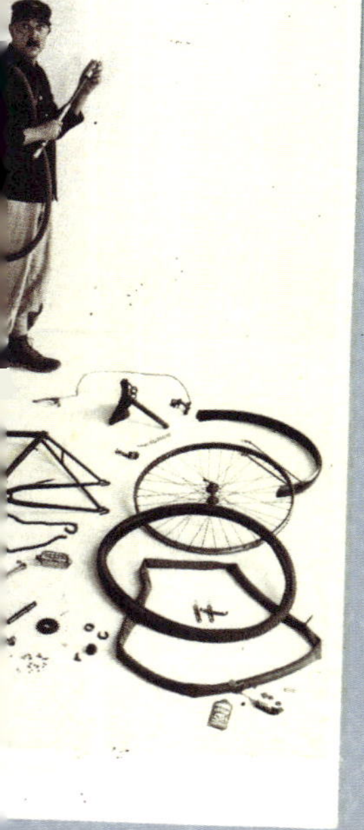

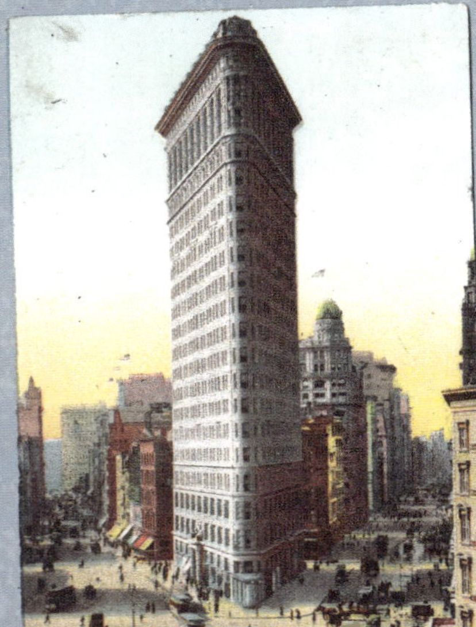

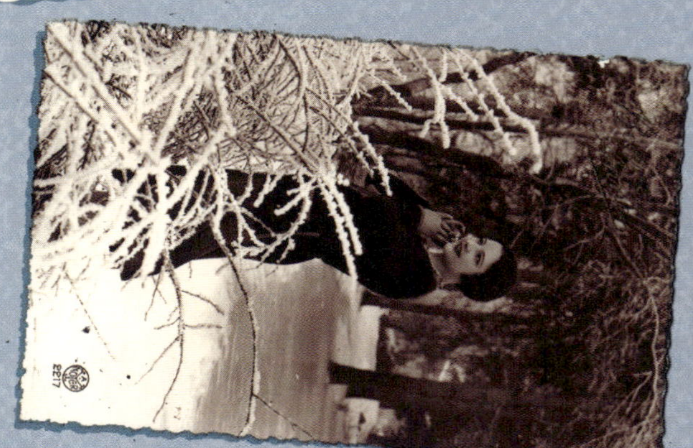

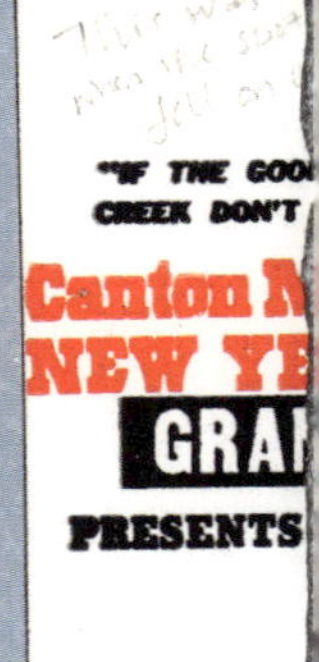


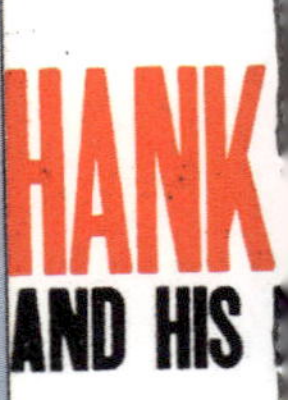

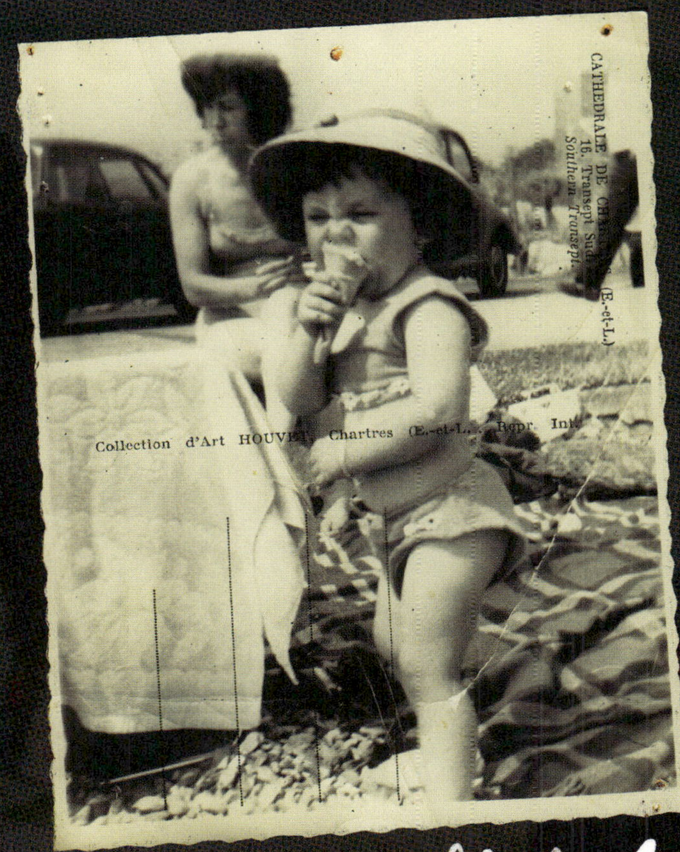


for sharon, lighthouse keeper & queen of darktown. i am the luckiest – jonny.

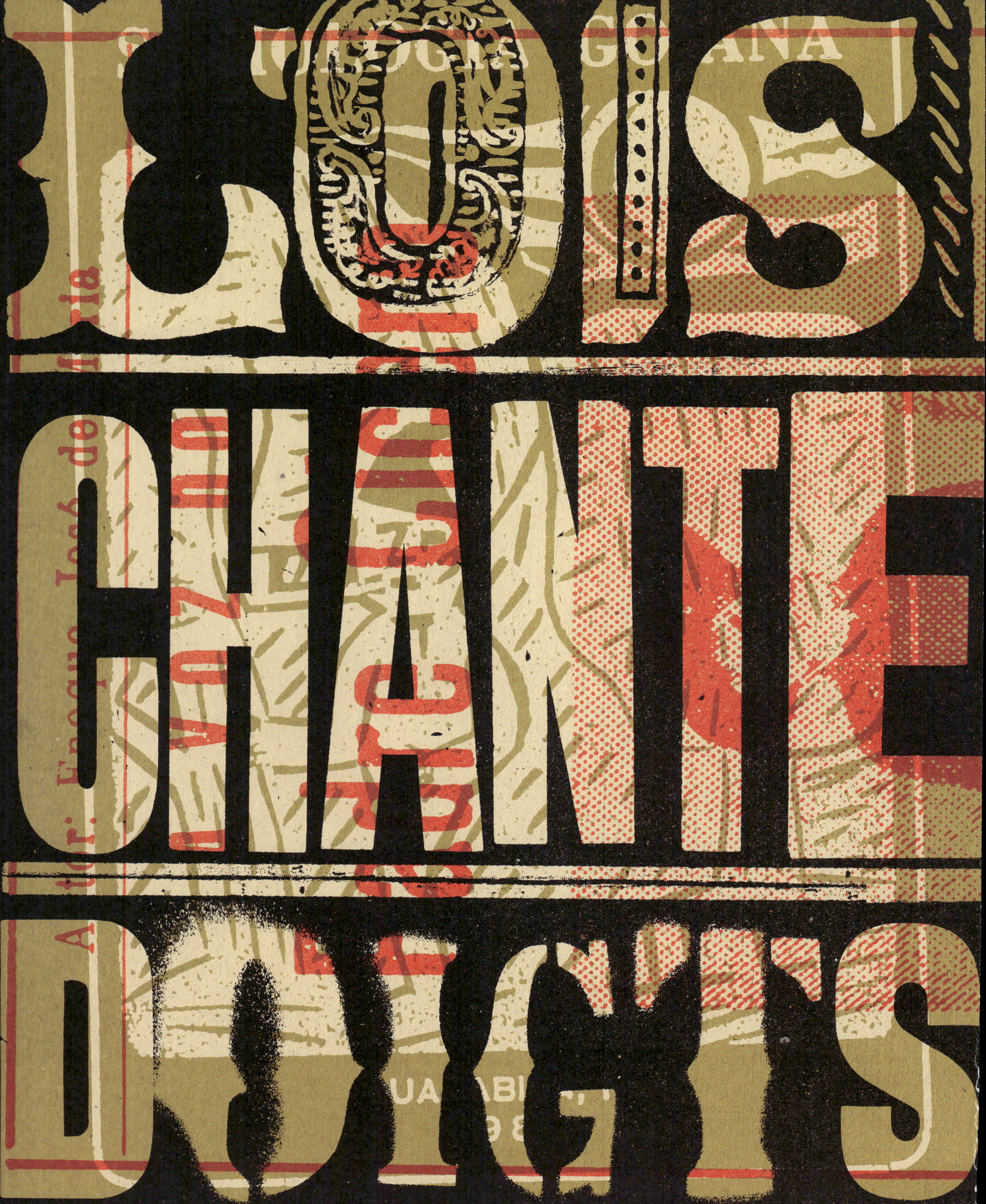

LOIS
CHANTE